PROGRESS IN CYBERNETICS AND SYSTEMS RESEARCH
Volume VII

General Systems Methodology
Organization and Management
Cognition and Learning

PROGRESS IN CYBERNETICS AND SYSTEMS RESEARCH

PROGRESS IN CYBERNETICS AND SYSTEMS RESEARCH
Volume VII
General Systems Methodology
Organization and Management
Cognition and Learning

Edited by

FRANZ R. PICHLER

Professor of Systems Theory
University of Linz, Austria

F. de P. HANIKA

Austrian Society for Cybernetic Studies

WITH INTRODUCTION BY
RENÉ THOM

HEMISPHERE PUBLISHING CORPORATION

Washington   New York   London

Hemisphere Publishing Corporation
1025 Vermont Ave., N.W., Washington, D.C. 20005

1 2 3 4 5 6 7 8 9 0   B C B C   8 9 8 7 6 5 4 3 2 1 0

Library of Congress Cataloging in Publication Data (Revised)

Main entry under title:

Progress in cybernetics and systems research.

Vol. 2 edited by Robert Trappl and F. de P. Hanika;
vol. 5 edited by Robert Trappl, F. de P. Hanika, and
Franz R. Pichler.
Papers presented at a symposium organized by the
Austrian Society for Cybernetic Studies beginning in
1972.
Sponsored by the Bundesministerium für Forschung and
others.
Includes bibliographical references and indexes.
1. Cybernetics—Congresses. 2. System theory—
Congresses. I. Trappl, Robert. II. Pichler, Franz R.
III. Hanika, Francis de Paula. IV. Österreichische
Studiengesellschaft für Kybernetik. V. Austria.
Bundesministerium für Wissenschaft und Forschung.
Q300.P75   001.53   75-6641

ISBN 0-470-88475-4 (v. I)
     0-470-88476-2 (v. II)
     0-470-26371-7 (v. III)
     0-470-99380-4 (v. IV)
     0-470-26553-1 (v. V)
     0-89116-194-5 (v. VI)
     0-89116-195-3 (v. VII)

Printed in the United States of America

Contents

List of authors

van Aken, J. E., N. V. Philips Gloeilampen-
fabrieken, Eindhoven, The Netherlands.
Andrew, Alex M., Department of Cybernetics,
University of Reading, Whiteknights, Berks,
England.

Banathy, Bela H., Far West Laboratory for Educa-
tional Research and Development, 1955 Folsom
Street, San Francisco, California 94103, USA.
Bandler, William, Department of Mathematics,
University of Essex, Colchester, England.
Ben-Eli, Michael U., General Systems Research,
Inc., 345 East 86 Street, New York, New
York 10028, USA.
Broekstra, Gerrit, Graduate School of Manage-
ment, Poortweg 6-8, Delft, The Netherlands.
Buchberger, Bruno, Lehrkanzel für Mathematik,
Johannes Kepler University, A-4045 Linz,
Austria.

Cavallo, Roger E., Department of Systems Science,
School of Advanced Technology, State Univer-
sity of New York, Binghamton, New York
13901, USA.
Chakraborty, Samir, Engineering Department, New
Brunswick Telephone Co. Ltd., 22 Prince
William Street, St. John, N.B., Canada.

DeGreene, Kenyon B., University of Southern
California, Los Angeles, California 90007,
USA.
Destouches, J. L., Université Pierre et Marie
Curie, 75230 Paris, France.

Elstob, C. M., Brunel University, Uxbridge,
Middlesex, England.
Espejo, R., University of Aston, Birmingham,
England.

Fevrier, Paulette, Université Pierre et Marie
Curie, 75230 Paris, France.

Gage, W. L., School of Management, London,
England.
Gagliano, Ross A., Georgia Institute of Tech-
nology, Atlanta, Georgia 30332, USA.
Gigch, John P. van, School of Business and
Public Administration, California State
University, Sacramento, California 95819,
USA.
Glanville, Ranulph, The Architectural Association,
School of Architecture, 34-36 Bedford Square,
London WC1B 3ES, England.

Haefner, James, College of Natural Resources,
Utah State University, Logan, Utah 84322,
USA.
Hanson, O. J., The City University, Business
School, London EC1M 7BB, England.
Hernandez-Chavez, F. J., Department of Cybernetics,
Brunel University, Uxbridge, Middlesex,
England.
Hirsch, Helmut, Federal Ministry for Trade and
Industry, 1010 Vienna, Austria.
Hough, Robbin R., School of Economics and Manage-
ment, Oakland University, Rochester, Michigan
48063, USA.
Huska, A. M., Building Economics and Organization
Institute, Bratislava, Czechoslovakia.

Jacak, Witold, Technical University of Wroclaw,
Wroclaw, Poland.
Johnson, L., Department of Cybernetics, Brunel
University, Uxbridge, Middlesex, England.
Jones, Alwyn H., The City University, Business
School, London EC1M 7BB, England.

Karayalcin, I. Ilhami, Faculty of Mechanical
Engineering, Technical University of Istanbul,
Gumossuyo, Istanbul, Turkey.
Klir, George J., Department of Systems Science,
School of Advanced Technology, State Univer-
sity of New York, Binghamton, New York
13901, USA.
Krippendorff, Klaus H., The Annenberg School of
Communication, 3620 Walnut Street, University
of Pennsylvania, Philadelphia, Pennsylvania
19174, USA.

Lebkowski, K. S., Georgia Institute of Technology,
Atlanta, Georgia 30332, USA.
Locker, A., University of Technology, Vienna,
Austria.
Lowen, Walter, Department of Systems Science,
School of Advanced Technology, State Univer-
sity of New York, Binghamton, New York 13901,
USA.

Malik, Fredmund, Management Center, St. Gallen
Graduate School for Economics, St. Gallen,
Switzerland.
Mayon-White, Bill, The Open University, Milton-
Keynes, England.
Mitchell, P. David, Concordia University, 1455
Maisonneuve Blvd. West, Montreal H3G 1M8,
Quebec, Canada
Mulej, Matjaz, Faculty of Economics and Commerce,
University of Maribor, Yugoslavia.

Nurmi, Hannu, Department of Political Science, University of Turku, Aurakatu 14B, SF-20100 Turku 10, Finland.

Pask, Gordon, Systems Research Ltd., 2 Richmond Hill, Richmond, Surrey, England.

Pavlidou, M., Ministry of Public Works, 67 Tsimiskistr. 67, Thessaloniki, Greece.

Priese, Lutz, Fachgebiet Systemtheorie und Systemtechnik, Abteilung Raumplanung, Universität Dortmund, Postfach 500500, 46 Dortmund, Federal Republic of Germany.

Quatember, Bernhard, Lehrkanzel für Systemtheorie, Johannes Kepler University, A-4045 Linz, Austria.

Reuver, H. A., Twenty University of Technology, Enschede, The Netherlands.

Revell, Norman, The City University, Business School, London EC1M 7BB, England.

Rudnick, Hans H., 112 Dogswood Lane, Carterville, Illinois 62918, USA.

Schmutzer, M. E. A., University of Vienna, Austria.

Shaw, Mildred L. G., Brunel University, Uxbridge, Middlesex, England.

Spear, R. G., The Open University, Milton-Keynes, England.

Staudigl, Peter, Technical University of Vienna, Austria.

Stolliday, Ivor, School of Business and Public Administration, California State University, Sacramento, California 95819, USA.

Tchon, Krystof, Technical University of Wroclaw, Wroclaw, Poland.

Watt, J., University of Aston, Birmingham, England.

Wedde, Horst, Institut für Information System-forschung, GMD, D-5205 St. Augustine 1, Federal Republic of Germany.

Willmer, M. A. P., Manchester Business School, Manchester M15 6PB, England.

Zehetner, Wolfgang, Federal Ministry for Trade and Industry, 1010 Vienna, Austria.

Preface

The European Meetings on Cybernetics and Systems Research have become something of a tradition since the first such event was organized by the Austrian Society for Cybernetic Studies in Vienna at Easter 1972, followed by similar meetings in 1974 and 1976. For 1978 the timing remained the same but, following a suggestion "to go to the country" for a change, Linz was chosen as the venue where the Johannes Kepler University cooperated by making appropriate facilities available.

More than 150 scientists from all over the world met there at Easter 1978 to work on current themes in cybernetics and systems research through formal presentations and discussion. The meeting also carried on a tradition which has characterized these meetings all along by fostering discussions among individuals both personally and jointly on social occasions. Some of these occasions were sponsored by the Governor of Upper Austria and the municipality of Linz, as well as by the Society.

The written report of the Linz meeting is again being published as for previous meetings (except the 1972 event taken care of by TRAN-SCRIPTA, London) by Hemisphere Publishing Corporation, Washington, D.C., to whom we are indebted for their positive and always helpful cooperation.

This seventh volume contains the contributions to the three Symposia:

GENERAL SYSTEMS METHODOLOGY
    Chairman: George J. Klir, U.S.A.
ORGANIZATION AND MANAGEMENT
    Chairman: F. de P. Hanika, Austria
COGNITION AND LEARNING
    Chairman: Gordon Pask, U.K.

As each of these Symposia carries its own introduction by the Chairman, there is no need to comment on them here.

There is call, however, to thank in this Preface all those who came from far afield to help make this conference the success which we have reason to believe participants rated it. At any rate, quite a number have notified their intention to participate once again at the meeting scheduled for Easter 1980 in Vienna.

Franz R. Pichler
F. de P. Hanika

PATRONS

Dr. Hertha Firnberg
Federal Minister of Science and Research

Dr. Josef Ratzenböck
Governor of Upper Austria

Franz Hillinger
Mayor of the City of Linz

CHAIRMAN

Franz Pichler
Austrian Society of Cybernetic Studies
Professor of Systems Theory, University of Linz

SPONSORS

Bundesministerium für Wissenschaft und Forschung
Linzer Hochschulfonds

PROGRAMME COMMITTEE

A. Adam (Austria)
H. Blomberg (Finland)
G. Broekstra (Netherland)
W. Güttinger (FRG)
F. de P. Hanika (UK)
G. Klir (USA)
P. K. M'Pherson (UK)
J. Milsum (Canada)
J. G. Miller (USA)
G. Pask (UK)

M. Peschel (GDR)
F. Pichler (Austria)
G. Reber (Austria)
L. Ricciardi (Italy)
N. Rozsenich (Austria)
R. Trappl (Austria)
T. Vamos (Hungary)
L. Zadeh (USA)
G. de Zeeuw (Netherland)

ORGANIZING COMMITTEE

I. Chang   J. Faffelberger   M. Günther   A. de P. Hanika   F. de P. Hanika   K. H. Kellermayr
C. Langhammer   I. Neumann   W. Ottendörfer   F. Pichler   B. Quatember   E. Reischl

PROGRESS IN CYBERNETICS AND SYSTEMS RESEARCH
Volume VII

General Systems Methodology
Organization and Management
Cognition and Learning

KEYNOTE INTRODUCTION

Systemic versus morphological approach in general system theory

RENÉ THOM
Paris, France

A System may be given two kinds of definitions: The first one is the algebraic, combinatorial one: a System is a set of elements interacting between themselves. The second is the morphological one: a system S is the part of the world contained in a specific domain D of space-time.

Both definitions have advantages and drawbacks. The second is in principle more precise, and localization in space-time is, for any entity, a good criterion for its identifiability. But it has the inconvenience of excluding "abstract" systems; for instance, an "economy" would be difficult to define in terms of spatio-temporal events alone. The first definition allows for "abstract" systems but raises, from a logical point of view, the suspicion of being tautological. For what is an element, if not a subsystem? To define this subsystem, one would have to introduce elements of second order, and so on ad infinitum. To be self-contained, the systemic approach has to start with well-defined elements (anagkê sthênai!); in most examples, these elements are spatio-temporally defined: they may be molecules or atoms in Physical Sciences, cells in Biology, of human individuals in Social Sciences. This inconsistency in the definition of system raises, in the systemic approach, a lot of difficulties to be considered later.

From the mathematical viewpoint, the systemic approach leads to a rather sketchy theory. Let (e_i) be the elements of our system (S); associate to any (e_i) a point c_i; if the element (e_i) acts on the element (e_j), draw an oriented edge $c_i \longrightarrow c_j$; we obtain that way an oriented graph (G), the graph of (S). The only mathematical construction to be applied to such an object is the following: define among the vertices of (G) an equivalence relation, as follows: $c_i \sim c_j$ if there exists an oriented path in G starting from c_i and ending at c_j, and if there exists an analogous inverse path leading from c_j to c_i. Denote by $[c_i]$ the equivalence class of the vertex c_i. It is easy to see that these equivalence classes [c] form themselves an oriented graph: draw an edge $a \longrightarrow b$ if there exists an oriented path joining a representative of a to a representative of b; such a graph $\hat{G}$ is then a tree; for if there would be a path in $\hat{G}$ leading from a representative of b to a representative of a, then a and b would define the same class in G. Hence this construction, which in some sense is nothing but Birkhoff's definition of wandering and non-wandering points, extracts out of (G) all of its irreversibility content: if $a < b$ in $\hat{G}$, then any element in a has some influence on an element of b, whereas no element of b can act on an element of a. See, for instance,

P. Delattre [1]. To get more precise mathematical structures, one has to make assumptions how to describe the "states" of the elements, and the mathematical nature of the actions $e_i \rightarrow e_j$. We shall come back later on the systemic formalism.

1. THE MORPHOLOGICAL APPROACH

Here the system (S) to be studied is this part of space contained in a domain (D) of Euclidian space. Many people require from a system that it should have a certain autonomy with respect to the outside universe, i.e. its temporal evolution should be relatively insensitive to perturbations coming from outside. This leads to considering that the system (S) should be enclosed in a box: the boundary of the domain (D) has to consist of fairly impermeable walls, which separate the inside of (D) from the perturbating influences from outside. There are many reasons not to accept this requirement; as we shall see later, a system is never completely independent from us, human observers (if it was, we had better to forget about it . . .); hence the walls of D have to be provided with windows, through which we may act on the system or, conversely, receive information about its inner state. This justifies introducing the notion of Input and Output of the system, or -- in slightly different terms -- of control parameters and of observables. If we accept the introduction of such notions as Input and Output, then there is no longer any necessity to enclose our system in a box. In fact, in the Catastrophe-theoretic approach, one admits that the boundary of D may be entirely fictitious; provided one can control with sufficient accuracy the fluxes (matter and energy) across the boundary D, then one is entitled to take these fluxes as Input and Output to the system. In the original form of Catastrophe Theory (the one which appeared in my book [2]), I considered in fact the spatio-temporal localization of (D) as the only "control" parameter of the system (spatio-temporal localization is obviously also an observable). The true -- nonspatial - observables could be described by a vector y in an auxiliary Euclidean space Y. This space being supposed independent from the boundary of D, unnecessary the global appearance of the totality of these systems generated by varying D, may be defined as follows: if E is Euclidean space, the global observable is a section of the bundle projection $p : E \times Y \rightarrow E$, this section may not be continuous (and thus defines natural walls in E).

From this viewpoint, this general catastrophe-theoretic approach is nothing but classical field theory (on space E).

The morphogenetic approach gives spatio-temporal coordinates a paramount importance; it may be that such an emphasis on space-time has no justification for the problem considered. But, in such a case, the methodology inspired by the catastrophe-theory of first type will have to be applied to other spaces, for instance the Input space U of our system. To explain that, we have to consider also two kinds of approaches for describing systems:

2. THE INTRINSIC ("IMMANENT") APPROACH

Here one supposes that the system studied is wholly transparent as a mathematical object, provided with its own explicit evolution law. The paradigm of this modellization is of course the classical mechanical system; its states are parameterized by the points of a smooth manifold S; and its (autonomous) evolution may be described by a differential system

$$ds/dt = F(s)$$

The observer identifies himself (w.r. to the system) as an omniscient God, who, having created the system with its own law, is no longer able to act on it; this is the situation described by classical Laplacean determinism.

3. THE EXTRINSIC (PHENOMENOLOGICAL) APPROACH

Here the system (S) is a "black box"; the observer knows something about (S) by feeding inputs into it, and observing outputs.

Let us admit that the input, at a given time t, is a vector $u(t)$ of some vector space U, the output being also a vector $y(t)$ of another vector space Y. Let us admit -- to simplify the matter -- that time is discrete and takes only integral values. The observer is able to choose arbitrarily the sequence $u(t)$ of inputs; he then observes the corresponding sequence $y(t)$ of outputs. Such a composed sequence $(u(t),y(t))$ will be called an history of the system. Each history defines a cloud of points in the product space $U \times Y$; by varying the input sequence $u(t)$, one may get an arbitrary large number of histories, hence we may construct a huge cloud of points in $U \times Y$.

It may happen (in fact, it is often the case) that the cloud of points exhibits some asymptotic properties. When one continues to add to it new histories, its density may, for instance, tend towards a probability distribution $m(u,y)$ independent from the sequence of inputs $u(t)$. In such a situation, the statistician may well feel satisfied with the knowledge of the limit distribution $m(u,y)$; if one knows $u = u_0$, one may derive a probability distribution $m(u_0,y)$ for the corresponding output; this is the general philosophy of the "frequentist" interpretation of probability, which is grounded on the belief that future has no reason to be different from past . . .

But Science cannot be satisfied with such an attitude; if man cannot hope to reach the absolute knowledge of Laplacean determinism -- incompatible, in fact, with his own free will -- he can nevertheless try to find local explanations of deterministic type, involving a deterministic model depending on the input he chooses. The ideal is to find, for a system (S) having Input space U, and Output space Y, an inner state space S, with an evolution law of type:

$$(oo) \quad \begin{aligned} ds/dt &= F(s;u(t)) \\ y(t) &= G(s(t);u(t)) \end{aligned}$$

where F and G are smooth maps $F:S \times U \to T_*S$, $G:S \times U \to Y$, T_*S tangent bundle to S.

In that respect, such a model incorporates the basic features of both approaches; constructing such a model from the data in $U \times Y$ given by the histories of the system is the task of the interpretative (hermeneutic) theory which is undoubtedly the final aim of Catastrophe Theory. I owe this far reaching generalization of my original theory to Christopher Zeeman, who in his models introduced the notion of control parameters, and state variables.

Of course, this "interpretation problem" is not easy. After all, transforming a passive observer into an omniscient God may well appear as a Promethean project, an apparently clear-cut case of what the ancient Greeks called hubris; but Modern Science taught us that the project has been successful -- in some cases, at least. There are phenomena -- those of classical Mechanics and Physics -- where the mechanisms leading to the observed outputs are sufficiently simple that the human mind is perfectly able to simulate them via models of type (oo). Hence one might hope that such a method can be generalized to less simple situations . . .

We are then led to consider the first steps of such a hermeneutic theory. Among the "black boxes", we first find those which have a very simple property: namely those for which the output $y(t)$ is defined uniquely by the corresponding input $u(t)$, irrespective of the past history of the system. We then say that the law $u \to y$ is given by a mapping $H : U \to Y$, for which we may postulate regularity properties (smoothness or analyticity). Such a situation, exemplified by the notion of function, seems to us very familiar; but it is astonishing to recall that such a notion was unknown to Greek Mathematics, it came slowly to maturation through the work of the Italian Algebraists of the XVI Century, unfolded itself through many special cases during the XVII Century, to get its final, modern form, in a 1695 article by Leibnitz; no doubt the appearance of the notion did play a fundamental role in the birth of Modern Science, with Galileo and Newton.

These systems -- for which the input u determines the output y -- may be considered as sheer transmission mechanisms from U to Y (even if these mechanisms may be quite complicated). Hence, for such systems, there is no need to introduce a state space. But this is an exceptional situation; in general, the value of the output $y(t)$ depends, not only on the corresponding input $u(t)$, but also on the whole past history of the system. As an intermediate case, we may consider those systems with the following property:

4. FINITE TYPE PROPERTY (Ftp)

To any given $u \in U$ there corresponds only a finite set of possible outputs $y \in Y$.

In other words: if we denote C (characteristic) the set of couples $(u(t), y(t))$ for all possible histories in the product $U \times Y$, then the projection $p : U \times Y \rightarrow U$ maps C onto U in such a way that the counter-image $p^{-1}(u) \cap C = c_u$ is always a finite set.

As a result of this hypothesis, if the characteristic C is a smooth submanifold (or more generally, a semi-algebraic or semi-analytic set), then (C) and (U) have the same dimension.

By imposing to the map $p : C \rightarrow U$ some local continuity properties (the local invariance of the total degree of the map $p^{-1}(V) \rightarrow (V)$ at any point of $p(V)$ for any small neighbourhood V in U), some topologists (R. Jerrard [3]) have been able to generalize the notion of mapping to the notion of an M-map : an M-map $F : X$ to Y has the property that $F^{-1}(y)$ is finite in X for all $y \in Y$, together with the above invariance of degree; M-mappings form a category, and it can be proved that M-homotopy classes of M-maps $F : S^n \rightarrow K$ to a polyhedron K naturally form a group, which is isomorphic to the standard homology group $H_n(K)$. Hence this notion appears as a natural generalization of the notion of map.

Let S be an Euclidean space of dimension N; let $W : U \times S \rightarrow R$ be a smooth proper real-valued function. It can be proved that for "almost" all W, the set -- denoted by Q -- in $U \times S$ defined by the vanishing of $\text{grad}_S W$, has the property that the projecting map $h : S \times U \rightarrow U$ restricted to (Q) is an M-map, having the Ftp property. This set Q is in that case a smooth submanifold of $U \times S$, of dimension equal to dimension of U.

Let us then admit that our System has (S) as state space, and that the dynamic in S is given by

$$ds/dt = - \text{grad}_S W(s;u)$$

u being fixed. The system reaches an equilibrium position given by a minimum of W; because W is proper, for any w, there are only a finite number of minima (generic, non degenerate) of W. Hence, for any u, the system has to choose among a finite set of possible stable equilibria, hence, for any observable $g(s;u)$, for a finite set of possible values. This is the framework of the so-called elementary Catastrophe Theory, which is now fairly well-known.

By imposing for any $u \in U$ a specific rule for the choice of the corresponding equilibrium (minimum of W), one is able to describe the topological structure of the set of points where some jumps occur from one minimum to another; these correspond to the so-called catastrophe points in U. There are two basic rules for that: either the "perfect delay rule", which states that an equilibrium remains valid when u varies as long as it does not become unstable by bifurcation; or "Maxwell's rule", which states that the dominating equilibrium above u is the point minimizing W on C_u. In both cases, one can describe the stable configurations of the catastrophe locus in U.

Of course, the hypothesis that the state dynamic is a gradient dynamic is a very restrictive one. But the Ftp hypothesis is somewhat more general; for instance if the state space S is compact, and if the dynamics F on S is structurally stable, then F can have only a finite number of attractors. If one averages any g function $U \times S \rightarrow R$ on such attractors, one gets only a finite number of possible outputs. The problem of describing the generic bifurcations between such attractors is mathematically difficult, but it is to be expected that the configurations found in E.C.T. may still keep some validity in this more general case.

What happens when the Ftp hypothesis is not satisfied? In such a case, the cloud of points in $U \times Y$ may be quite extended: the limit probability measure may have a support with nonempty interior. To get an idea about the internal mechanisms of (S), it is worthwhile, first, to play with the history input $u(t)$; experimentation may reveal critical histories, a small variation of which may lead to considerable variation in the output; such a search may greatly help to find the "catastrophe sets" in U, if there are any. In that respect, before attempting any statistical treatment, first look at your cloud of points, and try to identify its obvious morphological accidents: boundaries, folds, corners, cusps, etc. It should be observed that this methodology goes in the reverse direction of the standard statistical interpretation. In general statisticians interpret a cloud of points as arising through:

Deterministic Law + Noise

Here I advocate to interpret them by:

Noise seen through a deterministic law

the total effect being eventually blurred by secondary noise . . . Let, for instance, A_{u_0} be an attractor of the state dynamic for $u = u_0$, ergodic and mixing; suppose A_{u_0} is carried by a smooth manifold. Then any ^{0} observable mapping g, restricted to A_{u_0}, will have singularities, and their images ^{0} in $Y_g(\Sigma A_u)$ (critical values of $g|A_{u_0}$) will, in principle, carry an infinite density. Hence, they should be recognizable easily, despite local blurring due to secondary noise, or to some underlying quantum effects (like in Optics). If u varies, then we shall get in Y the envelope of all these sets $g(\Sigma(A_u))$.

These ideas, which I did propose for the statistical interpretation of clouds of points (or probability distributions) have not been accepted -- up to now -- by specialists; this may be due -- to a large extent -- to the artificial nature of the substrate space of statistical data -- where each coordinate axis has a specific meaning, and the notion of a group intermingling the coordinates has little relevance. But I feel confident that in the interpretation of more "natural" data, as in Geology, Geomorphology . . . etc., such methods may be very valuable.

5. RELATIONS BETWEEN THE SYSTEMIC AND THE MORPHOLOGICAL APPROACHES

Let us now come back to the systemic approach;

it may happen that the "systemic" analysis arises precisely from a morphological exploration of the system. The elements appear as isolated clumps (generally topological balls) connected by thread-like structures like wires, pipes...able to transmit fluxes from one element to another. In front of such a pattern, it is tempting to translate directly this spatial organization into a combinatorial graph of interacting elements. Such a description may be quite legitimate for structures built by human technology, where the connecting function -- like a telephone line -- of the "threadlike" structures is obvious. But for natural structures (in particular biological structures), more caution is necessary.

Putting together the "black box" approach, and the "systemic" description, one is led to the following general scheme: to any element (e_i) there corresponds a black box B_i, having Input space U_i and Output space Y_i; to any arrow connecting e_i to e_j, there is associated a map g_j^i from Y_i to U_j. If the evolution law of each element is known, according to a system of type (oo), then it is theoretically possible to extract from the reunion of these individual laws, plus the relations g_j^i a global evolution differential system for the whole structure. Here of course time may be discrete or continuous, according to need. That such a system is in general mathematically intractable is shown by the following simple example: suppose we have only one element, with no inner memory (state space), hence characterized by a map $G : U \to Y$ from Input space to Output space; suppose we create now -- with discrete time -- a feedback loop defined by a map $h : Y \to U$; then the dynamic of the system will be defined by iteration of the composed map $U \xrightarrow{Gh} U$. If such a map is smooth, one knows the difficulties of the problem, to determine the asymptotic regime of such a dynamic (strange attractors are defined that way, like the Hénon attractor). This primitive example shows how weak is the hope to have a model amenable to computation, if drastic hypotheses are not made on the nature of the elements and their interactions. (For instance, linear formalism...)

One could also imagine other complications for this scheme; for instance, one could have _global control parameters_ acting on the connexions g_j^i at the disposal of the macroscopic observer, or it could happen that the g_j^i may themselves depend on the inner states of the elements e_i, e_j.

As a continuous system is in general difficult to compute, most algorithms for computing a solution rely on a "discretization" of the system; one divides the substrate spaces into cells separated by ficitious walls, and one associates to each cell a "black box" (e_i). Here connexions g_j^i occur between contiguous elements. This is the principle of the so-called _finite element method_ in Applied Mathematics. Of course, convergence of the algorithm toward an effective solution when the diameter of the elements tends to zero may lead to tricky problems. The coordinate q of a wall between elements may also be considered as a control and input parameters for the limiting elements e_i, e_j; hence one has in general to require that the $g_j^i : q_i \to q_j$ be diffeomorphisms; if these diffeomorphisms had to depend on the inner states of the elements (for instance described by momenta coordinates p), one could obtain that way some possible way to interpret quantum indeterminacy...

Of course, in such examples, all elements have similar properties, which lead to better computational possibilities. This requirement, that elements are all alike, or belong to a few classes, seems to be necessary to have a manageable model. This is the case of systems of transformations used in chemical kinetics, and also in population theory. Except for these cases, where the underlying quantitative interactions are fairly simple, it is not obvious that the systemic approach has much predictive power.

At first glance, the data of the graph (G) of interactions in a system seems to bring a good understanding for the behaviour of the global system. In fact, this knowledge may be perfectly useless and illusory; this is often the case for biological systems; in Embryology, for instance, the embryo exhibits -- at a very early stage -- such huge regulative abilities that it may reconstruct itself after a through mixing of its cells. Such a behaviour of cells may be understood only if we admit that each individual cell has an inner template of the structure of the whole organism; in that respect, the element -- the cell -- may be considered as complex as the global organism itself. In such a case, the discrete systemic approach has certainly less relevance than the search for pertinent morphogenetic gradients. The theoretical stagnation of brain neurophysiology with respect to understanding mental processes is a clear-cut instance where the knowledge of the anatomy of a system is of little help to understand its physiology...

In some sense, the graph (G) of interacting elements brings information only if it is incomplete, i.e. if some arrows $e_j \to e_k$ are missing. In that case, one could try to generate the given graph by a smooth "catastrophic" procedure, on the model I gave for linguistic graphs [2] (predation graph, excision graph, etc.). In front of any such graph, it is always interesting to get back from the static observed structure to the dynamical process of its ontogenesis. Another approach consists, for any couple of elements e_i, e_j to measure by a positive scalar d_{ij} the relative strength of their reciprocal interactions. Then one could try to imbed the graph G in a finite dimensional Euclidean space E in such a way that the distance between the vertices c_i, c_j is measured by d_{ij}^{-1}; if it could happen that the graph G embeds in an intermediate low dimensional manifold, M, then this could give us a satisfactory of insight about the "deep" structure of the system, allowing to define meaningful perturbations or bifurcations of the system.

As a general conclusion, one should not be biased and reject a priori the discrete systemic, nor the smooth morphological approaches. Both may in fact help to a better modellization. As a general rule, discretization is necessary for computing, hence for quantitative prediction, whereas morphological - catastrophe theoretic methods may provide more intuition and global understanding -- without having, by themselves, any predictive power. The important point is not to express too many hopes on the power of such general methods; practical efficiency is always -- as one can judge -- limited to situations where one has "a priori" an exact quantitative model, such as the situations entirely described by mechanical and physical laws. This is the so-called miracle of Physics, and in no case should we extrapolate the validity of such models beyond their natural boundaries.

REFERENCES

1. DELATTRE, P., L'evolution des systêmes moléculaires, Malousie, Paris, 1971.
2. THOM, R., Stabilitê Structurelle et Morphogénèse, Intereditions, Paris, 1972.
3. MEYERSON, M. and R. JENARD, Homotropy with M-functions, Preprint.

GENERAL SYSTEMS METHODOLOGY

Introduction

GEORGE J. KLIR
School of Advanced Technology, State University of New York
Binghamton, New York USA

The Symposium on General Systems Methodology has become associated with the European Meetings on Cybernetics and Systems Research. Since 1972, the symposium has been a clear indicator of the status and trends in general systems methodology.

One topic that clearly dominated the 1978 symposium was the problem of reconstructability of multidimensional relations from their appropriate projections. Several papers discussing various aspects of the problems were presented by Broekstra, Krippendorff, Cavallo and Klir during the first session of the symposium. Different terms were used such as "structure identification," "constraint analysis," "spectral analysis," or "reconstructability analysis," but these authors were basically talking about the same problems with different viewpoints and emphasis.

The sentiment during the discussion involving these papers was that the problem is very important but, unfortunately, has been neglected by model-makers for a long time; although many models developed in various areas of social science, ecology, and the like are based on the assumption that the whole can be reconstructed from the knowledge of its parts (projections of the overall relation), no justification for the validity of this assumption is usually given.

The remaining papers presented in the symposium were less related and included descriptions of two new systems theories: a theory of infringements (Wedde) and a theory of eventistic systems (Jacak and Tchon); an exploratory study of the use of generative grammars in systems methodology (Haefner); computer oriented studies by Buchberger (investigations of universal models) and Priese (simulation of concurrent systems); and an attempt to characterize epistemological foundations for systems methodology (Van Gigch and Stolliday).

Two methods of constraint analysis

GERRIT BROEKSTRA
Graduate School of Management, Delft, The Netherlands

1. INTRODUCTION

It would appear that W. Ross Ashby has often been concerned with the natural connection between algebraic set and probabilistic information theoretical methods. He alluded to the relationship between the two theories on many occasions. For example, in his article on "The Set Theory of Mechanism and Homeostasis" [20], he stated that "one final advantage of the method (of set theory) is that it is ready at every stage to admit the various measures of the 'quantity of information', such as those of Shannon and McGill and Garner." Ashby himself made important contributions to the theory of the 'quantity of information' [15,17], which he regarded as being "basically just counting" [15], thus joining naturally to set theory.

I have been using the methods of information theory in connection with problems of searching for structure in systems of data, in particular, as posed by the hierarchy of epistemological levels of systems as devised by George J. Klir [2-10,21]. It was shown that probabilistic methods of constraint analysis could be applied successfully to the problem of structure identification. An interesting parallel of this type of research was indicated pertaining to the multivariate analysis of qualitative data from panel studies [7], where the data are in the form of cross-classifications.

It is the purpose of this paper to explore the compatibility of a non-probabilistic method of constraint analysis with these previous results. The constraint analysis of many-dimensional relations was developed to some extent by Ashby [1]. He used set theory and developed the important tool of p-th order cylindrical closure of a relation. In this paper I carried the development of set theoretical constraint analysis somewhat further by using the results of the probabilistic method as an analogy. The key notions which initiated the idea contained in this paper are the notion of a structure system as proposed by Klir [9,10] and its representation by means of elemental constraints as proposed by this author [8]. In Section 2 we intend to show the strong analogy between some fundamental concepts of set theory and information theory, such as variety, variability, independence, and constraint. Section 3 first reviews the (non)probabilistic concepts connected with the decomposition of the total constraint of a system (relation) into degrees of complexity. The second part of Section 3 contains the basic idea of this paper. It argues the plausibility of reconstructing a many-dimensional relation by intersection of lower-dimensional cylinders pertaining to elements of a

structure system only. In Section 4, a particular example of the identification of a structure system by both methods is discussed at some length. The results are quite remarkable and appear to have some interesting implications for practical research problems in discrete multivariate analysis, such as the problems associated with empty cells in multiway contingency tables, the definitions of (higher-order) interactions, and, in general, the importance of developing non-probabilistic methods of multivariate analysis, the necessity of which was recently urged by Kendall [22]. The latter issues are alluded to in Section 5.

2. VARIETY, VARIABILITY, CONSTRAINT

We commence by introducing the basic concepts of variety, variability, independence, and constraint. In his AN INTRODUCTION TO CYBERNETICS, Ashby considered the concept of variety of fundamental importance to his subject. He defined variety as the number of distinct elements of a set [11]:

Thus, if the order of occurrence is ignored, the set
    c,b,c,a,c,c,a,b,c,b,b,a
which contains twelve elements, contains only three <u>distinct</u> elements
    a,b, and c.
Such a set will be said to have a variety of three elements.

The concept of variety is a property of the set, and thus has little meaning for the individual elements.

If the number of distinct elements of a set S is denoted by N, the variety will be denoted by

var S = N .

Instead of obtaining a measure of variety by simple counting, one may also use the logarithm to the base 2 of N, denoted by lvar, as a measure of logarithmic variety, i.e.,

$$\text{lvar } S = \log N \qquad (1)$$

where, henceforward, it is assumed that the logarithm has base 2. Its unit is then the 'bit'.

Let X be a discrete variable which takes on values in a finite set $X = \{x_1, x_2, \ldots, x_N\}$. Here we will not be concerned with some (empirical)

13

meaning of X. Also, no metric is assumed over the set X. In order to bring out the abstract nature of X, we will usually specify the x_i's as elements of the set of nonnegative integers.

With a view to the probability model, which we will discuss later on, one may think of X as a discrete random variable which is defined as a function with the totality of conceivable outcomes (the sample space) of a random experiment as domain and the set of nonnegative integers as its counterdomain [12]. For example, let the experiment be the repeated tossing of a single coin. The sample space Ω contains two possible outcomes, Ω = {head, tail}. An equivalent set may be defined by a function X, such that X(head) = 1 and X(tail) = 0. As a matter of fact, X is a random variable, denoting the number of heads, with value set X = {0,1}. (Though somewhat loosely, the latter notation is preferred; actually, the set {0,1} is the range of the function X.) The variety of X, var X, equals 2 elements, or alternatively, lvar X = 1 bit.

Since we are usually interested in experiments with more than one variable, we consider n joint discrete (random) variables $X_1, X_2, \ldots, X_n$. An n-dimensional variable $X \equiv (X_1, X_2, \ldots, X_n)$ is assumed to take on values $(x_1, x_2, \ldots, x_n)$, or, in abbreviated form, $(x_i)_{i \in I}$, which is composed of one element x_i from each set X_i, where i is an element of the index set I, in an n-dimensional nonnegative integer space, defined by the Cartesian product $X = X_1 \times X_2 \times \ldots \times X_n$, or, briefly, $X = \prod_{i \in I} X_i$ (I = {1,2,\ldots,n}).

If the component variables could assume values independently, the variety of X would yield

$$\text{var } X = \prod_{i=1}^{n} \text{var } X_i \tag{2}$$

or, logarithmically,

$$\text{lvar } X = \sum_{i=1}^{n} \text{lvar}_i .$$

If, for example, the three lamps of a traffic light $X \equiv (X_1, X_2, X_3)$, where X_1, X_2, X_3 = {0,1} ('0' means unlit, and '1' lit) stand for Red, Yellow and Green lamps, respectively, could vary independently, eight distinct values of X could appear, i.e., var X = 8, or lvar X = 3 bits. Alternatively, Equation (2) may be conceived of as a (non-stochastic) definition of (joint) independence of n variables.

In most cases, however, an n-dimensional or n-ary relation, denoted by $R(X_1, X_2, \ldots, X_n)$ or, briefly, as R(X) is defined between the constituent variables of the n-dimensional space as a subset of the product-set $X = \prod_{i \in I} X_i$, i.e.,

$$R(X) \equiv R(X_1, X_2, \ldots, X_n) \subset \prod_{i \in I} X_i .$$

So a relation is the set of those n-tuples $(x_i)_{i \in I}$ that satisfy the relation [1]. In most cases of interest, viz., where R(X) is a proper subset of X, the var R(X) will be smaller than the var X, or

$$\text{var } R(X) \leq \text{var } \prod_{i \in I} X_i . \tag{3}$$

Assuming, for example, a Dutch traffic light, one will find that only three out of eight combinations are actually realized, that is,

$$R(X) = \{(1,0,0), (0,1,0), (0,0,1)\}$$

and, consequently, var R(X) = 3. Apparently, the lamps do not vary independently, since var R(X) is less than var X = 8.

This deviation of independence will be termed total constraint, denoted by $D(X_1, X_2, \ldots, X_n)$, or briefly by D(X). It is defined as a subset of X, i.e.,

$$D(X) = \prod_{i \in I} X_i - R(X)$$

which means the set of elements that is in X but not in R(X). The intensity of the constraint introduced by the relation R(X) is, of course, measured by the number (or the logarithm of the number) of distinct elements in D(X), that is, by its variety. However, in order to avoid confusion we will speak of the cardinality, denoted by card D(X), of the constraint, which commonly stands for the number of distinct elements in the set D(X). The intensity of the relation's total constraint is then given by

$$\text{card } D(X) = \prod_{i \in I}^{n} \text{var } X_i - \text{var } R(X) . \tag{4}$$

When R(X) = X the constraint is zero, i.e., D(X) = $\emptyset$, var D(X) = 0; as R(X) shrinks, so does the constraint become more intense. In our example of the traffic light, the intensity of the constraint equals 2x2x2-3 = 5 elements.

The concept of constraint was introduced by Ashby as "a relation between two sets, and occurs when the variety that exists under one condition is less than the variety that exists under another" [11]. The 'one condition' here is identified with that of independence and the 'other' with the actual relation. It is clear that D(X) is itself an n-ary relation in set theoretical sense, i.e., D(X) $\subset$ X.

So far, we have been concerned with the value set of one or more (random) variables, for which we defined the concepts of variety and constraint. We will now turn to the probabilistic counterparts of these fundamental concepts, by assuming a probability space for which a (joint) discrete density function is defined. Let us start again with one discrete random variable X with a finite range or value set X = $\{x_1, x_2, \ldots, x_N\}$, and a discrete density or probability function

$$f(x_i) \quad (i = 1, 2, \ldots, N; \quad \sum_{i=1}^{N} f(x_i) = 1) .$$

(Sometimes the notation $p(x_i)$ is used instead of $f(x_i)$, which is then reserved for continuous functions; for reasons of clarity we will also use the notation $f_X(x_i)$.)

The concept of variability is defined by the entropy functional

$$H(X) = -\sum_{i=1}^{N} f(x_i) \log f(x_i) \tag{5}$$

measured in bits. It is a property of the probability function and measures the degree of dispersion in the distribution of values. For the sake
of brevity, we will, somewhat loosely, speak of
the variability of the variable X. Its properties
are well known; it is a nonnegative quantity, assuming the value zero iff some $f(x_i) = 1$ ($f(x_j) = 0$,
$j \neq i$; by definition, $0 \log 0 \equiv 0$), while attaining
its maximum value if the x_i's are distributed
equally likely, i.e., $f(x_i) = 1/N$ ($i = 1,2,...,N$),
which yields $H(X) = \log N$. Comparing this latter
result with Equation (1), it is of interest to
note that for such a discrete uniform distribution
of values the more primitive concept of logarithmic
variety is equivalent to the variability concept.
Or, the epithet 'primitive' may be associated with
the state of knowledge about X, being of course
smaller without than with knowledge of the density
function defined on the sample space of X. It is
suggested that the above definitions enable a natural transition between the two states of knowledge.
We will return to this discussion below. As a
final remark, we note that the entropy function is
usually connected with concepts like uncertainty
and information. Since we are mainly concerned
with multivariate analysis, we prefer to abstain
from reference to the information theoretic meaning
of the concepts involved.

We will extend the definition of variability to
n discrete random variables defined on the same
probability space with an associated joint discrete
density function

$$f(x_i) \underset{i \in I}{} \equiv f(x_1, x_2, ..., x_n) \quad (\underset{i \in I}{\Sigma} f(x_i) = 1)$$

where the summation is over all possible values in
the set $\underset{i \in I}{\Pi} X_i$. We define the joint variability of
the discrete random variable $X \equiv (X_1, X_2, ..., X_n)$ by

$$H(X) \equiv H(X_1, X_2, ..., X_n) = -\underset{i \in I}{\Sigma} f(x_i) \, \log f(x_i) \quad (6)$$

where again the summation is performed for all
$(x_i)_{i \in I} \in \underset{i \in I}{\Pi} X_i$.

It is a well-known result that, in general,

$$H(X) \leq \overset{n}{\underset{i=1}{\Sigma}} H(X_i)$$

where $H(X_i)$ may be referred to as a marginal variability. The equality sign is valid iff the random
variables are jointly independent, i.e.,
$f(x_i)_{i \in I} = f(x_1) f(x_2) ... f(x_n)$ for all possible
values of x_j ($j = 1,2,...,n$). The difference between the joint variability and the sum of the
marginals is thus an indication of the deviation
of probabilistic independence [13] and is called
the joint or total (probabilistic) constraint, denoted by $T(X_1 : X_2 : ... : X_n)$, or, briefly, by $T(X)$,
and defined as

$$T(X) \equiv T(X_1 : X_2 : ... : X_n) = \overset{n}{\underset{i=1}{\Sigma}} H(X_i) - H(X) \quad (7)$$

It is a nonnegative quantity, which is usually regarded as a measure of the amount of structure, organization or law in a system of n variables [14,15].

In information theoretical jargon it is also termed
total transmission.

It is noted that there is some resemblance in
form between the nonprobabilistic identity (4) and
its probabilistic counterpart (7). We may assume
that this occurred to Ashby in developing a non-
probabilistic theory of constraint analysis, because he wrote: "The investigation... was originally undertaken to provide a clear framework for
studies of similar type, leading to a similar 'constraint analysis,' with quantitative methods based
on information theory, the idea being that the
total entropy $H(X_1, X_2, ..., X_n)$ corresponds to the
relation R, the maximal entropy $H(X_1) + ... + H(X_n)$ to
the set X, and the total transmission (their differences) to the constraint X-R" [1].

In the next section we will discuss the two
methods of constraint analysis.

3. CONSTRAINT ANALYSIS

3.1. Decomposition of Complexity

The purpose of this section is to introduce
briefly some concepts related to the decomposition
of the total constraints D(X) and T(X) into degrees
of complexity introduced by a relation (system) of
n variables (for further details one may consult
Ashby [1,15,16] and Broekstra [2-8]).

We commence with a brief review of some set
theoretic concepts. If $J \subset I$, where I is the index set, the projection operator pr_J is defined by
a mapping of $X = \underset{i \in I}{\Pi} X_i$ into $\underset{i \in J}{\Pi} X_i$, such that for
a typical n-tuple $(x_i)_{i \in I}$

$$pr_J (x_i)_{i \in I} = (x_i)_{i \in J} . \quad (8)$$

The projection $pr_J X$ is the set of all $(x_i)_{i \in J} \in$
$\underset{i \in J}{\Pi} X_i$ obtained by application of (8). If
$R(X) \subset \underset{i \in I}{\Pi} X_i$, then $pr_J R(X)$, $J \subset I$, is the set
of all those elements of $\underset{i \in J}{\Pi} X_i$ which appear in
$R(X)$, i.e.,

$$(x_i)_{i \in I} \in R(X) \rightarrow (x_i)_{i \in J} \in pr_J R(X) . \quad (9)$$

For the traffic light example we had the relation
$R(X) = \{(0,0,1), (0,1,0), (1,0,0)\}$. If $J = \{i\}$
($i = 1,2,3$) we find

$$pr_i R(X) = \{0,1\}$$

omitting the brackets (and comma's) in the subscript
notation, while for $J = \{i,j\}$ ($i < j$, $i,j = 1,2,3$),
the projection yields

$$pr_{ij} R(X) = \{(0,0), (0,1), (1,0)\} .$$

The second set operator which we will need is the
spreading or inverse projection operator pr_i^{-1},
which, when acting on a typical element $(x_i)_{i \in J}$,
$J \subset I$, will give all those elements in X that have
$(x_i)_{i \in J}$ as their components in J; thus

$$pr_i^{-1} (x_i)_{i \in J} = \{(x_i)_{i \in J}\} \times \underset{i \in I-J}{\Pi} X_i . \quad (10)$$

Similarly, the inverse projection of a set $B \subset \prod_{i \in J} X_i$ is defined as the set of all elements in X obtained by application of (10) to all $(x_i)_{i \in J} \in B$, i.e.,

$$pr_J^{-1} \; B = B \times \prod_{i \in I-J} X_i \, . \tag{11}$$

If the cardinality of J is equal to p, then the latter set will be termed an '(n-p)-dimensional cylinder' or a 'cylinder having (n-p) dimensions' on the p-dimensional base B.

If in our example we have, for instance, $B = pr_3 \, R(X)$, then it is easily shown that

$$pr_3^{-1} \; pr_3 \; R(X) = X$$

so that all possible eight combinations appear in the inverse projection of $pr_3 \, R(X)$. Likewise, it may be shown that, for instance,

$$pr_{12}^{-1} \; pr_{12} \; R(X) = X - \{(1,1,0), (1,1,1)\}.$$

The cylindrical closure of order p of the relation $R(X) \subset \prod_{i \in I} X_i$, denoted by $C_p R(X)$, is formed by projecting R(X) onto all p-dimensional subspaces of X, and intersecting all cylinders in X having these projections as bases. Thus,

$$C_p R(X) = \bigcap_J pr_J^{-1} \; pr_J \; R(X) \tag{12}$$

is a subset of X, for $p = 1,2,\ldots,n-1$, and card $J = p$, while by definition $C_0 \, R(X) = X$, and $C_n \, R(X) = R(X)$.

It may be shown that generally the sets $C_p \, R(X)$ $(p = 1,2,\ldots,n)$ form a nested set of 'approximations' to R(X), that is,

$$X = C_0 \, R(X) \supset C_1 \, R(X) \supset \ldots \supset C_n R(X) = R(X)$$

Finally, two more quantities may be defined, one of which is termed cylindrance of R(X), denoted by cyl R(X),

$$cyl \; R(X) = \min_p \; (p : C_p \, R(X) = R(X)) \tag{13}$$

and the other, the dimensional scope of R(X), denoted by scp R(X),

$$scp \; R(X) = \max_p \; (p : C_p \, R(X) = X) \tag{14}$$

Applying these concepts to our traffic light example, we find for the first-order cylindrical closure: $C_1 \, R(X) = X$; for the second-order cylindrical closure: $C_2 \, R(X) = R(X) \cup \{(0,0,0)\}$, so that $C_3 \, R(X) = R(X)$. This yields cyl R(X) = 3 and scp R(X) = 1.

By forming the sequence of cylindrical closures of a relation one obtains a decomposition of the relation's complexity. In particular, by defining the interactional constraint or interaction of order m-1 (or the m-factor interaction) as $D_m(X) = C_{m-1}R(X) - C_m R(X)$ $(m = 1,2,\ldots,n)$ the card $D_m(X)$ shows the intensity of constraint due to different degrees of complexity. The zero-order or one-factor 'interaction' $D_1(X) = C_0 R(X) - C_1 R(X)$,

for example, "shows how much of R's constraint is due simply to the fact that R's variables have domains that do not use all that is offered by the sets X_i. This constraint D_1 is thus that due to the properties that R imposes on the variables individually. D_2 shows the extent of R's constraint by binary relations. D_1's effect has been removed, so D_2 shows how much of R's constraint is due to the variables as unique pairs. D_3 shows how much of R's constraint is due to variables acting in triples, over and above the effects due to their actions in pairs; and so on" [1].

It may be shown that the total n-dimensional constraint D(X) is partitioned into the different degrees of complexity $D_m(X)$, $m = 1,2,\ldots,n$, such that,

$$D(X) = \bigcup_{m \in I} D_m(X) \tag{15}$$

$D_i(X) \cap D_j(X) = \emptyset$ $(i \neq j)$. Moreover, the intensity of the constraint is given by

$$card \; D(X) = \sum_{m=1}^{n} \; card \; D_m(X) \, . \tag{16}$$

Our traffic light example yields

$D_1(X) = \emptyset$;   card $D_1(X) = 0$
$D_2(X) = \{(0,1,1),(1,0,1),(1,1,0),(1,1,1)\}$;
                                  card $D_2(X) = 4$
$D_3(X) = \{(0,0,0)\}$;   card $D_3(X) = 1$

while $D(X) = D_1(X) \cup D_2(X) \cup D_3(X) = X - R(X)$, and card D(X) = 0 + 4 + 1 = 5 elements.

We will now deal very briefly with the decompsition of the total probabilistic constraint $T(X) \equiv T(X_1:X_2:\ldots:X_n)$ into different degrees of complexity. Without further proof (see Ashby [15, 17] and Broekstra [2-8]) it may be shown that

$$T(X) = \sum_{i<j} T(X_i:X_j) + \sum_{i<j<k} Q(X_i,X_j,X_k) \tag{17}$$
$$+ \sum_{i<j<k<l} Q(X_i,X_j,X_k,X_l) + \ldots + Q(X)$$

where $Q(X) \equiv Q(X_1,X_2,\ldots,X_n)$, $i<j<k\ldots = 1,2,\ldots,n$. The two-factor or first-order interaction, $T(X_i:X_j)$, as defined by Equation (7), is a measure of the constraint due to variables acting as pairs. The second-order interaction, for example, between X_1, X_2, and X_3, is defined as

$$Q(X_1,X_2,X_3) = T_{X_k}(X_i:X_j) - T(X_i:X_j)$$

where $i < j$; $k \neq i,j$; $i,j,k = 1,2,3$, while the so-called conditional first-order interaction $T_{X_k}(X_i:X_j)$ is obtained by subscripting all terms by X_k in an equation like (7). Similarly, higher-order interactions are defined as, for example,

$$Q(X_1,X_2,X_3,X_4) = Q_{X_1}(X_i,X_j,X_k) - Q(X_i,X_j,X_k)$$

for $i < j < k$; $l \neq i,j,k$; $i,j,k,l = 1,2,3,4$. The summations of two-factor, three-factor, etc., probabilistic interactions may be compared with $D_2(X)$, $D_3(X)$, etc., in Equation (16) respectively, while the summation of the latter may be compared with

the addition of the results of the respective summations in (17). Since the probabilistic decomposition has been applied by this author [3,5] as a
tool for the identification of a structure system,
it would be of interest to study the potential use
of the set theoretical constraint analysis also.
Moreover, the comparative study of the definitions
of interactional constraints may contribute to the
understanding of their respective meanings.

It is of some interest at this stage to discuss
a specific example. It concerns a four-variable
analogy of a three-variable illustration given in
Ashby's article [15]. Four spies (Mr.'s X_1, X_2,
X_3, and X_4) are suspected to conspire. They were
observed to visit on any one day either Amsterdam (A) or Vienna (V). It was ascertained that
the four spies were on any day distributed equally
likely according to the following eight combinations of locations:

X_1:   A   A   A   A   V   V   V
X_2:   A   A   V   V   A   A   V   V
X_3:   A   V   A   V   A   V   A   V
X_4:   A   V   V   A   V   A   A   V

Computations of the joint and marginal variabil-
ities yield $H(X_i) = 1$ bit, $H(X_i,X_j) = 2$ bits,
$H(X_i,X_j,X_k) = H(X_1,X_2,X_3,X_4) = 3$ bits ($i < j < k$;
$i,j,k = 1,2,3,4$). With these results we calculate
for the first-order interactions $T(X_i:X_j) = 0$
($i < j$; $i,j = 1,2,3,4$), i.e., each spy operates
independently of each other spy. Likewise, it is
found that the second-order interactions are equal
to zero, that is $Q(X_i,X_j,X_k) = 0$ ($i < j < k$;
$i,j,k = 1,2,3,4$; that is to say, each spy acts independently of any combination of two other spies.
Finally, $Q(X_1,X_2,X_3,X_4) = 1$ bit, and thus equals
$T(X)$. So all constraint is due to third-order interaction; given the location of any triple, the
location of the fourth spy is uniquely determined.
Hence, the suspicion appeared justified. The set
theoretical method yields analogous results. It
may be shown that the cylindrical closures are
$C_1R(X) = C_2R(X) = C_3R(X) = X$, where X stands for
the unconstrained set of 16 possible combinations.
Finally, $C_4R(X) = R(X)$, so that all constraint $D(X)$
is due to the third-order interaction $D_4(X)$.

Although it is of interest to explore the analogies much further, especially as far as less esoteric examples are concerned, we will abstain from
doing so. The above type of analysis is useful as
a second stage in a constraint analytic approach to
structure identification [6-8]. The first stage of
such an approach is characterized by a different
type of decomposition, i.e., in terms of disjoint
or non-disjoint subsystems. This will be the subject of the next section.

3.2. Structure of a System (Relation)

We will now reverse the order of discussion and
start with some remarks pertaining to the decomposition of the probabilistic total constraint in
terms of constraints of subsystems. At the end of
this section we will formulate some hypotheses as
to the decomposition of the set theoretical total
constraint.

A well-known type of probabilistic decomposition
in subsystems is obtained by partitioning the system
of variables in disjoint subsets [18]. Suppose, for

example, that a four-dimensional variable
$X = (X_1,X_2,X_3,X_4)$ is given. A possible decomposition yields

$$T(X) = T(X_1:X_2) + T(X_3:X_4) + T(X_1,X_2:X_3,X_4).$$

It is shown that the total constraint is composed
of additive combinations of: (i) the constraint
within the subsystem (X_1,X_2), (ii) the constraint
within (X_3,X_4), and (iii) the constraint between
the two subsystems.

The decomposition into subsystems has been extended by this author [7,8] to a more general version pertaining to non-disjoint subsystems. This
method was found particularly useful in connection
with the probabilistic representation of so-called
structure systems. These systems were defined by
Klir [9,10] as a result of establishing a hierarchy
of epistemological levels. Given an n-dimensional
relation with an associated probability function -
which pair is termed a generative system [10] - a
structure system is defined as a set of elements
together with a set of couplings. An element is
defined as a subset of variables which are all
directly related. The notion of a direct relationship may be defined rigorously in terms of probabilistic constraint analytic concepts [3,23].
Couplings between elements are defined as the intersections of the respective element sets. A
structure system may be regarded as an hypothesized
model which is to be tested to see how well it
fits the data (generative system [21]).

Suppose, for example, that a four-variable
structure system of three elements is used:
$E_1 = \{X_1,X_2\}$, $E_2 = \{X_2,X_3\}$, and $E_3 = \{X_2,X_4\}$,
or, in abbreviated notation, 12/23/24. This description entails that there exist direct relationships (defined probabilistically) only between
variables X_1 and X_2, X_2 and X_3, and X_2 and X_4.
The elements are coupled by the couplings
$C_{12} = C_{13} = C_{23} = \{X_2\}$. The block diagram of
this type of structure system, which may be considered as a candidate structure which is to be
tested for congruency with the data, is shown in
Figure 1(B) as type (4).

Figure 1(B) also shows some other block diagrams and their notations (disregard for the moment
the part of the notation between brackets below
type (1)). These structures may be ordered in a
lattice, as is shown in Figure 1(A). Since the
number of possible direct relationships between n
variables equals $\frac{1}{2}n(n-1)$, one may discern a number of $\frac{1}{2}n(n-1) + 1$ successive levels arranged
according to the number of direct relationships
which have been deleted, i.e., starting at the top
of the lattice, characterized by structures with
$0,1,...,\frac{1}{2}n(n-1)$ direct relationships missing.
Full descriptions of such lattices have been given
by Klir [9,10].

In the four-variable lattice of Figure 1 the
descriptions of the type of structure candidates
below the block diagrams (with inclusion of the
notation between brackets of type (1)) may be used
to specify the decomposition of the total constraint. It was proven by this author that the
total probabilistic constraint of a structure system could be decomposed into additive combinations
of constraints pertaining to elements, provided
that, in case pairs of elements are coupled by

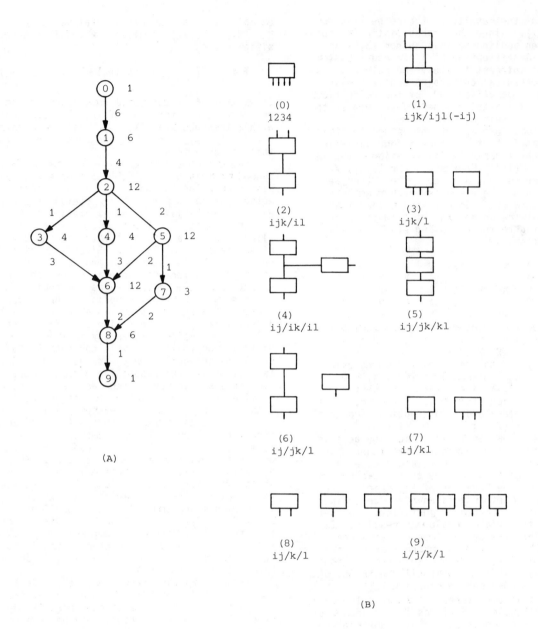

(A)

(B)

Figure 1

(A)   Hierarchy of structure candidates of a four-variable system; numbers within circles refer to the type (see B); numbers next to circles refer to the number of candidates of that type; numbers next to connections between circles refer to the number of immediate successors.

(B)   Block diagrams of type of structure candidates (from Klir [9]).

means of more than one coupling variable, a correction is subtracted amounting to the constraints between those coupling variables.

Let us consider, for example, structure type (4), $ij/ik/il$; it may be shown that

$$T(X) = T(X_i:X_j) + T(X_i:X_k) + T(X_i:X_l)$$

Similarly, structure type (8) yields:

$$T(X) = T(X_i:X_j)$$

where, evidently, the structural constraint has no meaning for individual variables. The description of type (1), notation ijk/ijl $(-ij)$, is read as

$$T(X) = T(X_i:X_j:X_k) + T(X_i:X_j:X_l) - T(X_i:X_j)$$

where the latter correction term is plausible, when

one realizes that the constraint between X_i and X is 'included' twice in the constraints referring to both elements. For a more rigorous exposition the reader is referred to the author's previous papers [7,8].

The above type of decomposition has some features in common with the methods of treating cross-classification tables as exemplified by Goodman [19] From a four-way table one can obtain two-way, three-way, etc. tables pertaining to pairs, triples, etc. of variables (ignoring the remaining ones). When a four-way table is replaced by three-way, two-way, or combinations of these tables, information may be lost about the relationships between the variables. The methods developed by Goodman for the log-linear model, and by Klir and myself for probabilistic models are used for determining whether the information can be ignored that may be lost by replacing, for example, a four-way table (structure system (0), notation 1234, in Figure 1) by tables of smaller dimension (elements of structure candidates). In the next section we will give an example of a method that searches for the most parsimonious model that still fits the data well. For a comparative study of both Goodman's method and the constraint analytic method one is referred to a previous paper [7].

Let us return now to a discussion of some similar ideas pertaining to a method based on set theoretic constraint analysis of a many-dimensional relation. It has been shown in the previous section that Ashby developed a method of determining the set of cylindrical closures of an n-dimensional relation. The concept of cylindrance was used to obtain an impression of the intrinsic complexity of such a relation. More specifically, if the cylindrance of a relation can be shown to be smaller than n, it is obvious that the n-dimensional relation might be replaced by combinations of lower-dimensional relations.

Considering the probabilistic methods of constraint analysis as used in the identification of a structure system, and reasoning by analogy, it occurred to me from the actual meaning of the outcome of intersecting cylinders, that the intersection of those cylinders which pertain to elements of a structure system only would yield the original relation, if it were originally composed that way. For example, we expected that if, given a four-dimensional relation of cylindrance two, a structure candidate like 12/23/24 would fit the relation well, the latter could be correctly reconstructed from two-dimensional relations pertaining to elements only, as follows

$$R(X) = \overset{-1}{pr_{12}} pr_{12} R(X) \cap \overset{-1}{pr_{23}} pr_{23} R(X) \cap \overset{-1}{pr_{24}} pr_{24} R(X)$$

It is noted that, knowing that the cylindrance of the relation is equal to two, i.e., $C_2 R(X) = R(X)$, the four-dimensional relation can be reconstructed, by definition, by means of intersecting all two-dimensional cylinders. However, this fact by itself neither does yield the structure of the relation nor a method for the identification of a structure which is congruent with the original relation. Moreover, if the dimensional scope of the relation is lower than its cylindrance, it is not clear how to go about in reconstructing the n-dimensional relation from relations pertaining to lower and differing dimensions.

Before turning to an example, we note that the n-dimensional relation should be a proper subset of the product set. Otherwise, the relation would be totally uninformative. In other words, at least some of the variables need to be 'relevant' to the relation [16].

With the above conjectures in mind, we speculated that also the identification procedure as applied to probabilistic structure systems would yield analogous results. In the next section, we will give a typical example of the application of both methods.

4. IDENTIFICATION OF A STRUCTURE SYSTEM

We will give an example of the identification procedures of a discrete four-variable structure system. We will consider only dichotomous variables. A (generative) system is supposed to be specified by a four-dimensional relation (in case of the non-probabilistic approach) and a joint discrete density function (in case of the probabilistic approach).

Example. A generative system was specified and composed for (X_1, X_2, X_3, X_4) by means of the following marginal and conditional (population) distributions for $X_i = \{0,1\}$, $i \in I = \{1,2,3,4\}$.

$$f_{X_2}(0) = f_{X_2}(1) = .5$$

$$f_{X_i | X_2}(0|0) = 0 \; ; \; f_{X_i | X_2}(1|0) = 1 \quad (i = 1,3,4)$$

$$f_{X_i | X_2}(0|1) = f_{X_i | X_2}(1|1) = .5 \quad (i = 1,3,4)$$

Table 1 gives the resulting four-dimensional relation $R(X)$ and associated joint probability function $f(x_i)_{i \in I}$.

Note: It is important to notice that the actual non-zero values taken by the probabilities may vary over a wide range; as long as the zero's are maintained for the same (conditional) probabilities, the resulting relation $R(X)$ will still be the same.

For purposes of comparison we will deal first with the results of the probabilistic method (I).

Method I. Table II shows some results which were obtained from a standard computer program. The table displays in the first column the number of the structure candidate, in the second column its description (see Figure 1), in the third column the total constraint in bits computed on the basis of this description for the hypothesized candidate (see previous section), and in the last column the so-called T-distance, denoted by Δ_i^0, defined as the difference between the total constraints of the candidate C_0 and C_1, and also measured in bits (for further details see references [6-8]).

From Table II it is seen that out of the set of successful (i.e., $\Delta = 0$) immediate successors of candidate C_0 one candidate, C_1, was chosen. Its immediate successors are C_7, C_8, C_{10}, and C_{11}, of which C_8 and C_{11} are congruent with the data ($\Delta = 0$).

Table I

Example of a four-dimensional relation $R(X_1,X_2,X_3,X_4)$
and probability function $f(x_i)_{i \in I}$.

$R(X_1,X_2,X_3,X_4)$	$f(x_1,x_2,x_3,x_4)$
0 1 0 0	.125
0 1 0 1	.125
0 1 1 0	.125
0 1 1 1	.125
1 0 1 1	.25
1 1 0 0	.0625
1 1 0 1	.0625
1 1 1 0	.0625
1 1 1 1	.0625

Table II

Probabilistic structure identification.
Candidates C_i, description of candidates, total constraints $T_i(X)$,
and T-distance $\Delta_i^0 = T_0(X) - T_i(X)$ computed for immediate successors
of successful candidates (indicated by *); see Table I.

C_i	Description	$T_i(X)$	Δ_i^0
0	1234	.7201	0
1*	123/124(-12)	.7201	0
2	123/134(-13)	.6013	.1188
3	123/234(-23)	.7201	0
4	124/134(-14)	.6013	.1188
5	124/234(-24)	.7201	0
6	134/234(-34)	.5146	.2055
7	123/14	.5645	.1556
8*	123/24	.7201	0
10	124/13	.5645	.1556
11	124/23	.7201	0
19	123/4	.5157	.2044
24	12/13/24	.5645	.1556
28*	12/23/24	.7201	0
33	13/23/24	.4576	.2625
44	12/23/4	.5157	.2044
45	12/24/3	.5157	.2044
51	23/24/1	.4088	.3113

Immediate successors of C_8 are C_{19}, C_{24}, C_{28}, and C_{33}, of which only C_{28} still fits the data. Since the T-distances of the immediate successors of C_{28}, viz., C_{44}, C_{45}, C_{51}, are unequal to zero, C_{28} is the 'best' (in the sense of most parsimonious) candidate. So, the four-dimensional probability function may be reproduced without loss of information from the three two-dimensional marginals pertaining to variables (X_1,X_2), (X_2,X_3), and (X_2,X_4). For the treatment of sample distributions one is referred to previous papers, where it is shown that adequate tests of the null hypothesis $H : \Delta = 0$ do not essentially complicate the above picture of an identification procedure using the

tools of probabilistic constraint analysis.
We will now turn to our main interest, the outcome of a similar but non-probabilistic procedure.

Method II. A computer program was written which calculated the projections, inverse projections, and cylindrical closures of order p $(p = 1,2,3,4)$ for $R(X)$ given in Table I. The dimensional scope was shown to be scp $R(X) = 1$, while cyl $R(X) = 2$, i.e., $C_2R(X) = R(X)$. The latter results indicate that the relation may be reconstructed from two-dimensional relations only. Next, the same procedure as for the probabilistic case was followed, by determining for appropriate structures of the lattice (see Figure 1) the projections of $R(X)$ on the element subsets of the structure system, forming the cylinders in X on the element projections as bases, and then taking the intersections of these 'element cylinders'. The results are given in Table III.

To clarify the notations, we will discuss a specific example. Consider structure candidate C_8. It consists of the elements $E_1 = \{X_1, X_2, X_3\}$ and $E_2 = \{X_2, X_4\}$, notation 123/24 (second column of Table III). The inverse projection $pr_{123}^{-1} pr_{123} R(X)$ equals the union of $R(X)$ and $\{(1,0,1,0)\}$, so that there are 10 elements in this cylinder, the nine constituting the original relation plus one more $(1,0,1,0)$; denoted by $R \cup \{(1010)\}$ in the table. Similarly, the cylinder of element E_2 was determined as $R(X) \cup \{(0,0,0,1),(0,0,1,1),(1,0,0,1)\}$. It is easily shown that the intersection of the two cylinders reconstructs the original relation $R(X)$ correctly; the intersection of the element cylinders is denoted in the fourth column of the table. Finally, a distance measure, denoted by d_i^0, may be defined as follows

$$d_i^0 = card \ (R(C_i) - R(C_0))$$

where $R(C_i)$ stands for the relation found by intersecting the cylinders of elements of candidate C_i, while $R(C_0) = R(X)$ (note that X refers to the unconstrained set of 16 members, i.e., $X = \prod_{i \in I} X_i$ $(I = \{1,2,3,4\})$. For instance, $d_8^0 = 0$ means that $R(C_8) = R(X)$, while $d_2^0 = 1$ means that the cardinality of the set difference $R(C_2) - R(X)$ is equal to one.

Comparison of the results of Table III with those of Table II shows a striking resemblance between them. In both cases, structure candidate C_{28} is identified correctly.

It is interesting to delve a little deeper into the similarities between the outcomes of both methods. It can be shown for structure C_{28} that, in general, first-order and second-order probabilistic constraints should satisfy the following inequalities:

$$T(X_1:X_2) \geq T(X_1:X_3) \ , \ T(X_1:X_4)$$
$$T(X_2:X_3) \geq T(X_1:X_3) \ , \ T(X_3:X_4)$$
$$T(X_2:X_4) \geq T(X_1:X_4) \ , \ T(X_3:X_4)$$
$$T(X_1:X_3:X_4) \leq T(X_1:X_2:X_3) \ , \ T(X_1:X_2:X_4) \ ,$$
$$T(X_2:X_3:X_4)$$

These inequalities are also intuitively plausible on closer inspection of the block diagram of C_{28}.

A non-probabilistic quantity which appears to display a somewhat related behavior might be defined by introducing the constraints $D(X_i, X_j)$ and $D(X_i, X_j, X_k)$ defined as

$$D(X_i, X_j) = \prod_{i \in I} X_i - pr_{ij}^{-1} \ pr_{ij} \ R(X)$$

$$D(X_i, X_j, X_k) = \prod_{i \in I} (X_i) - pr_{ijk}^{-1} \ pr_{ijk} \ R(X) \ .$$

The analogy with the total constraint $D(X) = X - R(X)$ is obvious. The above quantities might be considered as measures of constraints on subsets of variables induced by the overall relation.

The cardinalities, denoted by $cD(X_i, X_j, (X_k))$, of these quantities are given in Table IV, together with their probabilistic counterparts. It is shown that

$$cD(X_1, X_2) > cD(X_1, X_3) \ , \ cD(X_1, X_4)$$
$$cD(X_2, X_3) > cD(X_1, X_3) \ , \ cD(X_3, X_4)$$
$$cD(X_2, X_4) > cD(X_1, X_4) \ , \ cD(X_3, X_4)$$
$$cD(X_1, X_3, X_4) < cD(X_1, X_2, X_3) \ , \ cD(X_1, X_2, X_4) \ ,$$
$$cD(X_2, X_3, X_4)$$

which corresponds entirely with the above probabilistic inequalities.

Investigations on other types of structure yield similar results, indicating that the two methods are strongly compatible, although, of course, the non-probabilistic method gives a somewhat coarser picture of the intensities of the constraints. In view of the above note, one might even think of the non-probabilistic relation as representing a class of probabilistic structure systems specified by the same relation but widely different probability distributions defined on that relation. So the probabilistic method may be regarded as a refinement of the non-probabilistic method. Especially for systems containing a large number of variables, a non-probabilistic method might precede the probabilistic investigation.

Although the above results may at best be regarded as explorative, we intend to substantiate these findings in future publications. The idea of compatibility of the two methods appears viable enough to warrant a thorough examination.

5. CONCLUSIONS AND PERSPECTIVES

The identification of structure in a data system serves the purpose of locating the intrinsic complexities in the relation amongst the system variables. In this paper we have started to explore the (dis)similarities between a non-probabilistic and a probabilistic method of structure identification. From the example in the last section, and from many others as well, it appears that there are some interesting implications.

In a recent paper, Maurice Kendall [22] summed up ten groups of major unsolved problems in the treatment of multivariate analysis, with particular reference to contingency tables. The first one he discussed is the problem of empty cells or small frequencies which provide difficulties because they impair tests of independence. It is clear that non-probabilistic constraint analysis is only fruitful in the presence of empty cells. As a matter of fact, we performed a number of examples of the non-probabilistic identification of a structure system, which was characterized by a probability function with non-zero probabilities. By gradually deleting those elements of the original relation with the smaller probabilities we were able to identify the same structure as was identified by the probabilistic method. How to determine the cut-off point of omitting elements from the relation by an objective criterion rather than intuition still poses a problem.

Table III

Non-probabilistic structure identification.
Candidate C_i, description of candidates, element cylinders, intersection of element cylinders, and a distance measure $d_i^0 = card (R(C_i) - R(C_0))$; immediate successors of successful candidates are indicated by * (see Table I).

C_i	Description	Element Cylinders	Intersection	d_i^0
0	1234	R	-	0
1*	123/124	$R \cup \{(1010)\}$ / $R \cup \{(1001)\}$	R	0
2	123/134	$R \cup \{(1010)\}$ / X	$R \cup \{(1010)\}$	1
3	123/234	$R \cup \{(1010)\}$ / $R \cup \{(0011)\}$	R	0
4	124/134	$R \cup \{(1001)\}$ / X	$R \cup \{(1001)\}$	1
5	124/234	$R \cup \{(1001)\}$ / $R \cup \{(0011)\}$	R	0
6	134/234	X / $R \cup \{(0011)\}$	$R \cup \{(0011)\}$	1
7	123/14	$R \cup \{(1010)\}$ / X	$R \cup \{(1010)\}$	1
8*	123/24	$R \cup \{(1010)\}$ / $R \cup S_{24}$ [1]	R	0
10	124/13	$R \cup \{(1001)\}$ / X	$R \cup \{(1001)\}$	1
11	124/23	$R \cup \{(1001)\}$ / $R \cup S_{23}$ [2]	R	0
19	123/4	$R \cup \{(1010)\}$ / X	$R \cup \{(1010)\}$	1
24	12/13/24	$R \cup S_{12}$ / X / $R \cup S_{24}$ [1,3]	$R \cup \{(1001)\}$	1
28*	12/23/24	$R \cup S_{12}$ / $R \cup S_{23}$ / $R \cup S_{24}$ [1,2]	R	0
33	13/23/24	X / $R \cup S_{23}$ / $R \cup S_{24}$ [1,2]	$R \cup \{(0011)\}$	1
44	12/23/4	$R \cup S_{12}$ / $R \cup S_{23}$ / X [2,3]	$R \cup \{(1010)\}$	1
45	12/24/3	$R \cup S_{12}$ / $R \cup S_{24}$ / X [1,3]	$R \cup \{(1001)\}$	1
51	23/24/1	$R \cup S_{23}$ / $R \cup S_{24}$ / X [1,2]	$R \cup \{(0011)\}$	1

[1] $S_{24} = \{(0001),(0011),(1001)\}$ [2] $S_{23} = \{(0010),(0011),(1010)\}$ [3] $S_{12} = \{(1000),(1001),(1010)\}$

Table IV

Comparison of probabilistic constraints $T(X_i:X_j)$ and $T(X_i:X_j:X_k)$, and cardinalities (cD) of non-probabilistic constraints $D(X_i,X_j)$ and $D(X_i,X_j,X_k)$ $(i < j < k$; $i,j,k = 1,2,3)$ for structure C_{28} .

(i,j)	$T(X_i:X_j)$	$cD(X_i,X_j)$	(i,j,k)	$T(X_i:X_j:X_k)$	$cD(X_i,X_j,X_k)$
1,2	.31	4	1,2,3	.52	6
1,3	.05	0	1,2,4	.52	6
1,4	.05	0	1,3,4	.13	0
2,3	.20	4	2,3,4	.41	6
2,4	.20	4			
3,4	.03	0			

Kendall also referred to the problem of measuring the intensity of a relationship: "for the past thirty or forty years statisticians have been mainly concerned to test for independence and let it go at that, without paying much attention to the measurement of dependence." It was shown that both constraint analytic approaches provide such measures, be it that, as a matter of fact, the probabilistic measures are much more refined than the non-probabilistic ones.

Another problem which was listed by Kendall is that of finding a systematic way through the multiplicity of possible hypotheses "which enables us to discard a number of them." Klir's method of identification does satisfy this requirement. The non-probabilistic method also indicates by means of the concepts of cylindrance and scope at which

levels of a lattice one does not need to evaluate structure candidates. The selection of subsets of variables was another item on Kendall's list. It seems that a 'primitive' method like the set theoretical analysis would enable one to make a preliminary and quick survey of the dependencies between variables. Finally, Kendall also urged in general for non-probabilistic methods of structure analysis.

In summary, the non-probabilistic method of constraint analysis seems a promising enough tool for the identification of structure in complex data to warrant further elaboration. This is especially so because it evidently belongs to the expanding class of much-needed system methodological tools that "provide indications rather than conclusions" [16].

REFERENCES

1. ASHBY, W. R., "Constraint Analysis of Many-dimensional Relations," *General Systems, Yearbook of the Society for General Systems Research*, Ann Arbor, Michigan, 9, 1964, pp. 99-105.

2. BROEKSTRA, G., "Some Comments on the Application of Informational Measures to the Processing of Activity Arrays," *International Journal of General Systems*, Vol. 3, No. 1, 1976, pp. 43-51.

3. BROEKSTRA, G., "Constraint Analysis and Structure Identification I," *Annals of Systems Research*, 5, 1976, pp. 67-80.

4. BROEKSTRA, G., "Simplifying Data Systems: An Information Theoretic Analysis," in *Proceedings of the Third European Meeting on Cybernetics and Systems Research*, Vienna, April 1976.

5. BROEKSTRA, G., "Constraint Analysis and Structure Identification II," *Annals of Systems Research*, 6, 1977, pp. 1-20.

6. BROEKSTRA, G., "Structure Modelling: A Constraint (Information) Analytic Approach," in *Proceedings of the International Conference on Applied General Systems Research*, Binghamton, New York, 1977.

7. BROEKSTRA, G., "On the Application of Informational Measures to the Structure Identification Problem with an Example of the Multivariate Analysis of Qualitative Data from a Panel Study," in *Recent Developments in Systems Methodology for Social Science Research* (R. Cavallo, ed.), Martinus Nijhoff, Hingham, Massachusetts, 1979 (in press).

8. BROEKSTRA, G., "On the Representation and Identification of Structure Systems," *International Journal of Systems Science*, Vol. 9, No. 11, pp. 1271-1293, 1978.

9. KLIR, G. J. and H. J. J. UYTTENHOVE, "Computerized Methodology for Structure Modelling," *Annals of Systems Research*, 5, 1976, pp. 29-66.

10. KLIR, G. J., "Identification of Generative Structures in Empirical Data," *International Journal of General Systems*, Vol. 3, No. 2, 1976, pp. 89-104.

11. ASHBY, W. R., *An Introduction to Cybernetics*, Chapman and Hall, London, 1956.

12. MOOD, A. M., F. A. GRAYBILL and D. C. BOES, *Introduction to the Theory of Statistics*, McGraw-Hill, Tokyo, 1974, 3rd edition.

13. CONANT, R. C., "Laws of Information Which Govern Systems," *IEEE Transactions on Systems, Man and Cybernetics*, SMC-6, No. 4, 1976, pp. 240-255.

14. WATANABE, S., *Knowing and Guessing*, Wiley, New York, 1969.

15. ASHBY, W. R., "Measuring the Internal Informational Exchange in a System," *Cybernetica*, 8, 1965, pp. 5-22.

16. MADDEN, R. F. and W. R. ASHBY, "The Identification of Many-Dimensional Relations," *International Journal of Systems Science*, Vol. 3, No. 4, 1972, pp. 343-356.

17. ASHBY, W. R., "Two Tables of Identities Governing Information Flows within Large Systems," *Communications of the American Society for Cybernetics*, Vol. 1, No. 2, 1969, pp. 2-8.

18. CONANT, R. C., "Detecting Subsystems of a Complex System," *IEEE Transactions on Systems, Man and Cybernetics*, SMC-2, No. 4, 1972, pp. 550-553.

19. GOODMAN, L. A., "Causal Analysis of Data from Panel Studies and Other Kinds of Surveys," *American Journal of Sociology*, 78, No. 5, 1973, pp. 1135-1191.

20. ASHBY, W. R., "The Set Theory of Mechanism and Homeostasis," in *Automation Theory and Learning Systems* (D. J. Stewart, ed.), Academic Press, New York, 1967.

21. KLIR, G. J., "On the Representation of Activity Arrays," *International Journal of General Systems*, Vol. 2, No. 3, 1975, pp. 149-168.

22. KENDALL, M., "Multivariate Contingency Tables and Some Further Problems in Multivariate Analysis," in *Multivariate Analysis IV* (P. R. Krishnaiah, ed.), North-Holland Publishing Company, Amsterdam, 1977.

23. ABRAHAMSE, A. P. J., "Constraint Analysis in Structure Modelling: A Probabilistic Approach," in *Recent Developments in Systems Methodology for Social Science Research* (R. Cavallo, ed.), Martinus Nijhoff, Hingham, Massachusetts, 1979 (in press).

Systems with universal subsystems, realization and application

BRUNO BUCHBERGER* and **BERNHARD QUATEMBER****
*Institut für Mathematik
**Institut für Statistik und Informatik
Johannes Kepler Universität, Linz, Austria

1. INTRODUCTION

In this paper we study a possible realization of systems that are composed of, theoretically, infinitely many and, practically, a large number of subsystems. Each of these subsystems
- is identical
- essentially operates autonomously, however,
- at certain moments may communicate with other subsystems in its neighbourhood,
- is universal (in the sense of algorithm theory or, more practically, in the sense of computer science), and
- contributes to a common goal.

Thus, these systems share essential features with well-known other types of systems. On the other hand, however, they are distinct with respect to at least one feature from the systems studied so far. For instance:

Cellular spaces [1] consist of a large number of subsystems that communicate with subsystems in the neighbourhood. However, no single subsystem is universal. Furthermore, the operation of the whole system is synchronized.

Combinatorial switching circuits [2] may well be composed of identical components (see [3]) that operate asynchronously. Again the components are not universal.

Parallel computers [4] consist of a large number of processors that, normally, are not universal and do not operate autonomously.

Computer networks (see, for instance, [5]) consist of highly autonomous universal subsystems. However, only a few computers are combined in one system. Also, the communication between the subsystems occurs only for organizing the distribution of independent tasks among the subsystems, not for contributing to some common goal.

Hierarchical systems in the sense of Mesarović [6] consist of subsystems with a certain degree of autonomous behaviour contributing to a common goal. However, no emphasis is on universality and homogeneity. The same characteristics hold for structured software systems [7].

Universality of the subsystems is an essential enrichment of systems. Of course, a combination of universal systems cannot produce more than a universal system. However, the availability of universal subsystems may drastically influence the complexity of problem solving in a universal system (see Section 4).

2. SYSTEMS WITH UNIVERSAL SUBSYSTEMS

The concept of a system with universal subsystems (SUS) is a slight generalization of the concept of computer-trees introduced in [8].

The basic component ("module") of a SUS is a sequential universal automaton [9] with finitely many additional "in-lines" and "out-lines" (see Figure 1).

Every in-line and every out-line consists of: a data line; a sensing line + sensor bit; and a setting line (see Figure 2).

In fact, so far in-lines cannot be distinguished from out-lines. The difference can only be made after having introduced the identifier modification described in the later paragraphs. An out-line of one module may be connected with an in-line of some other module in the following way (see Figure 3).

An arbitrary number (even a potentially infinite number) of modules may be interconnected in this way in order to form SUS's of different structures such as trees and nets like this: (see Figure 4).

We assume the modules to be programmed in an ALGOL-like language. Then the functional characteristics of the in- and out-lines may be explained by describing the semantics of two additional language features:

(1) Sensor Instructions:

if S_1 then ...;   if S_2 then ...;   ...
if T_1 then ...;   if T_2 then ...;   ...
U_1 := true; U_1 := false; U_2 := true; U_2 := false; ....
V_1 := true; V_1 := false; V_2 := true; V_2 := false; ...

These instructions are used for communication with the sensor bits which are supposed to be designated like this: (see Figure 5).

Notice that each sensor bit has two designations depending on whether it is referenced by its own module for reading or by a neighbouring module for setting and resetting.

(2) Identifier (Address) Modification

Every identifier x is available in $k+1$ issues $x, x', x'', \ldots, x^{(k)}$ where k is the number of out-lines in the modules. A module C in the system, by means of identifiers of the types $x, x', x'', \ldots, x^{(k)}$ has access to its own storage and (via the data lines) to the storage of its first, second, $\ldots$, k-th neighbour $C', C'', \ldots, C^{(k)}$, respectively. Furthermore, if module C addresses a storage region of its neighbour $C^{(i)}$ by identifier $x^{(i)}$ then module $C^{(i)}$ may address the same

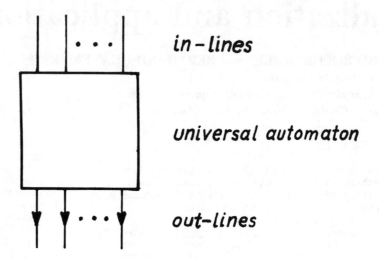

Figure 1. One module

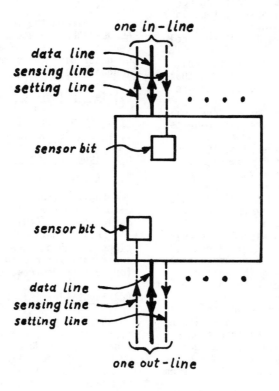

Figure 2. Structure of in- and out-lines

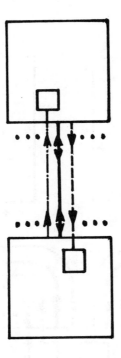

Figure 3. Connection between in- and out-lines

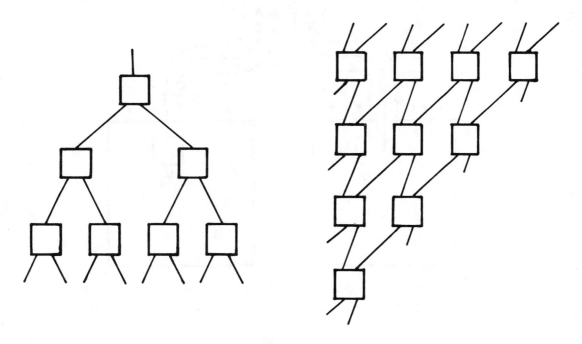

Figure 4. Different types of SUS's

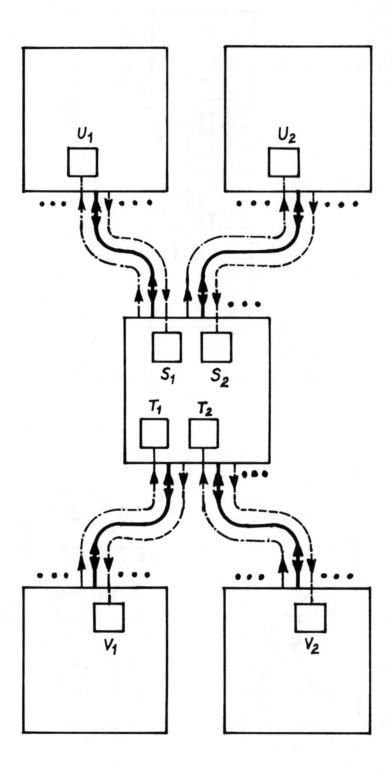

Figure 5. Designation of sensor bits

region by identifier x.

In a SUS all modules are started simultaneously and operate autonomously. However, by means of the two additional language features described above, at certain points of the computation neighbouring modules may communicate. Concurrent access to the same storage region is supposed to be excluded by an appropriate use of the sensor instructions.

Further, we add the following language feature:

(3) <u>Computed goto:</u>

goto a;

This jump-instruction uses the numerical value of variable a as a label. In order to avoid ambiguities we admit integer labels exclusively.

3. REALIZATION

It is easy to realize (finite approximations to) SUS's with present-day hardware components.

The modules may be realized by an appropriate combination of the following components: a micro-processor (μP), a data memory (DM), a program memory (PM), an interface (IF) -- containing the sensor bits and realizing the address modification.

The structure of one module is as follows (without loss of generality we consider only two in-lines and two out-lines): (see Figure 6).

The address modifications may be realized as follows: We divide the set A of addresses that are not needed for addressing PM or for other special purposes into three disjoint subsets A_0, A_1, and A_2 of equal size and define two bijective mappings:

$$f_1 : A_1 \rightarrow A_0$$

$$f_2 : A_2 \rightarrow A_0 .$$

(For example: $A : = \{0,...,3071\}$,
$A_0 : = \{0,...,1023\}$,
$A_1 : = \{1024,...,2047\}$,
$A_2 : = \{2048,...,3071\}$,
$f_1(a): = a - 1024$,
$f_2(a): = a - 2048 .$)

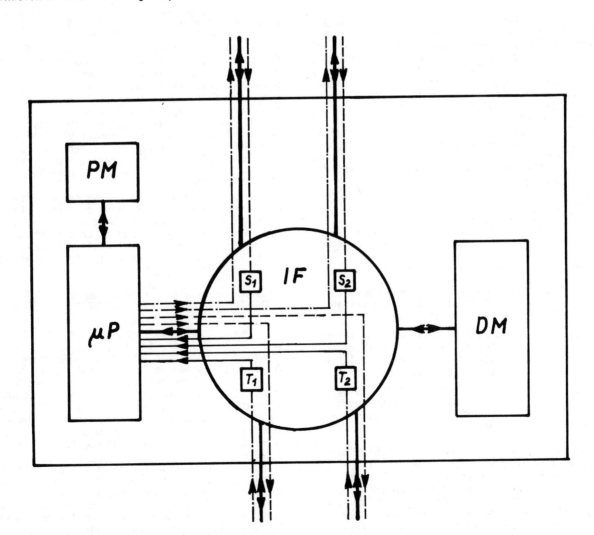

Figure 6. Structure of one module

The IF must realize the following function:

(1) An address a produced by the μP is analysed in the IF. Accesses to the DM of its own module or to the DM's of the first and second neighbour are, then, carried out according to the following rule:

If $a \in A_0$, then location a of the DM of its own module is accessed.

If $a \in A_1$, then location $f_1(a)$ of the DM of the first neighbour is accessed.

If $a \in A_2$, then location $f_2(a)$ of the DM of the second neighbour is accessed.

(2) An address a arriving at the IF via an in-line remains unchanged.

The sensor bits may be implemented by using bits of a fixed storage location outside DM. A concrete realization of this type has been carried out in collaboration with ICA-Company (Vienna) using the KIM-1 microprocessor (see [10]).

4. APPLICATION

Our main motivation for developing the concept of SUS's is the desire to exploit the parallelism inherent in the recursive formulation of certain algorithms in order to speed them up. The adequate shape of SUS's for this application is the (binary) tree. We have investigated this application in [8] by giving a number of typical examples which show that all types of recursions may be executed on SUS's in a natural way.

We first briefly summarize the discussion given in [8]. Then we pursue some aspects of this application in more detail.

Consider the tautology problem which is recursively defined by

$$taut(t,n) \leftrightarrow$$
$$n=0 \wedge true(t) \vee$$
$$n\geq 1 \wedge taut(\ subst(t,n,1),\ n-1) \wedge$$
$$taut(\ subst(t,n,0),\ n-1)$$

where we used the following abbreviations:

taut(t,n)   - the boolean expression t contains no more than n variables and is a tautology,

true(t)   - the boolean expression t does not contain any variables and the evaluation of t yields the truth value 1,

subst(t,n,x)   - the result of substituting the truth value x for the n-th variable in the boolean expression t.

This definition of the tautology problem may equally well be read as a recursive formulation of an algorithm for solving the problem. The execution of this recursive algorithm on an ordinary computer uses a stack mechanism which artificially sequentializes the simultaneous procedure calls taut(subst(t,n,1),n-1) and taut(subst(t,n,0),n-1). As a consequence, the execution time of this algorithm on a normal computer is $O(2^n)$. In fact, no essentially better algorithm is known for this problem at present time (see [11]).

However, we can solve the problem in $O(n)$ steps on the binary computer tree (Figure 4) by the following program:

```
1: if ¬ S₁ then goto 1;
   if n=0 then
            begin  y:= true(t); U₁:= true; goto 5
            end;
   if n≥1 then
            begin
              t':= subst(t,n,1); t":= subst(t,n,0);
              n':= n":= n-1;
              V₁:= V₂:= true;
   2:       if ¬(T₁∧T₂) then goto 2;
              y:= y'∧y";
              U₁:= true; goto 5
            end;

5: ;
```

If this program is loaded to all modules of the tree and all modules are started simultaneously, a "computational wave" is generated in the tree which first propagates downward until level n of the tree and then contracts again. Propagating downward it distributes sub-tasks to the modules, contracting upward it combines partial results in order to yield the final solution. The total amount of time for this computation is $O(n)$.

Of course the gain in time complexity must be purchased by an equivalent explosion of hardware complexity. (Note that this is very similar to what can be observed when passing from serial to parallel adders or from serial to parallel multipliers, see [3].)

In practical applications we can realize only a finite number N of levels in the tree. In this case, at the N-th level we must call a sequential procedure true(t,n) instead of true(t) which solves the tautology problem for the ultimate value of n (see [8]). The time complexity of the algorithm then is $= 2^{n-N}$. Hence,

$$\frac{\text{computation time on ordinary computer}}{\text{computation time on computer tree}} = \frac{2^n}{2^{n-N}} = 2^N.$$

This means that in any case we have a constant speed-up of 2^N. If, for instance, N = 15 (which seems to be realistic for present-day hardware) then a constant speed-up of approximately 30,000 is possible. This corresponds to what has been achieved by hardware improvement in one computer generation. Even though we cannot really convert $O(2^n)$ into $O(n)$, we could thus achieve a "one-generation speed-up" by introducing a new computer concept instead of developing new computer hardware.

Let us now pursue the above example in more detail. At the bottom level of the tree we have to execute the procedure true(t). Such a procedure is polynomial in the length of t (see [11]). However, we again can define a recursive procedure for this problem which may easily be translated into a computer-tree program that exploits the parallelism contained in the recursive formulation:

$$true(t) := \begin{cases} \underline{true}, & \text{if } t=1 \\ \underline{false}, & \text{if } t=0 \\ \neg true(\text{ opd1}(t)\text{ }), & \text{if } t \text{ is a negation,} \\ true(\text{ opd1}(t)\text{ }) \wedge true(\text{ opd2}(t)\text{ }), & \\ & \text{if } t \text{ is a conjunction,} \\ true(\text{ opd1}(t)\text{ }) \vee true(\text{ opd2}(t)\text{ }), & \\ & \text{if } t \text{ is a disjunction,} \end{cases}$$

where opd1(t) and opd2(t) denote the first and second operand of the boolean expression t, respectively.

A corresponding computer-tree program is:

```
3: if ¬ S₁ wait;                                    *)
   if t=1 then
          begin y:= true; U₁:= true; goto 4
          end;
   if t=0 then
          begin .....
          end;
   s:= true;
   while t is a negation do
          begin t:= opd1(t); s:=¬s
          end;
   if t is a conjunction then
          begin  t':= opd1(t); t":= opd2(t);
                 V₁:= V₂:= true;
                 if   (T₁∧T₂) wait;
                 y:= y'∧y"; if ¬s then  y:= ¬ y;
                 U₁:= true; goto 4
          end;
   if t is a disjunction then
                 begin .....
                 end;
4: ;
```

From this example we see that we can carry out the evaluation process in a time that is linear in the number of nested boolean operations in t. Furthermore, we wished to demonstrate how we can avoid the branching of the computation in the case where t is a negation. In general this technique may be applied whenever a recursive procedure is called only once in a certain part of the procedure body. This technique permits a saving in the number of modules needed in a given computation.

We now can combine the two programs for taut and true in a single one using the computed goto in order to switch control from one program part to the other. (Note that we cannot simply load the program for true to the n-th and the subsequent levels of the tree because the level n depends on the input data):

```
1: if ¬ S₁ wait;
   goto a;                                          **)
```

----
*) abbreviation for: 3: if S ¬ then goto 3;
**) a must be initialized with 2.

```
2: if n=0 then goto 3;
   if n≥1 then
            begin
            t':= ...; t":= ...; n':= n":= n-1;
            a':= a":= 2; V₁:= V₂:= true;
            if ..... goto 4
            end;
3: if t=1 then
            begin  y:= true; U₁:= true; goto 4
            end;
   if t=0 then ...;
   s:= true;
   while t is a negation do ...;
   if t is a conjunction then
            begin  t':= opd1(t); t":= opd2(t);
                   a':= a":= 3;
                   V₁:= V₂:= true;
                   if ....
            end;
   if t is a disjunction then ...;
4: ;
```

Of course, by the techniques given above we could also implement one of the more sophisticated methods for solving the tautology problem. These methods analyse the syntactic structure of t from the very beginning instead of first generating all combinations of truth values (see, for instance, [12]).

The above program for true also demonstrates one of the major practical problems using computer-trees: the computation of the procedure true may propagate very far in one branch of the tree whereas it terminates after a few levels in some other branches. Thus, in a concrete implementation where we have only a fixed number N of levels a given computation might be impossible, though there would still be a lot of modules available in the system. This problem could be solved if we had a hardware mechanism that would permit us to flexibly interconnect the modules during execution time.

There are two extreme possibilities for realizing such a mechanism: a time-shared bus for all modules or a complete interconnection between all modules. The first possibility does not work because it would be a bottleneck in the system that would artificially sequentialize the computational process which should be parallel. The second possibility is not realistic because of its complexity. Therefore a compromise has to be found. Recently, optimistic proposals in this direction have been made (see [13]).

The above example is also good for showing another practical problem: If a module calls its two offsprings it has to transmit the formal parameters which may be considerably long. Although, theoretically, this may only multiply the time complexity by a constant factor, in practice, such a factor can play an important role. We would not need transmitting formal parameters if we had a common storage for the whole system which could be accessed (at least for reading purposes) by all modules simultaneously. In this case we could simply transmit pointers to the information instead of the information itself. The same argument applies to the program memory. At present such memories are not available (see, however, again [13]).

In the above example one module combines the solutions of two subproblems in order to form the final solution of the problem. In some cases we actually need only the solution to one of the subproblems although we must start trying to solve all of them. This is typical for non-determinism in algorithms. Of course, we can also implement this type of control by an appropriate use of the sensor instructions. We can show this by considering the satisfiability problem:

given a boolean expression t of n variables,

decide whether t is satisfiable (i.e., whether there is an assignment of the truth values 1 and 0 to the variables of t such that the evaluation of t yields 1)

A suitable program for the computer-tree is:

```
if ¬S₁ wait;
if n=0 then
          begin  y:= true(t); U₁:= true; goto 2
          end;
if n≥1 then
          begin
              t':= subst(t,n,1); t":= subst(t,n,0);
              n':= n":= n-1;
              V₁:= V₂:= true;
          3: if T₁ then  if y' then
                  begin y:= true; U₁:= true; goto 2
                  end;
             if T₂ then  if y" then
                  begin y:= true; U₁:= true; goto 2
                  end;
             if T₁∧T₂ then  if ¬(y'vy") then
                  begin y:= false; U₁:= true; goto 2
                  end;
             goto 3;
          end;
    2: ;
```

So far we have only considered examples where the tree structure seems to be the appropriate type of SUS. However, it seems to be natural to use other types of SUS's for other types of algorithms. For instance, dynamical programming seems to be a possible field of application for which a connection schema of the type shown in Figure 4, right-hand side, might be appropriate (see [11], p. 68). However, we have not analysed this type of application so far. Also we think that such patterns may well be simulated in array processors (see, for instance, [14]). On the other hand, as far as we can see, computer-trees cannot be implemented in array processors without loss of efficiency.

CONCLUSION

We introduced the theoretical concept of systems with universal subsystems, in particular computer-

trees. Our main concern was the speed-up of algorithms by writing appropriate programs for computer-trees. In typical examples the gain in time complexity is exponential. This has to be purchased by an equivalent increase of hardware complexity.

Two major hardware problems were mentioned which have to be solved before we can gain a practical advantage from SUS's.

Recently, a number of similar proposals have been made in the literature (see [13-18]. In favour of our approach we would like to emphasize its simplicity and modularity and the easy availability of test hardware.

Acknowledgement: We thank Mrs. I. Chang for her help in preparing the English text.

REFERENCES

1. CODD, E. F., Cellular Spaces, Academic Press, 1968.
2. HARRISON, M. A., Introduction to Switching and Automata Theory, McGraw Hill, 1965.
3. LANGHELD, E., "Zellenlogik und algorithmischer Schaltungsentwurf I und II," Elektronik, Heft 1 (Jänner 1978), pp. 34-42, Heft 2, (Feber 1978), pp. 59-66.
4. ENSLOW, P. H., Multiprocessors and Parallel Processing, John Wiley, 1974.
5. ASHENHURST, R. L. and R. H. VONDEROHE, "A Hierarchical Network," Datamation, 1975.
6. MESAROVIC, D. MACKO and Y. TAKAHARA, Theory of Hierarchical, Multilevel Systems, Academic Press, 1970.
7. WIRTH, N., Systematisches Programmieren, Teubner, 1975.
8. BUCHBERGER, B., "Computer-Trees and their Programming," Proc. Troisième Colloque de Lile "Les arbres en algèbre et en programmation," 16-18 February, 1978.
9. BUCHBERGER, B. and B. ROIDER, "Input/Output Codings and Transition Functions in Effective Systems," International Journal of General Systems, Vol. 4, 1978, in press.
10. BUCHBERGER, B. and J. FEGERL, "A Universal Module for the Hardware-Implementation of Recursion," Bericht Nr. 106, Institut für Mathematik, University of Linz, 1978.
11. AHO, A., J. E. HOPCROFT and J. D. ULLMAN, The Design and Analysis of Computer Algorithms, Addison-Wesley, 1974.
12. SMULLYAN, R. M., First-Order Logic, Springer, 1968.
13. SULLIVAN, H., T. R. BASHKOW and D. KLAPPHOLZ, "A Large Scale, Homogeneous, Fully Distributed Parallel Machine, I and II," Conf. Proc., 4th Annual Symposium on Computer Architecture, ACM SIGARCH 5 (1977), 3, pp. 105-117.
14. HÄNDLER, W., "Aspects of Parallelism in Computer Architecture," in M. Feilmeier (ed.), Parallel Computers-Parallel Mathematics, North-Holland, 1977.
15. GLUSHKOV, V. M., M. B. IGNATYEV, V. A. MYASNIKOV, V. A., TORGASHEV, "Recursive Machines and Computing Technology," Proc. IFIP Congress, 1974.
16. SCHWENKEL, F., "Zur Theorie unendlicher Parallelprozessoren," Computer Science, 26, 1975.
17. GOSTELOW, A. and K., "A Computer Capable of Exchanging Processors for Time," IFIP Congress, 1977.
18. VORGRIMMLER, K. and P. GEMMAR, "Structural Programming of a Multiprocessor System," in M. Feilmeier (ed.) -- see reference 14 above.

The structure of reconstructable relations, a comprehensive study

ROGER E. CAVALLO and GEORGE J. KLIR
School of Advanced Technology, State University of New York
Binghamton, New York

1. INTRODUCTION

Simon [25] asserts that "the task of science is to make use of the world's redundancy to describe that world simply." A main emphasis of general systems research has been to focus attention on two related facts:

a. for many of the chunks of the world for which descriptions are currently desired, the derivation of simple descriptions is at best no simple task;

b. the derivation of meaningful or acceptable simple descriptions is not simple mainly because of the danger of treating cavalierly or discounting high order interaction effects.

The intuitive sense of these facts seems to crystallize most clearly in terms of the notion of structure which Webster, for example, defines as: the interrelation of parts as dominated by the general character of the whole.

This definition, and many similar ones, however, while adequately conveying a conceptual significance, do not provide much guidance as to how to implement or use this insight, especially at more general levels of systems investigations. Consequently, it must be a high-priority task of general systems methodology, parallel to Simon's characterization of the task of science, to clearly delineate issues involved in the identification or determination of structure, and to do this in a manner which supplies operational significance. In this latter sense, two notable examples of work which is similar in spirit to ours are Atkin's development of Q-analysis [4,5] and Ashby's studies of: (a) higher order interaction effects using information-theoretic measures [2], and (b) the reconstructability of higher-order relations from measurements in (or projections onto) lower order subspaces [1,3]. The developments of this paper specifically provide a framework which generalizes and encompasses both Ashby's work on interaction measures (as criteria for acceptability of structure systems when the overall system is defined probabilistically) and his work on reconstructability (which he defined in terms of cylindrance).

2. GENERAL DISCUSSION

To deal with ambiguity which is often found in systems literature, while at the same time not constraining perspective or utility by restricting systems descriptions to a particular form (e.g. differential equations, linear sequential machines),

Klir [6,9] has attempted to develop an epistemological-level hierarchy of general systems which is at the same time conceptually powerful, simple, and precise. This hierarchy forms the conceptual background for the ongoing development of a General Systems Problem Solver (GSPS) which is defined in Cavallo and Klir [11] and Cavallo [9]. GSPS is conceived as an organized problem-solving framework constituting a structured methodology (Cavallo and Pichler [13]; Pichler [24]) by which a spectrum of mathematical results can be brought to bear on systems -- and thus real world problems --with minimal modification of objects of study to fit available techniques. Within GSPS one kind of problem involves the derivation of systems defined at one level from systems defined at another. A special and important class of problems of this kind involves transitions from behavior systems to structure systems and it is to this class of problems that this paper is addressed.

To describe the problem we are dealing with, consider a system as represented by a set of variables $V = \{v_1, v_2, \ldots, v_n\}$, each of which may take values from an appropriate state set $V_1, V_2, \ldots, V_n$ respectively. A behavior system is defined either simply as a subset B of $V_1 \times V_2 \times \ldots \times V_n$ or as an assignment to each $x \in V_1 \times V_2 \times \ldots \times V_n$ of a nonnegative number $p(x)$ such that $\Sigma\, p(x)$ over all x is equal to 1. Behavior systems may either result from data-gathering and processing or (as in the case of design problems) may be given directly by a "client." Transition to a structure system involves a specification of a set of elements (or subsystems) and connections between them along with a suitable "composing rule" such that some criterion defined in terms of the behavior system and/or the resulting structure system is met. For the first type of behavior system this criterion ideally is that the set of overall states which are implied by the subsystem configuration along with the composing rule is precisely the set B (as in the case with Ashby's cylindrance [1,3] or with some problems of switching circuit design (Klir [17])). For behavior systems of the second type (where the state set is augmented by a probability distribution) the criterion is most naturally given in terms of the probability distribution (for example, as a distance measure (Klir [18]), or in terms of information lost in the transition (Ashby [2]; Broekstra [6,7]; Cavallo [9]; Conant [14,15]; Krippendorf [23])).

A useful way to consider a given structure system is as an hypothesis regarding the overall (behavior) system. The individual subsystems may be considered as generating their own combinations of states, either independently of other subsystems or constrained by them to the extent that they are connected or coupled. The "reasonableness" of the hypothesis then depends on the extent to which the overall system's behavior can be considered to result from the hypothesis.

Structure system determination of the form just described generally fits into one of two categories depending on whether or not so-called internal variables are allowed. We will not deal in this paper with situations which allow the use of internal variables, but we offer a few comments regarding these cases for purposes of comparison. These situations arise most often in problems of design and are also evidenced in some modelling approaches. If there is no restriction on the use of internal variables, the designer or modeller has much more freedom and, consequently, such cases admit much more easily of the derivation of acceptable structure systems. We can draw a parallel here between the work of a designer -- who has available for use in construction or design a set or store of available "elements" (whether these are actual or conceptual) -- and an investigator trying to develop a "theory" regarding some object of investigation. In this latter case the elements may be previously completed theoretical or empirical studies which overlap the domain of interest of the investigator. In this case, however, the use of these "elements" imposes significant constraint on the investigator and the approach becomes very similar to standard analytic procedures. On the other hand, it does not seem to be conceptually significant to allow the theory-builder general freedom in the use of internal variables as their use would then entail essentially no external reference. For these reasons, studies relating to the use of internal variables are quite tricky at the general level since there is no semantics which naturally accrues to them. We thus conceive that the use of internal variables implicitly defines a new system including these variables in the original configuration and we restrict our attention to structure determination which is always based on a fixed set of variables.

To motivate somewhat the discussion which follows, we briefly consider Ashby's concept of cylindrance through which he investigated the possibility of reconstructing n^{th} order relations (subsets of Cartesian products of n value sets) from projections onto n-1,n-2,...,2 dimensional subspaces. Ashby called the lowest dimensional subspaces from which it was possible to reconstruct the overall relation the cylindrance of that relation. Thus if a relation on six variables could be reconstructed by considering only three-dimensional subspaces, the system could be considered to be less complex than it might otherwise appear. While this concept provides a mechanism which is useful in different contexts (cf. Cavallo [9]), the cylindrance measure can be considerably refined.

For example, consider the following four relations (defined as lists) which are subsets of $V_1 \times V_2 \times V_3$ where $V_1 = V_2 = V_3 = \{0,1\}$.

I.	v_1	v_2	v_3
	0	0	0
	1	1	1

II.	v_1	v_2	v_3
	0	0	0
	0	0	1
	0	1	0
	1	0	0
	1	1	0

III.	v_1	v_2	v_3
	0	0	0
	0	0	1
	0	1	0

IV.	v_1	v_2	v_3
	0	0	0
	0	0	1
	0	1	0
	1	0	0

All four cases have cylindrance 2 by Ashby's definitions. This measure does not, however, convey all of the structural information which the data (relations) possess. To express this we utilize diagrams which use a box for each subset (subsystem) of the original set of variables with labelled lines indicating the variables relevant to that subsystem. For example, the diagram

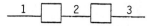

denotes the fact that the original three-variable system is broken up into two two-variable subsystems where the variable 2 is shared by both the subsystems.

For the four relations we are considering (all with cylindrance 2) we give the diagrams of the acceptable structure systems. The structure of relation I may be expressed by

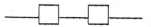

where any permutation of the three variables is acceptable. For relation II, the same structural form is acceptable -- but with only the one particular permutation of the variables which is shown in the following diagram.

For relation III, the following structure is acceptable:

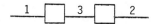

while for relation IV information regarding all pairs of variables must be retained and we may depict the structure by:

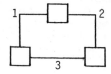

A proper interpretation, then, of the statement that a relation has cylindrance 2 is that there must be at least one two-dimensional relation present. The four examples illustrate that it is often possible to make much stronger statements than this.

In what follows we will characterize some meaningful classes of structure systems with the objective of forming a comprehensive methodological basis for the general reconstructability problem: Given a relation n, determine its properties of reconstructability from its nontrivial projection relations.

3. CLASSES OF STRUCTURE SYSTEMS

Let V be a set of variables which represents a system under investigation. Given the restriction regarding internal variables, subsystems (or elements of a structure system) can only be chosen from among subsets of the set V. In the most general case a structure system may be considered to be any family of subsets of V and we can define the set of all possible structure systems with respect to V as

$$S = \{S_i \mid S_i \subseteq P(V)\}$$

where $P(V)$ denotes the power set of V. As this general case, with no further restrictions, may not preserve the original conception of the object of investigation (if S_i does not constitute a cover of V), we only define this set for completeness and do not consider it further. We do observe, however, that for this most general set of structures (and similarly for all the subsets of it whose definitions follow) we can define a partial ordering on it which captures the concept of structure refinement. This ordering is crucial in that it allows us to generate the complete space of structure systems through local procedures based on immediate refinements. The ordering is obvious. Let S_i and S_j be elements of S. Then $S_i \leq S_j$ ("structure S_i is a refinement of S_j") if and only if for each set $E_a \in S_i$ there exists a set $E_b \in S_j$ such that $E_a \subseteq E_b$. Moreover, S_i is an immediate refinement of S_j if and only if $S_i \leq S_j$ and there is no S_k such that $S_i \leq S_k$ and $S_k \leq S_j$.

At the next lower level of generality we may define the set

$$S_\alpha = \{\alpha_i \mid \alpha_i \subset P(V) \text{ and } \cup E_a = V,$$

$$\text{where } E_a \in \alpha_i\}.$$

Elements of S_α will be called α-structures.[1] In this case, the level of generality is still higher than necessary for making significant statements regarding systems since there may be subsystems which contribute no information which is not present in some other subsystem (when there exist two subsystems $E_a, E_b \in \alpha_i$ where $E_a \subseteq E_b$). We thus

---

[1]The symbol α is used here to retain a connection with previous work (cf. Klir [18]; Klir and Uyttenhove [21,22]).

further restrict the set of possible structure systems by defining

$$S_G = \{G_i \mid G_i \subseteq P(V); \cup E_a = V, \text{ where } E_a \in G_i;$$
$$\text{for each } E_a, E_b \in G_i, E_a \not\subset E_b\}.$$

Thus, elements of S_G are structure systems (or families of subsets) of V such that each $v_i \in V$ participates in at least one subsystem and such that no subsystem properly contains all the variables associated with any other subsystem; these structure systems will be referred to as G-structures. In terms of the structure identification problem, our ultimate goal is a scheme which will allow consideration and evaluation of all elements of S_G. However, attempts to find a simple and direct procedure for generating all G-structures have as yet proven unsuccessful. We also observe that in many situations the context of the investigation will indicate large numbers of elements of S_G which it would not be necessary to consider. For these reasons the investigation of more restricted structure systems has been undertaken.

The addition of certain interpretively and systemically meaningful constraints to the set S_G will allow for the development of generally efficient and conceptually simple procedures for generating structure systems. The procedures which we refer to will in effect provide a way to get at all elements of S_G, but by dealing first with various subsets of S_G this will be accomplished in a more computationally efficient manner.

As a basis for the development of these procedures we consider that each family of subsets of V, and thus each structure system, defines a reflexive and symmetric binary relation on the set V, where two variables v_i and v_j are related if and only if they both belong to at least one of the subsets of V through which the structure system is defined. If, for example, the structure system under consideration is a G-structure, say G_i, then we denote the binary relation associated with G_i by $R(G_i)$. Thus R is to be considered as a function from S_α to the set of all reflexive and symmetric binary relations on V. The intention is to be able to utilize the relation representation of structure systems to systematically generate (and evaluate) all possible structure systems.

A main factor influencing the difficulty of this generation stems from the fact that the function R is not one to one, that is, that in general there exist many structures associated with each reflexive and symmetric binary relation on V. To deal with this problem, we define the following sets (which will allow concentration on manageable subsets of S with options for proceeding from results on these subsets to consideration of the most general cases):

a. S_M, consisting of elements of S_G which contain only maximal compatibility classes. We denote elements of S_M by M_i and refer to them as M-structures. An element G_i of S_G is also an M-structure if and only if, for each $E_a \in G_i$ there is no $v_k \in V$ such that $v_k \notin E_a$ and $(v_j, v_k) \in R(G_i)$ for all $v_j \in E_a$.

   b. S_C, consisting of elements of S_G which contain only and all maximal compatibility classes consistent with some relation $R(M_i)$. Such structures may also be considered as complete covers of V with respect to $R(M_i)$ and we refer to elements of S_C as <u>C-structures</u> and denote them by C_i. An important motivation for considering C-structures is that each reflexive and symmetric binary relation defines a unique C-structure. Hence, when R is restricted to S_C, it is both one to one and onto. We can take great advantage of this fact for defining an almost trivial procedure for generating immediate refinements of a given structure and, conversely, immediately less refined structures of (immediate aggregates) of a given structure. This is done simply by excluding (including) one pair of variables from (in) the relation $R(C_i)$ where C_i is the structure system which is the subject of modification.

   c. S_I, consisting of elements of S_M which are irredundant in the following sense. An element M_i of S_M also belongs to S_I if and only if for each $E_a \in M_i$ there exist v_j and v_k, where $v_j \neq v_k$, such that $v_j \in E_a$, $v_k \in E_a$, and there does not exist $E_b \neq E_a$ such that $E_b \in M_i$ and such that $v_j \in E_b$ and $v_k \in E_b$. We call elements of S_I <u>I-structures</u>. An obvious reason for the definition of the set S_I is -- in context of the overall identification problem and in keeping with the methodological orientation of GSPS, of which this problem is a part -- to take advantage of the extensive algorithmic work which has been done with respect to irredundant covers.

   d. S_β, consisting of elements of S_M which satisfy the following condition: an element M_i of S_M is also an element of S_β if and only if, for each $E_a \in M_i$, the transitive closure of $R(M_i - \{E_a\})$ is a proper subset of the transitive closure of $R(M_i)$. We denote an element of S_β by β_i, refer to it as a β-structure, and observe that elements of S_β have the property that removal of any subsystem of the structure disconnects at least two variables of the system which were otherwise connected (even if only indirectly, that is, through a sequence of subsystems).

   There is one further important subset of S_G which we will define, but before doing so we provide some commentary on the set S_β. Elements of set S_β have been studied extensively (see Klir and Uyttenhove [21,22]; Klir [20]; Broekstra [8]) and have proven reasonably accessible to computational procedures. They also represent an important meaningfully constrained subset of the larger set of interest, S_G, in that, given a β-structure β_i, each subsystem of β_i contains information regarding at least one pair of variables which not only is not contained in any other subsystem but which is also not obtainable through any other sequence of subsystems. Thus, in a well-defined sense, elements of S_β provide a crisper sense of structure than any of the other sets which have been so far defined. To slightly rephrase the characterization of S_β: given $\beta_i \in S_\beta$, each subsystem of β_i must contain at least one pair of variables which are not related through variables belonging only to other subsystems.

   This characterization is important since, in constructing a hypothesis about the structure of a system -- that is, in defining a structure system -- when dealing with a β-structure it is assured

that every subsystem contains some information which is not both part of the hypothesis and part of the empirical evidence as represented in the direct projections onto the subsystem. We observe, however, that the restriction of R to S_β is not onto the set of reflexive and symmetric binary relations. Thus, it is not easily possible to use this set in the generation of β-structures.

   In Klir and Uyttenhove [21] it was incorrectly thought that β-structures possessed the even more desirable property that they could <u>totally</u> distinguish hypothesis from empirical evidence. While this is in fact the case for structure systems defined on sets of five or less variables, this property is not guaranteed for β-structures containing six or more variables.[1] To resolve this potential difficulty we define our last subset of S_G:

   e. S_γ, consisting of elements S_M which satisfy the following additional condition: Let $M_i \in S_M$; for each pair $v_j, v_k \in V$ ($v_j \neq v_k$), let $E_{jk} = \{E_a \mid E_a \in M_i$ and $\{v_j, v_k\} \subseteq E_a\}$; then M_i is a γ-structure, γ_i, if and only if the pair v_j, v_k is not an element of the transitive closure of $R(M_i - E_{jk})$. γ-structures possess the important property that no pair of variables appears in the same structure in two different forms:

      i. as a relation supplying direct
   empirical information
      ii. as a relation which is a result of
   the structural hypothesis embodied in $\gamma_i \in S_\gamma$.
Thus γ-structures completely separate empirical from theoretical aspects of the system under investigation.

4. RELATIONSHIP AMONG CLASSES OF STRUCTURE SYSTEMS

   In considering further the rationale for the definitions of Section 3, we repeat that our goal is to delineate an overall procedure by which an investigator could conceivably "test" <u>every</u> structural hypothesis regarding his object of investigation. The subset characterizations which we have developed have been motivated by either: "meaningfulness," in context of possible interpretations of what subsystems may be; the fact that a particular characterization allows simplified computational procedures; some combination of the two motivations. Cavallo and Klir [12] contains a complete specification of the algorithms which have been developed based on this classification as well as proofs of all the technical results.

   There are many technical results which are associated with these definitions and which together provide direction for the operational procedures whose implementation constitutes a complete software package to aid an investigator in the identification and determination of structure. We also observe that it is basically unnecessary for a given investigator to be familiar with either the technical results or even the

---

[1] Investigations of H. Uyttenhove and G. Broekstra have implicitly assisted in the discovery of this fact.

technical definitions of Section 3. All that will be necessary for an investigator to profitably utilize this portion of GSPS is a general understanding of the distinctions which are represented by the definitions and a sense of how these characterizations relate to his own area of investigation and object-language problem (see Cavallo and Klir [11]; Cavallo [9]).

In this spirit we summarize some of the results in Figures 1 and 2. Figure 1 illustrates the connections among the various subsets which we have defined. This figure is the Hasse diagram of the partial ordering defined by the relation "is a subset of" on the set $\{S, S_\alpha, S_G, S_M, S_C, S_I, S_\beta, S_\gamma\}$. We remark that the elements of the ordered set

are sets of structures. Thus, although S_β and S_C are incomparable, there exist β-structures which are also C-structures.

Figure 2 presents this information in the form of a Venn diagram.

By looking at Figure 2 we can see that if we restrict ourselves to consideration of structures which belong to S_G there are eight non-empty categories of structures. These structure categories can be signified by concatenation of symbols which indicate that the category belongs to the relevant subset or by symbols with overbars indicating that the category does not belong to that subset. The eight categories along with the structure diagram of an example of each are given in Figure 3.

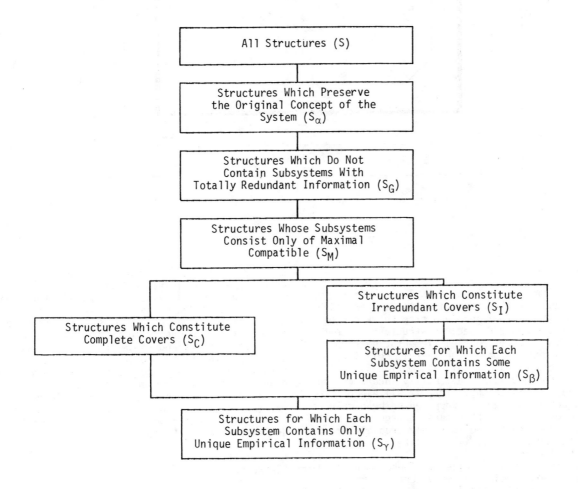

Figure 1.

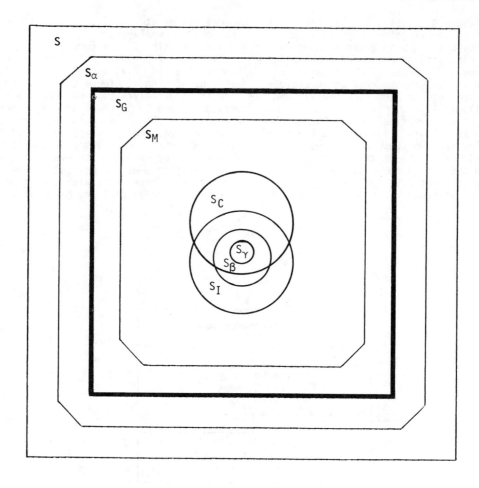

Figure 2.

5. CONCLUSIONS

Many systems models have recently been developed which are based on the assumption that the actual relation among a set of involved attributes can be reconstructed through a specific structure system; i.e., through a set of coupled elements, each representing a projection of the overall relation. It is quite clear that if this assumption is not warranted, the model is fundamentally incorrect and might be vastly misleading. Yet, if all elements of the structure system are represented by highly credible models, it is often taken for granted that the whole structure system is highly credible too. Although it may be so, it is more likely that this is only an illusion.

There are, of course, classes of phenomena for which each overall relation among certain attributes can be reconstructed from some specific projections of the relation. The problem of identifying the right set of projections in a particular application area is one of the most important problems of modelling. While the reconstructability properties are somewhat better understood in the natural sciences -- most notably in classical physics -- they have been largely unexplored in the social sciences, where they are often postulated in the most convenient manner and accepted without justification.

The problem has also unfortunately been too frequently avoided by systems researchers or, even worse, assumed not to exist. Attempts to develop means to deal with this situation have not been numerous and those contributions which do address the basic problem have all been restricted in some way (for example, Ashby's cylindrance or Klir's focus on β-structures).

In this paper we have provided a fundamental methodological framework for dealing with this problem in a manner which is as comprehensive and general as possible.

REFERENCES

1. ASHBY, W. R., "Constraint Analysis of Many-Dimensional Relations," General Systems Yearbook, Vol. 9, pp. 99-105, 1964.
2. ASHBY, W. R., "Measuring the Internal Information Exchange in a System," Cybernetica, Vol. 8, No. 1, pp. 5-22, 1965.
3. ASHBY, W. R., "Constraint Analysis of Many-Dimensional Relations," in: Progress in Biocybernetics, Vol. 2, N. Wiener and

CATEGORY

CATEGORY

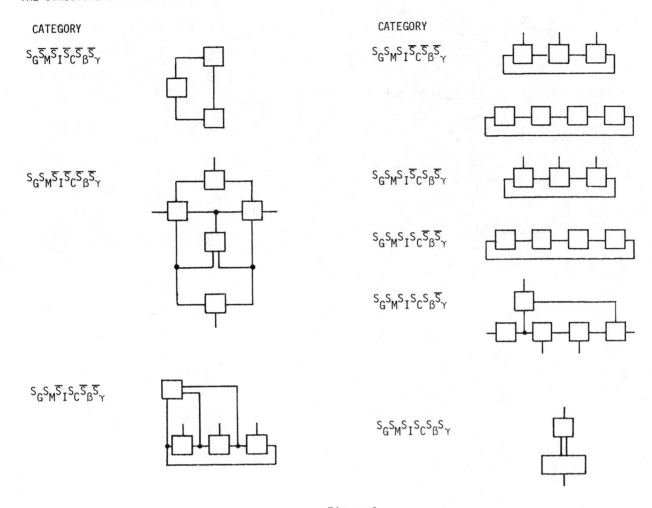

Figure 3.

J. P. Schade (eds.), Elsevier, Amsterdam, 1965.

4. ATKIN, R. H., *Mathematical Structures in Human Affairs*, Heinemann, London, 1974.

5. ATKIN, R. H., *Combinatorial Connections in Social Systems*, Birkhauser, Basel and Stuttgart, 1977.

6. BROEKSTRA, G., "Constraint Analysis and Structure Identification I," *Annals of Systems Research*, Vol. 5, H. E. Stenfert Kroese, Leiden, The Netherlands, 1976.

7. BROEKSTRA, G., "Constraint Analysis and Structure Identification II," *Annals of Systems Research*, Vol. 6, H. E. Stenfert Kroese, Leiden, The Netherlands, 1977.

8. BROEKSTRA, G., "Structure Modelling: A Constraint (Information) Analytic Approach," in: *Applied General Systems Research*, G. Klir (ed.), Plenum Press, New York, 1978.

9. CAVALLO, R., *The Role of Systems Methodology in Social Sciences Research*, Martinus Nijhoff, Leiden, The Netherlands, 1979.

10. CAVALLO, R. (ed.), *Recent Developments in Systems Methodology for Social Science Research*, Martinus Nijhoff, Leiden, The Netherlands, 1980.

11. CAVALLO, R. and G. J. Klir, "A Conceptual Foundation for Systems Problem Solving," *International Journal of Systems Science*, Vol. 9, 1978.

12. CAVALLO, R. and G. J. Klir, "Reconstructability Analysis of Multidimensional Relations: A Theoretical Basis for Computer-Aided Determination of Acceptable Systems Models," *International Journal of General Systems*, Vol. 5, pp. 143-171, 1979.

13. CAVALLO, R. and F. PICHLER, "General Systems Methodology: Designs for Intuition-Amplification," in: *Improving the Human Condition: Quality and Stability in Social Systems*, R. Ericson (ed.), Springer-Verlag, New York, 1979.

14. CONANT, R. C., "Detecting Subsystems of a Complex System," *IEEE Transactions on Systems, Man and Cybernetics*, Vol. SMC-2, No. 4, pp. 550-553, 1972.

15. CONANT, R. C., "Laws of Information Which Govern Systems," *IEEE Transactions on Systems, Man and Cybernetics*, Vol. SMC-6, No. 4, pp. 240-255.

16. KLIR, G. J., _An Approach to General Systems Theory_, Van Nostrand, New York, 1969.

17. KLIR, G. J., _Methodology of Switching Circuits_, Van Nostrand, New York, 1972.

18. KLIR, G. J., "Identification of Generative Structures in Empirical Data," _International Journal of General Systems_, Vol. 3, No. 2, pp. 89-104., 1976.

19. KLIR, G. J., "General Systems Concepts," in: _Cybernetics: A Sourcebook_, R. Trappl (ed.), Hemisphere, Washington, D. C., 1978.

20. KLIR, G. J., "Computer-Aided Systems Modelling," in: _Theoretical Systems Ecology_, E. Halfon (ed.), Academic Press, New York, 1978.

21. KLIR, G. J. and H. J. J. UYTTENHOVE, "Computerized Methodology for Structure Modelling," _Annals of Systems Research_, Vol. 5, Martinus Nijhoff, Leiden, The Netherlands, pp. 29-65, 1976.

22. KLIR, G. J. and H. J. J. UYTTENHOVE, "On the Problem of Computer-Aided Structure in Identification: Some Experimental Observations and Resulting Guidelines," _International Journal of Man-Machine Studies_, Vol. 9, No. 5, 1977.

23. KRIPPENDORFF, K., "A Spectral Analysis of Relations: Further Developments," this volume.

24. PICHLER, F., "Structured Methodologies for General Systems Research," in: _Recent Developments in Systems Methodology for Social Science Research_, R. Cavallo (ed.), Martinus Nijhoff, Leiden, 1980.

25. SIMON, H. A., "The Architecture of Complexity," _Proceedings of the American Philosophical Society_, Vol. 106, 1962.

Epistemological foundations of the systems paradigm

J. P. VAN GIGCH and IVOR STOLLIDAY
California State University, Sacramento, California USA

1. INTRODUCTION

This paper springs from consideration of the difficulties which attend the attempts to construct a workable systems theory for the 'soft' systems domains of society, social processes, history and the political, ethical and human sub-systems that comprise it. In short, the problems are those that inhabit the "inexact sciences" where human agency makes both prediction and the ascription of laws so difficult.

It may be both instructive and comforting to see that our problems are not new. Those who attempted to apply the methodologies of the traditional sciences to these areas found that their scientific machinery was haunted by ancient ghosts. Part of the purpose of this paper is to suggest that those same ghosts may be alive and well and living under the newer roof of systems theory. We must see if they are still as resistant to attempts at exorcism.

Our starting point, then, is that the attempt to apply the natural sciences to the areas of human agency has, with just a few exceptions, foundered on some ancient <u>philosophical</u> rocks. Now that general systems theory seeks also to chart those same seas, it must avoid the same rocks. We shall argue that the role of <u>epistemology</u> is crucial here. For if systems theory is, at meta-system level, to be more than a loose metaphysical construct, it must have an epistemology, or theory of knowledge. It has been said that "the job of a theory of knowledge is to make an honest woman of metaphysics" [1] and allow metaphysics to move from a descriptive account of the order of things in which, to some degree, 'anything goes', to one in which there are criteria for knowledge and thus some limits and control on ontology. If systems theory is to move successfully from a more menial role of co-ordinating areas of existing knowledge, to a more grand station of claiming to give new knowledge in inexact areas, it must have some epistemological foundations. Without these, it will have no means of deciding what does, or does not, exist, or what is, or is not, real. However, once it has invested in an epistemology, how can it avoid the annoying presence of our ancient ghosts, which have no business to be there but which still inhabit the science paradigm?

We shall approach these problems as follows.

Firstly, we will look at the historical context of our inquiry in terms of the development of science.

We will then look at the epistemological foun-c dations of the science paradigm that led both to its successes and to the entry of the problems.

Thirdly, we will attempt to list the problems themselves, to inquire whether systems theory could generate innovative epistemological approaches by which these problems can be solved or sidestepped.

2. THE HISTORICAL CONTEXT

The growth of the scientific method and the path to dominance of the science paradigm was not an even and uneventful process. In the collapse of the medieval world, we see a crisis of epistemology, accompanied by a breakdown of the systems of knowledge and belief. Until the reformation, faith and reason had been happily married and their issue had been a picture of the universe in which all was rationally ordered for divine purpose. The divorce of faith from reason saw both a new path for metaphysics and religion, and, crucially, a new role for reason in the development of science. The divorce was not without bitterness, expressed both in intellectual argument and systematic persecution. Luther said [2]: "We know that reason is the Devil's harlot, and can do nothing but slander and harm all that God says and does . . . Therefore keep to Revelation and do not try to understand."

But men continued to be seduced by reason, and developed two great engines of rational endeavour, which are still critically relevant for our debate today. We refer to the development of European rationalism, by Descartes, Leibniz and Spinoza, and the growth of empiricism, mainly in Britain with Locke, Berkeley and Hume. In the fusion of these two, and in their separate developments, we have the twin epistemologies on which science is built. On the one hand, formal deductive reasoning, from axiomatic premises, leading to the development of mathematics, and on the other hand, inductive reasoning from propositions whose ultimate verification rests only in experience. Both are fraught with problems which have been there since their inception, and it is these problems we will examine later, to see if systems theory can aid their avoidance. But problems or not, the two approaches led to amazing results. By the nineteenth century, as we all know, the science paradigm and its methodology had transformed the world of knowledge and our knowledge of the world. The transformation had occurred in the <u>physical</u> sciences, and the application of these to our world and beyond it to the cosmos. But the science of nature had yet to be completed by the science of man. A major theme of the last century has been the attempt to complete such a science. Darwin provided a science of human origins, and others wished to extend the use of the scientific method to encompass man's history, society, economy, morality and individual behaviour. Marxism may be seen as one of the bravest attempts to do just this, in a theory so broad that it stands itself almost as a meta-theory within which there can be individual key elements; from its roots in a science of history it develops into an economic science, a political science and a theory of the liberation or repression of the individual [3]. But for all its breathtaking scope, Marxism is still identifiable as almost symbolic of the great nineteenth century endeavour: to provide a science of man by subsuming his affairs under the science paradigm. In the preface to Capital, Marx states that his ultimate aim is to "lay bare the law of motion of modern society." Marx's own use of an analogy drawn from physics is itself instructive, and illustrates our point. But we know that those hopes have never been fully realised. Compared with the physical sciences, the social and human sciences are still in their infancy, and appear by now to be 'late-developers' of a rather acute kind. Economics has made some progress, but even this does not 'fit the facts' in the way we might have hoped. Psychology has given us new insights but little that is testable. As A. J. Ayer has stated [4]:

> All in all, the stock of generally accredited and well-tested theories that the social sciences can muster is comparatively small. The social scientist may well look on the garden of the natural sciences as an intellectual paradise from which he has lamentably been excluded.
> Buy why should this be so? Is it just that the factors which govern human behaviour are unmanageably complex? ... Or is there some more fundamental reason, some reason of principle, why the kind of success that the natural sciences have had is here unattainable?

In our time, extreme empiricists, and some others, argue for Ayer's first answer: that human affairs, although vastly complex, are potentially as amenable to science as any other. This is the view of all varieties of positivism, in which all the besetting problems are usually eliminated by the devastating expedients of denying the existence of many of the entities that cause the problems, such as mind, volition, etc., and applying a strict nominalist reductionism. This bold path may save the purity of a rigorous scientific method, but it has not done much to develop any social sciences. In mid-stream, some try to save a 'unity of method' for the physical and social sciences by arguing that the scientific method is not like we thought anyway, and looks just like social science after all. Popper, in both The Poverty of Historicism [5] and Conjectures and Refutations [6] and elsewhere, argues just this way. But this view may create more problems than it solves. It fails to give a thorough logical analysis of the process of science, unlike rationalism and empiricism. Moreover, if it claims that there is such a 'unity of method' between both social and physical science, it leaves unsolved our initial problem: Why does science work so well in the physical areas and yet so poorly in the human, 'soft' areas? Having seen

the historical context of our dilemma, we must now face up to the question itself and look for Ayer's "more fundamental reason, some reason of principle." We shall see that the difficulties of analysing the 'soft' domain lie in the epistemology of the science paradigm itself.

3. THE EPISTEMOLOGICAL FOUNDATIONS OF THE SCIENCE PARADIGM

We must be careful here not to attempt to debate the whole vast field of the theory of knowledge, with its constant attendants: truth, belief, universals, memory and ontology. Our questions are: What theory of knowledge underpins the science paradigm? And what problems are left over when we have put the scientific machinery together? We can then consider how far systems theory might help us with these.

There is no doubt that the development of Rationalism and the 'Geometric Method' gave the intellectual impetus to the development of science. In the philosophy of science, the hand of Descartes can be seen reaching through to Vienna positivists and beyond. Despite this, however, western science and its philosophy have become progressively more empiricist, and have abandoned the rationalists' insistence on truths made manifest to reason, and deductive inference from these to propositions capable of yielding new knowledge. The 'geometric' or deductive method beloved of the rationalists is reduced to application in formal systems, whose axioms are chosen, not given, and which are analytic in the Kantian sense, and which are tautological. Mathematics becomes the servant of science, but not the source of its truths. That prime place, in the empiricist world view, rests always with observation of the world and argument from this. Our science is founded on an increasingly rigorous empiricist epistemology, with statements of sensory experience as the ultimate sources of verification, and knowledge reduced to the consensus of experience and operational utility. By this means, positivist scientific theory has hoped to expel a number of metaphysical items, which since they cannot be verified by experience, are ruled to be unknowable and "literally meaningless", and thus are expunged from the ontologists' list of the things of the universe. Like the rationalists before them, the intention of the empiricists with their epistemology is to make easy and true the path of science. They might truly echo Hobbes, in Leviathan [7] in stating: "Reason is the pace; increase of science the way, and the benefit of mankind the end." But we have seen that despite the 'purifying' of the science paradigm into a rigorous positivist mould, with all the difficult 'metaphysical' concepts packed off into oblivion, none of these seems to have helped us make progress in the 'soft' domain of social science. Moreover, the metaphysical 'ghosts' keep returning to haunt the machinery, and the occasional heretic takes a serious swipe at the very foundations of the empiricist epistemology. If this epistemology and its superstructure of the science paradigm is so rigorous, why does it look so frail in places and why are we still unable to use it to solve some of our most pressing problems?

4. THE PROBLEMS OF THE SCIENCE PARADIGM

The epistemology of the science paradigm yields problems which could amuse us for lifetimes, but we cannot here spend an undue portion of our allotted space on them. Instead we shall simply try to isolate and list them, and then see what advance systems theory might make. Before we do so, however, it will be as well to reflect upon why any epistemology might fail since this will have relevance for our epistemology of systems theory.

Part of the problem lies in the way we set about doing the business of epistemology. There would seem to be two theoretical ways of doing so. On the one hand, we could specifiy in advance our ontology, listing carefully the items to which we would allow existence and claims of knowledge. (For example, trees would probably be in our list of items, while tree-spirits might not be.) We could then decide criteria for knowledge which would purchase for us the items on our ontological shopping list. What we might be doing is drawing out from our list the kinds of criteria which would justify their inclusion. In short, we would be teasing-out the epistemological assumptions in our common-sense view of the world. On the other hand, if we were courageous philosophers or systems theorists, we might proceed on another track. We might decide first some criteria for knowledge, and then see what things these allowed us to know of, and thus to grant 'existence' to, and then compare this list with our naive and common-sense view of what things there are. A rigorous positivist-empiricist epistemology does much of the latter, and we find that many of the major items of furniture of the soft systems domain have been cast into non-existence. In our common-sense world, however, we keep bumping into this furniture that has no business still to be there. The practical problems of doing epistemology are worsened by the way in which we adopt something of both approaches. We know that our naive epistemology is a loose result of previous philosophical assumptions, and yet although we may devise a new, purer, conceptual system, we test it against our old ontology. We are, instinctively, demanding that a paradigm or conceptual system is not only internally coherent, but in some way 'fits the world'. Here positivism fails, but it can rightly demand of us to describe which world it is that we wanted it to fit. We may well describe all manner of possible world, but which possible world do we happen to live in?

If the possible world offered by the empiricist science paradigm will not do, we must look and see which bits are left over on the garage floor when the empiricist machine has been built.

What are the problems of the soft systems domain that empiricism cannot cope with? We must ask what are the main questions which the systems paradigm must seek to answer before claiming to replace the science paradigm and becoming the methodology by which real-world problems in soft-systems domains can be solved.

5. THE QUESTIONS WHICH MUST BE ANSWERED

If the systems paradigm is to pretend to do better than the science paradigm it must work to resolve some of the long standing questions which our previous discussion has raised. It may be wishful thinking to expect that answers will be readily forthcoming when some of these questions have been under discussion for literally thousands of years. However, the systems movement will only remain an ephemeral passing fad unless it makes a contribution to their resolution.

In what follows we have borrowed Laszlo's [8] seminal presentation on the basic premises of systems philosophy but have turned his assertions into questions.

4.1. The Ontological Question

It is not clear whether the philosophy of systems should consider within its purview the problem of cognition or whether it will be able to make a contribution to it. Thus it may be that we ought to accept the existence of systems without asking the previous question. How do we know that they exist? But even if we jump this first hurdle the next one concerns the differentiation that can be made between natural systems, actual entities existing in nature as irreducible wholes, and contrived systems, the convenient entitities invented for ease of study by our imagination. In other words, are systems to be considered empirical facts proven by experience or just merely theoretical constructs? Answers to this question will depend, in part, on whether you belong to a school of thought such as Laszlo's, who proposes an ontological thesis whereby "sets of irreducibly different mental and physical events constitute an identical psycho-physical system, disclosed through the invariance of their respective theories" [8]. Thus the concept of system is tied here to that of theory invariance.

If you belong to a neo-rationalist school of thought, systems are to be considered as "extra-linguistic entities that are theorized about, for example, our solar system as opposed to theories describing its behaviour" [9]. And here we fall into the next problem which is not ontological but definitional: the problem of explicating the concept of system. A satisfactory answer to this question has been attempted, whereby a set-theoretical representation of a system appears to be able to handle the various contexts in which systems are described. It satisfies the following criteria:

A satisfactory explication will make clear:
(1) the basis for identifying and distinguishing between different systems;
(2) the basis for identifying and distinguishing between different kinds of systems; and
(3) will not result in everything being a system.
The definition given is:
  S is a system only if $S = \langle E,R \rangle$, where
    (i) E is an element set, and
    (ii) $R = \langle R_1,...,R_n \rangle$ is a relation set, i.e. $R_1,...,R_n$ are relations holding among the elements of E.   [9]

4.2. The Question of Knowledge

If you have answered to your satisfaction the previous questions of how do we know (the problem of cognition) and how do we know that we know (the problem of consciousness), presumably you are ready to ask the question of what constitutes knowledge and how do we acquire it, with the collateral question how do we validate trust in systems philosophy.

Here again you may be allowed to waver between answers which reveal your empiricist-inductivist bias or that of a neo-rationalistic reconstruction-ist. In the first instance you will insist on using induction and verification as the cornerstones of truth, whereas in the second you will require that theoretical constructs, built independently from sense-experience, be made to contain testable propositions which can be refuted. Refutation is to the reconstructionalist what verification is to the inductivists [10,11]. The question which we must settle is: which path should the epistemology of systems follow? There are obviously many philosophical postures such as the ones outlined above and many in between which can be adopted, but to date the systems movement has not clearly identified with any.

Many positions are viable depending on how you conceive that scientific knowledge grows. Laszlo has proposed using the previously mentioned concept of invariance as a powerful concept leading to the growth of knowledge; as an example insistence upon invariance is purported to have led to discoveries such as Einstein's Relativity Theory.

In this case, insistence on preserving uniformity led at the same time to a new discovery and to the enlargement of the principle of invariance over a larger set of transformations [12].

In Laszlo's philosophical world, invariance works hand in hand with evolution to provide a dynamic environment in which systems and systems science grow. However, if in spite of himself we could enlist Popper as an epistemologist of systems science--a role which he could, not so facetiously, be accorded--he would probably regard evolution as a "process", a "behavioural disposition" and not as an objective "product" of knowledge, or reputable theory upon which the growth of scientific knowledge could legitimately be built [13]. Therefore, it is not obvious how the systems movement has contributed any answers to the questions of how to validate truth and how the theory of truth connects to the theory of knowledge.

Collateral to the truth-knowledge question, and probably one which should be answered at the same time, is that which questions the ontological uniformity of domain among physical and social systems domains. Indeed an answer to that question will go a long way in determining the form of the scientific paradigm to which one will ascribe, where the concept of "paradigm" is to be given its most general meaning of "scientific research program" [8,10].

4.3. Three More Questions: Volition, Teleology and Action

If the systems paradigm is to be propounded as a problem solving methodology three additional related questions must be addressed:

(1) The first one relates to volition or the question of choice or obtaining an answer to the question whether systems are determinate or whether they can display free-will.

(2) The second one is called the teleological question and seeks to determine how the concept of goals relates to systems.

(3) The third question is the question of action. An answer to the third question caps the whole quest for an epistemology of systems, given that: (a) the answer to the question of choice is that there is no incompatibility between individual freedom and a social organization determined by environmental constraints, and that (b) the answer to the teleological question reveals that systems science has normative implications in the sense that the information it produces is valued for its appropriateness in improving the state of optimum adaption of system to its environment, then (c) we would be ready to assign an activist role to the systems scientist. Thus, systems philosophy yields a theory of action: Man is involved in changing the environment. He is a "part of it" [8].

Unfortunately, all three questions cannot be answered categorically as shown above.

The question of choice or volition admits other possibilities such as positing that systems have no choices available and that what happens is determined by the blind convergence of environmental forces over which the system or the human being has no control, or contrariwise, systems are entirely free to choose among alternative courses of action. There are no causal or deterministic factors responsible for choice and thus one cannot make predictions as to what will happen.

The teleological question also admits alternative answers which must be resolved before positing the systems paradigm as a useful problem-solving methodology. It is not at all certain that all recommendations derived from a systems paradigm can be valued either (a) by their appropriateness at improving the system's state of adaptation, or (b) that this state is necessarily to be valued for its own sake, or (c) that indeed systems naturally pursue this objective over others, or finally (d) that the morality of systems is automatically served by this imperative [15].

Finally, the question of involvement and playing an active part in designing a system requires a metasystem capability which is still beyond our grasp. Judging which criteria a system must satisfy can only be done at a level above that of the system itself. This is not only true of the system for which the design is intended but also applies to the choice of the paradigm or methodology by which it can be studied. To date we have hardly made any dent in the problem of defining the requirements which such a metaparadigm must meet. It is patently obvious that if the systems paradigm and attendant methodologies are to succeed, enough work lies ahead of us before they can claim a role in solving the problems of social science and social systems.

REFERENCES

1. HOLLIS, M., The Light of Reason, London, Collins-Fontana, 1973.
2. LUTHER, Martin, De Servo Arbitro (1483-1546).
3. BESANCON, A., Les Origines Intellectuelles du Léninisme, Paris, Calman-Lévy, 1977.
4. AYER, A. J., Metaphysics and Common Sense, London, Macmillan, 1969 (paperback, 1973).
5. POPPER, K., The Poverty of Historicism, London, Routledge and Kegan Paul, 1957.

6. POPPER, K., <u>Conjectures and Refutations</u>,
    London, Routledge and Kegan Paul, 1957.

7. HOBBES, T., <u>Leviathan</u> (1588-1679), Ch. 5.

8. LASZLO, E., <u>Introduction to Systems Philos-
    ophy. Towards a New Paradigm of Contemporary
    Thought</u>, New York, Gordon and Breach, 1972.

9. MARCHAL, J. H., "On the Concept of System,"
    <u>Philosophy of Science</u>, 42: 448-468, 1975.

10. LAKATOS, I., "History of Science and Its
    Rational Reconstructions," in: R. C. Buck
    R. S. Cohen (eds.), <u>Boston Studies in the
    Philosophy of Science</u>, Vol. 8, 1971,
    pp. 91-136.

11. MUSGRAVE, A., "Logical versus Historical
    Theories of Confirmation," <u>British Journal
    of Philosophy of Science</u>, 25: 1-23, 1974.

12. LASZLO, E. and H. MARGENAU, "The Emergence
    of Integrative Concepts in Contemporary
    Science," <u>Philosophy of Science</u>, Vol. 39,
    252-259, 1972.

13. POPPER, K., <u>Objective Knowledge</u>, Oxford,
    England, Oxford University Press, 1972.

14. KUHN, T. S., "The Structure of Scientific
    Revolutions," <u>International Encyclopedia
    of Unified Science</u>, Vol. II, No. 2, 2nd
    edition, Chicago and London, The Univer-
    sity of Chicago Press, 1970.

15. van GIGCH, J. P., <u>Applied General Systems
    Theory</u>, London and New York, Harper
    and Row 1974. (2nd edition, 1978, in
    process.)

Generative grammars and general systems

JAMES W. HAEFNER

Department of Wildlife Science, Utah State University
Logan, Utah USA

1. INTRODUCTION

The mathematics underlying most general systems theory and methodology are differential equations and automata theory. There are good reasons for this: the former is the basis of many important applications of systems research and the latter is the natural setting for a theory of computation, to which the applications are closely tied.

There are, however, other mathematical structures that warrant application to general systems research. One such mathematical structure is generative grammars. The purpose of this paper is to initiate an investigation of the role of generative grammars in general systems research.

2. A CONCEPTUAL SPACE FOR GENERAL SYSTEMS THEORY

The role of generative grammars can be best explicated by observing the relationships between all systems models. These relationships are defined in the space of all systems models on the basis of three properties: theoretical abstraction, idealization, and physical abstraction.

Any particular systems model can be communicated in a variety of languages ranging from natural languages to the abstractions of mathematical systems theory. These form a continuum of levels of increasing theoretical abstraction. They can be ordered on an axis and used to define and distinguish different systems models. Levels of theoretical abstraction form one dimension of the conceptual space (Figure 1).

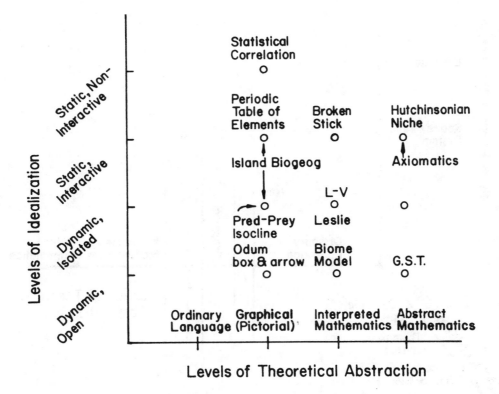

Figure 1.   A two-dimensional model of the conceptual space of systems models. Every point defined by the two axes is a class of models; examples are from ecology and population biology.   L-V = Lotka-Volterra predator-prey models; Broken-stick = MacArthur's random model of niche packing; Leslie = Leslie's age-specific population projection matrix; and G.S.T. = general systems theories.

Models also differ from one another by the particular hypotheses (assumptions) used in the models. These hypotheses form a continuum of idealization (Figure 1). Models are more idealized if the hypotheses apply to only a small set of systems (e.g., static, equilibrium, linear, etc.).

This basic model of the set of all systems models can be extended to include the models of any particular epistemic domain. For illustrative purposes the emphasis here is on ecology and population biology.

Levels of theoretical abstraction and idealzation, however, do not completely characterize the set of all models because they neglect certain aspects of human conceptual frameworks. Conceptual frameworks form a continuum from specific and detailed to general and abstract. At one extreme of the continuum of abstraction the conceptual framework is identical with the types of human knowledge ("modes of cognition") in the usage of Locker and Coulter [19]. We can identify three types of human knowledge: proprio-receptive, space/time, and language. This classification of knowledge is not necessarily exhaustive nor does it imply that mechanistic theories of human knowledge and cognition must describe three separate causal pathways.

Proprio-receptive knowledge is a name for learned responses that cannot be readily communi-

cated to others. This knowledge is identical to the "tacit knowledge" of Polanyi [12]; it is exemplified by physical skills (e.g., playing instruments), or discovery skills (e.g., patterns in chess, mathematical theorems). Since, by definition, proprio-receptive knowledge is not communicable to others and cannot form the basis for systems models, we will not consider it further.

Space/time knowledge is knowledge of systems or objects that are defined in physical space and time. This knowledge may concern physical, material objects as well as statistical relationships possessed by a collection of interacting objects (e.g., organisms). This type of knowledge can be represented by spoken language and is, thus, communicable to others. Consequently, it can form the basis for systems models. Most systems models attempt to represent space and/or time; thus, this model of cognition is predominant in general systems research.

Humans also have linguistic knowledge: knowledge of languages. Particular languages, as objects, can be described within a meta-language and consequently can form the basis for systems models. Languages that are known by humans include: natural languages (e.g., German), formal languages (e.g., mathematics), and esthetic languages (e.g., music).

Figure 2 summarizes these three properties of systems models and gives some examples of the

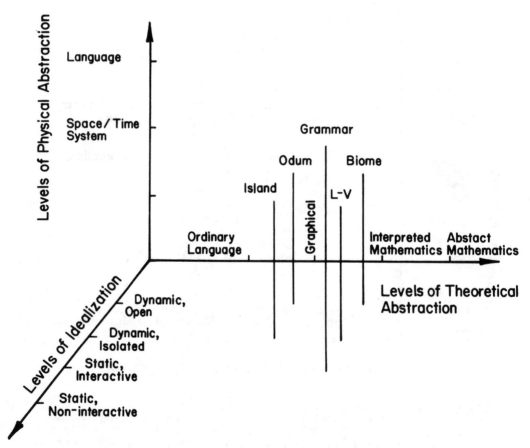

Figure 2.   A three-dimensional model of the conceptual space of systems models. Bottom axes as in Figure 1; the third axis corresponds to types of human knowledge. The relation of models based on generative grammars to the models of Figure 1 is shown.

models possible at different points in the conceptual space. An aspect not readily visualized is the incongruity between levels of idealization for different levels of physical abstraction (languages and space/time). A language model cannot represent system dynamics directly but may represent the results of the dynamics. Thus, static space/time models and static language models need not possess similar hypotheses. Accurate representation of the differences between models based on the language abstraction and those based on the space/time abstraction requires at least two interpretations of the idealization axis (not shown in Figure 2).

3. FORMALISM OF GENERATIVE GRAMMARS.

As used here a generative grammar is any rewrite device that distinguishes between terminal and non-terminal vocabulary items. The structure of the device is contained in rewrite rules having the form: $X+A+Y \rightarrow Y+B+Y$, where X and Y are unspecified variables, and A and B are related by the "substitution" relation. That is, "$A \rightarrow B$" is read as: "B substitutes for A". A terminal vocabulary item is any symbol that appears to the right of the rewrite arrow in at least one rule and not to the left of the arrow in any rule. A non-terminal vocabulary item is one that appears to the left of the arrow. Thus, A in the above rule is a non-terminal vocabulary item and B may or may not be terminal.

A grammar is a collection of rules. A grammar of a particular set of syntactic relations (e.g., a natural language) is a grammar where the vocabulary items have empirical interpretations (e.g.,

"Noun", "Verb Phrase", "sleep", etc.). A string (or sentence) is produced by a grammar when all non-terminal vocabulary items are replaced by terminal vocabulary items. Recording, for each string, the rules and non-terminal vocabulary items used in generating the string produces a derivation tree. Figure 3 and Figure 4 illustrate these relationships for an elementary grammar of English.

In addition to rewrite rules generative grammars may possess transformation rules. These rules operate not on vocabulary items (as do rewrite rules), but on the derivation trees produced by a set of rewrite rules. An abstract example is given in Figure 5. The effect of a transformation rule is to transform one derivation tree into another as indicated in the lower portion of the figure. The notation for this movement (upper portion of the figure) involves defining the tree as a set of labeled brackets. A bracket is labeled by the node that appears above it in the derivation tree. Nodes (e.g., X_1, X_2, etc.) can be manipulated relative to one another given this labeling and a left-to-right ordering. Figure 5 illustrates several types of movement: deletion (X_3), permutation (X_4 and X_5), and addition (X_6).

4. FORMAL DEFINITION

With these considerations and the mathematics of formal languages we can define a system generator (G) as a sextuple (S, V_N, V_T, P, $\emptyset$, I). Here S is a start symbol, V_N is a set of non-terminal vocabulary items, V_T is a set of terminal vocabulary items, P is a set of rules (rewrite and transformation), $\emptyset$ is the null set, and I is an

1. $S \rightarrow NP + VP$

2. $NP \rightarrow Article + \begin{cases} noun\text{-}sing \\ noun\text{-}plural \end{cases}$

3. $VP \rightarrow verb\text{-}sing + (NP) + (S)/noun\text{-}sing\underline{\quad}$

4. $VP \rightarrow verb\text{-}plural + (NP) + (S)/noun\text{-}plural\underline{\quad}$

5. Article $\rightarrow$ {this, that, a, some, the, every,...}

6. noun-sing $\rightarrow$ {dog, cat, chair, girl, shoe, boy, cabbage,...}

7. noun-plural $\rightarrow$ {dogs, cats, chairs, girls, men, boys, cabbages,...}

8. verb-sing $\rightarrow$ {kicks, found, ran, runs, hates, ate, sees, see,...}

9. verb-plural $\rightarrow$ {sleep, found, ran, run, hate, ate, eat, saw,...}

Figure 3.   A simple generative grammar of English. S = sentence, NP = Noun Phrase, and VP = Verb Phrase. Sentences are produced by obeying each rule as it occurs. The notation of Rules 5 to 9 indicates that one item of the list of terminal items is to be selected for each application of the rule.

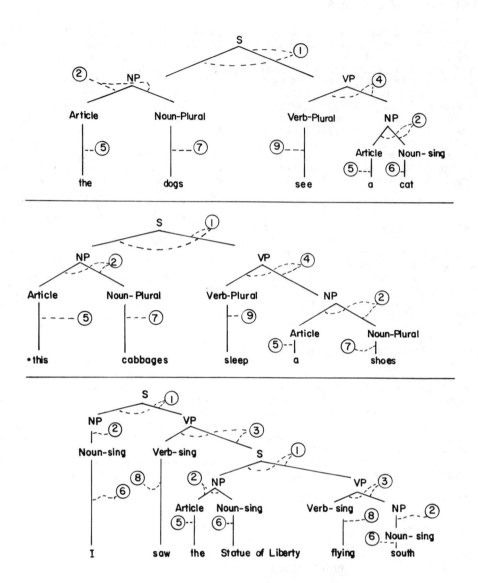

Figure 4.   Three examples of the derivation trees and strings produced
             by the grammar of Figure 3. Each node of the tree is a
             terminal or non-terminal vocabulary item of the grammar.
             Numbers indicate the rules (Figure 3) used to produce the
             strings. An asterix (*) indicates an ungrammatical string.

index set (e.g., I ⊆ N, the natural numbers). This
definition follows closely the definition of a
grammar (Hopcroft and Ullman [6]). A particular
production of a system generator is a <u>system</u> (structure plus behavior). The set of all productions
(equivalent to the language produced by a grammar)
will be termed the <u>system class</u>.

    In most applications of generative grammars
(e.g., natural languages) time is represented by a
left-to-right order of terminal vocabulary items.
For example, the time order of words spoken in a
sentence is equivocated with the left-to-right
order of the terminal items of a grammar production.
This approach can be generalized by introducing
additional structure to the basic definition. Let
the set of rules (P) be such that a special terminal

vocabulary item "x" ($x \in I$) is added to the right
of the terminal string whenever a grammaticality
criterion is met. An example of a suitable criterion is: a string is grammatical if all non-
terminal vocabulary items have been replaced by
terminal vocabulary items. Addition of an index
marker denotes the completion of a set of operations; thus, the string to the left of the index
is grammatical.

    Further, let $P \equiv P_1 \cup P_2$, such that P_1 and P_2
are a set of rules that apply before and after
(respectively) the addition of the index marker.
Let P_2 be such that its operation permits subsequent application by some members of P_1. This
is possible because of the use of variables in
transformation rules. As a result, the grammar

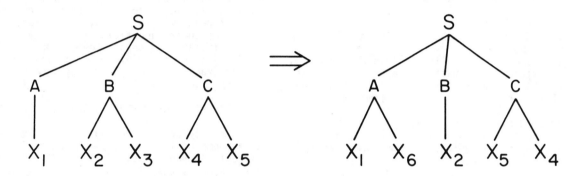

$$\left[X_1\right]\ \left[X_2 + X_3\right]\ \left[X_4 + X_5\right]$$

SD: 1   2   3 4 5 6   7 8

SC: 1 + X_6 2 ϕ 4 5 7   6 8

Figure 5.   An abstract example of a transformation rule. Portions of a
             derivation tree (lower half) are given a structural description
             ("SD": upper) by labeling brackets of nodes. The tree is
             transformed by defining a structural change ("SC": upper).

will cycle between P_1 and P_2. After the last application of a member of P_1 and before an application
of P_2 an index marker is added. Time is introduced
by interpreting the index marker as time. If the
string between two indices represents a grammatical
string (i.e., a system) at time t, then the next
grammatical string to the right is a system at time
t+1. A simple example is: "$x_1 + x_2 + ... + x_n$
(t_1) $x_1' + x_2' + ... + x_n'$ $(t_2) ...$ "

5. GENERAL SYSTEMS AS LANGUAGES

This representation of system structure and
dynamics as a production of a grammar is related to
definitions of general systems based on automata
theory (e.g., Wymore [15]). It is well known that
classes of formal languages are isomorphic to
classes of automata (e.g., Hopcroft and Ullman [6]).
This suggests that the formal language and automata
definitions of systems are isomorphic and that one
(usually automata theory) suffices as a general
framework. This seems to be the position of Pattee
[11] and Wymore [15]. They have given special
attention to the differences between machines and
formal languages.

Pattee [11] has emphasized that discrete representations of systems imply "infinitely fast"
dynamics in the sense that rates are not used in
the theory. This is also true of language theories,
as Pattee notes. This does not imply that the
semantic contents of automata theories and language
theories are equivalent. A fundamental distinction
in theoretical linguistics is relevant here. This
is the difference between performance theories
(language use, "speech") and competence theories
(language capabilities). The assumptions and
hypotheses of competence theories are not interpreted as approximations to the performance or
behavior of a machine that uses language. The
hypotheses of competence theories concern the
formal structure of a system of meanings, syntax,
and phonetics (Chomsky [2]). Humans (machines)
may or may not physically manipulate sound and
meaning as hypothesized by a competence theory.
The issue of rates and the discrete approximation
does not arise in considerations of competence,
although it is a legitimate concern of performance
models.

Because of the distinction between competence
and performance, language theories and automata
theories are not semantically equivalent, even
though they may be formally isomorphic. This difference is manifested in other aspects of languages
and automata. (1) Technically, the concept of
state does not apply to a grammar while it certainly applies to a machine. (2) Grammars do not
contain reference to the spatial position of an
object in the way that Turing machine instructions
refer to movements of the reading (or writing) head

(e.g. to the left or right). Further, in placing automata output on tapes the output is given an arbitrary, but significant (relative to automata operations), position in a fixed frame of reference (the tape). In grammars this constraint does not exist and only the relative position of the output is crucial. (3) In general (but this is not an absolute difference), grammars represent the generation of strings and automata the recognition of strings. Both operations are interchangeable in both grammars and automata, of course; nevertheless, the former interpretations of the operations are common. The "naturalness" of a formalism (automata or grammars) for a particular operation (recognition or generation) will be critical for general systems theories that seek to incorporate one or the other operation as a system property.

6. GENERAL SYSTEMS AND GENERATIVE GRAMMARS

General systems theory is still in a polyphonic (Klir [7]) state and no unified theory or collection of problems have dominated the field. Historically (Bertalanffy [1]) general systems theory was motivated by a search for laws common to all systems with emphasis on biological systems. Many systems properties of interest to the theoretician are manifested by biological systems: complexity, negative feedback, teleological (purposeful) behavior, replication, self-organization, and so on.

Certain features of the language formalism are particularly appropriate to the statement of laws of general biological systems. (1) The rewrite rule (i.e., the substitution relation) produces a hierarchical relation between system objects. This hierarchy requires the distinction between terminal and non-terminal vocabulary terms and the concept of the substitution class. Hierarchical structure is a significant aspect of all biological systems (Milsum [10]). Moreover, substitution classes represent equivalence of objects and subsystems. In linguistics substitution classes arise because many words (e.g., a subset of the class of nouns) can be interchanged without altering the grammaticalness of the sentence. For example, "the boys are noisy" and "the girls are noisy". Equivalence is important in ecological systems in the same way. For example, (a) different morphological structures can be used by different species to perform the same goal (e.g., feeding), and (b) different species can have the same effect on an ecosystem (e.g., man and elephants on grassland ecosystems).

(2) Another important relation between elements of a string, besides belonging to substitution classes, is the left-to-right order induced by the concatenation operator ("+"). This relation can be used to describe a time-ordered sequence of events, a property of obvious importance to general biological systems.

(3) The distinction between phrase-structure rewrite rules and transformation rules is important for stating significant empirical relationships between sentences in a language. In linguistics these are the relationships of synonymous sentences (e.g., the relation of the active and passive forms of sentences). A general definition of synonymous systems is two or more "different" systems that meet some criteria for similarity (e.g., identical meaning). Potential biological examples are analogous morphological structures and a species' functional role in an ecosystem.

(4) Recursive phrase-structure rules permit a grammar to produce a countably infinite number of strings. In general biological systems infinite languages are important in theories of evolving systems, since there do not appear to be limits on the number of possible species (Whittaker and Woodwell [14]).

(5) Transformation rules can be stated so that they contain variables corresponding to portions of derivation trees that do not affect application of the rule. As a result, transformation rules can be general and apply to many (often infinitely many) derivation trees. The same rule can apply to different systems. Thus, the systems, while retaining their superficial differences, are shown to be similar on a deeper level. An example that proved not to be useful theoretically is the geometric transformations of D'Arcy Thompson [13].

7. PROPERTIES OF GENERAL BIOLOGICAL SYSTEMS

Recently Locker and Coulter [9] have described a taxonomy of living systems based on fundamental biological properties. Important to the present discussion is the class of systems they called "organizational". An organizational system is one that can be described by a causal network and a system of goals. Locker and Coulter identify three types of organizational systems: teleonomic systems with externally derived goals, teleozetic systems with the capability to choose goals from an externally derived set, and teleogenic systems having the ability to internally formulate goals.

This classification can form the basis for theoretical studies of general biological systems. There are two basic approaches to pursuing this theory: (a) construct simple, abstract devices that produce behavior similar to teleonomy, teleozesis, and teleogenesis, or (b) incorporate the general biological properties into an empirically based theory of a particular class of biological systems. The first approach can be implemented with little biological structure. A finite automaton can be used to manipulate simple input to simulate the general properties (viz., choosing or creating goals). The second approach requires extensive biological structure and information. Rather than seeking elementary computational procedures that are mechanistic explanations of the properties, the second approach uses the general properties as hypotheses of biological processes and attempts to incorporate the properties (e.g., teleozesis) into a theoretical (mechanistic) explanation of particular biological phenomena (e.g., organic evolution, ecosystem dynamics, etc.).

The remainder of this paper describes a theory of ecosystem organization that implements some of the fundamental biological properties identified by Locker and Coulter. This theory and the biological properties are specified in the formalism of generative grammars.

8. ECOSYSTEM ASSEMBLY GRAMMARS

The application of generative grammars to eco-logical systems is described in Haefner [3]. The fundamental objective of this application is to describe all the possible ecosystems and none of the impossible ones. An ecosystem is defined as a set of interacting species and a set of abiotic environmental features. Ecosystems are described by a "matching" theory of ecosystem assembly. The matching theory is a generative grammar that repre-sents the temporal order of life cycles as a string of symbols ordered from left to right, and the spatial heterogeneity of the environment as a string of symbols. The grammar also has the ob-jective to transform one assembled ecosystem to another based on the mechanisms: predation, com-petition, and environmental alteration. These eco-system alterations are made operational with trans-formation rules. These rules constitute hypotheses of the mechanisms by which ecosystems are organized.

The grammar has two primary components: the species subgrammar (which produces a species pool) and the abiotic environment subgrammar (which pro-duces a spatially and temporally heterogeneous dis-tribution of abiotic environmental features). One derivation of each of these components produces a species pool with N species (where the number and characteristics of the species depend on the details of the derivation) and an abiotic environment with M environmental features (where the characteristics and patchiness of these features depend on the de-tails of the derivation). This grammar (Haefner [3]) is recursive, implying that an infinite number of derivation trees are possible.

Matching is achieved because the terminal vocab-ulary items are identical in the species and eco-system subgrammars. A simplified version of the subgrammars is given in Figures 6 and 7. Figure 6 shows the ecosystem grammar. Rule 1 decomposes the system ("S") into the abiotic environment ("eco-system"), the species pool ("Lexicon": species sub-grammar in Figure 7), and the set of "utilized" abiotic environments. The subsequent rules decom-pose the ecosystem into "environments". These have air, water, and soil components, each of which is described as a set of elementary, terminal features (e.g., $\{\alpha F_1, \ldots, \nu F_n\}$).

The species subgrammar (or Lexicon, Figure 7) has considerably more structure. The Lexicon (species pool) is decomposed into a finite set of Latin binomials (species: "LB" in Rule 1). Each LB is decomposed as a set of species types ("Σ"). These categories represent different "states" in which an individual of the species can exist and still be classified as a member of the LB. Examples of this optional behavior or structure are alterna-tive food bases, different reproduction activities (e.g., sexual and asexual), different developmental pathways, and so on. Each category of activities (e.g., "Developmental State": Rule 4; "Reproduction: Rule 5, etc.) is described by a collection of spe-cific activities not shown in Figure 7. Each of these are rewritten (Rules 7 and 8) as terminal habitat requirements. These terminal vocabulary items are identical to those in Figure 6. Conse-quently, the algorithm for ecosystem (matching) can be stated in set-theoretic terms: a species is in-serted into an ecosystem only if the set of terminal vocabulary items subsumed by at least one Σ (Figure 8)

is a subset of the terminal vocabulary items sub-sumed by "ecosystem" in Figure 6.

The basic structure of derivation trees pro-duced by the species subgrammar is shown in Figure 8. The very important process of generating species types (Σ) is a result of transformation rules (Haefner [3,4]). This is illustrated for the activity "Feeding" in Figure 9.

Successive application of the matching algo-rithm assembles ecosystems until no species in the Lexicon (species pool) possesses species types whose terminal strings are a subset of available resources. When this occurs additional rules (Haefner [3]) operate to eliminate competitively inferior species from the ecosystem; other rules permit ecological succession to occur. Space does not permit a full description of the grammar and the interested reader is referred to Haefner [3].

9. RELATION OF ECOSYSTEM ASSEMBLY GRAMMARS AND FUNDAMENTAL PROPERTIES

The above implementation of an ecosystem as-sembly grammar pertains to the three classes of organizational systems (Locker and Coulter [9]). The species subgrammar that generates a species pool is based on the observation that environmental requirements are dependent upon the specific activ-ities performed by species. These activities are organized in hierarchies. All species have mem-bers that can reproduce, but the hierarchy of activities that may be performed in fulfilling that goal varies between species. A grammar of species activities, as exemplified here, consti-tutes a theory of the structure of species goals created by evolution. The grammar (e.g., Figure 7) is one representation of a theory of general bio-logical systems based on teleonomy.

The basic teleonomic structure of a species is generated by phrase-structure rules (Figure 7). Many species have the potential to perform dif-ferent activities (with different environmental requirements). This property is made effective by applying transformation rules to activity struc-tures and, in this way, describing a Latin binomial as a set of species types ("Σ", Figure 9). This incorporates teleozetic systems because the grammar "externally" defines a set of goals (actually goal structures: species types) and lets the Latin binomial (the system) "choose" which structure is to be represented in the ecosystem. It is signif-icant that the representation of the process of system choice is passive. That is, a Latin binomial is not hypothesized to be a conscious system that actively evaluates possibilities and chooses one goal structure rather than another. The hypotheses of teleozetic systems can be implemented without attributing conscious powers to the system.

Teleogenesis is also represented by ecosystem assembly grammars, but not at the level of the species subgrammar. Goal creation requires (in ecosystem grammars) two levels of organization. Goals are only created in assembly grammars by con-sidering the set of goals extant at a moment of time. By altering the conditions of the ecosystem (e.g., the abiotic environment) different species are allowed to enter the system. Transformation rules governing the ecological interactions that delete species create new goal structures by

1. S $\longrightarrow$ ecosystem + utilized + Lexicon

2. ecosystem $\longrightarrow$ Environment (Environment) MORPH

3. Environment $\longrightarrow$ (Air)[(Water)(Soil)] (Environment)

4. Air $\longrightarrow \{\alpha F_1, \beta F_2, \cdots, \nu F_n\}$

5. Water $\longrightarrow \{\alpha F_1, \beta F_2, \cdots, \nu F_n\}$

6. Soil $\longrightarrow \{\alpha F_1, \beta F_2, \cdots, \nu F_n\}$

Figure 6.   A portion of a simple ecosystem assembly grammar. Shown is the description of ecosystems as a set of elementary abiotic environmental features (αF_1, βF_2, etc.) in Rules 4 to 6.

1. Lexicon $\longrightarrow$ LB(LB)

2. LB $\longrightarrow \Sigma(\Sigma)$

3. $\Sigma \longrightarrow$ Developmental Stage + Reproduction

4. Developmental Stage $\longrightarrow$ Activities + #Morphology#
   (Developmental Stage)

5. Reproduction $\longrightarrow$ Activities + Alternate Generation

6. Alternate Generation $\longrightarrow$ Reproduction

7. Activities $\longrightarrow$ Habitat Requirements

8. Habitat Requirements $\longrightarrow \{\alpha F_1, \beta F_2, \gamma F_3, \cdots \nu F_n\}$

Figure 7.   A portion of a simple ecosystem assembly grammar: the species pool. Shown is the description of the life cycles of N species. Terminal vocabulary items are habitat requirements that match the abiotic environmental features of Figure 6.

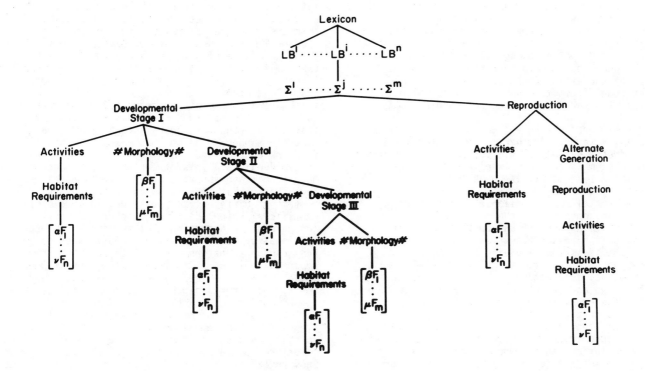

Figure 8.   An example of a derivation tree from the species subgrammar of Figure 7.

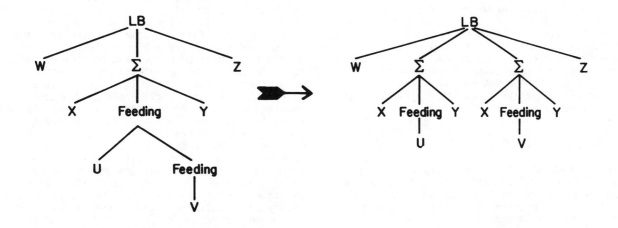

Figure 9.   A transformation of a derivation tree from the species
subgrammar. Shown is the creation of species types
(Σ, optional species goals) for different feeding
activities (U and V).

creating new "niches" (useable resources) for species in the species pool. Goal creation is not under the control of any particular component; teleogenesis is not global in that sense. Instead, control is dispersed among all of the components and interactions. Local events (e.g., species deletion and extinction, niche shifts, etc.) create the circumstances by which, relative to the system at a particular time, new species goals are created.

This is not the only interpretation of teleogenesis, however. Another procedure for studying teleogenetic systems within the context of ecosystem assembly grammars is related to self-organizing systems and is probably nearer to the original intent of Locker and Coulter.

The set of goals available to organisms and species is dependent on the phrase-structure and transformation rules of the species subgrammar (these define possible and impossible species). Teleogenesis is the unfolding of goals over time in response to the system's historic environments and internal interactions. This is also a description of the changes occurring in macro-evolution (e.g., the evolution of body plans, feeding structures and tactics, etc.).

Since these properties are described by the species subgrammar at an evolutionary instant in time, evolution can be modeled by the progressive alteration of a generative grammar. Thus, theories of teleogenesis are a description of a series of grammars. Since a grammar is a string of symbols, a grammar can be transformed by manipulations of that string. A meta-grammar is any rewrite device whose output is a grammar. A meta-grammar, when defined as a meta-system generator, is a description of grammar alteration and, thus, constitutes a theory of teleogenesis. When the system generator is an ecosystem assembly grammar the meta-grammar is a theory of evolution.

The precise form of a meta-grammar is very problematical at this time. This form must be constrained by both formal and empirical considerations. A superficially attractive definition of a meta-grammar is a generative grammar (as defined above) whose terminal vocabulary items are the elements of the rules in the object grammar (e.g., "$\rightarrow$", "+", the elements of V_N and V_T, etc.). There are, however, formal difficulties with this approach concerning the interpretation of non-terminal vocabulary items in the meta-grammar. Alternative approaches include control and associative grammars and these need to be explored.

10. METHODOLOGICAL ISSUES

Many methodological questions arise in the application of generative grammars to general systems theory. Space allows for a discussion of only a few. Especially important is the role of empirical studies in evaluating general systems theories: Are general systems theories testable in the ordinary sense? The view presented here suggests that these theories are testable, but only if they are given algorithmic representations in broadly-defined, but specific empirical domains. For example, the existence of teleozetic systems constitutes a significant empirical hypothesis of general biological systems only if it can be trans-

lated into a theory of a particular subdomain of biology. Goal selection in ecosystem assembly grammars is a crucial process for determining species lists. Incorporating teleozesis into the basic structure of a generative grammar permits the ramifications and implications of teleozesis to be explored in a systematic, rigorous, and testable manner.

There are many other conceptual frameworks such as that proposed by Locker and Coulter [9] that can be (and have been) investigated in a testable manner. One obvious example is negative feedback control and its stabilizing effects on system dynamics. This concept is the subject of much formal and abstract analysis in general systems theory, but it is also incorporated, using systems of differential equations, in models of specific empirical domains. Locker and Coulter are correct in observing that properties of organizational systems have not been formulated so that they can be transferred to and tested in particular empirical domains. The formal structure of generative grammars is ideally suited for this transferral and permits rigorous statement of interesting biological questions.

The application of generative grammars to linguistics has revealed that the formal theory constitutes a description of those human cognitive structures pertaining to language competence. Chomsky [2] and Harris [5] suggested that the application of "grammars" to other aspects of human behavior can also constitute explanatory theories of other cognitive structures. Locker and Coulter, considering the more general and abstract question of observer-defined systems, raised the same issue in the content of general systems methodology.

These observations plus the existence of a generative grammar of ecosystem assembly suggests further roles that grammars may play in general systems theory. An ecosystem assembly grammar can be interpreted as a theory of the competence of ecologists to distinguish possible and impossible ecosystems and species. We may generalize this to say that a grammar of any system class is a theory of human scientific cognitive structures relative to that system class. Grammars, therefore, are an indispensable tool for exploring in detail the observations made by Locker and Coulter concerning the relation of system objectivity and observer subjectivity. This has implications for the theory of model construction and self-organizing modeling systems. If a grammar is a theory of the cognitive structures involved in classifying (recognizing) a description as a member of a system class (e.g., grammatical sentence, possible ecosystem), then it is also a portion of a theory of model construction. System definition by identifying components and interactions is an essential aspect of modeling. The choice of necessary components and interactions is dependent on the objectives of the model and the modeler's internal conceptual framework. Generative grammars of the system class is one approach to studying these internal structures by identifying the modeler's decisions on possible and impossible system descriptions.

Grammars of cognitive structures do not describe the processes or dynamics by which these structures are employed (e.g., in language use).

Thus, another important theoretical tool is the simple, abstract models of these processes (e.g., switching network representations of the brain). Both the space/time approach and the language approach need to be pursued for a complete understanding of human cognitive structures. However, the empirical test of general systems theories is not well developed and future substantive advances of these theories must be accompanied by empirical examinations.

REFERENCES

1. BERTALANFFY, L., "The History and Status of General Systems Theory," pp. 21-41 in: G. J. Klir (ed.), 1972.
2. CHOMSKY, N., The Logical Structure of Linguistic Theory, Plenum Press, New York, 1975.
3. HAEFNER, J. W., "Generative Grammars that Simulate Ecological Systems," pp. 189-211 in: G. S. Innis (ed.), New Directions in the Analysis of Ecological Systems, Simulation Councils, Inc., LoJolla, Cal., 1977.
4. HAEFNER, J. W., "Ecosystem Assembly Grammars: Generative Capacity and Empirical Adequacy," Journal of Theoretical Biology, 1978 (in press).
5. HARRIS, Z., "On a Theory of Language," The Journal of Philosophy, 73: 253-276, 1976.
6. HOPCROFT, J. E. and J. D. ULLMAN, Formal Languages and Their Relation to Automata, Addison-Wesley, Reading, Mass., 1969.
7. KLIR, G. J., "The Polyphonic General Systems Theory," pp. 1-18 in: G. J. Klir (ed.), 1972.
8. KLIR, G. J. (ed.), Trends in General Systems Theory, Wiley-Interscience, New York, 1972.
9. LOCKER, A. and N. A. COULTER, "A New Look at the Description and Prescription of Systems," Behavioral Science, 22: 197-206.
10. MILSUM, J. H., "The Hierarchical Basis for General Living Systems," pp. 145-187 in: G. J. Klir (ed.), 1972.
11. PATTEE, H. H., "Dynamics and Language in Biology," pp. 199-200 in: Proceedings of IEEE Conference on Biologically Motivated Automata Theory, 19-21 June 1974.
12. POLANYI, M., Personal Knowledge, The University of Chicago Press, Illinois, 1958.
13. THOMPSON, D. W., On Growth and Form, MacMillan, New York, 1942.
14. WHITTAKER, R. H. and G. M. WOODWELL, "Evolution of Natural Communities," pp. 137-159 in: J. A. Weins (ed.), Ecosystem Structure and Function, Oregon State University Press, Corvallis, Oregon, 1972.
15. WYMORE, A. W., "A Wattled Theory of Systems," pp. 270-300 in: G. J. Klir (ed.), 1972.

Theory of eventistic systems, a survey

WITOLD JACAK and KRZYSZTOF TCHOŃ
Technical University of Wrocław, Poland

1. INTRODUCTION

A notion of events seems to be as well intuitively clear as difficult to be defined. "Events" appear in every system theory having a dynamical character, from Bogdanov's tektology [8] through Ashby's machines theory [1,2] and theory of dynamical systems [15] up to the inductive general systems theory [16,17]. According to these theories the event is an instantaneous state of some object, an appearance of attributes of the object, a collection of instantaneous values of parameters of the object, etc. Thus, in systems theory the event is always related to time and to something changeable in time. In physics the event is what has some space-time coordinates in four-dimensional space-time [30].

The notion of event has played a considerable role in the philosophy of being. From Whitehead's and Russell's philosophy [27,28] we can talk about the appearance of a philosophical view called eventism [4]. In accordance with eventism, the event is the only primitive entity to which the others--such as things, processes, time, space, etc.--may be reduced via definition. Eventism, as is usual in philosophy, has not been a homogeneous trend. It has not been elaborated to any homogeneous conception of event and has not made the reductions postulated by itself [4]. A certain success has been achieved only for the matter of eventistic definitions of time [3,4,21,29].

We would not like to discuss here the question, is eventism a "good" ontology from a philosophical point of view. However, we want to use some elements of a method of events description proposed by eventism, namely the assumption that the event is a primitive notion--not necessarily individual, and the axiomatic approach to the theory of events. Using such a conceptual framework we shall formulate our definitions of eventistic systems and present some fragments of theory of the systems. Of course, we shall not regard a consistence of our theory with some arguments of eventism as to be a fault of the theory, nevertheless we do not intend to clutch the assumptions of eventism.

As it follows from the above, we want to connect general systems theory with a theory of events and to propose a concept of system which is ultimately defined by events. Let us explain now how we understand the term "system." Well, in our opinion every system is a description of an arrangement or regularity inside a certain object. At this point we approximate Löfgren's conception of system [20]: a system is a description of an arrangement the antithesis of which is chaos.

To discover and describe the arrangement inside an object the object must be conceptualized. The conceptualization consists in a choice of the features, attributes, parameters of the object which manifest themselves inside the sought for arrangement as well as in a choice of an adequate method to draw up the arrangement.

In our considerations we shall assume that the object which can be called a systemic object is given as a set of events. We are not interested in how this set has been obtained. We shall also assume that some relations of conceptualizational type are defined on the set of events.

Our theory of events and theory of eventistic systems based on the former are some deductive theories. Set theory is our fundamental mathematical tool. We assume several essential axioms. To obtain stronger results for some special classes of systems we shall introduce some additional axioms and enrich the applied mathematical tools. The interdependence between theory of eventistic systems and a certain domain of reality is characterized by an interpretation of the theory.

We have accepted the deductive methodology but it does not mean, however, that we resign the intuition, some heuristic exemplifications of the concepts, and so on. Conversely, we regard them as very important for development of the theory. It should be just remembered that any exemplification used to explain a theory is neither necessary nor the only one.

2. EVENTISTIC SPACE

As stated above we shall assume that the systemic **object** -- a **thing**, process, phenomenon, a combination of things, **processes**, phenomena, etc. -- is a set of events. In order to **discover** and describe an arrangement inside this set it appears necessary to conceptualize the set. Such notions as time, states and eventistic lines are assumed to make possible the description. Each of the notions follows from a classification of events from a certain point of view.

Now let us go to a formalization. Let a nonempty set E be given. The set E will be called the set of events. On the set of events E the following binary relations are defined: a relation of events heredity, a relation of events precedence and a relation of events similarity. The properties of these relations are described by the following axioms [10,12].

(a) The relation of events heredity $H \subset E \times E$

is an equivalence relation.

(b) The relation of events precedence $P \subset E \times E$ is reflexive, transitive and connected.

(c) The relation of events similarity $S \subset E \times E$ is an equivalence relation.

3. TIME

It follows from axiom (b) that every event precedes itself, the relation P is transitive, and for every pair of events $e', e'' \in E$ we have either $e'Pe''$ or $e''Pe'$. In the set of events, some events e', e'' can be found for which it holds $e'Pe''$ as well as $e''Pe'$. One may therefore say that events e' and e'' are simultaneous [10,12,31,34].

Thus a relation of events simultaneity can be introduced. The relation $Q \subset E \times E$ is defined as an intersection

$$Q = P \cap P^{-1}. \tag{1}$$

where P^{-1} is the inverse relation.

One can easily show that Q is an equivalence relation. By means of Q we shall define instants of time. The set of instants is a quotient set

$$T = E/Q. \tag{2}$$

Hence, according to the definition, every instant is a non-empty set of simultaneous events.

The precedence of events induces a certain order in the set of instants. We may say that an instant $t' \in T$ precedes an instant $t'' \in T$ iff an event $e' \in t'$ precedes -- in the sense of the relation P -- an event $e'' \in t''$. Then the relation of instants precedence $\mathcal{P} \subset T \times T$ is defined as follows

$$t' \mathcal{P} t'' \Longleftrightarrow (\exists e' \in t')(\exists e'' \in t'')(e'Pe''). \tag{3}$$

Naturally, from (3) and the axiom (b), it follows that

$$t' \mathcal{P} t'' \Longleftrightarrow (\forall e' \in t')(\forall e'' \in t'')(e'Pe''),$$

which seems to agree with common sense. Moreover, it appears that the relation of instants precedence given by (3) is a linearly ordering relation on T. Therefore, $\mathcal{P}$ is reflexive, antisymmetrical, transitive and connected [31].

The linearly ordered set of events we propose to call time [4,10,12,22]. The time is an ordered pair in the form

$$\mathcal{T} = <T, \mathcal{P}>. \tag{4}$$

4. EVENTISTIC LINES - STATES

The quotient set E/Q will be called a set of instants. Quotient sets determined by the relations of events heredity and similarity will be treated as a set of eventistic lines L and a set of states C, respectively. Then we obtain

$$L = E/H \quad \text{and} \quad C = E/S. \tag{5}$$

Obviously, every eventistic line consists of hereditary events. One can explain the nature of events heredity by the relativistic notion of "genetic identity" of events belonging to a so-called world line which is related to a certain physical particle [5,6]. Considering general systems theory, in particular Klir's approach, an eventistic line would be related to appearances of an attribute of the systemic object [16,17].

The state $c \in C$ is a set of similar events. It seems to be obvious that the similarity of events does not mean either "to happen simultaneously" or "to happen at the same eventistic line". Moreover, an eventistic line should be "extended" in the time and the set of states. Therefore, the hereditary events should happen at least at two various instants and the classification obtained by the relation of events simultaneity must differ from the one due to the relation of events similarity. If for one moment we imagine the set of events as the Euclidean plane E^2, we may represent instants as some "vertical strips" consisting of events and states as some "horizontal strips".

These properties will be guaranteed by the following axiom (d).

(d) There exist both similar and non-simultaneous events as well as simultaneous events which are not similar,

$$S \cap (-Q) \neq \emptyset \quad \text{and} \quad Q \cap (-S) \neq \emptyset.$$

There exist some hereditary events which are neither simultaneous nor similar,

$$H \cap (-S) \cap (-Q) \neq \emptyset.$$

5. TRAJECTORIES

Having the instants, states and eventistic lines, we would like to describe a time evolution of the eventistic lines in terms of instantaneous states of the lines. To do it we must define the states.

Let us consider an eventistic line $l \in L$ and define a set $T_1 = \{t \in T: t \cap l \neq \emptyset\}$ which can be called a period of existence of the line l. Obviously, in general $T_1 \neq T$. The last inequality means that there exist some eventistic lines which at some instants are broken down.

Let $t \in T_1$. We shall say that the eventistic line $l \in L$ is at the instant $t \in T_1$ in a state $c \in C$ iff

$$l \cap t \subset c. \tag{6}$$

To describe the time evolution of eventistic lines we have to assume that every eventistic line at every instant of its existence is in a certain state. We shall formulate the above as a so-called axiom of the local determinism [12,31],

$$(e) \quad (\forall l \in L)(\forall t \in T_1)(\exists c \in C)(l \cap t \subset c).$$

Since the relation of events similarity S is an equivalence relation, every eventistic line at an instant $t \in T_1$ is in the only one state. Let us assign to an eventistic line $l \in L$ the set

$$f_1 = \{<t,c> : t \in T_1 \land c \in C \land t \cap l \subset c\} \qquad (7)$$

consisting of ordered pairs: <an instant of existence of l, the state of l at the instant>. From axiom (e) it follows that at every $t \in T_1$ the state c does exist and it is the only one. Then we see that f_1 is a function of time T_1,

$$f_1 : T_1 \to C. \qquad (8)$$

The function f_1 will be called a trajectory of the eventistic line $l \in L$. The trajectories are -- possibly partial -- functions of time. A set of trajectories is given by

$$F = \{f_1 : l \in L\}. \qquad (9)$$

By axioms (a - e) we have assigned to every eventistic line from the set L the trajectory being a function of time. Thus, we have described the classes of hereditary events in terms of their states at succeeding instants. The introduction of instants, states and eventistic lines may be interpreted as a representation of events at some resolution levels [16,17]. It can be also observed that the trajectory corresponds to one line in Klir's activity matrix [17].

The set of events E together with the relations of events heredity, precedence and similarity satisfying axioms (a - e) will be called an eventistic space [12]. Then the eventistic space is defined as follows

$$E = <E, H, P, S> . \qquad (10)$$

6. PROPERTIES OF TIME AND STATES

We have defined the time $\mathcal{T}$ as linearly ordered sets of instants (4). By the relation of instants precedence $\mathcal{P}$ a topology can be introduced into the set of instants T. Let $X \subset T$. Then we define a set

$$\overline{X}^{\mathcal{P}} = \{t \in T : A_p(t) \cap X \neq \emptyset\} . \qquad (11)$$

where $A_p(t) = \{t' \in T : t' \mathcal{P} t\}$. It can be easily shown that $^{-\mathcal{P}}$ is a closure-operation according to Kuratowski [19]. The topology introduced by the closure $^{-\mathcal{P}}$ is so-called left topology on T [7]. Substituting in (11) $A_p(t)$ by $P_p(t) = \{t' \in T : t \mathcal{P} t'\}$ we can obtain the right topology [7]. It can be only proved that the topological space $<T,^{-\mathcal{P}}>$ belongs to the class T_o [31]. Let us note that if $\overline{\overline{T}} \geq 2$ then the space $<T,^{-\mathcal{P}}>$ is not of the class T_1.

Now let us assume that $\overline{\overline{T}} \geq 2$. Then we can define an irreflexive ordering relation

$$\hat{\mathcal{P}} = \mathcal{P} \setminus id_T \qquad (12)$$

which is a non-empty relation. Let us introduce segments of time defined as follows

$$(t',t'') = \{t : t'\hat{\mathcal{P}} t \land t\hat{\mathcal{P}} t''\}, \qquad (13)$$

$$(t , \to) = P_p(t), \quad (\leftarrow, t) = A_p(t) .$$

The union of all these segments appears to be the basis of a topological space [7]. The topological space will be termed $<T, \tau\hat{p}>$. It can be proved that the space $<T, \tau\hat{p}>$ belongs to the class T_4 -- it is a normal topological space [7,31]. Obviously, the segments of time are open in $<T, \tau\hat{p}>$.

In the theory of time some ordered subsets of time are considered which are called time intervals [3,4,31]. We shall define a time interval with ends t', t'' $\in$ T as follows

$$[t',t''] = \{t \in T : t'\mathcal{P} t \land t\mathcal{P} t''\}. \qquad (14)$$

A time interval without ends t', t'' $\in$ T is given by

$$(t',t'') = \{t \in T : t'\hat{p} t \land t\hat{p} t''\}. \qquad (15)$$

Of course, the last intervals are some segments of time. Since $\overline{\overline{T}} \geq 2$, hence there exist time intervals of both types mentioned above.

Let us accept the last assumption. Then the time is a topological space. We shall consider some topological properties of the time [3,4,31].

It appears that from our definition of time we can prove that the topological dimension of the time -- the dimension in the sense of Menger-Urysohn [7,19] -- is equal to 0 or 1 and that the time is non-branched [4,31]. In general, however, we are not in a position to answer the questions of compactness, connectedness and infiniteness of the time [4,31].

It can be easily noticed that if we assume that in the set T there exists the first element, we shall obtain Mesarovic's time set from his theory of time systems [23].

In more specialized theories of systems two time sets -- sets of instants -- are used: the set of integers and the set of real numbers, both together with the natural order of numbers $\leq$. Then a question emerges concerning the existence of "numerical" representation for our time $\mathcal{T}$.

Let us define some mappings $\varphi_N : T \to N_0$ and $\varphi_R : T \to \mathbb{R}$ which establish an isomorphism of the structures $<T,\mathcal{P}>$, $<N_0,\leq>$ and $<T,\mathcal{P}>$, $<\mathbb{R},\leq>$, respectively. For denumerable sets of instants T which topological structures are trivial, the isomorphism φ_N is wholly sufficient as the mapping of the time into numbers.

In the case of higher cardinalities of the set T, however, we would like to obtain an isomorphism $\varphi_{\mathbb{R}}$ which is also a homeomorphism. In general the homeomorphism cannot be constructed because the topology on T is too weak. Thus we have the alternatives: to postulate the existence of homeomorphism $\varphi_{\mathbb{R}}$ or to impose on $\mathcal{T}$ some additional conditions which enable us to construct the appropriate $\varphi_{\mathbb{R}}$. We shall make use of the second method. Let $\overline{\overline{T}} = C$ and on the set of time intervals $J = \{[t',t''] : <t',t''> \in \mathcal{P}\}$ an equivalence relation $\sim_c \subset J \times J$ be given. For $I,J \in J$ let us define a relation "to have the end t in common" as follows

$$I \omega_t J \Leftrightarrow (\exists t',t'' \in T)(I=[t',t] \land J=[t,t'']) \qquad (16)$$

and let

$$I \omega J \Leftrightarrow (\exists t \in T)(I \omega_t J) . \qquad (17)$$

The relation $\sim_{\mathbb{C}}$ is called a relation of time congruence of intervals iff it satisfies the following axioms [31].

(a) $(\forall t \in T) (\exists I, J \in J) (I \sim_{\mathbb{C}} J \wedge I \, \omega_t \, J)$.

(b) $I \sim_{\mathbb{C}} J \wedge K \sim_{\mathbb{C}} L \wedge I(\omega \cup \omega^{-1}) K \wedge J(\omega \cup \omega^{-1})L \Rightarrow (I \cup K) \sim_{\mathbb{C}} (J \cup L)$.

(c) $I \subset K \wedge K \sim_{\mathbb{C}} J \Rightarrow (\exists L \in J) (I \sim_{\mathbb{C}} L \wedge L \subset J)$.

(d) $I \subset J \wedge I \sim_{\mathbb{C}} J \Rightarrow I = J$.

The fifth axiom (e) will be formulated further on.

Now we shall consider the most important concepts of the theory of time congruence. The details are included in [31]. Elements of the quotient set $J/\sim_{\mathbb{C}}$ will be called free intervals [3,4,31]. The set of free intervals: $J* = J/\sim_{\mathbb{C}}$. Let us define on the set J an ordering relation $\leq \subset J \times J$ which is as follows

$$I \leq J \Leftrightarrow (\exists K \in J) (I \sim_{\mathbb{C}} K \wedge K \subset J). \qquad (18)$$

where $\subset$ is the set-theoretical inclusion.

One can show that the relation $\leq$ is reflexive, transitive, and connected on J. Moreover, the relation $\leq$ is implied by the congruence $\sim_{\mathbb{C}}$. Hence

$$I \sim_{\mathbb{C}} J \Rightarrow I \leq J. \qquad (19)$$

and as a consequence of this

$$\sim_{\mathbb{C}} \subset \leq \cap \leq^{-i}. \qquad (20)$$

Now we can formulate the last axiom of the time congruence as follows.

(e) $\leq \cap \leq^{-i} \subset \sim_{\mathbb{C}}$.

The axiom (e), together with (20), gives the identity

$$\sim_{\mathbb{C}} = \leq \cap \leq^{-i}. \qquad (21)$$

Basing on the relation $\leq$ on J we can define an ordering relation $\leq*$ on the set of free intervals $J*$. We propose the following definition.

$$I* \leq* J* \Leftrightarrow (\exists I \in I*) (\exists J \in J*) (I \leq J). \qquad (22)$$

The so defined relation $\leq* \subset J* \times J*$ is a linearly ordering relation on J.

Now let us consider a relation $\oplus \subset (J \times J) \times J$ defined as follows. Let $I, J, K \in J$. Then

$$I \oplus J = K \Leftrightarrow (\exists I', J' \in J) (I \sim_{\mathbb{C}} I' \wedge J \sim_{\mathbb{C}} J' \wedge I'(\omega \cup \omega^{-1})J' \wedge K = I' \cup J'). \qquad (23)$$

It can be proved that the relation $\oplus$ is not a binary operation on J because there are a lot of "sums" $I \oplus J$ for the given I, J. It appears, however, that the relation $\oplus$ induces a well-defined binary operation on $J*$. The operation will be denoted by $\oplus*$ and defined as follows. Let $I*, J* \in J*$, $I \in I*$, $J \in J*$. Then

$$I* \oplus* J* = [I \oplus J]\sim_{\mathbb{C}} \qquad (24)$$

where $[I]\sim_{\mathbb{C}}$ is an equivalence class for $\sim_{\mathbb{C}}$ defined by I. The operation $\oplus*$ is associative, commutative, and monotonic with respect to the relation $\leq*$. In conclusion, from the axioms of congruence, it follows that the set of free intervals can be treated as an ordered commutative semigroup $<J*, \leq*, \oplus*>$.

Free intervals can be measured. A measure μ of these intervals is an isomorphism of structures $<J*, \leq*, \oplus*>$ and $<\mathbb{R}_0, \leq, +>$. We shall assume that $\mu([[t,t]]\sim_{\mathbb{C}}) = 0$. The measure μ enables us to metrize and coordinate our time [4,31].

A mapping $\rho : T \times T \to \mathbb{R}_0$ defined as follows

$$t' \, \mathcal{P} \, t'' \Rightarrow \rho(t',t'') = \mu([[t',t'']]\sim_{\mathbb{C}})$$

$$t'' \, \mathcal{P} \, t' \Rightarrow \rho(t',t'') = \mu([[t'',t']]\sim_{\mathbb{C}}) \qquad (25)$$

will be called a metric of time. The function ρ satisfies the axioms of metric and then the time T is a metric space $<T,\rho>$ [31].

In order to coordinate the time, let us establish an initial instant $t_0 \in T$. A mapping $\tau : T \to \mathbb{R}$ such that

$$t_0 \, \mathcal{P} \, t \Rightarrow \tau(t) = \rho(t_0,t)$$

$$t \, \mathcal{P} \, t_0 \Rightarrow \tau(t) = -\rho(t_0,t) \qquad (26)$$

will be called a system of coordinates for the time. The mapping τ appears to be isomorphism and homeomorphism of the structures $<T,\mathcal{P}>$ and $<\mathbb{R},\leq>$, therefore it is the required mapping $\varphi_{\mathbb{R}}$.

We cannot here be more engaged in the problems of time and this being so we leave open the question of existence of the congruence relation. It seems that the properties of time set considered by Windeknecht [32] and by Mesarovic for stationary time systems [23] are sufficient to define the relation $\sim_{\mathbb{C}}$.

We have presented a rather complicated way to obtain the isomorphism and homeomorphism $\varphi_{\mathbb{R}}$ between the structures $<T,\mathcal{P}>$ and $<\mathbb{R},\geq>$. Another more simple way is to introduce such a homeomorphism immediately using a concept of observable [26].

Let us remember that the observable on the set E is a mapping $f : E \to R$. The mapping f produces an equivalence relation $Z \subset E \times E$ defined as follows

$$e' \, Z \, e'' \Leftrightarrow f(e') = f(e'').$$

If the observable f concerns the events simultaneously, we can define by f the relation Q $(Q = Z)$ and introduce into the set of instants $T = E/Q$ a metric ρ_T. Let $e' \in t'$, $e'' \in t''$. Then

$$\rho_T(t',t'') = |f(e') - f(e'')| . \qquad (27)$$

Obviously, there exists a homeomorphism between

the set of instants T and the range of the observable f, $R(f) \subset \mathbb{R}$.

Similarly, we could metrize and topologize the set of states C. Let us take a set of observables $\{f_1, f_2, \ldots, f_n\}$ where $f_i : C \to \mathbb{R}$, for $i = 1, 2, \ldots, n$. Consequently, the relation of events similarity can be defined as follows

$$e' \, S \, e'' \Leftrightarrow (\forall i \in N_1^n) \, (f_i(e') = f_i(e'')) \,.$$

Let C = E/S. Then we can introduce into the set of states C a metric ρ_c. If $e' \in c'$, $e'' \in c''$ then

$$\rho_c(c', c'') = \sum_{i=1}^{n} |f_i(e') - f_i(e'')| \,. \quad (28)$$

The set C is then homeomorphic to the set $X\{R(f_i): i \in N_1^n\} \subset \mathbb{R}^n$.

6. EVENTISTIC SYSTEMS

We have described an arrangement inside the set of events in the terms of time, states and eventistic lines to which we have assigned trajectories being some functions of time. As a rule, the trajectories are partial functions. If the time and the set of states are topological spaces, it is possible to define a continuity of trajectories. For the discrete time the continuity can be defined by imposing on the set of states a certain tolerance relation [14,15].

The description of the arrangement which we have obtained is not complete. The description will be more complete if some interrelations among eventistic lines will be allowed for. We shall describe the interrelations in terms of some relations defined on subsets of trajectories [10,12,31].

At first let us define the subsets as follows

$$\mathcal{B} = \{f' : (\exists l \in L) \, (f' \subset f_l)\}. \quad (29)$$

Of course, all subsets of trajectories from the set F belong to the set $\mathcal{B}$. The subsets which are restrictions of trajectories to some time intervals are called segments of trajectories.

Now we shall define a generic set for eventistic systems [12,31] in the following manner

$$G = U\{XA \mid A \subset 2^{\mathcal{B}}\} \quad (30)$$

where XA is the Cartesian product of the family A, i.e.

$$A = \{A_i : i \in I\} \Rightarrow XA = \{\varphi : I \to UA :$$

$$(\forall i \in I) \, (\varphi(i) \in A_i)\}.$$

The generic set G contains tuples of subsets of trajectories. In other words, all the possible combinations of subsets of trajectories belong to the generic set. A subset of G consisting of the possibilities really realized we called a non-oriented eventistic system [10,12,31]. Then the non-oriented eventistic system ES is a non-empty proper subset of G,

$$ES \subset G \wedge ES \neq \emptyset \wedge ES \neq G. \quad (31)$$

The ordered pairs of elements of ES which "succeed" one another belong to an oriented eventistic system [10,12,31]. Then the oriented eventistic system $\overline{ES}$ is a non-empty binary relation on G,

$$\overline{ES} \subset G \times G \wedge \overline{ES} \neq \emptyset \wedge \overline{ES} \neq G \times G. \quad (32)$$

Let us take into consideration the inside of eventistic systems ES and $\overline{ES}$. The elements of ES which are tuples of subsets of trajectories will be called non-oriented activities, the elements belonging to $\overline{ES}$ the oriented ones. Therefore, eventistic systems are composed of their activities. Among activities of the non-oriented eventistic system there are tuples of varied cardinality. If all activities of the system ES have the same cardinality being equal to α then the system is called an α-homogeneous eventistic system [31]. Thus ES is α-homogeneous iff

$$ES \subset U\{X \, A: A \subset 2^{\mathcal{B}} \wedge \overline{\overline{A}} = \alpha\} \subset G \,. \quad (33)$$

It is easy to observe that the α-homogeneous system $ES \subset XA$ (for some $A \subset 2^{\mathcal{B}} \wedge \overline{\overline{A}}$ such that $\overline{\overline{A}} = \alpha$) is a general system according to Mesarovic [22,23,31]. Objects of this system are defined by subsets of $\mathcal{B}$. For $\alpha = n$ (n is an integer) we obtain: $A = \{A_1, A_2, \ldots, A_n\}$, $A_i \subset \mathcal{B}$ for every $i = 1, 2, \ldots, n$, and

$$ES \subset A_1 \times A_2 \times \ldots \times A_n. \quad (34)$$

By an appropriate specification of the eventistic systems we can develop our theory likewise Mesarovic's general systems theory. In particular, if $A_1 = A_2 = \{f \mid T_0 : f \in F \wedge f \mid T_0 : T_0 \to C\}$ and $T_0 \subset T$ has an initial element, then we obtain an eventistic system

$$ES_T \subset A_1 \times A_2 \quad (35)$$

which corresponds to Mesarovic's time system [23]. Therefore, we can develop the theory of eventistic system ES_T by introducing a concept of state objects as well as a dynamical system, etc., just as in Mesarovic's approach.

An important subclass of homogeneous eventistic systems is that one which corresponds to Klir's generative systems [18]. Indeed some analogies between eventistic systems and Klir's ones can be found at various epistemological levels; we shall confine ourselves to a correspondence at level 2 [18].

Let us assume that it is defined a congruence relation $\sim_c$ on the set J and consider a set of trajectories A where $A \subset \{f \in f : f : T \to C\}$ and $\overline{\overline{A}} = n$. A mapping

$$M : A \to J^* \quad (36)$$

will be called an "interval mask" [12,16,17]. The mask assigns to every trajectory $f \in A$ a free interval M(f) which the measure ("length") equals $\mu(M(f))$. We shall only consider the "interval masks" in the form (36) though using more extended and complicated definition it is possible to consider some more general masks.

Let $t_{01}, t_{02}, \ldots, t_{0n} \in T$ be some instants of reference. Then the first sample obtained by the mask M can be defined as

$$s_1 = \langle f_i \mid I_i^1 : i \in N_1^n \rangle \qquad (37)$$

where

$$I_i^1 = [t_{0i}, t_{1i}] \in M(f_i).$$

The sample s_1 contains segments of trajectories determined by the intervals $I_1^1, I_2^1, \ldots, I_n^1$. Having a sample s_k such that

$$s_k = \langle f_i \mid I_i^k : i \in N_1^n \rangle \qquad (38)$$

and

$$I_i^k = [t_{k-1i}, t_{ki}] \in M(f_i)$$

we can define a sample s_{k+1} as follows

$$s_{k+1} = \langle f_i \mid I_i^{k+1} : i \in N_1^n \rangle \qquad (39)$$

where

$$I_i^{k+1} = [t_{ki}, t_{k+1i}] \in M(f_i).$$

The presented procedure can be repeated for $k = 1, 2, 3, \ldots$.

Now let us define an n-homogeneous non-oriented eventistic system $ES_M = \{s_k : k \in N\}$. It is easy to verify that ES_M consists of tuples of subsets (segments) of trajectories from F. Thus $ES_M \subset G$ is a well-defined eventistic system. This system is related to a basic behaviour of Klir's generative system [12,17,18].

An oriented eventistic system $\overline{ES}_M = \{\langle s_k, s_{k+1}\rangle : k \in N\} \subset G \times G$ corresponds to a ST-structure according to Klir [12,17,18]. Therefore, some elements of Klir's methodology concerning the inductive systems theory seem to be relevant for developing a theory of eventistic systems ES_M and $\overline{ES}_M$.

In terms of eventistic systems not only the mentioned above systems can be reconstructed but also the others. A certain review of these problems one can find in [31].

Let us choose from the review a system which immediately related to Ashby's machine [1,2], or to so-called iterative system [25,33]. We shall consider an eventistic system $\overline{ES}_M^* \subset G \times G$ such that the ordered pairs $\langle$instant,state$\rangle$ belong to the domain and range of the system. These pairs can be called abstract events [31]. The abstract events are elements of the set $R = T \times C$ which is a systemic "time-space". Let T_0 be a denumerable subset of T and let

$$\mathcal{A} = \{\{\varphi : (\exists f \in F) \, (\exists t \in T_0) \, (\varphi = f \mid \{t\})\}\}.$$

Then we can define an oriented eventistic system $\overline{ES}_M^*$ as follows

$$\overline{ES}_M^* \subset \mathsf{X} \mathcal{A} \subset \mathcal{A}. \qquad (40)$$

(For $\mathcal{A} = \{A\}$ we assume $\mathsf{X} \mathcal{A} = \{\{a\} : a \in A\}.$)

It is easy to note that the system $\overline{ES}_M^*$ contains ordered pairs $\langle x, y \rangle$ where $x = \{\{\langle t, c \rangle\}\}$, $y = \{\{\langle t', c' \rangle\}\}$ for some $\langle t, c \rangle$, $\langle t', c' \rangle \in R$. Obviously there exists a one-to-one correspondence between the system $\overline{ES}_M^*$ and a relation $\overline{ES}_M \subset R \times R$ defined as follows

$$\langle r, r' \rangle \in \overline{ES}_M \Leftrightarrow \langle \{\{r\}\}, \{\{r'\}\} \rangle \in \overline{ES}_M^*. \qquad (41)$$

If the relation $\overline{ES}_M$ satisfies a condition: $\mathcal{D}(\overline{ES}_M) \cap \mathcal{R}(\overline{ES}_M) \neq \emptyset$, then $\overline{ES}_M$ will be called an eventistic machine. Let us observe that if $\mathcal{D}(\overline{ES}_M) = \mathcal{R}(\overline{ES}_M)$ and $\overline{ES}_M$ is a function, the eventistic machine $\overline{ES}_M$ strictly corresponds to Ashby's machine.

The machine $\overline{ES}_M \subset \mathcal{D}(\overline{ES}_M) \times \mathcal{R}(\overline{ES}_M)$ can be treated as Mesarovic's input-output system and as such a system $\overline{ES}_M$ has a global response-function [23]. Let U be a set. Then the global response-function $\varphi_M : U \times \mathcal{D}(\overline{ES}_M) \to \mathcal{R}(\overline{ES}_M)$ of the machine $\overline{ES}_M$ satisfies the following condition

$$\langle r, r' \rangle \in \overline{ES}_M \Leftrightarrow (\exists u \in U) \, (\varphi_M(u, r) = r'). \qquad (42)$$

We can treat the set U as an input set and the knowledge of which can be varied. If we have a complete knowledge of $u \in U$, the function φ_M is a parametric representation of the machine $\overline{ES}_M$. Whereas our knowledge concerns only a distribution of probability for $u \in U$, we say that φ_M is a probabilistic representation of $\overline{ES}_M$. As it will appear further on, eventistic machines are the eventistic systems suitable for computer simulation.

7. GOAL-ORIENTED EVENTISTIC SYSTEMS

A system (not necessarily an eventistic one) which controls its behaviour in order to achieve a certain goal we shall call a goal-oriented system. A notion of goal we shall treat as a primitive one. When we talk about goal-oriented eventistic systems we have in mind the systems composed of two subsystems: an eventistic system and a decision system. The goal-oriented eventistic system will be defined axiomatically [9, 11,13].

The goal-oriented eventistic system is an ordered quadruple in the form

$$ES_G = \langle \overline{ES}, G, V, \gamma \rangle \qquad (43)$$

where $\overline{ES} \subset G \times G$ is an oriented eventistic system and G is a non-empty set of goals. For every goal $g \in G$ a set of degrees of realization of g is defined. The set V in (43) is a union of V_g-s being the degrees of realization of g, $V = \mathbf{U}\{V_g : g \in G\}$. The last component of ES_G is a relation $\gamma \subset \overline{ES} \times V$ called a relation of goals realization.

If $v \in V_g$ and $\ll x,y \gg, v> \in \gamma$ then the pair $<x,y> \in \overline{ES}$ realizes the goal g to the degree v.

Some fundamental properties of goal-oriented eventistic systems are formulated in the following axioms [9,13,14].

(a) There are two binary relations defined on the set G: a relation of goals subordination $\pi \subset G \times G$ and a relation of goals collision $\kappa \subset G \times G$. The relation π is reflexive and transitive, the relation κ is irreflexive and symmetrical.

(b) Sets of degrees of realization are linearly ordered. The set V_g is ordered by a relation $\leq_g \subset V_g \times V_g$.

(c) Every goal from the set G can be extremely realized by an activity (or a set of activities [9,22]) of the system $\overline{ES}$. This condition can be written as follows:

$$(\forall g \subset G) \ (\hat{V}_g \neq \emptyset)$$

where $\hat{V}_g = R(\gamma) \cap UB_{V_g}(R_g(\gamma))$. (For $Z \subset X$, $UB_X Z = \{x \in X : (\forall z \in Z)(z \leq x)\}$ is a set of upper bounds of Z in X.) $R_g(\gamma) = V_g \cap R(\gamma)$.

Let us observe that it does not follow from the last axiom that there exists an activity $z \in \mathcal{D}(\gamma)$ such that $(\forall g \in G)(\forall \hat{v}_g \in V_g) \ (<z,\hat{v}_g> \in \gamma)$. The activity z satisfying the above condition realizes extremely all goals from G. This activity z satisfying the above condition realizes extremely all goals from G. This activity cannot exist if the relation of goals collision is non-empty, which is the matter of the next axiom.

(d) If two goals collide to one another then they cannot be extremely realized,

$$g' \kappa g'' \iff \neg (\exists z \in \mathcal{D}(\gamma)) \ (\exists v' \in \hat{V}_{g'})$$

$$(\exists v'' \in \hat{V}_{g''}) \ (<z,v'> \in \gamma \wedge <z,v'> \in \gamma).$$

Thus each of the goals can be realized only to a certain (compromise) degree.

Axioms a-d are a complete collection of axioms concerning goal-oriented eventistic systems [9,11]. These axioms have been inspired by Jaron's approach to his goal-oriented cybernetical systems [13,14].

We have assumed that some activities of a goal-oriented system $\overline{ES}$ realize all the goals from G. But for a given system and a given set of goals it may happen that no activity of the system realizes a goal $g \in G$, which implies that the corresponding system ES_G is not a goal-oriented one. What can we do in this situation?

In such cases we propose to introduce a concept of politics [9]. The politics intends to redefine the system ES_G so that a new system ES_G would be a goal-oriented one. The redefinition can be based on a modification of the set of goals G as well as of the system $\overline{ES}$. The modification must fulfill some additional conditions formulated elsewhere [9].

To find an activity $Z \in \mathcal{D}(\gamma)$ which realizes all the goals from G to as high as possible a degree, we must resolve a polyoptimization problem. For the empty relation of goals collision the problem can be stated in the following manner. Find $\hat{z} \in \mathcal{D}(\gamma)$ (if it exists) such that

$$(\forall g \in G) \ (\exists \hat{v}_g \in \hat{V}_g) \ (<\hat{z},\hat{v}_g> \in \gamma). \tag{43}$$

If the relation κ is non-empty, we must choose a suboptimal resolution of our problem. In this case an aggregation of goals [9] can be used. If every V_g is a metric space with the metric ρ_g then by the aggregation we can obtain a function

$$\Psi : \mathcal{D}(\gamma) \rightarrow \mathbb{R}_0$$

defined as follows

$$\Psi(z) = \sum_{g \in G} \lambda_g \cdot \rho_g \ (\gamma(z) \cap V_g, \hat{V}_g) \tag{44}$$

where

$$\gamma(z) = \{v \in V : <z,v> \in \gamma\} \ , \ \lambda_g \in \mathbb{R}$$

are such that

$$\sum_{g \in G} \lambda_g = 1$$

and for $A,B \subset V_g$, $\rho_g(A,B)$ is a distance between the sets A,B.

For the given function Ψ a suboptimal solution $\hat{z} \in \mathcal{D}(\gamma)$ is equal to

$$\arg \min_{z \in \mathcal{D}(\gamma)} \Psi(z)$$

More detailed consideration on the problems of optimization related to goal-oriented eventistic systems are included in [9].

There are well-known analytical methods of optimization theory which enable us to resolve some optimization problems. However, in some cases strong mathematical methods cannot be immediately applied. Sometimes it happens that the set of feasible decisions (in our case, the set of activities of an eventistic system) is defined only as some computational procedures.

For an eventistic system the above means that we have a simulational model of the system. The decisions which ensure a realization of the given goals are based on an analysis of the model [9]. The idea of a computer simulation of eventistic systems seems to be especially attractive because their exist so-called event-oriented programming languages (CSL, SIMON, etc.) suitable to simulate these systems.

It appears that for some eventistic systems the appropriate programs do exist; moreover, they are rather easy to write. A simulational model of the eventistic system is very helpful to analyse the behaviour of one system or a cooperation among a group of systems. Obviously, this model may be also a source of feasible decisions in some problems of optimum choice.

8. COMPUTER SIMULATION OF EVENTISTIC SYSTEMS

We shall say that a system has a simulational model (the system can be simulated) if for the system there exists a simulational algorithm. The algorithm is assumed to be a pair

$$A = <X, F> \qquad (46)$$

where X is a set of simulation states and F is a partial operation in X called a transition function [25,33]. A sequence $x_0, x_1 = F(x_0), \ldots$ $x_{n+1} = F(x_n)$ will be called a computation $COMP(A, x_0)$ of the algorithm A starting from an initial state x_0 [33].

Usually we have $X = T \times S$ and $F(x) = F(t,s)$ $= <\tau(t,s), \varphi(t,s)>$ where the function τ points out an instant of the next simulation event and the function φ a state of the event. The set X should have a numerical representation, as a rule $X \subset R^n$ for some n. We shall say that a system has a simulational model (and a simulation algorithm $A = <X, F>$) iff the system is isomorphic to the algorithm.

Let an eventistic machine $\overline{ES}_M$ be given along with its representation according to (42) for some $U \subset R = T \times C$ and let a mapping $\varphi_U : U \to U$ describe a determined or stochastic "mechanism" of changes of inputs $u \in U$. Therefore we can define an extended global response-function for $\overline{ES}_M$

$$\overline{\varphi}_M : U \times \mathcal{D}(\overline{ES}_M) \to U \times R(\overline{ES}_M)$$

such that

$$\overline{\varphi}_M(u,r) = \begin{cases} <u, \varphi_M(u,r)> \text{ if } crd' \; \varphi_M(u,r) \\ \qquad \hat{\mathcal{P}} \; crd' \; u \\ <\varphi_U(u),r> \text{ if } crd' \; u \; \hat{\mathcal{P}} \; crd' \\ \qquad \varphi_M(u,r) \\ <\varphi_U(u),\varphi_M(u,r)> \text{ if } crd' \; \varphi_M(u,r) \\ \qquad = crd' \; u \end{cases} \qquad (47)$$

where for $r = <t,c>$ we have $crd' \; r = t$.

It can be proved that an iterative system $M = <X', F'>$ where $X' = U \times (\mathcal{D}(\overline{ES}_M)) \cup R(\overline{ES}_M))$ and $F' = \overline{\varphi}_M$ is isomorphic to a certain simulation algorithm $A = <X, F>$. Then for an eventistic machine $\overline{ES}_M$ having an input set $U \subset R$ there exists a simulation algorithm [9].

Now let us consider a collection of eventistic machines $\{\overline{ES}_{Mi} : i \in I\}$ defined on R which have the extended global response-functions as in (47). We know that every machine $\overline{ES}_{Mi}$ has a simulational algorithm $A = <X_i, F_i>$. Now we are interested in an analysis of cooperation of the machines.

Let us form the Cartesian product

$$Y = \mathbf{X} \{ X'_i : i \in I \}$$

and let

$$\alpha : Y \to X'_0 \subset R \times R \qquad (48)$$

be a one-to-one correspondence. We shall assume that the cooperation of the machines is such that at every instant only one machine acts and its influence to the others is due to some special functions. Let

$$\Theta : Y \to I \qquad (49)$$

indicate a machine which is to act. Let some partial mappings

$$\Psi_{ij} : X'_i \times X'_j \to X'_j \; , \quad i,j \in I \qquad (50)$$

describe the cooperation. The mappings must be such that

$$\Psi_{ii}(x'_i, x'_i) = F'_i(x'_i) .$$

Therefore we can define an iterative system $M_0 = <X'_0, F'_0>$ such that for $\Theta(\alpha^{-1}(x'_0)) = i$

$$F'_0(x'_0) = \alpha(<\Psi_{ij}(crd^i \; (\alpha^{-1}(x'_0)),$$

$$crd^j \; (\alpha^{-1}(x'_0))) : \quad j \in I>) .$$

Let us see that the system M_0 is isomorphic to a simulation algorithm $A_0 = <X_0, F_0>$. The algorithm A_0 can be composed of the algorithms $A_i = <X_i, F_i>$. It is a simulation algorithm for the cooperation of machines $\{\overline{ES}_{Mi} : i \in I\}$ [9,33] on condition that the formulae (48) - (50) hold.

We have shown that the eventistic machines and their cooperation have some simulational models. The presented conception of the cooperation is based on [33]. Some more detailed considerations are included in [9].

If there exists an eventistic machine $\overline{ES}_{M0}$ such that $X'_0 = U_0 \times (\mathcal{D}(\overline{ES}_{M0}) \cup R(\overline{ES}_{M0}))$ and F'_0 is the extended global response function of $\overline{ES}_{M0}$, then $\overline{ES}_{M0}$ will be called a complex eventistic machine [9,31].

For a given cooperating eventistic machine $\{\overline{ES}_{Mi} : i \in I\}$ the machine $\overline{ES}_{M0}$ can be found (if it exists). A simulation algorithm for the machines $\overline{ES}_{M0}$ is also the algorithm of cooperation for machines $\{\overline{ES}_{Mi} ; i \in I\}$. The machines $\overline{ES}_{Mi}$ are related to $\overline{ES}_{M0}$ by the mapping α. The following problem was considered in [9]: The machines $\overline{ES}_{M0}$ and $\overline{ES}_{Mi}$, $i \in I$, and the function α are known. The simulation algorithms for $\overline{ES}_{M0}$ and $\overline{ES}_{Mi}$ are known too. Usually the algorithm (and a simulation program) for $\overline{ES}_{M0}$ is rather complicated and it seems to be natural to "compose" it of simulation algorithms (and programs) for the machines $\overline{ES}_{Mi}$. Is it possible to formulate any principles according to which such a program can be organized?

The answer is positive. For the simulation programs of $\overline{ES}_{M0}$ written in CSL, the simulation programs of $\overline{ES}_{Mi}$ can be treated as some subroutines or procedures of the whole program. The operations F_i are sequences of instructions of a corresponding routine. It is also possible to define a function which allows successively to call the subroutines as well as to determine the initial conditions for every subroutine. The operation F_0 of the algorithm A_0 is represented

by a sequence of instructions inside the loop
ACTIVITIES. Thus we are able to write the simulational program as a well-organized block
structure [9].

9. FINAL REMARKS

The presented review of the theory of eventistic systems contains the most important problems
and results obtained by us in this area. As it
can be easily observed, the theory has very differential form. In the theory of eventistic
systems there are some fully developed "subtheories" (e.g. the theory of time) as well as
"subtheories" which are not much advanced (the
theory of states, the theory of goal-oriented
eventistic systems), but a lot of questions are
open yet.

Irrespective of the actual state of the theory,
it seems to be worth emphasizing a considerable
unifying power of theory of eventistic systems.
The concept of eventistic systems corresponds to
many well-known types of systems belonging to
both deductive and inductive trends in general
systems theory.

The theory of goal-oriented eventistic systems is related to some general polyoptimization
problems.

To analyse some eventistic systems a method
of computer simulation can be used. For goal-
oriented eventistic machines and their cooperation the problem of choice of the optimum activity
can be reduced to a choice from computations of
the appropriate simulation algorithms.

Of course, we do not expect that so general
theory as the theory of eventistic systems will
resolve immediately any practical problems. In
our opinion the last requirement is an absolute
misunderstanding. Our understanding of general
systems theory and its relation to some special
systems theories is in line of Bogdanov's idea
of degression [8].

However, to resolve the practical problems one
must develop the relevant special systems theories
and among them some special theories of eventistic
systems. In this area a theory of discrete-
continuous eventistic systems and a theory of
fuzzy-eventistic systems seem to be an interesting
proposal [24].

REFERENCES

1. ASHBY, W. R., _An Introduction to Cybernetics_,
   Chapman and Hall, London, 1958.
2. ASHBY, W. R., "Principles of Self-Organizing
   Systems," in: _Principles of Self-Organization_,
   H. von Foerster and G. W. Zopf (eds.),
   Pergamon Press, New York, 1962.
3. AUGUSTYNEK, Z., _Properties of Time_, PWN,
   Warsaw, 1972 (in Polish).
4. AUGUSTYNEK, Z., _The Nature of Time_, PWN,
   Warsaw, 1975 (in Polish).
5. BASRI, S. A., _A Deductive Theory of Space and
   Time_, North Holland, Amsterdam, 1966.
6. CARNAP, R., _An Introduction to Formal Logic_,
   Springer, Vienna, 1973 (in German).
7. ENGELKING, R., _General Topology_, PWN, Warsaw,
   1975 (in Polish).
8. GORELIK, G., "Principal Ideas of Bogdanov's
   'Tektology': The Universal Science of
   Organization," _General Systems_, Vol. 20,
   1975.
9. JACAK, W., _Some Optimization Problems on the
   Basis of Definition of Eventistic Systems_,
   Doctor's Thesis, Technical University of
   Wrocław, Wrocław, 1976 (in Polish).
10. JACAK, W. and K. TCHOŃ, "Events and Systems,"
    Systems Science, Vol. 2, 1976.
11. JACAK, W. and K. TCHOŃ, "On Goal-Oriented
    Eventistic Systems," _Systems Science_,
    Vol. 3, 1977.
12. JACAK, W. and K. TCHOŃ, "On the Eventistic
    Approach to the Notion of System,"
    General Systems Depository, No. 071777
    (see International Journal of General
    Systems, Vol. 4, 1977).
13. JARON, J., "On Goal-Oriented Cybernetical
    Systems," _Systems Science_, Vol. 1, 1975.
14. JAROŃ, J., "The Goals-Space of the Cyber-
    netical System," _Proceedings of the
    International Congress of Cybernetics
    and Systems_, Bucharest, 1975.
15. KALMAN, R., P. FALB and M. ARBIB, _Topics on
    Mathematical Systems Theory_, McGraw-Hill,
    New York, 1969.
16. KLIR, G. J., _An Approach to General Systems
    Theory_, Van Nostrand, New York, 1969.
17. KLIR, G. J., "On the Representation of
    Activity Arrays," _International Journal
    of General Systems_," Vol. 2, 1975.
18. KLIR, G. J., "Identification of Generative
    Structures in Empirical Data," _Inter-
    national Journal of General Systems_,
    Vol. 3, 1976.
19. KURATOWSKI, K., _Topology_, Vols. 1-2, New
    York, 1966-1968.
20. LÖFGREN, L., "Relative Explanation of
    Systems," in: _Trends in General Systems
    Theory_, G. J. Klir (ed.), John Wiley,
    New York, 1972.
21. MEHLBERG, H., "An Essay on the Causal Theory
    of Time," _Studia Philosophica_, Vols. 1-2,
    1935-1937 (in French).
22. MESAROVIC, M. D. (ed.), _Views on General
    Systems Theory_, John Wiley, New York,
    1964.
23. MESAROVIC, M. D. and Y. TAKAHARA, _General
    Systems Theory_, Academic Press, New York,
    1975.
24. MUSZYŃSKI, W., _Theory of Fuzzy-Eventistic
    Systems_, Doctor's Thesis, Technical
    University of Wrocław, Wrocław, 1978
    (in Polish).
25. PAWLAK, Z., "On Programming Machines,"
    Algorytmy, Vol. 5, 1969 (in Polish).
26. ROSEN, R., "Structural Stability, Alternate
    Descriptions and Information," _Journal
    of Theoretical Biology_, Vol. 63, 1976.
27. RUSSELL, B., _Analysis of Matter_, Allen and
    Unwin, London, 1959.
28. RUSSELL, B., _Our Knowledge of the External
    World_, Allen and Unwin, London, 1959.
29. RUSSELL, B., "On Order in Time," _Proceedings
    Cambridge Philosophy Society_, Vol. 32,
    1936.
30. TAYLOR, E. F. and J. A. WHEELER, _Spacetime
    Physics_, W. H. Freeman and Co., San
    Francisco and London, 1966.

31. TCHON, K., _Event as a Primitive Notion in Systems Theory_, Doctor's Thesis, Technical University of Wrocław, 1975 (in Polish).

32. WINDEKNECHT, T. G., _General Dynamical Processes_, Academic Press, New York, 1971.

33. WINKOWSKI, J., _Programming of Processes Simulation_, WNT, Warsaw, 1974 (in Polish).

34. WOJCICKI, R., _Formal Methodology of Empirical Sciences_, Ossolineum, Wroclaw, 1974 (in Polish).

A spectral analysis of relations, further developments

KLAUS KRIPPENDORFF

The Annenberg School of Communications, University of Pennsylvania
Philadelphia, USA

1. INTRODUCTION

Part of my background is in the social sciences where the concept of "relation" is a central one. Almost anything social is said to be transacted and has relational qualities. Processes of communication are relational in the sense of connecting, however tenuously, two or more individuals. Authority, power and control can only be defined in relational terms. And the very notion of organization, social or otherwise, implies boundaries within which certain patterns of interaction are maintained and across which matter, energy and information are exchanged which in turn creates, maintains or destroys other patterns of interaction. While much of social science data contain evidence about relations, it is surprising that empirical techniques for analyzing complex relations are quite underdeveloped.

In a previous paper [9] I developed the idea of a spectral analysis of relations in part because I feel quite strongly that we might miss important insights if we restrict our vision through existing analytical techniques to very simple kinds of relations, correlations, associations, factor loadings, proximities, differences, causes, etc., all of which are <u>essentially</u> <u>binary</u> in nature. This restricted vision stands in marked contrast to ordinary conceptions of social life which recognize human communication as a multi-channel affair, social interaction to be rich and complex, and the environment of social organizations to be turbulent in the sense that feedback loops are multiple and intermeshed and rates of change are unequal and interdependent.

A spectral analysis of relations does not promise all the badly needed insights into what everyone agrees are deep and hidden complexities (see Simon [12], for example). For once, it is constrained by current computational limitations. But it does offer a modest improvement in analytical vision.

2. A SPECTRAL ANALYSIS OF RELATIONS

Generalizing from physics, one could say that a <u>spectral</u> <u>analysis</u> entails a calculus or accounting system for certain magnitudes such that the magnitude of a whole can be regarded as the algebraic sum of the magnitudes of its component parts. The decomposition of a source of light into additive spectra is a classical example but so is the Fourier analysis of oscillations, mechanical, musical, economic or social. I am applying the general idea to the study of relations.

The <u>relations</u> of interest in this paper are manifest in distributions of data in multivariate spaces. Illustrating this notion, we are all familiar with scatter diagrams of data points in a plane. One can easily extend this notion by visualizing a distribution of data points in a three or four dimensional space. But when more than four variables are involved other conceptual devices are needed. Nevertheless it should not be difficult to imagine that multi-variable distributions may assume very complex forms. Some distributions are inherently simple in the sense that either some variables are redundant or the whole distribution can be explained as a conjunction of distributions of lower ordinality. Distributions that represent linear relations are of this kind. They are usually depictable in a series of scatter diagrams each representing a binary relation. Figure 1 exemplifies such a case.

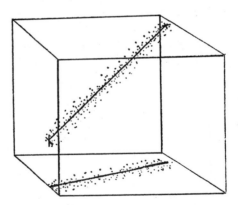

Figure 1. Example of a Linear Relation Typically Assumed in Social Science Methods

Some relations are inherently complex in the sense that all variables are needed, not in pairs, not in triples, all in conjunction, to account for that relation. Figure 2 depicts such a non-decomposable relation in three dimensions. Most non-linear relations are of this kind. Part of the aim of a spectral analysis of relations is to ascertain whether a multi-valued relation can be simplified without loss, where the non-decomposable complexities lie in the data, the ordinality of the explanation required, how much would be

lost if one were to impose an unjustified simplification on an empirical fact, etc.

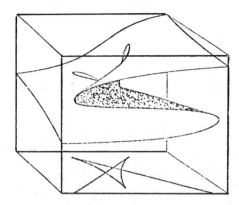

Figure 2. Example of a Non-Linear Relation
           of Concern to Catastrophy Theory
           Among Others

The qualitative components in the spectral
analysis of relations consist of all possible relations of equal or lower ordinality than are
inherent in a given data. Generally, for relational data within m variables there are:

1	zero-order relation
m	1st-order relations (properties)
$\frac{m(m-1)}{2}$	2nd-order relations (binary relations)
$\frac{m(m-1)(m-2)}{6}$	3rd-order relations (tertiary relations)
.	
.	
.	
$_mC_r = \frac{m!}{(m-r)!r!}$	rth-order relations
.	
.	
.	
1	mth-order relation
2^m	total number of possible relations

This can be a large number, even with a moderate
number m of variables. While the number of possible relations might set computational limits
for a complete analysis of relational data, this
fact can hardly serve as a justification for
statistical techniques in the social sciences to
assume as it were that social phenomena are essentially linear and, hence, decomposable into
binary relations or at best constrained by a
third variable.

The magnitudes in a spectral analysis of relations reflect deviations of observed frequencies
from what would be expected by chance. Again, we
are all too familiar with the two-variable case.
Two variables, A and B, are regarded as independent

when the joint probability distribution is fully
explainable from its individual probability
distributions, i.e., for all values $a \in A$ and
$b \in B$" $p_{ab} = p_a p_b$ or $p_{ab}/p_a p_b = 1$ where
$p_a = \sum_b p_{ab}$, etc. The extent of the deviation
of p_{ab} from $p_a p_b$ is taken to be indicative of
the strength of an association between the two
variables. In the literature I have found no
extension of this test to higher order dependencies. Bartlett [4] might be mentioned as an
exception. However, his test concerns only
2 by 2 by 2 contingency tables. In the spectral
analysis of relations the above comparison of
observed and expected probabilities is generalized by an expansion of the probabilities in distributions of varying ordinality into a series of
tests, each pertaining to a different subspace
of the original distribution, and all are logically
independent of each other (see (1) on next page).
The probability p_{abcd} of a data point in a four
dimensional space can be seen as the product of
the tests for the presence of one zero-order
relation (which is an artifact here and of no
consequence in the following), four unary relations (properties or distributions in one variable), six binary relations (involving all pairs
of variables), four tertiary relations, and one
qua ternary relation.

The accounting equation for the spectral
analysis of relations is obtained by first dividing both sides by the set of first order probabilities and then summing the average logarithm
of these probabilistic expressions for all data
points. While there are probably several tests
that could be employed to establish the presence
of relations of higher ordinality, the logarithmic
function is justified by Shannon's [11] proof
that it is the only function leading to additive
quantities. Thus, the fundamental accounting
equation for the spectral analysis of relations
is:

$$T(AB) \quad = \quad Q(AB)$$

$$T(ABC) \quad = \quad Q(ABC) + Q(AB) + Q(AC) + Q(BC)$$

$$T(ABCD) \quad = \quad Q(ABCD) + Q(ABC) + Q(ABD) + Q(ACD) + Q(BCD) + Q(AB) + Q(AC) + Q(AD) + Q(BC) + Q(BD) + Q(CD)$$

$$T(m \text{ variables}) \quad = \quad \sum_{r=2}^{m} \sum_{i=1}^{_mC_r} Q(\text{rth-order})_i$$

$$(2)$$

In it, the T-measures assess the total amount of
relation (relatedness, constraint, information
transmission, multivariate association, etc.) in
the data as a whole:

$$T(AB) \quad = \quad \sum_a \sum_b p_{ab} \log_2 \frac{p_{ab}}{p_a p_b}$$

(continued on p. 72)

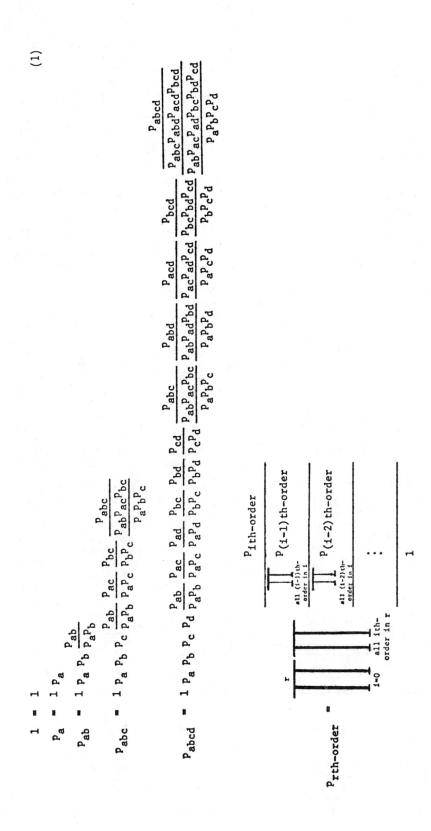

$$T(ABC) = \sum_a \sum_b \sum_c P_{abc} \log_2 \frac{P_{abc}}{P_a P_b P_c}$$

$$T(ABCD) = \sum_a \sum_b \sum_c \sum_d P_{abcd} \log_2 \frac{P_{abcd}}{P_a P_b P_c P_d}$$

etc.

And the Q-measures assess the unique contribution each relation makes to the total:

$$Q(AB) = \sum_a \sum_b P_{ab} \log_2 \frac{P_{ab}}{P_a P_b}$$

$$Q(ABC) = \sum_a \sum_b \sum_c P_{abc} \log_2 \frac{P_{abc}}{\dfrac{P_{ab} P_{ac} P_{bc}}{P_a P_b P_c}}$$

$$Q(ABCD) = \sum_a \sum_b \sum_c \sum_d P_{abcd} \log_2 \frac{P_{abcd}}{\dfrac{\dfrac{P_{abc} P_{abd} P_{acd} P_{bcd}}{P_{ab} P_{ac} P_{ad} P_{bc} P_{bd} P_{cd}}}{P_a P_b P_c P_d}}$$

etc.

Mainly because it will not cause confusion in this paper, my notation condenses the conventional forms established by Ashby [1,2]. Accordingly, T(ABC) = TA:B:C), Q(ABC) = Q(A:B:C), and in what follows H(ABC) = H(A,B,C), T($\overline{ABC}$) = T(A,B:C), etc.

Some of the properties of these measures have been discussed and exemplified previously [9]. Here I will state them very briefly.

<u>First</u>, the Q-measures are indicative of the magnitude of a relation. If such a measure turns out to be zero or approximately zero, then the relation so assessed contributes nothing to the data and may be ignored. If it equals the total then it is the only relation accounting for the data.

<u>Second</u>, all Q-measures are independent. The finding that all binary relations are absent does not imply anything about the presence or absence of a higher order relation in data and, vice versa, the presence of a higher order relation suggests nothing about the magnitude of any of its relations of lower ordinality.

<u>Third</u>, Q-measures assume negative values when its immediately lower-order relations overdetermine the distribution (include redundant accounts of the total) and they assume positive values when its immediately lower-order relations underdetermine the relation (are insufficient as aggregate account of the total). In other words, each Q-measure of a relation compensates for the errors of commission or the errors of omission committed by the conjunction of its component relations.

For examples, consider the four relations in a three dimensional space (see Figure 3). The values of all expressions of the accounting equation are computed under the assumption that the probability P_{abc} of the shaded cells is $1/n$ and the others are zero.

The leftmost distribution shows variable B to be redundant. The whole distribution can be explained in terms of A and C without loss of generality. This is indicated in the corresponding Q-measure. The accounting equation here reduces to T(ABC) = Q(AC), suggesting that explanations based on the pairs of variables A and B or B and C yield nothing. The next distribution is seen as fully explainable by the binary relations within pairs of variables. Actually only two such binary relations are required, the third is implied and redundant. Taken together, the three binary relations therefore overdetermine the whole. It is the amount of overdetermination which now appears as the negative value in the test for the presence of the tertiary relation. The third relation from the left shows the binary account for the distribution to be important but not sufficient to provide a complete account of that distribution. An attempt to describe the whole in terms of the three binary component relations will miss about one-seventh of the total amount of constraint in the data. The rightmost distribution is the more complex of the four. All projections of the distribution on the three

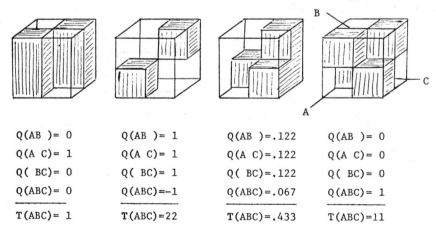

Q(AB)= 0	Q(AB)= 1	Q(AB)=.122	Q(AB)= 0
Q(A C)= 1	Q(A C)= 1	Q(A C)=.122	Q(A C)= 0
Q(BC)= 0	Q(BC)= 1	Q(BC)=.122	Q(BC)= 0
Q(ABC)= 0	Q(ABC)=-1	Q(ABC)=.067	Q(ABC)= 1
T(ABC)= 1	**T**(ABC)=22	**T**(ABC)=.433	**T**(ABC)=11

Figure 3.   Four Examples of Relations

two-dimensional planes yield uniform distributions. The Q-measure for all binary relations are all zero. A unique tertiary relation accounts for the total constraint in the data: T(ABC) = Q(ABC). This last example demonstrates the point made earlier that the presence or absence of a relation of one ordinality is independent of the presence or absence of a relation of another ordinality. The Q-measures are not ordered, do not imply each other.

The idea of representing a distribution of data in a many-variable space in terms of simple relations is based on Ashby's "Constraint Analysis of Many-Valued Relations" [1] which suggests a qualitative method for analyzing complex relations into simple ones. Ashby starts by identifying a relation with a proper subject of a product set. When an empirically obtained relation is projected onto several subspaces and reflected back into the original space, the conjunction of these reflections form a new relation that contains the empirically obtained one as a proper subset. The set-theoretical difference between the two subsets can be taken as the loss incurred by the projection. Constraint analysis simplifies a relation by identifying those subspaces for which the loss is minimal or absent. A spectral analysis of relations realizes many of Ashby's intentions in a probabilistic context. Transmission measures, T, clearly are measures of constraint:

$$T(ABC...) = H(A) + H(B) + H(C) + ... - H(ABC...)$$

$H(A) + H(B) + H(C) + ...$ is the maximum entropy in a multi-variable space that would be observed if all variables are independent and $H(ABC...)$ is the entropy actually obtained. In terms of the four examples given in Figure 3, the second from the left exhibits the largest constraint and the third from the left the smallest. It is the use of an accounting equation for separating the magnitudes associated with all logically distinct and unique contributions of each subset of variables that makes the spectral analysis different from Ashby's approach.

The quantitative part of this spectral analysis also owes much to the groundwork laid by Ashby in various extensions of information theory [2,3] which were influenced by McGill's work on multi-variate information transmission [10].

3. BASIC BUILDING BLOCKS OF ORDER

One of the interesting consequences of the accounting equation is that it points to the Q-measures as possible candidates of what one might call basic building blocks of order. While these measures are far from simple and quite removed from the entropies of a distribution, they are at least as appealing as entropy measures are because all information theoretical measures can be expressed as the <u>algebraic</u> <u>sum</u> of several Q-measures, whereas entropies require additions <u>and</u> subtractions. So, if one is willing and capable of computing all Q-measures for an empirically obtained distribution of data points, one can gain considerable insights into its relational properties which ordinary H-measures would hide. For example, in the five dimensional case of Figure 4, all possible Q-measures are seen as forming a lattice. In it one can identify all entropies, H, all information transmission terms, T, and all interactions, Q. The figure shows three examples. The Q-measures adding up to H(BDE) are connected by solid lines, those adding up to $T_A(BCD)$ by broken lines, and those adding up to $Q_B(ACDE)$ by a chain.

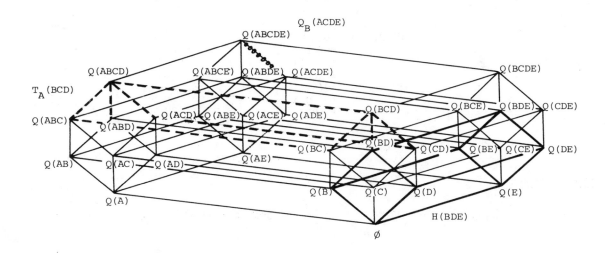

Figure 4. Lattice of Q-measures for Five Dimensions

The basic Q-measures are computable from entropies H:

$$Q(A) \;=\; -H(A) \;=\; \sum_a p_a \log_2 p_a$$

$$Q(AB) \;=\; H(A) + H(B) - H(AB) \;=\; H(A) + H(B) + \sum_a \sum_b p_{ab} \log_2 p_{ab}$$

$$Q(ABC) \;=\; -H(A) - H(B) - H(C) + H(AB) + H(AC) + H(BC) - H(ABC)$$

etc.

$$Q(m \text{ variables}) \;=\; \sum_{j=1}^{m} \sum_{k=1}^{mC_j} H(j \text{ variables})_k \; \Delta_{m-j} \quad \text{where } \Delta_x = \begin{cases} +1 \text{ for uneven } x \\ -1 \text{ for even } x \end{cases}$$

(3)

whereupon all entropies, information transmissions and interactions are expressable as the algebraic sum of these basic Q-measures:

Transmissions

$$T(m \text{ variables}) \;=\; \sum_{j=2}^{m} \sum_{k=1}^{mC_j} Q(j \text{ variables})_k \qquad (4)$$

e.g.:

$$
\begin{aligned}
T(ABCD) \;=\; & Q(AB\;\;) \\
& +Q(A\;C\;) \\
& +Q(A\;\;D) \\
& +Q(\;BC\;) \\
& +Q(\;B\;D) \\
& +Q(\;\;CD) \\
& +Q(ABC\;) \\
& +Q(AB\;D) \\
& +Q(A\;CD) \\
& +Q(\;BCD) \\
& +Q(ABCD)
\end{aligned}
$$

Entropies

$$H(m \text{ variables}) \;=\; \sum_{j=1}^{m} \sum_{k=1}^{mC_j} Q(j \text{ variables})_k \qquad (5)$$

e.g.:

$$
\begin{aligned}
H(BDE) \;=\; & Q(B\;\;) \\
& +Q(\;D\;) \\
& +Q(\;\;E) \\
& +Q(BD\;) \\
& +Q(B\;E) \\
& +Q(\;DE) \\
& +Q(BDE)
\end{aligned}
$$

Conditional Interactions

$$Q_{r \text{ variables}}(s \text{ variables}) \;=\; \sum_{j=0}^{r} \sum_{k=1}^{rC_j} Q(j+s \text{ variables})_k \qquad (6)$$

e.g.:

$$Q_{AB}(CDE) \;=\; Q(\;\;CDE) + Q(A\;CDE) + Q(\;BCDE) + Q(ABCDE)$$

Conditional Transmissions

$$T_{r\ variables}(s\ variables) = \sum_{j=2}^{s} \sum_{k=1}^{{}_sC_j} Q_{r\ variables}(j\ variables)_k \tag{7}$$

e.g.:

$$
\begin{aligned}
T_{AB}(CDE) = \ & Q_{AB}(CD\ ) = \ & Q(\ \ CD\ ) +Q(A\ CD\ ) +Q(\ BCD\ ) +Q(ABCD\ ) \\
& +Q_{AB}(C\ E) & +Q(\ C\ E) +Q(A\ C\ E) +Q(\ BC\ E) +Q(ABC\ E) \\
& +Q_{AB}(\ DE) & +Q(\ \ DE) +Q(A\ \ DE) +Q(\ B\ DE) +Q(AB\ DE) \\
& +Q_{AB}(CDE) & +Q(\ \ CDE) +Q(A\ CDE) +Q(\ BCDE) +Q(ABCDE)
\end{aligned}
$$

Conditional Entropies

$$H_{r\ variables}(s\ variables) = \sum_{j=1}^{s} \sum_{k=1}^{{}_sC_j} Q_{r\ variables}(j\ variables)_k \tag{8}$$

e.g.

$$
\begin{aligned}
H_{AB}(CDE) = \ & Q_{AB}(C\ \ ) = \ & Q(\ C\ \ ) +Q(A\ C\ \ ) +Q(\ BC\ \ ) +Q(ABC\ \ ) \\
& +Q_{AB}(\ D\ ) & +Q(\ \ D\ ) +Q(A\ \ D\ ) +Q(\ B\ D\ ) +Q(AB\ D\ ) \\
& +Q_{AB}(\ \ E) & +Q(\ \ \ E) +Q(A\ \ \ E) +Q(\ B\ \ E) +Q(AB\ \ E) \\
& +Q_{AB}(CD\ ) & +Q(\ \ CD\ ) +Q(A\ CD\ ) +Q(\ BCD\ ) +Q(ABCD\ ) \\
& +Q_{AB}(C\ E) & +Q(\ C\ E) +Q(A\ C\ E) +Q(\ BC\ E) +Q(ABC\ E) \\
& +Q_{AB}(\ DE) & +Q(\ \ DE) +Q(A\ \ DE) +Q(\ B\ DE) +Q(AB\ DE) \\
& +Q_{AB}(CDE) & +Q(\ \ CDE) +Q(A\ CDE) +Q(\ BCDE) +Q(ABCDE)
\end{aligned}
$$

Grouping of Variables in Interactions

$$Q(\overline{r\ variables} + s\ variables) = \sum_{j=1}^{r} \sum_{k=1}^{{}_rC_j} Q(j+s\ variables)_k \tag{9}$$

e.g.

$$
\begin{aligned}
Q(\overline{ABC}DEF) = \ & Q(A\ \ DEF) \\
& +Q(\ B\ DEF) \\
& +Q(\ \ CDEF) \\
& +Q(AB\ DEF) \\
& +Q(A\ CDEF) \\
& +Q(\ BCDEF) \\
& +Q(ABCDEF)
\end{aligned}
$$

It should be noted that the number of possible Q-measures equals the number of possible H-measures, and since all information theoretical measures can be expressed in either of the two kinds of terms, there seems to be no immediately apparent advantage. In fact, one might favour the entropies on account of their simplicity.

However, I am suggesting that Q- and H-measures provide complementary accounts of empirical facts. Q-measures approach an empirical phenomenon from the point of view of what can be explained within the set of observational variables. They locate the relations of different ordinality that account for given data. H-measures approach the same phenomena from the point of view of what can not be explained within these variables. They locate the uncertainties within different subspaces of a multi-variable distribution. The spectral analysis elucidates structure, pattern, dependency and constraint, whereas an account in terms of entropies emphasizes the freedom of variation,

uncertainty, lack of structure and error. Both are essential for gaining any understanding of systems.

4. BASIC BUILDING BLOCKS OF FUNCTIONAL COMPOSITION

Another interpretation of the results of a spectral analysis of relations is that it quantifies the extent to which functional components of varying complexity underlie a process that is responsible for the given data. $Q(AB) > 0$ indicates that there exists a binary relationship between the variables A and B that cannot be explained in terms of the properties associated with A and/or B. $Q(ABC) > 0$ indicates that there exists a tertiary relationship among the three variables A, B and C over and above what the three binary relationships between A and B, A and C, B and C, and the three properties in

A, B and C can account. Q(ABCD) > O indicates the
presence of a unique and non-decomposable quarter-
nary dependency between A, B, C and D, etc. All
variables among which a Q-measure exhibits a positive value could be said to stem from a single
source that maintains the pattern which the Q-
measure quantitatively assesses. Since the Q-
measure reflects the unique co-occurence of values
on all variables thereby assessed, it identifies
the coordinative effort by a source, an effort
that cannot be understood by fewer variables. To
make this correspondence between Q-measures and
functional components apparent, I am using Klir's
[8] graphical symbols:

Q(A) assesses a property   ≡ ─⊟ a single-valued component

Q(AB) assesses a binary relation   ≡ ═⊟ a two-valued component

Q(ABC) assesses a tertiary relation ≡ ≡⊟ a three-valued component

Q(ABCD) assesses a quarternary relation ≡ ≣⊟ a four-valued component

Q(ABCDE) assesses a quintenary relation ≡ ≣⊟ a five-valued component

etc.

By evaluating all components that could possibly
generate data of a given dimensionality and by
associating a magnitude with each, the accounting
equation in effect outlines the dependency structure (the wiring diagram) of the components of a
complex data source.

An accounting equation for m-valued data has
$2^m - m - 1$ distinct Q-measures. Since any one Q-
measure may be positive and since each configuration of Q-measures describes a different dependency structure, there are in fact $2^{2^m - m - 1}$ different dependency structures to be considered.
This can be a tremendously large number. Happily,
not all Q-measures need to be evaluated one-by-one.
Some can be evaluated en bloc, which provides the
basis of a more efficient algorithm.

The first such shortcut is suggested by
Ashby's [2] theorem stating that if a transmission term between two sets of variables is
zero, so are all Q-measures that make reference

to variables in both sets. Thus, if a set of
variables can be broken down into two, having,
say, r and s variables respectively, then
T(r variables + s variables) > O implies
$(2^r - 1)(2^s - 1)$ of the 2^{r+s} Q-measures are known
to be zero, leaving only $2^r + 2^s$ Q-measures to
be evaluated. This means a considerable saving
of computational efforts. To find independent
subsystems in the set of variables should be the
first and in a sense preliminary step of any
spectral analysis of relations. A system of,
say, five variables may be decomposed in the way
shown below.

In what follows I am therefore ignoring all
zero dependencies across independent subsystems
and focusing instead on the interdependencies
within a system of variables that cannot be
partitioned as shown below. I suppose this is
where the real power of a spectral analysis of
relations lies.

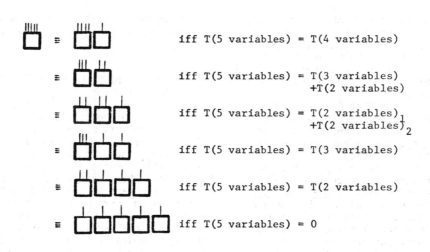

iff T(5 variables) = T(4 variables)

iff T(5 variables) = T(3 variables)
                    +T(2 variables)

iff T(5 variables) = T(2 variables)₁
                    +T(2 variables)₂

iff T(5 variables) = T(3 variables)

iff T(5 variables) = T(2 variables)

iff T(5 variables) = 0

The second shortcut is suggested by the way functional components are conceptualized. Suppose the lattice of Q-measures reveals that one relation is embedded in another. For example:

$$Q(ABC)>0$$

$$Q(AB\ )>0$$

This finding would suggest that a tertiary relation between variables A, B and C contains a binary relation between variables A and B. To realize (program or build) a functional component that would represent (generate or simulate) the given data would require a function of no less than three values or a box with no less than three variables attached. All constraints among these three variables will have to be programmed into that box, including any binary dependency that might be manifest in the data. Only if these binary relations are shared through communication with other components might they have to be considered separately. The example:

$$Q(ABC\ )>0$$

$$Q(AB\ )>0$$

$$Q(AB\ D)>0$$

leaves open where the binary relation is to be realized, in the ABC-component or in the ABD-component. The dependency structure is not affected in either case.

Summarizing, one can say that a relation is embedded in another when the set of variables in which that relation is manifest is a proper subset of the set of variables in which the other relation is manifest. If it is the task to identify dependency structures among functional components, then a spectral analysis of relations can stop with the location of postive Q-measures for relations none of which is embedded in another. If it is the task to quantify the information each functional component requires to generate given data, then the quantities associated with embedded relations need to be examined. Clearly, the task of identifying the dependency structure is prior to that of quantifying what is involved inside and across each component. The illustration to follow pertains to the structural identification task only.

A final and in a sense still preliminary point is that structural ambiguities may arise from the fact that Q-measures assess the extent of a unique relation among variables. To determine structure types requires suitable decision criteria. In the above example, if Q(ABC) were positive but very small compared with Q(AB) then one has the choice of representing the data either by the most inclusive positive relation, here involving A, B and C, or by tolerating the error Q(ABC) and representing the data in terms of the variables that dominate the total constraint, here involving A and B only. The choice of a suitable decision criterion is not a simple matter. But I am assuming here that such a criterion does exist. It disambiguates the emergence of structure types.

With these preliminaries, I will now exemplify the dependency structures a spectral analysis of relations will reveal. The two-variable case is actually of no particular interest. Assuming a suitable decision criterion given, a binary relation is either present in the data or it is not. A spectral analysis of a three-variable system, on the other hand, could result in any one of three dependency structure types which are listed together with the Q-measures of relations that are ignored for lack of statistical significance or overdetermination, and Q-measure configuration defining the structure. I am ignoring the permutations of variables throughout.

Statistically insignificant or negative Q-measures	Defining configuration, non-embedded	Q-measure, embedded	Dependency structure	Required components
	Q(ABC)	Q(AB) Q(A C) Q(BC)		1 tertiary
Q(ABC) $Q_B(AC)$	Q(AB) Q(BC)			2 binary
Q(ABC)	Q(AB) Q(A C) Q(BC)			3 binary

A spectral analysis of a four-variable system could
result in any one of the following fourteen dependency structure types:

Statistically insignificant or negative Q-measures	Defining configuration, non-embedded	Q-measure, embedded	Dependency structure	Required components
	Q(ABCD)	Q(ABC) Q(AB D) Q(A CD) Q(BCD) Q(AB) Q(A C) Q(A D) Q(BC) Q(B D) Q(CD)		**1** quarternary
Q(ABCD) Q_D(ABC) Q_C(ABD) Q_{CD}(AB)	Q(A CD) Q(BCD)	Q(A C) Q(A D) Q(BC) Q(B D) Q(CD)		**2** tertiary
Q(ABCD) Q_D(ABC) Q_C(ABD) Q_B(ACD) Q_{CD}(AB) Q_{BC}(AD)	Q(BCD) Q(A C)	Q(BC) Q(B D) Q(CD)		**1** tertiary **2** binary
Q(ABCD) Q_D(ABC) Q_C(ABD) Q_B(ACD) Q_A(BCD) Q_{CD}(AB) Q_{BC}(AD) Q_{AB}(CD)	Q(A C) Q(B D) Q(BC)			**3** binary
Q(ABCD) Q_D(ABC) Q_C(ABD) Q_B(ACD) Q_A(BCD) Q_{CD}(AB) Q_{BC}(AD) Q_{AC}(BD)	Q(A C) Q(BC) Q(CD)			**3** binary

$Q(ABCD)$ $Q_D(ABC)$ $Q_C(ABD)$ $Q_B(ACD)$ $Q_{CD}(AB)$	$Q(\ BCD)$ $Q(\ BC\ )$ $Q(A\ C\ )$ $Q(\ B\ D)$ $Q(A\ \ D)$ $Q(\ \ CD)$		1 tertiary 2 binary
$Q(ABCD)$ $Q_D(ABC)$	$Q(AB\ D)$ $Q(AB\ \ )$ $Q(A\ CD)$ $Q(A\ C\ )$ $Q(\ BCD)$ $Q(A\ \ D)$ $Q(\ BC\ )$ $Q(\ B\ D)$ $Q(\ \ CD)$		3 tertiary
$Q(ABCD)$ $Q_D(ABC)$ $Q_C(ABD)$	$Q(A\ CD)$ $Q(A\ C\ )$ $Q(\ BCD)$ $Q(A\ \ D)$ $Q(AB\ \ )$ $Q(\ BC\ )$ $Q(\ B\ D)$ $Q(\ \ CD)$		2 tertiary 1 binary
$Q(ABCD)$	$Q(ABC\ )$ $Q(AB\ \ )$ $Q(AB\ D)$ $Q(A\ C\ )$ $Q(A\ CD)$ $Q(A\ \ D)$ $Q(\ BCD)$ $Q(\ BC\ )$ $Q(\ B\ D)$ $Q(\ \ CD)$		4 tertiary
$Q(ABCD)$ $Q_D(ABC)$ $Q_C(ABD)$ $Q_B(ACD)$	$Q(\ BCD)$ $Q(\ BC\ )$ $Q(AB\ \ )$ $Q(\ B\ D)$ $Q(A\ C\ )$ $Q(\ \ CD)$ $Q(A\ \ D)$		1 tertiary 3 binary
$Q(ABCD)$ $Q_D(ABC)$ $Q_C(ABD)$ $Q_B(ACD)$ $Q_A(BCD)$ $Q_{CD}(AB)$ $Q_{BC}(AD)$	$Q(A\ C\ )$ $Q(\ BC\ )$ $Q(\ B\ D)$ $Q(\ \ CD)$		4 binary
$Q(ABCD)$ $Q_D(ABC)$ $Q_C(ABD)$ $Q_B(ACD)$ $Q_A(BCD)$ $Q_{CD}(AB)$ $Q_{AB}(CD)$	$Q(A\ C\ )$ $Q(A\ \ D)$ $Q(\ BC\ )$ $Q(\ B\ D)$		4 binary
$Q(ABCD)$ $Q_D(ABC)$ $Q_C(ABD)$ $Q_B(ACD)$ $Q_A(BCD)$ $Q_{CD}(AB)$	$Q(A\ C\ )$ $Q(A\ \ D)$ $Q(\ BC\ )$ $Q(\ B\ D)$ $Q(\ \ CD)$		5 binary

Q(ABCD)   Q(AB)   6 binary

Q_D(ABC)   Q(A C)

Q_C(ABD)   Q(A D)

Q_B(ACD)   Q(BC)

Q_A(BCD)   Q(B D)

                 Q(CD)

It should be noted that the algebraic sum of the defining Q-measures (of embedded and non-embedded relations incorporated in the dependency structure) equals the amount of transmission accounted for by the components of the structure. Thus, in the first dependency structure in this list (the un-differentiated case) this sum is T(ABCD) and in the last it is the sum of the six binary trans-missions between the four variables.

The aim of the above exercise was not to enumerate dependency structure types. Although these are far fewer in number than the configura-tions of possible Q-measures, they grow exponen-tially with the number of variables involved. A spectral analysis does not test for distinct struc-ture types. They simply emerge from or are implied by the configuration of statistically significant and non-embedded relations as represented by their Q-measures. The aim of the above was merely to show the correspondence between configurations of Q-measures and dependency structures, and to thereby demonstrate what a spectral analysis (of interconnected systems) of relations may reveal.

One way to organize dependency structure types is by the number of components required to repre-sent each structure. The above list is an example of this. Another and far more promising way is to follow the path of an <u>algorithm for structure identification</u> from the most complex component of the highest possible ordinality to the smallest set of least complex (binary) components all of which could conceivably represent the intercon-nections among the variables of a non-decomposable system. The algorithm iteratively evaluates the consequences of removing non-embedded relations (in decreasing order of ordinality) and brings thereby into focus those previously embedded re-lations that are now considered candidates of a more efficient representation of dependencies.

This algorithm is applied here to the four-variable system of the above example (see Figure 6). When the removal of a relation is indicated by the transition this invokes from one dependency struc-ture to the next, the following lattice emerges. It assigns each structure type a unique place. To enhance readability, the removal of the quarter-nary relation is indicated by a horizontal line, of a tertiary relation by a vertical line, and of a binary relation by a 45° line. The transitions are signed by the Q-measures representing the re-moved relation.

The first step of this algorithm involves testing for the statistical significance of the one quarternary relation encompassing the whole system. Its second and third steps involve de-ciding whether and which tertiary relations can be ignored as well. It might be noted that the removal of the second tertiary relation renders one of its embedded binary relations a component of the resulting structure. The fourth step

offers a choice between removing the one binary relation or one of the two tertiary ones; etc. The process continues until a structure type emerges that is maximally simple and represents the total with a minimum of loss.

The functional component interpretation of the results of the spectral analysis of relations invites comparisons with Klir's work [7,8]. Its aim is very similar if not identical, but it deviates from the approach taken by the spectral analysis in at least two ways. First, Klir uses the sum of the absolute differences between ex-pected and observed probabilities as measures of the degree to which a relation is approximated by the conjunction of its components. While this approach is well grounded in the tradition of statistical testing (e.g. x^2 methodology), it is biased towards a binary notion of constraint. In terms of the spectral analysis, the binary notion of constraint is implicit in the T-measures of information theory. But no longer in third or higher-order Q-measures. The fact that Klir's approach cannot lead to a calculus of additive quantities for many-valued relations need not be a disadvantage.

Second, Klir [8] adopts two rather stringent "axioms of structure candidates" that limit the structure types his procedure is able to differ-entiate. As a consequence, circular dependencies, e.g.:

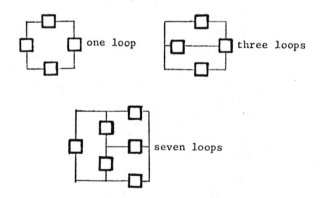

one loop

three loops

seven loops

cannot be identified if they exist in the data. In the above example of an interconnected system of four variables, nine out of the fourteen structure types include circular or indirect mutual dependencies. Klir's approach would identify only the first five on the list of dependency structure types (not to be confused with the steps of the algorithm). The others are forced into these five types. The major advantage and presumably the reason for adopting this somewhat more restricted concept of

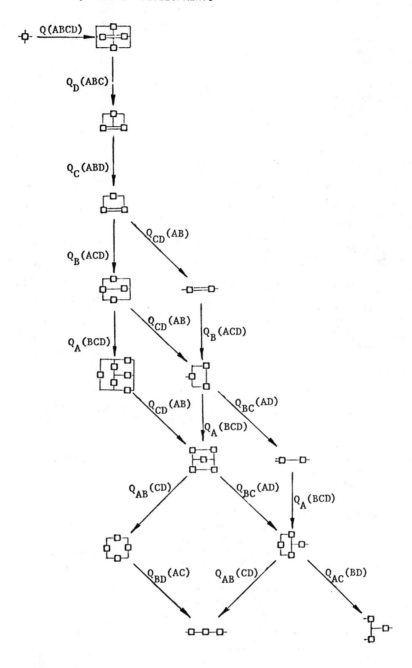

Figure 6. Lattice Resulting from Structural
Identification Algorithm

structure is computational efficiency which is still a problem with spectral analysis. At this point, I cannot say how important it is and what it implies that the spectral analysis of relations identifies so many more alternative structures.

I should also acknowledge here recent work by Broekstra, who was so kind to supply me with copies of his work [5,6] after the presentation of this paper in Linz. Like myself, he approached the problem of structure identification from information theory. He too encountered the power of the Q-measures. But, unlike myself, he adopts a notion of structure that includes only binary relations and can be depicted as graphs between variables, although his second publication expands this notion to give a quantitative account of Klir's structure types. I believe the key to the difference between the spectral analysis approach and his lies in divergent generalizations of "statistical independence." The tests for the absence of a relation adopted by spectral analysis are spelled out in (1). His generalization of statistical independence to more than two variables is, in effect:

$$P_{ab} = P_a P_b$$

$$P_{abc} = \frac{P_{ac} P_{bc}}{P_c}$$

$$P_{abcd} = \frac{P_{acd} P_{bcd}}{P_{cd}}$$

etc.

In transmission terms, this condition is respectively: $T(AB) = 0$, $T_C(AB) = 0$, $T_{CD}(AB) = 0$, etc. He correctly argues that a direct dependency between two variables (represented by a graph) is born out by data only if the conditional (on all other variables) transmission between the two variables is positive. His approach does allow for circular dependencies to be detected. But this representation of structure is limited to binary relations only.

One of his examples may aid the comparison. From data he presented in [5, p. 76] as Case VI, he finds that the five binary transmission measures $T_{WX}(YZ)$, $T_{WY}(XZ)$, $T_{WZ}(XY)$, $T_{XZ}(WY)$, $T_{YZ}(XW)$ are positive while $T_{XY}(WZ)$ is zero, and concludes that of the six possible direct connections between the four variables only the W-Z connection is absent. In terms of his graph of

binary dependencies, the result is:

From Broekstra's data:

$$Q(WXYZ) = -.0014$$
$$Q_Z(WXY) = .0192$$
$$Q_Y(WXZ) = -.0011$$
$$Q_X(WYZ) = -.0045$$
$$Q_W(XYZ) = .0192$$
$$Q_{YZ}(WX) = .0248$$
$$Q_{XZ}(WY) = .0510$$
$$Q_{XY}(WZ) = .0000$$
$$Q_{WZ}(XY) = .1065$$
$$Q_{WY}(XZ) = .0451$$
$$Q_{WX}(YZ) = .0510$$

Following the algorithm for structure identification, the spectral analysis of relations would start with the following:

Statistically Defining configuration, non-embedded	Q-measure, embedded	Dependency
Q(WXYZ)=-.0014	Q(WXY)= .0206	
	Q(WX Z)= .0003	
	Q(W YZ)=-.0031	
	Q(XYZ)= .0206	
	Q(WX)= .0053	
	Q(W Y)= .0349	
	Q(W Z)= .0042	
	Q(XY)= .0667	
	Q(X Z)= .0053	
	Q(YZ)= .0349	
total:	T(WXYZ)= .1883	

Removing the three relations that are overdetermined as indicated by negative (conditional) Q-measures and the one that is zero would zield the following dependency structure and quantitative account:

Q(WXYZ)=-.0014	Q(WXY)= .0206	Q(WX)= .0053		
Q_Y(WXZ)=-.0011	Q(XYZ)= .0206	Q(W Y)= .0349		
Q_X(WYZ)=-.0045		Q(XY)= .0667		
Q_{XY}(WZ)= .0000		Q(X Z)= .0053		
		Q(YZ)= .0349		

equals: T(WXY)= .1275
         -T(XY)=-.0667
          T(XYZ)= .1275

total: .1883

In this special case, the two tertiary components fully account for the total amount of transmission in the data. This need not, of course, always be achievable. There may be losses and redundancies. The example further illustrates the role of the embedded relations in the representation of data by functional components. The relation X-Y may be realized either in the WXY-component or in the XYZ-component. Since T(XY) is included in both transmission measures, it is redundant in the sum T(WXY) + T(XYZ) and must therefore be subtracted from the account.

If one were to further simplify the representation of the data, for example to the point of Broekstra's method, one would have to accept losses as evident in the account below. Evidentally,

the tertiary relation that cannot be depicted in the form of a graph with variables at its nodes are removed in this result as a consequence of which about 22% of the accountable transmission in the system is lost.

In conclusion, let me say that my spectral analysis of relations is far from a state of completion. What I have learned is that while it may be difficult to conceptualize higher-order relations, when they are manifest in data, they cannot be analysed into pieces. Perhaps much of systems research into reality hangs on the ability to cope with relations of different (and usually higher) ordinalities. The spectral analysis of relations may be regarded as a stepping stone in this direction.

Removed	Non-embeded	Embedded		Dependency structure
$Q(WXYZ) = -.0014$	$Q(WX\ ) = .0053$	–		
$Q_Z(WXY) = .0192$	$Q(W\ Y\ ) = .0349$			
	$Q(\ XY\ ) = .0667$			
$Q_Y(WXZ) = -.0011$	$Q(\ X\ Z) = .0053$			
$Q_X(WYZ) = -.0045$	$Q(\ \ YZ) = .0349$			
$Q_W(XYZ) = .0192$	$T(WX\ ) = .0053$	–		
	$T(W\ Y\ ) = .0349$			
$Q_{XY}(WZ) = .0000$	$T(\ XY\ ) = .0667$			
	$T(\ X\ Z) = .0053$			
	$T(\ \ YZ) = .0349$			
	$\underline{.1471}$			

REFERENCES

1. ASHBY, W. R., "Constraint Analysis of Many-Valued Relations," General Systems, 9, 99-105, 1964.
2. ASHBY, W. R., "Measuring the Internal Information Exchange in a System," Cybernetica, 8, 1, 5-22, 1965.
3. ASHBY, W. R., "Two Tables of Identities of Governing Information Flows Within Large Systems," American Society for Cybernetics Communications, 1, 2, 3-8, 1969.
4. BARTLETT, M. S., "Contingency Table Interactions," supplement to the Journal of the Royal Statistical Society, 2, 248-252, 1935.
5. BROEKSTRA, G., "Constraint Analysis and Structure Identification," Annals of Systems Research, 5, 67-80, 1976.
6. BROEKSTRA, G., "Constraing Analysis and Structure Identification II," Annals of Systems Research, 6, 1-20, 1977.

7. KLIR, G. J., "Identification of Generative Structures in Empirical Data," International Journal of General Systems, 3, 89-104, 1976.
8. KLIR, G. J., "Structural Modelling of Indigenous Systems," paper presented to the 22nd Annual Meeting of the SGSR, Washington, February, 1978.
9. KRIPPENDORFF, K., "A Spectral Analysis of Relations, Foundations," paper presented to the International Congress on Communication Sciences, Berlin, May 1977.
10. McGILL, W. J., "Multivariate Information Transmission," Psychometrica, 19, 1954.
11. SHANNON, C. E. and W. WEAVER, The Mathematical Theory of Communication, Urbana, University of Illinois Press, 1949.
12. SIMON, H. A., "The Architecture of Complexity," pp. 84-118 in his The Science of the Artificial, Cambridge, Mass., MIT Press, 1969.

On the concept of simulation in asynchronous, concurrent systems

LUTZ PRIESE
Fachgebiet Systemtheorie und Systemtechnik, Universität Dortmund
Federal Republic of Germany

1. INTRODUCTION

Recently several models for asynchronous, concurrent systems have been proposed. Among them are Petri-nets [26,14,4], Generalized Petri-nets [10,16], Coordination nets [22], Vector-Addition and -Replacement Systems [15,16], Flow Graph Schemata [15,33], Semaphores [5], Speedindependent Modules [17], APA-nets [28], asynchronous cellular automata [21,27,7,8], asynchronous graphs [32], etc. Those concepts have been frequently compared according to their "modelling abilities", "computational power", "synchronizing abilities", etc. Arguing on a formal level one needs a conception of simulation to compare those "abilities" of different systems; a conception of simulation that reflects the systems' behavior of interest. Such a conception of simulation should be formalized precisely -- as otherwise the behavior to be compared remains obscure -- and carefully -- as otherwise one may compare those systems according to some unnecessary features. As simple as this statement is, the conceptions of simulation in the theory of asynchronous systems -- and, to some extent, also in General Systems Theory and the theory of non-deterministic automata -- have been somewhat neglected. One can find articles, comparing different systems, without any clear notion of simulation at all [2,23,19,9]. One may eventually drop a simulation conception [6] for some explicitly stated constructions for some normal-form-theorems as these constructions tell implicitly what features of interest are transferred. However, sometimes even impossibility results, such as "simple Petri-nets [1] are a proper subclass of Petri-nets" or "Petri-nets are less powerful than combinatorial Petri-nets" [23,19] have been proven without any conception of simulation -- and thus without any notion of "as powerful as". Some authors operate with some informal conception (such as "to have the same input-output behavior", etc.) [17,35,21], while other authors present some formal definitions of simulation (often via some generated languages) [1,3,10,24, 20]. We will discuss some of those conceptions that are attached to "computational" comparison. It should be noted quite carefully that nobody can prove a definition of simulation to be incorrect. Any such definition is a "definiendum" of a certain (mathematical) situation, the "definiens", that shall become a precise conception through the

definiendum. This step, from a definiens to a definiendum, is no subsect for mathematical proofs but allows certain arbitrariness. For example, most people agree that "recursiveness" is a reasonable definiendum of "computability" [13], as all different formal concepts for "computability" turned out to be equivalent to recursiveness. But this is no proof. In this paper we will discuss some features of existing simulation conceptions and will point to some irritating aspects that shall suggest further research on these conceptions. For example, one should agree that simple Petri-nets are "less powerful" in their computational abilities than arbitrary Petri-nets (as Patil's argumentation [23] is certainly true). However, for most existing conceptions of simulation it holds that simple Petri-nets can simulate arbitrary Petri-nets. This is one approach for our criticism.

We are mainly interested in the "computational" aspects and thus have to develop a conception of simulation where a system B, simulating a system A, simulates the computations of A. As Patil's and Kosaraju's [23,19] results show some computational limitations they shall be true with respect to the conception of simulation to be developed. In addition, as both results are generally accepted, we have a certain right to criticize existing simulations that violate both results.

The discussions on simulation conceptions were quite fruitful in the theory of linear, or just deterministic, automata [11,30,12] and have led to several well-accepted definitions. However, in General Systems Theory and the theory of non-deterministic automata, the existing definitions may deserve some reconsiderations as will be indicated in the final chapter.

2. SIMULATIONS WITH LANGUAGE CONCEPTIONS

Let A and B be some systems in some models of asynchronous, concurrent concepts; i.e. they may be Petri-nets, Vector-Replacement Systems, nets of Keller's speedindependent modules, etc. One usually defines a class C_1 of such systems to be "richer" (or "more powerful") than a class C_2 if for any system A of C_2 there exists an equivalent (or simulating) system B of C_1. Two conceptions of "equivalence" -- with lots of modifications -- are frequently used:

Conception I: Two systems A and B are equivalent if they have

---

[1] Definitions for Petri-nets and simple Petri-nets can be found in the Appendix.

the same input-output-behavior.

Conception II: Two systems A and B are equivalent if they "generate the same language".

To make the following arguments more intelligible, we will consider both conceptions with respect to Petri-nets only. However, all arguments do also hold -- with some minor modifications -- for different models of asynchronous, concurrent concepts. In the theory of Petri-nets the mentioned generating language (sometimes called Sim-Set [24]) of Conception II is the set of all possible firing-sequences (mainly of transitions, seldom of markings) from a given initial marking. This is frequently modified by regarding only firing-sequences that lead to some final markings or by intersecting them with a set T of some distinguished transitions. Often Sim-Set contains not sequences of transitions but of names of transitions, where different transitions may be named equally or receive no name at all (λ-transitions).

Conception I is sometimes used in exactly our formulation; i.e. "input-output-behavior" remains undefined. Conception I seems to be adopted from the theory of sequential machines, where the allowed input-output-procedures are known. However, for asynchronous, concurrent systems it is by no means evident what "input-output-procedures" are allowed, except in some very special cases. For example, one might use the input-places of a Petri-net, N, in such a way that one only applies an input-token to a specific input-place if a certain place of N carries no token. With such a tricky

input-procedure one obtains the computational complexity of combinatorial Petri-nets with inhibitory arcs. Such a trick is certainly not intended and has to be excluded from reasonable input-output-behaviors. One may request that the allowed input-output-procedures are of no more "complexity" than the class of Petri-nets under research; i.e. inputs and outputs have to be managed by a further, "surrounding" Petri-net of the same class. This leads to a treatment of closed Petri-nets where, on a formal level, the generated language is intersected with some "input-output" - transitions or states. Conception I turns in this way into Conception II. A different way of how one can manage an understanding of "input-output-procedures" is shown in the Appendix.

However, even if the allowed input-output-procedures are unambiguously known, Conception I has a further important disadvantage. Two Petri-nets, A and B, may be equivalent via Conception I although B allows for hang-ups; i.e. in B occur some computations that cannot be continued -- while A has no hang-ups. Figure 1 gives some examples of Petri-nets that are all equivalent with respect to a "same input-output-behavior": it is not allowed to look into the "black boxes". Nevertheless, their intuitive behavior is quite different: N_1 is a prompt net, N_2 is non-prompt, and N_3 contains a hang-up.

For any Petri-net N one can construct a simple Petri-net N' with the same input-output-behavior: simply hide all wrong computations of N' in hang-ups! Thus Conception I is incompatible with Patil's impossibility result. One might try to escape this criticism by looking also into the black boxes. This is done in Conception II, where also "inner" transition-sequences are considered.

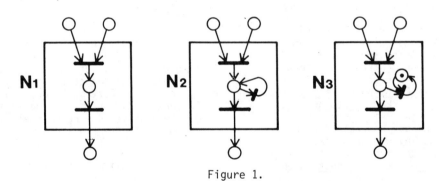

Figure 1.

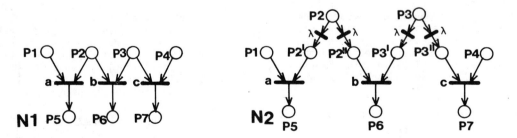

Figure 2.

However, the same criticism also holds for Conception II. Figure 2 shows two Petri-nets, N_1 and N_2, where in N_2 λ-transitions are allowed that generate the same language (of transition-sequences). But N_2 computes by "guessing" as it can easily run into hang-ups: if, e.g., P_2 sends a token to P_2'' although P_3 carries no token but P_1 does, no further computation is possible. Note that nevertheless both generated sets of transition-sequences are equal.

Following this idea one can show that language conceptions usually allow hang-ups to be hidden. As N_1 is a non-simple Petri-net "equivalent" to the simple Petri-net N_2, Conception II also violates Patil's result. This seems to be true for most language conceptions, where as language conceptions that prohibit hang-ups to be hidden are severely restricted and don't allow for some constructions that are intuitive simulations. A further serious disadvantage of Conceptions I and II is that they allow no statements about prompt, real-time simulations; see, e.g., the net N_2 of Figure 1.

3. SIMULATION IN STATE SYSTEMS

For an easier understanding of further discussions, we will propose a skeleton for a simulation definition that shall overcome the mentioned difficulties and needs only a minimal logical apparatus. The following State-Systems are very closely related with Keller's Transition Systems [16]. They are needed only for a common definition of simulation for several classes of systems. We try to abstract as much as possible to receive a simulation conception of large generality.

A State System A is a pair $A = (S, \rightarrow)$ of a set S (of states) and a recursive relation $\rightarrow \subseteq S^2$. For two states $s, s \in S$ we write $s \rightarrow s'$ for $(s,s') \in \rightarrow$ and read s' to be a direct successor of s.

We need the transitive closure of $\rightarrow$ with some additional properties:

For a State System $A = (S, \rightarrow)$, states $s, s' \in S$, a set $K \subseteq S$ of states, and an integer $n \in \mathbb{N}_0$, we define:

(a) $s \xrightarrow[K]{n} s'$ if there exist states $s_1, \ldots, s_n \in K$
such that $s_1 = s$, $s_n = s'$ and $s_i \rightarrow s_{i+1}$
holds for all i, $1 \leq i \leq n$.

(b) $s \xRightarrow{n} s'$ if $s \xrightarrow[S]{n} s'$.

(c) $s \xRightarrow[K]{} s'$ if there exists an integer m with
$s \xrightarrow[K]{m} s'$.

(d) $s \Rightarrow s'$ if $s \xRightarrow[S]{} s'$.

We also add sometimes an index A to $\Rightarrow$ to indicate that $\Rightarrow$ refers to the State System A.

For two State Systems $A = (S_A, \rightarrow_A)$, $B = (S_B, \rightarrow_B)$, an integer $n \in \mathbb{N}_0$, we say that the properties P1,P2,P3,P4 and P5 are true if there holds:
For all states $s \in S_A$ there exists a non-empty subset $K_S \subseteq S_B$ such that for all $\bar{s} \in K_S$ and s, $s' \in S_A$ there holds (respectively i) for Pi:

(a) $s \rightarrow_A s' \Rightarrow \exists \bar{s}' \in K_{S'} : \bar{s} \Rightarrow_B \bar{s}'$

(b) $\forall \bar{s}' \in K_{S'} : \bar{s} \Rightarrow_B \bar{s}' \Rightarrow s \Rightarrow_A s'$

(c) $\forall s^0 \in S_B : \bar{s} \Rightarrow_B s^0 \Rightarrow \exists s^+ \in K^+ : s^0 \Rightarrow_B s^+$
where $K^+ = \bigcup_{s \in S_A} K_S$

(d) $\exists n \in \mathbb{N}_0 : $ (i) (not $s \rightarrow_A s'$) $\Rightarrow$
$(\forall s^+ \in S_B : \forall d \in \mathbb{N}_0 : d > n \Rightarrow$
not $\bar{s} \xrightarrow[K_S \cup K^0]{d} s^+)$ and (ii) $s \rightarrow_A s' \Rightarrow$
$(\forall s^0, s^1 \in S_B : \forall d \in \mathbb{N}_0 : d > n \Rightarrow$
not $(\bar{s} \xrightarrow[K_S \cup K^0]{} s^0 \ \& \ s^0 \xrightarrow[K^0]{d} s^1))$ where
$K^0 = S_B - K^+$

(e) $s \rightarrow_A s' \Rightarrow \exists \bar{s}' \in K_S : \bar{s} \xRightarrow[K]{} \bar{s}'$, with
$K = K_S \cup K_{S'} \cup K^0$.

We say that B is:
i.   a <u>simulation</u> of A if P1,P2 and P3 hold;
ii. a <u>prompt simulation</u> of A if P2,P3 and P4 hold;
iii. a <u>homomorphic simulation</u> of A if P2,P3 and P5 hold.

If P3 is not fulfilled, we use the above notations with the term "<u>weak</u>" added.

One may also define combinations of these simulation conceptions. A <u>weak, prompt, homomorphic simulation</u>, e.g. requires P2,P4 and P5 to be true. P3 is left according to the term "weak", P1 is left as P5 implies P1.

The properties P1 up to P5 may be interpreted as following, using the term "<u>computation</u>" for the $\Rightarrow$-relations:
P1 requires that any (one-step) computation of A, $s \rightarrow_A s'$, can also be fulfilled in B, $\bar{s} \Rightarrow_B \bar{s}'$, but may require more steps, as $\Rightarrow$ is used instead of $\rightarrow$. Such intermediate steps are quite common (see, e.g., λ-transitions in Conception II or most definitions in automata theory). The states $\bar{s} \in K_S$ are the states of B "equivalent" (or better "attached") to the state s of A. K^+ is the set of all states of B being attached to some states of A while K^0 denotes the remaining states of B. K^0 contains the "intermediate states" of B that cannot be attached to some states of A, or where there is no need to attach them to A.

P2 operates only on states of K^+: if $\bar{s}'$ is attached to a state s' of A and can be derived in B from any state $\bar{s} \in K_S$ then s' could also be derived from s in A.

If one drops P2 and uses only P1, any State System $A = (S_A, \rightarrow_A)$ could be "simulated" by the State System $B = (S_A, \rightarrow_B)$ with $\rightarrow_B = S_A^2$ via the canonical state-correspondence $s \rightarrow K_S : s \mapsto \{s\}$. Informally speaking, P2 requires that B cannot compute more than A if B starts only with states attached to some states of A.

At first glimpse one might regard P1 and P2 to be a reasonable formalization for simulation. However, we call this only a weak simulation, motivated by the fact that any Petri-net N can be weakly simulated by a simple Petri-net N'. A proof may follow the simple plan to hide all incorrect computations of N' in the intermediate states of K^0 in such a fashion that they can never be prolonged to some states of K^+. One can mask in such a way all incorrect computations of N' in hang-ups that cannot be found in K^+, without thus violating both properties P1 and P2. Note, P2 doesn't care about states in K^0. This idea was used in [18] to prove how to "simulate" finite automata with very poor primitives. Property P3 just excludes such masked hang-ups: all intermediate states in K^0 that are derivable from K^+ can be prolonged by a further derivation to K^+ again. P1, P2 and P3 just define "hang-up-free" simulations, but we have dropped the term "hang-up-free" as all simulations allowing for some masked hang-ups seem to be somehow "incorrect" and will be explicitly denoted as weak simulations.

Property P4 introduces a substitute for "time": For a prompt simulation there exists an integer n such that B needs at most n steps to compute one step of A. The cases $s \to_A s$ and not $s \to_A s$ are distinguished: in the $s \to_A s$ case any computation in B, starting with a state $\bar{s}$ attached to s, may run in K_S without any such bound n as each of these computations in K_S may simulate one $s \to_A s$ step of A.

It should be noted that it is often quite difficult to construct hang-up-free and prompt simulations. For example, Hack's proof [10] that General Petri-nets can be simulated by Petri-nets involves a non-prompt construction. It is also easy to find a prompt weak simulation. To construct a prompt, hang-up-free simulation is possible, using some ideas of Keller [17], but quite difficult and lengthy [29].

The final property for homomorphic simulations is motivated by the following observation: Let A and B be the State Systems A = ({1,2,3}, $\to_A$), B = ({1,2,3}, $\to_B$) with $1 \to_A 2$, $1 \to_A 3$ and $2 \to_A 3$ and $1 \to_B 2$ and $2 \to_B 3$; i.e. $1 \to_B 3$ doesn't hold. Figure 3 gives a graphical representation.

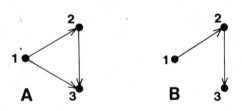

Figure 3.

With the correspondence, $s \to K_S : i \mapsto \{i\}$, $1 \le i \le 3$, B becomes a (prompt) simulation of A, but no homomorphic simulation. One might demand a simulation to be homomorphic if one is used to simulation conceptions via graph-theory. It is possible to define a "time-graph" for State Systems A and B -- essentially the $\Rightarrow$-relation -- and "blockings" on $\Rightarrow_B$ -- essentially the sets K_S -- and call B to be a <u>U-simulation</u> of A if the time-graph of A is isomorphic to that of B divided by the blocking [7]. In this sense our simulation conception would not necessarily be a U-simulation, but our homomorphic simulations would. Those conceptions involving "time-graphs" have another disadvantage: one has to define which states of the time-graph

of B divided by a blocking have circular arcs of length 1; this may be required by the states s of A, as $s \to_A s'$ is possible. This definition seems to need a formalization very closely related to our properties P1 up to P5, and thus leads to no simpler conceptions. Another difficulty in this graph-theoretical conception is the need to distinguish intermediate states of K^0, but this can be done without too much formalism [8].

The need for intermediate states of K^0 is very often overlooked but is quite important, as the following example shows:

Let A and B be the State Systems with $S_A = \{0,1,2,3\}$, $\to_A = (0,i'; 1 \le i \le 3$, and $S_B = \{0,0',1,2,3\}$, $\to_B = \{(0,3),(0,0'),(0',1),(0',2)\}$, represented by Figure 4.

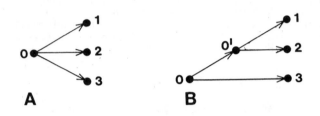

Figure 4.

B uses only local interdeterminism with two alternatives and should certainly be regarded to be a simulation of A. But any state-correspondence $S_A \to P(S_B)$, $s \mapsto K_S$, that makes B a simulation of A requires intermediate states. One easily finds out that, up to renaming the states, the states i of A have to be attached to the one-elementary sets $K_i = \{i\}$. Suppose the state $0'$ of B can be attached to the state 0 of A, i.e.: $K_0 = \{0,0'\}$. In this case P1 would require $0' \Rightarrow_B 3$, as $0 \to_A 3$ holds. Suppose $0'$ is attached to the state 1, i.e.: $K_1 = \{0',1\}$. But this contradicts with P2: $0' \Rightarrow_B 2$, $0' \in K_1$ would imply $1 \Rightarrow_A 2$.

4. DISCUSSION AND CONCLUSIONS

We have proposed some properties for State Systems that should be fulfilled in simulation conceptions. If one argues formally, we have proposed no definitions for the mentioned models of asynchronous, concurrent systems, as the step from these mentioned systems to State Systems was left undefined. One can always use some straight-forward translation to State Systems. A Petri-net N, for example, becomes a canonical State System N' by declaring $\mathbb{N}_0^r$, where r is the number of place in N, to be the set S of states (S is thus the set of all "markings" of N) and $s \to_N s'$ shall hold if there exists an s-enabled event that changes the marking s to s' by firing. Things become more complicated if N is a Petri-net with inputs and outputs and the constructions for a net M, simulating N, involve some allowed input-output-procedures. In this case one also has to translate these input-output-procedures in the State Systems (see Appendix).

One may criticize our simulations in that there are no restrictions for the state-correspondence $s \mapsto K_s$. This is certainly true as one should not accept some exotic state-correspondences for the input-output-behavior. However, we just wanted to point out -- on a very abstract level, without specifying the very type of systems under consideration -- what situations have to be taken into account. The Appendix also shows how such exotic state-correspondences can be easily excluded for specified systems. We will formally prove in the Appendix that our simulation conception is compatible with Patil's impossibility result: not any arbitrary Petri-net can be simulated by a simple Petri-net if the simulation doesn't code the inputs and outputs.

A further criticism may deal with the accentuation of the computational behavior in our simulation conception as one may argue that the synchronizing abilities of those asynchronous, concurrent systems are of "more importance". One may try and subsume this aspect in our conceptions, maybe by generalizing State Systems to Transitions Systems. Without such a speculative argument one may better regard this paper to be a contribution to the computational aspects.

The properties P1 up to P5 may also be used for some clarifications of simulation conceptions in General Systems Theory and automata theory. Let us define a __system__ A to be a tuple $A = (X_A, Y_A, S_A)$ of __inputs__ X_A, __outputs__ Y_A, and __transitions__ $S_A \subseteq X_A \times Y_A$ and define a system $B = (X_B, Y_B, S_B)$ to __simulate__ A if there exist mappings $a : X_A \to X_B$, $b : Y_B \to Y_A$ such that for all $x \in X_A$ and $y \in Y_A$ with $x S_A y$ there exists a $y' \in Y_B$ with $a(x) S_B y'$ and $b(y') = y$ [25]. This definition is also generalized for systems with states, etc., in the same style 25. Such kinds of definitions contribute only to P1 and violate even P2. We might call them "__very weak simulations__". As mentioned before, $A = (X, Y, S)$ can always be simulated very weakly by the "universal" system $A^+ = (X, Y, X \times Y)$, that fulfills all possible computations.

If one regards simulation definitions in the theory of __non-deterministic automata__ only P1 and P2 are usually requested (although these properties remain quite obscure in current definitions). Starke [34], for example, regards only non-deterministic automata with non-deterministic transitions of the type (__input__, __state__) $\to$ P((__state__, __output__)) $- \emptyset$. These automata don't allow for a composition theory as, by compounding automata, signals may in general enter a loop without being able to leave that loop again (a hang-up). If one develops a theory of __non-completely defined, non-deterministic automata__, an asynchronous composition theory can also be developed [31,27,18]. In this case properties P1 and P2 are again not sufficient for simulations (note: one operates only with sequential machines, no concurrency is involved), as one may non-deterministically "find" the correct computations and all incorrect computations are again masked by hang-ups that cannot be managed by P1 and P2 without P3! In the synchronous case P3 may be dropped for prompt simulations; if, after a certain limited time, no correct output arrives, a hang-up is recognized.

APPENDIX

The intention of this Appendix is threefold: We will give an exact definition for (safe) Petri-nets (to make this article intelligible for a reader being not familiar with the concept of Petri-nets); we will indicate how to describe input-output-procedures in State Systems; and we will present a formal proof that simple Petri-nets cannot simulate Petri-nets in general.

Definition 1.

A Petri-net, N, is a tuple $N = (P_N, E_N, F)$ of a finite set P_N of places, a finite set E_N of events and a relation $F \subseteq (P_N \times E_N) \cup (E_N \times P_N)$ that connects the places and events. In the graphical representations places are denoted by circles, events by bars and F by arcs. If for some place p and event e of N pFe holds, p is called an input-place of e and e an output-event of p; if eFp holds, p is called an output-place of e and e an input-event of p. $I(e)$, $O(e)$, $I(p)$ and $O(p)$ are the sets of all input-, output-places of e or input- and output-events of p, respectively. p is an input-place of N if $I(p) = \emptyset$ and an output-place of N if $O(p) = \emptyset$. I_N and O_N denote the input- and output-sets of N. We further assume that $I_N \cap O_N = \emptyset$ for all Petri-nets N.

N is called a simple Petri-net if any event of N possesses at most one shared input-place. A place p is called shared if $\# O(p) > 1$.

A state (marking) of N is a mapping $s : P_N \to \mathbb{N}_0$. $\mathbb{N}_0$ is the set of all non-negative integers. For $r = \# P_N$ any such state is isomorphic to an r-vector of $\mathbb{N}_0^r$. S_N ($\approx \mathbb{N}_0^r$) denotes the state-set of N. A state s' is a direct successor from a state s if there exists an event $e \in E_N$ such that there holds:

(a) $s(p) > 0$ and $s'(P) = s(p) - 1$ $\forall p \in I(e)$;

(b) $s'(p) = s(p) + 1$ $\forall p \in O(e)$;

(c) $s'(p) = s(p)$ $\forall p \in P_N - (I(e) \cup O(e))$.

$\to_N \subseteq S_N^2$ is the relation: $s \to_N s'$ if s' is a direct successor of s.

Definition 2.

An input-output-procedure (I-O-Proc) P for a Petri-net N is a subset $P \subseteq S_N^2$ such that for all s, $s' \in S_N$ with sPs' there holds:

(a) $s'(p) \geq s(p)$ $\forall p \in I_N$;

(b) $s'(p) \leq s(p)$ $\forall p \in O_N$;

(c) $s'(p) = s(p)$ $\forall p \in P_N - (I_N \cup O_N)$.

Note that any sub-set P' of an I-O-Proc P is also an I-O-Proc.

Definition 3.

For a Petri-net N (with an I-O-Proc P, resp.) the State System N ((N-P), resp.) is defined as: $N = (S_N, \to_N)$ (($N-P) = (S_N, \to_N \cup P)$, resp.). The transitive closure of $\to_N \cup P$ is denoted by $\overrightarrow{P_s^N}$

We always refer to the State System N ((N-P) resp.) if we talk about simulations of N (with the input-output-procedure P, resp.).

Definition 4.

Let N and M be two Petri-nets with $I_N = I_M$ and $O_N = O_M$. A mapping $K : S_N \to P(S_M)$, $K : s \mapsto K_s$, is called a simulation-mapping if the properties P1, P2 and P3 hold. A simulation-mapping K is called true if there holds:

(a) $\forall p \in I_N \cup O_N : \forall s \in S_N : \forall \bar{s} \in K_s :$
$$s(p) = \bar{s}(p);$$

(b) $\forall s, s' \in S_N : \forall p \in P_N - (I_N \cup O_N) :$
$$s(p) = s'(p) \to \forall \bar{s} \in K_s :$$
$$\exists \bar{s}' \in K_{s'} : \forall p \in P_M - (I_M \cup O_M) :$$
$$\bar{s}(p) = \bar{s}'(p).$$

If K is a true simulation-mapping we say that M simulates N truly.

Note that in a true simulation the input- and output-places and their markings are not coded by K. This is just for convenience for the following and the property "true" can certainly be weakened without the following theorem becoming false.

Theorem: <u>There exists a Petri-net that cannot be truly simulated by a simple Petri-net.</u>

We prove this theorem with the help of the following lemmata.

Definition 5.

Let N be a Petri-net with an I-O-Proc P. (N,P) is called strong if there exists a sub-set P_1 of P, a state $s_0 \in S_N$ and an output-place $P_0 \in O_N$ such that for all $s' \in S_N$ with $s_0 \xRightarrow[P_1, N]{} s'$ there holds:

(a) $\forall p \in I_N : \exists s'' \in S_N : s' \xRightarrow[P_1, N]{} s''$ and $s''(p) > 0;$

(b) $s'(p_0) = 0;$

(c) $\exists s''': s' \xRightarrow[P, N]{} s'''$ and $s'''(p_0) > 0.$

N is called strong if there exists an I-O-Proc P for N such that (N,P) is strong.

Lemma 1: Let M be a true simulation with the true simulation-mapping K. For any I-O-Proc P for N define a relation $P^K \subseteq S_M^2$ by: $\forall \bar{s}, \bar{s}' \in S_M :$ ($\bar{s}\ P^K\ \bar{s}' : \Longleftrightarrow \exists s, s' \in S_N : sPs'$ and $\bar{s} \in K_s$ and $\bar{s}' \in K_{s'}$ and $\forall p \in P_M - (I_M \cup O_M) : \bar{s}(p) = \bar{s}'(p)$). Then there holds:

(a) P^K is an I-O-Proc for M;

(b) $\forall s, s' \in S_N : \forall \bar{s} \in K_s : \forall \bar{s}' \in K_{s'} :$
$$\bar{s} \xRightarrow[P^K, M]{} \bar{s}' \to s \xRightarrow[P, N]{} s';$$

(c) $\forall s, s' \in S_N : s \xRightarrow[P, N]{} s' \to \forall \bar{s} \in K_s :$

$\exists \bar{s} \in K_{s'} : \bar{s} \xRightarrow[P^K, M]{} \bar{s}';$

(d) $\forall s \in S_N : \forall \bar{s} \in K_s : \forall s_1 \in S_M : \bar{s} \xRightarrow[PK, M]{} s_1 \to$
$$\exists s' \in S_N : \exists \bar{s}' \in K_s : s_1 \xRightarrow[PK, M]{} \bar{s}'.$$

The proof for Lemma 1 is quite straightforward. The hang-up-freeness property P3 is required for (d)!

Lemma 2. Let N be a strong Petri-net and M be a Petri-net simulating N truly. Then M is also strong.

Sketch a proof: There exists an I-O-Proc P with a sub-set P_1, a state s_0, an output-place p_0, such that Definition 5 is fulfilled. With the help of Lemma 1 it is not too difficult to show that Definition 5 also is fulfilled by M, the I-O-Proc P^K for M, the sub-set P_1^K, the same place p_0, and any state $s_0 \in K_{s_0}$. Thus (M,P^K) is strong.

Lemma 3. (a) There exists a strong Petri-net. (b) There exists no strong simple Petri-net. The theorem follows immediately from Lemma 2 and Lemma 3. Proof for Lemma 2:
(a) Let N be the Petri-net of Figure 5 (Patil's 3-smoker problem). Regard S_N to be $\mathbb{N}_0^6$

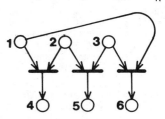

Figure 5.

with $s_i = s(i)$ for $s \in S_N$. N is strong with respect to the place $p_0 = 6$, initial marking $s_0 = (0,0,0,0,0,0)$ and the two I-O-Proc P and P_1, $P_1 \subseteq P$, with the relation

(0,0,0,0,0,0) P_1 (1,1,0,0,0,0)	}	input-
(0,0,0,0,0,0) P_1 (0,1,1,0,0,0)		procedure
(0,0,0,1,0,0) P_1 (0,0,0,0,0,0)	}	output-
(0,0,0,0,1,0) P_1 (0,0,0,0,0,0)		procedure
(0,0,0,0,0,0) P (1,0,1,0,0,0)	}	input-proc.
(0,0,0,0,0,1) P (0,0,0,0,0,0)	}	output-proc.

as can be seen immediately.

(b) Let N be a strong Petri-net that shall be strong with respect to the place p_0, the initial state s_0 and the I-O-Proc P, P_1 with $P_1 \subseteq P$. We define for this proof: An s_0-derivation, d, in N,P', for an I-O-Proc P' for N, is a finite sequence $d = (s_0, s_1, \ldots, s_n)$ with $s_i \to_N s_{i+1}$ or $s_i P' s_{i+1}$ for all i, $1 \le i \le n$. The length, $l(d)$, of d shall be n and the last state, s^d, of d be s_n. Note that $s_0 \xRightarrow[P', N]{l(n)} s^d$ holds for any s_0-derivation d. d puts tokens on the places of $\mathbb{P}(d) := \{p \in P_N; s^d(p) > 0\}$. Let P'/d be the set of s_0-derivations in P', N that may be prolonged from d: $d' \in P'/d$ if there exist states $s_1, \ldots, s_n$, $s_{n+1}, \ldots, s_{n+m}$ with $d' = (s_0, \ldots, s_n, s_{n+1}, \ldots, s_{n+m})$ and $d = (s_0, \ldots, s_n)$; m = 0 is allowed.

$$\mathbb{P}(P'/d) \underbrace{\quad}_{d' \in P'/d} \mathbb{P}(d') \text{ is the set of all}$$

places that may receive a token by prolonging d in P', N.

Let us assume that N is a simple Petri-net. We will construct a contradiction by the following inductive construction (that follows exactly the original proof of Patil [23]) of s_0-derivations d_n:

$n = 0$: $d_0 := (s_0)$

$N \Rightarrow n+1$: Let d_n be the s_0-derivation constructed in the n-th step. Define for all $p \in P_N - \mathbb{P}(P_1/d_n)$, $L(p) := \infty$ if $p \notin \mathbb{P}(P/d_n)$ and $L(p) := \min \{ l(d') ; p \in \mathbb{P}(d')$ and $d' \in P/d_n \}$, else.

Define $L := \min \{ L(p) ; p \in P_N - \mathbb{P}(P_1/d_n) \}$.

$L(P_0) < \infty$ implies $L < \infty$. Let $\bar{p}$ and $\bar{d}$ be a place and an s_0-derivation with $\bar{p} \in P_N - \mathbb{P}(P_1/d_n)$, $L(p) = L = l(\bar{d})$, $\bar{p} \in \mathbb{P}(\bar{d})$, $\bar{d} \in P/d_n$.

There holds: $l(\bar{d}) > l(d_n)$, as $\bar{p} \in \mathbb{P}(\bar{d})$, $\bar{d} \in P/d_n$ and $\bar{p} \notin \mathbb{P}(d_n)$. Thus the s_0-derivation d^+ with $l(d^+) = l(\bar{d}) - 1$ and $\bar{d} \in P/d^+$ (i.e.: $\bar{d} = d^+, s^{\bar{d}}$)) is also in P/d_n.

Regard the last state s^{d^+} in d^+. There must hold either $s^{d^+} \to_N s^{\bar{d}}$ or $s^{d^+} \, P \, s^{\bar{d}}$. Suppose $s^{d^+} \, P \, s^{\bar{d}}$ holds. This implies $s^{d^+}(\bar{p}) \geq s^{\bar{d}}(\bar{p})$, as $\bar{p}$ cannot be an input-place of N according to property (a) of Definition 5 and $\bar{p} \notin \mathbb{P}(P_1/d_n)$. We thus found an s_0-derivation $d^+ \in P/d_n$ with $\bar{p} \in \mathbb{P}(d^+)$ and $l(d^+) < l(\bar{d}) = L(\bar{p})$, contradicting the definition of $L(p)$. Thus $s^{d^+} \to_N s^{\bar{d}}$ is true.

There exists an event $e \in E_N$ with $\bar{p} \in O(e)$ and $s^{d^+}(p) > 0$ for all $p \in I(e)$ that led to the derivation $s^{d^+} \to_N s^{\bar{d}}$, with $\bar{p} \notin \mathbb{P}(d^+)$ and $\bar{p} \in \mathbb{P}(\bar{d})$. Let us assume that $I(e) = \{ i_1, i_2 \}$ (the general case is analogical). Assume $i_1 \notin \mathbb{P}(P_1/d_n)$. This contradicts the definition of L as $i_1 \in \mathbb{P}(d^+)$, $d^+ \in P_1/d_n$, $l(d^+) < L$, thus $L(i_1) < L$. Therefore, $i_1, i_2 \in \mathbb{P}(P_1/d_n)$ holds. As N shall be simple at most one input-place of e might be shared. We thus assume that i_1 is a non-shared place: $O(i_1) = \{e\}$. Let d^0 be the shortest s_0-derivation in P_1/d_n such that $i_1 \in \mathbb{P}(d^0)$. There are two possibilities:

(1) $\cdot i_2 \in \mathbb{P}(P_1/d^0)$,

(2) $i_2 \notin \mathbb{P}(P_1/d^0)$.

For (1) we chose a shortest s_0-derivation d^1 in P_1, N with $i_2 \in \mathbb{P}(d^1)$ and $d^1 \in P_1/d^0$. As $O(i_1) = \{e\}$, a token on i_2 could only be taken away by a firing of e. This implies $i_1 \in \mathbb{P}(d^1)$; i.e., $i_1, i_2 \in \mathbb{P}(P_1/d_n)$, as $d^1 \in P_1/d_n$. Thus, $s^{d^1}(p) > 0$ for all $p \in I(e)$ ($= \{i_1, i_2\}$), and by firing e we receive a state s with $s(\bar{p}) > 0$, $(d^1, s) \in P_1/d_n$, thus $\bar{p} \in \mathbb{P}(P_1/d_n)$, a contradiction.

Thus (2) is true. Define the n+1-st constructed s_0-derivation to be d^0. As $i_2 \in \mathbb{P}(P_1/d_n) - \mathbb{P}(P_1/d_{n+1})$, $d_{n+1} = d^0$, $\mathbb{P}(P_1/d_n) \subsetneqq \mathbb{P}(P_1/d_{n+1})$ holds. This construction cannot be continued infinitely often. There exists a construction-step n where (2) must be true, implying a contradiction.

REFERENCES

1. AGERWALA, T. and M. FLYNN, "Comments on Capabilities, Limitations and 'Correctness' of Petri-nets," Proceedings of the 1st Annual Symposium on Computer Architecture, ACM, New York, pp. 81-86, 1973.

2. BANNING, J. P., "Asynchronous Modular Systems," Technical Report 116, Princeton University, Department of Electrical Engineering, 1973.

3. CHANDRA, A. K., "The Power of Parallelism in Programming," Information Processing 74, North-Holland Publishing Company, 1974.

4. DENNIS, J. B., "Modular Asynchronous Control Structures for a High Performance Processor," Record of the Project MAC, Conference on Concurrent and Parallel Computation, ACM, New York, pp. 55-80, 1970.

5. DIJKSTRA, E. W., "Cooperating Sequential Processes," in: Programming Languages, F. Genuys (ed.), Academic Press, New York, pp- 43-112, 1968.

6. FURTEK, F., "Modular Implementation of Petri-nets," MS Thesis, Department of Electrical Engineering, MIT, Cambridge, Mass., 1971.

7. GOLZE, U., "(A-) synchronous (non-) deterministic Cell Spaces Simulating Each Other," Journal of Computer and Systems Science, 1978.

8. GOLZE, U. and L. PRIESE, "Petri-net Implementation by a Universal Cell Space," to appear.

9. GRANDONI, F. and P. ZERBETTO, "Description and Asynchronous Implementation of Control Structures for Concurrent Systems," in: International Computer Symposium, A. Gunther (ed.), North Holland Publishing Co., pp. 151-158, 1974.

10. HACK, M., "Petri-net Language," Computer Struc. Group Memo 124, Project MAC, MIT, Cambridge, Mass., 1975.

11. HARMANIS, J. and R. E. STEARNS, Algebraic Structure Theory of Sequential Machines, Prentice-Hall Inc., Englewood Cliffs, 1966.

12. HERMANN, G. T., "Every Finite Sequential Machine is Linearly Realizable," Journal of Computer and Systems Science, pp. 489-510, 1971.

13. HERMES, H., Aufzählbarkeit, Entscheidbarkeit, Berechenbarkeit, Springer Verlag, Heidelberg, New York, 1971.

14. HOLT, A. W. and F. COMMONER, "Events and Conditions," Record of the Project MAC, Conference on Concurrent and Parallel Computation, ACM, New York, pp. 3-52, 1970.

15. KARP, R. M. and R. MILLER, "Parallel Program Schemata," Journal of Computer and Systems Science, 3, pp- 167-195, 1969.

16. KELLER, R. M., "Vector Replacement Systems: A Formalism for Modelling Asynchronous Systems," Technical Report 117, Department of Electrical Engineering, Princeton University.

17. KELLER, R. M., "Towards a Theory of Universal Speed-Independent Modules," IEEE Transactions Computing, C-23, pp.21-23, 1974.

18. KOERBER, P., "Simulation endlicher Automaten durch Netzwerke," MS Thesis, Department Math. Logik, Münster, 1971.

19. KOSARAJU, S. R., "Limitations of Dijkstra's Semaphore Primitives and Petri-nets," Technical Report 25, Johns Hopkins University, Baltimore, Md., 1973.

20. LIPTON, R. J., L. SNYDER and Y. ZALCSTEIN, "A Comparative Study of Models of Parallel Computations," _Proceedings of the 15th Annual Symposium on Switching and Automata_, IEEE, New York, pp. 145-155, 1974.

21. NAKAMURA, K., "Asynchronous Cellular Automata and Their Computational Ability," _Systems, Computers, Controls_, 5, pp. 58-66, 1974.

22. PATIL, S. S., "Coordination of Asynchronous Events," Ph.D. Thesis, Department of Electrical Engineering, MIT, Cambridge, Mass., 1970.

23. PATIL, S. S., "Limitations and Capabilities of Dijkstra's Semaphore Primitives for Coordination Among Processes," Computer Struc. Group Memo 57, Project MAC, MIT, Cambridge, Mass., 1971.

24. PETERSON, J. L. and T. BREDT, "A Comparison of Models of Parallel Computations," _Proceedings of IFIP Congress 74_, North Holland Publishing Co., pp. 446-470, 1974.

25. PICHLER, F., _Mathematische Systemtheorie_, de Gruyter, Berlin, New York, 1975.

26. PETRI, C. A., "Kommunikation mit Automaten," Ph.D. Thesis, Bonn, 1962.

27. PRIESE, L., "Reversible Automaten und Einfache Universelle 2-dimensionale Thue-Systeme," Zeitschr. Math. Logik Grdlgf., 22, pp. 353-384.

28. PRIESE, L., "A Note on Asynchronous Cellular Automata," _Journal of Computer and Systems Science_ (to appear).

29. PRIESE, L., "Asynchronous, Modular Systems," in preparation.

30. REUSCH, _Lineare Automaten_, Bibliographisches Institut, Mannheim, 1969.

31. RÖDDING, D. and W. RÖDDING, "Networks of Finite Automata," _Progress in Cybernetics and Systems Research_, 3, Advance Publication Limited, 1978.

32. ROSENTIEHL, P., "Intelligent Graphs: Networks of Finite Automata Capable of Solving Graph Problems," in: _Graph Theory and Computing_, R. C. Read (ed.), Academic Press, New York, pp. 219-265, 1972.

33. SLUTZ, D. R., "The Flow Graph Schemata Model of Parallel Computation," Ph.D. Thesis, Department of Electrical Engineering, MIT, Cambridge, Mass., 1968.

34. STARKE, P., _Abstrakte Automaten_, VEB Deutscher Verlag Wissenschaften, 1969.

35. YOELI, M., "Petri-nets and Asynchronous Control Networks," Research Report CS-73-07, Department of Applied and Analytical Computer Science, University of Waterloo, 1973.

The literary work of art as a system

HANS H. RUDNICK
Department of English, Southern Illinois University
Carbondale, Illinois USA

Any attempt to investigate the possibility of a systems approach to the literary work of art is at this time usually met with an emotional reaction. It is a reaction of disbelief and doubt since most literary research is limited to the study of individual works and the particulars contained therein. Therefore, the average critic objects by saying: "How can the literary work of art be adequately represented and described by a 'mechanical' system? Don't you remember that Norbert Wiener himself spoke of cybernetics as only dealing with 'regulation and communication with regard to animals and machines (die Regulation und Kommunikation bei Tier und Maschine)'? How in your right mind can you bring a product of man's ingenuity into this context and disregard the individuality of a literary work of art? You are trying to force the work of art into the straight jacket of a system which will disallow any consideration of the creativity which has been invested by the artist in his particular work of art."

Without being presumptuous, please allow me, in all humility, to draw attention to some of the difficulties that faced the pioneers of our modern image of the world. At that time, during the fifteenth and sixteenth centuries, it is the time of the setting in of the "dissociation of sensibility" as T. S. Eliot called it, when the foundations for the scientific revolution were laid, the almighty sciences of today were just beginning to struggle for their right of existence and proper recognition. You all know of the disbelief, skepticism, and castigation which were encountered by the clearly proven and scientific findings of Copernicus, Galileo, and Johannes Kepler in those days, and the findings of Darwin and Einstein closer to ours. Any attempt to synthesize a large number of phenomena which were believed to be unrelated because the integrating criteria have not yet been conceived within a theory, seems to run into major opposition. A groundshaking discovery of the magnitude of the Copernican revolution, where suddenly a world picture is turned upside down by shifting the center of the universe from the earth to the sun, is a traumatic experience for those who have to revise the image of the world which they have held to be permanent. Doubtlessly, the understanding of the world has to be justified on the basis of reason and experience. Theories have to be established through scientific induction and have to be proven by putting them to the test. Bacon's inductive method permitted the separation from the world view of scholasticism, but it did not lead much farther since it did not make use of mathematics. However, Copernicus as well as scientists and philosophers from Descartes and Leibniz to Max Planck and Heisenberg used mathematics for their revolutionary discoveries.

Apparently aware of a continuing "dissociation of sensibility" wherein the natural sciences (Naturwissenschaften) become increasingly dominant over the humanities (Geisteswissenschaften), Leibniz attempted in the early eighteenth century to reintegrate physics and metaphysics, philosophy and theology in his Versuch über die Theodizee. Further integrating systematics are expressed in his famous Monadologie in which a hierarchy of monads, i.e. fundamental substances of mind and matter, finds its unity in the "preestablished harmony" of the universe. Toward the end of the eighteenth century it is Kant who recognizes the danger of the one-sidedness of human perception. He develops in response his well-known "Kritizismus" which demands that human knowledge has to be scientifically verified beyond any doubt by drawing its arguments for truth and proof from the areas of human experience (Gegenstände der Erfahrung). In his Critique of Pure Reason (1781) Kant makes the crucial statement about what we could call in modern terms his concern about our closed mode or system of cognition. Kant says in the next-to-the-last sentence of the "first critique": "the critical path is the only one which is still open (der kritische Weg ist allein noch offen)." Such a statement is an attempt to preserve the freedom of thought and creativity wherein man can and must establish his own existence and find his own intellectual home. If everything were regulated and communicated over and over again in the same way, there would be no freedom at all and, as a consequence, man would lose his primacy among the creatures of this world. While Linné's Systema Naturae (1735) developed for the field of botany a simple but not yet quite "natural" system of classification, it is no longer a surprise when Darwin's On the Origin of Species (1859) provides an evolutionary system which is not only based on clearly prevailing rules but which allows for built-in quirks which provide for variety through unforeseeable, i.e. "unsystematic" mutations."

The intellectual consequence of such findings is an awareness of the absolute necessity for open systems in order to accommodate for the creative aspects which exist above and beyond the general systematic base of any ordered and sensible human existence. In a world which appears to be founded on binary relations it is imperative that the coexistence of closed systems (i.e. "regular" systems) and open systems (i.e. "irregular" systems, but functioning on a "regular" base) be recognized and further explored. A synthesis of both types of systems which outlines the interrelational base and identifies the range of variety must be provided by man about his activities in the same way as Linné and Darwin have provided the perimeters of their systems through observation, analysis, and conclusions for the worlds of the plants and animals respectively.

In the nineteenth century several serious and specific attempts to establish such a system were made. Besides Christian Hermann Weisse's System der Ästhetik als Wissenschaft von der Idee der Schönheit (1830), which develops a partially Hegelian method of the internal self-development of an idea, Johannes Immaneul Volkelt's System der Ästhetik (1905-1914) must be mentioned above all. Volkelt's system strives to account for the independent nature of aesthetics in which the "plenitude and range of its freedom (Fülle und Weite seiner Freiheit)" can unfold.

Through the work of Ludwig von Bertalanffy, John Sutherland, and Ervin Laszlo, systems thinking has not only maintained its influence on the life sciences but has also found its way into sociology, music, and global concerns as they e.g. sponsored by the United Nations and the Club of Rome. The humanities have generally kept themselves, skeptically, at a distance. Only Roman Ingarden, the Polish phenomenologist, began to imply the significance of systems thinking for literature and aesthetics in his The Literary Work of Art (1931), The Cognition of the Literary Work of Art (1968), and Der Streit um die Existenz der Welt (Polish 1947 and 1948; German 1964). Today, eight years after Ingarden's death, as the limitations of prevailing formalistic approaches to literature become more evident, some scholars begin to turn to the more encompassing statements of philosophers dealing with the broad issues that are related with and incorporated in literature. Ingarden has made some of the most fertile observations in this regard. His ingenious division of the sciences actually places literature and biology in the same category. Since they are in contrast to the apriori sciences of mathematics and logic both fact-related sciences (Erfahrungswissenschaften), an important axiom for a systems approach to literature has been formulated by Ingarden. Such an axiom provides the possibility for the development of a system of literature. The biological sciences to which a systems methodology was first applied with all its initial flaws can serve as an adequate model.

Besides Ingarden's outline of a systematic "Poetik" (1940/41), recent publications like Literaturtheoretische Modelle und kommunikatives System (1974), edited by Walter Krolls and Aleksandar Flaker, Offene Systeme (1975), edited by Ernst von Weizsäcker, and Janusz Slawiński's Literature als System und Prozess (1975) have provided further significant stimuli for a more confident venturing of literary theorists into this hitherto untouched taboo-area of literary study.

In order to establish a comprehensive approach to literary activity within the framework of an open system, and in order to provide authority to literary study, we must define the characteristics and cultural implications of literary activity. Only the existence of such criteria can enable the literary scholar to function in and contribute to the mainstream of scientific research. Only under

such conditions can the profoundly humanistic discipline of literary studies obtain recognition as a science (in the sense of an open system) which knows about the general criteria that regulate its making and communication processes. As to the terminology with which we name our dealings with literature, the English language, for example, will only speak vaguely of "criticism", whereas the German language, perhaps overly ambitiously, speaks of "Literaturwissenschaft." The inadequacy and vagueness of both terms in both languages hints at the basic problem of literary studies. We are neither dealing with an objective "Kritizismus", nor are we dealing with a pure "science." We are not dealing with a "closed" system of the kind that underlies mathematics and logic; we are dealing instead with a system, an "open" system, which is also very much in Wiener's sense "regulated" by certain forms and conventions that make effective communication between human beings, not animals and machines, possible. There is no doubt that such criteria for regulation and communication exist. How else could literature be a viable means of communication between human beings? So that the regulating powers involved in the literary communication process can be identified, we must investigate all the factors affecting how a literary work of art is created, how the work of art itself exists as a structured independent entity, how it is received by the reading public for which, we must assume, it has been created, and how it is judged by critics as representative of the general literary, social, and cultural environment which influences and surrounds the reception of the work of art at a certain time.

An investigation of these criteria, which all together affect the creation and constitute the environment of the literary work of art, can at this early time not be as detailed as one would wish. Because this is the first comprehensive attempt to come to grips with such an immense task, this paper can only identify the foundations for more detailed research along these lines of thought. When the phase of more detailed investigation is reached, it must, however, never be forgotten that the detail has always to be related back to the context of the entire literary system. If this important caveat is not kept in mind, the ensuing diversification will create spin-offs which will forget that they are parts of a larger system. We have observed and are still observing, for example, the consequences of one such development which began when the Linguistics Departments became independent from their parent departments, the English Departments. The result of such diversification has created pluralism and confusion which have affected the writing abilities of students disastrously since the teaching of literature and linguistics is generally no longer done in one department.

Turning our attention now to the outline of a systems approach to literature, we must first talk about the author who is the creator of the work of art and, therefore, responsible for its existence. The author's genetic capacity is the pre-condition for his personal development which, during his lifetime, will build his personality like a superstructure over this genetic human capacity. Influences beyond his personal control are at this early stage history, the milieu, and those moments of importance in one's life that are significant enough to be part of the learning process. Once the person becomes more aware of his potential control of the environment by ordering it according to intentions and by directing his own development in this or that direction, a distinct learning process sets in which develops judgment through selection or preference. The result is an intentional personal development which endeavors to achieve an understanding of the environment through a synthesizing activity called "understanding" by associating and grouping facts that have been acquired.

When a basic understanding of the literary environment has been obtained, the development of the artistic creativity can begin. The hallmark of creativity is self-awareness which not only recognizes the uniqueness of the artistic individual but also understands the place of this individuality within the larger context of society, the creative person (author) will concentrate on communicating his inner experience through the medium of written language. He will be concerned with his effectiveness as a writer and, considering the ability of his readers to understand him, he will modify his freedom of self-expression accordingly. Such expression of the author's imagination may be called his "valuation" at a certain point in time. As time continues, revelations will occur because of self-criticism or change in attitude. Even external influences coming from friends, critics, editors, readers, and other general changes in environmental, social, and political conditions will have their impact and, consequently, will be reflected in the work of art.

The second stage in this system of the literary work of art after its creation by the author is the literary work of art itself. The literary work of art, as any work of art, has an existence independent of its creator and its audience. This existence rests in the medium of language which all human beings share to a certain degree. We are relatively well informed about language on the levels of formal and structural function, we are less sure about associative and psychological uses of language, at least as far as its poetic uses are concerned. There is no doubt that the specific language contained in a work of art reflects the author's experience of the world. The ideas which are carried by this language also project the author's sentiments about himself, the world, and the interrelation between both. So that the work of art can make sense, it must offer a full complement of related ideas and feelings which together constitute the existence of the work of art as a system. If such a system would not underlie the work of art, the audience (its readers) would not be able to reconstruct the experience of this work of art from the language it contains. The capability of being reconstructed by a reader could be called the work of art's "potential" which allows the reader to re-know and re-feel the thoughts and feelings of the author. Such a communication between author and reader through the language of the work of art establishes an interest on the side of the reader to partake in the author's views and insights. The reader's interest is the result of a feeling of sympathy and value toward the work of art. The reader wants to share and partake in the communication offered by the author.

Turning now to the third state in this system of the literary work of art, we have to take a closer look at the audience, which is the reader, who re-creates the already once created work of art. The genetic capacity of the reader has preconditioned him to read on the same grounds of experience and potential insight as the writer has been preconditioned to communicate on. Reader and writer meet in the medium of language. Such an encounter is possible because both, reader and writer, share their common human background and their ability to express and receive communication via written language. The personal development of reader and writer has followed a largely identical course of human development. They have both been subjected, as already mentioned in the case of the author, to history, the socio-cultural milieu, and those unique events that occur in any individual's life. Also in the same way as the author, the reader has personally developed himself intentionally through learning, judgment, and the synthesis of understanding.

As the reader encounters literary works of art he engages the re-creative activity which he originally learned for the purpose of executing simple communication; but now, under the influence of the literary work of art, he will develop this communicative faculty into a form of edification, a process of quiet learning and participation on the human level through re-creation. During this re-creative activity the reader must suspend his regular criteria for judgment to some degree in order to remain open to the ideas and feelings contained in the literary work of art. This open-mindedness allows him to expose himself to the author's world and translate the symbols, images, and characters of the fiction into concrete and familiar terms and experiences which are meaningful to him as a human being. Only in this way can the individual reader apprehend the significance of the communication contained in the literary work of art and make it a meaningful part of his life. Meaning will always have to remain something which has a personal and subjective basis. Only after having been perceived on personal grounds, meaning can obtain an objective status; otherwise meaning would be lacking the necessary component of understanding. In its objectivized form meaning finds its way as communication into literature. In this objectivized form meaning becomes a communication directed at other individuals who concretize this meaning on the grounds of their own experiences. The range and depth of such a "concretization", to use Ingarden's term, depends on the reader's range of experience and intellect. It must, however, also be pointed out, that the meaning of a work of art will never be fully exhausted by any single concretization. Because of the different perspectives and experiences which are applied to the concretization process, different solutions to problems in the reader's environment may be forthcoming, depending on the emotional and physical conditions which control the reader's interpretive powers. In any such interpretation, however, the artistic fiction is related to reality experienced in human action.

The fourth and final part of the literary system is the critic who, obviously, also shares the same human conditions of learning, education, and development as the author and the reader. On the other hand, he is distinguished from the author and the reader, the other human beings involved in the literary system, by the responsibility he has toward the work of art as well as toward the world of culture and tradition as historical components. The critic's responsibility rests on his sense of priorities. He must first judge what is important about life before he can judge what is important in art. He must know what function art serves before he can judge the value of a particular work of art. The critic is responsible for knowing as much about the world as possible. He must take a stand on the kind of life man ought to live. He must explain his standards of quality so that others may recognize the standards his criticism articulates. He must fight for quality on an objective level by insisting that certain standards must be maintained for the benefit of all.

The critic must also be a student of human society and its inner workings. He must know how one person relates to another, how a person relates to a group, and how a person relates to the institutions of society. Moreover, the critic must be aware of cultural distinctions and determinations. The critic must analyze a person's relation to his culture, he must inquire how one culture interacts with another, and how a particular culture contributes to world affairs.

Once the critic has obtained an understanding of the world system, both physical and ethical, he can turn to the task of evaluating individual works of art as objectively as possible on the basis of the acquired knowledge. First in the evaluation process the critic must place the work of art under consideration into its various contexts. He must identify the work of art as a product of a specific limited and limiting socio-cultural milieu, he must understand it as a part of a historical situation, and he must identify the artistic context of the work of art as to influences and effects which have shaped the work of art and which, in turn, the work of art itself will shape. Then he must articulate the purpose for which the work of art has been written. This must state what the author intended to achieve with this particular work in light of his previous works, whether he used the most effective style to achieve that particular purpose, and to what extent the content of the work has actually realized this purpose. Finally, the critic must judge the overall quality of the work of art and its potential impact on contemporary society and subsequent societies. For this purpose he must look at the reception of the work by contemporary critics and audiences, as well as at reception history in general. He must furthermore assess the contribution the work has made to the advancement or refinement of style, genre, topic, culture and to the amelioration of contemporary problems.

The above sketch of a system existing around and within the literary work of art can at this point only highlight the potential development of a detailed system. However, it appears to be evident from the preceding that the development of such a system focusing on the artist, the work of art, the audience, and the critic is no longer a hypothesis but well within the range of possibility without causing harm to the nature of the literary work of art as many scholars in the field have feared.

Fundamentals of a theory of infringements

HORST WEDDE
Gesellschaft für Mathematik und Datenverarbeitung
St. Augustin, Federal Republic of Germany

1. INTRODUCTION

Large real systems -- computer operating systems or networks, economical production combines or a state administration -- are normally <u>distributed</u>. Their subsystems (modules, production units like factories or departments of administration) have a relative independence in practice; so they have a partial control of their activities, a certain responsibility of planning their production, or a certain authority, respectively. It is well-known in many fields of scientific interest that this phenomenon causes enormous difficulties in describing and analyzing the cooperation and coordination of processes in different subsystems. This paper is a contribution in finding general formal models which especially enable us to speak about the cooperation of partially independent processes in basic terms. Thus we get an adequate fundament to study the extremely complex structure of the behaviour in such systems.

Every coordination of activities in different subsystems leads to a restriction of the behaviour in at least one subsystem. In our approach we develop an event-oriented specification method for describing these constraints in a systematic and consistent manner. The first step is to come to a formal and general concept of <u>infringements</u> on such constraints. The idea is then that in systems described this way all activities are admitted in a given situation except those which would infringe on prespecified constraints and so would lead to undesirable follower situations (e.g. violations of law). On doing so, we have been guided by the following two observations: Firstly, in many interesting fields of application the occurrence of a change normally depends on some <u>attendant circumstances</u> which are necessary to get a full understanding of this change (e.g. the constraints in physical or biological experiments). The second observation is that in diverse fields, e.g. in legal affairs or in technology, the number of attendant circumstances which are necessary to characterize when a change is <u>forbidden</u> is often much smaller than any corresponding set of circumstances under which this change <u>may occur</u>. As a very simple example, assume that a man is driving a car with a damaged headlight. A policeman watching this is enabled by this single circumstance to decide that the car driver has violated a law (on the necessary equipment of cars). On the other hand, when looking at an arbitrary car the same policeman would need a lot of examinations to be sure that this car is driven legally. In the sequel we shall develop an axiomatic frame for infringements which will be used then as a convenient tool to generate a systems concept.

2. LOOSELY COUPLED SYSTEMS

Assume that we have two jobs J_1 and J_2 each of which executes several tasks, mainly under its own control. Between the tasks there is a precedence relation specified as shown in Figure 1. Furthermore, assume that J_2 during its section 4 of activities (see Figure 1) updates a parameter which is at the same time used by J_1 in its section 3. In addition to that, let J_1 update some data in its section 2 which are then used by J_2 in section 5. To describe this interaction between J_1 and J_2 we only need the sections $1,\ldots,5$ but not the task structure. These sections are called <u>phases</u> and are denoted by $p, p_1, p_2, \ldots$. We then describe J_1 and J_2 (and so system components or production units) by formal objects called <u>parts</u> which are subsets of phases. Denoting them by $b, b_1, b_2, \ldots$ and the set of phases (parts) by P (B) we have:

$$\mathop{\forall}_{b\in B} \; b \subseteq P; \quad \mathop{\cup}_{b\in B} b = P; \quad \mathop{\forall}_{b_1, b_2 \in B}$$

$$(b_1 \neq b_2 \Rightarrow b_1 \cap b_2 = \emptyset).$$

We assume that every part has at least two phases. By a <u>configuration</u> we mean a subset $k \subseteq P$ with: $\mathop{\forall}_{b\in B} |k \cap b| = 1$. An <u>elementary change</u> is a pair (k_1, k_2) of configurations such that: $\mathop{\forall}_{b\in B} |k_1 \cap b| = |k_2 \cap b|$ and $|k_1 \backslash k_2| = |k_2 \backslash k_1| = 1$. ($k_1 k_2$ is the set theoretical difference of k_1 and k_2.) Let (k_1, k_2) be an elementary change, i.e. a single phase transition in some part, and let $\{p_1\}: = k_1 \backslash k_2$, $\{p_2\}: = k_2 \backslash k_1$; $\{q_1,\ldots,q_m\}: = k_1 \cap k_2$. For the matter of convenience we shall then use the notation: $p_1 \rightarrow p_2 \,|\{q_1,\ldots, q_m\}$. The phases $q_1,\ldots,q_m$ are assumed to remain constant under the change (k_1, k_2) and are called <u>side-conditions</u> of (k_1, k_2).

Looking at our example in Figure 1, we see that J_1 must be prevented from entering its section 3 and so from using the parameter mentioned above as long as J_2 is updating its value (in section 4). Using our formal language we can state that $1 \rightarrow 3 \,|\, \{4\}$ (and similarly $5 \rightarrow 4 \,|\{2\}$) would be infringements in the parts b_1 and b_2, respectively (see Figure 2). Infringements with only one side-condition are called <u>elementary</u>, and instead of $1 \rightarrow 3 \,|\, \{4\}$ we shall write $1 \rightarrow 3|4$. We formulate as a thesis:

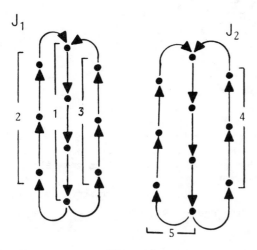

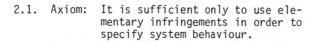

Figure 1.

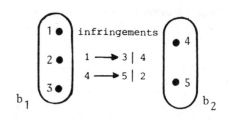

Figure 2.

2.1. Axiom: It is sufficient only to use elementary infringements in order to specify system behaviour.

It will come out later that more general infringements can be represented by means of elementary ones. As we understand infringements as changes which lead to undesirable situations (that have to be avoided), we have:

2.2. Axiom: Let $p_1 \rightarrow p_2|q$ be an infringement; $p_1, p_2 \in b$. If $p_3 \in b\backslash\{p_1, p_2\}$ then $p_3 \rightarrow p_2|q$ is also an infringement.

Going back to Figure 1, let us assume that at some time J_1 is allowed to be in section 3 and is using the latest parameter value generated by J_2. Now J_2 cannot go into section 4 without heavily disturbing J_1. So, if it is left to J_2 to enter section 4, it is the <u>right</u> of J_2 eventually to prevent J_1 from entering section 3. But at the same time J_2 must have the <u>duty</u> not to disturb J_1, and to ensure that J_1 can <u>rely</u> on using the parameter value without confusion, we specify $5 \rightarrow 4|3$ to be an infringement. This motivates:

2.3. Axiom (equilibrium property): Let $p_1, p_2 \in b$; $q \in b'$. If $p_1 \rightarrow p_2|q$ is an infringement and $q' \in b'\backslash\{q\}$ then $q' \rightarrow q|p_2$ is also an infringement.

This property seems to be characteristic for infringements in many fields of scientific interest. To demonstrate this we try to describe the kinematic aspects of a stamping machine. A strongly idealized schema is found in Figure 3: A disk Sch is driven by electric power with a constant speed. The mechanism connected with this disk consists of two link rods and a punch St. It eventually works against the power of a spring F. St stamps material placed on a table T. An interposer part I may eventually be pulled down (dotted position) by switching electromagnetic power on (Sw). Depending now on whether the interpower part I is in its upper position (4)

or in its lower (5) the link L is moved along the path between the positions 1 and 2 or between 1 and 3, respectively. By construction it is impossible to pull I into position 5 as long as L is in position 2. So, representing L by a part b_1: = {1,2,3}, I by a part b_2: = {4,5} we know that $4 \rightarrow 5|2$ is an infringement. At the same time the machine cannot stamp as long as l is in position 4. So also $1 \rightarrow 3|4$ is an infringement. By axiom 2.3 we can formally derive the infringements $1 \rightarrow 2|5$ and $5 \rightarrow 4|3$. But these have a very natural semantics: $1 \rightarrow 2|5$ would be a violation of a physical law, and if $5 \rightarrow 4|3$ would be allowed it could not be guaranteed that the stamping procedure (L is in phase 3!) can be finished in an ordinary way because the stamping mechanism would no longer be stable. Altogether, we have, for this machine, the same specification as for the interaction between J_1 and J_2 (see Figure 2).

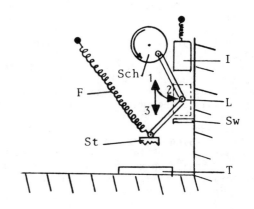

Figure 3.

It is now easy to derive from the axioms:

2.4. Proposition: Let $b_1, b_2 \in B$; let $p_1, p_2 \in b_1$; $q \in b_2$; $b_1 \neq b_2$. $p_1 \to p_2 | q$ is an infringement iff p_2 and q exclude one another.

Thus we introduce mutual exclusion relations $K\langle b_1 b_2 \rangle \subseteq b_1 \times b_2$ as a shorthand description for the given infringement structure concerning b_1 and b_2. Of course we have $K\langle b_1 b_2 \rangle = K\langle b_2 b_1 \rangle^{-1}$. For $K\langle bb \rangle := (b \times b) \backslash id\langle b \rangle$; $K := \bigcup_{b_1, b_2 \in B} K\langle b_1 b_2 \rangle$.

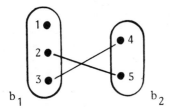

Figure 4.

The coupling structure corresponding to Figure 2 is to be found in Figure 4. We formalize the concept of undesirable situations:

2.5. Definition: A phase subset mc is a miscase iff: (1) $\bigvee_{b \in B} |mc \cap b| = 1$; (2) $\underset{p_1, p_2 \in mc}{\exists} (p_1, p_2) \in K$.

This means (see 2.4) that miscases are those maximal configurations which are the result of some infringement. Instead, we have:

2.6. Definition: A phase subset c is a case iff it is a maximal configuration and not a miscase.

The set of cases is denoted by C. To clarify our language we formulate:

2.7. Assumption: For $b_1, b_2 \in B$; $b_1 \neq b_2$ and $p \in b_1$ there is $q \in b_2$ such that $(p, q) \notin K$.

This is not really a loss of generality. If a phase P is coupled with all phases of another part it cannot be contained in any case, i.e. it can never hold.

2.8. Definition: Let $c \in C$; $p_1, p_2 \in b$ and $p_1 \in c$. $p_1 \to p_2$ is called an elementary event in c iff, for every $p_0 \in c \backslash \{p_1\}$, $p_1 \to p_2 | p_0$ is not an infringement.

Thus elementary events normally depend on $n-1$ side-conditions where $n = |B|$. It is easy to see that $p_1 \to p_2$ is an elementary event in c iff $[(c \backslash \{p_1\}) \cup \{p_2\}] \in C$. So we have a case graph with the cases as nodes and an edge between any two cases which differ in only one phase (indi-

cating an elementary phase transition). The case graph corresponding to Figure 4 is in Figure 5. Remembering that in Figure 4 the infringement structure of the stamping machine is represented we see from Figure 5 that we have covered its relevant kinematic aspects by only specifying two infringements in a very simple part structure.

Figure 5.

A quadruple (P,B,C,K) with the properties listed above is called a <u>Loosely Coupled System</u> (LCS).

2.9. Definition: Let $p_1 \to q_1$ and $p_2 \to q_2$ be elementary events in $c \in C$. They are <u>concurrent in c</u> iff $(q_1, q_2) \notin K$.

So concurrency is a very basic property in LCS. At the same time we have:

2.10. Proposition: $p_1 \to q_1$ and $p_2 \to q_2$ are concurrent in c iff there is $c_3 \in C$ such that the diagram

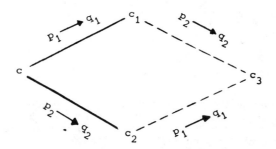

has the dotted commutative completion.

The proof is not difficult. 2.10 shows that by our definition 2.9 we have got quite a "normal" concept of concurrency. As an example let us discuss DIJKSTRA's philosophers' problem for three philosophers sitting around a table and having only one fork in between (see Figure 6). As it is well-known the only "correct" solution is to regard eating (i.e. having one fork in each hand) as an indivisible operation. The corresponding LCS and its case graph are also found in Figure 6. The phases a_i represent "thinking", the b_i "eating". We see at once that in the case a_1, a_2, a_3 there is a conflict between every two transitions $a_i \to b_i$. By removing the coupling edge (b_2, b_3) we come to another LCS (Figure 7) where $a_2 \to b_2$ and $a_3 \to b_3$ are concurrent in a_1, a_2, a_3 (see 2.9). Remembering the semantics

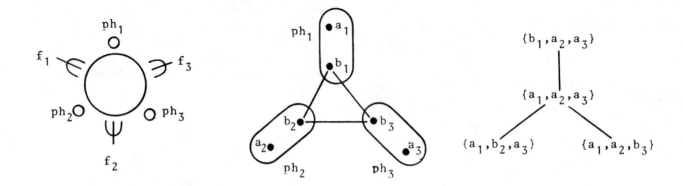

Figure 6.

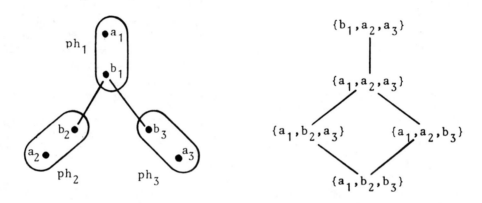

Figure 7.

Remembering the semantics of the coupling edges this can be achieved by adding one fork f2' between ph2 and ph3 (see Figure 6). So we see that instead of <u>deciding</u> <u>conflicts</u> (which is basic, e.g. in programming languages) the basic solution in LCSs is to <u>avoid</u> <u>conflicts</u> (by adding further resources). On doing so one follows, by the way, one of the intentions for <u>look-ahead</u> strategies in resource allocation problems.

One of the basic questions for the formal study of LCSs is the following: Let, for an LCS (P,B,C,K), $p_1 \in b_1$; $p_2 \in b_2$ and $(p_1,p_2) \notin K$. Is there a case $c \in C$ such that $\{p_1,p_2\} \subseteq c$?

A positive answer would tell us that a necessary condition for concurrent reachability of p_1 and p_2 (see 2.9) is satisfied. It is out of the frame of this paper to report the very complex investigations to answer this question in general (see [3]). But it is perhaps worth mentioning that this problem was found to be also fundamental for the studies of algorithms in picture processing (see [2]).

Given parts b_1, b_2, b_3 as shown in Figure 8, assume that being in phase 3,6,8, respectively, means to use a common resource. Furthermore, the resource be limited such that at most two of

interested processes in b_1, b_2, b_3 may use it at the same time. So we have the infringements listed in Figure 8 which are <u>not</u> elementary.

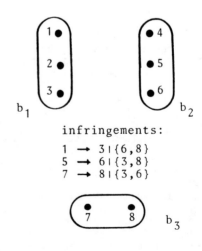

infringements:

$$1 \rightarrow 3 \mid \{6,8\}$$
$$5 \rightarrow 6 \mid \{3,8\}$$
$$7 \rightarrow 8 \mid \{3,6\}$$

Figure 8.

The idea how to represent them by means of elementary ones (see 2.1) is the following: The
<u>minimal</u> <u>function</u> of any <u>control</u> which guarantees that the limitations given by the infringements are respected is eventually to prevent one of the b_i to come to its "critical" phase. We think of the control to be part of the system, and so we represent it by a part cp. cp has exactly three phases, and in each of them it prevents one of the b_i to go to the critical phase. This is achieved by the coupling structure shown in Figure 9.

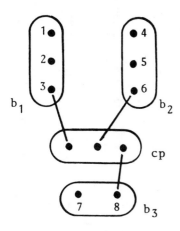

Figure 9.

In this LCS again every phase transition in the b_i is an elementary event which is not a prespecified infringement (compare 2.8). So these general infringements can be integrated consistently into the language of LCSs as defined before. Finally, the example in Figure 8 nearly completely explains the method how to derive general infringements from elementary ones. Therefore axiom 2.1 is justified.

3. GENERATING CONTROL MECHANISMS

Assume that we have production units $M_1,\ldots,M_5$ each of which may produce different products. At

some time M_1 and M_2 process some common raw materials into intermediate products which are then composed by M_5 with intermediate products produced both by M_3 and M_4. The production plan is found in Figure 10. Assume furthermore that the intermediate products are perishable goods or that there is no storage capacity available for them. Let the production rate of M_3 and M_4 be twice as high as that of M_1 and M_2 if M_3 and M_4 both work together. Then we must be careful that when M_1 and M_2 cooperate as described above at most one of the units M_3, M_4 is allowed to produce goods for M_5 while the other one has to do some different work. In our language we describe the production units by parts M_i; $i = 1,\ldots,5$ which have a special phase p_i representing the section of activity mentioned above. We arrive at the LCS shown in Figure 11, and we see at once:

3.1. Proposition: (a) $c \overset{\vee}{\in} C$ ($p_1 \in c \wedge p_2 \in c \Rightarrow p_3 \notin c \vee p_4 \notin c$).
(b) As long as the premise of the formula in (a) does not hold every event may occur in the M_i which does not lead to a situation c where the premise holds.
(c) In a situation like that preassumed in (b) we can reach at a case c where the premise of (a) holds, namely by first going to a case c' where the conclusion of (a) holds.

The semantical background for this special type of construction was already given before (see Figure 9). An advantage of the property 3.1 (c) comes out as follows: Let b_1,b_2 be two hardware components which admit at some time a transition $p_i \rightarrow q_i$ but never $q_i \rightarrow p_i$; $i = 1,2$. Furthermore $p_1 \rightarrow q_1$ enforces $p_2 \rightarrow q_2$ after a certain while. Constructing an LCS as shown in Figure 12 (which is a specialization of the construction in Figure 11) we ensure (see 3.1 (c)) that between $p_1 \rightarrow q_1$ and $p_2 \rightarrow q_2$ there is a transition $1 \rightarrow 2$ in the part D. So D works as a <u>delay</u> with the delay time which is needed for $1 \rightarrow 2$. Assume that in our example represented in Figures 10 and 11 there is a need to double

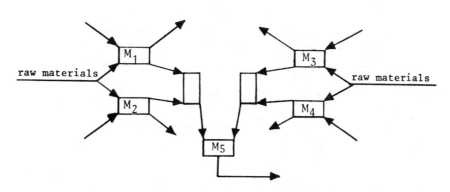

Figure 10.

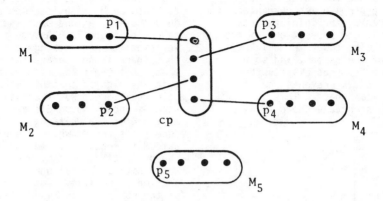

Figure 11.

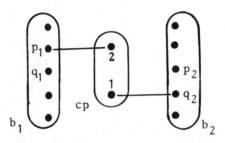

Figure 12.

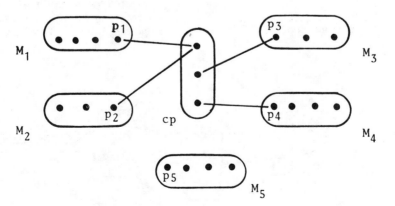

Figure 13.

the production rate of M_1 and M_2, e.g. because the demand for activities different from p_1, p_2 has grown up to that extent. At the same time the flow capacity between M_3, M_4 and M_5 cannot be increased. To represent this restriction we now need an LCS where, instead of 3.1 (a), the following holds:

3.2. $\bigvee\limits_{c \in C} (p_1 \in c \vee p_2 \in c \Rightarrow p_3 \notin c \vee p_4 \notin c)$

The corresponding construction is found in Figure 13. For this LCS 3.1 (b) and (c) are still valid.

Before enlarging the production rate M_1 consisted of the machines E_1, E_2; M_2 consisted only of E_5. In the changed system M_1 now consists of $E_1, \ldots, E_4$; M_2 consists of E_5, E_6. The corresponding sections of activities in the E_i previously described by p_1, p_2 are represented by $q_1, \ldots, q_6$ (see Figure 14). Substituting $z_1 := \{q_1, \ldots, q_4\}$; $z_2 := \{q_5, q_6\}$ we have for the LCS in Figure 14:

3.3. $\bigvee\limits_{c \in C} (z_1 \subseteq c \vee z_2 \subseteq c \Rightarrow p_3 \notin c \vee p_4 \notin c$

(Compare 3.2.) Again, 3.1 (b) and (c) hold for this LCS.

By the construction techniques found in this section the behaviour of system parts was restricted in a systematic way. To describe this

formally we define:

3.3.   Definition: Let (P, B, C, K) and (P', B', C', K') be LCSs. A mapping $f : P \rightarrow P'$ is an <u>allomorphism</u> iff f preserves parts, and if mc is a miscase in (P, B, C, K) $f(mc)$ cannot be contained in a case.

So every mapping which preserves parts and coupling edges is an allomorphism. If one couples a new part to a given LCS the inclusion map is an allomorphism. Especially the realization of the restrictions in Figure 11 and Figure 13 is an allomorphic construction. The system in Figure 11 is mapped by an allomorphism onto that in Figure 13, and the "substitution" of M_1, M_2 (see Figure 14) is an allomorphic extension of the LCS in Figure 13. Allomorphisms normally change the event structure (instead of preserving it). This motivates the name.

4.   FURTHER COMMENTS

Global constraints associated with the function of systems and the cooperation of their components can already be formulated at a very early stage of system design. Our method admits then to design an LCS the behaviour of which is only governed by the given set of restrictions. If

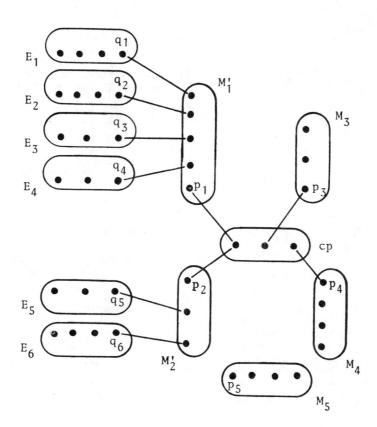

Figure 14.

104

later on further restrictions have to be imposed, this can be done by merely extending the LCS construction so far reached at, without any change of the previous structure. In [1] it has been shown that an important class of synchronization mechanisms can be generated by elementary constructions like those in Figure 11 and Figure 13.

By the substitution technique as introduced in Section 3 (see Figure 14), we could reach at a deeper level of representation, but again without essentially changing the LCS as constructed so far and without any need to leave the representation level. The common mathematical tool for modelling and changing the system structures in this manner is a new type of morphisms, namely allomorphisms. They are of special use for the formal study and characterization of the processes which may run in LCSs. This is mainly shown in [4].

The main thesis for our formal approach is that a set of prespecified constraints which partially <u>determine</u> the behaviour of a system to be modelled describe at the same time an <u>independent formal aspect</u> of this behaviour. The result in following this thesis was the formalism of LCSs. But we may also add, to a given LCS structure, further information about processes in some parts. One way to do so is shown in the example in Figure 15.

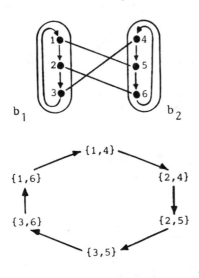

Figure 15.

Here a precedence relation for possible steps in b_1, b_2 is introduced. This induces an orientation in the corresponding case graph such that the behaviour of the whole system now looks like a (computer) clock with six times. If this precedence relation is slightly changed, as shown in Figure 16, the same system behaves like a network consisting of three sources and three sinks only.

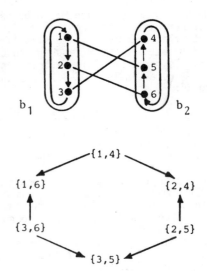

Figure 16.

Unfortunately, the introductory character of this paper does not leave enough space to show in more detail that our method is especially useful and adequate in formalizing construction principles which are, up to now, used by technicians in a more or less informal way (e.g. the interposer technique in Figure 3). Besides the chance so e.g. to contribute to a theory of technical mechanics, this would give rise to introduce new construction ideas, e.g. to the computer science field: In technical mechanics the interaction between system parts is very often implemented independently from a special direction of processes. So the stamping machine in Figure 3 works meaningless whether the upper disk is driven lefthand or righthand. Organizing the cooperation of processes in computer systems in a similar way, we would in general be allowed to use backtracking techniques and so practically to solve a lot of problems in connection with error detection.

REFERENCES

1. LAUTENBACH, K. and H. WEDDE, "Generating Control Mechanisms by Restrictions," in: <u>Lecture Notes in Computer Science</u>, Vol. 45, Springer Verlag, Berlin-Heidelberg-New York, 1976.
2. MONTANARI, U., "Networks of Constraints: Fundamental Properties and Applications to Picture Processing," <u>Information Sciences</u>, 7, American Elsevier Pub. Co., 1974.
3. WEDDE, H., "Lose Kopplung von Systemkomponenten," <u>GMD Report</u> No. 96, Bonn, 1975 (German).
4. WEDDE, H. and J. WINKOWSKI, "Determining Processes by Violations," in: <u>Lecture Notes in Computer Science</u>, Vol. 53, Springer Verlag, 1977.

ORGANIZATION
AND MANAGEMENT

Introduction

F. DE P. HANIKA, R. R. HOUGH and F. PICHLER

The wide scope offered by a Symposium on Cybernetics and Systems Research in Organization again found its usual response of rather more than two dozen papers, whittled down to just below that number in the event.

Ranging from the abstract ideas to downright practical application, they reflect the growing trend already noted in my introduction to Vol. V of this series, which reported on the Proceedings of the Third European Meeting on Cybernetics and Systems Research, held in Vienna in 1976. There the trend from emphasis on speculative papers as to what might be done with cybernetics and systems research in the fields of management and administration became evident. Gratifyingly, the theorists and philosophers in the field are still with us, for as we said there, nothing is as practical as a sound theory, but on this occasion the majority of the material presented directly related to, outlined, demonstrated or reported applied ideas and work, simultaneously with a clear trend to treat organization more and more in social science terms.

The growing penetration of the whole field of organization, in the broadest sense of that term, by cybernetic/systems research thinking is further evidenced by the groupings of the papers for presentation, which on this occasion filled (in addition to an opening plenary meeting: "Cybernetics in Management") eight half-day sessions in parallel, clearly showing the "Progress in Cybernetics and Systems Research" in the field of Organization and its Management, viz. Management Information Systems, Quantitative Analysis, Organization Research, Ris and Uncertainty, Decision Making, Social Systems I and II, Organization and Management (Practice).

The "Progress" element in these biennial reviews of scientific and applied work is further underlined by the fact that many of the contributors on this occasion had contributed to more than one of the European Meetings organized by the Austrian Society for Cybernetic Studies, on the evolving State-of-the-Art in their field, flanked by newcomers attracted to join in as the standing of these biennial events becomes more widely known.

A system approach to control and coordination in complex organizations

J. E. VAN AKEN
N. V. Philips' Gloeilampenfabrieken, The Netherlands

1. INTRODUCTION

Throughout the history of mankind the phenomenon of organization, i.e. the willingness of two or more human beings to combine their efforts through a relatively stable network of social relations, has always been (and still is) one of the most important factors in society. Organizations range from small ones such as families, football teams and drugstores to large ones like universities, armies, nations and economic or military alliances. The structures of these organizations are often only partly the result of deliberate design; in many cases they are rather the result of an evolution process: unsuccessful structures disappear while successful ones survive and proliferate. However, as organizations have to adapt their activities continually to their changing environment, it may be desirable to control such evolutionary processes and to use an explicit design approach for finding suitable organization structures. Design aims at making artifacts with desired properties. One can distinguish three phases in the design process (see e.g. Simon, 1969 [4]):

- determination of the function of the artifact to be designed
- information gathering and search for alternative solutions
- evaluation of alternatives.

Once the function of the artifact is specified the design process moves between two poles: the synthesis of solutions and the evaluation or analysis of these solutions. These synthesis-analysis iterations continue until a satisfactory solution is found.

The representation of the design plays a key role in this iterative procedure. Only with the aid of an adequate representation can the designer draw up, analyse and modify his design.

This paper will develop a system of concepts concerning organizational control and coordination (a more comprehensive discussion is given in van Aken, 1978 [1]). We will define these concepts and we will discuss for several cases their functions in the process of control and coordination. This conceptual system can be used to represent (elements) of organizational structures and thus to support the process of designing them. Furthermore, the discussion of their functions can guide the application of these elements in the design.

As we will use a system approach, we will start by introducing some, for the greater part well known, concepts from system theory.

2. SYSTEMS

There are several possibilities to define a system. In this paper we define a system as a set of elements with a set of relations between them, the relations having the property that all elements are directly or indirectly related. Coherence is thus a defining characteristic of a system. The set of relations form the structure of the system.

The elements are the smallest entities used in the argument. They may be abstract, in which case the system is an abstract system. If two or more elements represent empirical objects the system is a concrete one. If two or more elements of a concrete system represent human beings we will call it a social system. A concrete element may be divisible, but in the system analysis in question it is treated as an opaque unit, as a "black box". The elements may have various properties or attributes associated with them; the above-mentioned relations form one kind of such attributes.

The environment of a system consists of all elements outside the system; if there are no relations between internal and external elements the system is closed; if there are such relations the system is open.

A system can be studied by making subsystems or aspect systems. A subsystem of a system consists of a subset of its elements with all their original attributes, while an aspect system of a system consists of all its elements with only a subset of its original attributes.

An important class of systems consists of hierarchic systems. With respect to this concept the ideas of Simon [4,5] will be followed. A hierarchic system is a system the elements of which are themselves systems and may in turn also be hierarchic systems. Although we will use this concept in the discussion of organizational structures, the concept itself should be seen as "totally divorced from its original denotation in human organizations of a vertical authority structure" (Simon, 1973 [5], p. 5). It is the "parts-within-parts" structure which is the defining characteristic of a hierarchic system in this paper. With the aid of a hierarchic description, a system can be analysed at various levels of resolution. As the whole system is described at each level, we may regard the levels of a hierarchic system as aspects systems of it.

Another class of systems consists of stratified systems (van Aken [1]). A stratified system is a system the elements of which are ordered, individually or combined to subsystems, according to a given priority criterion. There are many possible priority criteria. For example, a school can be represented as a stratified system in which the pupils are ordered by classes, while a project can be described as a stratified system consisting of elementary activities, ordered according to priority in time as determined by technical considerations.

As will be described in Section 7, the classical structure of line management has two defining characteristics, viz. hierarchy and stratification; these two characteristics form two distinct design issues.

3. ORGANIZATIONS

We will use Luhmann's [3] concept of position as elementary unit of any organization. A position is a set of addressable role expectations with the following three properties: it is to be occupied by a person, it is to carry out a programme, and it is to have limited communication possibilities with other positions (this last property means that there is no all-channel communication network between positions).

This concept can be generalised to a compound position: a compound position is a set of addressable role expectations, to be occupied by a number of persons, to carry out a programme (or set of programmes) and having limited communication possibilities with other compound positions. The individual position can be seen as the limiting case of a compound position. Departments and divisions of a company are examples of compound positions.

Now an organization can be defined as a system of occupied positions with their physical means of operation. An organization is thus conceptualised as a concrete system, consisting of human beings and e.g. buildings, machines and materials, but with the abstract system of (compound) positions as its defining characteristic. It should be noted that the organization's participants belong to it only in their organizational roles.

As the positions form a system, every position is directly or indirectly related to every other position. The relations between the positions form the organization structure. These relations can be e.g. of a technological nature (resulting from interdependence between the programmes of the positions in question) or of a control nature (see below).

The definition of organization given above is of a rather wide applicability: not only formal organizations like armies, companies or universities can be conceptualized as systems of occupied (compound) positions, but also a family, a tribe, a national economy or the EEC.

The wide applicability of this concept of organization can be compared with that of the concept "system": (almost) any sector of the real world can be described as a system, viz. as a set of elements with mutual relations. Whether it is worthwhile doing so depends on the problem involved and the degree of coherence between the elements in question. Likewise (almost) any set of human actors with social relations between them can be described as an organization in the sense defined above and again the question as to whether it is

worthwhile doing so depends on the problem involved and the degree to which the activities of the actors show coherence. As we will see below, this degree of coherence often depends on coordination: in most cases it is only useful to describe a social system as an organization if there is some coordination mechanism.

4. CONTROL

An organization is an open system, which must be able to secure its resources (manpower, money and material resources) from its environment: it must maintain various resource equilibria. Resources are usually acquired in exchange for a certain output (goods and/or services); in that case the organization must also maintain an output equilibrium, i.e. the output it offers must on the average be equal to that demanded by its social environment.

In a dynamic environment these equilibria are also dynamic. The activities of the actors in the organization must be controlled in order to make output disposal and resource acquisition respond adequately to threats and opportunities.

Control can be defined for a wide range of applications (including both technical and social ones) as the use of interventions by a controller to promote preferred behaviour of a system-being-controlled. In technical systems the controller can be a distinct subsystem; in organizations it is always an aspect system, because every actor is engaged in control (at least of the execution of his own programme).

The process of control can be described as an equilibrium-seeking process by introducing the concept of interference reduction (the subsequent discussion on interference reduction and transfer of interference is based on ideas put forward by De Sitter [6]). An interference can be defined as an event causing a disequilibrium in the system-being-controlled, i.e. a departure of its state from the state(s) preferred by the controller. Organizational controllers are to a large extent free to define (subjectively) their preferences, but for viable organizations these preferences should also include several "objective" criteria like the maintenance of output and resource equilibria.

Control, or interference reduction, is the process of restoring equilibrium by changing the state of the system-being-controlled, the controller preferences or both. The changes in controller preferences (e.g. the preferences with respect to the output level may change with the external demand) adapt the organization's activities to changing circumstances. It should be noted that not only threats but also opportunities can produce interference with an organization.

The programmes of the various (compound) positions are often technologically interdependent. The reduction of an interference somewhere in the organization may therefore cause interference with connected suborganizations. We can call this phenomenon transfer of interference.

An interference generated somewhere in a compound system consisting of rigid subsystems with rigid connections will be propagated throughout the whole system. In organizations, however, the situation is quite different, because their sub-organizations often have the capacity to absorb (part) of their interferences. In other words, they often have the choice between internal and external reduction of interference: in the first case they reduce their interferences in such a way that this does not cause interference to connected suborganizations, while in the second case they do cause interference elsewhere. For example, an interference to a TV picture-tube factory consisting of a machine breakdown can be reduced externally by simply cutting the deliveries to customer TV factories (causing expensive interferences there) or internally by using overtime after the machine has been repaired to make up for the lost production or by using other buffers such as an intermediate stock of picture-tubes. Similarly, an interference consisting of an increase of the prices of some materials may be reduced externally by increasing the price of the end products or internally by more efficient use of the materials in question.

5. COORDINATION

The positions of an organization are usually arranged in a hierarchic system of compound positions, which is the well known phenomenon of departmentalization (the reasons for using a hierarchic structure are discussed in Section 7). The activities of the actors assigned to these (compound) positions are at least partially controlled by those actors themselves: this mode of control will be called selfcontrol.

A key issue in organizational control is the problem of integration of control: the control interventions applied in the various parts of the organization must be selected in such a way that the organization as a whole responds adequately to internally and externally generated interferences. Resource and output equilibria should not only be maintained for some occupied compound positions but also for the organization as a whole. The suborganizations should not transfer the burden of their interferences wholly to connected ones, but should absorb (part of) them themselves.

The integration problem can be solved partly by selfcontrol: problems arising from interactions between suborganizations can to some extent be solved by direct bargaining between the parties involved. However, these interactions can be very complex (e.g. because there are many suborganizations involved) and can cause acute conflicts between the interested parties (which will tend to be settled in the interests of the most powerful party if only selfcontrol is operative). Therefore, the solution of the integration problem cannot be left wholly to selfcontrol; this activity has to be supplemented by a certain amount of coordination. From a control viewpoint the "raison d'etre" of coordination is its capacity to improve the behaviour of the organization as a whole.

Coordination in organizations is the control of the execution of the programmes of (compound) positions by coordinators, i.e. actors in (compound) positions with the task of controlling the activities of other actors. It will be recalled that, according to the definition of control given in Section 4, control does not necessarily mean complete determination of behaviour, but refers to any promotion of preferred behaviour. The activities of actors in organizations are thus controlled by a combination of selfcontrol and coordination. To paraphrase George Orwell, coordination means that "everyone controls but some control more than others".

6. COORDINATION MODES

Coordination is the control of people by other people. The "levers" of coordination are influence and power. We will use the following definitions of these concepts here. A social system has influence over another, if it is able to induce behaviour of the latter which deviates from the behaviour without intervention, but is still in agreement with the latter's preferences. A social system has power over another if it is able to induce behaviour which is in conflict with the latter's preferences. Power is thus seen as the capacity to make people do things they dislike.

Coordination using power will be called stratified coordination, while coordination using only influence will be called non-stratified coordination.

Coordination can be direct, intervening directly in the process of decision-making by selfcontrol or indirect, preparing decision-making by selfcontrol through instructions, regulations, indoctrination, etc.

The combination of these classification criteria produces four coordination modes:
- Mode 1: stratified direct coordination
- Mode 2: non-stratified direct coordination
- Mode 3: stratified indirect coordination
- Mode 4: non-stratified indirect coordination

Mode-1 coordination is the traditional, powerful and well tested mode of coordination by line management, almost as old as the phenomenon of organization itself. This mode is the backbone of the whole coordination structure in many formal organizations.

Mode-2 coordinators have no official power over the coordinated groups, but they influence decision-making by participating in various formal and informal control procedures. Examples in formal organizations are planning departments, liaison officers, product managers, committees consisting of managers of equal rank, etc., etc.

Mode-3 coordination is indirect; it uses regulations, instructions, standards, etc. to modify decision-making by selfcontrol. It is a stratified mode, which means that the instructions, etc. are backed by a coordinator with the power to impose them. For example, the personal policy of large formal organizations is often largely governed by mode-3 coordination.

Mode-4 coordination is also indirect, but does not constrain unduly the exercise of discretion by selfcontrol as it is non-stratified. It uses e.g. intra-company training, indoctrination or a system of incentives rewarding behaviour in the best interests of the whole to modify selfcontrol.

The actual organizational operations will be controlled by a combination of selfcontrol and one or more of these coordination modes; we will call this combination the coordination mix.

The coordination mix to be used depends on the situation, i.e. on the organization's environment and technology. For formal organizations it will almost always contain a fair amount of mode-1 coordination; but for most complex or geographically dispersed organizations or organizations facing uncertain situations, mode 1 will have to be largely supplemented by other coordination modes. If the need for coordination is due to complexity and/or uncertainty one has to make ample use of non-stratified coordination modes, because these permit the organization to make better use of the discretion involved in self-control (mode-1 coordinators are often not in the best position to judge the local circumstances and they may also hamper a quick local response to interference). On the other hand, if the need for coordination is due to conflict, one will need more stratified (in particular mode-1) coordination in the coordination mix.

The various coordination modes are also found in other areas than formal organizations. For example, pollution control (which can be seen as modification of the selfcontrol of industrial companies by government agencies) can also choose between these modes. Mode 1 would mean a permit system: for each discharge the company in question has to apply for a permit from a pollution agency. Mode 2 would mean that companies have to report intended discharges, whereupon the pollution agency can advise them e.g. on the timing of the discharge. A general prohibition by law of discharges above a certain amount per period would be mode-3 coordination and a tax on discharges, creating a pressure to decrease discharges, would be a form of mode-4 coordination.

Another example is the coordination mix men have used throughout the ages to ensure fidelity in their wives: keeping rivals away by (the threat of) force (with the harem as the extreme example) is mode-1 and using persuasion is mode-2 coordination. Forbidding adultery by law is an example of mode-3, while social norms producing a conviction that adultery is immoral can be seen as mode-4 coordination.

7. ORGANIZATION DESIGN

The essence of organization design is the creation of an effective control structure, enabling the organization as a whole to respond adequately to threats and opportunities through a cooperation between selfcontrol and coordination. This applies both to the static control and coordination relations between the various (compound) positions and to the control procedures such as budget and planning procedures.

As said above, the backbone of the organizational coordination structure is often mode-1 coordination (line management). This structure has two characteristics, viz. hierarchy and stratification.

Hierarchy refers to the arrangement of the compound positions (departments) in a parts-within-parts structure. This arrangement has both technological and coordination aspects. It has technological aspects because it determines the allocation of programmes over the various (compound) positions, or, in other words, because it determines

the intra-organizational division of labour. One generally tries to form the compound positions in such a way that they have as homogeneous a technology and environment as possible at each level of the hierarchy. The hierarchic structure has also coordination aspects, not only because each compound position has usually a mode-1 coordinator assigned to it but also because its use can strongly reduce the complexity of the coordination problem: at each level of the hierarchy the coordinators can concentrate on controlling the input and the output of the suborganizations at that level (i.e. they control the output produced, the resources needed to produce it and the technological interactions between the suborganizations), while leaving the intricacies of the interactions within the suborganizations veiled under the cover of selfcontrol.

Stratification, the second characteristic of line-management, refers to the organizational power structure. One aspect of this is the difference in the amount of power to be used for the mode-1 coordination of different compound positions (for example, one often uses less power on research departments than on commercial ones, see Hofstede [2]). Sometimes one uses a special kind of stratification, viz. a matrix structure (each compound position being coordinated by two or more mode-1 coordinators; a project organization with project managers next to functional managers is an example).

As we mentioned above, mode-1 coordination will generally be supplemented with other coordination modes; room must be made for them during organization design. Remaining coordination problems might be solved by using adequate control procedures (e.g. by specifying that some issues have to be subjected to coordination, while others may be left to selfcontrol).

Efficient use of these coordination modes other than mode 1 in designing a coordination structure is essential in complex and uncertain situations. In those cases the central problem is in our opinion not how to find the best coordination decisions, but rather how to make the best use of the discretion involved in self-control. It is fairly easy to stifle selfcontrol by using too much stratified coordination; it is much more difficult to stimulate selfcontrol in such a way that it benefits the organization as a whole.

Human cooperation and the accompanying coordination mechanisms are not phenomena confined to formal organizations. The coordination of the activities of economic agents in a national economy, the administration of a federal state or the adjustment of the economic policies of the member states of an economic community like the EEC can also be seen as organizational problems. An organization-design approach to such problems may contribute something to their solution.

REFERENCES

1. AKEN, J. E. van, On the Control of Complex Industrial Organizations, Leiden, Martinus Nijhoff, to be published, 1978.

2. HOFSTEDE, G., "Cultural Elements in the Exercise of Power," in Y. H. Poortinga (ed.), <u>Basic Problems in Cross-Cultural Psychology</u>, Amsterdam, Swets and Zeitlinger, 1977.

3. LUHMANN, N., "A General Theory of Organized Social Systems," in G. Hofstede and S. M. Kassem (eds.), <u>European Contributions to Organization Theory</u>, Amsterdam, Van Gorcum, 1976.

4. SIMON, H. A., <u>The Sciences of the Artificial</u>, Cambridge (Mass.), MIT Press, 1969.

5. SIMON, H. A., "The Organization of Complex Systems," in H. H. Pattee (ed.), <u>Hierarchy Theory</u>, New York, George Braziller, 1973.

6. SITTER, L. U. De, "A System Theoretical Paradigm of Social Interaction: Toward a New Approach to Qualitative System Dynamics," <u>Annals of Systems Research 3</u>, 1973, pp. 100-140.

Preliminary analysis (PA) in managerial problem solving

SAMIR CHAKRABORTY
New Brunswick Telephone Co., Ltd.
Saint John, New Brunswick, Canada E2L 4K2

1. INTRODUCTION

A Managerial Problem Solving Methodology (MPSM) has been developed [1] and extensively used [2,3,4, 5,7] to solve Process Problems. A Process is defined as an operational combination of man-machine systems. These systems perform functions which transform basic (to the Process or Organization) inputs ($'s) to primary (for survival) outputs (products/services). A problem is defined when the actual values of state-space constraints [1,8] of a Process fall outside a predetermined range of acceptable values.

The solution of Process problems requires that people representing different interdependent organizational constituencies, professional disciplines, experience and knowledge be organized into problem solving teams. These teams identify and minimize problem constraints through the manipulation of Process design and performance variables.

Their basic activity involves collecting, analyzing, creating and communicating information about the Process. This information loaded activity is subject to the constraints posed by:
- the dynamics of differentiation, selection [13] and communication [6,7] in human Processes;
- the increasing complexity of the Processes;
- the volatility/uncertainty of the Process environment/context.

These constraints, together with economic/financial constraints, require that the problem solving effort meet increasingly stringent performance requirements.

This can be achieved by reducing the entropy [6] associated with the problem solving Process, in part, through:
- utilizing a problem solving methodology (see Section 2.1) which guides the effective and efficient identification and minimization of problem constraints;
- utilizing a framework (Section 2.2) into which Process information is structured and through which it is acquired and communicated.

This framework and methodology have been developed and form the basis of the MPSM [1]. Preliminary Analysis (PA) is the first step in the MPSM and results in proper problem definition.

The fact that a problem unstated is a problem unsolved is often ignored by problem solvers. Design and implementation activities begin before the key causal relationships and constraints surrounding a problem are defined and understood. The results are cost overruns, missed schedules, dissatisfied customers/users, and endless series of what we euphemistically call "bugs" and "system maintenance".

The roots of these problems lie in the fact that the problem solvers have not been able to present themselves with:
- a common understanding of the essential facts about the Process, its environment/context, constraints, design requirements, etc.;
- an exposition and reconciliation of their individual predilections and preemptive assessments about the problem causes and solutions;
- a common understanding of the key assumptions which will form the basis of later problem solving activities; this lack of appreciation and understanding severely affects both the efficiency and the effectiveness of the problem solving activity.

We know from experience that Process problems are complex and ill defined. Complexity is an inherent fact of life which the manager/problem-solver must face. But, poor problem definition is the result of inadequate attention and poor methods. The former can be handled by disciplined and exacting management [6] of the problem solving activity, the latter by methods for Preliminary Analysis (PA), which is the subject of this paper.

Section 2 will briefly review the relevant concepts which form the basis of the PA activity. These include concepts of the MPSM [1] and the Hierarchy of Epistemological Levels (e-levels) of Systems [11,12]. Section 3 outlines the PA procedure, while Section 4 describes the PA framework. Sections 5 and 6 mention the outputs of the PA activity and its applications.

2. RELEVANT CONCEPTS

2.1. The Managerial Problem Solving Methodology

The Managerial Problem Solving Methodology (MPSM) [1] consists of the following activities to be performed by the problem solving team:

Preliminary Analysis (PA). Identify (and form a common understanding about) the Process under study, its environment/context, its key constraints, assumptions, and define the requirements the problem solving activity must satisfy.

Synthesis [1,10]. Model the actual-Process by defining a hierarchy(ies) of actual-systems (a-systems) up the e-levels defined on the Process.

Analysis [1,10]. Describe the ideal-Process by defining a hierarchy(ies) of ideal-systems (i-systems) down the e-levels of the Process.

Constraint Identification and Minimization [1, 8]. Sequentially, move up the hierarchy(ies) of a-systems, identify at each e-level all relevant constraints of the a-systems and minimize them, using the various scientific disciplines (engineering, economics, OR/MS, management, etc.) related to type of constraint source and within the limits of the environmental constraints.

Design Modification. Based on final constraint minimization, define the hierarchy of modified-a-systems up the hierarchy of e-levels of the actual-Process to give a modified-actual-Process, while satisfying performance and design constraints.

Recommend, Approve and Implement. The modified-actual-Process subsequent to testing against the key constraints and assumptions.

Monitoring and Maintenance. Define procedures for the adaptive monitoring and maintenance of the Process.

2.2. The Hierarchy of Epistemological Levels of Systems

All relevant information concerning the Process is structured during its acquisition, manipulation/interpretation and communication in the framework provided by the Hierarchy of Epistemological Levels of Systems [11,12]. This framework satisfies the following criteria [1]:
- is universal, unrestricted and compatible with any language;
- allows all information regarding the Process to be included;
- allows all levels of knowledge to be expressed fully and accurately;
- represents the hierarchical nature of the information generating mechanisms;
- allows synthesis and analysis to be performed on the information contained in it.

When applied to a Process, in the context of the MPSM, the hierarchy of e-levels of systems is defined as follows:

e-level	System Name	Contents of System Set
0	Source	(Variables, space-time resolution level)
1	Data	(Source Systems, activity matrix)
2	Functional	(Data Systems, time invariant relations/generating behaviour)
3	Micro	(Functional Systems, coupling variables/relations)
4	Operation - I	(Micro Systems, Managerial System - I)
5	Operation - II	(Operation - I Systems, Managerial System - II)
↓	↓	↓
x	Operation - y	(Operation - (y-1) Systems, Managerial System - (y))

The systems defined at e-levels 2 and 3 are, in fact, equivalent to the Generative and Structure Systems [11,12], respectively. The systems defined at e-levels 4 to x correspond to the hierarchy of Meta-Systems [11,12], where the system defined at e-level x is the Process itself. These systems defined at the various e-levels represent "snapshots" of the Process at various levels of knowledge about it.

The Managerial System at an e-level is defined as the set (or subset in a specific case) consisting of the following management information: Objectives, Tasks, Responsibilities, Decision Procedures, Information Flows, Measurements, Personnel, Feedback/Control Mechanisms, Performance-Reward Mechanisms, Hiring-Training Mechanisms, Corporate Culture, Ethics, etc.

The notation -I and other such numbers, which appear after the entries: Operational and Managerial System, is meant to represent the organizational level of management hierarchy corresponding to a given e-level which controls systems at the lower (previous) e-level.

3. PRELIMINARY ANALYSIS (PA)

3.1. The PA Procedure

PA reflects the first look by the problem solvers at the Process and its problems. It forms the basis for all subsequent information gathering, analysis, design, testing and acceptance activities. It integrates the overview information that is required to define the scope and depth of the problem solving activity and the performance and design constraints that must be satisfied. In addition, assumptions held by individual team members regarding the Process, its problems and associated causal relations get stated, examined and reconciled (where required). This is to minimize downstream conflict between team members and avoid faulty design.

The PA Procedure is executed in an iterative manner until sufficient and complete information is acquired, structured and documented. The main steps in the PA Procedure are outlined as follows:

(0) Define overall performance requirements on the problem solving task.

(1) Identify the Process under examination at a boundary level.

(2) Identify the environment/context of the Process at the boundary level.

(3) Identify the constraints [1] on the Process at the boundary level.

(4) Identify the problem constraints on the Process at the boundary level. These will be reflected in problem symptoms that appear at the Process boundary and should be a subset of Item 3.

(5) Identify the assumptions associated with Items 0 to 4.

(6) Integrate Items 1 to 5 to present an overview of the "area of interest" to the problem solvers.

(7) Identify potential cause and effect relationships for the problem, at a level compatible with those for Items 1 to 6.

(8) Define the generic form of the Function-framework (Ff) using the hierarchy of e-levels (Section 4.1).

(9) Define the generic form of the Problem-framework (Pf) using the hierarchy of e-levels (Section 4.2).

(10) Define the generic form of the Requirements framework (Rf) using the hierarchy of e-levels (Section 4.3).

(11) Identify the functions/sub-Processes of the Process. This is done by a combination of

synthesis and analysis on the Process. The functions are identified as being the smallest, homogeneous, man-machine units that can be defined using an agreed upon set of discrimination rules. These discrimination rules are derived by subjecting the Process to a layered categorization by grids representing types of management activities, scientific/technical disciplines, flow of work and organization structure that are used to create and manage the Process.

(12) Identify the environment/context of the functions of the Process.

(13) Identify the constraints of the functions of the Process.

(14) Define the working form of the Function-framework using information from Items 11 to 13 and the generic Ff. Note: It is generally accepted that the scope and depth of information regarding the functions, context and constraints will not be of equivalent detail.

(15) Identify the constraints that are analyzed to be associated with problems of the functions of the Process.

(16) Identify potential cause and effect relationships for those functions of the Process that are problem constrained (from Item 15).

(17) Define the working form of the Problem-framework using information from Items 15 and 16 and the generic Pf.

(18) Identify requirements that must be satisfied by the functions, both in terms of performance and design.

(19) Define the working form of the Requirements-framework using information from Item 18 and the generic Rf.

(20) Identify the relevant Assumptions that accompany the working frameworks - Ff, Pf, and Rf.

(21) Review together the Overview (Item 6), Ff (Item 14), Pf (Item 17), Rf (Item 19) and Assumptions (Item 20) for completeness, logical consistency and accuracy (where possible). If required, iterate through the stages of PA from 0 to 21 until satisfactory results are achieved.

(22) The PA-framework (Section 4) is now ready for further MPSM activity.

4. THE PRELIMINARY ANALYSIS (PA) FRAMEWORK

The PA-framework is defined as the set = (Overview, Function-framework, Problem-framework, Requirements-framework, Assumptions).

4.1. The Function-framework (Ff)

The generic form of the Ff is defined as follows, using the hierarchy of e-levels:

e-level	System Name	Contents of System Set
0	Source	((Variables: Function, Context, Constraints), space-time resolution levels)
1	Data	((Source Systems: Function, Context, Constraints), activity matrices)
2	Functional	((Data Systems: Function, Context, Constraints), time invariant relations/ generating behaviours)
3	Micro	((Functional Systems: Function, Context, Constraints), coupling variables/relations)
4	Operation-I	((Micro Systems: Function, Context, Constraints), Managerial System-I)
5	Operation-II	((Operation-I Systems, Managerial System-II)
↓		

and so on

The Managerial System is defined here as the set = (Decision Procedures, Control Mechanisms).

4.2. The Problem-framework (Pf)

The Pf is in fact a "problem" subset of the Ff, as all the information in the Pf is contained in the Ff. It is extracted by applying some cause-effect analysis. Its generic form is defined as follows, using the hierarchy of e-levels:

e-level	System Name	Contents of System Set
0	Source	(Subset of Ff - Source System Set)
1	Data	(Subset of Ff - Data System Set)
2	Functional	(Subset of Ff - Functional System Set)
3	Micro	(Subset of Ff - Micro System Set)
4	Operation-I	(Subset of Ff - Operation-I System Set)
5	Operation-II	(Subset of Ff - Operation-II System Set)
↓		

and so on

Each System Set (at given e-level) is supplemented with notes identifying problem associated causal relations.

4.3. The Requirements-framework (Rf)

The Rf is defined on a subset of the Ff. It represents the imposition of performance and design constraints on the identified Operation Systems of the Process. The generic form of the Rf is as follows:

e-level	System Name	Contents of System Set
4	Operation-I	(Ff - Operation-I System Set, Requirements)
5	Operation-II	(Ff - Operation-II System Set, Requirements)
↓		

and so on

Requirements is defined as the set = ((Performance: Variables, Value Range), (Design: Varibles, Value Range)).

5. PA OUTPUTS

The PA Procedure described should result in the following:

(1) An identification of the overview of the Process, its environment and its constraints.

(2) A hierarchically organized identification of the functions of the Process, its environment/context and its constraints (the Ff).

(3) A hierarchically organized identification of the problematic cause and effect relations of the functions of the Process (the Pf).

(4) A hierarchically organized identification of the requirements on the functions of the Process (the Rf).

(5) A hierarchically organized identification of the assumptions underlying the PA and its framework.

The documentation would consist of a set of hierarchically organized system diagrams [1,5] and matching system notes [1,5].

5.1. PA Applications

Since early 1974, the PA concept as part of the MPSM has been adaptively developed by the author and used to successfully solve problems for several categories of Processes in the author's company. The Processes have included those for:
- provisioning of equipment capactiy [2,5];
- provisioning and maintenance of service on equipment capacity made available to customers [3];
- design and implementation of advanced technology systems [4];
- organizational change [7].

6. CONCLUSIONS

The PA presented here has passed [2,3,4,5,7] the acid tests of:
- Technical Feasibility
- Operational Feasibility
- Financial Feasibility

With further development and use, the PA Procedure could become more efficient, especially in the area of documentation.

The key to effective and efficient problem solving for Processes lies in the proper front-end statement of the problem and a coming together of the problem solvers' ideas. The significance of the methods here lies in the fact that individual problem solvers are aided not only in their thinking but also in their ability to communicate with each other. It is hoped that the PA Procedure presented here has added a little towards enhancing managerial problem solving capacilities.

REFERENCES

1. CHAKRABORTY, S., "A Managerial Problem Solving Methodology," Applied General Systems Research (G. Klir, ed.), Plenum Press, New York, 1978.
2. CHAKRABORTY, S., "Problem Solving for the Central Office Equipment Provisioning Process," Project Report No. AS1, NBTel, 1974.
3. CHAKRABORTY, S., "Problem Solving for the Maintenance Process," Project Report No. ASE2, NBTel, 1975.
4. CHAKRABORTY, S., "Problem Solving for the Switched Network Analysis Centre Interface System and Test Board System," CSE Project Guidelines, NBTel, 1976.
5. CHAKRABORTY, S., "Problem Solving for the Station Equipment Provisioning Process," SEPS Feasibility and Implementation Report, NBTel, 1976.
6. CHAKRABORTY, S., "Management Performance - the Acid Tests," Position Paper No. MRE, NBTel, 1976.
7. CHAKRABORTY, S., "Considerations and Notes on Proposed Organization Change," Organization Change Project Report, NBTel, 1977.
8. FRIEDMAN, G. J., "Constraint Theory: An Overview," International Journal of Systems Science, 1976, Vol. 7, No. 10, 1113-1151.
9. JOLLYMORE, P. G., "Memo - Engineering Technical Committee," TCTS Memo, NBTel, 1974.
10. KLIR, G. J., An Approach to General Systems Theory, Van Nostrand Reinhold, New York, 1969.
11. KLIR, G. J., "Identification of Generative Structures in Empirical Data," International Journal of General Systems, Vol. 3, No. 2, 1976, pp. 89-104.
12. KLIR, G. J. and H. J. J. UYTTENHOVE, "Computerized Methodology for Structure Modelling," Annals of Systems Research, 5, 1976, pp. 29-66.
13. ROSEN, R., "Complexity and Error in Social Dynamics," International Journal of General Systems, 1975, Vol. 2, pp. 145-148.

Application of multilevels system theory to management and organization

J. L. DESTOUCHES
Pierre and Marie Curie University, Paris, France

Every knowledge about a system can be obtained only be means of measurements. But generally one cannot perform on a system the measurements of all the observables which are to be known if one wants to make predictions. Measurements are restricted to the accessible observables. Moreover, in general a measurement perturbs the observed system. Therefore measuring a certain observable at a certain time prevents from knowing the values of other observables at the same time. This is related not only to the measurements made by means of apparatus, but chiefly to the socio-economical observables which can be reached only by means of inquiries or questionnaires and so on, and have to be known in management and organization. The model of a system must take into account these conditions brought in by the measurements taken in a broad meaning as I have mentioned above.

Besides, it can happen that a coherent and adequate model of a system fulfilling the conditions on the measurement above mentioned cannot be built up, and that only practical models describing adequately a part of the system can be constructed.

Let S be the system for which we try to elaborate a model and M_1, M_2,...,M_n the partial models that we are able to construct. Each one of them describes partly the system S and the partial description is adequate for an aspect of the system.

If two of these partial models are compatible, eventually after slight modifications they can be reduced to a single model including the two initial partial models. On the contrary, if two models, even after having been modified but nevertheless remaining adequate, are still incompatible, these two partial models are called irreducible.

Irreducible partial models are incompatible. A single coherent model including all of them, or even a coherent model including only two of them, cannot be elaborated. In the case where, for a system S, only n partial models M_1,M_2,...,M_n irreducible two by two have been constructed, I call such a system S an n-levels system. In particular a system is a two-levels system when the partial models needed for its description can be reduced to two, that is M_1 and M_2. These last two partial models are incompatible and contradictory; otherwise a coherent model M (non-contradictory) could not be built up, M_1 and M_2 being its parts.

The first example of such two-levels systems have been provided by physics, in kinetic theory of gases and in classical or quantum statistical mechanics, where two-scales descriptions occur, one scale being microphysical, the other macrophysical. The coherence between the two descriptions is not feasible at first sight. But such a situation appears in many other domains.

Taking into consideration multi-levels system can be useful to describe concrete systems, especially in management and organization. Indeed, facing tasks or prescriptions which at first sight include contradiction, one can use a successful method by describing coherent partial systems using models M_1,M_2,...,M_n which cover the various aspects of the system S. In the following step, two or more among these partial models are connected. Taking into consideration the presuppositions above, such connections can be established without contradiction, but only in the following way:

(1) either by a modification of logic [1] making weaker the rules of reasoning in order to eliminate the initial contradictions (this is in particular the case when there are non simultaneously measurable observables); or

(2) by replacing certain functional relations involving contradictions by stochastic relations, that is by introducing random variables.

In the practical cases dealt with in management, it is preferable, because more adequate, to keep up the classical bivalent logic in the partial models M_1,M_2,...,M_n, and to introduce random variables to connect them together. Making the partial models compatible by means of stochastic relations instead of functional ones, a global model M describing the system as a whole can be set up.

In every particular case it is advisable to choose carefully the way of introducing the random variables and the conditions to be assigned to them.

Among the examples that we have met of such problems, most typical are that of the management of a hospital, dealt with by P. Février and F. Doare [2], and that of the decentralization of a system by D. Leccas [3]. But the above method can be applied in many other cases.

REFERENCES

1. FEVRIER, P., "Adéquation et développement dialectique des théories physiques," C. R. Acad. Sc. Paris, 224, 807, 10 mars 1947.
2. FEVRIER, P., "An Application of Two-Levels System Theory to a Problem of Management and Organisation".
3. LECCAS, D., "Application of System Theory to Problem of Decentralization".

Management information systems, a system for design

R. ESPEJO and J. WATT
University of Aston, Birmingham, England

INTRODUCTION

This paper aims to give direction to MIS design research rather than to provide a "solution". It gives a brief review of the evolution and current state of MIS design attempting at the same time to support the need for a true systemic approach. Such a systemic approach forms the basis for the main part of the paper which focuses on certain crucial aspects of systemic design.

THE PROBLEM

After at least a quarter of a century of conscious effort there is to be found little evidence that we are able to design and implement management information and control systems possessing a minimum predictable level of effectiveness. This is not to say that there do not exist some apparently satisfactorily effective systems. (When Bleriot's machine flew across the Channel there were many more designs which did not even leave the ground.)

The information systems we shall be referring to here are those above what is commonly called "operational level". Operational level is generally taken to mean the activities at the periphery of the production and managerial levels where there is in a limited sense a one-to-one matching of variety; for each order there is an invoice, for each worker there is a pay slip, for each product, a stock card. Above this level we have:

a. an increasing difficulty in perceiving the states of the system that leads to;

b. an increasing need for reduction of variety, that is an increasing degree of selection, blocking and filtering.

We would suggest that the problem with design arises from our failure to develop a true general theory of system design that maps usefully onto the real world and more specifically our failure to come to terms with the questions of variety and viability in systems.

1. THE EVOLUTION OF MIS DESIGN APPROACHES

A brief review of MIS design approaches is necessary to place the main message of this paper in context. We can perceive two main streams; the first, which we will call the applied approaches, focuses on the machine together with systematic guidelines for analysis; the second stream, which might be termed the theoretical approaches perhaps mainly because they have had small impact upon applications, focuses upon the organisation.

The first computer applications in business from the early 1950's till the early 1960's were essentially mechanisation of existing clerical systems, a few steps beyond the punch card systems of the time. They were involved almost entirely in facilitating the activities at the operational level that we have previously defined. From such applications various collations of "management information" could also be derived; frequently this was complete listings rather than exceptions or "distillations". By the early 1960's such applications were sufficiently numerous and complex to make it obvious that some systematisation of the "design" process was necessary and there rapidly grew, starting in external consultancies, a variety of "systems approaches". The basis of these approaches is a methodical check list of project steps or phases usually coupled with a breaking down of the organisation into functions such as production planning and control or distribution for which packaged designs can be produced. Typical of this approach is the framework outlined by Optner [18]. Add to this the data base approach of the late 1960's and you have the basic of most MIS design work being carried out in practice.

By and large these designs support the generation of whatever information could come out of already existing operational applications instead of asking first what information is relevant to management so that consequent systems could be designed. In this context MIS, instead of filtering relevant information out of the large complexity of organisational situations, are proliferating data of perhaps irrelevant (for management) operational dimensions. Ackoff's analysis of management mis-information systems [1], Beer's contention that present systems are doing precisely the wrong thing for management, i.e. proliferating variety where it should be filtered [7], or Simon's empirical observation that by and large MIS are not used by managers [20] are but a few of the references to this unfortuned evolution of information systems.

With the increased use of exception reporting techniques and the enquiry facilities of on-line date-bases this problem is somewhat reduced. Nevertheless, it is clear from the literature that data-base has not satisfied the need for effective information at higher levels of management (Alter [2]; Appleton [4]), and some of the logical and unavoidable reasons for this can be found in a recent paper by Crowe and Jones [11]. The second stream of approaches dates back in the main to the mid-1960's when, with the availability of larger machines, organisational data processing swung towards centralised systems. Computers were to provide the sort of control for larger organisations that the small business under one man had always had. Manifestly this dream did not materialise but concurrent with move towards centralisation came an increased awareness of the organisation as a whole. At that point it was perceived that MIS were closely inter-related to organisational changes and that they could not be viewed any longer independently of organisational behaviour. We see a rapid growth in the literature dealing with behavioural approaches to the implementation of effective systems and "system approaches" attempting to provide models of organisational structure and/or behaviour for MIS design.

The behavioural or organisational development response is well illustrated by Demb [12] which gives a summary of expert opinion in the field. Centralised systems are held, among other things, to lead to rigidity and inflexibility in the organisation, to give inadequate response to local needs, to decrease incentive and job satisfaction at local level, to increase communication and co-ordination difficulties and to increase problems associated with data security and system failure.

The parallel response involving the attempts to develop organisational models for MIS design have implicit in them the realisation that most MIS design approaches do not give significant attention to the intended function of these systems within the organisation (Zani, [23]).

Examples of such approaches can be found in Blumenthal [9] and Schoderbek et. al. [21] and the extent to which the need is seen by business is shown by the extensive literature on corporate modelling; useful surveys of modelling literature and model applications are to be found in Naylor [17] and Grinyer and Wooller [15].

What is of most concern to us is that even for those information systems in which there is a clear awareness of their organisational embedding the underlying organisational models supporting design are chiefly empirical, thus unconcerned with the basic principles and laws relevant to systems striving for their viability in complex, uncertain environments. It is our view that because of this very fact MIS have had little, if not negative, impact upon organisation effectiveness. It is our contention that a conscious effort toward a general theory for effective design of MIS implies understanding and applying principles supporting self-regulation and self-organisation in complex organisations. In this direction, Beer's design of a regulatory system for the Chilean economy [8] is perhaps the most outstanding, if not unique, applications of this organismic approach. It is our aim in this paper to build upon that design.

2. A SYSTEM FOR DESIGN

2.1. A Conceptual Framework

It is the complexity of the whole and not of management alone that defines the level at which environmental complexity is matched by the

organisation, i.e. its level of performance. For management it is important to understant that complex systems are by and large self-regulating and self-organising. This is in itself a powerful way to increase managerial capacity to handle information for control purposes, yet it may not be enough. Designing information systems may be a necessary addition if managerial control capacity is going to support effectively the organisational response to present environmental challenges.

2.1.1. Self-Regulation

Self-regulation means that as long as there are some references for organisational behaviour the different organisational parts will develop naturally the relevant information flows to control each others' behaviour. This is imminent to the purpose of viability of complex organisations. However, because social organisations are artificial systems, i.e. design is necessary to achieve desirable outputs (Simon [19]), it is not enough to rely on self-regulation. It is necessary to design regulation capacity consistent with a desirable level of performance. Failing this, the Law of Requisite Variety (Ashby [3]) will assert itself and tasks will be achieved only at a level consistent with the existing organisational complexity.

Information systems that do not recognise self-regulating processes may constrain or disturb this imminent control capacity, thus reducing the complexity of the organisation and hence its effectiveness in achieving tasks. We recognise that this interference in the internal organisational processes is likely to spring back in the form of human frustration, a hallmark of our present institutions.

Thus, we suggest that information systems design should take into account these natural processes. If so, a first task is to recognise the internal regulatory processes in a complex organisation. Beer's second model [6] of the organisation structure of viable systems is a platform for this purpose (see Appendix for a brief description of this model). It is a model of the many regulatory loops that are necessary and sufficient to make a system viable. For each of these loops it is necessary to design:

a. _Requisite Variety_: The level at which balance should be achieved between interacting systems. The information system should be designed consistently with the agreed references for system behaviour.

b. _Channel Capacity_: Regulatory capacity is limited to the variety that can be handled by the available communication channels. They should be designed so that requisite variety between interacting systems is made possible.

c. _Transduction Capacity_: Regulatory capacity is not only limited by channel capacity but also by the capacity of a system to interpret the variety of its regulator. Thus, transduction capacity should be designed wherever information crosses a system's boundary.

In the end the overall complexity of information systems is a function of the references for behaviour, i.e. what the organisation chooses to do. More complex tasks imply a larger information handling capacity. Definition or identification of these references permits the development of measures of performance considering both the present and future viability of the organisation. These measures are in permanent change due to environmental disturbances. Monitoring performance is the focus of our design.

2.1.2. Self-Organisation

Further information design criteria spring out of self-organisation. While self-regulation concerns the performance of the system with respect to a given set of references, the organisational capacity to structure and change these references involves the process of self-organisation. This is a mechanism for survival in the long run. Organisational mechanisms emerge to cope with the several areas of complexity that are perceived as relevant. The organisational structure is continuously adapting. One of the most powerful mechanisms permiting adaptation is the allocation of discretion to organisational parts. If this allocation of discretion implies to give a relative autonomy to the parts so that they are able to respond to unforeseen situations, de facto, the system is structuring within itself a new systems level. This new level is logically faced with the same managerial problem as the overall system; it has to develop a viable organisation.

Self-regulation and self-organisation are necessary at this new level as well. The new system is recursive to the original one. The unfolding of recursion levels is a major design mechanism to make viable artificial systems.

It follows then that the design of information systems that support the achieving of effective interactions between system levels is of paramount relevance. It is in a way supporting the level of synergy that the parts may achieve in the context of the whole. The higher is the autonomy of the sub-systems the more complex they are and therefore the larger is the demand over the systems control capacity. This is a consequence of the Law of Requisite Variety. However, if control, in these conditions, is actually achieved the higher will be the synergy of the system. The more we impose constraints over the sub-systems autonomy the lower will be the synergy of the system. However, too much autonomy without matching control capacity destroys synergy. Information systems which increase management control capacity may support a higher level of organisational synergy.

3. THE FRAMEWORK; FOCUSING ON SOME ASPECTS OF DESIGN

So far it has been suggested that information systems design cannot ignore self-regulation and self-organisation processes in social organisations. Both are natural processes in complex systems, however, because of the artificial character of social organisations design should facilitate their development. As said before, this proposition is not new. It underlies Beer's design for Allende's Government in Chile (Beer [7,8]; Barrientos and Espejo [5]; Schwember [22]).

Beer's concern was designing a comprehensive regulatory system for the Chilean economy. His conception was not of a management information system for top decision makers but a comprehensive design of information flows, communication channels and transducers for the multiple layers of management in that complex situation. It does not seem necessary to repeat in the present context its design logic and practical implementation. The reader is referred to the above mentioned publications. We shall assume the reader's acquaintance with this work and draw upon that experience to do an in-depth analysis of one particular aspect of the design vital to make it practical; we are referring to structuring "indices" to control organisational behaviour in real time and by exception.

Beer's design is indeed very powerful as long as it is understood how to design meaningful indices. They are in his framework the elementary bricks supporting the building of information for organisational management. They have the meaning of physiological measures like the body temperature of the blood pressure; they have a profound systemic meaning.

Perhaps it is convenient to say a few words about these indices before we get involved in their analysis. Essentially they are measures of performance relevant to any organisational operation. In Figure 1 we have a diagrammatical definition of these indices.

What is done today, the actuality, is compared with what could have been done, considering present level of resources and operational constraints, if everything had been optimally organised, i.e. the capability. This gives the so-called index of productivity. If we remove constraints and allocate resources we should acheive a better value than capability. This is potentiality. The index of latency is a measure of possible organisational development considering resources that are present but not yet active. The index of performance integrates present behaviour with future possibilities. A detailed analysis of these indices is in Brain of the Firm (Beer [6]), so we shall not go deeper in their definition. It just seems necessary to point out the relevance of capability as a "systemic" concept central to to the definition of indices. While potentiality is basically a normative value, and actuality is a fluctuating value, capability is a measure of the present organisational resources. Its value can only be defined once it is understood the way other systemic activities affect the particular activity being measured. Thus, the designed capacity of a machine is not its capability if, for instance, other machines (interacting with this one) do not permit it to reach that value.

4. ON THE NATURE OF OBJECTIVES

We shall relate the concept of indices to the widely used concept of system objectives. In this discussion we aim to elucidate some systemic characteristics of objectives and problems related to their measurement.

The idea of system objectives has pervaded most of the literature concerned with planning and management of complex organisations. Systems are designed to achieve objectives. Though there are good reasons to think in this way in most real world situations objectives seem to be very

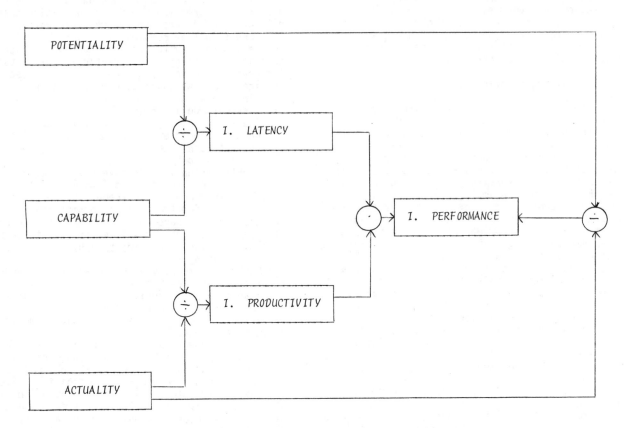

Figure 1.   Measure of Performance: Beer's Indices

elusive. It is common experience to find a sub-stantial gap between objectives as stated and real behaviour. This perception has led in some cases to the view of questioning the usefulness of the concept of objectives in systems analysis (Checkland [10]); social systems are "soft" as opposed to the "hardness" natural, for instance, to engineering designs, and only for the latter are objectives meaningful.

In our view, the apparent shortcoming of the concept is more because we have failed to under-stand its systemic meaning than to its limitations in modelling real behaviour. It is precisely because of the sheer complexity of social organ-isations that we think objectives are necessary in any managerial process. This is implicit in the ideas of self-regulation and self-organisation. Management cannot possibly get into the details of the system under its concern. It is to a larger or lesser degree a black box. The variety or number of possible states of this box is far greater than that of management, yet, because of the Law of Requisite Variety, both varieties should be matched. Otherwise the box is out of control. Managerial strategies to cope with this situation are simultaneously to reduce the com-plexity of the box and increase its own complexity. Objectives are an instrument to reduce situational variety. Of the multiple possible alternatives just a few are chose for Figure 2.

Objectives have two apparent characteristics in this model:

a. They are references for systems behaviour. Self-Regulation in the black box should permit the achieving of outputs as close as possible to the references defined by the objectives. Objectives so defined are instruments for the control of systemic behaviour. Management does not need to get into the black box as long as there is a feed-back mechanism capable of changing inputs so that outputs keep close to objectives.

b. They are focused in the receiving systems, i.e. environment (Morasky [16]). Objectives imply a change in the environment. The extent of this change is a result of the reciprocal interaction between the system and its environment. More than defining objectives, the managerial problem is _to find_ them out for control purposes. Implicit in this statement is the recognition that objectives are what the system _is doing_ now and not its intentions or aims as they are normally considered. Managerial capacity to define objectives is in decisions that lead to new levels of output either by changing capabilities and/or organising better system activities.

Yet there is another characteristic of objec-tives not apparent in the above model. This is a logical conclusion of the recursive nature of Beer's model (see Appendix). If the black box under managerial concern is a viable system, it must have sub-systems that are also viable systems. At this new level management itself and therefore the logical necessity for objectives is the same as before (see Figure 3).

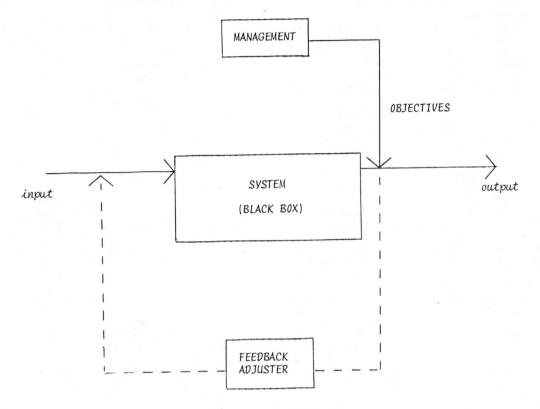

Figure 2. System Objectives

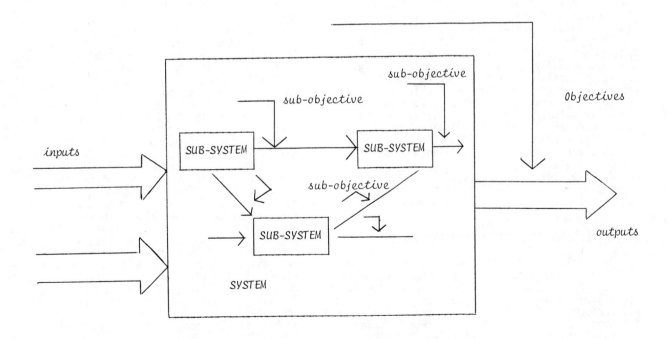

Figure 3. Principle of Decomposition of Objectives

The unfolding into sub-objectives, and of sub-objectives into sub-sub-objectives, is referred here as the principle of decomposition of objectives. This principle has important implications, as we shall see later, in the process of defining indices. It gives us a systemic tool to aggregate and disaggregate objectives. It is clear that objectives at one level of recursion are a function of objectives at the lower level, and the other way around.

To. sum up, we may say that management is on the one hand in the continuous process of monitoring system's behaviour around objectives or states of the structural stability and on the other to adapt and change objectives in response to environmental disturbances. Perhaps it is necessary to reinforce the idea that when we refer to management we are thinking of the several managerial levels implicit in the recursive logic of our organisational model. Thus, the control of behaviour around objectives implies a complex web of references pervading the whole organisation. We are clearly not thinking in a top-down or bottom-up approach as it may be inferred from the logic of objectives unfolding. The states of structural stability are the result of multiple interactions over time and not of sequential processes. In our social organisations it is not uncommon that objectives are not formally defined; there are even cases of complete unawareness of what these objectives are. It may be the role of a systems scientist to make them apparent by studying the particular organisation as a viable system.

Following the above argument we do not agree with those suggesting that a necessary characteristic of objectives is that they must be formal, explicit statements (Morasky [16]). Because they are of a systemic nature, evolving over time, any formalisation even if there is a good systemic understanding is bound to be outdated soon by the natural process of adaptation to environmental disturbances. Perhaps exception to this proposition are "goal oriented systems". In this case it is clear that there is an explicit aim to have a large degree of control over the environment, so that the objective is achieved as defined, e.g. public programs. However, in general we may expect that a formal statement of objectives introduces an unnecessary rigidity to organisational capacity for adaptation. It is not unusual to see managers sticking to out-dated objectives. This is particularly clear if we think in traditional planning systems, with fixed horizons (Espejo [13]).

Once we study the concept of "indices" we shall come back to objectives so that we can finish our discussion of their systemic nature.

5. PROBLEM-SOLVING AND INFORMATION SYSTEMS

Discussing the nature of objectives has helped us to focus managerial concerns on the concept of references for behaviour. Continuous monitoring of sub-systems interactions, as well as their individual performance is central to the managerial control function. Decisions and control are two fundamental dimensions of this activity. Decisions imply "many to one" transformations. The multiple possible states of each sub-system are finally reduced to one state, e.g. a planning decision. Control, on the other hand, implies "one to many" transformations, i.e. high variety specific to the situation to be controlled. There are several different ways to do these transformations, and they are by no means equally effective. If some ways are more effective than others it is worth having criteria of effectiveness. Our contention is that control in real time and by exception of references for behaviour or objectives using Beer's indices is a powerful paradigm for these purposes. In Simon's terminology it is a powerful way to increase problem solving capabilities of humans in non-programmed situations (Simon [20]).

We have several reasons supporting this contention:

a. Indices are effective means to attenuate situational variety. This is in much contrast to the more popular practice of over-loading management with indigestible data. Indices play a similar role to vital signals in the human body, e.g. blood pressure. They are continuously integrating a large amount of physiological data. Only if necessary, i.e. when indices get out of their physiological limits, the brain becomes aware of the need for problem solving. Clever computer design may increase brain capacity to detect "would be" problems by using short term forecasting techniques (Beer [8]).

b. Indices operating in real time increase brain capacity for pattern recognition. A set of indices permits the appreciation of complex situations as a result of their synergistic interaction in managers' brains. Time is a major dimension along which variety proliferates. Indices measuring in real time several activities of a system imply a powerful filtering of the multiple possibilities implicit in the dynamics of each of these activities. The transformations happening within the system become potentially more transparent to management, thus increasing its capacity for pattern recognition.

c. Exception reports of indices behaviour provide management with a powerful search tool. Instead of designing information systems to collect all the data that might be necessary, indices point out over time the particular dimensions for which "one to many" transformations are necessary, i.e. high variety specific to the problem under concern.

d. Indices of performance related to the several sub-systems of a given level of recursion can be effective instruments to support self-regulation. This is because indices follow a systemic logic (principle of decomposition) thus permitting to each sub-system to know in real time and by exception relevant changes of other sub-systems. In our present organisations this problem of sub-systems co-ordination is by and large left to mechanisms lacking in requisite variety, e.g. periodical meetings (while changes happen all the time) and to informal information transfer mechanisms. A consequence of this behaviour is the need for large "slack resources" reducing organisational performance. Effective problem solving implies dissolving problems, i.e. effective self-regulation.

6. MEASUREMENT, INDICES DESIGN

Our previous discussion related organisational objectives to indices of performance. In addition, we have suggested that indices may have a fairly important role in problem solving and controlling organisational operations. Our task now is studying the design of indices for real situations. We shall rely for this purpose on the Chilean project. However, we should say from the outset that the problem of defining indices with a systemic logic still requires further research and experiment.

A simplified methodology for indices design is suggested in what follows:

a. Organisational Modelling: Supported by Beer's model the recursive structure of the organisation under concern is defined. For instance, for a firm a first level of recursion may be defined by the divisions "doing" what the firm is all about. Within each division we may have several plants, they define the second level of recursion. Within the plants we may have several sections "doing" what the plants are supposed to do. The break-down is done as many times as it is necessary for design purposes. (See Figure 4.)

b. Operational Modelling: This implies the "doing" of each recursion level. At this step modelling is focused on the different processes producing organisational output at each recursion level. These models are expressed by "quantified flowcharts". Their sophistication may vary from highly sophisticated simulation models to very crude observational modelling. However, their usefulness depends upon the definition of indices which gives true measure of internal activities. (See Figure 5.)

c. Choosing Indices: The idea of references for behaviour is helpful to understand the nature of the control function in complex organisations. They give a focus to choose indices. There is no simple rule to choose them. The set of necessary indices to support control at any given time is basically a learning process. The more we understand the nature of interactions between a system and the receiving systems, i.e. environment, the better prepared we are to choose relevant indices. In the end we have to design as many indices as it is perceived necessary to control the balanced interaction of the system and its receiving systems. Certainly transformation of references into indices implies a good understanding of "doing" processes and their "metabolism". Indices of productivity are measures of what the system is doing and could be doing in relation to its receiving systems. For management the internal transactions of the black box are of no interest as long as it can keep control of the critical variables. Because output is multi-dimensional we may need several indices to support effective control. For instance, even for very simple processes, we may want to know about quantity, quality and cost. That immediately suggests three sets of indices to control that process. In the Chilean project five to ten sets of indices were designed per black box. Concern was in production output and not in financial performance. Thus, mainly production indices were designed.

d. Atomic Indices: Indices are first defined for the elementary processes in the organisation.

There are a number of problems involved in this definition. We have to answer properly questions like:

What do we measure?
How often do we measure?
Which are the references for measurement?

When it is suggested that indices are related to the output of processes it is not necessarily meant that we are measuring outflows. In practice it may well be that the variety of outputs makes impossible the task of reducing them to a set of consistent indices. The problem is to measure whatever gives a natural integration of multiple states. As long as we measure something that reflects the black box level of activity we do not need to be concerned with the large variety in which this activity might finally be expressed, i.e. many different products. For instance, in a textile factory, with a large variety of outputs in each process, it does not make sense to structure indices for each of these outputs. Considering that changes in product mix are happening all the time fluctuations in the behaviour of the indices would make impossible the idea of indices with a stable behaviour to support control by exception (we say that these indices do not have a physiological behaviour). Instead, it is possible to define few indices related to basic operations that are common to all products, e.g. use of looms; measured by the number of elementary operations in a given time, registered by inbuilt counters. By the same token measures of daily output in a tyre plant, with a large variety of products, are poorly reflected by the actual number of tyres produced. The physiology of that plant is better represented by elementary operations in the process, e.g. use of tyre presses, for which a clear capability can be defined.

In general, a systemic understanding of operations is necessary before reliable indices can be defined. A trivial example, however illustrative, is measuring the output of production by the number of items arriving at a warehouse. Unless we are talking of a continuous process, that measure would be non-physiological, just because it may well be that production is delayed outside the warehouse, while inside we are reporting a drop in production.

The overall problem of "where" to measure and "what" was considered in the Chilean project as part of the necessary concern for "integrity of the input" to the information system. Several trials were necessary for each index before achieving a "physiological" measurement. Historical time series help in this task.

How often do we measure? No doubt a third dimension to the "integrity of input" is "how often" do we measure. In theory for a system in real time, measures are done all the time and exceptions reported as soon as something happens. In practice for non-continuous processes this is impossible. Thus understanding the natural rhythm of a process is necessary. In the Chilean project most of these measures could be done on a daily basis, i.e. that was their natural rhythm, or in other words, it was found that daily measures had a structural stability around a mean value. However, for other operations, i.e. timber production, it was found that the natural

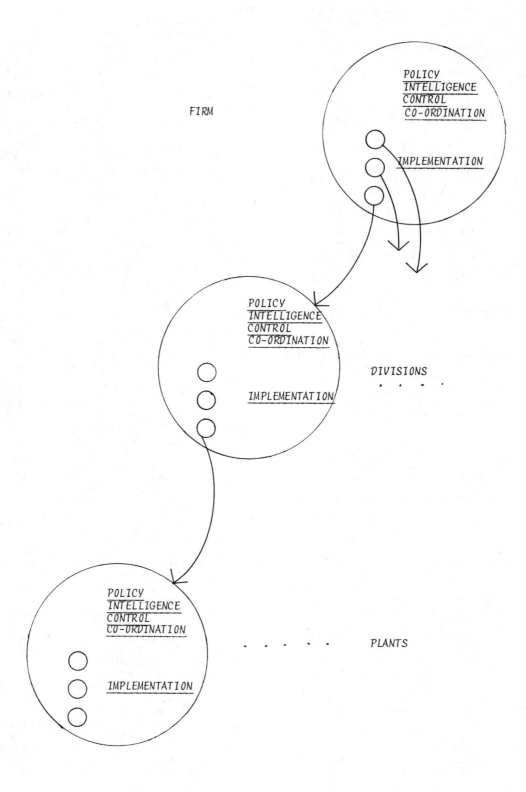

Figure 4. Organizational Modelling

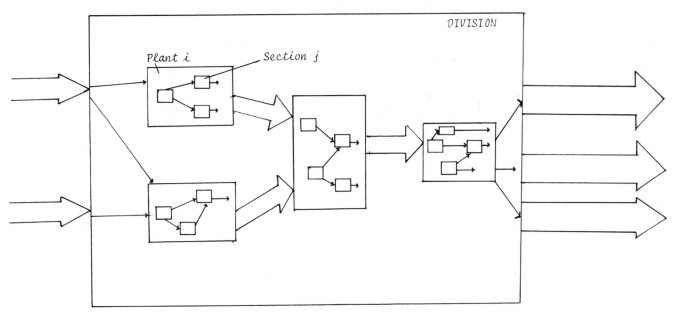

Figure 5. Quantified Flowchart

rhythm was every two or three days. In addition
to these variations, for each index it was
necessary to consider organisational factors,
e.g. the number of working hours was not the
same each day.

Yet another factor central to indices and
their physiological behaviour is the definition
of "capability". Because it is a "systemic"
value its definition implies a good understanding
of "relationships" relevant to the process under
concern. It should not be confused with "capacity",
essentially a "design" value that is not necessarily concerned with the organisational context
in which a process is done. Capability aims to
capture the idea of functional capacity of a
process. This is a physiological measure taking
into account resources, technology and organisation. If resources and technology are optimally
organised (for the given process) we have the
value of capability. Because capability is defined
by a given organisation it does not necessarily
have a constant value over time, e.g. for a
machine, programmed maintenance is clearly an
organisational aspect to be considered in defining
capability. For practical purposes we can say
that capability is the best ever measure of a
variable representative of a given process.
However, this crude definition has to evolve in
parallel to a better understanding of the systemic
nature of the process. This understanding is
partly achieved in the process of structuring
indices from the point of view of their physiology.
Once an index is defined -- the integrity of its
input and the value of its capability studied --
its behaviour over time should be fairly stable
around a mean value. Of course, changes in the
mean or significant trends departing from it are
"relevant" information for management.

If, on the contrary, it is recognised that the

behaviour of the index does not follow any stable
pattern, it should be studied again until a
physiological behaviour is found (see Figure 6).
In the Chilean project for most of the indices
it was necessary several iterations before a
reasonable behaviour was found.

e. Molecular Indices: Atomic indices are
defined for simple operations at low recursion
levels. However, implicit in the model we have
unfolded is the possibility of defining indices
of the same nature, i.e. physiological, for
higher recursion levels. They are measures to
control outputs of more complex operations.
Early in the Chilean project the need to aggregate atomic indices into molecular ones was
discussed. Some people had the idea that with
present computer capabilities it was not necessary to do this aggregation. However, that view
did not take into account the structural implications of that alternative. Recursion levels are
not arbitrary definitions. They are the result
of an organisational strategy to deal with
environmental complexity. The limited control
capacity of each managerial level is amplified
by the distribution of discretion to lower system
levels. This empirical limitation is responsible
for systems within systems and therefore for
references for behaviour at multiple structural
levels. Thus, measurement to support control
is necessary. The alternative, i.e. only
atomic indices, would imply either that higher
recursion levels cannot benefit from this regulatory system or the belief that control can be
exercised with only one unfolding of objective
into sub-objectives. The latter view is contrary
to our empirical observation. Thus, it is necessary to tackle the problem of aggregation. This
was, in the end, what was done in the Chilean
project. There is no simple algorithm or rule

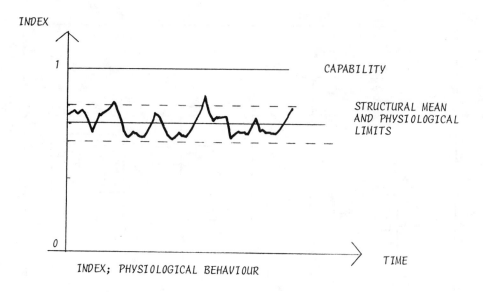

INDEX; PHYSIOLOGICAL BEHAVIOUR

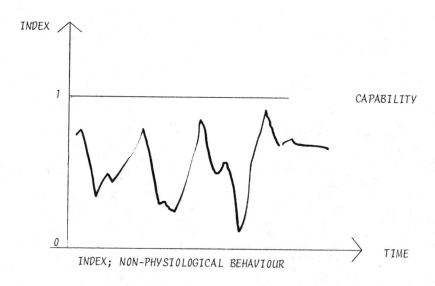

INDEX; NON-PHYSIOLOGICAL BEHAVIOUR

Figure 6. Index Behaviour

for this purpose. As we move to higher levels of recursion it is more difficult to do the "many to one" transformations. Physiological behaviour of indices is a useful approach to validate whether aggregations have followed systemic criteria.

For some production processes the problem is easier than for others. For instance, in Chile for the textile industry it was fairly easy to develop molecular indices. The main processes, i.e. weaving, spinning, are in a single line within each firm and the different firms of the industry had little connectivity. This is

explained in the flow chart of Figure 7.

Molecular indices for the whole industry could be structured just by addition.

Another simple situation for aggregation is provided by production processes with fixed bottlenecks. They define the capability for the whole system.

However, the most general situation is that of several processes, producing several services and/or products, with a complex network of relationships. For this situation the capability is a function of the particular product mix

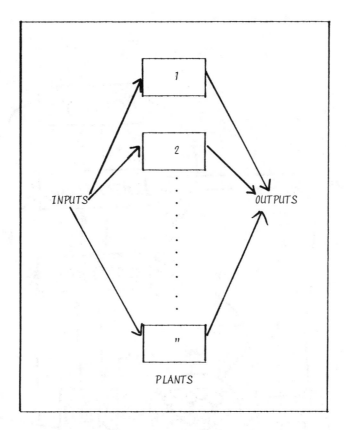

Figure 7. Aggregation: Parallel Processes

in process and also is very sensitive to different organisational arrangements. Bottlenecks, if any, may be a function of the product mix. In this situation capability is defined by a complex algorithm function of several parameters changing over time. Several of these algorithms were developed in the Chilean project (Gabella [14]). These algorithms are context bound and each one by itself could be the subject of a paper.

7. DISCUSSION

Our logic for designing information systems is resting with the systemic fact that references for behaviour are necessary at all levels within an organisation. These are our objectives.

In some managerial situations it may happen that there is no awareness of references for behaviour, though objectives in their traditional sense may well be defined by several plans. We think that in this situation management may have difficulties in exercising effective control. Dimensions of control are blurred by the organisational complexity.

Objectives or references for behaviour as presented here support one fundamental point; what matters is what the system does and not what it claims. In the end we are saying that references for behaviour are the systemic expression of objectives and their control is facilitated by indices measuring what the organisation does:

This gives a platform for adaptation.

It is clear that objectives are normally perceived as aims related to given time horizons. In practice they are either general statements that imply nothing or if they are specific enough to permit interpretation there is a tendency in management to stick to them as if they were "objective" statements of unchangeable truth:

This gives a platform for maladjustment.

In our organisational model (Appendix), while the future is the concern of the intelligence function at each level of recursion, the present is the concern of the control function. The effective integration of these two concerns implies a policy process. This is the process by which future and present capabilities are integrated in a permanent adaptation to the environment. In the end we know that organisational performance is a function of the effective transformation of policies (perhaps the so-called objectives) into operational capacity. This implies a continuous adaptation of system capabilities to the nature of the tasks in order to preserve viability. In this context references for behaviour are continuously changing. Our information system is an instrument to control this adaptive process. Thus, an objective -- measured by indices -- while defining the situation as it is now, is implicitly supporting a continuous assessment of the situation's future.

It is interesting to see that for "goal oriented" systems we have the other side of the

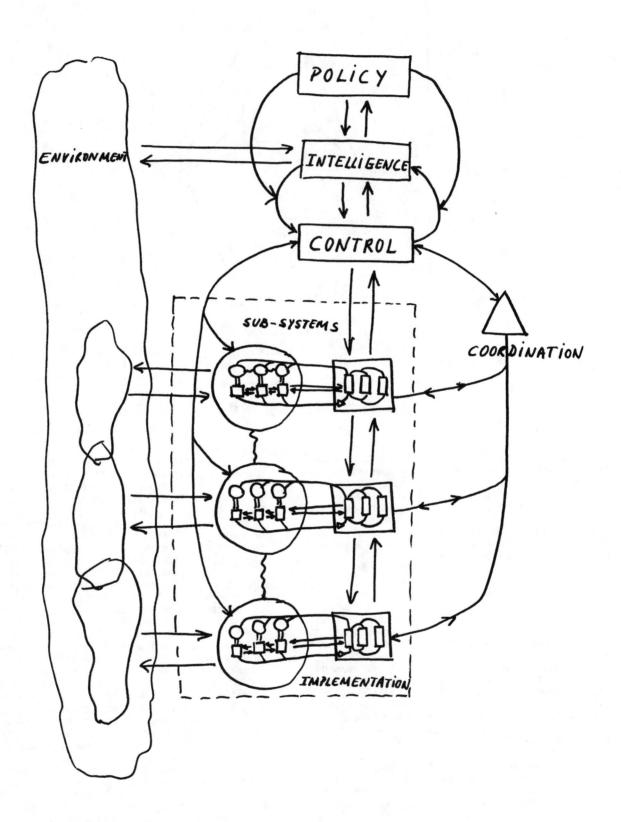

Figure 8.   (see Appendix)

coin, the organisational capabilities are changed so that "objectives" are achieved as defined.

A practical application of the framework presented in this paper was the "regulatory" system designed for the Chilean economy. However, it is clear that still there are several design aspects that need further research. We pose the problem of how practical is this approach for systems "softer" than manufacturing activities. For instance, it may be quite difficult to design indices for a "social services" department in a local authority. Yet, from the conceptual point of view, it is equally true that also in these services managers should aim to control situations that are far more complex than management itself. Thus, the need for references for behaviour . . .

APPENDIX

Beer's Model of the Organisational
Structure of Viable Systems

A very short summary of Beer's model is presented in what follows. A system is viable if it is capable to respond to environmental changes even if they were not foreseen at the time the system was designed.

If a system is to be viable it needs to develop five basic functions:
- a. Policy
- b. Intelligence
- c. Control
- d. Co-ordination
- e. Implementation

These are necessary and sufficient for systems viability. The policy function implies a systemic capacity to choose few among the multiple possible responses to environmental disturbances. For this purpose it needs an intelligence function scanning the environment, structuring problem situations, identifying opportunities and threats. However, it is not enough for the policy function to have a good filter of environmental situations. It also needs information about the internal situation of the system. This information is provided by the control function. The effective implementation of policies is the responsibility of this function. In this sense it should support policy decisions well rooted in reality. The control of the implementation of policies implies the responsibility for resource allocation, and of course the control and monitoring over time of implementing activities. A major organisational strategy to make viable the policies of a system is to give discretion to sub-systems for carrying out particular areas of policy. These sub-systems, actually doing what the system is supposed to do, are the parts of the implementation function. What is central to this function is the degree of autonomy that sub-systems can exercise while implementing policies. The extremes of centralisation and decentralisation are clearly non-viable. The autonomy of sub-systems implies that they themselves have to develop viable organisations. The control function cannot possibly consider in advance their response to all environmental disturbances. The complexity of the environment is too large. Sub-systems should develop internal capacity to respond to

all environmental disturbances. The complexity of the environment is too large. Sub-systems should develop internal capacity to respond to unforeseen situations, i.e. they should develop a viable organisation. Finally, sub-systems, to a larger or lesser degree, are operationally interconnected. Because of their autonomy they are bound to take unco-ordinated decisions. There is no mathematical algorithm or computer capacity to predefine with complete precision their interfaces. As an on-going process this is the role of the co-ordination function. It is a damping mechanism.

Perhaps the most central aspect of this model is the replication of the overall organisational structure in each of the parts, i.e. the sub-systems. This is the recursive property of this model. This implies that the whole is encapsulated in the parts.

The linkages between the five functions, and the interaction of the system with its environment, are schematically presented in Figure 8. These linkages and interactions define the multiple regulatory loops that should be carefully considered to understand systems behaviour.

REFERENCES

1. ACKOFF, R., "Management Mis-information Systems," Management Science, December, 1967.
2. ALTER, S. L., "How Effective Managers Use Information Systems," Harvard Business Review, November-December, 1976.
3. ASHBY, W. R., An Introduction to Cybernetics, London, Methuen, 1964.
4. APPLETON, D. S., "What Data Base Isn't," Datamation, January, 1977.
5. BARRIENTOS and ESPEJO, "A Cybernetic Model for the Management of the Industrial Sector," National Research Institute, Review Number 4, June, 1973 (in Spanish).
6. BEER, S., Brain of the Firm, London, Allen House, 1972.
7. BEER, S., "Cybernetics of National Development," The Zaheer Lecture, Zaheer Science Foundation, New Delhi, December, 1974.
8. BEER, S., Platform for Change, London, Wiley, 1975.
9. BLUMENTHAL, S. C., Management Information Systems, Prentice-Hall, New Jersey, 1969.
10. CHECKLAND, P., "The Problem of Problem Formulation," Applied General Systems Research, Plenum Press, New York, 1977.
11. CROWE, T. and J. H. JONES, "Potential Fallacies in the Design and Use of Data Basis," Computer Bulletin, December, 1974.
12. DEMB, A. B., "Centralised versus Decentralised Computer Systems: A New Approach to Organisational Impacts," CISR Report 12, Sloan W. P., 818-75, Cambridge, Mass., 1975.
13. ESPEJO, R., "A Cybernetic Paradigm for Organisational Assessment," Proceedings of Third European Meeting on Cybernetics and Systems Research, Vienna, 1976.
14. GABELLA, H., Tecnica de la Flujogramacion Cuantificada, CORFO Press, Chile, 1973.
15. GRINYER, P. and T. WOOLER, Corporate Models Today: A New Tool for Financial Management,

Institute of Chartered Accountants, London, 1975.

16. MORASKY, R. L., "Defining Goals - A Systems Approach," Long Range Planning, Volume 10, Number 2, 1977.

17. NAYLOR, T. H., "A Conceptual Framework for Corporate Modelling and the Results of a Survey of Current Practice," Operational Research Quarterly, 17 (3), 1976.

18. OPTNER, S. L., Systems Analysis for Business Management, Prentice-Hall, New Jersey, 1975.

19. SIMON, H., The Sciences of the Artificial, M.I.T. Press, 1969.

20. SIMON, H., The New Science of Management Decision, revised edition, Prentice-Hall, New Jersey, 1977.

21. SCHODERBEK, P. P., KEFALAS, A. G. and C. G. SCHODERBEK, Management Systems: Conceptual Considerations, Business Publications Inc., Dallas, 1975.

22. SCHWEMBER, H., "Project Cybersyn: An Experience with New Tools for Management in Chile," in Computer Assisted Policy Analysis, Bossel (ed.), Birhauser Verlag, Basel.

23. ZANI, W. M., "Blueprint for MIS," Harvard Business Review, November-December, 1970.

An application of Destouches' two-levels system theory to a problem of management and organization

PAULETTE FEVRIER
Pierre and Marie Curie University, Paris, France

In order to build a model for the management of a huge hospital which is also a Research Institute, we use a particular two-levels system in Destouches' meaning.

Our problem is the following: The individual handling of patients involves presently complications and errors in management; we seek a better method which would provide the following advantages:

- simplify the connections between the hospital and the social health insurance (which in France is a national institution)
- avoid handling in detail the case of each individual patient
- be less expensive, owing to the establishment of a contract

By a contract we mean an agreement between the hospital administration and the national health insurance administration, about average evaluations of the expenses concerning the patient.

The problem above is equivalent to that of finding out an adequate form for such a contract.

The main difficulties arise from the fact that, presently, the management of the hospital includes two separate parts which evolve independently and cannot be prevented from evolving independently; that is, on one hand, the so-called hotel-running (or hospital care), and on the other hand, the medical acts. Hence a two-levels model, the evolution of each part of it being described by means of a different time variable.

Let t be the time variable for the hotel-running and T the time variable for the medical acts, both being connected with the same elements of the system, that is, the patients.

These times are discontinuous and vary by units: for t the unit is the day of hotel-running, for T it is one medical act, whatever it is, performed inside the hospital.

We can consider on one hand observables connected to the patients at each level -- for instance the number n of the days of hospital care for the patient j; on the other hand consider observables connected to the hospital -- the number $L(t)$ of beds occupied on the day t, and the number $A(t)$ of medical acts performed on the day t. But here occurs one of the main difficulties preventing our solving the problem in a satisfactory way. Indeed, actually, $A(t)$ cannot be measured, because the number of medical acts performed by each physician is only known globally at the end of large periods of time, for instance one year. The medical acts are not registered both per day and per patient and are still less predictable in individual cases.

We have the relations:

$$\left.\begin{array}{l} \sum_j n_j = \sum_t L(t) \\[2ex] \sum_j N_j \qquad \sum_t A(t) = T_1 \end{array}\right\} \begin{array}{l} T = T_1 \text{ on one} \\ \text{year, for instance} \end{array}$$

As in Hydrodynamics, we can in principle take either Euler's method or Lagrange's method, that is, either look at the flow on a certain point and consider functions such as $L(t)$ and $A(t)$, or follow the elements according to time--that is, consider the patients. But in fact this last method only is feasible by use of the individual records showing for each patient the number of days of hospital care and the number of medical acts. $\sum_t A(t) = T_1$ is the only possible relation connecting the time scales of t and T.

As there is no connection between the number of days of hospital care and the number of medical acts for a given patient, we are led to take one of the two time scales as a reference, and represent the other time by a random variable. It is more convenient to take t as a fixed variable and T as a random variable.

Using the second formula above, one can define an average time $\overline{T}$ by

$$\overline{T} = \alpha t$$

A standard deviation σ_T can be estimated, using statistics from preceding years. Large gaps appear between the numbers of medical acts for different patients, therefore σ_T is very great and, looking at it on the last ten years, for instance, appears as increasing historically. At a first approximation, the increase is proportional to time, that is

$$\sigma_T = \beta t$$

It is not possible to divide, at a given time, the various patients into subsets, because their future treatment is not known; it is not known at all when a patient enters the hospital, and even after the first medical acts it is still not predictable, even sometimes for a very near future.

But one can divide the medical acts into subsets according to their rate of repayment, that is: to split up the observable T into several observables $T_1, T_2, \ldots, T_k$, according to the number of medical acts belonging respectively to the classes $1, 2, \ldots, k$. The cost of the medical acts ranges from 1 to 1000, and their number by patient can range from 1 to 100. Hence it is difficult to estimate the average cost of the medical acts.

In the model presented here, the cost c of one day of hospital care, which is fixed for a given period, is taken into account; the dates of admission and leave of the patients are fixed, hence the hotel-running expenditure:

$$d_h = c(t_1 - t_a)$$

but the medical acts are also registered, though in a different way not connected with the hotel-running, that is on the individual patient record; hence N_j is known when the patient j leaves the hospital. The aim of the needed improvement in the management methods is to avoid computing in detail the particular expenses for each patient. Such a computation is actually, indeed, the origin of many drawbacks, errors and extra expenses in connection with the national health insurance formalities.

We can see that, because of the management methods presently used, there are non-simultaneously measurable observables in the system. About a patient j, one cannot know what is the number of medical acts undergone T on a given day t, neither d_h simultaneously with the cost p of the medical acts. Therefore our model must include indeterminism. Because of the great variability of the number N for the various patients and of the cost p of a medical act, the total amount S of the repayment for one patient is submitted to large variations and a formula of average value cannot be used, that is we cannot write

$$\overline{S} = \overline{p} \cdot \overline{N}.$$

Nevertheless one seeks a means of establishing such a contract $\overline{S}$ because it would provide a reduction of 20% on the management expenses.

Three processes are proposed in order to formulate such a contract:

(1) The amount of the repayment S by the national insurance to a patient j would be given by the sum of the hotel-running related to him and of the average value $\overline{s}$ of the medical acts for one patient computed out of the total expenditure of the hospital for medical acts for all patients. That is,

$$S = c(t_1 - t_a) + \overline{s}.$$

But this process is not satisfactory because of the large differences between the prices of the various medical acts.

(2) One would use the average price $\overline{p}$ of a medical act obtained by dividing the sum of the prices of all the different kinds of acts by their number, and use the number $\overline{n}$ of medical acts per day in the hospital in one year. This process would be expressed by the formula:

$$S = [c + \overline{p} \cdot \overline{n}] \quad (t_1 - t_a) ;$$

$\overline{n}$, the average number of medical acts per day, is $\overline{N}/365$ if $\overline{N}$ is the average total number of medical acts in one year calculated out of the last five years.

This method would introduce fewer gaps because of a certain correlation between N and $(t_1 - t_a)$. However, the gaps would still be too great to provide a satisfactory evaluation of the contract.

(3) The set of the acts would be divided into subsets according to the expenditure. A distinction would be introduced between acts both cheap and frequent on one hand and acts both expensive and rare on the other hand, these last ones being charged individually, while the first ones would be evaluated by means of an average value $\overline{p}_1$ per day. So we should have the formula:

$$S = [c + \overline{p}_1 \cdot \overline{n}] \quad (t_1 - t_a) + S_{exc} .$$

Such a solution introduces complexity but prevents large gaps.

A definitive choice between these various methods has not yet been made. For the time being, the managers are dividing the patients into 5 subsets, using the process (1) above and attributing 5 different values to $\overline{s}$. But it is an obvious mistake to divide the patients into subsets, because, as already remarked, a patient can at any moment pass from one subset to another, and this should compel the manager to look at the detail of the medical acts.

This problem, presently submitted to specialists inquiries, is in particular studied through the two-levels system model by Mme F. Doare [1], who is in the same time putting it in a suitable form, gathering the needed information and trying to solve it, that is to find an adequate definition for the required contract.

[1] Thesis in preparation, Universite Pierre et Marie Curie, Paris; Hôpital et Institut Gustave Roussy, Villejuif.

Why managers want interrogation facilities in management information systems

W. L. GAGE

School of Management, Polytechnic of Central London; and Harold Whitehead & Partners Ltd., England

It is apparent to those concerned with systems theory that cybernetics provides the framework for the analysis and synthesis of management information systems. It may not be so apparent to the incumbent manager, especially one who is learning empirically about management systems without having received training in systems theory. The vision of Stafford Beer [1] and Jay Forrester [2] may not have been imparted. This paper offers a reconciliation, and concentrates mainly on explaining the trend to interrogation capability in management information systems (MIS).

1. PLANT AND PROCESS CONTROL

The achievements of the process control engineers offer the most convincing evidence, for management, in favour of cybernetics. The mathematical analysis of stability requirements in a sophisticated petroleum or metal refinery is perceived to have great value, at least in the industries concerned. At first the design of such systems may have been regarded as a matter for the technical people. But the introduction of third generation computers for on-line control of plants provided the power to use some of the same measurements, the same channels of communication and the same computers for production control.

For engineers aware of these developments, the road to an understanding of systems theory must be easier than for managers with other professional backgrounds. Indeed, many of the texts dealing with cybernetics and systems theory use either James Watt's mechanical governor or the thermostat as their first model of control through feedback. Keith Lockyer [3], in his Production Control in Practice, points out that a feedback circuit is a very familiar idea for an electrical engineer and by page 3 he is exploiting the idea of a thermostat to introduce the philosophy of production and inventory control.

2. OPERATIONAL CONTROL SYSTEMS

An industrial engineer is bound to use cybernetics. If the rejection rate due to scrap in a process is targetted at 2%, the industrial engineer will ensure that feedback about actual rejection rates is presented to the works manager. The story he tells to the works manager will reflect their agreement on design for their control system. It may be expressed by the works manager in such terms as:

- I want the figures every week.
- Convert the loss into $ at sales value.
- Show me the trend on your graph.

Are they aware, these two, when they make a change in the procedure, of the theoretical basis for its features -- optimal frequency of measurement, standard units of measurement, predictive model building? And would it help them if they were able to make an analysis by reference to general systems theory?

A brand manager is bound to use cybernetics. If the Neilson [4] report on his market share shows a decline, he must present a report to the marketing manager. His presentation will imply some agreement about sales control in the enterprise. If the marketing manager reacts to the relative decline in this way,

- Don't just stand there moaning about your market share report! Tell me what you are going to do about it.

then he is showing an intuitive grasp of the requirement to close the feedback loop by corrective action. It is suggested that the nature of this control loop may not have been made explicit in the marketing department unless consultants are used to construct a marketing model.

The engineer's scrap analysis or the brand manager's market share variance may or may not be displayed as computer output. Even if they are, the information may or may not have been processed by the computer's arithmetic unit. There can be manual preparation of data for computer retrieval, as used by the DANA Corporation [5] to provide the database for extraction of their management control information.

3. MANAGEMENT INFORMATION SYSTEMS

In local government the budgets assistant may be expected to present a half-yearly report to the chief administrator and department heads at City Hall. By custom he comments on every code for which the actual expenditure exceeds the budget by $2000 or more. He is providing feedback, and in this case he is probably aware of his role in the cybernetics loop. He has probably read T. G. Rose's classic 1934 book [6] on Higher Business Control or perhaps during his training as a cost accountant he used Anthony's [7] Planning and Control Systems. Yet, when he goes home, late, after the meeting, he kicks the dog and scolds the children because he doubts whether corrective action will be taken so as to justify his work in reporting. He wonders if the bureaucrats will summon up the energy to reduce costs in the second half-year in order to compensate for the drift he detected. He wonders if the Councillors will interpret their political aims in such a way as to frustrate the department heads looking for savings. Perhaps a change in national government policy will over-ride the response decided on locally.

The most widespread and satisfactory management information systems reside in the historical accounts and the budgets. The outlines of these MIS were largely designed by 1922 by people who would have smiled indulgently to hear cybernetics discussed. Various refinements such as D. C. F. and inflation accounting are continuously applied. The flexibility and the rapid response of modern ledger-based management information systems, with codings arranged as a model of the organisation for responsibility, would have delighted McKinsey or Rose [8].

4. DATABASE AND INTEGRATED MANAGEMENT INFORMATION SYSTEMS

It is said that balance sheets, periodic financial accounts and periodic budget variance analyses are insufficient for steering the enterprise. Perhaps we lack chief executives of the type who list in Who's Who the recreation of reading variance analyses? One or two of the obituaries of the late Lord Thomson of Fleet referred to the myth that his Who's Who entry lists "reading balance sheets". A balance sheet is certainly an extremely useful low frequency report to someone at Roy Thomson's level, as well as a legal requirement. Even so, there will be a demand for such measurements as
- sales in kilogrammes
- output in automobiles
- yield of each ton of plastic in finished toys
- standard hours achieved as a percentage of flexi-time clocked
The systems developed by leading organisations such as the National Goal Board or Texas Instruments Ltd. provide computer reports of their operation as well as their money results, the operations information systems and the management information systems being integrated and reconciled. Reports of different levels in Anthony's hierarchy (strategic, management, operational, prime) could conceivably be found from the same program suite, although it is more likely that strategic reports and the ledger accounts will be separate.

5. BUSINESS (PLANNING) MODELS

In an article [9] for the Operational Research Quarterly, Dr. K. D. Tocher points out that if the result of corrective action by the manager is to be predictable, there must be a predictive model of some kind, explicit or implicit. Strategic decisions in large scale enterprise justify considerable effort in predictive model building, in which field the author's colleagues of Harold Whitehead and Partners have been heavily involved [10].

From our early work in the baby food market, the marketing directors in consumer goods have encouraged the development of this class of cybernetics system in the food industry, in pharma-

ceuticals, drinks and tobacco; wherever, in fact, advertising expenditure and promotion costs are likely to be so heavy that they must be carefully and continuously tuned to the feedback from the market. Many of the models tend to be broad brush in their treatment of costs or margins, and to ignore manpower planning or industrial relations constraints. They can be faulted for failure to reconcile with the accounts. But they have overriding virtues. Their construction forces the management to analyse its marketing systems more meticulously than ever before, and they concentrate on the lifeblood decision areas of marketing management.

6. UTOPIAN ENGINEERING

Cyberneticians tend to be better known for their vision than for their restraint. Stafford Beer is associated with his assessment of the potential for computers in International Publishing Corporation Ltd., for his rousing addresses and stimulating books. Gordon Pask is recognised for the sweep of his research in the field of Computer Assisted Instruction. Less is known about their "shop floor" achievements and their counsel against over-elaboration.

The systems research workers are assumed to be devising a "proposed model for optimising investment decisions in a multi-national corporation" or "a proposed model for a generalised industrial organisation as a dynamic system" [11].

The cybernetics practitioners are aware of the danger. Three quotations will illustrate the kind of thinking that acknowledges the needs of managers, over and above the services already packaged:

What (matters) is not the feedback information itself, but the value of the information. (Leon Brillouin, who worked for IBM, in 1962 [12])

If any (management) action is taken, the result ... must be predictable and compared with alternatives and the objective. (K. D. Tocher, who worked for British Steel Corporation, in 1971, [9])

Consider
- what decisions have to be taken
- how their results are measured
- how important to company results
(Maurice Blackman, who works for Arthur Anderson, in 1975 [13])

The intention of this paper is to press the point a little further, and acknowledge the individual manager's perceived needs.

7. OBJECTIVE AND SUBJECTIVE REQUIREMENTS

The managing director of a retail store group said, "Get that computer off the back of my merchandise."

During the test period of the merchandise stock replenishment system, he complained about the slow response of the system, which allowed fast moving items to go out of stock before the open-to-order signal appeared in the printout. A better analysis of peak demand, response time and procurement lead time would have avoided this fault.

The retail director also complained about being expected to read, every month, 5 printouts each about 1 metre long, showing the stock-outs and stock status of the class A merchandise in each store. This also could have been corrected, but was it a fault? The systems analyst, if correctly trained, starts with management requirements expressed as system outputs, or as management specification. It might be better to use the expression manager requirements.

The researcher in cybernetics and systems is bound to work to a general statement of output requirements in a management application until he meets the man who has authority to take corrective action and close the loop.

That man or woman will possess strong views on the units, format and frequency of the measurements he wishes to have fed back to him. He may say that he is helpless without the up-to-date turnover figures for all major items of merchandise. People like Baron Bich, Sir Halford Reddish and Anton Philips are considered to have imposed their leadership style on the companies they steered. They demand the information they need as steersman. It will be to some extent subjective, and it may change faster than software can be revised and tested.

(On a very grand scale the giants of management may be able to accept the general, theoretical reports appropriate to their multinational conglomerates. A. P. Sloan [14] appears to have done this in General Motors, implementing a standard form of budgetary control advocated by J. C. McKinsey [8] in the profit centres of one of the world's largest corporations. Texas Instruments provide a standardised unit statistics report to all their operations.)

8. INTERROGATION MODE

Not many managers would claim the skill and authority to dominate the design of cybernetics systems intended to provide them with information for decisions. But there are subjective requirements, due perhaps to conditioning. At one period in Rank Hovis McDougall the sales of Mother's Pride bread were measured for management reports not in money, nor loaves, nor even in bakers' dozens, but "sacks". The "sack" was the quantity of bread traditionally produced from a sack of flour. No other measure provided for the senior managers, brought up in flour milling, the kind of information they could use.

It seems unlikely that the subcontract systems analysts and programmers on Route 128 will prepare sales analysis output reports in sacks. But a reconciliation between standard computer systems and individual information needs is available when the manager can use a terminal capable of interrogation. Such equipment offers a bridge between computer suites (designed to fulfill theoretical systems requirements) and the individual manager. It would provide for interrogation of a standard sales analysis programme:

    TØTAL SALES RGN 3 MØNTH 2 ?
    86800 LØAVES

and it would even present in sacks where 128 converts loaves to sacks: ÷ 128 = 67.7 .

This example is a trivial illustration of the way that a special measure can be extracted, either on a teletype terminal or a visual display unit. Interrogation is extensively used for information retrieval, the most familiar examples being airline allocation systems and automobile manufacturer's networks which permit all subscribing parts stockists to search for a spare engine for a Land Rover.

Such an interrogation capability which avoids excessive noise in the feedback is an attractive idea! Nancy Foy [15] writes ruefully: "A decade ago, oracular voices (among them mine) proclaimed that every manager would soon have a computer terminal on his desk, giving him instant access to ... information about his organization." Ms. Foy goes on to say: "Walk into any executive suite today. See all the terminals? In 99 cases out of 100 there will be no evidence at all of computers." This is not denied. A terminal until very recently was a machine both noisy and ungainly in an elegant office. But it is hasty to talk of pendulum swing and attribute to today's top executive the statements: "The kind of information I need to run my organisation doesn't come through computers." Shell have just placed an order worth over $£1 \times 10^6$ to provide terminals for management of marketing, distribution and inventories. Honeywell have increased their investment in the TABOL package [16] because of its popularity as a business information system. Of the total installed value [17] of computers in France at 1.1.77, half is universal in application (including payroll and stocks) and a further quarter is for management applications only. Only automation applications and certain replenishment systems exploit the computer to take corrective action.

But the information needed, the extrapolations and alternative predictions for many decisions in most large organisations does come through computers. The Shell investment confirms their belief in providing terminals for interrogation which can improve management information. To obtain the measurement required, without redundant information, at the right time for corrective action, is good cybernetics. Interrogation of computer information would appear to provide the manager with what he wants. Distributed computer peripherals and kindly software are available to provide for interrogation.

When market models and corporate planning models are prepared by the OR consultants at Whiteheads, the requirement is normally for interactive facilities so that "what if" questions may be asked. On receipt of the latest Neilson report on brand share the marketing manager is able to predict the consequences of increased advertising, lower relative price, or whatever options are open to him for corrective action.

9. ADAPTIVE MANAGEMENT BEHAVIOUR

The importance of OR to cybernetics lies in this ability to change complex information being fed back to the manager so that it suits him and is predictive.

The best work done by OR scientists in functional applications has the quality of being adaptive, as when stock control packages programs modify the forecast and update it as soon as new postings are recorded; and indeed they may modify the predictive model itself. In manpower planning models, provision is made for detecting a change in natural wastage of employees (such as occurs when jobs are scarce), so that fresh projections are computed for residual staff five years hence.

The greater challenge, posed by applying cybernetics to the total firm, is to make the enterprise adaptive. To look through the file of Management Today discloses that continued interest in articles about the recovery of a company under the leadership of a particular personality. He got the message, and he took action.

This challenge was discussed at the 1976 European Meeting as a result of the paper presented by the St. Gallen team [18]. Fred Malik and his colleagues argued that it was necessary for an adaptive enterprise to inculcate the OR approach in the whole management team.

The client management team is advised and helped to identify a model of its sales/promotion system, and make the model as explicit as possible as time goes by. It is claimed that a determination to improve a mathematical model (of response by the company to change in its environmental trading conditions) implies a determination to cope with the changes which have hurt a great many European companies in the last few years. The management team, rather than its Operational Research boffins, is expected to maintain commitment to the model in its detail. Dr. Malik stressed repeatedly that the intention is not to use OR to solve the next problem (for example, devising the least cost physical distribution system for a greatly reduced volume of sales), but to inculcate a problem solving capability which is enduring, and which keeps on trying to update and improve a model of the market-manufacture-inventory system as a whole. This aim brings OR close to OD.

10. ORGANISATION DEVELOPMENT

For many enterprises, and even more public organisations, it is considered that the management information systems supply adequate feedback information, but the organisation finds difficulty in responding by taking action. The organisation is identified as an interacting system, its members needing to participate in the decision to grasp the tiller and change course. Organisation Development equally aspires to help the client to generate a reforming ability in the management team, although the teething ring problem-solving exercises used by OD tutors would be thought trivial by management scientists who attach as much importance as St. Gallen to designing a predictive model.

If the organisation aspiring to adapt is in the public sector, the OD approach is very attractive because two conditions are met. First, decision making is indeed difficult when feedback signals come in -- when, for example, cash control limits have been exceeded. Secondly, it is very difficult to build a comprehensive model of the services-to-costs relationship in a large borough. If an empty area of dockland is to be redeveloped to meet the needs of the local community, its larger borough, minority conservationists, and the water authority, then whoever is responsible for planning have a pretty intractable problem. If a borough's

social services are to be maintained as completely as possible through several years of control by cash limit, then the Director of Social Services has a problem. Whilst a good deal of work has been done to provide useful mathematical models for these problem owners, the most enthusiastic advocates of cost benefit analysis would hesitate to contend that they had provided a solution to these soft, unstructured public problems.

The OD consultant helps his client to examine qualitatively the processes whereby the organisation learns (to adapt), and then endeavours to develop the power to exploit this knowledge when future or continuous change is needed.

The concept of a model is in constant use during OD assignments, although generally in the sense of analogy or illustration or flow diagram.

11. SUMMARY

The brief descriptions of some identifiable applications of cybernetics may suggest that system design for better control of an organisation may be a matter of choosing horses for courses. Often it means the addition of one more feedback loop to the large number already in use. Sometimes it seems more difficult to dismantle part of the old system, or indeed graft on to it.

So from necessity and by default large organisations have many control loops -- hierarchies of feedback at various frequencies from automation to the balance sheet.

The idea of corrective action implies a manager and/or a group who alter course. Concentration on the former, with assumptions about responsibility and authority, leads to the construction of systems which defer to subjective needs for information, and hence to his interrogation facility.

Concentration on the management as a team leads towards the ideas of organisation development, or to the sophisticated assignment where OR and OD are not easily distinguished.

This sketchy analysis is itself defective, perhaps, in that it defers to the existing organisation of people rather than deriving an optimum organisation of people. It is hoped, however, that it may offer some reconciliation between the characteristic assignments of the consultant mathematician and the consultant behavioural scientist. Practising managers are impatient with competing packages which disparage each other's contribution to management development.

REFERENCES

1. BEER, S., Decision and Control, Penguin, 1966.
2. FORRESTER, J., Industrial Dynamics, MIT Press, 1961.
3. LOCKYER, K. G., Production Control in Practice, Pitman, 1966.
4. NEILSON, A. C., "Corporation" (the company produces a bi-monthly report, Neilson Researcher, but the reference is to a client of their market research service).
5. FOSTER, G., "DANA Corporate Management," Management Today, September 1976.

6. ROSE, T. G., Higher Control in Management,
    Pitman, 1934.
7. ANTHONY, R. N., Planning and Control Systems,
    H. U. P., 1975.
8. McKINSEY, J. O., Budgetary Control, Ronald
    Press, 1922.
9. TOCHER, K. D., "Paper on Control," ORQ,
    Vol. 21, No. 2, 1971.
10. MULVANEY, J. E. and C. MANN, Practical
    Business Models, Heinemann, 1976.
11. CHECKLAND, P., Proceedings of 3rd European
    Meeting, A.S.C.S. (in the opening address
    Checkland appealed for no more "proposed
    models").

12. BRILLOUIN, L., "Science and Information
    Theory," Science Research Associates,
    1956.
13. BLACKMAN, M., The Design of Real Time
    Systems, Wiley, 1975.
14. SLOAN, A. P., My Years with General Motors,
    Doubleday, 1972.
15. FOY, N., "The Communicating Computer,"
    Management Today, September 1977.
16. HONEYWELL NEWSLETTER, August 1977.
17. MALIK, F., Proceedings of 3rd European
    Meeting, A.S.C.S.

Cybernetics and a general theory of organization

ROSS A. GAGLIANO* and KRZYSZTOF S. LEBKOWSKI**
*Engineering Experiment Station
**School of Information & Computer Science
Georgia Institute of Technology, Atlanta, Georgia USA

1. INTRODUCTION

In 1948, Wiener defined Cybernetics as "the science of control and communication in the animal and the machine" [1]. Three major concepts were therefore indicated: system, feedback, and regulation. These concepts have been further elucidated by others; for example, Ashby [2], Pask [3], and Klir and Valach [4]. However, the most widely recognized abstraction of these concepts is generally referred to as the "black box" (BB). Moreover, the BB analytical aspects have been linked to systems theory (either general or mathematical). Since in the BB approach outputs are sampled and controlled by manipulating the inputs, ergo, the basic advantage becomes a major drawback in that the internal mechanism is unaccessible. Consequently, there have been many attempts to extend the methodology from this thermostat-like setting to more general applications.

Prior to the recent efforts in General Systems Theory, there were two significant attempts to develop a more general theory. In the 1920's, Bogdanov [5] published a treatise on the theory of complexes of Tektology (from the Greek τεκτον or builder) which is the science of building either artifacts or phenomena. This theory hypothesized that out of chaos arises (or is built) structure, or organization, exhibiting the functions of ingression, egression, and disingression with respect to a tektological boundary.

Later, Rashevsky [6] proposed a concept of organismic sets through which a strong analogy could be made between a cell, the interaction of genes, and society, the interaction of people. Thus, organizational concepts such as centralization, specialization, and division of labor could be formalized.

Needless to say, neither of these paradigms has attracted strong cybernetic following, although many of the theoretical constructs can now be accounted for within the general systems approach. For example, a principle of evolution has been indicated by Braham [7] who, like other general system theorists, envisioned that living organisms follow cyclic patterns in which the emergence of successively more complex forms can account for change, mutation, and evolution. Others, like Esposito [8], took a more formal approach in order to establish a connection to well developed theories, particularly those in physics and thermodynamics. In this way, the concepts of entropy and information have been linked, and shown to be useful in biology, communication theory, and other areas. For further discussion of these and other modern paradigms, see [9].

Suffice it to say, despite these and numerous other efforts, Cybernetics remains an evolving, inter-disciplinary activity, one that has not yet assumed its full potential. In light of this fact, we pose the following question: Are the concepts of Cybernetics sufficient to deal with the problems of organization? This question automatically causes another difficulty, however, in that the reference to organization requires additional clarification, at least with respect to how it relates to systems. Ideally, we would like to refer to a general concept of system or organization, if one were agreed upon. However, as is usually the case, we must address only a specific set of issues. Most systems are dealt with by models. For more discussion on a taxonomy of system models, see [10].

In any event, since Cybernetics is concerned with how "systems" regulate, reproduce, evolve, and learn (hence, "organize"), our task becomes clearly one of examining organization as a phenomenon. It may well be, as Bertalanffy [11] has observed, that the problem of life is that of organization. As a result, the need for a General Theory of Organization, or GTO, is an obvious necessity. And, for the convenience of discussing GTO and demonstrating its applicability in this paper, we shall distinguish between "organizational systems" and "cybernetic systems."

2. A GENERAL THEORY OF ORGANIZATION (GTO)

Only a brief description of GTO will be rendered here; a more thorough discussion can be found in [9]. The fundamental concept of GTO is that of conditional mediation, which is based upon the dual relations: commonness and conditionality. Commonness is a mutual transitivity relationship between two objects; the degree of conditionality is expressed by a satisfaction function (σ). The first principle of GTO is that of a Basic Organization Molecule (BOM); objects A, B, and C constitute a BOM if and only if B satisfies A to the degree C.

Since a single BOM may not be able to fulfill complicated functions, complexes of BOM's form (what is termed) organizational cells which require cooperative interaction. This is accomplished in the following way. Suppose that there exists: goal, g; condition, c; and product, p. Then, the goal "unites" with the condition to cause a product, as shown in the following operation:

$$g * c \rightarrow p \qquad\qquad (1)$$

which is called <u>forward mediation</u> or FM.

For some BOM's, we must assume that the reverse operation is possible; namely, <u>backward mediation</u> or BM:

$$|p| \leftarrow c' * p \qquad\qquad (2)$$

where $|p|$ is the evidence of p, and c' is an alternate condition, perhaps different from c.

After operations (1) and (2) are performed, $|p|$ is matched against g to determine if p <u>satisfies</u> g, and to what degree. Thus, we have

$$g \Leftarrow p \equiv (g, c, c', |p|) \geq \tau(g, c, c') \qquad (3)$$

which implies that g is satisfied by p if and only if the satisfaction value generated by σ equals or exceeds the threshold value generated by the tolerance function τ.

FM and BM are shown in Figure 1, and the satisfaction relationship and its value are shown in Figure 2.

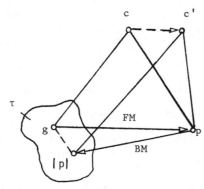

Figure 1

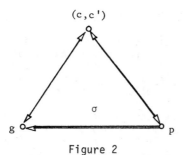

Figure 2

The uniting operation (*) is determined by commonness, or, in this case, the overlap of c and c'. And, a satisfaction function is constructed by a unique observer through "shared awareness" (c and c'), since self-organization implies a relation between observer and assembly [3]. Organization is then created by a concatenation of specialized BOM's listed below.

Notationally, c(X) stands for a condition of an X category molecule; and $|X|$ stands for a representation of X, where all X are referred to as mediators.

I. <u>Planning Molecules</u>
1. <u>Function Planning molecule</u> (FP)

$$g * c(FP) \rightarrow |f|$$

where f stands for function, which brings about a product p satisfying g;

2. <u>Structure Planning molecule</u> (SP)

$$|f| * c(SP) \rightarrow |s|$$

where s stands for structure, a vehicle for function f;

3. <u>Material Planning molecule</u> (MP)

$$|s| * c(MP) \rightarrow |m|$$

where m stands for material which satisfies structure s;

II. <u>Implementing Molecules</u>
4. <u>Material Implementation molecule</u> (MI)

$$|m| * c(MI) \rightarrow m$$

5. <u>Structure Implementation molecule</u> (SI)

$$|s| * c(SI) \rightarrow s$$

6. <u>Function Implementation molecule</u> (FI)

$$|f| * c(FI) \rightarrow f$$

III. <u>Performance molecule</u> (P)
7. $f * c(P) \rightarrow p$

IV. <u>Total Evaluation molecule</u> (TE)
8. $p * c(TE) \rightarrow \sigma$

where c(TE) stands for the total evaluation conditions represented by the cumulative satisfaction function, and which operates on the overall cellular structure; and σ stands for the total satisfaction value over a set of cellular parts.

Cells are then composed of molecular parts in a ring-like structure, which consist of a combination of eight categories of molecular parts. However, multi-ring branching may occur if the condition c(X) is insufficient to bring about satisfactory results. The molecules actually present in a cell depend upon the availability of the mediators provided by the cooperating cells. Nevertheless, the basic ring of a cell can be constructed into the "ideal" cell, as represented in Figure 3a.

Cellular parts can be represented even more conveniently if all the condition vertices are concentrated in the center of the ring, thus forming its <u>nucleus</u> (Figure 3b).

A particular order of mediation within and between cellular parts can be described by a Markov-like process, where the conditional probabilities are replaced by the conditional satisfaction values which determine the efficiency and effectiveness of transitions.

Wholes are then constructed out of the cellular parts where the resulting structures are

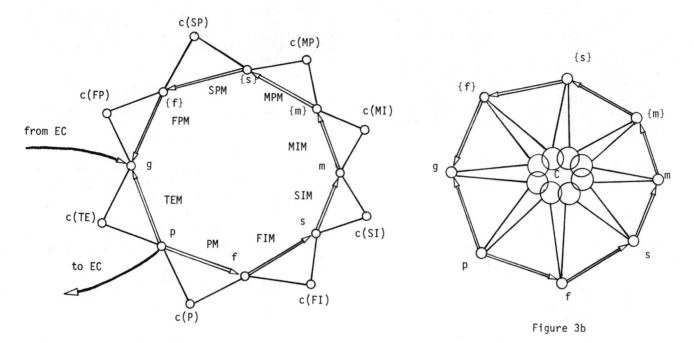

Figure 3a

Figure 3b

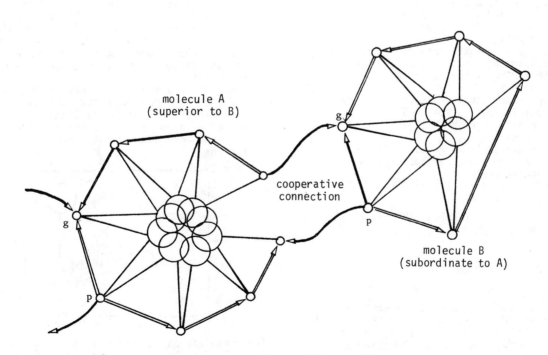

Figure 4

functional hierarchies of cellular chains. Structures originate from an initial set of goals and
conditions, and differentiate into more specific
molecular and cellular parts, which finally con-
verge into a final product set. These two sets,
initial and final, can be shown to have a satisfaction relationship to each other. Figure 4
illustrates a simple, two-molecule whole.

Thus, in the synthetic view of wholes, any
organization can still be modeled as a triangular
structure, as shown in Figure 5.

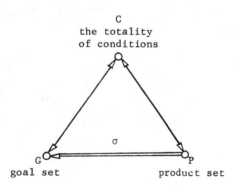

C

the totality
of conditions

σ

G   P

goal set   product set

Figure 5

Finally, a more formal definition of organizational σ-sets is given by:
<u>Definitions</u>: Let L be a set such that
1. $G \subset L$ and is a goal set;
2. $C \subset L$ and is a condition set;
3. $M = L - C$ and is a mediation set;
4. $P \cup |P| \subset L$ is the product set and its
    representation set;
5. PRS_L is a potential residence space (PRS)
    set associated with set L;
6. $PRS_L^G \subset PRS_L$ is the subset of PRS_L associat-
    ed with set G;
7. ARS_L is an actual residence space set
    associated with a set M - G;
8. $\sim PRS_L^G \Leftarrow P \equiv \sigma(PRS_L^G, C, |P|) < \tau(PRS_L^G, C)$;
    then a set
    $\theta \equiv \{(g,c,p,\sigma)_j \mid j \in (1,...,n),$ where $n \neq 0\}$
    is a finite number of applications of the
    following operation:
    $(M*C)^n \rightarrow p^{(n)}$ and $|P|^{(m)} \leftarrow (C*P)^{m \leq n}$
    so that
    $PRS_L^G \Leftarrow p^{(n)} \equiv \sigma(PRS_L^G, C, |P|^{(m)}) \geq \tau(PRS_L^G, C)$
    is an <u>organizational σ-set</u>.

3. CYBERNETIC AND GTO CONCEPTS

With the minimal framework for GTO just provided, let us examine some relative concepts of
Cybernetics and GTO. The most important issue is
probably that of conditionality which is best
illustrated through the role of the observer.
Thus, the lucid box (LB) versus the black box (BB)
approaches can be explained, and the dichotomy of
outside/inside is also enjoined. From these
issues, many other topics can be discussed.

Naively, let us now distinguish: simple

systems; cybernetic systems; and organizational
systems. The simplest system is usually an input-
output process, in which the transformation (T) is
defined in terms of inputs (I) and outputs (O),
as shown below.

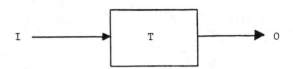

The cybernetic system, in the BB methodology,
expands upon the simple system by the addition of
a feedback loop and the use of a regulator (R),
shown below.

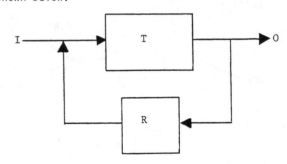

The usual sense of regulation implies that:
the observer is <u>outside</u> the BB, or unable to
deal with T; only the inputs can be manipulated;
and the levels of goals cannot be adequately
addressed. For example, suppose that the regula-
tion is sensitive to condition; say $|y - y_0| < \varepsilon$,
where y is the output, y_0 is the reference value,
and ε is the threshold value difference; then the
questions arise as to where do y_0 and ε come from.
However, perhaps more importantly, the goal of the
system and the goal of the observer are not easily
differentiated.

Thus, by placing the observer <u>inside</u> the box,
we can use the LB approach and apply some of the
GTO principles. The organizational system, as
shown below, also has inputs and outputs (interface to the environment) but places the observer
in the box.

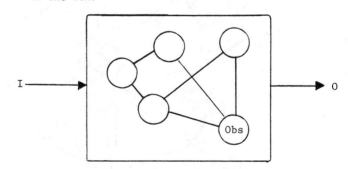

The immediate advantages are that: an inability
to deal with the inputs (environmental condition)
may be overcome and the process of evolution can
be pursued, at least from the distinction of
"system-in-being" (present) versus the "one-that-
is-becoming" (future). Clearly, in the last

instance, the problem of accounting for the <u>organon</u> (noun) and the <u>organizing</u> (verb) aspects is facilitated.

Thus, the implementation of GTO concepts in the LB methodology provides for an observer (conditionality): within a group activity (commonness); with the ability to distinguish individual and group goals (satisfaction); capable of contributing to the change process (mediation); and as a participant in the evolutionary mechanism at two different levels which are as part of the system transformation (internal) and as the observer (external). GTO thereby provides a potential for considering an organization as a complex of interacting (cooperating and competing) components while avoiding the dilemma of considering them as "systems of sub-systems." Further, GTO allows for these additional properties: micro-macro level distinction; cooperative-competitive phenomena; synergy (see [12]); purposiveness; and others.

4. APPLICATION OF GTO

To provide an appreciation of how GTO can be employed, the following three examples are presented. For a more detailed discussion of their implementation by computer, see [13]. For several related implementations, see [14,15,16].

Example 1.

Consider the Tug-of-War (or Rope) Game (see Figure 6), in which each of two goups or individuals at opposite ends of a rope attempt, by coordinated efforts, to pull the other group across a fixed line in between. For simplicity, let us focus on one side of the rope such that there are n individuals, and a meter joined by a rope to a fixed wall.

Thus, the task is to maximize the reading on the meter by the interaction of all n members pulling to the right and hopefully <u>in unison</u>. If n is small, the coordination function is somewhat easy. As n increases, it is obvious that the resultant measure of effort may be less than optimum; in fact, it may be negligible.

In accordance with GTO, each member is considered to be an observer whose: range of observation is several adjacent neighbors (<u>commonness</u>); <u>conditionality</u> is expressed as the desire to minimize the difference between the response time

that each individual predicts and the time that the next group "pull" actually occurs; <u>satisfaction</u> is brought about through a mechanism which rewards the individuals who are the more successful in establishing a "rhythm" (closest to center relative frequency, for example).

Space restrictions preclude further elaboration here; nonetheless, the significance of this example is that, even with its simplistic structure, organization emerges. In other words, a collection of random "pullers" can organize themselves through competitive/cooperative interaction in satisfying individual goals and mediating group goals. For application to other social issues, see [17].

Example 2.

By extending the single dimension (rope) to a topological space, let us look at a collection of "firers" instead of "pullers" which could be neurons. Thus, it is possible to study the communication and control mechanisms of an organ like the mammalian heart. The relative frequency of "firing" resembles the pressure of volumetric measure such as is described by an electrocardiogram (EKG). Obviously, the wave form of the EKG is more complex since it also measures physical functions as muscular response, etc. For more discussion of this subject, see [18,19,20].

Example 3.

Finally, by extending to another dimension, we can investigate several problems described as social imitation [21]. Extensive investigations have been made into the syncrony of the mating activity of the pteroptyx malaccae [22], for example, and other synergetic social behaviors; viz. schools of fish, flocks of migrating birds, and other territorial species. Of current interest in the United States is the application of these techniques to voting, buying, and other human preference behaviors.

5. CONCLUSIONS

The development of a General Theory of Organization (GTO) may assist in the further development of Cybernetics. Although still in its formulative stages, GTO attempts to identify fundamental issues in the system-organization

Figure 6.

distinction because the phenomenon of organization appears inappropriate, if not prior, to a discussion of systems.

The need for GTO was, in part, motivated by an apparent insufficiency of cybernetic concepts which can be demonstrated by the inability to deal with organizational issues with the black box methodology. Therefore, a lucid box approach has been suggested which utilizes the GTO concepts of conditional mediation, the Basic Organization Molecule, and a satisfaction function (σ-sets).

Three examples were briefly indicated to show the range of possible future applications: (i) the Tug-of-War or Rope Game; (ii) the mammalian heart; and (iii) the process of social imitation.

REFERENCES

1. WIENER, N., Cybernetics, New York, John Wiley and Sons, 1948.
2. ASHBY, W. R., Introduction to Cybernetics, London, Chapman and Hall, 1956.
3. PASK, G., An Approach to Cybernetics, New York, Harper and Brothers, 1961.
4. KLIR, G. J. and M. VALACH, Cybernetic Modelling, London, Iliffe Books, 1967.
5. BOGDANOV, A., Tektology: The Universal Science of Organization, Moscow, Izdatelstvo, Z. I. Grschebina, 1922.
6. RASHEVSKY, N., "Organismic Sets: Outline of a General Theory of Biological and Social Organisms," in: General Systems, Vol. XII, pp. 21-27, 1967.
7. BRAHAM, M., "A General Theory of Organization," in: General Systems, Vol. XVIII, pp. 13-23. 1973.
8. ESPOSITO, J. L., "Remarks Toward a General Theory of Organization," International Journal of General Systems, Vol. I, pp. 133-143, 1976.
9. LEBKOWSKI, K. S., "Towards a General Theory of Organization," MS Thesis, School of Information and Computer Science, Georgia Institute of Technology, Atlanta, March 1978.
10. GAGLIANO, R. A. and K. B. LANGSETH, "Towards a Taxonomy of Modeling Techniques," Proceedings of the Eight Annual Pittsburgh Conference on Modeling and Simulation,
University of Pittsburgh, pp. 1013-1016, 1977.
11. BERTALANFFY, L. von, Problems of Life, New York, Harper, 1960.
12. HAKEN, H., Synergetics: Nonequilibrium Phase Transitions and Self-Organization in Physics, Chemistry, and Biology, Springer-Verlag, 1977.
13. GAGLIANO, R. A. and K. S. LEBKOWSKI, "Models of Organization," Proceedings of the Ninth Annual Pittsburgh Conference on Modeling and Simulation, 1978.
14. WINDEKNECHT, T. G. and H. D'ANGELO, "The Stereotype Approach to the Modeling and Simulation of an Elementary School," IEEE Transactions on Systems, Man, and Cybernetics, pp. 216-225, March, 1975.
15. GAGLIANO, R. A. and T. G. WINDEKNECHT, "A Disaggregated Model for Neighborhood Dynamics," Proceedings of the Fifth Annual Pittsburgh Conference on Modeling and Simulation, University of Pittsburgh, pp. 41-46, 1974.
16. GAGLIANO, R. A., "Some Reflections on Societal Modeling," Proceedings of the Seventh Annual Pittsburgh Conference on Modeling and Simulation, University of Pittsburgh, pp. 766-770, 1976.
17. BUCKLEY, W., "Society as a Complex Adaptive System," in: Systems Behavior, J. Beishon and G. Peters (eds.), London, Harper and Row, 1972.
18. WILSON, H. R., "Cooperative Phenomena in a Homogeneous Cortical Tissue Model," in: Synergetics: Cooperative Phenomena in Multi-Component Systems, H. Haken (ed.), Stuttgart, B. G. Teubner, 1973.
19. ADAM, G., "Cooperative Transitions in Biological Membranes," in: Synergetics: Cooperative Phenomena in Multi-Component Systems, H. Haken (ed.), Stuttgart, B. G. Teubner, 1973.
20. TOMITA, K., "A Model for Muscle Contraction," in: Synergetics: Cooperative Phenomena in Multi-Component Systems, H. Haken (ed.), Stuttgart, B. G. Teubner, 1973.
21. CALLEN, E. and D. SHAPERO, "A Theory of Social Imitation," Physics Today, pp. 23-28, July, 1974.
22. BUCK, J. and E. BUCK, "Synchronous Fireflies," Scientific American, Vol. 234, 5, pp. 74-85, 1976.

Societal systems modeling, systems analysis without social systems theory

KENYON B. DE GREENE

University of Southern California, USA

1. INTRODUCTION

It is self-evident that from the perspective of man and his artifacts the world is increasingly complex, whether determined by the number of relevant elements; the number of combinations and interactions among elements; the degree and rapidity of social and technological change and of environmental impact; or the nature and variety of emergent forms. Not only is man's world becoming more complex, but belatedly his recognition of that complexity has increased. Attempts to manage complexity are reflected in the familiar rationalized methods of applied science -- operations research, management science, systems engineering, and systems analysis. Nevertheless, human capability for handling complexity has not kept up with the increase in complexity itself.

There are several reasons for this. First, rationalized approaches, although perhaps originally rooted in the scientific method, have become more ad hoc. Second, highly theoretical and mathematical approaches appear to be limited in applicability to the sub-subsystems of society. Third, the different disciplines have progressed at different rates and with different degrees of conceptual and practical mastery over problem areas. Indeed, relationships among the disciplines purporting to study society remain discordant. And fourth, attempted objective analysis almost always becomes bogged down in the unwieldy, even corrupt political system of bureaucratic organizations.

The key to these and other difficulties not mentioned here lies in the present deficiency of theoretical explanations of complex societal processes. Perhaps even more serious is the apparent lack of progress in advancing the theory of sociotechnical macrosystems. In the absence of such theory, most efforts to confront the exploding problems of world society, whether by engineers, behavioral and social scientists, planners, or politicians, are likely to be fragmented, mutually contradictory, simultaneously delayed and hasty, wasteful, and indifferent or even dangerous in the long run.

Granted that an integrated, all-encompassing theory of societal macrosystems, not limited by disciplinary bias, is scarcely just around the corner, is applicable or potentially applicable theory entirely lacking? The answer to this question must necessarily be in the negative. The focus of this paper is on computer simulation models of complex societal systems. Certainly cybernetic theory, hierarchy theory, and economic theory underlie the structure of some of these models. Nevertheless, these theories are only fragments of the necessary theory.

In the remainder of this paper we shall discuss: (1) the relationship between the theory and modeling of society; (2) the traditional behavioral and social science approach to modeling; (3) present modeling approaches as theories of society, with an emphasis on systems dynamics; and (4) implications of the "modeling movement" for human and societal limits.

2. THEORY VERSUS MODELING OF SOCIETY

A theory is usually regarded as a statement of apparent relationships of observed phenomena which is based on considerable supporting evidence and has been verified to some degree. A model is most simply a convenient analogy of the real world. Sometimes "model" is synonomous with "orientation." However, these brief definitions do not convey the operating relationships between theory and model, especially with regard to which comes (or should come) first, which is subordinate, and which receives priority at given stages in the development of ideas. Different practices of course obtain within the various scientific disciplines, and, indeed, the words "theory" and "model" mean different things at different times and places.

A model may in one context be a construct which helps the scientist devise a theory to explain a given domain. In another context a model may be simply a means of ordering a large amount of descriptive data. To some authors models are temporary constructs which aid in the partial validation of theories. In such a sense models are not direct analogies of the real world, and we can speak of models of a theory. To still other workers models presuppose theories.

In this paper modeling is held to be subordinate to theory, and theory should antecede modeling. A model is considered to be a formalized (computer) application of a theory or part thereof for purposes of theory development and systems analysis, design, evaluation, or management. Model results, whether explicit or implicit, intended or side-effect, when fed back can and should lead to continual improvement of theory. Thus, theory-building and model development are iterative, should proceed at least in parallel, and should eventually be convergent. In reality, this is not the situation with regards to major societal modeling efforts.

Several reasons apply, which are discussed through-out this paper:

1. No model is based on an inclusive theory or theories of societal systems, and especially of the macrosystem, because such does not exist.

2. Some models were originally based on portions of systems theories, for example, informa-tion feedback theory and multilevel, hierarchical theory, but: (a) These theories, assuming they are valid unto themselves, explain only a limited number of societal processes. (b) These theories appear frozen in the time of one to two decades ago, and not modified through feedback from the actual modeling experience.

3. Most models incorporate elements of economic theory, or at least economic hypotheses, explanations, rules, or algorithms (e.g., the Cobb-Douglas production function).

4. Models incorporate psychological, socio-logical, and cultural factors only at the most superficial, aggregated, or rationalized levels, if they do even this.

5. Models imperfectly if at all handle societal phenomena which are latent, discontinuous, suddenly restructuring, and emergent.

To recapitulate: We are stressing large-scale computer simulation models of societal systems. Obviously, catastrophy models, for example, indicate that the fifth point is not wholly generalizable, and models of the psychiatric interview and of drug addiction show progress along the lines of the fourth point.

Nevertheless, the present author holds (De Greene [4,5,6,7,8] that, because of the above limitations, large-scale societal models lack fidelity, and are prone to misunderstanding and misuse that are potentially harmful and even dangerous. The fourth and especially the fifth points are scarcely acknowledged in the literature on modeling. As far as this author knows, he was the first to identify the fifth point.

The nature of most of the objections raised above is straightforward, once the problems have been identified. Such problems are remediable through such methods as better rapproachment among the disciplines, better evaluation of basic assumptions in given modeling efforts, and better comparison of theoretically predicted and actual model outputs. The fifth point requires a radical restructuring of our thought processes. We shall devote the rest of this section to this point.

Theory of societal systems should be based on an understanding of psychological, sociological, cultural, political, historical, economic, tech-nological, and environmental forces, and on the field performance of these forces. Performance should especially emphasize properties of latency, criticality, threshold, coalescence, symbiosis, discontinuity, and emergence. The terms "force" and "field" are used in the field-theoretic sense.

Although field theory remains important in physics, it has lost much of its vitality in behavioral and social sciences. This author (De Greene [4,5,6,7]) has recently reexamined field theory in the light of recent developments in several sciences and in qualitative mathematics. Broadly generalizable approaches such as those of critical phenomena in physics, the emergence of collective or cooperative behaviors in several fields of science, catastrophe theory, and the

symbiotic and hyperbolic growth relationship between society and technology from the Paleo-lithic to the present were discussed. The field theoretic frame of reference also permitted con-sideration of more specific theoretic advances by individual authors. These included Emery's and Trist's theory of causal texture of the environ-ment (especially the turbulent-field environment), Emery's concept of futures we are in, Platt's concept of hierarchical jump, Simon's theory of the role of hierarchy in the evolution of complex organization, and Georgescu-Roegen's concept of the role of exosomatic organs in societal evolution.

This author believes that field theory pro-vides the most important frame of reference for the eventual definition, measurement, and control of societal forces. Especially important is an understanding of conversion of continuous to suddenly discontinuous system behavior, incipient change and early-warning signs, threshold behavior, splitting and clustering, reversibility/irreversibility of behavior, and emergence of new properties.

An example of the type phenomena we are con-sidering would be the psychological state or level of a population. The level could be, for instance, that of frustration, potential aggres-sion, kinetic aggression, alienation, achieve-ment motivation, and the like. The societal dynamics also include expectations, achievements, disparities between the expected and the actual, persuasiveness of messages, social contagion, and the like. Riots and revolutions exemplify some of the most dramatic resultant behaviors. These phenomena have long been studied by behavioral and social scientists, and explanatory theories offered.

As constantly reiterated by the present author, these phenomena and theories are not in-corporated into the mainstream of societal modeling. However, Zeeman et. al. [13] provide an example of the modeling of explosive changes in behavior, consequent to changes in psycho-logical states which lead to the exceeding of critical thresholds. This is a cusp catastrophe model of disturbances in institutions, particu-larly of riots in prisons. Fifty-two weekly totals of about 25 indices were factor analyzed to suggest two major control variables, aliena-tion and tension. An on-going monitoring system is being developed as an aid to predicting when, as a function of alienation and tension, disorder will break out.

In concluding this section, a comment should be made regarding an apparent contradiction of concepts, viz, field theory and causality. The layman finds it necessary to explain happenings in terms of causes. Even sophisticated modelers use words like "cause-effect," "causal model," and "causal diagram." Field theory states that Event A does not cause Event B in any simple determinate manner. Rather, Event A may lead to Event B as a function of a field of forces. We shall continue to employ the word "cause" only with reservations and only because it is so embedded in common usage. It is interesting to note that Coyle [3] uses "influence diagram" rather than "causal diagram."

3. TRADITIONAL SOCIAL SCIENCE MODELS

In this section we shall make no attempt to summarize the large literature on modeling and simulation in the behavioral and social sciences. Numerous models have of course been designed over the last two decades. These models differ by hierarchical level, degree of complexity, being static or dynamic, being deterministic or stochastic, discipline involved, and so on. Pertinent aspects of this literature have been reviewed elsewhere (De Greene [5]). Most of these models are small, one-of-a-kind designs, limited in scope, greatly aggregated, or static, or they possess other limitations rendering them beyond the scope of this paper. We shall consider only the fairly recent "social indicator models" as representative of traditional social science modeling. We suggest these to be the most "modern" approaches and potentially the easiest to reconcile with mainstream societal modeling.

Any meaningful scientific description or prediction of the states of a societal system requires both a set of measured indicators and a theoretical framework for interrelating these indicators. In any practical sense the framework must permit the manipulation of relevant variables to determine effects on policy. For our purposes the framework must be generalizable and not limited to specific societal subsystems.

The economic and social indicators movements represent large-scale efforts to sense and measure the pulse of society. In this paper we are concerned mostly with the social indicators.

A simple definition of a social indicator considers it to be a time series in some demographic or institutional variable. Superimposed on this are usually normative values of what is "good" for people. An excellent source of social indicator data and trends, mostly for the United States but also to some extent for certain other countries, is Social Indicators 1976 (Federal Statistical System [9]). However valuable such a compendium is in indicating certain features of certain states of society at a given time and as viewed from a certain perspective, it does not represent a theory of society, an indication of the underlying structure of society, or a statement of the cause-effect relationship of society. A framework is needed to tie things together.

Land [10] has provided the concept of a "social indicator model." He defines three major kinds of social indicator models: replication models, longitudinal models, and dynamic models. Replication models deal with macro-data from different individuals taken on the basis of two or more cross-sectional surveys. Longitudinal models are based on repeated micro-data from the same individuals. Dynamic models are of course time-dependent, and are the major concern of this paper.

Not all social statistics are relevant as social indicators; many social data are collected for routine administrative purposes. Nor can social indicators be equated to "quality of life" measurements, to any given hierarchical level of society, to implied "goodness" or "badness", or to application to immediate or short-range policies. Land [10] indicates three criteria for social indicators: (1) capability of collection in a time-series form; (2) possibility of aggregation or disaggregation to a desired level of analysis; and (3) identification as elements of a social system model.

Land differentiates among several types of or approaches to social indicators, organized within the context of a social system model somewhat as follows:

1. Exogenous variables: (a) Policy instrument descriptive indicators which are manipulable by social policy. (b) Nonmanipulable descriptive indicators which are not manipulable by social policy. Descriptive indicators are viewed as general measures of social conditions and changes.

2. Analytic indicators which are elements of the conceptual models of social processes. These are parameters which stem from the system of relationships connecting all other variables. Second-order impact analytic indicators derive from the interactions of output and side-effect descriptive indicators.

3. Endogenous variables: (a) Output or end-product descriptive indicators which define the social condition being measured and are the results of the social processes intrinsic to the model. (b) Side-effect descriptive indicators which influence or are influenced by, but do not define, the relevant social conditions and processes.

Although a simple conceptual model when compared to systems dynamics and other approaches to large-scale societal modeling, Land's model nevertheless far transcends actual social indicators work. Most modeling efforts have been at the subsystem level, and have attempted especially to relate nonmanipulable indicators to either output or side-effect indicators.

The heart of the dynamic modeling of complex societal systems can be expressed in terms of four questions: (1) What are the subsystems of concern, i.e., what are the categories for which indicators must be provided? (2) How are these subsystems organized hierarchically, i.e., what are the various levels of indicators required? (3) What are the forces, functions, or variables the behavior of which is indicated? (4) How is the totality interrelated causally? Modeling approaches based on existing (government) statistics will be of limited value, mostly because such statistics offer limited if any measures of actual subsystem performance.

Land [10] integrates earlier concepts of his and of other authors, viz, (1) definitions of the basic functions of society specified as types of activity such as reproduction; (2) organization as social indicator content areas, in which activities are related to institutional organizations like health care and the distributive consequences of such institutions, e.g., in relationship to morbidity and health at the level of the individual; (3) the societal life-cycle ordering of such distributed social attributes; (4) social stratification; (5) nebulous but extremely important "soft" factors such as aspiration, expectation, alienation, and morale; and (6) an individual life-space consisting of the three greatly aggregated and successively refinable measurement domains of (a) objective conditions, (b) subjective value-context (e.g., the subdomains of beliefs, expectations, and aspirations), and (c) subjective well-being (e.g., satisfactions, frustrations, and alienation derived from the factors in (a) and (b)).

In considering how social indicators might aid the understanding of social change, Land [10] classifies social indicator models in terms of three types of social transformations and two types of data used. Cohort change refers to that (decomposed) portion of a total observed historical change in the values of a social indicator due to the replacement of older cohorts in the population by younger cohorts. Cohorts are aggregates of persons who experience the same event, most often birth, within the same time interval. Life-cycle change refers to that portion of a total historical change due to the aging of cohorts. Period change refers to that portion of a total historical change due to the unique characteristics of the given observation period. Data types are macro-data and micro-data. A fourth change, socio-structural change, that portion due to changes in the efficacy of social institutions for various distributional processes, was not included in the classification.

There are three traditional reasons for social indicators: social reporting, social change, and social policy. Land states that a social indicator model can be transformed into a social policy model through use of an appropriate objective function and an optimization criterion. Such an operations research approach has not proved to be harmonious with systems dynamics or most other large-scale modeling efforts, and we suggest following it would be another step down the wrong pathway.

Stinchcombe and Wendt [11] discuss the theoretical domain, or set of possible uses of a concept and its measures, in terms of four elements:

1. The unit of analysis or most fundamental choice of a theory, and a boundary within which invariant causal interrelationships obtain. In social science the three main units of analysis have been the act or decision, the individual, and the group.

2. A set of environments within which invariances hold. e.g., closed systems or, alternatively, all possible environments.

3. A set of concepts or names of theoretical variables.

4. A set of functional forms for the invariant relations between concepts. These are usually divided according to the role of change in them (deterministic vs. stochastic) and the role of time. The latter is of particular interest to our concern with dynamic models in this paper.

Relationships in a system of equations or laws which relate the concepts of a theoretical domain can be stated in terms of a spanning set of concepts. A causal locus refers to a set of variables having the same causal relations to other variables in a domain. Two or more variables having the same causal locus are caused by the same phenomena and cause the same phenomena in the same proportions. A measure is valid in proportion to its identifying a unique causal locus, and different measures of the same concept should occupy the same locus.

The lack of specific theory about functional and termporal forms in most behavioral and social science theory, e.g., the lack of appreciation of the distribution of time differentials, renders

formulation of causal relationships very difficult. For example, the ordinal, or before-and-after (pulse) treatment, concept of time and cause-effect, emphasized in experimental psychology, had led to dead-end arguments as to which came first causally in many Western societies, capitalism or Protestantism. This concept overlooks mutual causality. Stinchcombe and Wendt [11] redefine the problem in terms of a pair of differential equations in time and several causal variables. Essentially, the rate of growth of capitalist socioeconomic relations depends on the level of Protestantism and certain other variables (taken from Max Weber), and the rate of growth of Protestantism depends on the level of capitalism and on several other influences on Protestantism. Neither one of the major variables precedes the other in time and they both grow together.

Note the (inadvertent) analogy to systems dynamics. This analogy is furthered by Stinchcombe's and Wendt's concern with equilibrium and comulative concepts, that is, where time enters as the span of an integral. An equilibrium relation predicts the cumulative change in a dependent variable as time approaches infinity.

Social variables predicting cross-sectional correlation often do not predict completely or at all changes over time. Causes found in longitudinal studies are usually different from those in cross-sectional studies. That is, studies before and after an event will not identify the same causes of changes in a dependent variable as will a cross-sectional study at a given time. Stinchcombe and Wendt interpret this disparity in terms of variability's being the end result of an equilibrating type of causal system. The causes that operate via equilibrium relations are (temporarily?) quiescent and their effects have already been manifested. This situation obtains especially when the causes are relatively permanent characteristics of the units of analysis and require a long time to reach an equilibrium effect. There may be very little of the equilibrating process between successive surveys, yet much of the cumulative results of this process in the variability among individuals at a given point in time. This is because the periods of oscillations associated with permanent causes in equilibrating processes are large compared to the time between surveys, but small compared to the span of values for these causes.

Stinchcombe and Wendt [11] summarize six different roles of time in the causal relating of variables:

1. Ordinal time, where the cause is an event. Periods before and after the event are identifiable, and changes that occur after the event or pulse are considered to be effects. This is the dominant approach to causation in behavioral science and history, but it has little meaning in the serious study of complex realworld social systems.

2. Instantaneous time, a linear of polynomial regressional analysis approach, in which causal invariables determine dependent variables without significant time lags. There is always a 1:1 relationship between the values of the causal and dependent variables.

3. Permanent time, in which causal variables

do not change appreciably, and regression analyses are also justified. Constancy pertains to any and all points of time, not just to a current state as for instantaneous time.

4. _Time as differential_, in which the rate of change of a variable is considered to be determined by its causes. In the differential equation time enters explicitly in the definition of the dependent variable. This approach has not been widely accepted among social scientists, because they perceive causality in terms of 1:1 mappings without time as an interacting variable.

5. _Time as a transient in equilibrating processes_, in which the full effects of causes in determining equilibria are manifested only after considerable time ("infinity"). In one form of equilibrating theory, which has seen application in relating public opinion and opinion compatible with current government policies, the causal force pushing a variable toward the equilibrium is proportional to the distance from that equilibrium. The value of the variable will keep changing until the disparity between that value and the equilibrium value of the variable equals zero, that is, until the value reaches its equilibrium value. The farther the variable is from its equilibrium value, the faster will be the approach. Further, the greater the strength of the equilibrating causal process, the less the time lag.

This conception of time with its cybernetic implications can obviously be related to systems dynamics, and also to other approaches to large-scale societal modeling, and to mathematical and non-mathematical field theoretic approaches reviewed earlier by this author (De Greene [4,7]).

6. _Time as a measure of changes in contextual variables_, which is not a conception of how causes operate over time. Rather, time may operate as a proxy for other variables.

Coleman [2] describes another approach to dynamic modeling relevant to the theme of this paper. It is based on the birth and survival matrix commonly used in demography, coupled with vectors which move given cohorts into and through various system states. The matrix of probabilities in the discrete-time version carries the population between ages 14 and 80 forward for a given time period (e.g., one year). There are several states for each age, and each stage represents an occupation (white-collar work, blue-collar work, education, the military, etc.) in which a person may be found. The model considers not only such direct changes in transition probabilities, but also factors determining these transition probabilities. Thus, in the continuous-time version it is able to provide a system of _flows_ among occupations in the context of a _causal_ model making these flows functions of variables at the level of the individual. The transition rates now are a function of age or of other characteristics of the individual and his job. The transition rate varies continuously with age, for example; hence, only one estimate over all years is necessary. For transition probabilities, on the other hand, separate estimates are required for each time period.

Coleman believes this modeling approach is quite general, and applies to educational states, health states, states in a "criminal justice" system, and states in other societal subsystems. As an accounting scheme for tracing the birth of

members of a population into and progressively through the states of a system, it is a policy-manipulable model. Changing underlying variables or parameters that govern the flow of people through states in the social subsystem will affect the transition rates among states. Coleman believes this approach represents the maturity of the social indicators movement.

To conclude this section, a few words should be said about the approach to societal problems in the traditional social sciences, especially sociology:

1. The level of emphasis is the individual, the group, the small formal organization, or the community rather than the society.

2. Cross sectional studies in frequency far surpass longitudinal studies; emphasis in these studies is on the present.

3. Discrete-data models are used far more often than are continuous-data models.

4. Multivariate (usually regression) analysis is the most commonly used methodological tool.

5. Scant attention has been paid to multiple, mutual causality.

6. Structural models are seldom employed.

We argue, nonetheless, that the social indicators/ social indicator models approach is complementary to the systems engineering/ economics approach characteristic of mainstream societal modeling. Both provide valuable concepts and elements of theory. The former can provide insight into behavioral/social relationships as well as a plethora of data. The latter provide superior structure, as well as a superior dynamic approach. As an example of complementarity, consider the following. Several large-scale societal models possess labor sectors or labor submodels. Yet so far these appear to be crude, mechanistic aggregations. Behavioral and social scientists have studied occupational mobility and achievement, the behavior of women and minority groups in the workplace, the role of labor unions, the impact of technological change on work, alienation from work, and so forth. Use of these findings could greatly refine the grossly oversimplified societal models.

Finally, for our purposes indicators need necessarily have no normative or value implication. They must be available for all the relevant hierarchical levels of society. They must apply both to obvious and convert phenomena. They must be capable not only of aggregation and disaggregation, but also of dissection to remove confounding causes and effects and, contrariwise, integration to indicate emergence. They must be relatable in terms of constructs and theory. These and other requirements are discussed more fully elsewhere (De Greene [5,6]).

---

[1] The feud between systems dynamicists and econometricians is again acknowledged. Indeed, econometric models have more in common with traditional models in sociology than they do with "state variable" models. Many of the criticisms of econometrics vouchsafed by systems dynamicists also apply to other behavioral/ social science models.

4. PRESENT MAINSTREAM MODELING APPROACHES

A continual comparative analysis and evaluation is being made of mainstream approaches to the computer simulation modeling of complex societal systems. "Mainstream" models are large dynamic models, in the public eye, the main raison d'etre of which is influencing the policy process. Five approaches have been evaluated or are in the process of ongoing evaluation: systems dynamics (e.g., the Limits models and the U. S. national socioeconomic model); hierarchical, multilevel systems model (Mankind at the Turning Point); SPECULATER/SAM (Interdisciplinary Systems Group of the University of California at Davis); the Latin American (or "Bariloche") World Model; and the Dutch Model of International Relations in Agriculture (MOIRA).

Comparative analysis of designer-produced documentation, the general literature, and listings and tapes if available includes some relatively straightforward areas of which the following ten are illustrative:

1. Underlying philosophies and basic assumptions.
2. Basic structure and structural units.
3. Origin and nature of major variables.
4. Nature of simulation -- discrete, continuous, or both.
5. Simulation languages used.
6. Definition, nature, origin, and use of data.
7. Fitting of parameters.
8. Concepts of and attempts toward verification and validation.
9. Sources of formal or substantive error.
10. Nature of user interaction, if any, including definition of words like "scenario".

In addition, special attention is being paid to the following areas:

1. Theoretical underpinnings.
2. Feedback of model results to original theory, if any.
3. Nature and degree of incorporation of behavioral/social theory, factors, findings, and data.
4. Flexibility in modeling societal processes other than those associated with the primary structural units, e.g., modeling of discontinuous and emergent processes.
5. Main policy applications.
6. Potentiality for misuse for advocacy or power-driven purposes.
7. Dangerous impacts or side-effects, assuming the model is accepted and used by policy- and decision-makers.

A number of evaluative comments and interpretations about the five modeling approaches have been made elsewhere (De Greene [4,5,6,7,8]). Others will be published later. For the purposes of this article the most serious deficiencies of mainstream modeling can be summarized as follows:

1. All models lack fidelity, because of lack of any real incorporation of behavioral and social theories, findings, and data.
2. All models lack fidelity, because their structures capture only one major type, if that, of societal process.
3. All models are on shaky footing because, lacking full theoretic grounding and the incorporation of human factors in models that purport to deal with human society, there is overreliance on the judgments of experts, on scenarios, or on exogenous inputs (see especially De Greene [4,6]).
4. Most models, especially those that deal with the world food problem, have inherent in them the possibility of dangerous technological impacts with the opening up of a Pandora's box of new crises.

It was concluded that systems dynamics possesses the least objections and is the most valuable approach so far for the modeling of complex societal systems. The capabilities and limitations of this approach are discussed in the following subsection.

4.1. Systems Dynamics and the Theory of Society

In this section we shall discuss: (a) the strengths and potentially rectifiable limitations of system dynamics; (b) the conceptually major limitations of systems dynamics, which may be difficult or impossible to rectify; and (c) systems dynamics as a partial theory of society.

Strengths and potentially rectifiable limitations. The major beauty of systems dynamics lies in its generality and flexibility. It is unquestioned that cybernetic systems exist at all hierarchical levels of living systems, both natural and man-made. The information-feedback loop, as the basic structural unit, permits the construction of models in all areas and at just about any level of complexity. The last two decades have witnessed applications ranging hierarchically from glucose metabolism within the human body to the spread of heroin addiction in a community and desertification in the Sahel to the dynamics of industries and cities to the dynamics of the United States economy and of the world. The behavior of feedback loops has been worked out in great detail, and the dynamic behavior of systems such as growth, oscillatory, and overshoot and collapse behavior explained in terms of these loops.

Two major limitations of systems dynamics are the lack of rapprochement with behavioral and social science and the subjective underpinnings. Both these limitations can be considered manageable. The present paper and other cited writings of this author are steps in this direction. Several examples of psychological level variables and associated dynamics have been offered earlier. There is a vast amount of potentially useful attitudinal and social indicator data. There are, however, different degrees of sophistication in applying the outputs of behavioral and social science.

At the lowest degree of sophistication social indicator data, for example, are unquestionably better than no data at all and the handling of behavioral/social factors either not at all or by crude oversimplifications and aggregations. Social indicator data may be either objective (e.g., conditions in the workplace, reported crimes, or labor force participation by various cohorts) or subjective (e.g., attitudes about "quality of life" dimensions such as the home or the neighborhood, and confidence in various societal institutions). Many indicators can be

directly expressed as level variables, and time
series and trends permit the estimation of rates
and some functional relationships. There are many
sources of error in societal simulation models.
We argue that using even crude social indicator
data would not add to the error already introduced
from other sources, and would actually reduce
error through refining concepts like "production,"
"labor," and "workforce."

The main deficiency of social indicators is
that cause-effect relationships are difficult or
impossible to detect. A higher degree of sophistication involves determining or estimating such
relationships. Two methods could be used iteratively and in conjunction: (1) path analysis and
the multivariate analysis and related methods
long used in social science, and (2) small systems
dynamics modules the output of which could be
fitted to actual data. We are not suggesting a
return either to reliance on correlational
methods or to the rigorous testing of confidence
limits so beloved by generations of statisticians
and behavioral and social scientists. We are
indicating a refinement on the otherwise subjective
relating of variables, especially in multiplier
curves (such a "fine tuning" was followed by the
modelers at U. C. Davis, by the way; for references
to such original literature see the cited
publications of this author). The better the
understanding of behavioral/social relationships,
the less the reliance on subjective underpinnings.
Such reliance is considered to be the second
major manageable limitation of systems dynamics.

The greatest degree of sophistication in
using extant behavioral and social science data
deals with discontinuities and sudden, unexpected
reconfigurations associated with volatile societal
processes. An example, which we are proposing to
model in detail is the rioting and looting
behavior in July 1977 which was triggered by a
several-hour-long electric power failure. Doubt-
less few researchers, if anybody, had systematically related rioting and looting as dependent
variables to electric power failures as an
independent variable. There is, of course, much
informal knowledge derived from experiences in
establishing martial law following floods and
other natural disasters. At any rate the statement
of the problem above is incorrect, as would be the
terms cause-effect. Once again, a field-theoretic
orientation is necessary. This discussion will be
continued in the next section.

Conceptually major limitations. There are two
major conceptual limitations to systems dynamics.
First, as a cybernetic model it is only a partial
model of society among a family of known models.
Second, systems dynamics may be unable to handle
catastrophe-theoretic and emergent phenomena now
on the frontiers of knowledge.

Three examples of alternative theoretic
approaches should suffice. In the first case,
systems dynamics modeling is deterministic, but
many processes in complex systems--and most likely
most of the interesting ones in society--are
probabilistic. Systems dynamics handles probabilistic inputs as noise inputs, but the relationships between variables remain deterministic.
"Probabilistic systems dynamics" is a blend of
systems dynamics and cross-impact analysis,
whereby probabilities of events and of effects

of events on trends and the like can be studied.
Systems dynamics could be made to handle additional
probabilistic situations. However, systems
dynamicists apparently do not feel it is worth
the effort, especially considering the subjective
assumptions underlying the theory and applications
of probability.

A second example derives from the confusion in
systems dynamics between open/closed and open-loop/
closed-loop systems. Even when the distinction is
clear the model may appear wrong, because: (1)
feedback loops do cross the purported closed-loop
system boundary, and/or (2) no important living
system in the real world and no systems dynamics
model is a closed system (the cloud symbols show
people and materials crossing the system boundary).
More significantly, the organizational and dis-
organizational (entropic) properties of open
systems are not handled by feedback dynamics.
Open systems models are currently of particular
importance to organization theory. Systems
dynamics models do not typically come to grips
with the environmental impact, qualitative
growth, structural differentiation, establishment
of new levels of control, dissociation of parts,
and increasing randomness characteristic of open
systems. Of course different models could be
built for qualitatively different stages of
system development, or SWITCH or CLIP functions
could be used to open up new loops of greater
diversification or turn on different levels of
control at future times. Nevertheless, this
would only approximate open systems properties.

As a third example, all non-trivial realworld
systems are hierarchical. Yet simulation models
handle hierarchy differently from natural hierarchies. Natural hierarchies require that certain
criteria be met. Mankind at the Turning Point is
formally defined in terms of multi-level hierarchical control as its basic structure. But
even this model does not satisfy all criteria
for natural hierarchies (De Green [4,7]). Systems
dynamics handles hierarchy in a loose sense.
Truly enough, modules or submodels can be successively assembled. But there is no intrinsic
vertical organization in systems dynamics. There
is only one kind of level variable. An n-th
order system means that there are n level variables and (often) delays, not that there are n
hierarchical levels of control each with qualitatively different emergent properties. Control
rests in feedback loops, and gives the impression
of casual horizontal arrangement more than of
vertical organization. Dominance is not necessarily implicit in a systems dynamics feedback
loop, and may shift from one loop to another as
a function of certain (but not most) parameters,
policy changes, exceeding limits, etc. Using
the mammalian organism as an analogy, systems
dynamics control appears more like the shifting
dominance in endocrine control (cf. the relationship between the anterior pituitary and the
gonads or adrenal cortex or thyroid) than the
normal hierarchical control of the brain over
lower nervous centers. Stafford Beer's [1]
approach may be more realistic than that of
systems dynamics in this theoretic sense.

Systems dynamics and field theoretic systemic
phenomena. We have previously identified a
number of field theoretic phenomena which we

believe are representative of the most important in Nature and Society (De Greene [6,7]). A model of society represents a filter, and that filter in turn reflects perspective, bias, and ignorance. Systems dynamics deals with only a few (e.g., feedback relationships, lead/lag situations, the quantitative features of growth) of the indicated phenomena. Systems dynamics may lack fidelity for two reasons (in addition to those discussed earlier). First, a wide variety of phenomena, which can collectively be lumped together under the term "morphogenesis" are not handled at all. Quantitative growth need not go on forever, level off at asymptote, collide with an absolute limit, or overshoot a limit and collapse. It can lead to diversification and splitting into qualitatively different forms. Second, by extracting certain phenomena (e.g., feedback loops) from the field in which they usually operate, these phenomena may be reduced to hollow caricatures of reality. In the real world there is not just one form of information feedback. In organizations there are at least three forms of communication: conscious and formal, conscious and informal, and unconscious. And how realistic are the familiar sales-inventory-production-workforce relationships which lie at the heart of all industrial dynamics and many other systems dynamics models? Do labor unions play no role? Do threats of production cutoffs not affect worker attitudes toward their jobs and hence productivity? Do older generation workers with certain values come from the same clouds outside the system boundary as do the new generation with different values--and more women and minority groups! (Cf. the 1972 strike at the Vega plant in Lordstown, Ohio.)

Coyle [3] suggests that systems dynamics may be inappropriate for situations, for example, interpersonal relationships, which are fluid and evolving. He believes there is no unambiguous and effective language to describe such situations. Suppose we were to exclude from systems dynamics the volatile processes which we argue are the most important and most interesting dynamic processes. What would be left? Much of the reason for systems dynamics lies in the identification and rectification through policy changes of time lags or delays between such things as accounting for sales, restocking inventory, and stepping up production. Yet this is conceptually old stuff. For example, at the level of retail stores and supermarkets which use automatic checkout counters and possess well-stocked warehouses and high-speed communications with distributors, time delays are reduced to truck delivery speeds. With improvements in computer-communications systems and management information systems, there is no conceptual impediment to applying these systems to successively higher levels of production industry. Should this be true, it is likely that systems dynamics would be relegated to becoming just another routine management science tool--highly abstracted, rationalized, and inapplicable to really complex problems.

It can thus be seen that much systems dynamics philosophy and application stems from an era in which things were different. In the example above the level of automation was much less. Unfortunately, the literature does not provide much evidence for qualitative changes in systems

dynamics. Nor is there much evidence for the validity of the process (as opposed to unlimited debate on the validity of model structure and output). We know of no examples of experimentally controlled studies in which systems dynamics has been compared with other approaches, or behaviors of systems have been compared with and without systems dynamics. The difficulty and cost of such studies is of course acknowledged.

Clearly, systems dynamics and other modeling approaches must evolve to handle different and more complex situations, or be replaced--if possible--by other approaches. How might systems dynamics evolve? Of the field theoretic phenomena mentioned in this article or in the cited references, several fit into the category of catastrophe theory, where elementary catastrophe theory could be considered to be a theory of catastrophes induced by a field of gradient dynamics. A readable description of catastrophe theory and analysis of its strengths and limitations and contrasting of viewpoints of the leading protagonists, together with applications to various sciences, is provided by Zeeman [13]. We perceive systems dynamics and catastrophe theory to be harmonious, and catastrophe theory to provide an infusion of new thought into systems dynamics for several reasons:

1. Both are built on the concept of continuous processes, but catastrophe theory carries on to deal with suddenly divergent, discontinuous, and jumping behavior produced by continuous causes.

2. Both aim toward refinement of formalization of loose conceptual models.

3. Both deprecate overreliance on statistics, and premature quantification and validation through small isolated experiments.

4. The elementary catastrophes, like feedback loops, provide a means of synthesizing many ideas. Elementary catastrophes could provide building blocks (Thom's "phonemes of the language") for construction of successively more complex hierarchies.

5. Delays play an important role in both types of models.

One possibly promising area for examination of a rapproachment between systems dynamics and catastrophe theory is that of economic cycles, especially in terms of stock market crashes such as that associated with the Great Depression. The Systems Dynamics National Model proposes that the Great Depression followed a period of overexpansion of the capital sectors of the economy, accompanied by widespread speculation and eventually severe decrease in investment opportunities. Zeeman's catastrophe model employs a cusp catastrophe in which excess demand represents a normal factor and proportion of the market held by speculators a splitting factor. Crash can be precipitated by reduced demand coupled with a large share of the market being held by speculators. Recovery is slow because of delays in the feedback loops. In pursuing this example the modeler must ask if the concepts of divergence, split, discontinuity, and sudden drop from the top to the bottom sheet provide any useful further precision in understanding.

System dynamics as a partial theory of society. We should like to argue that systems dynamics, in spite of the limitations just discussed, does indeed represent a partial theory of society. Our argument derives from the basic truism of systems science: the whole is greater than the sum of the parts. Thus, systems dynamics as a body of modeling experience has provided new insights, now--in retrospect--almost self-evident. We suggest this knowledge could not have been inferred prior to development of and experience with actual models. These insights now familiar to most readers include:

1. Counterintuitive behavior of complex systems: the correct policies tend to be opposite to those dictated by common sense; causes and effects are not closely related in space or time, but people have the tendency to choose causes that happen to be conveniently but only coincidentally related to effects.

2. Insensitivity to different values of parameters: the basic psychological and biological dynamics are almost invariants in different social systems.

3. Resistance to policy changes, deriving from the first two features.

4. Sensitivity to some parameter changes producing pressure points in unexpected places, leading to the radiation of large changes throughout the system.

5. Corrective programs counteracted by the system's behavior: system balance shifts so as to swallow up such attempts.

6. Long-term reactions much different from short-term reactions to policy changes.

7. Drift over time to system low performance: because, especially of the first and seventh features, policy- and decision-makers attempt "more of the same" rather than innovative new approaches.

A computer simulation model can, therefore, be interpreted and evaluated according to different criteria of usefulness, effectiveness, or validity at several different operating levels. A model, embedded in a social system of application, may produce valuable, even unexpected new insights associated with emergent properties, even though it fails all the usual validity tests at lower levels. This is but another example in which human creations, at certain levels, assume a life of their own.

5. CONCLUDING REMARKS: IMPLICATIONS FOR HUMAN AND SOCIETAL LIMITS

The theoretic considerations discussed in this paper have several further implications for the fidelity and usefulness of computer simulation models. One important area concerns the rate and nature of growth itself.

Evidence from studying the symbiotic relationship between society and technology suggests that sociotechnical evolution is not exponential but hyperbolic (see the discussion in, e.g., De Greene [4,7]). The rate of growth of human population and of social and technological change themselves appear to be increasing. The Forrester/Meadows concept of limits to population, economic, and associated growth, which seemed so bold in the early years of this decade, now appears antiquated and oversimplified. Not only are most physical

limits probably more imminent than any present simulation model would forecast, but the very nature of interactions, impacts, and side-effects is in all models grossly oversimplified. The complexities of ecologies and of human societies appear to be unappreciated. For example, land is cleared and fertilizer applied to increase crop yields per hectare to provide additional nutrients for growing populations. But what about the effects of land clearance on desertification, the water table, wildlife protection, flood control and avoidance, local temperature and atmospheric moisture condensation, and so on and so on? Realworld experience provides numerous examples of systems, organizations, and applications that have failed or have introduced serious and unanticipated side effects (cf. the Aswan High Dam, the Sahel, worldwide destruction of the tropical rain forests, the Green Revolution, and so on). Further, what about the now nourished citizen who demands, in the political as well as the economic sense of the word, a color television set, a motorcycle, a car, and so on (see De Greene [6])?

In short: The impression is generated that mainstream societal models do not reflect real-world frustrations and failures, and remain rooted in the concepts of abstracted living systems and of the rational man that characterized operations research and systems analysis in the 1950's and 1960's. This is paradoxical, considering that computer simulation modeling is supposed to be at the vanguard of methods in futurology. A next stage in serious modeling should, therefore, be: Given that the major policy recommendations of the five or so mainstream modeling approaches have been implemented, what are the likely states and behaviors of the world sociotechnical system?

In a sense, then, some of these models are technologically obsolescent, reactive to serious problems defined a decade or two ago rather than anticipatory of emerging societal configurations and problems. Considering the unmanageability of nations, economies, governments, and social bureaucracies in general, one must seriously question whether computer simulation modeling is augmenting human cognition, which like physical processes and the manageability of institutions may be fast approaching a limit. That human intelligence and problem-solving ability may be approaching their limits, especially under increasing time pressures, promises to be a proposition even less palatable than was the original limits to growth.

In conclusion, if computer simulation models are to live up to their promise in a timely manner, the following requirements must be fulfilled:

1. Models must be more fully and more dynamically related to theory itself.

2. Models must incorporate a much broader range of theories, both vertically (hierarchically) and horizontally (e.g., based on disciplines).

3. Models must make vastly greater use of behavioral and social science outputs.

4. Behavioral and social science must become more real world-oriented and more involved with the "big picture."

5. The systems development time for models must be greatly reduced to bring it more in tune with the actual rapidly changing state of society and to permit realtime changes in concept and structure.

6. Models must be designed and implemented so as to minimize deliberate misuse and unexpected technological impact.

REFERENCES

1. BEER, S., Brain of the Firm: A Development of Management Cybernetics, New York, McGraw-Hill, 1972.

2. COLEMAN, J. S., "Analysis of Occupational Mobility by Models of Occupational Flow," in Social Indicator Models, K. C. Land and S. Spilerman (eds.), pp. 319-334, New York, Russell Sage, 1975.

3. COYLE, R. G., Management Systems Dynamics, New York, Wiley, 1977.

4. DE GREENE, K. B., "Problems of Modeling Emergent Phenomena in Complex Societal Systems," in Proceedings of the International Symposium SIMULATION '77, M. H. Hamza (ed.), pp. 370-374, Anaheim, California; Calgary, Alberta; and Zurich, Switzerland: Acta Press, 1977.

5. DE GREEN, K. B., "Investigation of Means of Incorporating Behavioral and Social Variables into Dynamic Computer Simulation Models of Complex Societal Systems," Research Proposal Submitted to National Science Foundation, Washington, D. C., August 1977.

6. DE GREENE, K. B., "Problems in the Incorporation of Behavioral and Social Factors into Models of Complex Societal Systems," in Avoiding Social Catastrophes and Maximizing Social Opportunities: The General Systems Challenge, pp. 66-72, Washington, D. C., Society for General Systems Research, 1978.

7. DE GREENE, K. B., "Force Fields and Emergent Phenomena in Sociotechnical Macrosystems," Behavioral Science, 23 (1), January, 1978.

8. DE GREENE, K. B., "Progress and Set-Back in the Modeling and Computer Simulation of Complex Societal Systems," Progress in Cybernetics and Systems Research, Vol. V, Washington, D. C., Hemisphere, 1978.

9. Federal Statistical System, Bureau of the Census, Social Indicators, 1976, Washington, D. C., U. S. Government Printing Office, December, 1977.

10. LAND, K. C., "Social Indicator Models: An Overview," in Social Indicator Models, K. C. Land and S. Spilerman (eds.), pp. 5-36, New York, Russell Sage, 1975.

11. STINCHCOMBE, A. L. and J. C. WENDT, "Theoretical Domains and Measurement in Social Indicator Analysis," in Social Indicator Models, K. C. Land and S. Spilerman (eds.), pp. 37-73, New York, Russell Sage, 1975.

12. ZEEMAN, E. C., Catastrophe Theory: Selected Papers 1972-1977, Reading, Massachusetts, Addison-Wesley, 1977.

13. ZEEMAN, E. C., et. al., "A Model of Institutional Disturbances," in Catastrophe Theory: Selected Papers 1972-1977, pp. 387-401, Reading, Massachusetts, Addison-Wesley, 1977.

The problem of providing and assessing feedback in an educational system

O. J. HANSON
The City University Business School, London, England

1. INTRODUCTION

Whether a University course should prepare a student for a vocation, or deliberately avoid doing so, has often been debated in British academic circles. Academic respectability is the aim of some highly respected University course designers, rather than the provision of a sound education in a practically useful area. This has recently been criticised by the British Government, and in the present period of high graduate unemployment students themselves are turning more and more to courses of study that will given them a good chance of getting a job on graduation.

In Hanson [1] it was made clear that systems feedback and design methods are not easily applied to courses that do not have well-defined objectives. The type of course that is susceptible to systems analysis was described in Hanson [2] as being practically oriented. This does not exclude any other type; the test is whether objectives that are measurable can be laid down. Judgements here are often not absolute, but depend on subjective opinions. Even so, unless these judgements are made, systems techniques will not be able to operate, due to the lack of feedback to allow decisions to be modified in the light of experience. The making of feedback decisions in cases of uncertainty is the theme of this paper, and although a great deal of statistical analysis has been carried out in interpreting the data presented, it is recognised that social systems are not fully predictable -- except perhaps in the sort of future conceived by Asimov [3].

The first problem to be solved is that of the desired "output" from a course. When this has been decided on, it is possible to determine the type of "input" that is required; in this paper the student intake is the input examined. The progress of students and staff is then followed by the use of a number of techniques that allow for feedback and adjustment during the course.

At the end of each year the success of the course is reviewed, and changes aimed at improving it are introduced. This process, and the techniques employed in measuring it, are described below.

2. DEFINING SUCCESSFUL OUTPUT

The ultimate test of an educational course is the success in their chosen field of past students. This presents difficulties if students go back to very different careers, as is often the case. The Diploma in Systems Analysis has had members of the British Civil Service on all the first five courses, and in the longer run it is hoped to analyse the success of students in the Civil Service. The intention to do this was stated in Hanson [4], when the course was first described, and discussed in [1], when the first results of the course were presented. Up to the present, however, insufficient data is available for meaningful analysis.

A student who graduates from a course should have acquired a number of new capabilities as a result of the period of study he has followed. These will include:
(a) An understanding of the tasks to be carried out by a person working in the field he has chosen; examples might be:
 (i) The principles of stock control
 (ii) Critical Path Analysis, its benefits and the ways of applying it
 (iii) The steps involved in analysing a business system
(b) Techniques to be used; these might include:
 (i) Procedural flowcharging
 (ii) Fact-finding interviewing
 (iii) Statistical examination of data
(c) Skills to be developed in the student:
 (i) Confident verbal presentation of information
 (ii) Sympathetic handling of people from shop-floor level to Board members
 (iii) The ability to write concise, logical reports in a language that will be understood by the recipient.

As it is not yet possible to give practical results of the application of these skills, the next best alternative is to use the overall Diploma results that involve student performance in tests of the capabilities given above.

The author discussed the validity of examinations in assessing the student in [5]. Harrell [6] pointed out that the ATGSM -- now described as GMAT -- test results were not highly correlated with future success of graduates, but that first degree results were even less successful.

Appropriate examinations are very widely taken as proof of ability in fields requiring skill, and are legally necessary before professions such as medicine may be practised. For that reason, "success" of students on the Diploma has been taken to be reflected by their final mark, which is made up of contributions from coursework, case studies, interviewing exercises, presentations and final written examinations. This is discussed in greater detail in [4].

The use of final examination results to measure student ability is an act of faith; however, it has been possible to check the _consistency_ of these results in two years. In 1974/75 it was possible to compare the results of students in the Diploma overall, finishing in June (as described in [4]) with their marks in the BCS examinations, held in April, and set and marked by a different board of examiners. The results are given in Table 2, and the regression line for the two examinations is shown in Figure 2. The correlation coefficient is 0.81, and use of Student's Test shows that this is significant at better than the 0.1% level.

In 1976/77 ten students sat a "mock" BCS examination, using questions from the actual BCS papers of 1976, but marked by the Diploma teaching staff. The results are given in Table 1B. The regression line for these results is also plotted in Figure 2, and shows a close correspondence with that for the 1974/75 group. The correlation coefficient is 0.7, and has a probability of about 1% of occurring by change alone.

These two comparisons do not indicate that the final results of the Diploma predict future success; however, they do show that those final results are consistent and repeatable, and thus are a useful form of feedback. Incidentally, they indicate that the BCS examinations have the same desirable properties.

3. DECIDING ON STUDENT INPUT

Candidates for the Diploma show a very wide range of age, expertise in data processing, and prior qualifications. These three are shown in Tables 1A and 1B for the years 1975/76 and 1976/77. Details for earlier years are given in [1]. Figure 1 shows the age and experience spread for all four years in histogram form. Prior qualifications vary from "0" level to master's degrees, and the breakdown by year has been presented in [7].

In addition to these three personal attributes, candidates were expected to sit the ATGSB (now GMAT) test in 1973/74 - 1975/76, and a number of candidates also took the test in 1976/77. Results are given in Tables 1A and 1B, and in Tables 4A and 4B of reference [1].

Civil Service candidates were subjected to controlled and extensive exploratory interviews. The results of these can also be obtained from the sources given above. Private candidates were interviewed over so long a time-span that it was expected consistency might differ from that for Civil Service candidates, and too few results are available for these students as yet to decide whether this is so. Assessment of interviewing is therefore restricted to Civil Servants.

Before it was possible to examine the value of the factors discussed above as predictors of performance in the Diploma total lists, it had to be decided whether the four years results could be handled as a whole or needed to be split up. Table 4 shows six groups. In 1973/74 one student was unable to study full time and failed the Diploma very badly. This student is included in group 1, but excluded from 1'. In 1976/77 one student did not learn the English language properly due to living with the family and speaking a foreign language. Group 4 includes this student,

while 4' does not. Average Diploma totals ($\bar{x}$), numbers of students (N), sample variances (S_s), sample standard deviations (σ_S), and best estimates of population variances ($\hat{\sigma}^2$) are given in Table 4.

Table 5 shows the results of comparing the variances and means of the six groups (1 and 1' were not compared, nor were 4 and 4'). Best estimates of population variances were analysed by finding the ratio $\hat{\sigma}_A^2 : \hat{\sigma}_B^2$, and determining the significance with reference to Snedecor's F test [8,9]. Significance figures are given in percentages.

The means of the various groups were compared by the use of the null hypothesis. A best estimate of the standard error of the difference, σ_ω, was arrived at as follows

$$\hat{\sigma}^2 = \frac{N_1 S_{1s} + N_2 S_{2s}}{N_1 + N_2 - 2}$$

$$\sigma_\omega = \hat{\sigma} \sqrt{\frac{1}{N_1} + \frac{1}{N_2}}$$

Significance was tested using the equation $t = (\bar{x}_1 - \bar{x}_2) \sigma_\omega$. The probability p that the difference between the means, $(\bar{x}_1 - \bar{x}_2)$, was significant is given in Table 5 as a decimal, where $1 > P > 0$.

Only groups 1 and 2 had both variances and means that were close enough to allow them to be combined for analytical purposes. However, the form of the final examination changed markedly between the two years. For that reason it was decided to treat the four years as separate groups.

3.1. GMAT/ATGSB Test

Table 6A shows the coorelations observed between ATGSB test results and Diploma totals in the four years analysed. In 1973/74 and 1976/77 (on a very small sample) significant correlations were observed, but in the intervening years this did not apply. As the test is unreliable, attempts are being made to develop a combined aptitude/English language test more tailored to the needs of systems analysts (Hanson [7]).

3.2. Interview Assessments

Table 6B gives the performance of interviewing as a predictor of success in the four years examined. In 1973/74 and 1974/75 the overall results should be attributed merely to change, although one or two very good predictions were made in this time. The 1975/76 results were remarkable for a non-parametric method of assessment (the Kendal rank correlation test [10]); it is extraordinary that the _actual_ interview marks yielded a correlation coefficient of 0.88 with Diploma totals, showing a significance of better than 1/1000.

On a smaller sample in 1976/77 the significance had dropped to about one-in-five probability. Overall results suggest an improvement with experience. Interviewing is unlikely to be reliable unless interviewer and interviewee have sufficient common ground to allow fair assessment (Eysenck [11]). Within this limitation it appears that the systems analytical staff of The City University Business School are improving their interviewing performance as time goes on.

An overall ranking list of all candidates on the basis of interview results is still not likely to be very useful, and the main function of interviewing is seen to be the assessment of whether a candidate is capable of taking the course or not. Prediction of poor candidates has been fairly accurate in every year; prediction of good candidates has been accurate except in 1973/74.

From this experience, interviewing can be recommended for use as a "suitable"/"unsuitable" discriminator in cases where the conditions discussed in [11] and mentioned earlier in this paper are met. More detailed predictions based on interviewing rankings are not likely to be justified.

3.3. Prior Qualifications

These have been discussed fully elsewhere (Hanson [7]). The average result for the various groups is rather similar, with the exception of students who came to The City University possessing professional qualifications. They have done rather less well than other groups. However, as only four students have been in this category, and one of these was not typical (student 11, ref. [1]), the sample is too small to draw definite conclusions.

3.4. Age and Experience

Figure 1 shows the range of age and experience of students in the first four years of the Diploma. The course is intended for people with two or more years practical experience in data processing, but a number of candidates without this have been accepted in 1975/76 and 1976/77. There is no age limit. In reviewing this policy there are a number of problems. The first is that age and experience are not unrelated. The youngest students cannot have had a very long period of experience, and older students will on average have had more. However, a definite group of older students wishing to re-train, and hence without previous experience, also has to be considered.

This group of older, re-training students will be considered first. In 1975/76 a student of 45, without prior experience, passed the Diploma with an average mark less than one standard deviation below the mean. In 1976/77 student 7, who spoke English only during teaching hours, was 42 years old and without previous experience, obtained a mark 2.64 standard deviations below the mean. In a one-tailed test this implies 4 chances in a thousand that the student was "typical" of that year's course. It seems likely that language, rather than age or experience, is the reason for this result. Excluding this student (see Table 4, group 4'), student 12 was 1.93 standard deviations below the mean. In a group of thirteen students this is not unlikely, and suggests that his result, although low, was not sifnificantly so.

On this basis it is intended to continue accepting a few older students without previous experience. If the course were mainly made up of inexperienced students, however, the very important transfer of knowledge and experience from student to student would no longer occur, so the number accepted will remain low.

Age and experience were then examined both separately and together, to determine whether they had a general effect. Table 6D shows the multiple regression equations obtained for the four years. Table 7 gives individual regression results for age and experience, while Table 6C shows the relationship between the two.

In most cases the multiple correlation figures showed a greater standard error of the estimate than did simple correlation results. The only exceptions were the complete 1976/77 student group, and the reduced group (less students 7, 11 and 12).

In general it seems likely that simple regressions are more useful, particularly as a multiple regression equation between dependent variables is invalid. The simple regression of Diploma results with age (Table 7) show that any effect is both small and not statistically significant. For this reason no new guidelines on age will be applied, and students will be accepted without reference to age.

The simple regression of Diploma results with experience does show a significant trend. Only in 1975/76 was the regression coefficient negative, and even then the standard error of the regression coefficient was only 1.15, and there was a 15% probability that this was a negative coefficient due to chance alone. For every other group experience was an advantage, with benefits ranging from 1.8 to 12 marks out of 400 for each year of experience. There are two things to note about experience: first that it does appear to benefit students; second that its influence is important, but not vital, and that a determined student without it can still pass a course of this type. However, there is no intention to allow students without experience to become a majority, as this would affect the structure and depth of the syllabus.

4. MONITORING COURSE PROGRESS

The overall structure of the course has been described previously [4,1]. Methods used to provide feedback on student's progress can be divided into quantitative and qualitative:

Quantitative techniques include marked coursework on a two-week cycle of assignments, and the interview of presentation marks given during case-study and TV studio. Any variation in the marks obtained that pushes a student's average mark below 50%, or a lack of work handed in due to inability to finish it, can be quickly noticed, and leads to a counselling interview between the student and a member of staff.

A great deal of reliance can be placed on both coursework and Communication marks, as they have consistently shown high correlation with Diploma totals. The figures are given in Table 8. This is understandable in the sense that they are not independent variables; each makes up one-eighth of the total Diploma mark. However, this close correspondence far exceeds the expected level due to their lack of independence. They have one further advantage, which is that they allow for positive feedback by providing a way of enabling staff to monitor and motivate students throughout the course. It is a great help to be able to point to past correlation between these factors and the final Diploma total in the course of a counselling interview, and it reassures students that additional work put into these activities will be to their benefit.

Qualitative techniques are mainly aimed at allowing students to express their views, or at arranging informal staff/student contact. Both the personal tutorial system and the staff/student "complaint" meetings, at which students raise any points that are worrying them, have been described elsewhere [4]. In 1975/76 weekly student reports on staff performance were instituted, as students felt staff were not always preparing for lectures fully enough, nor always keeping to a high standard of communications performance. As this is a skill that staff teach, it was important to ensure that they could also do it!

The form of the report is shown in Figure 3. Staff were each given a copy of the report compiled at the end of each week. Over a period staff were able to compare their own performance both with their own earlier work and with that of their colleagues. It certainly seemed to improve staff performance, the author concluded, and provided to staff the type of feedback that the tutorial and case-study programme provides to the students.

5. END-OF-COURSE FEEDBACK

Apart from the Diploma results themselves, two types of feedback from students are employed. The first is a questionnaire filled in by students that allows them to say how useful, relevant, and well-taught each part of the course is. Some parts of the course have been redesigned every year due to student comments. In one case a course of lectures was originally held in the first few weeks of the Diploma. Due to student requests it was then altered to the second term, back to the beginning of the course, dropped, and finally (1977/78) re-instated. This is exceptional. In general the students' suggestions have helped to improve the course considerably.

The second is a questionnaire sent out to students after some years away from the University. This too has included suggestions that have been incorporated into both the syllabus and the structure of the course. It will be reported on in more detail at a future time.

6. CONCLUSION

This paper has described the methods of feedback used in deciding on student intake to the Diploma in Systems Analysis and the MSc in Business Systems Analysis and Design of The City University Business School, London. It has gone on to look at feedback techniques used during the course, and has shown how the results of that feedback are quantified and analysed. Individual conclusions have been given in the appropriate sections.

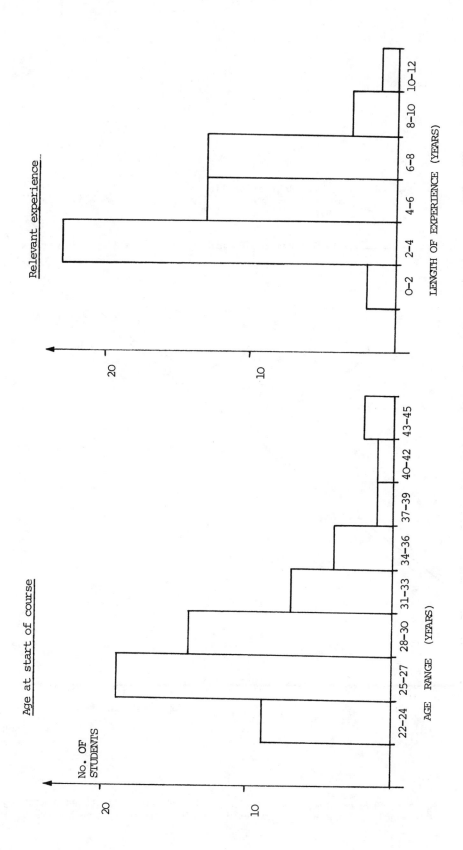

Figure 1. Histograms of Student Age and Experience

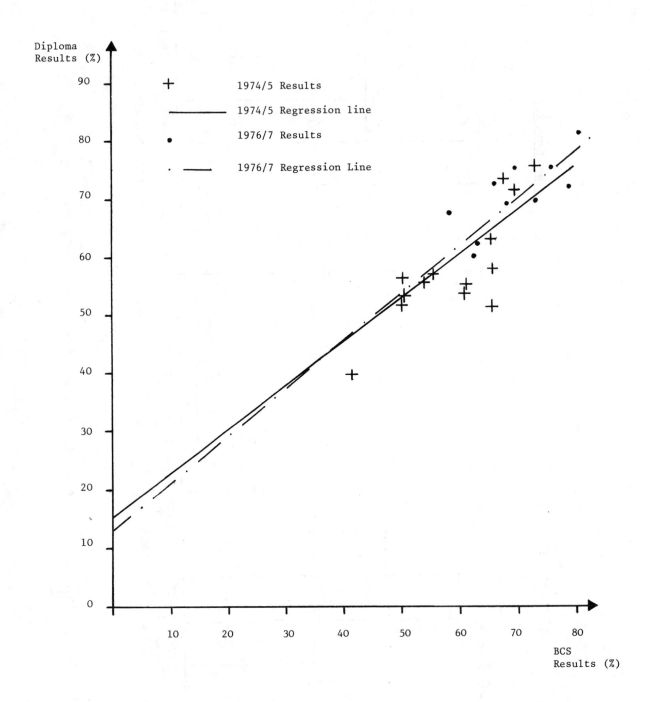

Figure 2. The relationship between results obtained by students sitting
BCS examinations and <u>total</u> marks in the Diploma in Systems Analysis

Week ending 21/5/76

Lecture Period	Lecturer (initials)	Subject of Lecture	Main (stated) relevance Enter "DIP" or "BCS" or "BOTH"	CONTENT Amount/weight of material in relation to time allocated — Too Little	About Right	Too Much	PRESENTATION Evidence of preparation Mark 0 – 10	Delivery Mark 0 – 10	Interaction with the Group Mark 0 – 10	COMMENTS (qualifying/ amplifying specific grading(s) or general comments)
1	PM & DB	Budgetary Control	Dip.		✓		7	7½	8½	2 comments Relevant & Useful.
2	A.E. M.K.M.	Industrial Relation	"		✓		7	8½	6	2 Favourable comments 2 criticised lack of question time.
3	N.R.	Online Systems Design	"		✓		6½	6½	7	
4	A.H.J.	Creativity	"		✓		7½	7	7	
5	O.J.H.	Direct File Timing	"		✓		6½	6	6	
6	N.R.	Online Systems Design	"			✓	6½	7	6½	2 comments about running out of time

Notes on relevant factors

(i) Evidence of Preparation: Balanced structure; consistent level of detail; good visuals/handouts (ii) Delivery: Coherence; pace; enthusiasm; smooth linkage (iii) Interaction: Handling of questions (flexible? defensive?); Fostering of genuine participation.

Figure 3. Systems Analysis Course: Students' Assessment of Lectures

Table 1A.   1975/76

STUDENT	INTERVIEW		ATGSB			DIPLOMA				PREVIOUS		
	Score	Rank	Verbal	Num.	Total	Comms.	C.W.	Total	Rank	Q	Age	Exp.
1	50	4	41	29	589	33	36	264	5	2(1)	38	8.5
2	60	3	44	38	665	25	25	203	15	4	29	7.5
3	–	–	28	34	524	30	34	237	10	5	33	9.5
4	50	4	31	26	497	33	31	266	4	3	23	2.5
5	50	4	26	33	494	30	26	228	12	3	23	3.5
6	80	1	43	47	707	30	27	269	2	4	22	2.5
7	40	10	26	31	486	25	35	244	8	6	27	3.5
8	–	–	–	–	–	30	33	248	7	7	29	2.5
9	45	9	34	31	551	28	33	223	13	6	25	2.5
10	70	2	–	–	–	33	33	251	6	4*	27	2.5
11	50	4	29	41	570	35	37	270	1	3	27	5.5
12	40	10	23	33	478	30	29	239	9	4	26	4.5
13	–	–	30	31	513	28	31	234	11	1	45	NIL
14	50	4	39	36	615	33	29	268	3	4	30	5.5
15	40	10	21	17	360	30	29	218	14	1	34	7.5

*Teachers certificate

Table 1B.   1976/77

STUDENT	MOCK BCS	INTERVIEW		ATGSB				DIPLOMA				PREVIOUS		
		Score	Rank	Verbal	Num.	Total	Rank	Comms.	C.W.	Total	Rank	Q	Age	Exp.
1		–	–					42	35	238	12	5	31	3.5
2	80.3	80	1	44	32	621	1	41	44	324	1	1	35	9.5
3		–	–	30	35	543	4	41	33	293	3	6	31	10.5
4	57.9	50	4					45	37	270	9	3	25	6.5
5	62.6	45	5					32	34	239	11	4+5	26	3.5
6	72.5	70	3	32	35	552	3	42	38	278	6	6	31	6.5
7		–	–					28	25	145	14	7	42	NIL
8	69.7	40	6	24	41	531	5	42	42	300	2	6	24	4.5
9	78.9	80	1	41	26	560	2	40	45	288	5	2*	29	6.5
10	68.2	40	6					39	40	274	7	2	31	6.5
11	63.1	–	–					36	36	247	10	2	25	6.5+
12		–	–					28	25	213	13	6	43	0.5
13	65.8	35	9					45	43	290	4	4	26	4.5
14	71.8	40	6	30	32	515	6	39	36	271	8	1	30	7.5

* Scottish 'A' levels   + As as operator

Table 2. Exam Consistency Figures 1974/75

BCS Exam	Diploma Result
73.00	75.50
50.00	51.50
54.00	55.50
50.50	53.25
55.50	57.00
69.50	71.50
41.50	39.75
62.25	62.75
50.25	56.25
61.00	53.50
65.50	51.50
67.50	73.50
65.75	57.75
61.25	55.00

Table 3. Interview Correlation Data

1973/4		1974/5	
Interview	Diploma Result	Interview	Diploma Result
01	12	01	09
02	04	02	04
03	11	03	12½
04½	06	04	01
04½	07½	05½	02
06	09	05½	12½
07	10	07	11
08	05	08	08
10½	01	10	05
10½	02	10	06
10½	03	10	07
10½	07½	13	03
13	13	13	10
		13	14

Table 4

Year	1973/4		1974/5	1975/6	1976/7	
Group Analysed	1	1'	2	3	4	4'
Group Members	ALL	Minus Student 11+	ALL	ALL	ALL	Minus Student 7
$\bar{x}$	232.1	241.9	232.6	244.1	262.1	271.2
N	14	13	14	15	14	13
S_s	1938.6	729	1406.5	403.6	1833.8	838.1
σ_s	44.0	27	37.5	20.1	42.8	28.9
$\hat{\sigma}^2$	2087.7	789.8	1514.7	432.4	1974.9	907.9

+   The data was presented in TABLE 4A, reference 1.

Table 5

Group	Tested Property	Group					
		1	1'	2	3	4	4'
1	Variance	*	*	–	1%	–	~5%
	Mean	*	*	–	.82	.96	.99
1'	Variance	*	*	~10%	~12%	5%	–
	Mean	*	*	.76	0.6	0.91	0.99
2	Variance	–	~10%	*	1%	–	–
	mean	–	0.76	*	0.84	0.96	0.996
3	Variance	1%	~12%	1%	*	1%	~7%
	Mean	0.82	0.58	0.84	*	0.91	0.995
4	Variance	–	5%	–	1%	*	*
	Mean	0.96	0.91	0.96	0.91	*	*
4'	Variance	~5%	–	–	~7%	*	*
	Mean	0.99	0.99	0.996	0.995	*	*

Table 6A. GMAT/ATGSB Correlation

Year	Group No.	Correlation r	Coefficient t	Significance
1973/4	14	0.624	2.77	better than 1.5%
1974/5	14	0.250	0.89	-
1975/6	15	0.029	-	-
1976/7	6	0.812	2.78	better than 5%

Table 6B. Interview Correlation

Year	Probability of this Agreement by chance
1973/4	0.48
1974/5	0.53
1975/6	0.022
1976/7	0.19

Table 6C. Age/Experience Correlation

Year	Correlation Coefficient	Significance
1973/4	$r = 0.475$	$(t = 1.93) < 7\frac{1}{2}\%$
1974/5	$r = -0.026$	Nil
1975/6	$r = 0.225$	Nil
1976/7	$r = 0.431$	~10%
1976/7+	$r = 0.6$	Signif $(t = 2.37) < 5\%$

+ excluding students 7 & 11

Table 6D. Multiple Regression

FORM: MARK = CONST + α AGE + β EXPERIENCE

1973/4:	MARK = 234 - 1.94 AGE + 13.06 EXP S.E. OF E. 45.5
1973/4+	MARK = 186.5 + 2.16 AGE - 0.58 EXP S.E. of E. 32.3
1974/5	MARK = 225 - 1.13 AGE + 9.45 EXP. S.E. of E. 43.5
1975/6:	MARK = 262 - 0.45 AGE - 0.95 EXP. S.E. of E. 22.0
1976/7:	MARK = 268 - 2 AGE + 10.3 EXP. S.E. of E. 23.8
1976/7*	MARK = 270 - 1.5 AGE + 8.3 EXP. S.E. of E. 23.8

* Excluding students 7, 11, 12.
+   "   student 11, Ref.'

S.E. OF E = Standard error of the estimate

Table 7

Y E A R

Factor Compared	Data Description	1973/4		1974/5	1975/6	1976/7	1976/7 Less Students 7 & 12
A G E	Number in Sample	14		14	15	14	12
	Intercept	187		267	260	392	201
	Standard error of the intercept	57		90	27	56	65
	Regression Coefficient	2.04		-1.23	-0.54	-4.25	2.6
	Standard error of the Regr. Coeff.	2.12		3.23	0.92	1.70	2.24
	Probability of a sign change	0.17		0.35	0.28	0.006	0.12
	Correlation	0.28		-0.11	-0.16	-0.57	0.34
	Standard error of the estimate	28.20		40.20	21.30	38.10	25.20
	Significance	-		-	-	5%	∿15%
E X P E R I E N C E	No. in Sample	14	13+	14	15	14	11*
	Intercept	185	234	194	249	196	234
	Standard error of the intercept	25	23	38	11	16	19
	Regression Coefficient	12.13	1.79	9.54	-1.15	12.02	7.00
	Standard error of the Regr. Coeff.	5.80	5.10	8.80	2.10	2.60	2.90
	Probability of a sign change	0.018	0.36	0.14	0.29	0.0000012	0.008
	Correlation	0.51	0.10	0.30	-0.15	0.80	0.63
	Standard error of the estimate	40.7	29.1	38.6	21.3	27.4	20.5
	Significance	-	-	-	-	better than 0.1%	2%

* Excluding students 7, 11, 12.

\+ Excluding student 11, ref. 1

Table 8. Correlation Between Given Factor and Diploma Total

Coursework

Year	Correlation Coefficient	Significance
1973/4	0.94	0.0001
1974/5	0.73	0.002
1975/6	0.43	0.05
1976/7	0.79	0.0005

Communications

Year	Correlation Coefficient	Significance
1973/4	0.74	0.002
1974/5	0.61	0.01
1975/6	0.73	0.002
1976/7	0.77	0.001

REFERENCES

1. HANSON, O. J., "A Systems Methodology for the Design, Assessment and Development of Training Courses," presented at EMCSR, March 1976.
2. HANSON, O. J., "The Role of Systems Analysis in Designing Systems and Methods of Training using Systems Techniques," presented at the 2nd Conference on Design Methodology, Warsaw, December 1974.
3. ASIMOV, I., Laws of Psycho-History, in The Foundation Trilogy, Panther Books (U.K.) and Double Day (U.S.).
4. HANSON, O. J., "A Systems Approach to the Training of Systems Analysts," Progress in Cybernetics and Systems Research, Vol. 2, Hemisphere, 1975.
5. HANSON, O. J., "A Methodology for Analysis of the Success of Educational Systems,"

presented at the IEEE Conference on Systems and Cybernetics, Dallas, Texas, October 1974.
6. HARRELL, T. W., "Predicting Job Success of MBA Graduates," Research and Development Brief No. 1, Princeton ATGSM (now GMAT) Program.
7. HANSON, O. J., "The Problem of Providing Effective Feedback Criteria in Handling Selection of Candidates for Education Systems," presented at the Third Polish National Design Conference, Wroclaw, September 1978.
8. MORONEY, M. J., Facts from Figures, Pelican.
9. CHAO, L. L., Statistics: Methods and Analyses, McGraw Hill, 1974.
10. KENDALL, M. G., Rank Correlation Methods, Charles Griffin & Co., 1970.
11. EYSENCK, H. J., Uses and Abuses of Psychology, Penguin Books.

Decision making in state administration and business management

HELMUT HIRSCH
Federal Ministry for Trade and Industry, Vienna, Austria

1. INTRODUCTION

In many countries, the feeling has grown during the last few years that something is wrong with state administration. The state bureaucracy becomes the target of attacks of increasing vigour and is accused of inefficiency, dictatorial control of society or lack of concern for the population's needs.

In this situation, there are two questions which come to mind, namely (a) what is really wrong with state administration, and (b) where is the public's perception of state administration wrong and in need of being modified? As a first step in answering these questions, a comparison with private business management seems highly relevant; after all, it is very often pointed out that if only state bureaucrats would work according to the same principles as business managers, all problems would be solved.

It has to be constantly borne in mind that increasing efficiency is not the sole goal of any reforms of state administration; indeed, there exists a double challenge of rapid technical and economical development on the one hand, and mounting pressure by the public for participation in control and decision making on the other. The first necessitates considerable planning efforts that reduce the degrees of freedom of democratic decision making and require flexible administrative structures adapted to rapid changes; the second has led to growing suspicion -- if not distrust -- in "technocratic" planning.

In this report, only the main points of discussion in the workshop will be highlighted. Due to the complexity of the topic, it will not be attempted to present them within a rigid scheme. Both the points where agreement was reached by the workshop participants as well as those issues where some variety of opinion persisted will be described.

2. NATIONAL DIFFERENCES

As the system of state administration and its relation to industry in Hungary, the U.K., the U.S.A., and Austria was discussed, it emerged very clearly that parallels and differences between state administration and business management vary strongly from country to country, according to the strength or weakness of the private sector; it is of particular importance whether there is competition, actual or potential, between the state and the private sector in areas which are traditionally state controlled, such as the social services. This situation exists in the U.S.A., where large, potent firms exist which are ready and able to take over anything the state cannot or does not want to handle. There remains the basic difference, however, that state administration by law has to serve the whole population on an equal basis, whereas a business manager has some choice in the clients he is dealing with and may also treat them with different priorities.

Regarding the situation in the U.K., M.A.P. Willmer (University of Manchester) described the main problem as the lack of public control over an administration which is self-controlling, self-preserving and self-renewing. The civil servants within a department can -- while always appearing loyal to the minister in front of the public -- seriously hamper the implementation of new policies by the minister and influence and control his work very effectively by control of the information flow. The minister has negligible possibilities to determine salary levels and to hire and fire employees compared to those of the board of directors in a large private firm. Recruitment, creation of posts and pay schemes are tightly controlled by administration itself; a recruitment system which applies criteria very fairly to candidates but by the appropriate choice of criteria guarantees that a certain type of people (usually with Oxbridge background and education in classical fields) is favoured perpetuates the state of affairs. As a result, payment in the civil service is now considerably better than in private industry which leads to a drain in industry's personnel resources.

On the other hand, the minister's formal power of delegation of tasks are also very limited; the full ministerial responsibility to parliament severely limits the scope for introducing systems of accountable management. This is an example of external political control complicating the patterns of internal control which is fairly typical for state administration in many countries.

In the discussion, it was pointed out that such an extreme situation of lack of control over state administration does not exist in other countries; in Austria, e.g., the position of a minister is considerably stronger. Firstly there is not one senior civil servant just below the minister, responsible for the whole department (like the "permanent secretary" in Britain); the ministry is, from the top, divided into several sections whose heads ("Sektionschefs") each hold a far weaker position than the permanent secretary (who is even directly responsible to parliament in budgetary matters, which further strengthens his independence) and may be played out against each other by the minister. Secondly, contrary to the situation in the U.K., party politics influence the Austrian civil service to a large extent, which gives the minister, backed by his party, the opportunity to, e.g., control personnel policy to some extent and fill key positions with people of his own choice.

R. R. Hough (University of Michigan) presented a problem which seriously affects state administration in the U.S.A. All complaints concerning the administration are usually passed to the highest political level -- the President and Congress -- where they lead to overloading with information. Furthermore, these complaints usually concern details, necessitating "fine tuning" of criteria such as changing the limits for eligibility for social benefits. However, they are not forwarded to the appropriate administrational level (e.g., cabinet officers regarding objectives; program managers regarding criteria; supervisors regarding boundaries, etc.) but are dealt with right at the highest level, which in principle should be concerned with goal-setting only. Thus, as complaints on minor matters pile up on congressmen's desks, the

end result is not adequate response by revising details but simply resetting goals -- such as changing the whole system of social welfare legislation -- which shakes the working of the whole machinery from top to bottom and necessitates a new build-up of detail regulations from the beginning.

He therefore proposed a system based on a clear hierarchical structure of the different levels of decision making and an according structure of the levels of administration (see Figure 1).

As can be clearly seen, the line of command extends downwards in this structure; assignment of capacity for the basic units actually dealing with clients, assessment of the number of potential clients, formulation of criteria on who is eligible for certain benefits, etc., are each in turn taken care of by a different level in the administration. Complaints have to be forwarded along different channels; clients may complain by writing to their Congressman but contact is usually made for them by organized reform groups, public interest groups, programme advocates, and associations (including an association for the civil servants themselves).

This system was designed by experts with considerable experience in private business

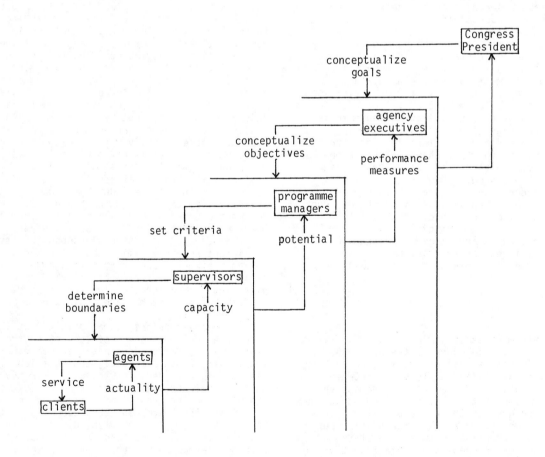

Figure 1. Desired System of U.S.-Administration (Hough)

management and therefore reflects, pointedly expressed, the private manager's answer to inefficient state bureaucracy.

G. Horvath (Budapest) described the Hungarian system of planning and control of industry by state organs. Multiple control is exerted by the competent industrial ministry, the ministries for finance, planning and development, and the "People's commissions" which consist mainly of experts from firms. Overall control is in the hands of parliament. Trade unions are involved in matters concerning social security, etc.

A notable change occurred in 1968, when the old system of direct control was changed to a new system of indirect control (see Figure 2).

It is evident that emphasis has shifted away considerably from central, authoritative planning to allow considerable freedom to the single firm. Its policy is mainly influenced by guidelines and the intensification of information flow. The new system takes into account the higher state of development which Hungary's economy reached in the mid-sixties, which renders too schematic and rigid planning schemes obsolete.

The problem of integrating private industry into state planning hardly exists in Hungary as only a comparatively small number of very small private firms exist.

3. CONTROVERSIAL ISSUES

As the different contributions were scrutinized and discussed in detail, the scheme presented in Figure 1 was criticized by some workshop participants. Clearly, it can only function adequately if the different levels of tasks depicted can be separated neatly so that each could be treated on a different level of a multi-level hierarchical organization without overlap

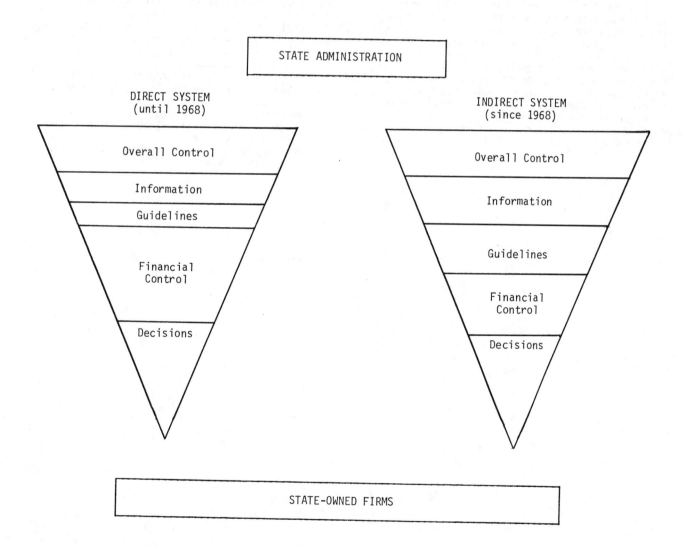

Figure 2. Direct and Indirect System of Control in Hungary (Horvath)

and fuzziness. Some participants did not accept the positivistic thinking implicit in this concept -- namely, that the formulation of value judgements on the one hand and their application in the gathering, classification and interpretation of data on the other can be performed completely independently. They pointed out that such a structure might not work at all or, worse still, turn into a straight-jacket for individual initiative and creative action. Further, it was said that, as control in such a system is strictly one-way (from the top downwards), the demands on an additional, external control-structure providing the counterweight in the flow of control (from the bottom upwards) will be very great and the external control might not be applied to a sufficient degree. On the other hand, well-organized citizen groups and Congress in many cases seem to be able to fulfill this function to some extent.

Closely linked to this controversial point was the discussion on the merits and shortcomings of the extensive use of numerical statistics and of quantification of job descriptions, criteria, guidelines for work, etc. While some participants considered it as highly beneficial, indeed absolutely necessary, for the running of large, centralized systems, others questioned the advantages of centralisation and/or saw dangers in the inevitable loss of "soft" information and possibly also in concern and interest for the individuals involved.

With reference to the last two points, it was stated that work in the civil service requires a certain amount of idealism and readiness to appreciate the clients' problems, not only those voiced in complaints but especially those left unvoiced. The fact that the possibilities for making complaints which highly organized management systems offer are mostly taken advantage of by the vocal, whereas the shy and less educated hardly do so, does not promote this objective. If the performance of a civil servant is measured by the number of cases treated, he will not readily go out of his way to discover a person's queries and wishes but will deal with each individual in the shortest possible way. In private industry, dissatisfaction with a product will be clearly demonstrated by the consumer's not buying it; if a "consumer" of some service of state administration is not satisfied with what he gets, and also not sufficiently eloquent to voice his protests, he will simply turn away, which will not manifest itself in any sales statistics. Statistics and numbers may be useful for giving an indication of the problems existing; but to get to their roots and to solve them, certainly more than this will be required.

Workshop Chairman and Reporter: Helmut Hirsch, Federal Ministry for Trade, Commerce and Industry, Vienna.
Workshop Co-Chairman: Wolfgang Zehetner, Federal Ministry for Trade, Commerce and Industry, Vienna.
Workshop Secretary: Hildegard Müllner, University of Vienna.

Family communications, educational outcomes, and the evaluation of delinquency prevention programs

ROBBIN R. HOUGH
School of Economics and Management, Oakland University
Rochester, Michigan USA

1. INTRODUCTION

The purpose of the paper which follows is to provide and show empirical support for a framework for the evaluation of programs which attempt to prevent juvenile delinquency. More specifically, the paper will (1) set forth a specific conception of the setting in which delinquency behavior germinates, (2) develop the linkages between educational performance and delinquent behavior, (3) define a set of evaluation measures which can be used to judge the performance of prevention programs, and (4) outline the policy implications of the framework developed including its implications for the development of preventive programs.

2. A DESCRIPTIVE VIEW

The basic premise proposed here is that the nuclear family is the key societal unit with which delinquency prevention and rehabilitation must deal. It is assumed that the needs of youth are best met and the values of the society best transferred between generations when the development of youth is guided by their intimate interaction with adults who shoulder the continuing responsibility for their well-being.

Of fundamental importance to this conception is the view that the family is a primary problem-solving unit in the society. That is, the family must somehow obtain and distribute the necessaries of life among its members. The term "necessaries," of course, encompasses a wide range of the goods, ideas and relations which are important to the emotional and physical well-being of the family members. In so providing and distributing, the family inevitably encounters a range of problems which must be solved if the members of the unit are to be sustained. By watching the family's adults cope with these problems and by learning to shoulder increasing responsibilities themselves, the young are able to grow into capable problem-solving adults.

Research carried out at Oakland Youth Assistance on a sample of "normal" families suggests that there are two alternative central strategies which families adopt in their problem-solving interaction (Hough [4]). In one type of family a mutualistic model prevails. That is, chores are shared and the activities which lead to problem-solving are undertaken jointly. In the second type of family there is also a great deal of mutualism; however, internal disputes over a variety of matters means that problems are solved only when accompanied by a great deal of conflict. Yet, in both cases, so long as it can be assumed that the benefits of participation exceed the costs of participation, the family will continue to engage in productive problem-solving behavior.

When the costs of interaction exceed the benefits of interaction, each central strategy breaks down. Among families in which conflict prevails, individuals are likely to withdraw or even leave the family entirely (migration). Among families in which mutualism prevails, certain members may come to feel and act as though they alone bear the burden of the family problem-solving activities (parasitism). The evidence suggests that the conflict and migration strategies are closely linked with high levels of alienation in the sense of role dissatisfaction with adults and in the sense of powerlessness among youth [4]. The link between the pressures bearing on the family and the probability of "delinquent behavior" can thus be made in a most straightforward way. The lay-off of working family members, prolonged youth contact with destructive peer groups, or stressful family relations with peer families may contribute to an increase in alienation (Bronfenbrenner [3]). The resulting powerlessness and role dissatisfaction lead to conflict as to who shall do what for whom in the problem-solving process.

The results are evident in the kinds of statements (defensive or supportive) which characterize the discussions of families. As is illustrated in Figure 1, members of "delinquent" families are far less supportive of one another in their discussions than are "normal" families (Alexander [1]).

The evidence suggests that the delinquent behavior which grows out of the pressures on alienated families may be contrasted with the impact of external pressures on non-alienated families. Conflict is directed outward and demands the attention of others. Parasitism, while seeking the attention of others, does not easily capture or hold that attention. Whining, complaining and self storying soon isolates this individual from others. Millendorfer's work on the mechanisms of socio-psychological development, in pointing to a similar contrast, suggests that the levels of external aggression and internal (self) aggression are substitutes for one another at a given level of stress [5]. It

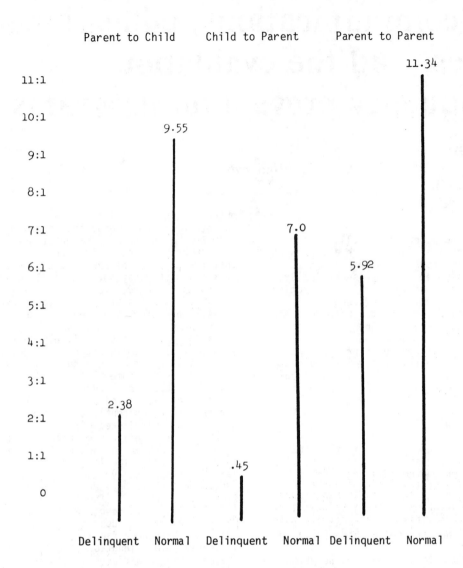

Figure 1.   Supportive Statement to Defensive Statement Ratios for
Delinquent Families and Normal Families

is here suggested that the substitution of external aggression (conflict) for internal agres-
sion (parasitism) is accompanied by growing
alienation.

One of these four strategies must also come
to characterize a youth's individual approach to
problem-solving. Indeed, the central strategy
which grows out of family interaction can be expected to dominate the youth's behavior in an
educational or other social setting. If home
problems are solved through conflict, a youth
may act as though school problems can be solved
through conflict. When conflict exceeds socially
acceptable thresholds it is labelled incorrigi-
bility, vandalism, or . . . Yet within the family
framework, the level of conflict chosen by the
youth may well be acceptable in the home environment. That is, suppose that arguments, tantrums,
toy breaking and physical abuse are part of a
family's approach to problem-solving. Their
children's teachers may find themselves frequently
confronted with attempts to initiate similar

sequences. Unless the teachers understand such
confrontations, the delinquent labelling may follow.
Similarly, migration is labelled absenteeism or
running away, even as the act itself signals a
severe breakdown in the family's problem-solving
processes. In essence, the costs of conflict
have some to exceed the rewards of conflict,
hence, migration.

In the last analysis, the social viability
of the youth's problem-solving strategy is
tested in the educational setting. If there
is an acceptable correspondence between a youth's
behavior and that youth has the necessary academic ability, able problem-solving will lead to
the achievement of 12th grade status.

In summary, (1) a variety of outside pressures and comparisons confront family members;
(2) the resultant is a vector of problem-solving
behaviors caricatured by migration, conflict,
mutualism and parasitism; (3) youth carry the
family's problem-solving style into the educational setting; and (4) academic success and

failure is strongly influenced by the problem-solving strategy used.

In the section which follows the evidence which supports this view will be outlined. As will be seen, the models which result closely fit the data available on 27 school districts in Oakland, Michigan.

3. TOWARD MODEL OF DELINQUENCY GENERATION

It is always useful to have an "utterly naive" model against which to contrast later results. Figure 2 simply plots 1/13th of the total 1974 enrollment in the 27 school systems against the 12th grade enrollments in those same systems. The model expresses the idea that most everyone makes it into the 12th grade. While the errors (as measured by the vertical distance from the points to the line) are large, the model is sophisticated enough to serve as a benchmark against which to visually compare other models. An obvious deficiency of the model is that it does not correct for growth induced differences in the age distribution of a community. This deficiency will be remedied somewhat further along in this section.

A "Socratic" model is displayed in Figure 3. This second model expresses the idea that the educational process involves the time and energies of students and faculty in a process which has 12th graders as its end product. It is further assumed that the process is subject to diminishing returns. Thus, an increase in students with the number of teaching faculty held constant will result in a smaller percentage of the total students reaching the 12th grade. Statistically, the "Socratic" model is a small improvement over the "utterly naive" model. However, since the error terms are still large, the essential character of the process has not yet been fully specified. Indeed, it might be suggested that the Socratic model is simply a statistical fluke. In order to insure the validity of the model it would be necessary to show that the error terms (represented by the distance from the points to the line) have real educational significance. Where the points lie above the line the Socratic model overestimates the number of 12th graders that are produced by the school system. Where the points lie below the line the model underestimates the number of 12th graders that are produced.

The Michigan Educational Assessment Program is a uniform test that has been administered for several years across all 27 community school systems in Oakland County. These assessments are administered to all fourth and seventh grade students under Act 38 of the Public Acts of 1970 and the policies of the Michigan State Board of Education. School district level summaries of the results are available for each of the 27 school districts served by OCYA. As put by John W. Porter, the Superintendent of Public Instruction for the State of Michigan, "The attainment of these minimal skills (in reading and mathematics) is considered to be critical to student success, not only in school, but in later life as well." The tests are not normalized but are scored on the basis of the absolute number of objectives achieved.

If, in fact, the inability of the Socratic model to predict 12th graders is related to educational outcomes, the error terms for the points in Figure 3 should closely relate to the MEAP scores of system students. As is shown in Figure 4, there is a very strong positive correlation between the error term and the percentage of the systems 1974 eighth graders achieving 70% of the reading objectives. Thus, in fact, the number of students achieving 12th grade status depends upon the resources available to reach that end (the student-faculty ratio) and when such a model fails to predict, real and measurable educational outcomes are clearly involved. The points in Figure 5 show the nature of the improvement achieved by correcting for the MEAP scores of the students and for the differential rates of growth experienced in the different communities. The latter correction is based on the observation that fast growing communities tend to have relatively more younger children than their slow growing or declining counterparts.

Of central concern to us here, success in reaching the 12th grade is dependent upon the resources allocated to the community school system and the set of influences which become evident in the MEAP scores as early as the fourth grade. The next important question is, of course, what are the influences that produce the MEAP score differentials? As nearly as can be determined there are two major influences operating. The first influence is the economic stress of relatively high unemployment and of relatively low income. The second influence is the degree of family disorganization as measured by the relative incidence of divorced, separated and single parent families. The effects of economic stress and family disorganization must be treated with considerable care. As might be expected, economic stress reduces the probability that a youngster will reach the 12th grade. Family disorganization, on the other hand, would appear to be beneficial if it does not operate to the economic determent of the youth involved.

As can be seen by comparing Figure 6 with Figure 5, the substitution of economic stress and family disorganization for the % achieving 75% of the MEAP reading objectives results in an even closer prediction of the number of 12th graders. The regression results which flow from treating MEAP reading objectives as the dependent variable and economic stress and social disorganization as independent variables further support the inference above. The signs of the raw correlation coefficients and slope behave in a similar fashion. Over 50% of the variance in the dependent variable is "explained" by the variation in the independent variables.

We are led to conclude on the basis of community level data that the same forces which Bronfenbrenner has identified as producing alienation in the family also help to generate reading shortfalls measurable through MEAP scores and eventually produce failure to reach 12th grade. This result is of central importance, if the linkages between these educational outcomes and delinquency can be further substantiated. If the linkages are to be made, however,

it will be necessary to use OCYA referral rates
as the basic indicator. It is important, therefore to understand precisely what those rates
mean. The next section will set forth a framework for the utilization of those rates.

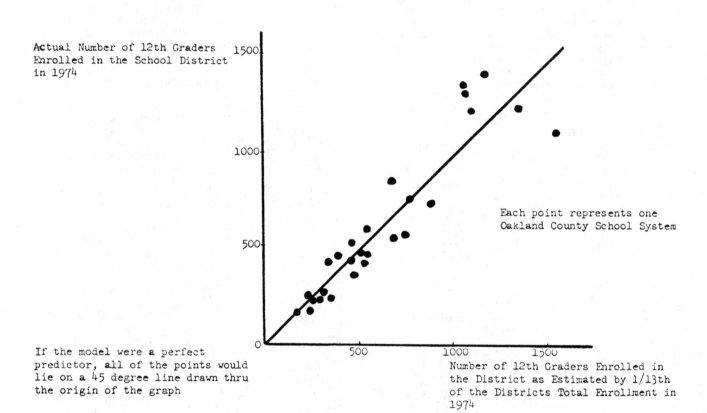

Actual Number of 12th Graders
Enrolled in the School District
in 1974

Each point represents one
Oakland County School System

If the model were a perfect
predictor, all of the points would
lie on a 45 degree line drawn thru
the origin of the graph

Number of 12th Graders Enrolled in
the District as Estimated by 1/13th
of the Districts Total Enrollment in
1974

Figure 2. The "Utterly Naive" Model

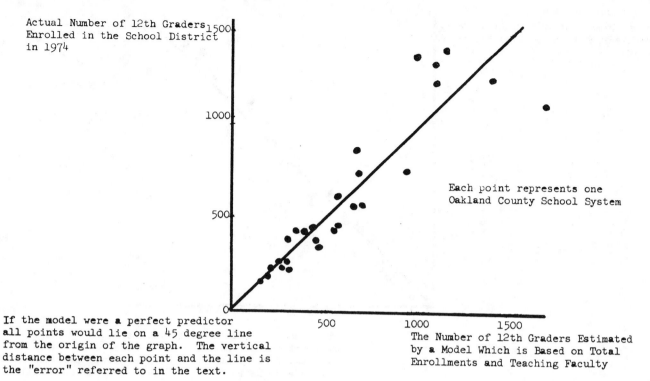

Actual Number of 12th Graders Enrolled in the School District in 1974

Each point represents one Oakland County School System

If the model were a perfect predictor all points would lie on a 45 degree line from the origin of the graph. The vertical distance between each point and the line is the "error" referred to in the text.

The Number of 12th Graders Estimated by a Model Which is Based on Total Enrollments and Teaching Faculty

Figure 3.   The Socratic Model

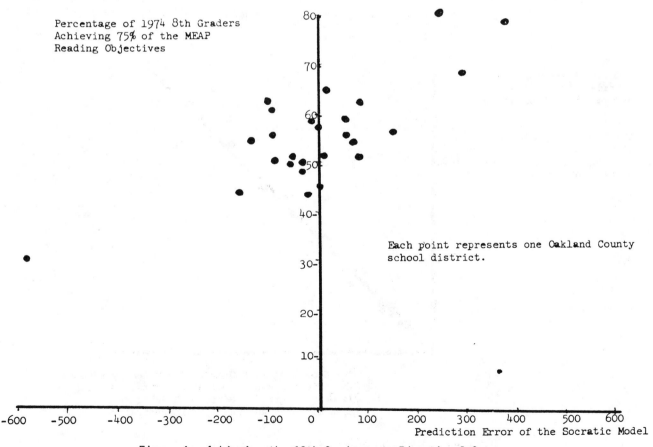

Percentage of 1974 8th Graders Achieving 75% of the MEAP Reading Objectives

Each point represents one Oakland County school district.

Prediction Error of the Socratic Model

Figure 4.   Achieving the 12th Grade as an Educational Outcome

Actual Number of 12th Graders
Enrolled in the School District
in 1974

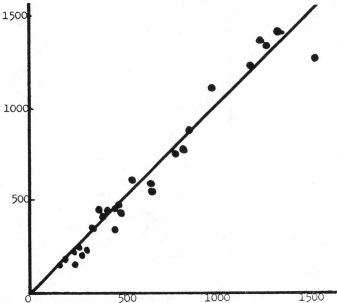

The Number of 12th Graders Enrolled in the School
District in 1974 Estimated by a Model which is Based
on Total Enrollments, Teaching Faculty, Migration
Ratios and the Percentage of the Students that Failed
to Achieve 75% on the MEAP Reading Objectives in the
Fourth Grade.

Figure 5.   The Corrected Socratic Model

Actual Number of 12th
Graders Enrolled in the
Community School System

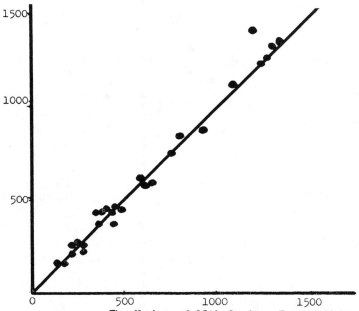

The Number of 12th Graders Estimated by a Model
Which is Based on Total Enrollments, Teaching
Faculty, Migration Ratios and Indicies of
Economic Need and Family Disorganization

Figure 6.   Educational Outcomes and Family Needs

4. MEASURING ORGANIZATIONAL PERFORMANCE

Without getting down to the specifics of any particular community, there are a series of ideas which will help us to deal with the problem of measuring the performance of an organization like OCYA or its General Citizens Committees. [1] There are in total six ideas which when linked together give a simple and straightforward conception of performance. We shall treat each of these ideas in turn (Beer [2]).

In a given community there is a pool of "high-risk" youngsters (like those with MEAP scores between 25% and 75%) that, in the absence of any intervention by helping agents, would be likely to come into conflict with their parents, the police, or school officials. Let us call this pool of young people the potential of a community. [2]

In contrast to the potential, the capacity of the community is measured by the pool of volunteer or other resources which could be brought to bear on the potential. Just as there exists a collection of high-risk youngsters there exists a collection of talented individuals with time, energy and resources that might serve the high risk youngsters.

Next, it may be observed that a specific series of programs is offered in each community during a given year. The high-risk youngsters that are reached by the program are the actuality of the programs.

We thus have three closely related ideas for measuring important facets of the delinquency problem in a community -- the potential, the capacity, and the actuality. Through these ideas an overall measure of the performance of the programs in a community can be derived. Ideally, an operating program would reach all of the youngsters in the potential. Under such circumstances the potential, the capacity, and the actuality would all be equal. If the program falls short of reaching all of the potential we should like to have a measure of performance which would show that shortfall. However, we should also like to be able to distinguish between those situations in which there is insufficient capacity to perform and those situations in which the capacity is underutilized. Suppose that latency is defined as the ratio of capacity to potential. Values of the resulting variable will fall between 0 and 1. Either increases in capacity or declines in potential will move the value of the latency toward 1. Suppose further that productivity is defined as the ratio of actuality to capacity. The values of this second variable will also vary

between 0 and 1. Either increases in actuality or decreases in capacity will move productivity toward 1. By definition, the product of latency and productivity is a variable which will range between zero and one. As given the capacity of the system changes in either latency or productivity will be reflected by changes in the product. The product, therefore, is an excellent measure of the performance of the system. The uses of the performance measure will be discussed in a later paper. At present, our concern is with developing a way in which to interpret OCYA referrals which, in the sense used above, are measures of actuality.

These concepts may now be applied in the following way. Caseworkers frequently comment that the number of clients expands to fill the available time. If, indeed, the potential number of clients exceeds the capacity of the community to serve the clients, the worker's observations are justified. Assume for the moment that the social worker is the primary capacity available to serve clients. The number of youth assistance referrals (the actuality) per potential referral should relate the community's potential referrals per worker in the way that is shown in Figure 7. Figure 7 is amenable to a simple and direct interpretation. Suppose that a full-time social worker (capacity) can handle a constant 120 referrals per year. Figure 7 simply shows that as the potential rises the percentage of the potential that one worker can handle declines so as to reflect the constant capacity of the worker. Thus, by our analysis, the raw number of referrals received by the YA office in a community is not at all helpful unless it is placed in context with the relevant potential and capacity measures.

Moreover, as OCYA volunteers are well aware, there are two sides to OCYA programming -- casework services and volunteer-manned prevention programs. Insofar as a caseworker is engaged in the delivery of organizing assistance to volunteer programs, the casework capacity of the community is reduced. If the volunteer programs are successful, the referrals per unit of potential will decline. A function such as that in Figure 7 thus provides a boundary measure against which to view the operation of OCYA programs.

The analysis of this and preceding sections now provide a basis for examining the linkages between educational performance and delinquent behavior. It is to that task that the next section of the paper will turn.

5. EDUCATIONAL OUTCOMES AND DELINQUENT BEHAVIOR

The key problem was to provide a measure of potential. With that measure in hand, capacity and referral rates may be used to provide a graph of actuality per potential and potential per capacity which can be compared to the construct of the previous section.

Table 1 lists the average number of students in the grades from 4-9 for 1974 in column 1. In column 2, the percentage of the 4th grade students that achieved between 25% and 75% of the

---

[1] General Citizens Committees are volunteer organizations that provide organizational support to Youth Assistance social workers and operate a wide range of delinquency prevention programs.

[2] Those youth with MEAP reading scores that fall below 25% would not appear to be included in the "high-risk" population. They are dramatically under-represented in the random sample of OCYA cases.

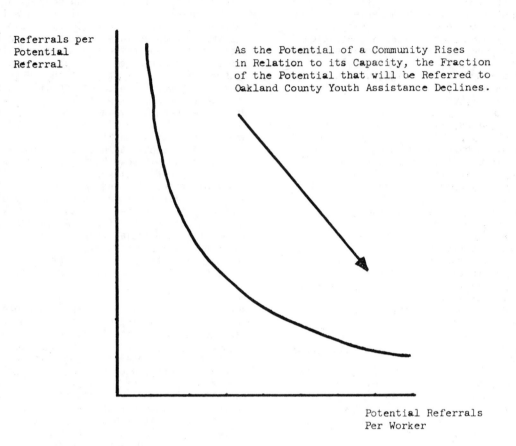

Referrals per
Potential
Referral

As the Potential of a Community Rises
in Relation to its Capacity, the Fraction
of the Potential that will be Referred to
Oakland County Youth Assistance Declines.

Potential Referrals
Per Worker

Figure 7.   The Community Service Capacity Frontier

MEAP reading objectives is listed. On the basis
of a study which is now underway at OCYA, but not
yet completed, it is the youth who achieve in the
25% to 75% range that are the high risk youth.
On incomplete returns for a large sample, there
are no youths on the OCYA caseload that achieved
below 25% of the MEAP reading objectives and
only one youth that achieved above 75%. Given
the percentages of column 2 this result is remarkable even in a sample of only about 40 scores,
if the scores achieved by referrals are distributed
as the scores of the rest of the population.

Eventually, it might be expected that all of
these youths would have problems coping with their
environment. However, as can be seen in Table 2,
referrals in a given year are not evenly distributed across the ages or grades. Rather the
peak referrals occur among 15 year olds.

If we suppose that all of the 10th graders
with 25% to 75% scores encounter problems and
that other classes encounter problems in proportion, we can estimate the size of the potential

for a given year in a given community. That
result appears in column 3. The 1976 capacity
of each community on the basis of 120 cases per
worker appears in column 4. The actuality as
measured by referrals appears in column 5.

As is shown in Figure 8, the relationship
between the two ratios computed on these measures
corresponds quite well to the theoretical construct set out in the last section. Thus both
by this exercise and by the preliminary results
from the project now underway, the educational
outcomes evident in 4th grade MEAP scores seem
to provide a firm basis for estimating the
potential delinquency problem in a given community. The final link in this complex structure
will be put in place in another forthcoming
study which examines family communications in
the families of youth referred to OCYA.

Given the results to date, it is important
to explore some of the policy implications of
the framework within which the results have
been generated.

Table 1.

Community	Ave. Students Grades 4-9	% MEAP 25-75	Estimate of Potential	Casework Capacity	Referrals (Actuality)
Avondale	303	27.45	239	60	51
Berkley	511	25.35	372	48	74
Birmingham	1004	19.18	553	120	89
Bloomfield Hills	712	15.85	324	60	38
Brandon & Clarkston	759	27.83	607	72	73
Clawson	319	26.28	241	120	57
Farmington	1196	24.73	850	120	171
Ferndale	514	27.78	410	120	118
Hazel Park	501	35.80	515	120	121
Holly	345	26.00	258	48	49
Huron Valley	764	31.98	702	120	114
Lake Orion	502	26.05	376	72	77
Lamphere	378	28.83	313	120	44
Madison Hgts.	327	32.50	305	120	65
Novi	203	24.11	141	48	55
Oak Park	316	24.00	218	48	21
Oxford	278	26.48	212	48	42
Pontiac	1532	30.03	1322	360	349
Rochester	811	24.15	563	120	79
Royal Oak	1097	25.78	813	120	120
South Lyon	321	29.33	271	120	102
Southfield	1089	25.15	787	120	125
Troy	669	24.00	461	120	96
Walled Lake	916	26.95	709	120	102
Waterford	1374	30.58	1207	120	161
West Bloom.	453	25.85	336	72	54

Table 2.   Age Distribution of the OCYA Caseload (1974)

Age	Frequency	Decimal Fraction
7	1	.004
8		
9	3	.013
10	3	.013
11	12	.053
12	14	.062
13	36	.159
14	47	.207
15	79	.348
16	29	.128
17	3	.013
	227	1.000

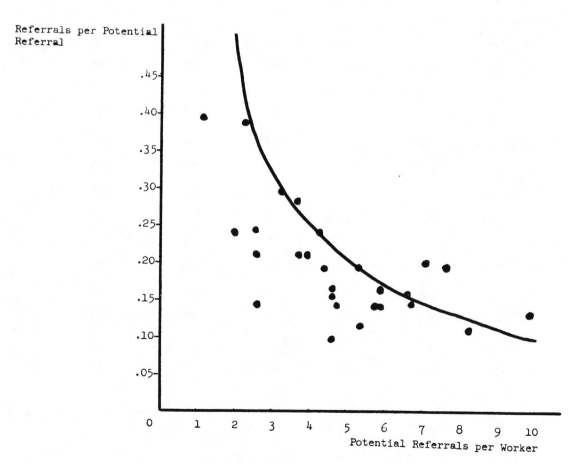

Figure 8.   The 1974 Utilization of Community Capacity

6. POLICIES FOR THE PREVENTION OF DELINQUENCY

Without going into the details of the programs, the findings of this paper have a broad range of implications for programs. The paragraphs following will briefly list some of the most important.

1. The close connections which have been established between educational outcomes and delinquent behavior suggest the need for close cooperation between community schools and organizations engaged in prevention efforts.

2. At the latest, preventive programs should target 4th graders. Given proper identification procedures, programs might well be aimed at even younger children.

3. The obvious direct impact of absenteeism on school performance and its probable connection with truancy and the breakdown of family problem-solving mechanisms mandates programs aimed at reducing absenteeism in the community schools and carefully directed efforts at helping families deal with the problems which produce absenteeism.

4. Attempts to counsel certain classes of individual referrals should eventually be supplanted by family therapy approaches or the obtaining of the kinds of specific services and assistance that will allow the family to confront and solve its problems.

5. Family education programs should be implemented which aim at: creative family problem-solving, conflict management, and improving communications between parent and teacher.

6. The important positive role of conflict in the family setting must be recognized and curricular-pedagogical changes must be made to accommodate the classroom setting to that role.

7. Noncompetitive recreational programs will be extremely important in the building of skills and confidence in marginal youth.

8. Contact with skilled, caring adults in diversion-competitive programs will also enhance the skills and confidence of marginal youth.[1]

9. Any projected revision of the Michigan Juvenile Code should be made in light of the important role of the family and the linkages between educational performance and delinquent behavior (Hough [4]).

10. The research implications of this paper are manifold. Several studies are currently underway at Oakland County Youth Assistance which will further explore particular aspects of the work. These include:

a. A family communications study which involves a large sample of the OCYA caseload.

b. A longitudinal study which aims at estimating recidivism and sibling delinquency rates for OCYA communities. In addition, the study will yield further information on the educational outcome and delinquent behavior questions raised in this paper.

c. An instrumentation study which links the models developed here to population models, enrollment models, and an economic model of Southeastern Michigan. The purpose of this study is to provide detailed delinquency potential forecasts by community.

7. CONCLUSION

This exercise on applied systems analysis has hopefully linked youth and family to the broader organizational and community forces which are of profound importance to them. If so, it has succeeded.

As is discussed in the previous section, the implications of the study are far reaching, and yet even more is at stake. The results suggest that the behavioral and in all probability the nutritional environment provided by the family have profound and quantifiable effects on the educational performance of the young. These environmental forces will have to be accounted for in any final resolution of the dispute between ecologists and socio-biologists. (See, for example, the controversy which has arisen over Paul Erlich's Population Bomb.)

The much larger and ultimately much more satisfying task is that of equipping and affirming high risk youth to cope with the demands of a complex and changing society. The habits that they have already learned may or may not have survival value. We must learn to distinguish the one kind of habit from the other and learn to help the young, despite the stylistic obstacles which they may place between us.

---

[1] The preliminary evidence available suggests that "high-risk" youth may find competitive programs to be just one more place in which they are failures.

REFERENCES

1. ALEXANDER, James F. and Barton COLE, "Behavioral Intervention with Families of Delinquents: Therapist Characteristics, Family Behavior, and Outcome," paper presented at the National Convention of the Association for the Advancement of Behavior Therapy, Chicago, November, 1974.

2. BEER, Stafford, A Platform for Change, New York, Wiley, 1976.

3. BRONFENBRENNER, Urie, "The Origins of Alienation," Scientific American, pp. 53-61, August, 1974.

4. HOUGH, Robbin R., "Alienation, Achievement Motivation and Problem-Solving Ability: Observations on the Human Family as a Complex System," Proceedings of the Third European Meeting on Cybernetics and Systems Research, Hemisphere Publishing Corporation, 1976.

5. MILLENDORFER, Hans, "Mechanisms of Socio-Psychological Development," Studien Gruppe for Internationale Analysen, 1976.

Extreme management as a special case of situational management

AUGUSTIN MARIAN HUSKA
Building Economics and Organization Institute
Bratislava, Czechoslovakia

This contribution only deals with the part of management information system of a modern factory that faces an extraordinary situation. The solution is built on consistent differentiation of normal and extreme situations and procedure of extreme management at differentiated levels of enterprise and utilizes a time-space building-block principle (TESPA). The extreme management is understood as a reserve management of normal management. The solution connects autatomized and organical (vital) management in an interface way.

1. METHODOLOGICAL STARTING POINTS AND A PRACTICAL BACKGROUND OF SOLUTION OF EXTREME MANAGEMENT

The complex multielemental enterprise system fails partly as a result of physical failing of its elements and partly as a result of decreasing its information reagent. Thus, the enterprise gets to a zone of permanent, word of word, chronical failing and its everyday management turns into a form of permanent reflexive improvisations at "extinguishing" the situations (the method known as a "muddle through"). If the system cannot increase its stock or reservation of logistic-productional reliability and flexibility arbitrarily (it is given by the limitation of system profitableness), then, in our opinion, it can at least increase its stock of intelligent or management flexibility.

The system ought to be intelligently foreseeable in facing the situation that occurs unforeseenly. An increasing of negative influence of the physical system failing arises in practice and is in coincidence with the negative influence of intelligent failing. We even know from the live systems the following kind of dependence: if degradation of physical functions arises then as a result of some disturbing interference [4] arises inclination to the functional degradation of management system.

The management system also ought to include the strategy and defence elaborating of planned goals by strengthening of means. For the extreme situation, therefore, it is necessary to have the extreme, i.e. strengthened management, at hand [2].

For the methodological starting point the following principle is used: For foreseeable facing the unforeseen disturbances it is necessary to have the integrated conception of management in extremity. Then the need results in: (a) clear and differentiated definition of normality and extremity, and (b) clear leveled differentiating of management functions that can be mobilized at the occurrence of extreme situation and integrated into the whole management system.

The introduced condition may come out from this working definition:

The normal situation. Such a configuration of situational ingredients that does not require corrective intervention and, therefore, the normal management is sufficient; the normal situation does not have a form of point, but that of span. It presumes the possibility of actual course oscillation round the thought median.

The failure situation. Such a configuration of situational ingredients in which the failed ingredients press down the normal course to its boundaries; it requires the strengthening of normal management by contra-disturbance intervention.

The crisis situation. Such a configuration of situational ingredients that shifts aside the managed course from the normal span. The crisis situation arises double dealing: It has already left the normal situation and has caused retardation that requires the contra-crisis intervention; or it has not reached the normal zone yet, is on trial running and requires the revivifying intervention (resuscitation).

The crashing situation. This arises when the unfavourable situational ingredients come into the absolute domination. Their coincidence provokes the state of functional paralysis and leads to the progressive degradation of functions. The crash situation often has no limitation and requires a massive intervention. (Herbert Grosh: "Matters may get worse without limitation" [1].)

2. POSTULATES OF THE EXTREME MANAGEMENT

It is necessary to choose an approach that utilizes the interval of span through the TESPA parameters in the characteristic of state or process. We come out of the fact that each state has its own scale shape and, therefore, we define:
- the span of normality, and the span of disturbances in it
- the span of extremity, and two sublevels of span in it
- the critical or crisis span and the crashing span

It is also necessary to define a unique leveled management competence for each processing scale (normality and extremity). An example of spans determining is given in Table 1.

Table 1.

Survey of the span of normality and extremity and the coordinated types of management

Situational criterions of span	Levels of dividing lines and zones of situations	Code index	Span max	Span min	Management type normal	Management type extreme
	upper crashing zone	007	007	005	X /passive/	massive supressive intervention
	upper divided line between critical and crashing zone	005				
	upper divided line between critical and normal zone /with disturbing zone in it/		005	001	X	corrective intervention
	upper divided line between normal and disturbing zone	001				
		003	001	003	X	contra-disturbance intervention
	non-disturbed normality		003	004	normal active management	X observation /neutral-passive/
	lowe divided line between normal and disturbing zone	004				
	lower divided line between normal and critical zone		002	004	X	contra-disturbance intervention
		002	006	002	X	corrective intervention
	lower divided line between critical and crashing zone	006				
	lower crashing zone	008	008	006	X	massive intervention of revivifying

Span of disturbances — upper / lower

Span within the framework of normality

crisis spans

Crashing spans — upper / lower

Table 2.

Types of characteristics and parameters of situation and its management

Span (maximum – minimum)	Substantial symptoms of situational state and intervention			
	Symptom of structure /p$_1$/	Symptom of content or kind /p$_2$/	Symptom of extent /p$_3$/	Symptom of time /p$_4$/
007 – 005	whole system failing through destruction of existential function	loss of functional qualities /functional paralysis/	extently non limited increasing of crash	terms and intervals of failing
008 – 006 /Crash/	structure of crashing management strategy	kind identification of crash and kind selection of operation facing the crash	extent calculation of structure-creative factors for stopping and revivifying	terms and interval of contra-crashing intervention
005 – 001	whole system retardation through subsystem failing	retardation of functional qualities	extent of breakdown and damages	terms and interval of crisis
006 – 002 /Crisis/	tasks of structure of crisis management	kind identification of crisis and kind selection of policy facing the crisis	extent calculation of corrective means	terms and intervals of contra-crisis intervention
001 – 003	disturbance of elements	disturbance of functional qualities	extent of disturbing factors	terms and intervals of disturbances
002 – 004 /Disturbance/	normal management structure strengthened by the structure of contra-disturbance intervention	kind identification of disturbance and kind selection of strategy facing the disturbance	extent calculation of contra-disturbances costs	terms and intervals of contra-disturbances intervention
003 – 004	whole system normal functioning	equilibrium of operating functions	span of normal courses	terms ans intervals of normal courses
/Absolute normality/	normal structure of management process	planning of kinds of courses and their ensuring	calculation of normal costs and sources	calender of time ensuring

To understand the situation in its basic and determinative features, it is necessary to choose such a language of management that reduces unsubstantial sides and explains the substantial ones in so-called unity of substantiality, i.e., in the consistence of substantial sides.

For this purpose the time-space building-block principle (TESPA) is used describing the situation by four parameters:

· parameter of morphogenetical or topological characteristic (symbolic $\langle p_1 \rangle$ - symptom of structure)
· intention parameter or qualitative-comprising characteristic (symbolic $\langle p_2 \rangle$ - symptom of content or kind)
· extention principle or quantitative characteristic (symbolic $\langle p_3 \rangle$ -symptom of extant)
· protention principle or temporal characteristic (symbolic $\langle p_4 \rangle$ - symptom of time)

An example of characteristic types and parameters of situation and its management is given in Table 2 (on previous page).

There is a need to renew the unity of management will in the management system through:

· the consistent coupling of horizontal and vertical management
· the consistent coupling of common and special management
· the consistent coupling of automized and organical management

If in the span of non-disturbed normality the real state is identified then the algorithms of higher types of management (optimization) are activated in the framework of normal management.

If in the span of framework normality the real state is identified but, owing to the disturbances, is pressed to the top or bottom of divided line, then as the strengthening of normal management algorithms of contra-disturbing management are activated.

If the real state comes to the position of crisis span then through the algorithms of corrective intervention the extreme management is activated.

If the real state comes to the position of crash then the algorithms of the massive intervention are activated. The extreme management has a following course in the crash situation: at first has a suppressive and then a revivifying character.

3. THE MODEL OF EXTREME MANAGEMENT

The model of extreme management is integrated into the whole management system as follows:

(a) Two types of tasks must be ensured in all the time horizons of management model: the task of normal and extreme management.

(b) The management model must consist of two standardized and compatible parts:

· SOFTWARE (automized functions of the model ensured by computer)
· ORGANWARE (non-automized or ante and post automized functions ensured by a "live" (i.e. organical) management)

(c) The users handbooks in this management model are divided into:

· ORGANWARE MANUALS for all the areas of organical management in the departmental structure with specification of normal and extreme tasks
· SOFTWARE OPERALS for attendance of computer with indicating of inputs ensuring for the normal and extreme tasks
· a register of scenarios for overcoming the crisis and crashing situations (in the form of management by committee this type creates a reserve of departmental management, shadow crisis staff in informal-gremial structure)

4. DISCUSSION

Alvin Tofler [7] introduces a very interesting Professor Miler's attempt with three groups of people. These groups solved the same problem under various circumstances: the first group solved the problem under the normal conditions, the second one under the strong time limitation, and the third group consisted of hospitalized schizophrenics. The attempt showed a high correlation between results of the second and third groups. Thus, a lesson follows from this fact: -if we want to avoid the schizoid process in management model, it is necessary to anticipate (ex ante) all the foreseeable situations and to prepare the algorithms of solutions both the automized (for computer) and organical functions (with aid of manuals, procedure cards, check lists and decision tables) for extreme situations too. It is illusion to rely on the fact that the extreme situation will not happen. Apparently, the first Murphy's law of informatics is in operation: "If something is to happen, it is quite sure it will happen in the most unfavourable time."

Therefore, it is not effective to rely on a reflexive, elemental facing the situation. In alarm situations the manager stretches out his hand for all the disposable resources, without consideration of sequence and extent [6].

The growing systems complexity causes the growth of functional systems failing that are in serial, monotonous connecting. Parallelization and reserving strike against the hard barrier of system profitableness [5].

The management mainly can face this development with flexibility. The flexibility is inherent in redundance of management algorithms so in the software area as in the organware one. Thus, in spite of lowered functional logistic reliability grows the intelligence reliability of system. This fact gives the chance for surviving [3].

REFERENCES

1. CARLISLE, H. M., "A Contingency Approach to Decentralization," _Advanced Management Journal_, No. 3, 1974.
2. HUSKA, A. M., "TESPA Management Model as a Complex Type of Management Information System," paper fair for XIII TIMS Meeting, Athens, July 1977.
3. HUSKA, A. M., "Model dispečingu ako interface

medzi jednotlivymi typmi ASR" ("Dispatching model as an interface between individual types of MIS"), Monthly: <u>Podniková organizace</u>, No. 3, Prague, Cyechoslovakia, 1977.

4. CHARVAT, M., <u>Zivot, adaptace a stres</u> (<u>Life Adaptation and Stress</u>), Akademia Prague, 1972.

5. NEUMANN von, J., "Pravdepodobnostná logika a výstavba spolahlivý organizmov," in <u>Ekonomika a kybernetika</u> (Oskar Lange), Svoboda Prha, 1965.

6. Ředitel výsadkář, Monthly: <u>Moderní řízení</u>, No. 1, 1976.

7. TOFLER, A., <u>Die Zukunftschock</u>, Scherz Verlag, München Bern, 1971.

Control checking as a dynamic component of operational information systems

ALWYN H. JONES

The City University Business School, London, England

1. INTRODUCTION

In a previous paper [5] the author explored how certain system design principles for dealing with the need for longer life in computerised information systems could be evolved from aspects of systems theory. To summarise these, they include the following proposed outline techniques:

Control checking. If a living system loses the use of internal negative feedback channels and these are not restored within a certain period of time, it begins to decompose and eventually yields control to its own suprasystems. It was proposed that a conscious policy of control checking should be developed for computerised information system design and that the establishing of this policy be the responsibility of the original system designers.

Phased consolidation. A living system will evolve by adding weaker bonded components to those that exist already and are strongly bonded. It was proposed that a policy of periodic consolidation be incorporated into systems design so that this process can be facilitated in otherwise non-evolving information systems.

Crisis balancing. The need to maximise the receipt of relevant information during crisis while avoiding damage due to lack of control was considered. The most important need was identified as that of maintaining internal structure, especially horizontal channels of communication, and deliberate maintenance of these was a key proposal here. Others will need to be formulated to develop a sound control system for sophisticated crisis balancing.

Scanning. The ability to scan its environment is an essential life supporting component of any complex system. The importance of formally incorporating it into information systems design was emphasised. The more open end of the spectrum -- intelligent surveillance as opposed to automated monitoring -- was seen as the aspect most in need of attention.

Memory sub-systems. It is usual to find that contemporary information systems accentuate the importance of acquiring current data and monitoring it in up-to-date form. The importance of holding information in time-depth is too often relegated to the practical question of how to store, and when to destroy, "old" data on, say, magnetic tapes. The proposal here was that more formal consideration be given to this question of "archival" data with a view to meeting future system memory recall demands.

Discrepancy. Finally the need to recognise and to formally monitor the gap between what the system can actually accomplish and the complex reality of the system it attempts to model was identified.

All these design principles need to be clarified and specified in greater detail. When this has been achieved, it is intended that research be conducted into actual purported long-life systems to attempt to establish in terms of these principles their strengths and limitations. The aim is ultimately to produce a number of quite practical rules which will act as sound design guides to would-be designers of longer life information systems. In this paper the first of the above, control checking, is examined in some detail, and possible approaches to actual design practice proposed.

2. THE NEED FOR CONTROL CHECKING

The implication from a study of living systems, as outlined above, is that system integrity is dynamically maintained by internal feedback loops which constitute a hierarchy and network of homeostats. We must first ask whether we believe that information systems bear sufficient resemblance to living systems to justify stressing the equal importance of homeostats in their case. This is a fundamental question that at present can be better answered from a basis of faith than from one of strict scientific evidence. Applications in cybernetics sometimes show that although living systems can often provide the clue to an important principle of system structure, the detailed mechanism is more economically designed without too much direct mimicry of living systems (see Fairhurst [2] for example). So must it be in considering control checking. It is the general principle of "homeostat within homeostat" that we want to carry over into information systems design rather than operational copies of living mechanisms.

The justification for carrying this through into workable principles for systems designers must await supportive study of actual systems using these principles as means of evaluation and comparison. However, it is important to emphasise that the ultimate objective is to make the use of a control checking discipline an accepted element of the design process for computerised information systems design.

3. OUTLINE PROPOSAL FOR A CONTROL CHECKING PROCESS

A number of factors need to have clearly

separate existence if a thorough-going process of control checking is to occur both in the design and the implementation of systems at an organisational scale of operations. These may be recognised as follows (see Figure 1).

A control-checking policy. Management support is clearly essential if resources are to be expended upon control checking. This means it must take its place as part of management policy.

A control-checking discipline. Systems designers must be both urged by management policy and also convinced by their own understanding if they are to give attention and apply skills to a conscious control-checking process.

A control-checking framework. If control checking is to be more than a hap-hazard activity there must be some "framework of application." This must be general enough to carry over from system to system yet sufficiently adaptable to be able to catch hold of the specific needs of individual systems.

A control-checking methodology. At the root of the process there needs to be a methodology, again both generally applicable and yet sufficiently adaptable, which will act as a criterion for the designer to be able to feel satisfied that a total control check of the system has been properly completed.

4. A POLICY AND A DISCIPLINE

We can for the time being consider these together since both must in general await evidence of the genuine effectiveness of the approach. There is no reason why a policy could not be instigated as a matter of faith, of course, and indeed it is true to say that the general principle of applying controls is already widely accepted by data processing management. This comes under the general heading of system audit which is concerned with responsibility for checking that the quality of system fabric and processes is of an acceptable standard. This audit process will no doubt provide the proper "home" for control checking administration but it does not at present contain an acknowledged detail procedure for the specific checking of system homeostats' existences and qualities. It is with this detail that we are concerned here.

Acceptance by practising systems analysts is similarly in a state of emergence only. Some practitioners and many educationists pay a good deal of lip-service to "controls" and their importance but fail at present to bring this to a stage of an applicable methodology. Again this is less true of the more general level than at the detailed level whereby, for example, if a control-checking policy existed it would be regarded as equally reasonable to enquire of an analyst for a specification of his control structure as it would to ask for sight of, say, the system flowcharts.

5. A FRAMEWORK FOR CONTROL CHECKING

The following description is proposed for an information system's control framework. Controls associated with a system may be termed either external (associated with human participants) or internal (programmed, automatic).

The external controls may be classified under two headings: general users and systems management. These can then be related as shown in Figure 2. All controls will be said to be homeostats comprising three main channels: goal information (G), performance information (P), and feedback information (F). Control checking is then the design activity of checking the feasibility, viability and ultimate quality of these channels for each potential occurrence of the homeostat.

5.1. The User Frame

The user frame can be analysed into sub-classes as follows (see Figure 3):
  U.1 Systems departments (or equivalent "immediate" management)
  U.2 Other departments (within the same organisation)
  U.3 Other organisations (affected by, or relating to, the system)
  U.4 Government(s)
  U.5 General public (as directly or "socially" implicated)

Each of these will have to be sub-divided into separate unit occurrences according to the nature of the actual system being considered. For example, we might find the following sub-divisions appropriate for U.1:
  U.1.1 Resource management responsibility
  U.1.2 Data input section
  U.1.3 Financial control system

But much would depend upon the actual organisational management structure of the case in question.

The sub-divisions for U.2 and U.3 would clearly be a matter for careful identification. Similarly with U.4, except that information flows between the system and government(s) would not be optional and therefore presumably would be more clearly specified.

The general public may be direct users of the system and are then obviously important control participants. But it may also be felt relevant to include a "public opinion" element of control where a system has social implications in the wider sense. A company could see it as part of their public service to monitor public and private comment about their operations, for example, even though these do not interact directly with the general public.

5.2. The Management Frame

As Figure 2 indicates, the management frame encloses both the system itself and the system-user interaction. We can therefore propose two main classes of control within the management frame:
  M.1 Intrinsic quality control
  M.2 Control of the system-user controls (i.e. meta-controls)

It could be argued that if all system-user controls are operating and are properly monitored by the M.2 meta-controls then there is theoretically no need for any other management controls since stability is inevitable. But this point of

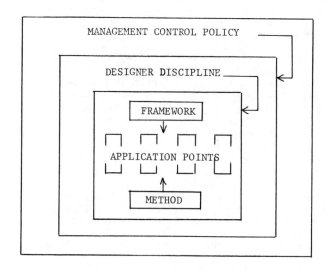

Figure 1.   Basic Features in the Control Process

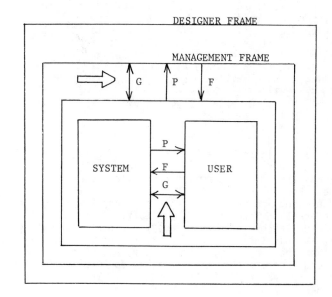

Figure 2.   Control Checking Framework

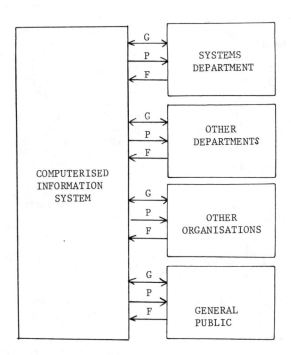

Figure 3.   The User Frame

view neglects the importance of wear and tear to system fabric itself and periodic review of this system quality is essential. It is a monitoring and integrative control which all too often is absent, or is present only in the sense that notice is taken immediatel something is obviously amiss. These intrinsic quality controls could be sub-classified as follows:

    M.1.1 Overall system behaviour
    M.1.2 Personnel
    M.1.3 Software
    M.1.4 Hardware

It would be necessary to devise for each of these the specific G, P and F channels and in such a way that the information was suited to management control needs. For M.1.3 and M.1.4 this would require specialist knowledge and a willing cooperation from operational staff. Clearly each of the latter three sub-classifications, although it is only their part in the system under consideration that is relevant here, must be part of a broader management responsibility for the information-processing services as a whole. This implies a need for a coordination of standards of performance which we can only mention in passing here. It emphasises the importance of the points raised in Section 4 earlier since without support from both management policy and working discipline accepted by the designers such coordination will be impossible.

5.3. The Internal Frame

If analysed fully, the nests and nets of homeostats within the information system proper would present a picture of great complexity. Such detailed analysis is beyond the scope of this paper but what we can do is to propose that actual analysis for homeostat sub-structure be introduced as a required element of the design process and added to the list of standard sections within a fully documented specification of the system design. Thus an analysis of all internal, automatic control loops could appear perhaps in diagrammatic form (supported by descriptive material) in much the same way as the system flowcharts which describe the flow of computer operations are now widely accepted as a standard element of documentation.

A first-level sub-classification could be the following:

    1. Input controls
    2. File/Database controls
    3. Output monitoring controls
    4. Special process controls
       (e.g. for security)

The fourth item is very general and indeed the very partitioning in the way shown may not be the most convenient. It is intended that further work be done in this area to investigate how a frame acceptable to a wide range of designers might be evolved.

6. A METHODOLOGY

In so far as we have described a reference framework providing a check for the designer as to where, in and around the system, homeostatic processes might be established, thus we have

determined a basic methodological approach. Now we turn to the question of how the designer is to enquire into the actual design qualities for these controls. The approach suggested is to present this as a process of checking (hence the title "control checking" is adopted). Justification for this is that controls are very often (and perhaps ought always to be) an integral part of the output from the design process. It is far more economic of design effort therefore to establish a proper quality for the homeostatic sub-structure by post hoc checking in the manner of an inspection process.

Using frameworks of the kind already described it is suggested that the designer work methodically through an outline design specification (or through an implemented system specification if the wish is to evaluate an operational system) performing the checking process as summarized in Figure 4. (This process is indicated diagrammatically for external control checking by the broad arrows in Figure 2.)

The first stage in the checking process results in either a need for evaluation of the existing homeostat or in the second-stage question of whether in fact there should be a homeostat present if there is not one. The rejection of the need for a homeostat may be based on any number of arguments; they might be logical, economic, technical or sociological. The vital important aspect from the point of view of our control-checking methodology is that the system specification henceforth indicate that a proper control check has been carried out and that the rejection decision was made consciously and rationally. This will provide both a useful strength to the control-checking discipline and also a vital element of documentation when future evaluations and amendments to the system arise.

Where a homeostat does finally exist within the proposed or implemented design there comes the difficult question of evaluation. In respect of internal controls this is again a matter of such diverse and potentially complex techniques that it can be a matter of reference only in this paper. Gilb and Weinberg [3] provide a working reference for the input controls aspects mentioned in Section 5.3. The present writer [4] has offered some ideas with respect to output controls, and the book [1] in which that paper appears is itself a useful summary of actual control techniques. Controls for files and programs have appeared in many texts but the subject is too vast to be taken further here.

The external controls, except as they come under the general concept of system audit, have been less well attended to and therefore a few general observations will be made here. We need to recognise that the closing of a feedback loop by human procedure is a very precarious one with the possible exception of where the human is an operator of a machine with a specified panel of controls. In the more general cases a number of further control check questions need to be put in order to evaluate the process. The following is a short list in no particular sequence but which may provide the basis for a more established list after further work.

What channel noise levels will apply?

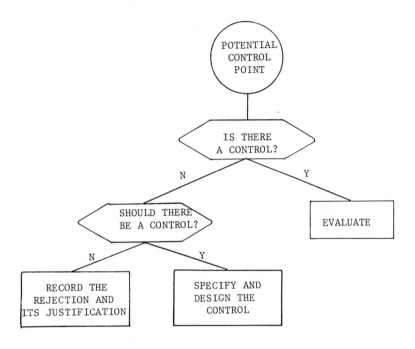

Figure 4. The Checking Process

· How will the channels be administered?
· To what extent will the flows be routine?
· What time lags will necessarily exist?
· What are the resource implications
  now and for the future?
· Is an online implementation feasible?
  Ability to answer all of these questions with
some accuracy and confidence would certainly put
one well on the road to a sound qualitative evaluation of the process. Inability to answer any one
will, however, inevitably present a designer with
a classically difficult problem of selecting
design options using compromise and trade-off.
  Finally, we can consider what actual vehicles
we may select by which external control channels
may operate. The following is again merely a
first offering but should help to focus the
attention on the practical options available:
· Operational statistics
· One-off surveys
· Questionnaires
· Education/training programmes
· Tests, routine and non-routine
· Complaints and suggestions monitoring
· User meetings, conferences, etc.
· Information services

It may be possible to specify which of these
is appropriate for each of the sub-classes U.1 to
U.5 in Section 5.1, but it is probably better to
leave the options open and let the designer make
the appropriate choice in the context of an
actual system. Also, with the increasing use
of on-line communication between user and system,
any one of these contains the major option of
being implemented as an on-line program. Gilb
and Weinberg [3] are again especially helpful
in this context.

REFERENCES

1. CHAMBERS, A. D. and O. J. HANSON (eds.),
    Keeping Computers Under Control, Gee & Co.,
    1975.
2. FAIRHURST, M. C., "Cyclic Activity in Infor-
    mation Processing Systems," Journal of
    Cybernetics, 7, 1977.
3. GILB, T. and G. WEINBERG, Humanized Input,
    Winthrop Computer Systems Series, 1977.
4. JONES, A. H., "Output Controls" in [1].
5. JONES, A. H., "Some Systems Ideas Applied to
    the Design of Computerised Information
    Systems," submitted for publication.

Development of a set of control criteria and a controlled systematic procedure for organizational design process

İ. İLHAMI KARAYALÇIN
Faculty of Mechanical Engineering, Technical University of Istanbul
Istanbul, Turkey

1. A CONTROLLED SYSTEMATIC PROCEDURE FOR ORGANIZATIONAL DESIGN PROCESS

We will try to build a schematic model for organization design process by interconnecting the following organizational parameters and variables: (a) activities, (b) functions, (c) standard positions, (d) necessary connections, (e) organization criteria, (f) organizational forms, (g) managerial objectives, (h) organization policy, (i) environmental parameters, (j) management tools and techniques, (k) system variables, (l) system parameters, (m) time element, (n) system's managerial skill and power, (o) characteristics of personnel, (p) organizational experience and know-how, (r) measures of organization effectiveness (see Figures 1 and 2).

In this design, major factors are:[1]
1.1. Basic management functions
1.2. Necessary business activities
1.3. Systems parameters
1.4. Variables of the system
1.5. Organizational design process
1.6. Control system of the organization structure

1.1. Basic Management Functions

Basic management functions which are interconnected within organizational network are reclassified. Functions which are typed with capital letters are defined by the author based on his specific observations, research and experience in industry. These management functions, which are interlinked by organization charts, are:
1. Determining objectives
2. SETTING CONTROL CRITERIA
3. Setting measurement standards
4. FORECASTING AND ANALYZING RESOURCES
5. IDENTIFYING RESTRICTIONS
6. Formulating business policies
7. Designing organization structure
8. Staffing and organization chart
9. Planning and programming
10. Setting systems and procedures
11. Developing management models and methods
12. COORDINATING AND INTEGRATING ACTIVITIES
13. COMMUNICATING AND TRANSPORTING
14. Leading, orienting and directing people
15. TRANSFORMING AND CONVERTING RESOURCES
16. Measuring, controlling and revising activities
17. Motivating, training and activating people
18. Executing and operating systems
19. IMPROVING AND DEVELOPING SYSTEMS
20. Making decisions

These twenty basic functions can be easily subclassified but for our purpose here, instead of sub-dividing, we will break down according to managerial levels which they can be delegated as: I. Board of Directors, II. President - Vice Presidents, III. General Manager, IV. Division Directors, V. Section Managers, IV. Middle Management, VII. Supervision; and also:
1. Staff type A - research and development
2. Staff type B - analyzing planning, designing
3. Line type A - executing directing
4. Line type B - operating supervising
5. Supporting
6. Servicing
7. Controlling
8. Relating
9. Motivating
10. Commanding

1.5. Organizational Design Process

Then a self controlled systematic procedure for organizational design process which is based on system dynamics principles is developed and implemented in more than forty companies during the last ten years. The procedure to be followed influences the effectiveness of the organization structure considerably. There are several procedures given in management literature, but usually they do not consider a certain set of control criteria in general. The one proposed here is based on a self-controlling and correcting flow (see Figure 3). Steps in this proposed procedure can be summarized as follows:
1. Determining the need for redesign by using statistical control charts such as P chart, C chart and (x, σ) charts, based on sample surveys, and performance analysis.
2. Determining restrictions, parameters and variables and overall characteristics of the system with a pilot study.
3. An analysis to determine objectives, subobjectives to be achieved in this work, weights and priorities of organizational criteria to be selected for this specific case.
4. Determining long range objectives of the

---

[1] 1.2, 1.3 and 1.4 will not be discussed here in detail due to limitation on length of paper, instead they are given in Schematic Models.

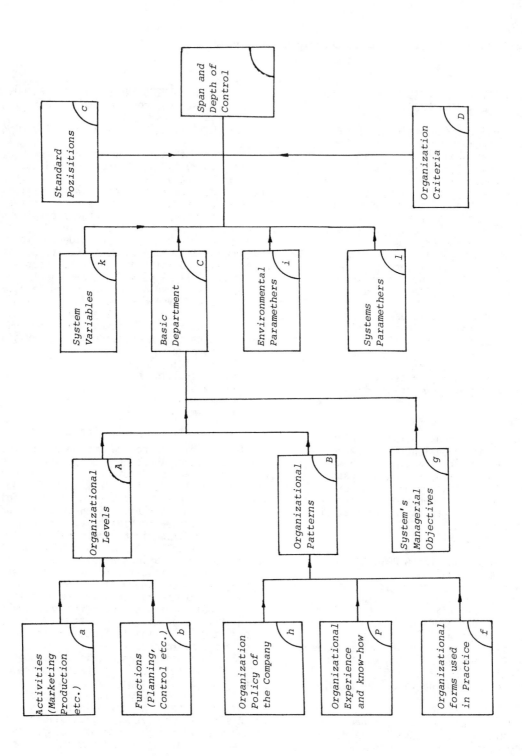

Figure 1. Schematic Model for Standard Procedure

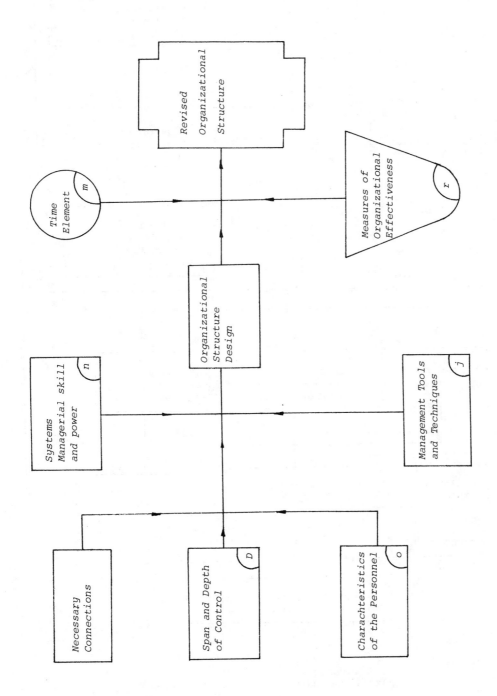

Figure 2. Continuation of Schematic Model in Figure 1

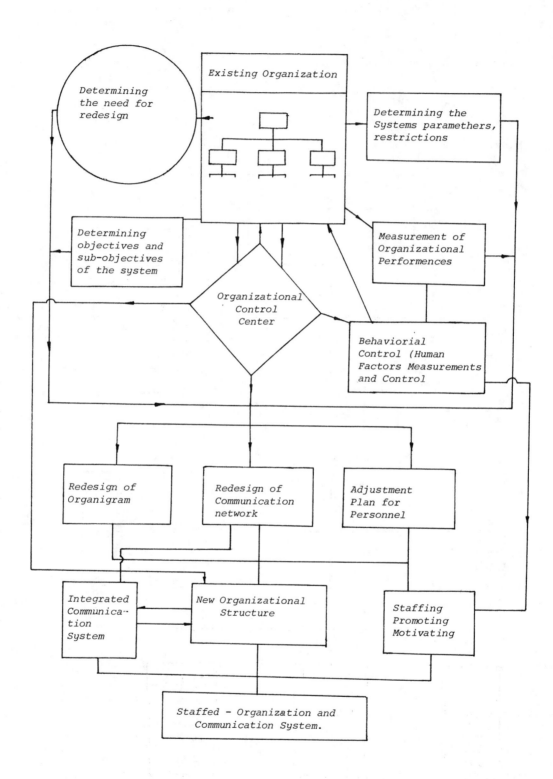

Figure 3. Detailed Design Procedure Model

system, business policies adapted for the period in question, and an inventory of available resources of the system.

5. Analysis and evaluation of the existing organizational structure, here functional and departmental analysis will be carried together with activity analysis.

6. Activity flow charting for basic functions and activities, such as planning, controlling, decision making and purchasing, producing, etc.

7. Work, task, function distribution charts to be made together with an analysis of authority and responsibility and relationship distributions for existing organization.

8. Designing an ideal organization by making a selection among the alternatives, considering both the organization criteria and characteristics of the system.

9. Describing the key jobs and job specifications for managerial positions.

10. Staffing the organization by assigning people to positions and analyzing significant differences and modifying the chart within the basic restrictions.

11. Checking the positions of command, planning, control and coordination centers and their interconnections in vertical and horizontal directions.

12. Effectiveness, efficiency, cost and managerial load analysis for this new organization chart.

13. Analyzing communicational circuits, information feedback flows and activity cycles to diagnose the operational defects of the organization.

14. Vectorial analysis for authority and responsibility allocation with vertical, horizontal and cross relations.

15. Designing "Regulator," "Transformer," "Redresser," "Adaptor" types of organizational tools to be built in the system, such as committees.

2. A SET OF CONTROL CRITERIA FOR ORGANIZATIONAL DESIGN

In another research of this author [8] forty different organizational criteria are analyzed and also ranked with a special technique. As an extension of this work, more attention is given to control criteria which should be used on organizational design. The criteria discussed with system approach are:

1. A unity of command should exist.

2. Execution and controlling should be separated functions.

3. Planning, execution and control functions should be coordinated with an upper level of position.

4. A person should never be a controller and also advisor to the same positions.

5. A control center should exist within the organization.

6. Span of control should be limited.

7. Missing functions should be minimized.

8. The distances of positions to the control centers should be optimized.

9. Effectiveness of the organization should

be measured.

10. Communication channels should be open for two ways of information flow.

These ten criteria, some of which introduced by the author himself, are descriptive in nature. So to make one step more, we tried to define some new control criteria in addition to these.

1. Vertical and horizontal communication deviations in two directions should be minimized.

2. Content of control activity carried by each unit should be as homogeneous as possible.

3. Horizontal control units for different activities should be coordinated at an at least one level upper center.

4. Vertical control units in the same area should be interconnected.

5. Standards, measurement, inspection, control and revision activities should be coordinated.

6. By continuous participation and rotation, control network should be revised.

7. Control network should be self-controlled.

8. Control network within the organization should be integrated with planning, directing and improving networks for mutual effects.

9. Permanent control departments should be interconnected and coordinated with control committees.

10. Long term - short term, strategic - tactic, preventive-corrective-predictive tpyes of control units should be coordinated with a permanent committee.

In this paper these ten criteria are analyzed with schematic models and flow charts with control engineering and cybernetic approach (see Figures 4, 5 and 6).

REFERENCES

1. BYRT, W. J., Theories of Organizations, McGraw-Hill, 1973.
2. EMERY, J. C., Organizational Planning and Control Systems, Macmillan, 1969.
3. FINCH, F. E., R. H. JONES, and J. A. LITTERER, Management for Organizational Effectiveness, McGraw-Hill, 1976.
4. FORKNER, I., and I. McLEOD, Computerized Business Systems, John Wiley, 1973.
5. HICKS, H. G. and C. R. GULLETT, Organizations: Theory and Behavior, McGraw-Hill, 1975.
6. KARAYALCIN, I. I., "Organizasyon Planlamasi," Istanbul Teknik Üniversitesi, 1965.
7. KARAYALCIN, I. I., "A Quantitative Approach to Span of Control," 35th Conference of ORSA, 1969.
8. KARAYALCIN, I. I., "Evaluation of Organization Criteria," 35th Conference of ORSA, 1969.
9. KARAYALCIN, I. I., "Introduction to Production Management and Industrial Engineering," Bosphorus University, Istanbul, 1974.
10. KARAYALCIN, I. I., "Integration of Productivity Oriented Engineering Disciplines for 'Built in Productivity Concept'", paper read at Congress of the European Federation of Productivity Services, Vienna, April 1977.

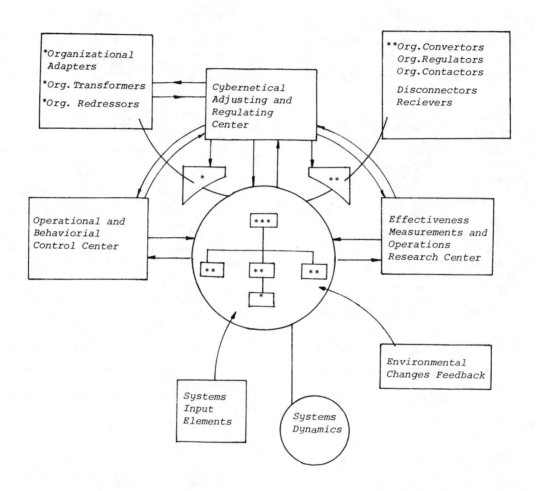

Matrix Analysis of Control Elements and Managerial Levels.

1. Types of Control :   2. Levels of Management: 3. Activities :

   . Overall Control   . Board of Directors   . Designing

   . Partial Control   . President   . Planning

   . Special Control   . General Directorate   . Procuring

   . Corrective Control   . Managerial Level   . Producing

   . Preventive Control   . Middle Management Level   . Transporting

   . Predictive Control   . Supervisory Level   . Servicing

   . Adaptive Control   . Operational Level   . Distributing

Figure 4. Continuously Controlled – Cybernetized Organizational Structure

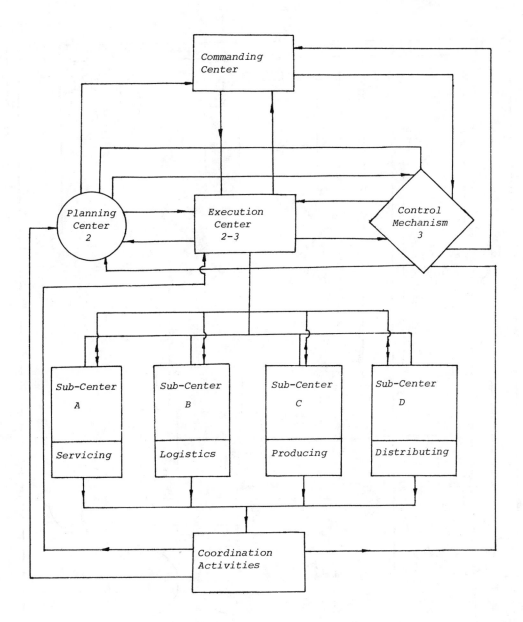

Figure 5.

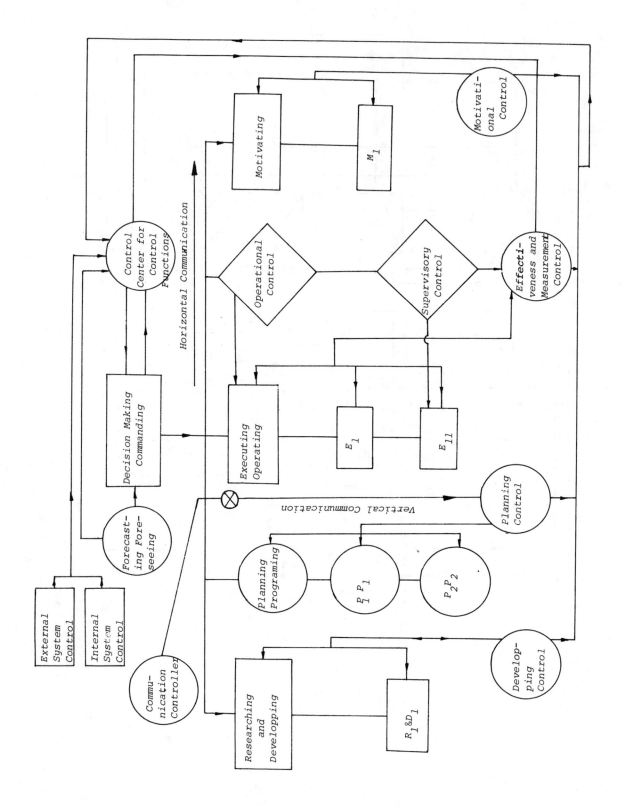

Figure 6.

Management decisions—theory and practice, a monitoring problem

FREDMUND MALIK
St. Gall Graduate School of Business Administration, Economics and Public Administration
St. Gallen, Switzerland

1. INTRODUCTION

This paper deals with the widening gap between the so-called theory of decision and the actual practice of managerial decision making. Despite the very intense interest in the theory of rational decision documented by a never-ending stream of publications on this topic, experience in the context of consulting and management development shows that in management practice serious efforts to apply decision theory are very rare. It would be too easy to argue that management practice still lags very much behind theory and that it is simply a matter of time and education until decision theory will be applied widely and successfully. I think that the reasons for the reluctance of managers are quite different and have more to do with a feeling -- perhaps only a very vague and inarticulate feeling -- that decision theory is fundamentally inadequate to deal with their problems. A closer look at two basic paradigms of decision making or, more general, of problem solving on the one hand and at two intimately related basic approaches towards social systems on the other hand will show that we have to take those feelings very seriously.

2. CONTROL OF COMPLEXITY

Complexity is the very problem of today's management. To cope successfully with complexity we have basically two possibilities: (i) organization or order, and (ii) problem solving. As Figure 1 shows, both may be looked at in two very different ways: An organization or order may be conceived either as <u>made</u> or <u>designed</u> or <u>taxical</u> on the one hand or as <u>grown</u> or <u>spontaneous</u> or <u>self-organizing</u> on the other. Problem solving can be understood either as <u>analytic/constructivist</u> or as <u>evolutionary</u>.

3. TWO KINDS OF PROBLEM SOLVING

Let us first have a look at problem solving. The predominant paradigm of problem solving/decision making is the analytic approach (Steinbruner [19]) or as Hayek called it the constructivist approach [11]. It is based upon the notion of rational choice of one of several alternative courses of action in order to optimally achieve a set of preconceived consistent objectives. The central elements of analytic decision models are: (i) preconceived and prioritized sets of operationalized objectives in stable preference orders; (ii) a comprehensive analysis of all possible courses of action and their consequences; (iii) the assumption that decision making is the allocation of means to ends; (iv) sufficiently operationalized and stable evaluation criteria; (v) the concepts of certainty, risk and uncertainty together with either the frequency calculus of probability or the theory of subjective probabilities. There is, of course, a rather wide variety of analytic models with several refinements, but the basic approach remains unchanged.

The analytic approach has been and still is very much criticized (e.g. Lindblom [13,14]; Braybrooke and Lindblom [7]; Steinbruner [19]; Hayek [11,12]; Simon [17]). The main stream of critical arguments against the analytic approach is focused at the limited capabilities of human and also computer information processing (for the latter, see Ashby [3]; Bremermann [8]; Beer [4]). It is shown that the analytic approach would constitute indeed a paradigm of rational choice if only the information processing requirements were fulfillable but that analytic decision making is in fact impossible due to the rather severe limitations of real decision makers. There are also critics who argue that even under ideal circumstances the analytic approach would not really solve the problem it claims to solve, namely the problem of rational choice. This argument has been developed into a new theory of rationality (Aldrup [1]).

The opposite of the analytic paradigm has been called "cybernetic paradigm" (Steinbruner [19]) or evolutionary approach (Hayek [11]). It is indeed the theory of evolution or, as one might say, the theory of the cybernetics of evolutionary processes which contributes most to an entirely different approach towards managerial decision making, the improvement of its effectiveness and its monitoring or control. An evolutionary process is an open ended and, in its results and details of working, largely unpredictable process in which trial and error, or as Campbell put it "blind variation and selective retention", plays an important part (Campbell (1974); Popper [16]). In such a process what is optimized is not some specific result but only the chance that a problem solution will be found the details and often even the type of which we cannot know in advance and which may very often surprise us as completely unexpected. Rechenberg [18] has even shown that an evolutionary strategy is not only some strategy but that it is also the optimal strategy for the adaptation of organisms and systems in general.

Now it must be frankly admitted that in the area of management our knowledge of the achieve-

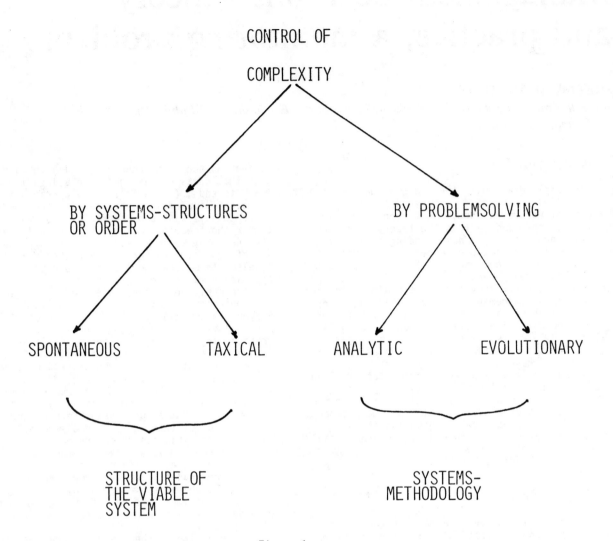

CONTROL OF

COMPLEXITY

BY SYSTEMS-STRUCTURES
OR ORDER

BY PROBLEMSOLVING

SPONTANEOUS   TAXICAL   ANALYTIC   EVOLUTIONARY

STRUCTURE OF
THE VIABLE
SYSTEM

SYSTEMS-
METHODOLOGY

Figure 1.

ments of the theory of evolution is still very small. Particularly the theory of evolution of social systems (see, for example, Hayek) is still widely unknown. Therefore the difficulties of applying results of the theory of organic or biological evolution in the field of management and of transferring the main lines of thought must not be underestimated. A first though very modest step towards the design of evolutionary problem solving processes is the expansion of any kind of problem solving schema with a simple trial and error process as shown in Figure 2. The control-oriented systems-methodology for organic problem solving developed and discussed elsewhere is another attempt (Gomez, Malik and Oeller [9]). Recently I have attempted to transfer some results of the theory of evolution to the problem of strategic management [15].

4. TWO KINDS OF ORDER

    Let us now have a look at the second major way to cope with complexity. A made or designed or taxical order is one which results from explicit command and human making. A spontaneous order or self-organizing system results from the intense interaction of its elements obeying certain abstract rules of conduct. Such an order may evolve to quite different and much higher levels of complexity than any taxical system ever can achieve since its mode of working allows it to utilize the greatest possible amount of knowledge (or information) available in dispersed form to its elements or members. There is no place here to elaborate on the very interesting issue of rule-guided action and of the detailed working of abstract rules (see Hayek [10,11]). It needs to be emphasized, however, that the elements of a spontaneous order need not "know" the rules they follow in the sense that they could articulate them in words. It is sufficient that the behaviour of the elements in fact follows the rules. Table 1 may serve to make these ideas more clear.

    To avoid misunderstandings, it should be noted that a system which is the result of

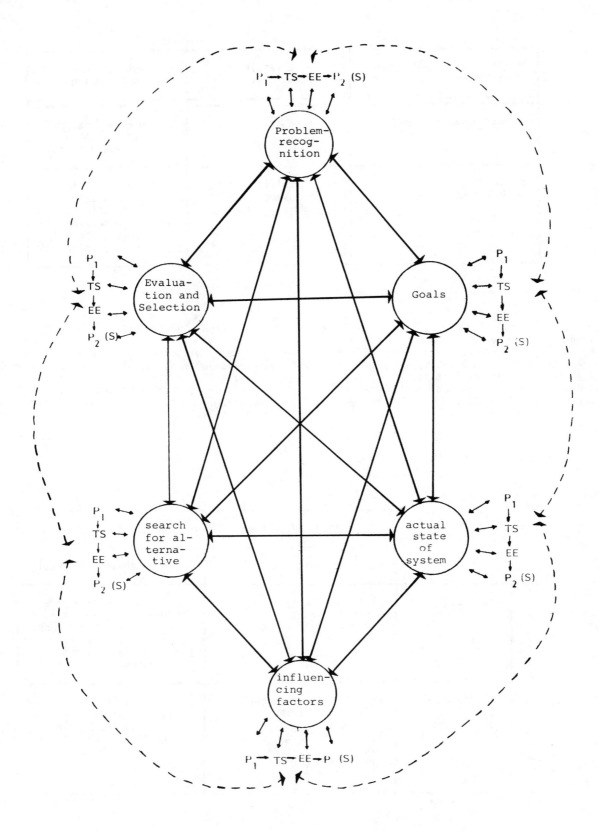

Figure 2.

Table 1.

Origin of different types of system or order	as a result of human design	not the result of human design
without human action	none	prehuman natural systems; e. g. planetary systems
as the result of human action	technical systems and very simple social systems	complex social systems and institutions; language, law, family, society, company, etc.

human action but not of human design (this phrase was coined by Adam Fergusun and has been made public by Hayek [10]) need not result only of human action (other than human actions, e.g. those of machines may play an important role) and that human design may be a very important ingredient but that the result as a rule does not correspond to the preconcieved design.

5. STRUCTURE AND PROCESS

If we now combine kinds of order or system with kinds of problem solving, we arrive at the following (Table 2).

In order to achieve a symbiosis of self-organizing, spontaneous systems with evolutionary problem solving processes a certain amount of

Table 2.

		Kinds of problem solving or decision making	
		analytic/constructivist	evolutionary/cybernetic
Kinds of order or system	taxical	classical theory of management and administration	attempts to make given forms of organization more flexible and more adaptive; organizational development, job-enrichment, etc.
	spontaneous self-organizing	this depicts the actual situations; business firms are in fact largely self-organizing but they degenerate under the impact of analytic methods	properly understood managerial cybernetics, evolutionary problem-solving in the context of viable systems

analytic and taxical intervention are necessary. The problem is to <u>design</u> self-organizing systems and evolutionary processes in the field of management out of existing structures and the given managerial culture.

To <u>design</u> a <u>self-organizing</u> system may at first sight seem to be completely contradictory; but it is not really, as cybernetics and social theory have shown provided that we distinguish <u>object-level</u> and <u>meta-level</u>. In his opening address to the 2nd EMCSR 1974, Stafford Beer has dealt with this apparent contradiction of designing a self-organizing system and he pointed out that one can design a free, self-organizing, spontaneous system by using a higher order language and by intervening at the metasystemic level (Beer [5]). At the metasystemic level you may operate on the system in a taxical way without destroying its freedom and spontaneous forces at the object level. This does not mean, of course, that <u>any</u> metasystemic intervention preserves the self-organizing capability of the system, but I would uphold the working hypothesis that <u>only</u> metasystemic intervention or design leaves the system basically, i.e. systemically, intact.

The same holds for the design of evolutionary problem solving and decision making processes. So we arrive at Figure 3, and here we have a classical situation of a homeostatically coupled system in which structure and process depend on each other in an autopoietic relationship.

If we want to understand and improve the cybernetics of practical decision making, we must operate on the basis of this fundamental autopoiesis. One has to initiate exactly such problem-solving processes which support and develop a viable structure; and one has to design exactly such structures which make possible evolutionary problem solving.

From this point of view the old and widely cherished managerial dogma that structure follows strategy appears somewhat obsolete. Even the question of what comes first, structure or strategy, or what is more important, seems ill-conceived if not completely irrelevant, since one cannot break up the close interdependence without destroying the most vital characteristics of an integral viable system.

6. THE STRATEGIC PROBLEM

One of the most important problems any viable system and therefore also the business firm has to solve is the problem of finding a viable position within the environment. This problem is called the strategic problem of the firm (Ansoff [2]) and it only very rarely has a lasting solution. Rather it demands a continual stream of decisions and of adaptations to position and reposition the firm in its environment. This problem certainly belongs to what has been labelled ill-structured problems. It demands preserving traditional, well-adapted and proven solutions as well as exploring completely unknown fields. It is therefore in many ways typical for a lot of other managerial problem situations. The means of the business firm as well as of any other system to solve this type of problem are of course strategy and structure as explained above.

Now, what is really important from the point of view of viability is not so much the specific content of the problem at a certain point of time, or the specific shape and content of a strategy chosen for a definite period of time. The really important problem is to keep the system permanently alert to the continually changing relationship with its environment and to keep the decision process of defining and redefining the firm's position active and adaptive. There are very great dangers that the process will peter out, that the attention and interest of the decision makers fade away to more specific or more urgent or more comfortable or simply easier problems or that the process runs in one fixed direction, thereby losing its adaptiveness.

There is now a growing number of business executives who are at least vaguely aware of the strategic problem as such and of the dangers just mentioned. They are looking actively for help to initiate a system capable to tackle the strategic problem and from my experience in consulting and management development analytic decision methods and the widely praised computer play at present a very minor role in all this. The major objective is to design and maintain structures and processes which force people to think permanently and continually about the strategic problem, to communicate effectively each other's opinions and arguments, to listen to criticism and counter-arguments, and to hammer out a shared opinion which utilizes all the relevant information which is available at the moment. In other words, the objective is to install a nucleus of multiply-connected brains with a maximum of freedom to think on the one hand but sufficient discipline and monitoring intervention on the other so that the whole process does not run out of control. Stafford Beer called this kind of system a <u>multinode</u> and located it in the highest echelon of his viable systems-model, i.e. in System Five (Beer [4]). Experience shows that it is even better to involve people lower down the hierarchy (Systems Three and Four) since this dissolves much of the problem of communicating and implementing the chosen policy.

In the last few years some instruments have been devised which have proved useful in monitoring a multinode and in preparing its way to successfully dealing with the strategic problem. The main elements of this monitoring system are shown in Figure 4 (Ulrich [21]; Ulrich and Krieg [22]). This is of course only a static picture showing nothing of the dynamics of the process. These elements together with the temporal sequence of applying them and several additional handling rules is constituted by the people who have gathered to deal with the strategic problem, their minds, their knowledge, feelings, opinions, and above all the intense discussions which are initiated and kept alive by metasystemic impulses.

If the monitoring is done well the process follows the lines Beer and Tarr [4,6,20] have discussed in several places and which are depicted in Figure 5. Variety is cut down step by step with respect to alternative courses of action and with respect to the specification of the tentative and temporal strategic posture. If an agreement is reached, information is used up

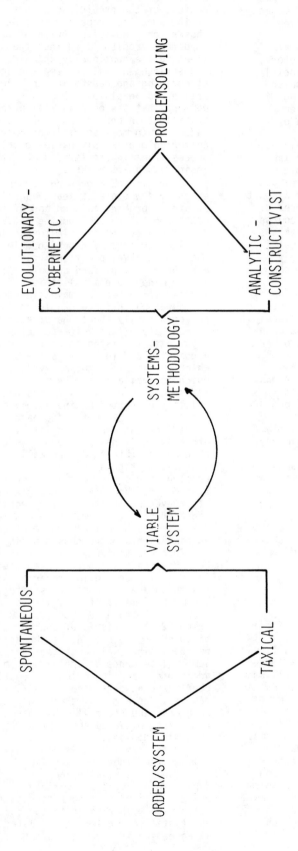

Figure 3.

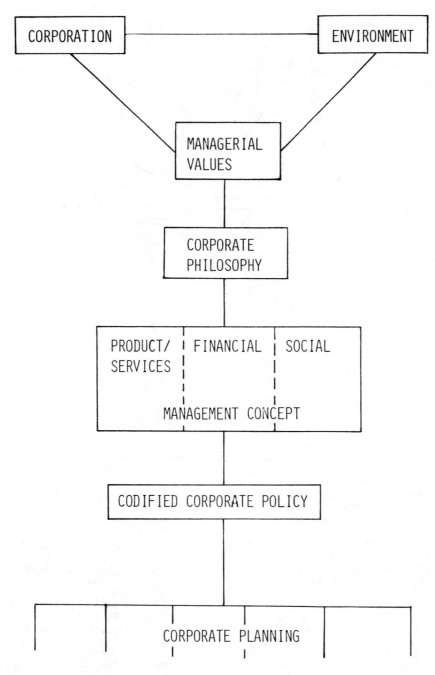

Figure 4.   The Corporate Decision-Making Process

and people feel rather exhausted. There is of course no guarantee that an agreement will be reached or that the chosen strategy will turn out to be successful. This is exactly what calls for continual revision of any decision as far as possible. Sometimes the group of executives constituting the multinode faces a fundamental uncertainty and begins to oscillate between several equally meaningful and plausible alternatives. If there is no possibility to resolve the uncertainty because no one has any further relevant information, the process must be postponed until more knowledge is available.

For the monitoring as such this is not surprising since there is no way of knowing in advance which information will prove to be relevant in the course of the process. The multinode, if properly monitored, will find out what it knows and what not, the latter being equally interesting for further search activities.

Metasystemically, a certain logical and temporal sequence of activities is suggested, but experience shows that the multinode has its own largely unpredictable logical and temporal sequence

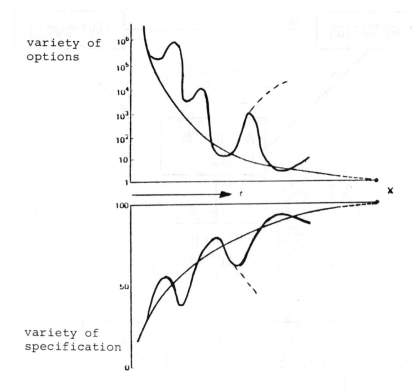

Figure 5.   Reduction of Complexity in a Properly
Monitored Decision Process

of touching issues. It often jumps from one issue to another in a way which, to an outside observer, seems to be entirely irregular. It is even a very common observation that such a group of executives acts illogically in the sense that it accepts propositions which are not deductible from previously discussed and accepted propositions.

The metasystemic monitoring of such a spontaneous and largely self-organizing system where control and relevance and attention, critical information, convincing power and consensus jumps irregularly from element to element, must be concentrated on leaving as much freedom as possible while nevertheless putting enough guiding constraints over the system by sequencing the process and drawing attention to the strategically relevant methodical aspects that the process comes in great discursive spirals (see Figure 6), either to shared opinion and a climate of common belief or to the discovery of open controversies which at the moment cannot be settled.

7. SUMMARY

I started with a critic of the analytic paradigms of decision making. It is quite possible that analytic decision methods may be applied to certain subproblems within the total problem solving process. But they are certainly not adequate to comprise the decision making process as a complex self-organizing system; they are not very useful in monitoring the working of a multi-node. In this sense a rather wide portion of

decision theory seems to be rather irrelevant to managerial practice.

REFERENCES

1. ALDRUP, D., Das Rationalitätsproblem in der Politischen Ökonomie, Tübingen, 1971.
2. ANSOFF, H. J., R. P. DECLERCK and R. L. HAYES, From Strategic Planning to Strategic Management, London, 1976.
3. ASHBY, W. R., "Some Consequences of Bremermann's Limit for Information Processing Systems," in: Cybernetic Problems in Bionics, H. Oesterreicher and D. Moore (eds.), New York, 1968.
4. BEER, S., Brain of the Firm, London, 1972.
5. BEER, S., "On Heaping Our Science Together," Proceedings of the 2nd EMCSR, 1974.
6. BEER, S., Platform for Change, London, 1975.
7. BRAYBROOKE, D. and Ch. LINDBLOM, A Strategy of Decision, London, 1963.
8. BREMERMANN, H. J., "Optimization Through Evolution and Recombination," in Self-Organizing Systems, M. Yovits, O. Jacobi and O. Goldstein (eds.), Washington, 1962.
9. GOMEZ, P., F. MALIK and K. H. OELLER, Systemmethodik - Grundlagen einer Methodik zur Erforschung und Gestaltung komplexer soziotechnischer Systeme, Bd. 1 und 2, Bern u. Stuttgart, 1975.
10. HAYEK, F. A., Studies in Philosophy, Politics, and Economics, Chicago, 1967.
11. HAYEK, F. A., Law, Legislation, and Liberty,

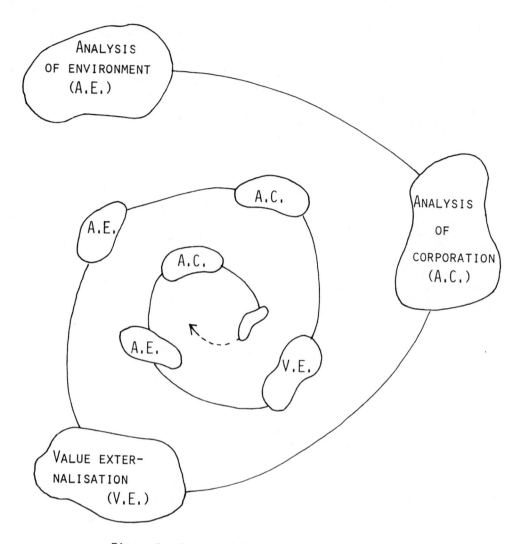

Figure 6. Spiral of Complexity Reduction

Vol. I: Rules and Order, London, 1973.

12. HAYEK, F. A., Law, Legislation, and Liberty, Vol. II: The Mirage of Social Justice, London, 1976.

13. LINDBLOM, Ch., "The Science of Muddling Through," Public Administration Review, 19, 2, 1959.

14. LINDBLOM, Ch., The Intelligence of Democracy, London, 1965.

15. MALIK, F., Kybernetische und Methodische Grundlagen des Strategischen Managements, forthcoming.

16. POPPER, K. R., Objective Knowledge, London, 1972.

17. SIMON, H. A., The New Science of Management Decision, New Jersey, 1977.

18. RECHENBERG, I., Evolutionsstrategie, Stuttgart, 1973.

19. STEINBRUNER, J., The Cybernetic Theory of Decision, Princeton, 1974.

20. TARR, G., The Management of Problem-Solving, London, 1973.

21. ULRICH, H., Die Unternehmung als produktives soziales System, Bern u. Stuttgart, 1970.

22. ULRICH, H. and W. KRIEG, St. Galler Management Modell, Bern u. Stuttgart, 1974.

Definition of objectives
and the dialectical systems theory

MATJAŽ MULEJ
School of Business Economics, University of Maribor
Maribor, Yugoslavia

1. STARTING POINTS

The systems theory started its way of development in the middle of this century without any explicit knowledge of the materialistic dialectics. The research of the natural and social life, however, brought the system theory to quite similar basic ideas; contrary to the narrow specialisation in metaphysics, the systems theory opens the idea of the whole, the open system concept and dynamics. The common point for all specialised sciences is found in the definition of the term "system" based on mathematics: a system is made up of two sets (compounds, relations). This fact makes a basic isomorphism of all kinds of subjects possible, it makes the research much more precise, but it also makes an important mistake: in order to have a common definition for every feature it leaves the contents aside and retains only the form. As the form is only one part of the properties, the feature as a whole considered and presented by "system" is no more the whole. Thus the term "system" is misused and therefore the system is no more a system but a subsystem or a partial system. According to my research this results from the lack of materialistic dialectics.

My attempt to find the way out of this problem has shown that a systems theory cannot be a bridge between specialised sciences and practices with a merely formalistic approach to their subjects; as too many important properties are ignored it is not realistic any more and cannot be used. We should realise the following fact:

According to the above mentioned mathematically based definition every system as viewed from the formal side is a whole; but according to the properties of the real object that is taken as a system, we must realise that only a part of these properties is taken into consideration because nobody is able to observe all the properties at the same time. Therefore, from the aspect of the contents, a system is only a onesided picture of the observed object.

Which part of the existing properties is to be considered depends on the aspect that has been selected. This conclusion brings our attention to the "starting points" from which the observer begins when he selects his aspect. Why? Things move successively, the previous phases influencing the later ones. Therefore, we can speak of the natural hierarchy of the succession. This puts the first phases of every process in a much more important role than people realise.

People only think of satisfying their own needs in the first place. But in order to fulfill this people need the results of their work based on the tasks that have previously derived from the defined objectives. According to this fact objectives are essential for the grade and the method of satisfying our needs.

Objectives, in the same way of thinking, cannot be said to appear all by themselves like plants in nature. Neither can they be merely identified with the feelings and wishes of the person involved. In such a case the objectives could hardly be achieved and/or they could hardly have a real basis for their achievement. It is also a fact that wishes emerge from the needs of the person who defines the objectives. But these needs are normally more numerous and diversified than the possibilities to satisfy them. For this reason we must be very careful about the phases before making the final definition of the objectives. In these previous phases some needs are to be selected from the whole list of the needs felt. These needs are relatively most important ones and they deserve preference. On the other side, and in a close mutual interdependence with the process of defining preferential needs, also a list of possibilities that go along with the preferential needs. The contents are obviously different in every case.

The conclusion is therefore as follows: There must be something that happens before the process of checking the lists of the needs and of the possibilities. This influences the selection of the aspect. Later on the aspect influences the selection of the preferential needs and corresponding possibilities, influencing in the further phase the definition of the objectives. They influence the tasks and the tasks influence the work, which again influences the results. There must exist some criteria at the beginning of this series: (1) some values (attitudes), (2) some knowledge on the subject, and (3) some knowledge on the methods. These three together could be given the common name "starting points."

The three compounds of the starting points complement each other:

The knowledge about the subject raises the issues, i.e., opens the questions about the possible objectives.

The values (attitudes) select the issues into a group that is to be taken in account and into the other group that is to be put aside.

The knowledge about the methods enables us to find an answer to the questions.

These findings lead to the conclusion that the objectives are very important, but the starting points are even more important. As the starting points also do not grow like plants, this fact opens the question of the pahse of creating the starting points.

The series of these findings can be presented in the following scheme:

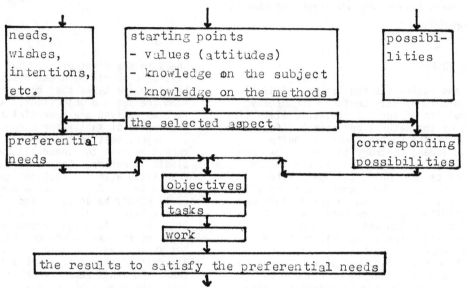

Figure 1. Hierarchy of Succession and the Objectives as Realised with the Dialectical System Theory

2. TEN THESES ON THE DEFINITION OF THE STARTING POINTS

The process presented in Figure 1 shows that the phases of analysis (studying) and the synthesis (building, producing) are unseparately interdependent and they follow each other. I attempted to show in my paper to the previous EMCSR 1976 in Vienna that the systems theory alone cannot cover analysis and synthesis well enough. This is due to the fact that the definition stating that everything can be defined as a whole, i.e. as a system, remains too far away from the real whole of the properties of the object in question. Nevertheless, the systems theory with its precise formal language and approach makes a very good synthesis of the system as a model possible. In order to have a realistic analysis the materialistic dialectics is unavoidable. It makes the consideration of all properties, circumstances, dynamics, etc., much more feasible. These, as the shortest possible summary, were the main reasons for me to propose the dialectical systems theory. It is supposed to be a bridge between the specialised disciplines of science and practice in the role of general methodology, which, in every single case of research, is to be combined with the specific methods of the specific fields according to the selected aspects.

The findings of my research, summarised in this paper, show -- among other results -- the fact that in most cases people do not care enough about the way of how to define the starting points.

They simply do not think enough about the first phases of the process of their work when they want to produce something in order to satisfy their needs of any kind. The dialectics of life shows that the life moves on in a continuous, never-ending process of changing and of development. Therefore something else should be considered before defining the starting points because it influences their contents: the specific quality of the starting points appearing in all three compounds (values, knowledge on the subject, knowledge on the methods) as interdependent subsystems of the system of starting points.

The routine work is here less interesting than the creative work for the following main reasons:

The creative work has much more influence on the final results than the routine work because it brings new points into the process of work; the creative work is more the responsibility of the worker and depends more on his personal "starting points"; this fact also depends on the creative work.

Thus I have confined myself to the creative work, and my research and its practical uses in different activities (maintenance, marketing, organising in industries and social activities) have shown that the following ten theses on defining of the starting points are to be taken in account:

2.1. Revolutionarity

In order to make work creative we must start from revolutionarity in values and knowledge because they contain a tendency towards new, better solutions, a tendency to change the old, existing situation. In order to produce this we need science, but also the will and values are important because they are dialectically inter-linked. Values and knowledge are unseparable parts of the same system and they must be progressive, revolutionary, not conservative. In the opposite case, we cannot search for the natural truth and produce new results as the truth is normally not finite.

2.2. Methodological Knowledge

For creative work also a corresponding methodological knowledge is necessary, i.e., the capacity to learn, use and develop the methods of work. As a part of starting points general methodological knowledge is necessary. It is very close to the theory and offers a general methodological orientation of the research and of creation and measurement of its results.

2.3. Clear Definition

In every day creative work on such a basis a clear definition of the issue must be made in the first place. Also the tasks must be specified in order to make it clear as to what must be done and produced. This again depends on the objectives dependent on the preferential needs and corresponding possibilities. Their selection depends on the values and knowledge, on the starting points because they define the aspect.

2.4. Delimitation of the Phases

For this reason, according to the starting points, also the basic phases of work have to be delimited, in advance, roughly said: (1) the definition of the problem, (2) the synthesis of the model, (3) the analysis of the problem in the model, (4) the synthesis of the results and findings on the problem and on the methods of work. As we see, all the work that follows depends on the starting points.

2.5. Clear and Realistic Starting Points

The starting points therefore must be clear and realistic. For this reason they must provide for as many aspects of the observation of the defined problem as possible. They have to be interlinked because they are interdependent. From each single aspect the same object shows more or less only one part of its properties. Therefore no single aspect can show the whole truth, not even the most important part of it.

2.6. Mutual Understanding

Because of this fact we need the possibility and capacity for mutual understanding and the collaboration of specialists with different knowledge and experience, will, intentions and values.

2.7. Interdisciplinarity

Therefore the capacity for such definition of starting points is necessary as to enable an interdisciplinary cooperation. The consideration of creative and other capacities and activities of other men, of their own processes and ideas, i.e. not only those in which we have specialized inside a part of the whole, must be made possible. The whole does not disappear because of the specialization, but it is frequently forgotten.

2.8. Modernising

These findings are results of the modern, very specialized and fast life and work, which is very different from the "good old times". This is why the old methods cannot be used any more. The starting points of the past time cannot be used either because they reflect the characteristics which have no relevance to the present time. So the starting points must be adapted to current processes over and over again and modernised.

2.9. Extreme Interconnection of the Starting Points with Values and Knowledge

Because of all findings described above the definition of the starting points is extremely interconnected with: (1) the values, and (2) the knowledge.

2.10. Complicated Definition of Starting Points

All these facts appear exceptionally complicated when the defining of the starting points themselves is in question as the method of defining the starting points is less formal and precise and it mostly depends on intuition. This means that it depends on values, general methodological knowledge, and the theoretical framework of knowledge and attitudes of the man who is entitled to define the starting points. The exact technical work starts much later and leads to the results which have been foreseen as objectives according to the starting points. So, if the starting points are conservative, they will direct all the work towards a mere renewing of the old situations, without searching for new and better solutions. In such a case there would be no creative work. Last but not least, the starting points, no matter whether conservative or revolutionary, have to enter the consciousness and even the subconsciousness through education and experience.

The conclusion that the starting points have an essential role could be shown by the scheme presented in Figure 2.

3. DIALECTICAL SYSTEMS THEORY AS A METHODOLOGICAL PART OF STARTING POINTS

The systems theory has ruined the metaphysics as a methodology over the last decades. But in some specific cases in the recent years it has been transformed into a formal science on common characteristics of features of different types.

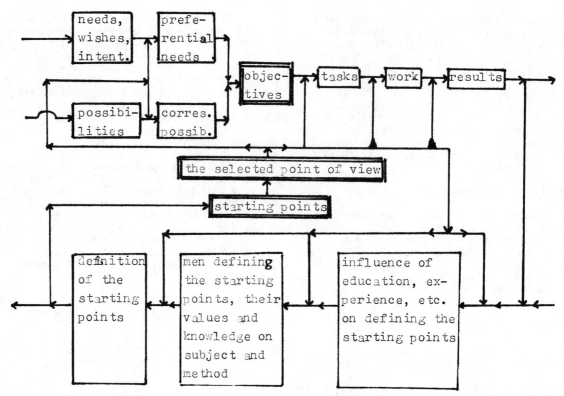

Figure 2.   The Central Role of the Starting Points

Therefore it has become uncapable of forming efficient starting points. If we accept the definition that the system is a whole made up of a set of compounds and a set of their relations (which is mathematically exact) as the only possible definition, the misuse of the term system becomes possible. On this basis, however, the term system can be used in a narrow, onesided sense, i.e. metaphysically. This fact leads to a loss of two most important advantages of the systems theory: (1) the wholeness and complexity, and (2) open and not isolated system concept. In view of this the systems theory alone cannot be used in the role of the methodological part of the starting points, particularly not for creative work.

On the other hand dialectics, even materialistic dialectics alone, is not enough. It can be very useful in the phases of analysis, but it is not clear enough in the phases of the synthesis of models and the synthesis of results, for here very clear borders have to be defined.

Thus, materialistic dialectics is useful in the phases of analysis above all. Systems theory is, however, useful in the phases of synthesis. Synthesis and analysis are two interdependent parts of the same work. Therefore materialistic dialectics and system theory if put together produce the dialectical systems theory. This is a general methodological science and the methodological part of the starting points, especially for creative work. (I speak of the methodological part of the starting points because I realise that

only here we can make a bridge between different specialized sciences. They are specialized according to their knowledge in different aspects, and in methods they have special aspects too, but here also a commom moment can be found.)

My research showed the following ten rules:

3.1.   Wholeness

This means that we must take into account that the system as a formal whole, in its contents is only one out of a series of possible onesided pictures (models) of the observed feature. So, only a series of such systems, interlinked into an interdependent complex of many of them -- only such a dialectical system of systems that have been introduced from many different aspects -- can assure wholeness in observation, and in research and at its end realistic findings.

3.2.   Open System Concept

This means that it is not enough to isolate an interesting feature out of its environment and to observe it only from the aspect of the properties viewed from such narrow starting points, as this shows only one part of reality.

3.3.   Dynamics

We must never cease, when we have come to a result. It will have changed in the meantime.

On the other hand, this rule means also that we must take into account that other men could have come to other findings resulting from other points of view that may be even a more important part of the truth.

3.4. Interdisciplinarity

Normally no feature can be understood or mastered well from only one aspect, dictated by any kind of specialization.

3.5. Probability

There is probably no observation or management without any risk. Another aspect can show some other insight, another part of the truth and the first one will no more be complete or finite.

These five rules may be beyond doubt and are necessary parts of general methodological subsystem of the starting points. They only impose demands. Thus the question arises of how should they be answered. The answers are given by the following five rules:

3.6.

In the phases of analysis we must use methods of materialistic dialectics in order to be able to assure real wholeness, open-system-concept, dynamics, interdisciplinarity and probability. This is the way to take the real interdependence and succession into account as unity of adverse and genesis. This interdependence of the features and parts of features and processes means also an interdependence of findings produced by the analysis (studying).

3.7.

In the phases of synthesis of the starting points, models (systems) and results we cannot use dialectecs so well, because with it things would become too complicated. Here we must start from the mathematically exact, strict and precise delimitation of precisely defined types of systems, in order to realise in advance the borders of the properties involved in analysis, as well as the borders of the validity of the reached results as a part of the truth. Here the typology of systems and models is to be used.

3.8. Realistic Generalisation

The generalisation of results from onesided systems and models (as a second rate type of systems) would lead to wrong opinions because it would lose the connection with reality. Thus, instead of the formal generalisation with elegant formal models quite far away from reality, the opposite of this is more important: to keep the relatively close contact with the reality.

3.9. Dialectical Systems

In view of rule 3.8., the findings from one-sided systems and models (which are unavoidable because of the necessary specialization) must be interlinked in a synergetic interdependence. This means that we must observe the object from all the possible aspects (in an ideal situation, from all of them), using interdisciplinary cooperation. In this way we have to produce a dialectical system of systems, interlinked in a synergetic way instead of relying on a single system.

3.10.

Therefore, the analysis and synthesis must be two interdependent sides and phases of the same process of creative work.

General systems theory and especially cybernetics, include among their basic terms the feedback. We do not include it into the basic terms of the dialectical systems theory although I have a great respect for it and the results of its proper use. However, the feedback cannot be considered a general property of a system of any kind. It is more a specific property of those (closed) systems that have the special (important, but not general) ability of self-regulation for an automatic renewal of the former state, but without development.

4. FINAL CONCLUSIONS

Metaphysics was the way of thinking that was very useful with its emphasis on analysis. Its weak side was the total concentration on analysis. That is why, since the time of its appearance in the medieval age, it has become too narrow and rigid because life has changed; insight into parts with considering the whole and the development is not enough any more.

Systems theory ruined metaphysics at first, but later the overemphasis on the formal definition of "system" brought it back to the old method of creative work and slowed down its successful development. My analysis of this fact showed in synthesis that this problem is particularly acute if we concentrate on the problem of creative work and especially on the definition of objectives.

My conclusion is that, however, we could save the useful elements and the basic progressive ideas of the systems theory (wholeness, open system concept, clearness, preciseness, general use) if we combine these elements with the materialistic dialectics. Thus, the idea of the dialectical systems theory as a general methodology has been born.

Along with its elaboration a new finding has appeared, on the essential importance of the proper definition of starting points. There is also the finding on the rule of hierarchy of succession. According to these rules the starting points have an essential and unavoidable influence on all further processes and on the results. Further research has produced ten theses on the issues which have to be considered for an effective definition of starting points for creative work. It also produced the finding that the dialectical systems theory might be a bridge between specialized sciences in the role of the general methodological subsystem of the starting points. For this reason, further research also produced ten rules of the

dialectical systems theory as a general methodological part of the starting points, including
the forming of starting points for the definition
of starting points for actual work.

Last but not least, I can say that these
ideas in one year's time of practical approba-
tions proved their usefulness: they make people
think in a different way, they make them realise

that they have used to overlook some properties
which are important, bring new insights and new
ways for the solving of old problems. Their
direct effect in industries has reached more
than half a million dollars. This knowledge
(including many further details) has in every
case been used as a bridge between specialists
and in combination with their own knowledge and
values.

Modelling impreciseness in human systems

HANNU NURMI

Department of Philosophy, University of Turku, Finland

1. INTRODUCTION

The aim of this paper is to discuss the sources as well as the modelling devices of the impreciseness that surrounds systems consisting of human components. In particular, the mathematical theories or structures purporting to model the impreciseness are focused upon. No attempt is made to discuss the theories in extenso, but only outline their main principles along with the intuitive background or motivation of their construction.

The second aim of the paper is to give a systematic account of the notions pertaining to impreciseness, such as vagueness, ambiguity, randomness, etc. Conceptual clarity is always, ceteris paribus, a good thing and is by no means excluded by the fact that the concepts involved have imprecise references.

Thirdly, an attempt is made to discuss a problem related to measuring imprecise properties, viz. their representation by means of various mathematical relational systems. This problem is tackled with respect to two impreciseness notions only: fuzziness and randomness. This part of the paper is a continuation of one of my previous articles [14].

2. THE SOURCES OF IMPRECISENESS

I am using the concept of impreciseness as a general one. In this usage it refers to all sorts of things (i.e. events, properties, etc.) that cannot be exactly determined, as well as to concepts that either lack univocal meaning or are otherwise ridden by problems of application to specific cases. It should be observed at the outset that impreciseness of concepts does not entail the impreciseness of the things referred to. For instance, one may talk about exactly determinable properties or events using imprecise concepts. On the other hand, the fact that the events or properties are imprecise in an objective sense -- for example, irreducibly random events -- does not exclude the possibility of talking about them by using precise expressions. Indeed, this is what the mathematical theories of modelling impreciseness purport to do. In the human sciences the motivation for developing mathematical theories of impreciseness is, however, not always to find a precise way of modelling imprecise phenomena, but the theories are often directed at discovering precise ways of handling imprecise concepts. In particular, this

is the case when ordinary language is being modelled. The expressions of ordinary language are generally somewhat imprecise.

2.1. Randomness

By far the most commonplace source of impreciseness is randomness, if one bases this judgement on the nature of the mathematical description apparata currently in use in the social sciences. Random variables and stochastic or probabilistic models are well known to every student of the social sciences. Randomness is the sort of impreciseness that is taken care of by probabilistic notions. In what sense these notions "take care of" randomness will be discussed later on. For the moment it suffices to point out some properties commonly thought of as characterizing randomness as distinct from other types of impreciseness.

Intuitively, randomness is related to uncertainty concerning the occurrence or nonoccurrence of an event of some sort. "Essentially randomness has to with uncertainty concerning membership and nonmembership of an object in a nonfuzzy set. Fuzziness, on the other hand, has to do with classes in which there may be grades of membership intermediate between full membership and nonmembership" [1]. Or, in the words of Negoita and Ralescu, "Randomness involves uncertainty about the occurrence of an event precisely described. Fuzziness deals with the case where the object itself is intrinsically imprecise..." [11]. The "event" in question may be anything describable by means of a set of variables. The uncertainty concerns the specific values of the variables in an "experiment" (natural or man-made). One crucial characteristic of randomness in contradistinction to other sources of impreciseness is that after the experiment has been performed the uncertainty vanishes entirely: the values of the relevant random variables in that particular experiment are now known. They may not be directly observable, though. Nonetheless, it still is the case that when randomness is involved, the trial is assumed to completely determine the values of the variables.

In the case of randomness one can legitimately say that the impreciseness is reflected in the uncertainty concerning an event. It is, however, not the case that uncertainty would always be due to randomness. In the most straight-forward case (the one mentioned in the previous paragraph) the uncertainty pertains to a chance setup and a specific trial to be performed in the future. But, of course, we can speak of random events also when the uncertainty concerning a specific trial has completely disappeared. Indeed, what is sometimes called a statistical explanation takes particular advantage of the properties of random events in an effort to explain their occurrence in specific cases [8,16]. In general any attempt to account for random events presupposes that the randomness is somehow patterned and that the investigator is able to gain knowledge of the pattern. This much is generally agreed upon. As to the source of randomness, views differ. One school of thought claims that the source is in the phenomena themselves, i.e. that randomness is of an objective nature. The representatives of this school can be further divided into two groups: (1) the frequentists, and (2) the advocates of the propensity view [15,7]. The criterion of this subdivision is whether the properties of randomness upon which we base our accounts of phenomena are derivable from observation of a sequence of trials or whether the properties of the chance setup are the sole determinants of the phenomenon [14]. The other school of thought takes its point of departure from the notion of uncertainty which is conceptually related to knowledge. This school maintains that randomness is always knowledge-relative. Hence, it is elliptic to speak of randomness without mentioning either the agent or the corpus of knowledge with respect to which the events are random.

From the point of view of the present paper it is worth noticing that the views of the nature and source of randomness are all compatible with the same formal system or -- more precisely -- are admissible interpretations of a particular formal system, viz. that of A. N. Kolmogoroff. This compatibility guarantees that for each of the interpretations of randomness, we can find a measure of the uncertainty involved.

2.2. Fuzziness

In some cases the uncertainty concerning the prevailing state of affairs does not vanish when an experiment is conducted and its result is observed. This is the case in particular when the impreciseness takes the form of fuzziness in the sense suggested by the quotations in the preceding section. According to them fuzziness has to do with the sort of impreciseness that presupposes the possibility of borderline cases in the application of the concept. A fuzzy concept is, eo ipso, vague. It is not, however, necessarily ambiguous. The ambiguity of a concept implies that the concept refers to different things. A concept may be entirely precise (that is, nonfuzzy) in referring to two or more different entities. In other words, there need not be any borderline cases of the application of the concept. On the other hand, fuzziness in the sense of intentional vagueness presupposes that there are possibly borderline cases. If the concept, moreover, is extensionally vague, there, in fact, are some borderline cases [6].

Conceptually, then, randomness is a property of events that are unambiguously classifiable so that one can always, in principle, say to which class a given event belongs. On the other hand, fuzziness turns on the issue of classification: some events are not unambiguously classifiable, but it seems that their belonging to various classes is a matter of degree (degree of membership in a fuzzy class or set).

From a methodological point of view there is a further difference between fuzziness and randomness. In the case of randomness we can speak of probabilities of events and assign specific probability values to various events on the basis of our knowledge concerning the pattern of randomness involved. Regardless of the interpretation of randomness chosen, there is no way in which an observation concerning the result of an experiment or trial could challenge our value assignment (disregarding the degenerate case in which the assigned value is 0 or 1 and the event occurs or does not occur, respectively). In contrast, the investigation of the event and that only can determine the justifiability of a given membership degree assignment. Experiment is, thus, directly relevant in the latter case, whereas its relevance is of an indirect nature in probability assignments.

When testing probability statements one usually calculates relative frequencies. In the limiting frequency interpretation the link between probability and frequency is an even more direct -- indeed a conceptual -- one. Therefore, it may be of some interest to notice that fuzziness does not seem to have any connection whatsoever with frequencies. These remarks may be sufficient to suggest that intuitively fuzziness and randomness can be kept distinct.

2.3. Complexity

The third type of impreciseness relates to the structural aspects of the objects of study. It is sometimes argued that the sheer complexity of the systems under study makes it impossible to give accurate predictions of their behavior or to describe their behavior in detail. In these allegations the complexity serves as an explanatory factor; it is a source of uncertainty. Recently a number of publications dealing with complexity have been published [13, 19]. I shall touch upon the complexity-uncertainty relationship only as it seems most pertinent in the present context [13].

In an article that in many respects was ahead of its time, Weaver discussed the notion of complexity and pointed out that the methodology of knowledge production is based on the assumption that the objects of study are either deterministic and simple or disorganized and random in character [21]. Objects that can be characterized as organized complexities were in Weaver's view beyond the reach of our methodological apparata. Thirty years later the situation is not much better: in some specific aspects of complexity only are we anywhere near the exactness of the concept of probability.

Whereas randomness and fuzziness relate to the outer aspects of events or behavior of systems, complexity often refers to the underlying structure. To focus, thus, on a different aspect of the systems is compatible both with randomness and fuzziness in the sense that both in outer behavior can be due to the complexity of the system refers to the number of its components as well as to their interdependence [19]. There are other senses in which the concept of complexity has been used. In particular, information theory contains a specific definition of complexity or information content. Similarly, the computer scientists have constructed various measures of computational complexity [18]. The latter has to do with the number of stages or the amount of working space required in the computation of a given function for a given argument. Complexity is then seen as a machine-relative notion, i.e. it varies both with the computational task and with the computing device. The ideas are not, however, easily transferable from formal languages to the language in which the social systems are usually described. The information-theoretic complexity concept, in turn, is defined in terms of probability. Therefore, turning now to the measurement problems related to impreciseness, I shall restrict myself to fuzziness and probability only.

3. MEASURING IMPRECISENESS

Despite the conceptual differences of randomness and fuzziness touched upon above, it may be claimed that a reliable way of determining whether two distinct notions are really needed is to find out whether the corresponding measures differ. In other words, we should investigate whether the ways in which we conceptualize the measurement of probability and fuzziness are sufficiently different to warrant the employment of the concepts. In my opinion there is much to be applauded in this view although I do not agree with giving the measurement properties a decisive role in making the conceptual distinction. The formal properties of probability can be given interpretations that have nothing to do with what we mean by probability. So, the identity of formal properties does not imply that the methods in the study of probability and fuzziness would be the same. On the other hand, if the formal properties of the concepts differ, it is, at least in principle, possible to find cases in which the property referred to by one of the concepts is measurable while the property to which the other one refers is not.

3.1. On Measurement

It is well known that measurement is essentially an assigning of numbers to empirical phenomena. From a foundational point of view measurement involves proving a representation theorem and a uniqueness theorem. In proving the former, one establishes a "natural" way of assigning numbers to phenomena so that their empirical relationships are adequately reflected in the numerical apparatus employed. In order to solve the representation problem we have to formalize the empirical relationships investigated. Moreover, one has to show that the formal relationships are isomorphic with certain numerical relationships [10,12]. Expressed in a more exact fashion, the solution of the representation problem amounts to the following. An ordered n+1-tuple $U = (A, R_1, \ldots, R_n)$, where A is the set of empirical objects or properties investigated and where

R_i ($i = 1, \ldots, n$) is a relation on A, is an empirical relational structure. The relational structure $V = (Re, S_1, \ldots, S_n)$ is a numerical relational structure if Re is the set of real numbers. A function from A into Re is a homomorphism if for all i ($i = 1, \ldots, n$) and for all k-tuples $(a_1, \ldots, a_k) \in A^k$, the following is the case:

$$R_i(a_1, \ldots, a_k) \quad \text{iff} \quad S_i(f(a_1), \ldots, f(a_k)).$$

If f is a bijection U and V are isomorphic. Now, proving a representation theorem means that one shows that if the empirical relational structure satisfies certain properties, there is a homomorphism from the empirical relational structure into a certain numerical relational one. The latter, then, represents the former in the sense that the objects and relations of the empirical relational structure have their counterparts in the numerical one. It is obvious that if we want to use a given numerical structure, then not all empirical relational structures can be represented by it. The choice of the numerical structure is mostly dictated by convenience.

The second problem related to measurement deals with uniqueness: proving a uniqueness theorem involves involves establishing the transformations of the homomorphism f that are permissible. Permissibility, in turn, has to do with what is customarily referred to as the scale of measurement: the transformation of the homomorphism f into f' is permissible exactly when f and f' are both homomorphisms into the same numerical relational structure [10]. One notices immediately that what counts as a permissible transformation of a measurement scale depends on the nature of the empirical relations we are interested in. Moreover, the establishment of a uniqueness theorem presupposes the solution of the representation problem. Given a solution, there is no way of distinguishing measurement scales which are obtained from each other via permissible transformations.

3.2. Measurement of Probability

In establishing the representation theorem for probability we are interested in finding out the conditions under which we can numerically measure probability. In other words, we are interested in the conditions under which the relation "is at least as probable as" defined on a set of events can be represented by means of a numerical relational structure.

We call a non-empty collection F of subsets of a set X a set algebra or algebra of sets on X, if the following conditions are met for all A, B ∈ F:
1. -A ∈ F (-A is the complement of A);
2. A ∪ B ∈ F. If, moreover,
3. A_i ∈ F for all i = 1, ..., n implies that $\bigcup_{i=1}^{\infty} A_i$ ∈ F, we call F a σ-algebra.

Let G be an algebra of sets on non-empty X and let ≥ be a 2-place relation in G (≥ can be interpreted in the fashion suggested above). ≥ is realizable if there exists a mapping P : G → Re such that:
1. (X,G,P) is a finitely additive probability

space, i.e. for all $A, B \in G$:

    i. $P(A) \geq 0$,

    ii. $P(X) = 1$, and

    iii. if $A \cap B = \emptyset$, then $P(A \cap B) =$
        $P(A) + P(B)$.

2. For all $A, B \in G$, $A \geq B$ iff $P(A) \geq P(B)$.

We are now looking for the conditions under which this relation $\geq$ in G is realizable. Necessary conditions for realizability were set forth by de Finetti as follows. If X, G and $\geq$ are as above, then the conditions

1. $\geq$ is complete,
2. $\geq$ is transitive,
3. $A \geq \emptyset$,
4. not $\emptyset \geq X$, and
5. if $A \cap C = B \cap C = \emptyset$, then $A \geq B$,
    iff $A \cup C \geq B \cup C$,

are necessary ones for the realizability of $\geq$.

The necessary conditions for the existence of (comparative) probability measure 1-5 are not, however, sufficient for the existence of an additive representation. In the literature quite a number of different conditions have been discussed. In this context I shall take up only one, viz. that proven by Savage [17]. We define first what is meant by the statement that a structure is fine and tight. $(X, G, \geq)$ is fine and tight iff for all $B, C \in G$ such that not: $B \geq C$, there is a partition of the set $X = \{X_1, \ldots, X_M\}$ = such that not: $X_i \cup B \geq C$, for all $i = 1, \ldots, M$. That is, we can divide the set X into (arbitrarily) many equiprobable parts. Savage's theorem now states that if $(X, G, \geq)$ is fine and tight, then $\geq$ is uniquely realizable. In other words, there is one and only one probability measure that represents $\geq$ in G.

3.3. Measurement of Fuzziness

Let X be a set as above and let L be a lattice. We denote by L(X) the set of all mappings from X into L. L(X) is called the set of all fuzzy sets in X. As has been pointed out by De Luca and Termini, we can induce a lattice structure upon the set of mappings L(X) by means of two binary operations $\wedge$ and $\vee$ such that for all mappings f and $g \in L(X)$ we define the composition of mappings as follows:

$$(f \vee g)(x) =_{def} 1.u.b \{f(x), g(x)\}$$

$$(f \wedge g)(x) =_{def} g.1.b \{f(x), g(x)\}$$

In the following we assume that $L = [0,1]$. Then we can define the composition as follows:

$$(f \vee g)(x) = max \{f(x), g(x)\}$$

$$(f \wedge g)(X) = min \{f(x), g(x)\}$$

We now try to construct a measure of fuzziness of the fuzzy $f \in L(X)$ following De Luca and Termini [3,4] and Capocelli and De Luca [2]. First we require that the measure denoted by d(f) be dependent on f in X only. Furthermore, it should satisfy the following requirements:

1. $d(f) = 0$ iff f in X has the values 0 and 1 only,
2. $d(f)$ has its maximum value iff for all $x \in X$: $f(x) = 1/2$,

3. $d(f)$ should be less than $d(f')$ where f' is "sharper" than f in the sense that $f'(x) \geq f(x)$, if $f(x) \geq 1/2$, and $f'(x) \leq f(x)$, if $f(x) \leq 1/2$.

Now, these plausible requirements are fairly mild, and consequently, a large number of functionals d satisfy them. De Luca and Termini have primarily studied a measure which bears a close resemblance to probabilistic entropy measures. In particular, the following functional satisfies the above requirements:

$$d(f) = k \sum_{i=1}^{N} S(f_i),$$

where $f = f(x_i)$, N is the cardinality of X, and k is a positive constant. S is Shannon's function

$$S(x) = -x \ln x - (1-x) \ln (1-x).$$

d(f) defined in this fashion has the plausible property that

$$d(f) = d(\bar{f})$$

where $\bar{f}$ is the complement of f defined as follows

$$\bar{f}(x) = 1 - f(x) \text{ for all } x \in X.$$

This measure, moreover, has the following property:

$$d(f \vee g) + d(f \wedge g) = d(f) + d(g).$$

Hence, d(f) is called a nonnegative valuation on L(X).

We have restricted our discussion to the case of finite sets only. In this case the above definition of d(f) gives us a measure of fuzziness. De Luca and Termini also consider a more general class of measures of fuzziness [14], viz. the following:

$$d(f) =_{def.} \sum_{i=1}^{N} T(f_i) \text{ where}$$

$$T(x) =_{def.} h(x) + h(1-x).$$

h may be any strictly increasing and continuous function in the interval [0,1] such that

$$\lim_{x \to 0} h(x) = \lim_{x \to 1} h(x) = 0.$$

Also this definition of d(f) satisfies the requirements 1-3 above.

In a recent paper De Luca and Termini give necessary and sufficient conditions for the convergence of

$$d(f) = \sum_{i=1}^{\infty} S(f_i)$$

in the case of denumerable support [5]. The logarithmic entropy series $k \sum_{i=1}^{\infty} S(f_i)$ converges and consequently the measure exists iff

i. $\displaystyle\sum_{i=1}^{\infty} (f_i \wedge \bar{f}_i) < +\infty,$ and

ii. $\displaystyle\sum_{i=1}^{\infty} (f \wedge \bar{f})_n^0 \ln n$ converges.

$(g)^0$ means the fuzzy set obtained from a fuzzy set g so that for all n, $g_n^0 \geq g_{n+1}^0$ and $\displaystyle\sum_{i=1}^{\infty} g_i = \sum_{i=1}^{\infty} g_i^0$.

Another interesting result has been achieved by Knopfmacher [9]. It states that if certain conditions are met, we can extend our considerations to the case in which X is infinite and set forth some additional intuitively plausible requirements on d(f) and still end up with a definition of d(f) that covers the case. In other words, Knopfmacher states a sufficient condition for the existence of d(f) satisfying certain conditions in the case of infinite X. Knopfmacher restricts himself to the case in which (X,F,u) is a measure space such that F is a σ-algebra on X and $0 < u(x) < \infty$. $f \in L(X)$ is assumed to be a measurable function. Now, Knopfmacher's requirements are the following:

1. d(f) = 0 ff f : X → (0,1) with a finite number of exceptions (almost everywhere),
2. d(f) is at a unique maximum iff f(x) = 1/2 almost everywhere,
3. $d(f) \geq d(f')$ if $f' \in L(X)$ has the property that $f'(x) \geq f(x)$ if $f(x) \geq 1/2$ and $f'(x) \leq f(x)$ if $f(x) < 1/2$,
4. $d(f) = d(\bar{f})$
5. $d(f \vee g) + d(f \wedge g) = d(f) + d(g)$,
6. d(f) is a continuous function of f,
7. $d(f_a)$ is a strictly increasing function of a for $0 \leq a \leq 1/2$ where $f_a(x) = a$ for all $x \in X$,
8. $d(f) = 1/u(x) \int t(f(x))\, du(x)$, where t is a real-valued function of $a \in [0,1]$ such that t(0) = t(1) = 0, t(a) = t(1-a) and t is a strictly increasing function of a.

The result of Knopfmacher's paper is that the definition 8 satisfies the properties 1-7 if the above assumptions concerning (X,F,u) hold.

We immediately notice that the result -- as the author himself points out -- presupposes that (X,F,u) be a probability space. Hence, in order to define a measure of fuzziness in the sense of the previous definition, we have to assume that a probability measure already exists. Similarly, in the case of the logarithmic entropy measure as well as the generalized entropy measures mentioned above in the case of finite X, we have to assume that a probability measure exists. In other words, it is always the case that when we can define a probability measure over a set, we can also define a measure of fuzziness over that set. The question now becomes: what then distinguishes the two notions?

4. COMPARISON AND INTERPRETATION

In comparing the concepts of probability and fuzziness an obvious distinction -- that pertains to the remarks made in the previous paragraph -- has to be pointed out at the outset, viz. proba-bility and fuzziness refer to different levels of reality in some usages. It can be said that the former is a property of an element of a set, whereas the latter is a property of a set in toto. Another way of saying this is that fuzziness is a property of mass events only while probability may refer to a property of single events. Hence, there is no risk of confusing probability and fuzziness as they belong to different levels of analysis. Indeed, one easily notices that the d(f) measure above is a function f. And it is f that comes close to probability intuitively speaking. Alternatively, it is not probability that one may confuse with fuzziness but random-ness, which is similarly a property of sets of events as fuzziness is. Therefore, in comparing the two concepts we must be careful to pay due attention to the fact that both fuzziness and randomness can, thus, be discussed on two levels.

Let us first focus upon the aggregate level concepts, i.e. on fuzziness and randomness as properties of sets. On this level the two concepts are indistinguishable as one readily notices upon inspecting, for example, the loga-rithmic entropy measure of fuzziness outlined in the previous section. Indeed, if one equates randomness with entropy, the indistinguishability becomes a conceptual matter.

In this connection one notices that the so-called limiting relative frequency interpretation defines probability as a property of mass events, i.e. definable for event classes rather than events. It has been pointed out by Salmon that this interpretation is an admissible one, that is, it satisfies the Kolmogoroff axioms of probability [15]. As the other main interpreta-tions are also admissible in this sense, there are no formal differences between them. The dif-ferences are a matter of interpreting formal properties. And in just this sense fuzziness differs from probability in the relative fre-quency sense: frequency is related to the inter-pretation of formal measurement-theoretic proper-ties. As I have argued, fuzziness differs from the frequentist view of probability in that it has nothing to do with frequencies. But I want to emphasize that this is a matter of methodo-logical difference, not a formal one.

What, then, about the relationships of fuzzi-ness and probability on the "lower" level, i.e. on the level in which these two notions are applicable to events instead of classes? On this level the issue becomes one of relating member-ship degree measures to probabilistic ones. It is, I think, here that we encounter the most interesting demarcation problem. We observe that the measurement-theoretic considerations per-taining to fuzziness of sets have very little bearing upon the present problem. Fuzziness of sets is definable and measurable only on condi-tion that we can define a membership function. And now we are faced with linking the latter with probability. The issue is relatively easy to settle once one has a similar definition of mem-bership function as of fuzziness of sets. Terano and Sugeno propose a definition of what they call a fuzzy measure (membership function) [20]. I present the definition in somewhat modified form in the following. Consider a σ-algebra H on the finite set X. If there is function f with the

following properties, we call f a fuzzy measure:
1. $f(\emptyset) = 0$, $f(X) = 1$,
2. if $A,B \in H$ and $A \in B$, then $f(A) \leq f(B)$.
Now (X,H,f) is called a fuzzy measure space. Upon confronting this definition with the definition of the finitely additive probability space given earlier in this paper, we notice that the conditions are almost identical with those characterizing a finitely additive probability space with the exception of 2. Condition 2 states that the membership degree of an element in a subset of a set cannot be greater than its membership degree in the set itself. The "corresponding" condition for finitely additive probability space is that for all $A,B \in H$, if $A \cap B = \emptyset$, then $P(A \cup B) = P(A) + P(B)$. In the case of fuzzy measure we have monotonicity, whereas in that of probability we have additivity. Now, we know that additivity is a special type of monotonicity. Therefore, it is straightforward to argue that from a measurement-theoretic point of view, fuzziness is a more general property than probability as the measure of the latter can be derived as a special case of the measure of the former.

Now one could object that this conclusion depends on the concept of probability as an additive measure. Were we to employ a nonadditive probability measure, we would end up with a different conclusion. To this objection there is an obvious reply: dropping the assumption of additivity would be tantamount to giving up the axiom system of Kolmogoroff. There is no a priori reason why we whould not do that. The crux of the issue is, however, that it is a matter of interpretation which formal properties we want our probability measure to possess. Of course, we can construct many types of measures and call them probability measures. Similarly, we can interpret our probability measures in such a way that they have nothing to do with out intuitive notion of probability. The same applies, of course, to fuzzy measures.

In conclusion, it remains to be said that in terms of formal properties there are similarities as well as differences in fuzzy and probability measures. At least in the finite case, we can agree with Terano and Sugeno in arguing that a fuzzy measure is a generalization of a probability measure. On the other hand, when the concepts are defined on sets of events, the concept of entropy appears to cover both the case of randomness and that of fuzziness. We pointed out, moreover, that fuzziness measures on this level presuppose the existence of probability ones. In this paper I have not discussed the problems related to the decidability of fuzzy vs. probabilistic concepts. Yet I think it is in those problems that the differences and similarities are most important.

REFERENCES

1. BELLMAN, R. and L. A. ZADEH, "Decision-Making in a Fuzzy Environment," Management Science, 17, 141-164, 1970.

2. CAPOCELLI, R. and A. DE LUCA, "Fuzzy Sets and Decision Theory," Information and Control, 23, 446-473, 1973.

3. DE LUCA, A. and S. TERMINI, "A Definition of a Nonprobabilistic Entropy in the Setting of Fuzzy Sets Theory," Information and Control, 20, 301-312, 1972.

4. DE LUCA, A. and S. TERMINI, "Entropy of L-fuzzy Sets," Information and Control, 24, 55-73, 1974.

5. DE LUCA, A. and S. TERMINI, "On the Convergence of Entropy Measures of a Fuzzy Set," Kybernetes, 6, 219-227, 1977.

6. FINE, K., "Vagueness, Truth and Logic," Synthese, 30, 265-300, 1975.

7. HACKING, I., Logic of Statistical Inference, Cambridge, Cambridge University Press, 1965.

8. HEMPEL, C., Aspects of Scientific Explanation, New York, The Free Press, 1965.

9. KNOPFMACHER, J., "On Measures of Fuzziness," Journal of Mathematical Analysis and Applications, 49, 529-534, 1975.

10. KRANTZ, D., R. D. LUCE, P. SUPPES and A. TVERSKY, Foundations of Measurement, Vol. I, New York, Academic Press, 1971.

11. NEGOITA, C. V. and D. A. RALESCU, Applications of Fuzzy Sets to Systems Analysis, Basel, Birkhäuser Verlag, 1975.

12. NIINILOUTO, I., "Todennäköisyyden lajeista" ("On Types of Probability"), in: Yhteiskuntatieteiden Eksakti Metodologia (The Exact Methodology of the Social Sciences), R. Tuomela (ed.), Helsinki, Gaudeamus, 1975.

13. NURMI, H., "On the Concept of Complexity and Its Relationship to the Methodology of Policy-Oriented Research," Social Science Information, 13, 55-80, 1974.

14. NURMI, H., "Probability and Fuzziness," Sixth Research Conference on Subjective Probability, Utility, and Decision Making, Warszawa, September 6-9, 1977.

15. SALMON, W., The Foundations of Scientific Inference, Pittsburgh, University of Pittsburgh Press, 1967.

16. SALMON, W., "Statistical Explanation," in: Statistical Explanation and Statistical Relevance, W. Salmon (ed.), Pittsburgh, University of Pittsburgh Press, 1971.

17. SAVAGE, L., The Foundations of Statistics, New York, Wiley, 1954.

18. SALOMAA, A., Formal Languages, New York, Academic Press, 1973.

19. SIMON, H., "How Complex Are Complex Systems," in: PSA 1976, Vol. 2, F. Suppe and P. Asquith (eds.), East Lansing, Philosophy of Science Association, 1977.

20. TERANO, T. and M. SUGENO, "Conditional Fuzzy Measures and Their Applications," in: Fuzzy Sets and Their Applications to Cognitive and Decision Processes, L. Zadeh, K-S. Fu, K. Tanaka and M. Shimura (eds.), New York, Academic Press, 1975.

21. WEAVER, W., "Science and Complexity," American Scientist, October, 1948.

Integrated systems planning of construction operations

MARIA PAVLIDOU

School of Engineering, University of Thessaloniki, Greece

Construction operations are distinct from production activities by the fact that each project has unique characteristics, even when industrialized building is used. Differences are to be found in the kind of inputs to be used, the conversion processes to be selected, and the kind and quality of the finished output. The environment of each project is another unique feature.

We consider the following system components for each project:

a. inputs
b. outputs
c. conversion processes
d. environment - physical and social
e. the human factor - including managerial actions

The last system component, the human factor, serves as a catalyst in the process of creating the desired output in a particular environment, using components (a) and (c) in such a way as to achieve a minimum cost and the desired timeliness for the execution of the project.

While we will not restrict our analysis on specific types of projects, we will mainly have in mind civil engineering constructions, since they usually have a greater variety of operations and situations to be planned and controlled than the constructions of buildings.

The construction operations planning phase deals with the formulation of the strategy by which the objectives and goals of the construction project will be accomplished. The plans prescribe both the ends and the means for a successful project accomplishment. The planning phase deals to a great extent with how resources will be allocated to support their most fitting usage for the implementation of the project.

Experience, as well as systemic analysis, shows that the planning and execution phases of construction operations are by necessity intermingled to a considerable extent. Therefore, by integrated planning we include in part some management processes. We do not mean, of course, a Construction Management Information System, which contains information essential for the effective control of the project. This is expected to provide the means to the people responsible for the decision-making procedures to make and implement their decisions.

The planning phase may be considered to follow two procedural modes. After the first mode, the operation is preplanned according to an advance planning and scheduling program. The resources needed, the conversion processes to be used, and the environmental factors are considered ahead of time. The operations are then performed on the basis of a detailed schedule. This mode of action is inflexible to conditions that may be different than the ones considered at the planning-scheduling phase, as well as to field and environmental situations. Moreover, any detailed schedule cannot take due consideration of human problems and especially of the specific needs of the working force in the project.

Planning Mode I → advance preplanning and scheduling

Planning Mode II → instantaneous decisions by managerial and administrative staff

Figure 1.

After the second mode, there is no preplanning. The operations are performed on instantaneous decisions taken by the project manager, the supervising engineer, the foreman or the technician in charge. The people who make the decisions take into consideration all existing conditions and constraints. While this second mode of action is most flexible, it may account for a considerable waste of resources, for longer time periods, for the execution of activities due to lack of coordination, as well as for an atmosphere of nervousness and uncertainty at the construction site, which affects the productivity and the spirit of cooperation between the workers and craftsmen.

Between the two extremes there is an infinite variety of possibilities of partial preplanning and partial at-the-site decideing for the execution of construction operations. The mode of planning, which is most appropriate for each situation, depends on many factors. However, even though we can identify the most influential ones, it is very hard, if not impossible, to determine numerically the degree of interdependency and to estimate coefficients, so that we may formulate an analytic function. The main reason for this difficulty is the fact that each project is completely different from any other. Even when the same project is constructed under the same design more than one time, overall conditions may differ because of different location, economic or political conditions, etc.

The factors considered to influence the outcome of the one or the other mode of planning most strongly are the following:

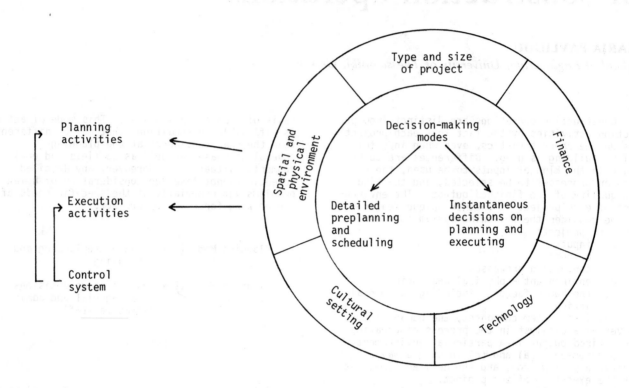

Figure 2. Overview of Construction Operations

1. TYPE AND SIZE OF PROJECT

The type of project determines to some extent the mode of planning. A building complex is more fit under the well-preplanned scheduling mode than a flood control project or a highway maintenance project. The size of the project is also another important factor. The smaller the project the less the needs for a detailed advance scheduling. However, it is not rare that for small and medium-sized projects detailed scheduling turns out to be more effective. This is due to the fact that scheduling difficulties are fewer than in large-size projects.

2. SPATIAL AND PHYSICAL ENVIRONMENT OF THE PROJECT

This is a major factor influencing the outcome of one or another planning mode. The more concentrated the project, e.g. a building or a dam, the easier the planning and scheduling and the more successful the advanced detailed planning. However, when a project is dispersed the planning and scheduling needs are greater. Preplanning is more essential, since the people in charge would not be able to take into consideration all existing conditions and constraints on instantaneous decisions because of the dispersion of activities.

Highway constructions, irrigation schemes, gas-pipe constructions and flood control projects are some examples of dispersed projects, where detailed preplanning would be more essential.

3. THE TECHNOLOGY USED

The more advanced the technology the more essential is detailed preplanning. This is due to the fact that the more advanced the technology the more intense the use of machinery and equipment. Management science techniques become of considerable importance and, as we know, preplanning is essential for their use. Conversely speaking, traditional technology will involve a considerable manpower force. Their efficient management cannot be achieved with technological methods alone; behavioral approaches are absolutely necessary as well.

4. THE CULTURAL SETTING

It has been repeatedly noted that similar methods and techniques have a different outcome under different circumstances. One of the most important factors which differentiates this outcome is the cultural setting of the project. It affects both the manpower participating at all levels and aspects of realization of the project, as well as the social environment which affects the project planning and execution.

5. FINANCIAL POLICY

Last, but not least, is the financial policy toward the project. While proper financing cannot account for an actual improvement of the execution or the control activities, it may account for a deficient planning process. Inadequate financing creates, besides the inadequate planning scheme, greater uncertainty about the project and makes the risk issue more important.

As we said before, we could not estimate coefficients of an analytic function, which would give the most fit planning mode according to an interdependency combination of the above factors, based on their specific characteristics. However, we conducted a field research in order to empirically assess the impact of the different factors on the mode of planning, as well as the social and economic effectiveness of the different modes. The construction sites, which were scattered all over Northern Greece, were selected at random. We made an effort to analyse conditions and behavior at different sites of the same contractor in the same area. A basic outcome was that when conditions were different, planning and execution modes were also different, even when the contractor's planning attitudes were similar.

The number of the sites which were analysed is not good enough to help formulate a general theory. However, we give the up to now results of this survey, because we consider them a quite good indication of the way the Construction Industry carries out its operations.

1. Financial matters affected 80% of the sites as far as planning and execution modes are concerned. The sites visited were both public works and private construction, mainly industrial and domestic complexes. People in charge argued that when uncertainty over the financing of the project is great, they usually have a frame-plan and decide on each occasion in a rather instantaneous manner. They consider the financial uncertainty the worst advocate of planning.

Some of them even argued that they were worse off when they had a detailed plan and had also to fight with severe financial uncertainties, because both consciously and unconsciously they had the feeling that planning would account for quite a good part of the scheduling activities and thus were less prepared and alert for reasonable instantaneous or intuitive decisions.

2. The impact of the type and size of the project was considerable. However, it can be said that to a quite considerable extent this impact intermingled with the technology used and the spatial environment of the project. Therefore, we tabulated the survey results in the following way:

	5 4 3 2 1 0	
	Detailed preplanning	Instantaneous decisions
Infrastructure large size	XXXXXXXXXXXX	
Infrastructure small size	XXXXXXXXXXXXXX	
Maintenance of infrastructure	XXXXXXXXXXXXXX	
Buildings large	XXXXXXXXXXX	
Buildings small	XXXXXXXXXXXXXXXX	

The impact of the spatial and physical environment is very hard to assess. In our research the area of the construction sites visited was not diverse enough to allow for considerable results. Some comments, though, that can be given out of observations of that area are the following:

Mountainous areas where bad weather conditions prevail were reported to discourage contractors from detailed preplanning. However, they admitted that scheduling and frequent careful updating is most useful, because they must make the most of the days when weather conditions permit full-scale work. Similar observations were reported in construction at ports or under the sea, where physical and weather conditions are most important.

4. The impact of technology in construction is manyfold. In the area where the construction sites were examined there were cases of advanced technology and cases of less advanced technology as far as mechanization is concerned. However, there were not cases of traditional labor-intensive construction. The impact was therefore categorized on the basis of the degree of mechanization.

Degree of mechanization	5 4 3 2 1 0	
	Detailed preplanning	Instantaneous decisions
High	XXXXXXXXXXXXXX	
Medium	eeeeeeXXXXXXXXXXXXXX	
Low	XXXXXXXXXXXXXXXX	

Note: eeeee means few cases of construction sites.

5. The cultural setting is the factor affecting the behavioral aspects of the construction operations. Since the most crucial system

component of the Construction Industry is the human factor, the behavioral aspects may differentiate a lot the final outcome. Three kinds of settings were considered:

a. urban setting - workers origin from urban and industrial environment

b. urban or industrial setting - workers origin agricultural

c. rural setting - workers origin agricultural

The survey outcome could be tabulated as follows:

Setting	5 4 3 2 1 0	
	Detailed preplanning	Instantaneous decisions
Urb. - Urb.	ooooooooooooooooooo	
Urb. - Agr.	ooooXXXXXXXXXXXXXXXXXX	
Rur. - Agr.	XXXXXXXXXXXXXXXXXXXXXXXX	

Note: oooo means that we did not have enough statistical inference.

A first-hand result of this survey is that the less urban or industrial the origin of the manpower, the less they are adaptive to detailed scheduling, discipline, charts, frequent reporting and updating. On the contrary, they would rather have more responsibility and self-management.

This field research is not yet completed. It will be followed by surveys in various kinds of sites in other parts of Greece. However, it would be most useful to have similar survey results from other countries, so that generalizations would be possible. Informal talks with construction people from other countries show that there must be a considerable similarity in observations, but we cannot make any definite statement before we have actual research results.

Some implications of the approaches adopted in the design of data base systems

NORMAN REVELL

The City University Business School, London, England

1. INTRODUCTION

The need for a systems approach to the design of information systems was discussed by the author in a paper of the EMCSR '76 Conference in which the approach of the author and his colleagues in the Systems Division at City University Business School was outlined.

One of the areas singled out for research was that of data base, partly because being a new field in its practical application, little fundamental work had been done on it, and partly because of its increasing importance. The availability of mini-computer systems now means that organisations without any computers at all can go immediately for a data base system, rather than being able to develop a data base system from existing computer based information systems in an evolutionary manner. It has been debated [2] whether organisations can make the "quantum leap" to data base at all as opposed to developing through the phases identified by Nolan [3] in an evolutionary manner. In an earlier publication [4] the author claims that at whatever stage in development the transition to data base is made it will represent a "quantum leap" as compared with a conventional data processing approach. The aim of the research is therefore to develop an overall design methodology for data base systems, that would be relevant for organisations at all stages of information systems development. A major part of the project has been the conducting of a survey of organisations that were actively involved in developing data base systems. It is not proposed to go into the details of the survey here since that has already been covered by Sherif [6] and by the author [5]. Instead, those results which have a bearing on the overall design of data base systems will be discussed.

One of the reasons why many organisations adopt data base systems is to simplify the design of individual information systems. With a data base approach there is potentially a significant saving in total design effort of individual information systems since the bulk of design effort is concentrated on the data base itself. As far as the purely technical aspects of design (files, programming, etc.) the justification for adopting a data base approach can be made in terms of the responsiveness of the individual information systems to their environment, if not in financial terms as well. However, at an organisational level the effects of a data base system can be far reaching throughout the organisation, and may indeed also have an effect on its future development. It is because of this that the question of data base design must be viewed in other than just purely technical terms. Further, since all information systems will use the data base, the scope for management "misinformation" is amplified. A simple model using reliability theory may be constructed to illustrate this point. If for the 'i'th information system the programs have a correctness factor of p_i (defined here as the probability of the program logic being correct) and the files have a correctness factor of f_i (defined as the probability of any element of information stored on that file being correct), then a measure of the utility of the system to management is given by $p_i f_i$. This is illustrated in Figure 1.

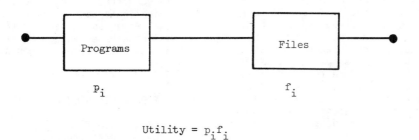

$$\text{Utility} = p_i f_i$$

Figure 1. A Conventional Information System

The average utility is simply the arithmetic mean:

$$\sum_{i=i}^{i=n} \frac{p_i f_i}{n} = \overline{p_i f_i}$$

For a data base system the files are combined as is shown in Figure 2.

Each information system has a utility of $p_i \times \pi f_i$ and is "weighted down" by the other files within the data base. Thus the mean utility is similarly "weighted down". In practice it is unlikely that the files would be so integrated that the data base could be analysed as a chain; however, there will be some degree of integration (otherwise it isn't a data base!).

The environment of the data base in an organisation is shown schematically in Figure 3. The physical data base is simply the computer hardware and file structures, etc., used to store and retrieve the information. The logical data base represented by the "data model" is the user's view of the data base base. The interface between the logical and physical data base is provided by the data base management system (DBMS) which translates the user's view of the logical data base into the physical reality of files, etc. So far the emphasis on development has been on the DBMS and data model. Both of these were necessary to make data base a practical possibility. In contrast very little work has been done on the interface between the organisation and the data model. The only attempt to define this interface has been to create a function, namely that of data base administration. Little attempt has been made to define this function except in very general terms, though it is equally important as the DBMS or data model. The function can be defined so as to include application systems analysis and physical data base engineering, or it can be restricted solely to the one interface. Defining a human function has tended to conceal the need for methodologies in this area and instituted the "folkloric" approach to data base. Whilst in the absence of anything better this is no bad thing, the latent dangers of this approach as already discussed in [1] cannot be overestimated, especially for the case of data base, on account of the significant investment made by organisations in a data base system, and also the far-reaching implications of such a system. It is not surprising that there has been more concentration of research on the two areas of data model and DBMS, since, as previously mentioned, both these are necessary in order to set up working data base systems upon which further research work can be performed. What is disappointing, though, is that it is now 10 years since this former work started, for example Codd's first paper on the relational data-model was published in 1967 [4], whereas until comparatively recently little work had been done on the practical data base environment.

It is extremely unlikely that an abstract or theoretical methodology will be developed for design of the total data base system in its environment since the methodology will need to take account of the complexity and variety within the organisation, and since as yet there are no theoretical models which represent organisations in the real world with sufficient accuracy, then it is not possible to develop a theoretical methodology for data base design. Instead the emphasis of the research project has been to develop a pragmatic approach based on actual recorded experience. Whilst not producing an "elegant" methodology, at least an approach is produced which is sensitive to the organisation's needs.

2. APPROACHES TO DATA BASE DESIGN

There are two basic reasons for adopting a data base system. These have been identified by the author [5] as the "Functional Approach" and the "Strategic Approach." Organisations may opt for data base in order to satisfy either of these needs or indeed a combination of both. The "functional approach" uses a data base system in order to derive some short or long term technical advantage such as better file handling or ease of handling terminals, etc. The "strategic approach" uses a data base system in order to derive organisational benefits, usually in the medium to long term. It is important to make the distinction between the two, since "functional approach" doesn't really have any organisational implications, being purely internal to the data processing function of an organisation, and consequently doesn't need any general methodology other than those already in existence for non-data base systems, e.g. file design, etc. The "strategic approach" is closely related to the organisation and its goals and does need a systematic design methodology since there is no obvious "springboard" as there is with a "functional approach". Further, there is a danger of an organisation drifting from an initial implementation of a "functional approach" to a "strategic approach" as it develops. Worse still there is a danger of an organisatin believing itself to have fully adopted a data base approach by implementing the former, and not even considering the potential benefits of a "strategic approach". Perhaps the problem lies in the blanket use of the term "data base system" to cover both possibilities.

Designing the data model is a very precise task, involving such techniques as the construction of Bachman diagrams, normalisation of data structures, etc., and so too is the task of physical data base design. There is a danger of these two areas dominating the design of the total data base system, or at least proceeding the less well defined organisational design process.

3. APPROACHES ADOPTED IN THE U. K.

In this section some of the practical results of the research project are discussed in the light of the preceeding sections.

The classification of data base systems into "functional" or "strategic" approaches has been found to be a very useful analysis of the U. K. data base systems so far studied. About 25% of organisations can be identified as clearly

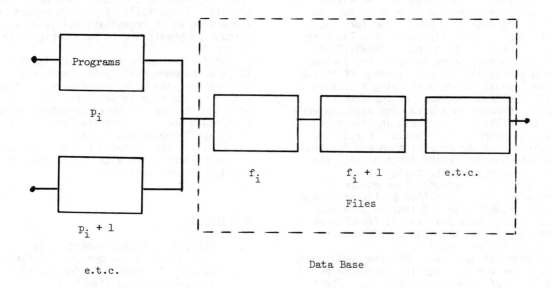

Figure 2. A Data Base System

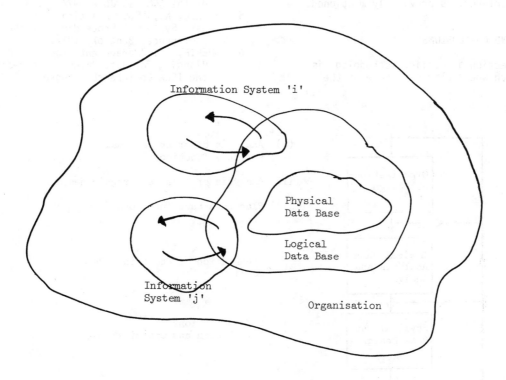

Figure 3. The Data Base Environment

belonging to each of these approaches, whereas the remaining 50% have elements of both. Thus the majority of organisations have opted for a functional, or part functional, approach. The extent to which this represents either a "static" or "dynamic" picture is being investigated further; i.e., do organisations generally progress through a functional phase before developing a strategic approach? The fact that most of the problems encountered in adopting a data base approach were found to be "political" rather than "technical" would tend to support this thesis. For these organisations, the majority of them had located the data base administration function with the data processing department, seeing it as a specific technical function. In considering the importance of this function as the interface between the organisation and logical data base in the total data base environment (see Figure 3) it is not surprising that most problems have turned out to be "political".

A few organisations have made the decision to build their own DBMS, though the overwhelming majority have opted for a standard one. Apart from the high cost involved in adopting the former approach there is an inherent danger and the emphasis of the project becomes distorted towards the technicalities of building a DBMS at the expense of wider aspects of the data base approach.

Another result that reinforces the previous point is that in most organisations the decision to adopt a data base approach came from within the data processing function. Both these latter points go some way explaining the nature of the problems encountered, as previously mentioned.

4. SUMMARY AND CONCLUSIONS

In this section an outline methodology is presented which would eliminate some of the

problems found in the U. K. data base research project. Essentially it is a "top-down" design commencing at an organisational level and working through to physical-data base design (see Figure 4).

Whilst the contents of this figure would seem to be a "commonsense" systems approach to data base design, the U. K. experience has shown this not to be the case in practice, and thus it is important to present here the general methodology that would work for both the "functional" and "strategic" approaches to data base.

Finally, the author would welcome contact and/or collaboration with anyone working in this field in other countries.

REFERENCES

1. REVELL, N., "An Assessment of Systems Techniques in the Design of Information Systems," European Conference on Systems and Cybernetics, Vienna, 1976.
2. SPROWLS, C. W., "Can Developing Nations take a Quantum Jump in Utilising Computers," Proceedings of the ICCA Conference, Bangkok, 1977.
3. GIBSON, F. F. and R. L. NOLAN, "Managing the Four Stages of EDP Growth," Harvard Business Review, Vol. 52, No. 1, Jan/Feb, 1974.
4. CODD, E. F., "A Relational Model of Data for Large Shared Data Banks," Communications of the ACM, 13 June 197/, p. 377.
5. REVELL, N., "Some Practical Aspects of Data Base Systems," Proceedings of the ICCA Conference, Bangkok, 1977.
6. SHERIF, J., "Management Experiences in Planning for Data Bases," Proceedings of the ICCA Conference, Bangkok, 1977.

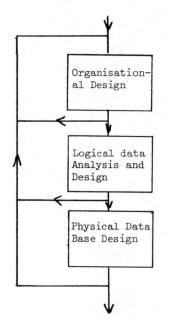

(i)   Analysis of organisational strategy function.

(ii) Analysis of data base requirements

(iii) Plan Data base functions

Translation of above into data model

(i)   DBMS Selection
(ii) File Design and Optimisation.

Figure 4.   Design Methodology for a Data Base System

Risk, the organisational response and inquiring systems

R. G. SPEAR

Systems Group, The Open University, London, England

1. INTRODUCTION

Flixborough, the ACMH report, and the Health and Safety at Work Act are manifestations of difficulties organisations have in coping with physical risk. Since the Rasmussen report there has been an increase in public and institutional pressure particularly in the chemical and nuclear industries culminating in the recent public inquiry on the Windscale processing plant. The work of Kletz (I.C.I.) and Farmer (UKAEA) can be interpreted as a recent attempt to cope with this environmental pressure.

This paper examines the basic similarities in the underlying assumptions of these organisational responses and determines to what extent they are appropriate given the state of empirical research on physical risk (e.g. Green).

The paper continues by considering the degree to which this kind of organisational response is consistent with a systems view of organisational decision taking drawing on the early work of Cyert and March, etc., and more recent developments; and finally what implications this has for the design of inquiring systems.

2. THE DIFFICULTIES

"Mad as a hatter" is a phrase derived from effects of mercury poisoning on members of the workforce in hat factories in Victorian England. Things have changed a bit since then, jokes are not cracked about people suffering from asbestosis, although it took about 50 years from the time the disease had been identified until an arguably adequate (Threshold Limit Value) safety level was set; up until that time there had been flagrant infringements which were apparently tolerated by the workforce, the TUC, and the Factory Inspectorate to the extent that powers of compulsion and mass action were not used. The vinyl chloride case where workers contracted liver cancer has been studied by the Committee on Scientific Freedom and Responsibility (of the A.A.A.S.); their report documents the suppression of carcinogenicity data by the Manufacturing Chemists Association.

The explosion of the Nyproplant at Flixborough in 1974 had as its immediate cause the failure of a temporary pipe installed by a maintenance crew. The court of inquiry found that "the unlicensed storage of large quantities of fluids had no effect upon the disaster," however, I understand the "fluid" was not recovered intact after the blaze. The court did find that at the time of the explosion and for a substantial period before hand there was no mechanical engineer on site with sufficient qualification or authority to deal with complex or novel engineering problems and insist on necessary measures being taken.

Risk levels at work are still high compared to environmental risk levels (a comparison of various environmental and occupational standards for various chemicals gives an average ratio of about 130 [1].

The examples illustrate that risk is a very complex phenomenon; important long term hazards are ignored (asbestosis) or suppressed (vinyl chloride); causes are often difficult to predict (Flixborough); and attitudes to the risks are not solely related to the risk level (FAFR or exposure rate) as a comparison of occupational and environmental standards illustrates.

In recent years there seems to have been an increase in interest in physical risk shown by the public and by various institutions. (Physical risk is here referred to as the probability that physical harm will occur.) This may be due to the general desire for an improved quality of life, to the shifting of ground in the battle between the counterculture movement and the military-industrial complex (energy issues used to be the battle front) to the issues themselves (nuclear power, cancer, genetic engineering) which are important and sensitive, to academic/media exploitation of the issues or to the fact that modern society seems to be developing a susceptibility to major hazards (as Kates [2] indicated, when referring to control over natural hazards, this effort has led to fewer disasters but it results in larger consequences when they do occur (Seveso, Minamata and Michigan provide examples for man-made hazards).

Whatever the underlying causes, the result has been considerable public and institutional activity. In the USA, the establishment (in 1975 by Congress) of the Office of Technology Assessment in the legislative branch of government (as opposed to the regulatory agencies in the executive branch) is an attempt to formally consider future problems; environmental impact statements and technology assessments are becoming more common and federal projects that are deemed to involve environmental impact are subject to environmental impact statements.

In the UK, 1974 saw the passing by Parliament of the Health and Safety at Work Act [3], which imposed duties of anticipation on every person whose activities at work could lead to health and safety risks, in all employment except private domestic.

In 1976, the Advisory Committee on Major Hazards [4], set up after the Flixborough disaster, completed their report recommending the establishment of a new category of major hazard installations with a corresponding requirement for more stringent regulatory and planning controls.

The Council for Science and Society, an influential lay group, set up a working party on the acceptability of risk which in 1977 produced a report intended to raise the level of public (and decision maker) debate [5].

I have only identified certain landmarks and certain issues in the general activity associated with physical risk. Not all of the activity is aimed directly at the organisational originators of this risk; nevertheless it constitutes a considerable challenge to these organisations.

A challenge in terms of their strategic objectives of prestige and social responsibility, the legal requirements they have to meet, economic considerations (for instance, in negotiations with planning authorities for expansion, etc.), as well as the problems of identifying, estimating, evaluating and managing the risks.

3. THE ORGANISATIONAL RESPONSE

Many organisational responses to this challenge may well take the form of procrastination, suppression of information, minimisation of the problem, etc. However, there have been serious attempts to come to grips with the problem, notably in the chemical and nuclear power industries (for example, Kletz and Farmer [6,7]).

It is no accident that these are both relatively "new" industries in the major hazard league; so it is to efforts in these industries that I turn my attention now.

In discussing the organisational response, it is perhaps appropriate to distinguish the following categories:

Risk estimation: The identification and quantification of risk.

Risk evaluation: Determination of social value, i.e., defining the "acceptability" of risk.

Risk management: The use of reliability technology, etc., to modify the estimated risk, i.e., to improve safety.

3.1. Risk Estimation

This involves the identification of events and their associated harmful consequences and an estimation of their probability and the severity of the consequences.

There are various probabilities that can be estimated, but a common one is to relate the frequency of occurrence of the event to the consequences. Where a complex set of interlinked events and consequences are involved (for instance in a nuclear power plant), it is usual to model the process and its failure modes so that the probabilities of the failures can be estimated. Calculation is usually based on the failure of individual components and there are various techniques available to assist in risk estimation of a process (for instance FMEA-failure modes and effects analysis, FTA-fault tree analysis).

Critchley [8], in discussing nuclear power

safety, has identified the following criteria upon which a meaningful application of the above modelling techniques are based:

(a) performance requirements for the plant and its subsystems must be clearly and finally specified;

(b) manufacture and construction of the components, sub-assemblies and the plant must be verified by inspection to be according to specification;

(c) the materials used in all aspects and phases of manufacture and construction must comply with relevant specifications and come from quality-assured supply;

(d) failure rate data must be drawn from verifiable sources, established by user experience and/or realistic and reproducible tests;

(e) such data when it is drawn from inferences deriving from observation of the performance of analogous systems does not meet criterion (d) and therefore must have an appropriate uncertainty factor attached to it;

(f) the sources of all data must be accessible for verification and the confidence limits or uncertainty factors must be stated;

(g) an independent analyst using the data must compute a similar figure or figures; and

(h) there must be enough user experience so that all credible faults and failures have occurred or the sequences leading to them have been identified.

As a caution to the application of these modelling techniques where inappropriate, he also pointed out that where operating data is limited as in experimental and prototype plant the data base for predicting probabilities and identifying "rogue" events (such as those that caused the Flixborough and Browns Ferry failures) is of uncertain usefulness. The Rasmussen group has received similar criticism.

3.2. Risk Management

This involves modifying risk to accord with "acceptable" levels. A study is usually carried out, modelling the process using risk estimation techniques; unsatisfactory aspects of the study are identified and a safety philosophy is employed to reduce the risk. This safety philosophy holds that: "Important equipment must be designed and inspected so that it does not fail or the plant as a whole must be designed in such a way that failures of individual components can be accepted (by providing diversity of measurement and function, and redundancy in response)" [7].

Again, employment of these modelling techniques rests on certain assumptions which could lead to the "effect of directing design and quality of construction downwards to some quantitatively assessed level of adequacy" and which could lead to misplaced confidence in the safety of plant by decision makers and politicians based on confidence in the internal logic and power of the techniques rather than on adequate knowledge of their applicability [5].

2.3. Risk Evaluation

This involves the determination of acceptable

levels of risks. There are a variety of approaches that can be adopted, for instance:

Cost effectiveness methods. Based on life values or on the cost of saving a life in conjunction with other criteria such as "with best practical technology" [9,1].

Natural risk levels. Of natural disaster or of disease. These are used as threshold levels on the basis that we accept these levels possibly as "acts of God" (an example is the risk of being hit by a meteor) [1].

Experimental testing of human activities. To develop a model of people's preferences; there is still the problem of relating attitudes to behaviour [10,11].

Use of societal behaviour statistics. Often referred to as the revealed social preferences method [10]. This, of course, is based on statistics of past social-behaviour and does not necessarily represent present behaviour, nor does it necessarily represent socially acceptable risk levels.

To determine acceptability the risk statistics may be compared "en masse" or the risks categorised according to various factors (the situation, the activity, etc.) and the appropriate categories then compared or the categories used in more sophisticated comparative methods [1]. Although there are various workers in the field (e.g. [11]), the state of empirical research still seems to be as stated (in [10]) in 1975: "There has been little research in the behavioural sciences on attitudes and beliefs with respect to the perception and acceptance of technological risks. As a result there is no body of behavioural theory from which to seek guidance."

Nevertheless it is still possible to comment on the various approaches (as one briefly above) so that a framework can be developed for considering the appropriateness of the various approaches to risk evaluation, for it seems (e.g. as stated in [11]) that "a semantic fog is descending about the word 'acceptable'." Thus, when considering the approaches to risk evaluation one would expect the following factors to be debated: academic rigour and empirical validity; economic cost; social equity; legal norms.

3.4. Overview

This section has attempted to examine how the organisation is responding to quite a complex problem -- the problem of how to deal with physical risk and cope with the environmental pressures associated with it. In reviewing the organisational response in the three areas of risk estimation, management, and evaluation it seems that the response could be characterised as follows: a general attempt to reduce the complexity of the situation by concentrating on those aspects of the situation that can be quantified (components not humans) despite methodological problems thus engendered; an avoidance of difficulties by concentrating on mechanical safety devices possibly at the expense of emphasizing "eternal vigilance" [5], a much more difficult concept to deal with; the history of the organisational response has in general been characterised by a minimisation of the problems and procrastination in dealing with them, and changes based on the concept "as little

as necessary" rather than any concept of optimality, etc. This represents a particular kind of model of organisational decision making, and seems to best fit the actual behaviour of the organisation in responding to physical risk.

The problem situation, as stated earlier, is very complex with a high degree of uncertainty as to goals, consequences of decisions, attitudes available, etc.

We can further comment on the overall response with reference to the above factors (i.e., how adequate or appropriate it is with regard to academic vigour and empirical validity, economic cost, social equity, legal norms); but we can also usefully examine the characteristics of the Inquiring System [12] adopted by the organisation in making its response. For inevitably when tackling a complex problem of this kind the organisation will adopt some kind of inquiring system.

The characteristics of the inquiring system adopted by the organisation to tackle the problem appear in sharp contrast to the actual behaviour (see especially Critchley's comments in Section 3.1). The inquiring system seems to have been based on the assumptions that:

(a) There is complete knowledge of the consequences of each alternative decision.

(b) Goals are clear and can be ranked in order of performance as a basis for selecting an alternative (and its consequences).

(c) There is comprehensive survey of the range and variety of alternative decisions and the means for achieving them.

This kind of inquiring system has been described by Lindblom [14] as the "synoptic ideal". Now these assumptions are obviously inappropriate in this kind of complex problem situation, indeed the approach is derived from "algorithmic" type problems and seems to face considerable difficulties in more complex problems. The difficulties it faces include the following [14]: man's limited intellectual capacities, inadequacy of information, costliness of analysis, failures to construct a ranking of goals, the close intertwining of fact and value, the levels of complexity of open systems, the difficulties of tackling problem messes involving multi-organisational systems.

Note that although I have been fairly critical of the particular inquiring system employed in this case, I am still maintaining the need for a normative approach to decision making; this is necessary, if we are to retain some concept of progress in human affairs. Thus an inquiry system is a normative approach to decision making and should be distinguished from a descriptive approach that builds up models of how decisions are actually made.

To summarise, the section has examined the characteristics of the organisational response to the risk problem and in particular the kind of inquiring system employed by the organisation in its response; it then attempted to determine how appropriate or effective the (normative) inquiring system is for the kind (or model) of organisational decision taking that actually takes place.

The next section will explore the organisational response in terms of various models developed, and the final section will return to the discussion on appropriate inquiring systems for types of organisational decision taking. The final section is based on the contention that the design of inquiring systems should be enlightened by the complexity of the problem and by the realities of decision making (based on available models), as well as other considerations such as the internal rigour of its methods, etc.

4. THE ORGANISATIONAL RESPONSE AND ORGANISATIONAL MODELS

This section examines to what extent the organisational response to the risk problem is consistent with the various (systems) models of decision making.

First a brief (individualistic) review of the models of decision making (based on [13,14,15,16, 17,18]).

4.1. Objective Rationality Model

Variations on this have been labelled as "synoptic," "economic man," "analytic paradigm," etc. It is characterised as behaviour that correctly optimises certain goals in a given situation based on a ranking of the goals, comprehensive knowledge of means, alternative decisions and consequences. It is the basis for much of economic theory of a free market economy.

4.2. Cybernetic Model

Variations on this have been labelled as "administrative man," "organisational process," "behavioural theory," etc. Organisational behaviour is characterised as involving quasi-resolution of conflict. This is the process by which an organisation thrives despite its internal conflicting interests. That is, by a subsystem solution of sub-problems according to the organisation's "acceptable level decision rules" (low enough to permit an outcome), and the sequential attention to problems and goals. Uncertainty avoidance: the organisation reacts to information and problems immediately rather than by developing long-term strategies and attempting to stabilise relationships. Problematic search: the search for solutions to problems is restricted in time (to the duration of the crisis situation; out of sight out of mind) and scope (not too different from the status quo). Organisational learning: organisations adapt their goals, search rules, etc., according to the assessment of past performance.

It regards "rationality" as being "bounded" by the human limitations of perception, knowledge, etc. Nevertheless it describes a powerful logic that copes with complexity by an organised process of decision, feedback and learning. The model has been further refined by the "garbage can" analogy of organisational processes [18].

4.3. Bureaucratic Politics Model

(Lindblom's mutual adjustment model seems to have many similarities to this model.) Basically it emphasises bargaining and gaming as processes of consensus building where conflict is high due to differences about goals, alternatives and consequences. This model is covered in detail in [16]. It has been developed for the study of multi-organisational systems.

4.4. Cognitive Model [15]

This attempts to expand cognitive theory to the collective level of explanation and thereby modifies the cybernetic model in very complex situations. It suggests different patterns of thought: "grooved thinking," "uncommitted thinking" (based on a variety of belief patterns), and "theoretical thinking" (based on generalised, highly deductive belief patterns). Though overlapping and interacting, these patterns of thought will modify (constrain) the organisational learning process.

The above summary is laughably brief and the different models involve many different assumptions about our notion of goal, rationality, decision, etc. However the main purpose here is to remind the reader of these different models so that this study may continue.

The models are very much my own interpretations of the work [13-18], in particular not all the writers would regard all the models as still valid in terms of their explanatory powers of organisational behaviour. However I would regard the models as complementary in explaining organisational behaviour in different situations; for instance in very simple (algorithmic-type) problem situations, the first model seems perfectly adequate; and there seems a progression in the first three models in terms of the degree of complexity of the situation each can explain. Each one seems adequate within a certain kind of problem situation complexity. The fourth, the "cognitive" model, modifies models two and three.

If we now consider the organisational response to risk, the "cybernetic" model seems the best fit; there seems to be a limited amount of multi-organisational interplay and thus the "bureaucratic politics" model is of limited use. It also seems that the modifications of the "cognitive" model may be relevant specifically in terms of "grooved thinking" and a predominance of "theoretical thinking" particularly in the use of quantitative techniques.

5. INQUIRING SYSTEMS AND ORGANISATIONAL RESPONSE

In this section I want to explore the relationship between an inquiring system and an organisational response with particular reference to the organisational models referred to above. I have shown above a situation where organisations have responded to the problems associated with physical risk by adopting a "synoptic" inquiring system; this had a number of drawbacks as the problem situation was quite complex and the organisational behaviour could be best described as fitting the "cybernetic" model.

Now if we wish to retain some notion of progress in human affairs, can we offer any advice on what would have been a better inquiring system for the organisation to have utilised in this situation?

5.1. Advice

Various advice has been offered on the design of inquiring systems [12] and it is further contended here that the design of inquiring systems can be enlightened by reference to both the complexity of the problem and to the realities of decision taking -- in particular by reference to the descriptive models of organisational decision taking outlined above.

As Lindblom [14] has stated, "the usefulness of an analytical method cannot be understood in isolation from the social processes through which it is applied."

Let's begin by examining to what extent many of the available inquiring systems relate to the realities of organisational decision taking. Most of the "synoptic" type (for instance, O. R. methodologies) tack an activity on the end, called "implementation," thus making all kinds of assumptions about the unitary nature of values, control, structure, etc.; for example, in a multiorganisational system "implementation" (with this inquiring system) would be dependent upon centralised decision taking. Further aspects of inquiring systems have been developed by Simon, etc., in the work on heuristics; however, most of this seems to assume an "objective rationality" model of decision taking with clearly ranked goals, etc. It is usual for the problem type to be a major consideration for inquiring systems, though there are more than a few instances of problems adapting to techniques; some of the more sophisticated techniques (for instance in policy sciences) recognise some elements of the realities of organisational decision taking (for example, a plurality of goals), but in most cases this is taken to be an elaboration of the "synoptic" type inquiring system.

All in all, scant attention is paid to the realities of organisational decision taking, despite the fact that the relevant model of organisational decision taking is bound to heavily influence the way a particular inquiring system actually works; and despite the fact that inquiring systems can surely learn from the way organistions work, after all a major "raison d'etre" of organisations is their ability to cope with complexity.

5.2.

Now for some contentious views on the matching of inquiring systems and models of organisational decision taking. They have a much more limited usefulness in situations where the other organisational models apply; for instance, the Roskill commission of inquiry into the third London airport used a synoptic type IS (cost benefit analysis) in a situation where the "bureaucratic politics" model applied; they spent several hundred thousand pounds on a discarded exercise. The "synoptic" type IS fits well with the "objective rationality" model because they make similar assumptions and use the same kind of logic for coping with complexity.

Now the "cybernetic" model uses a different kind of logic for coping with complexity -- an organised process of decision, feedback and learning. It seems to me that if we want to improve this kind of decision taking we should direct our attention to the logic used and design an inquiring system that turns its attention to the way the process of decision, feedback and learning is organised. It is for this reason that I believe the Checkland methodology (which I regard as directing the study to the functioning of the organisation) is an important step in the right direction. This kind of approach also seems to embody a broader definition of the problem thus any progress made using the inquiring system will not only benefit the tackling of the problem in hand but it will also improve the organisation's capabilities with similar problems in the future.

In the case of the "bureaucratic politics" model where there are very complex problems and decision taking behaviour, we have a situation of separated organisations sharing power with decisions emerging from a bargaining game -- the game being structured by certain processes that bring issues to the point of choice. In this kind of situation the use of a "synoptic" IS to carry out a policy study would result in material useful in the bargaining game.

It is difficult designing an inquring system for this model. Lindblom [14] proposes the method of "successive limited comparisons" which seems a rather unsatisfactory rationalisation of what exists rather than an IS strongly oriented towards progress. I would favour an IS that directed its attention to the processes and rules of the game (and how they develop) and to the ways in which the world views (and ideologies) of the organisations develop on the basis of experience. But the appropriate IS for this kind of model of organisational decision taking is still very much an open question.

Finally, I would like to make it clear that I regard the inquiring systems as complementary in the same sense that Singerian inquiring systems [12] employ different inquiring systems for different aspects of the problem situation and to different aspects of the inquiry.

Further considerations for the design of inquiring systems are: to what extent they can benefit from a similar kind of structure (as the organisational model) in order to better handle complexity.

What is the nature of the systemic relationship between the IS and the organisation? Further work needs to be done on the models, especially the later ones, and the implications of the "cognitive" model for these models and for inquiring systems needs careful consideration.

REFERENCES

1. ROWE, W. D., An Anatomy of Risk, Wiley, 1977.
2. KATES, R. W., "Natural Disasters and Development," Wingspread Conference Background Paper, Racine, Wisconsin, October, 1975.
3. HMSO, Health and Safety at Work Act, 1974.
4. HMSO, First Report of the Advisory Committee on Major Hazards, 1976.
5. Council for Science and Society, "The Acceptability of Risk, Report of a Working Party," 1977.
6. KLETZ, T. A., "What Risks Should We Run?"

New Scientist, 12 May 1977; also various other papers.

7. FARMER, F. R., "Experience in the Reduction of Risk," I. Chem. E. Symposium Series, No. 34, London, 1971.

8. CRITCHLEY, O. H., "Correspondence - Risk Prediction, Safety Analysis, and Quantitative Probability Methods - A Caveat," Journal of British Nuclear Energy Society, Vol. 18-20, 15 January, 1976.

9. SINCLAIR, C. G., P. MARSTRAND, P. NEWICK, Innovation and Human Risk, S.P.R.U., University of Sussex, 1972.

10. OTWAY, H. J., P. D. PAHNER and J. LINNEROO, "Social Values in Risk Acceptance," IIASA RM 75-54, 1975.

11. GREEN, C. H., "Motherhood, Apple Pie and Safety: Problems in Valuing Safety"; "Which Acceptable Safety: A Question of Justice"; "Certainly, One Football Team = Three Cabinet Ministers = One Princess of the Blood Royal? - Metrics for Societal Safety"; "Where Three are Gathered Together: Social Welfare and Safety"; "Life Safety: What it is and How Much is it Worth?", Faculty of Environmental Studies, Duncan of Jordan - Stone College, Perth Road, Dundee, U. K., 1977.

12. CHURCHMAN, C. W., The Design of Inquiry Systems," Basic Books, 1971.

13. SIMON, H. A., Administrative Behaviour, Collier MacMillan, 2nd Edition, London, 1965.

14. LINDBLOM, C. E., The Intelligence of Democracy, Free Press, New York, 1965.

15. STEINBRUNER, J. D., The Cybernetic Theory of Decision, Princeton University Press, New Jersey, 1974.

16. ALLISON, G. T., Essence of Decision, Little, Brown & Co., 1971.

17. CYERT, R. M. and J. G. MARCH, A Behavioural Theory of the Firm, Prentice Hall, 1963.

18. MARCH, J. G. and J. P. OLSEN, Ambiguity and Choice in Organisations, Universitets forlegt., 1976.

19. CHECKLAND, P. B., "Towards a Systems-Based Methodology for Real World Problem Solving," Journal of Systems Engineering, Winter, 1972

Approaches to social status

M. E. A. SCHMUTZER* and W. BANDLER**
*Breitenfurterstrasse 510, Vienna, Austria
**Department of Mathematics, University of Essex, Colchester, England

1. INTRODUCTION

Social status is a concept dear to sociologists, although there exist various difficulties in dealing with it. It is quite clear that it has something to do with prestige and even with privilege, which may explain why in the camp of Marxist sociology the concept itself enjoys little esteem. It would, however, be much too simple to think this to be the whole story. Marxists apply a different concept, familiar to us all: that of class. In some respect, the two concepts exhibit common features, although it is an almost trivial range which is covered by them both.

It is not the intention of this contribution to elaborate the differences between the two concepts, but one aspect seems to bear on what follows, so it should be mentioned. Both concepts share an intrinsic methodological function: they chop up societies into chunks of people drawing borderlines according to preestablished rules. But drawing borders can have consequences which are sometimes detrimental. Such consequences will be one of the main concerns of this paper, in which our emphasis will remain with the concept of status exclusively, for, as will become apparent, this is alone of ample complexity.

2. THE NOTION OF STATUS

Social status constitutes a method of social stratification for and by means of social evaluation (Schmutzer [19]). It makes various parts of society distinguishable by differentiating them, using mechanisms of evaluation. Talking about status consequently means talking about fragmentation and evaluation at the same time. It will prove useful to keep the two activities clearly separated.

The consequences of cutting an entity into portions can be more than quantitative; they can be qualitative. Evidence for this is provided by the common experience of trying to cook a favourite meat dish in another country. Wiener Schnitzel is only Wiener Schnitzel near Wien; anywhere else it is less successful, not because the meat is inferior, but because the cut is different.

Similar things happen if we chop up societies for or by evaluation. In our present society, it is rather customary to think in terms of individual status, that is, status granted to single individuals. At other times and in other societies, other customs prevail. Max Weber [22], one of the most highly reputed sociologists of our century, declares that in mediaeval society and in those of India, the carrier of status was a group, be it a professional guild or an aristocratic family. The member individual was merely part of this group in the form of a representative. He was granted the total of its group status, much as we still find in the context of official state visits, where the honoured personality receives deferential treatment not in view of his or her personal achievements, but in view of the relations between the two countries at large.

The previous example of state visits makes also clear that status granted from outside needs not correspond to that granted within a social setting.

The official visitor may enjoy far less status at home than he does abroad. The consequence of this observation is that status is not just variant in relation to social settings, but also variant over time. Not only may status be accumulated like capital over time, above and beyond this it may be subjected to sudden switches, in relation to environmental conditions, which may be temporal, social or local. To illustrate this, we may refer to the institution of Mothers' Day (Muttertag) which proves to be one of those strage occasions where all of a sudden a person frequently ignored, as housewives are, becomes the centre of attention and deference. Social status, as we see, takes many different forms. It may be individual status granted through achievement, or group status granted to an individual, but not as recognition of some personal achievements, but rather in recognition of the social context to which the individual belongs. Over and above all this, it will be variable over time; sometimes in a continuous manner, sometimes in irregular ways. Status enjoyed within a group will quite possibly differ from that enjoyed or missed beyond the group's frontiers (Laumann [12]).

These observations are made at the beginning, since they are neither selfevident, nor are they always taken into due consideration by social scientists. However, after so many words, we still have not provided clear definition of what status actually means. This deficiency shall be made up in a moment: At the beginning of this section we said that status is a method of stratifying society for and by evaluation. This statement suffices to note that status is intrinsically related to value. Status someone enjoys is simply the expression of the value this someone enjoys, whereby "someone" may be a person or a congregation

of persons, as we said before. Value is a fairly
lofty concept. It is hard to perceive. Consequently, it is in want of some mode of transport
or of a perceivable representative. And this is
actually how it is. Value is made visible through
the application of signals, which exhibit usually
all those properties thought essential by information theorists; above all they are scarce. This
is not to say that they are "naturally scarce", as
is frequently proposed; on the contrary, they are
made scarce, to serve the needs of signification.
But scarcity alone will not do the trick. The
letter 'z' is fairly scarce in the English language; nonetheless it does not serve as "status
symbol". Which would not mean that it could not
do the job, as "Zorro" demonstrated with great
ingenuity. One might say, potent status symbols
are scarce, but in addition they need also "mpf".
Where do they get it from? They gain it by affiliation with highly valued objects and/or persons.
This is clearly a circular argument, but circularity will not shock an assembly which has been
nurtured by feedbacks and loops (Bandler and
Schmutzer [1]; Berger et. al. [3]).

Summarizing the argument so far, we may say
status is value conferred upon persons by affiliation with valued objects, persons or actions
(Fararo [5]). It should be stressed that this
transfer of value is in many respects of a kind
contrary to what exchange theorists and economists
usually preach (Blau [4]). It is a process which
does not reduce the value of the original carrier,
just as knowledge or illness is not reduced by
transferring them to other persons. Psychologists
coined a term for processes of this kind; they
call them the "halo-effect". We prefer a more
pictoral expression, which came across in an
article by Leik and Nagasawa [14]; it is simply
"rub-off".

By now it is clear that our notion of status
differs from the so-called "socio-economic status".
It is certainly not just a question of possessions.
This may be contrary to the personal experience of
some. In our view, such experiences are not
invalid, but form as we will see later, peculiar
societal pattern.

The next section will be an attempt to incorporate various aspects of what we have said so far
in a simple input-output model, as was first suggested by Hubbell [10]. This model will not
satisfy our needs completely. It turns out,
however, to be a useful instrument to start with,
particularly as it has roots in the tradition of
social choice matrices (Moreno [17]). Social
choice is, if nothing else, at least the beginning
of social contacts, affiliation and rub-off.
Hence its suitability for a start in our approach.

3. AN INPUT-OUTPUT MODEL OF SOCIAL STATUS

As indicated above, our starting point is a
model proposed some time ago by Hubbell [10]. It
is an application of social choice matrices to an
input-output model of the usual type. The matrix
differs somewhat from traditional choice matrices
in that it is no longer a zero-one matrix, but a
matrix the components of which are non-negative
numbers, equal to or smaller than one. In the
tradition of social choice theory, the main

diagonal consists of zero's. The rationale behind
this is obvious: no one chooses himself. According to Hubbell the matrix components represent
weights, granted to the chosen person out of a
stock of unity. The model reads as follows:

$$S = E + WS.$$

The symbols stand for the following concepts:
  S - status vector with n components,
      given a group of members;
  E - vector of external contributions to
      the status of each person;
  W - weighted normatized choice matrix.

The intrinsic meaning of the model is clear.
The status of a person is the result of an external input of values into the group plus the
status gained through affiliation with persons
in the group. To render the system of equations,
soluble various constraints were imposed. The
first condition demanded is so-called "openness"
of the group. This condition is satisfied if at
least one member of the group abstains from
spending all his "capital" within the group. It
means that the sum of its components in at least
one column vector should be greater than zero.
A second condition to be met by the matrix is
strong connectedness. This amounts to saying
that between any pair of group members at least
one path must exist along which they may reach
each other. If these conditions are met, the
system of equations has a guaranteed solution.
If they are not, we are at loss. However, Hubbell
is quick to state that this will not be the case,
because in our present societies, closed systems
belong to an extinct race. This is a point of
disagreement between Hubbell and ourselves.
Another point concerns the static approach in
Hubbell's model. The lack of dynamics in the
model is not unconnected to the postulate of
permanent openness. The sociologically sensible
question of when and under what conditions a
group must be thought of as being open or closed
is distorted into an "either/or" and then decided
arbitrarily, "weil nicht sein kann, was nicht
sein darf!"

Drawing the boundaries of groups is a delicate
matter in itself. Is a person 900 miles from
home still a member of his domestic group? Is a
person leaving a closed meeting for a minute
still a member of the group? Is the closed meeting still closed under such conditions? These
are intricate questions of definitions which have
to be decided every now and then new, and on
which we will touch again later. One thing is
clear: there do exist closed groups, as the
election of a new Pope in Rome demonstrates
beyond all doubts. Whether we shall draw the
borders according to Gluckman's [9] suggestion
through the points where gossip ends, or rather
where names end or idioms, as Marsh et. al. [15]
suggest, must remain undecided at the moment.
The personal experience of university seminars,
of work hours in factories, or of hospital wards,
provide ample evidence for the actuality of
borders and barriers to communication.

To summarize Hubbell's achievement, his
model is a useful, but limited instrument. Its
most important contribution is its escape from

such narrow concepts as socio-economic status. One might make the point that socio-economic status is a special case in Hubbell's model, the case where the matrix W is a straightforward zero matrix, reflecting by this the solipsistic perspective of the ideology of individualism. Thinking in the tradition of social psychologists, Hubbell broke through the wall of isolated vanity, putting the individual into a social context. However, his model remains social-individualistic, as the solutions to his equations demonstrate. Each individual receives, in the tradition of personal property and achievement, his own special piece of the cake. Situations which do not allow for this kind of performance are not part of a cognitive world where society is like a gas with molecules drifting around at random. Alternative states are expelled from perception, as "all perception comes from wanting to perceive," as the Austrian novelist H. Broch once put it. Approaching the borders of this particular way of perception makes people shudder, as it means indeed breaking through into another universe. This is, however, exactly our aim.

4. THE PROBLEM OF CLOSED GROUPS

Our model reads

S(t) = F(t)S(t) + E(t),

where t is the time interval, S and E are, as before, a status vector and an external value-input vector respectively, but now the square matrix F is no longer Hubbell's choice matrix, but one representing relative communication frequencies. We have thus passed from mere intentions to actual outcomes. The weights in F are time periods of communication from person to person, normalized so as to make the columns sum to 1, thus standardizing the amount of time spent in sending information.

What happens in this model if an open group becomes closed? For simplicity, let us consider a group of two persons. The process is shown in Figure 1: the status of both persons approaches infinity. This might be interpreted to mean that at the moment of closure personal differences vanish, as the group fuses into a new unit. Referring to the ancient story of love, when a couple becomes so involved with each other that they have neither eyes nor ears for the outside world, it really does happen that the outside world responds by recognizing them as a new perceptual unit. There are of course other, duller examples to which we will refer later, of the fusion of individuals into a closed group. Are these cases so rare or peripheral that they can be ignored with impunity? We think definitely not. A satisfactory model must then be able to handle closed groups as well as open ones.

We must then look more closely at what goes wrong in the matrix model when a group becomes closed. Take the model in the form

(I - F)S = E.

When a group closes, I - F becomes singular; unless, by a coincidence which there seems no sociological

reason to expect, certain compatibility conditions are met, this precludes the solution of the equations. In other words, individual status is no longer determined. There is one very important partial exception, which occurs if the group is hierarchically organized, which in the language of linear algebra means that the matrix can be rearranged so as to be upper triangular. In this case, almost all the equations can be consistently solved, which is to say that individual status can still be assigned to most members of the group (except two).

Like all economics-based models, the above model is an _equilibrium model_; its failure is a failure of _stability_. When the rank of the matrix drops, the assignment of a well-defined status to the individual members of the group can no longer be made in a way which remains consistent over time, but tends to exceed all allowable bounds or to oscillate unacceptably. The certainty of the status-assigning process has been breached, and it is not difficult to see why this should be so. The closing of the group means precisely that its communications to the rest of society have been shut off; on what basis then can the society allot its members status? How can individuals from whom no signals are received be distinguished?

In this situation individual status will no longer be awarded, but instead _group status_ will be given indiscriminately to the members. We thus do find _group status as a result of the breakdown of the machinery for awarding individual status_. We will find a dual to this conclusion later, but meanwhile we can check with history that individual status came into being through the opening of groups and the gradual construction of the appropriate machinery. Medieval society was typically composed of tightly closed groups, each bearing its collective status. The Renaissance and Mercantilist periods created the individual and conferred his labile status upon him (Martin [16]).

When, however, a closed group is hierarchical, individual status is still feasible. This is instructive and in accord with sociological observation. In the hierarchical case, transitions from open to closed and vice versa may take place with relative smoothness. In the non-hierarchical case of a closely-connected group, on the other hand, such transitions are difficult and involve traumatic switches in the quality of the status system. In one direction, the communal control of group status symbols has to be individualized; in the other, individual control of status symbols must be abolished or socialized. Both of these are troublesome.

In terms of model building, the failure of stability and the element of suddenness which we have found naturally suggest recourse to catastrophe theory. This is therefore our next step.

5. CATASTROPHE MODEL FOR THE OPENING AND CLOSING OF GROUPS

It is an uphill process to emerge from the protective anonymity of a group and earn or usurp individual prestige. In contrast, sinking into a share of undifferentiated acclaim of

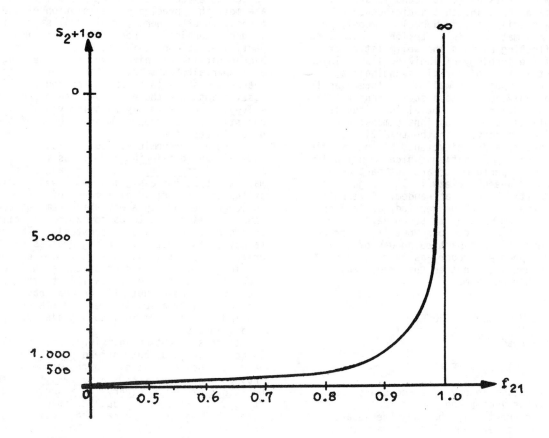

Figure 1.

scorn can sometimes happen overnight. One of the standard "landscapes" of catastrophe theory (Thom [20], perhaps more accessibly Waddington [21]) fits these historical observations very well. It has the form (see Figure 2) of a breaking wave (but is not to be confused with the explanation of the breaking of the wave). In the base plane, from left to right is the axis of openness-closedness, while from near to deep in the picture-plane hierarchicalness increases. Of course, as will be more explicitly gone into later, this continuity implies that neither openness nor closedness nor hierarchy are absolute, but come in degrees. The height of the figure above base level represents the difficulty of attaining the given position, not the status associated with it, which is not shown directly. On the lower fold, group status is awarded, on the upper fold individual status; the re-entrant overhang is not to be stably occupied. The interpretation is as follows:

The more open the group and less hierarchical, the slighter the distinction between group and individual status. If the more open group becomes more hierarchical, then a smooth transition to individual status (now differentiated) takes place. For closed groups, however, if they are not hierarchical, there is only group status to be had, on the lower fold. When they become sufficiently hierarchical, there can be an upward catastrophic jump to the individual-status fold. When they are on the individual-status fold, this is safe and stable in the background; if, however, the group loses hierarchicalness, there is a sudden descending catastrophe to group status.

The Middle Ages were inside this pocket below the overhang, with group status as the rule. The way out to individual status was not by the sudden catastrophic jump, but by the long way around through opening the groups and then achieving individual status, with perhaps a modern return to more closedness and more hierarchy on the upper fold. This is the Pilgrim's Progress of the ex-member of a guild, discarding its regalia and donning Puritan garb for his ascent to the heights of Capitalist prestige, followed by a few steps to the right. Just so, too, does it require time and a patient commitment to hoisting the correct signals to outsiders for members of an immigrant community to become perceived as individuals. An outstanding example of the energy demands of a hysteresis loop around this surface is that of the Japanese in California during and since the Second World War: from such individual status as they had attained, they were plunged by Pearl Harbour into (very negative) group status in prison camps, followed after

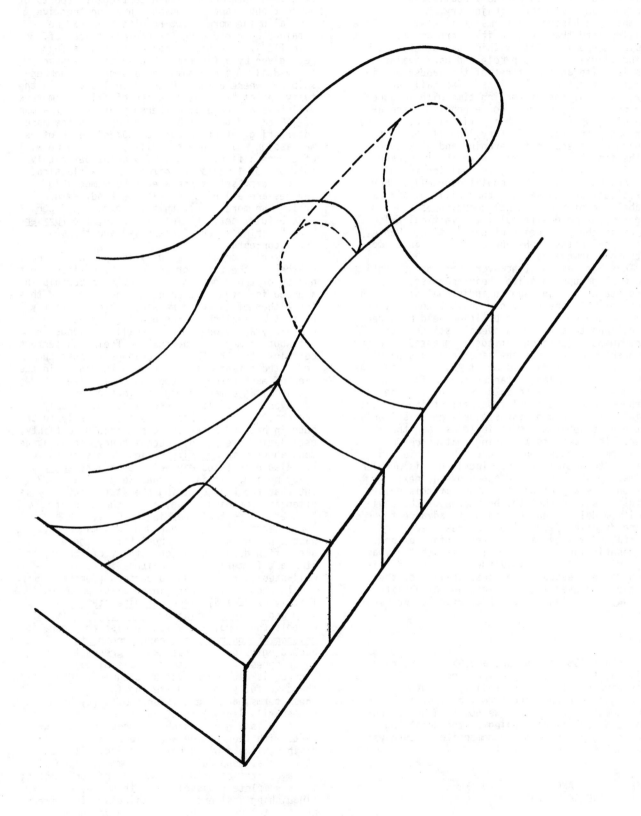

Figure 2.

their release by slow re-individualization in a laborious and roundabout trajectory.

While in historical terms it is easier to lose individuality than to gain it, there are many regular periodic shifts within our society from an individual to a group role and back again. This is quite another facet of the landscape, in a different set of dimensions. The daily and weekly alternation of working time with leisure time brings many of us a corresponding alternation of group status with individual status. The work group on, say, a factory line closes in the morning and opens in the evening and at weekends; at the same time the world in which the worker has his individuality is there waiting for him and does not need to be rebuilt diurnally. For this situation the same picture will do, with a relabelling of the vertical coordinates. Up no longer means more difficult; the vertical axis now bears the projection of cyclic time. Hence, the "happy" catastrophe upwards can be as common as the one downwards.

This last example, however, reminds us that some work groups, despite their openness, enjoy group status in addition to individual status. A nearby example are certainly Anglo-Saxon Universities where not just the position held by a person defines this person's overall status, but where in addition group status is granted through membership. It is not the same to be a student or a professor at Harvard or at Arizona State University. Similar instances can be found in Japanese firms and also in this country. The truth -- and a good model must reflect it -- is that individual and group status widely co-exist, only that one is sometimes more in focus than the other. This amounts to saying that we return to the incumbent questions of group boundaries in relation to social status. Tackling this problem ultimately shall be the concern of the next section. By way of brief summary at this point, we must conclude that the breakdown of the equilibrium model has encouraged us to advance towards a more dynamical model, here represented in a qualitative way by paths on the surface of an "epigenetic landscape". It is clear that anyway a dynamic model will avoid the self-contradiction which was expressed by the insolubility of the equations, converting this into an instability in an always-existing output. For example, we might go over to

$$S(t) = F(t-1) + E(t).$$

Pinkava [18] has shown, and Gaines [8] has utilized, the fact that various logical antinomies are equivalent to the instability of automata. But rather than entering into the minutiae of an improvement of this sort, we now turn our attention to a further broadening of the modelling process, to bring into the composite picture yet more aspects of reality.

6. FUZZINESS AND ITS ROLE IN THE AWARDING OF STATUS

There is a well worked out mathematical concept of fuzziness, which we owe to Zadeh (Zadeh [23]; for bibliography see Gaines and Kohout [7]).

It covers both inherent and contingent aspects of human thought and reasoning, in a constructive way, allowing more exact results than can be obtained by pretending its non-existence (cf. Klir [11]). The basic idea is that of a fuzzy set, given by a function which assigns to each individual of the population a degree of membership somewhere between 0 and 1 inclusive. In the fuzzy set of "tall men", a man of height 2 meters will have a degree of membership of, say .9, a man of 130 cm a degree of 0, and so on. In the more interesting set of "beautiful women", each of us may assign what degrees we like, in which we will of course differ. A vote of 0 means definitely out, one of 1 means definitely in. A classical or non-fuzzy set is one where the membership degrees are all of these extreme kind, either 0 or 1. The more nearly this is so, the crisper is the fuzzy set; the less it is so, the fuzzier. Thus "fuzziness" and "crispness" are themselves fuzzy concepts.

A social group is a fuzzy set par excellence. Whether as theorists or as ordinary citizens, our notion of the degree of somebody's membership in a group is often neither nought nor one, and this for either of two good reasons, or both: it may be that we feel the corresponding degree of uncertainty as to whether he "really" belongs or not, but it may also be that we feel with perfect certainty that he "really" belongs to just the indicated extent. There is such fuzziness in the view of each observer, upon which is piled the likely disagreement among distinct observers.

Even more so is a person's status a fuzzy concept. Not only, again, is there likely to be both in his and other persons' minds uncertainty, oscillation over time, inconsistency and disagreement about some definite notion of his status, but also his status may well be an inherently fuzzy notion. It is not that we guess at 94,7, but that the kind of thing the status actually is often is something vague, as in the case of "a pretty important chap in the City," or "a lousy dentist," or someone who "was mixed up, wasn't he, with those terrorists?". There is also often downright inconsistency of status, as at least formerly in the United States in the well-studied case of Negro doctors (Lenski, 1954).

It seems clear that (in an axiom purposedly fuzzily expressed): more definite status is accorded to more definitely perceived entities. Of this the corollary which we wish to pursue is: crisper groups receive clearer group status. We accordingly look at what causes groups to vary in crispness. One factor we have already considered is closedness versus openness. Now is the time fully to recognize the fuzziness of these terms, and the existence of a (by no means necessarily linear) continuum between them. At one pole is a group which has reduced its contacts with the outside world to nil; it is invisible, like a black hole in space. At the other is a group which in its communication plays no favourites as between members and non-members; it is completely dissolved, with no way of distinguishing insiders from outsiders. In between are all the real groups, which we encounter.

The more closed a group is, the sharper are its boundaries, to the extent that non-members have very low or actually zero degrees of membership. "Partial", "lukewarm", "part-time" members, however, may well exist with membership degrees well below 1. A reduction of this type of penumbra requires coherence of the group, which may be brought about by strong connectedness or in other ways, for example by large absolute contributions to the group. We thus find a new independent variable coming to the fore: coherence. In the sense intended here, coherence is marked by the extent of "active" or "intense" membership, with degrees near one. We may say: closedness makes a group exclusive; coherence makes it inclusive. Both of them sharpen the borders (from opposite sides), that is, they both enhance the group's crispness.

It now follows that: closed, coherent groups are perceived most crisply and will receive the most definite group status, while open and incoherent groups are perceived most vaguely and receive the haziest group status. We thus arrive at the promised dual to a proposition of the previous section, namely: individual status comes about as a result of excessive fuzziness in group status.

This leaves us with a problem to unravel. As a group opens and becomes less coherent, so that the awards of group status to its members blur more and more, and all that is left is to go over to individual status, is there some accompanying process that puts the individuals into better focus, so that in fact this new status is awarded to them, or do they remain so dimly perceived that finally no status is awarded? Either can in fact happen. The latter process is examplified, not rarely, by the uncommunicative member of a vanishing group, who used to receive his share of its status, but as the County Archaeologists dissolve, is left unperceived, with neutral status. The former and more meaningful process occurs when not apathy but energy directed elsewhere cause the opening and incoherence of the group: members are increasing their communications with non-members, and thereby their noticeability and hence eligibility for receiving individual status.

Where does hierarchical organization of the group fit into this scenario? As reflected in the communication matrix, hierarchy means communication upwards, which may vary from a full upper triangle -- indicating a tightly knit hierarchy -- to a mere fringe along the diagonal -- indicating a weak although unidirectional order. Thus between the poles of coherence-incoherence, the hierarchical groups can occupy any position, as they can between closedness and openness. If we are right in believing them to have a special role, a suitable locus for them on a sphere of coherence-incoherence or of closedness-openness would be as a sort of International Date Line, across which transition between group and individual status takes place imperceptibly in either direction.

The dilemma of the individual left without a group has very widely spaced horns indeed. Near one extreme is the stranger killed because he does not fit into the local kinship system; near the other the successful untrammeled tycoon who has cut his ethnic ties. Societies vary in their willingness to perceive individuals. Our modern Western World asserts itself to be at the peak in this respect, but it could be persuasively argued that in fact it accords group status, if not more

often, at least to more people, than it treats as individuals. This is surely so outside itself: the greatest kindness of many busy Westerners to the victims of a far-away famine is to award blanket status. But it may be so internally also: with every stereotype of the Coalminers, the Trade Unionists, the Politicians, the Students, the Political or Social Scientists . . . goes an award of group status. From the morning paper through the shared grumblings at lunch to the evening news, of how many persons do we think as individuals, of how many only collectively?

7. SOME CONCLUDING REMARKS

It is fashionable nowadays in some quarters to make mathematical models in the social sciences. Mathematicians, system theorists and cyberneticians are frequently quick in drawing one or another out of their sleeves. The social sciences are, however, the sciences of fuzzy concepts. Mapping social systems into formal ones needs more than just the skilled eye of eager mathematicians; it needs above all a careful study and concern for reality, and on top of this the openness of mind to accept the intrinsic necessity of the fuzziness of social concepts. This openness of mind is frequently lacking, not only among the above-mentioned group, but among the social scientists themselves, to a deplorable degree. The present contribution is an effort to amend this.

We have another criticism of much of the modelling that goes on. In some areas of the social sciences it is extremely fashionable to indulge in empirical research and to impose on the findings models borrowed from the well-reputed sister-science, economics. The model is then often taken as the reality itself, because of its data-bearing aura. This involves distortion and falsification to a positively dangerous extent.

REFERENCES

1. BANDLER, W. and M. E. A. SCHMUTZER, "The Valuton: An Automation Model of a New Theory of Value Genesis," Theory and Decision, XI, 1, 1979.
2. BENDIX, R. and S. LIPSET (eds.), Class, Status and Power, New York, Free Press, 1966.
3. BERGER, J. (B. P. COHEN), M. ZELDITEH, and B. ANDERSON (eds), Sociological Theories in Progress, Vol. 1, New York, Houghton Mufflin, 1966.
4. BLAU, P. M., Exchange and Power in Social Life, New York, Wiley, 1964.
5. FARARO, T. J., "Status, Expectation and Situation," Quality and Quantity, pp. 37-97, 1972.
6. FARARO, T. J., "Theory of Status," General Systems, XIII, pp. 177-188, 1968.
7. GAINES, B. R. and L. J. KOHOUT, "The Fuzzy Decade: A Bibliography of Fuzzy Systems and Closely Related Topics," International Journal of Man-Machine Studies, 9, pp. 1-68, 1977.

8. GAINES, B. R., "Nonstandard Logics for Data-
    base Systems," EUROCAMP 78, 1978.
9. GLUCKMAN, M., "Gossip and Scandal," Current
    Anthropology, pp. 307-316, 1963.
10. HUBBELL, Ch. H., "An Input-Output Approach
    to Clique Identification," Sociometry
    XXVIII, pp. 377-399, 1965.
11. KLIR, G. J., "Identification of Generative
    Structures in Empirical Data," Inter-
    national Journal of General Systems, 3,
    pp. 89-104, 1976.
12. LAUMANN, E. D., Prestige and Association in
    an Urban Community, Indianapolis, Bobbs-
    Merrill, 1966.
13. LAUMANN, E. D., The Logic of Social Hier-
    archies, Markham, 1970.
14. LEIK, R. K. and R. NAGASAWA, "A Sociometric
    Basis for Measuring Social Status and
    Social Structure," Sociometry XXXIII,
    pp. 55-75, 1970.
15. MARSH, P., E. ROSSER, and R. HARRÉ, The
    Rules of Disorder, London, Routledge &
    Kegan, 1978.

16. MARTIN, A. v., Soziologie der Renaissance
    - Zur Physiognomie und Rhythmik bürger-
    licher Kultur, F. Enke, Stuttgart, 1932.
17. MORENO, J. L. (ed.), The Sociometry Reader,
    New York, The Free Press, 1960.
18. PINKAVA, V., "On the Nature of Some Logical
    Paradoxes," International Journal of
    1977.
19. SCHMUTZER, M. E. A., Social Crystallization
    - Variations on a Structural Theme,
    University of Essex, G.B., Ph.D. Thesis,
    1975.
20. THOM, R., Structural Stability and Morpho-
    genesis, Benjamin, Reading, Mass., 1975.
21. WADDINGTON, C. H., Tools for Thought,
    Jonathan Cape, London, 1977.
22. WEBER, M., "Class, Status and Party," in:
    Class, Status and Power, R. Bendix and
    S. Lipset (eds.), New York, The Free
    Press, 1966.
23. ZADEH, L., "Fuzzy Sets," Information and
    Control, 8, pp. 338-353, 1965.

System uncertainty and leadership strategy

M. A. P. WILLMER
Manchester Business School, Manchester, England

1. INTRODUCTION

No executive can operate effectively in a vacuum. Whether he works in Government service, nationalised or private industry; whether his organisation attempts to control crime, or manufacture motor cars or plastic buckets, the executive who wishes to be successful needs good, reliable information. Regardless of whether the state of affairs under consideration is "good" or "bad"; regardless of whether the future looks bleak or rosy, executives need the truth.

Unfortunately one of the dangers which beset the top echelons of management when they seek information about the general state of their organisation and its environment is that often they drown in too much data [1]. For this reason data have to be selected and processed, frequently at several different levels, in order to reduce to manageable proportions the quantity of information that finally reaches the executives. Such operations, however, can lead to important information becoming lost or distorted.

Figure 1 shows diagrammatically the links between the parts of an organisation which can all receive information from the environment and from each other. Each link can be thought of as a simple communication channel with a transmitter, a receiver and a distortion generator (see Figure 2). The distortion generator represents the factors which cause information to become lost or modified. The reader may be reminded of the Christmas party game where guests are placed in a line. The person at one end whispers a message into the ear of the person next to him. This process continues until the message reaches the person at the other end of the line. The received message and the original one are then compared, often with humorous results. Reference [2] describes a psychological experiment based on the party game: there are six persons in the chain along which a story about an uncanny adventure to an English gentleman in India has to be passed. The variations between the initial and final versions of the story have been analysed and used to illustrate how people react to discontinuities and apparent illogicalities in messages.

The more removed the executive is from the source of information, the less certain he can be

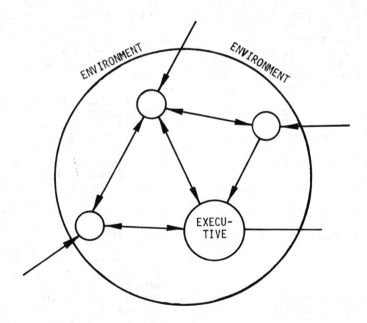

Figure 1.   Simplified Diagrammatic Representation of the
Information Links Between the Parts of an Organisation

253

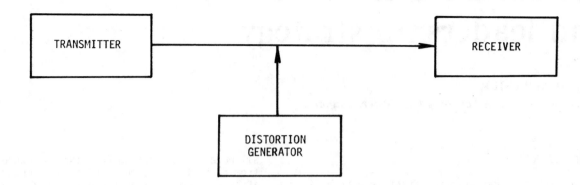

Figure 2. Diagrammatic Representation of the Information
Link Between Two Parts of an Organisation

about its accuracy. This applies to all types of
information ranging from raw data to refined intelligence, statistical or non-statistical. (In terms
of the Christmas party whispering game, the further along the line you are from the start the
less certain you are that the right message has
been received and transmitted.) Distortion factors affect the chances of the executive mis-
interpreting the content and significance of the
original message. Sometimes his uncertainty level
may increase. On the other occasions he may
believe that he is certain of the meaning of the
information but his interpretation may be wrong,
i.e., there is an increase in what may be termed
pseudo-certainty.

At each link of the communication process
information is received, processed and transmitted and, in considering the causes of the distortion of information in an organisation, it is
helpful to deal with each stage in turn. The
existence of an organised management information
system does not necessarily mean that these
causes have been entirely eliminated. Any system
may suffer from faults of design or operation and
amongst the most common, as noted in [3], are:

1.1. Reception Stage

a. The attention of an observer is focused
on the wrong subject.
b. Information is submitted in the wrong
form.
c. The speed at which information is received
is inappropriate.
d. The receiver allows personal factors to
affect his interpretation of information.
e. The response of the receiver is unsuitable.

1.2. Processing Stage

a. Information, when it is received by someone in the system, is wrongly classified or
catalogued.
b. Storage and retrieval facilities may be
inadequate.
c. Information may be dealt with too hastily
or too slowly.
d. The channels of communication may be

overlooked leading to information being lost.
e. The full significance of a piece of information may not be recognised and thus the
appropriate action may not be taken.
f. Decisions may be taken before the necessary facts have been considered.
g. The aims of the organisation may be inappropriate or badly defined.
h. Although the aims may be changed in the
light of experience, the new objectives may be
as muddled or as inappropriate as the old ones.

1.3. Transmission Stage

a. Persons or machines may be wrongly
directed.
b. A wrong response may be given because
either a person has been poorly trained or a
machine has been set up badly.
c. The reaction of a person or a machine
may be out of balance with the message or instruction received.
d. Reactions may be subject to outside
interference.

A considerable amount of distortion is caused
unintentionally rather than by design. ·Often by
sensible study of the organisation's communication problems, by making employees in the various
branches more aware of each other's problems and
by the introduction of better equipment, the
level of unintentional distortion can be greatly
reduced. In many cases, however, there is a
clear need for the development and integration
of an effective Business Intelligence System into
the existing information activities and processes [4].
On the other hand, some distortion is undoubtedly caused deliberately. For instance, it
has been suggested that in the budget game,
managers will attempt to obtain slack budgets
by influencing the budget process and that this
is achieved by understating revenues and over-
stating costs [5,6]. Another example of bias
is given by Lowe and Shaw [7], who found that
line managers introduced bias into sales forecasts. This type of bias has also been investigated experimentally [8].
Motives for distorting information are both

many and varied. They may be well-intentioned. In
reply to a question concerning the risks involved
in letting Gandhi travel third class to live in a
colony of Untouchables, a Congress Party member is
reported to have replied: "Before he travels -- and
he has no idea we do it -- we select his compartment,
have it cleaned out. We select the people that are
going to travel in it and dress them as Untouchables. When he gets up to Delhi, we take him to
the Bangi Colony which we have thoroughly cleaned
out before he arrives, and the people who live
with him are very carefully chosen but dressed
appropriately. It's quite an expensive game.
You've no idea what it costs the Congress Party
keeping that old man in poverty" [9].

On the other hand, the motives may be essentially personal -- to achieve an ambition, to satisfy
some greed, to obtain a quiet life, or even just
to survive. Over the years many dictators have
found to their cost [10] that the truth is something which often eludes them. Further, the
greater their powers the more likely are their
staff to tell them what they think their leaders
want to hear. If a powerful leader is not careful
he may well find himself operating in a vacuum,
out of contact with reality [11]. The more powerful a person becomes, the greater the tendency for
him to become isolated from the facts.

In government and business organisations senior
executives normally have considerable power over
their subordinates. They are often able to influence a person's type of work, place of work, pay
and bonus, hours of work, promotion prospects, etc.
It is not surprising, therefore, that the way in
which the performance of employees is appraised has
a significant effect on the reliability of information flows. Whatever measure of performance is
used, it is only human nature that some employees
will attempt to make it appear that their assessments are higher than their efforts truly warrant.
Considerable care has to be exercised, therefore,
when the method of appraisal is given a dual role:
to encourage both the faithful transmittal of
information and an increase in output from subordinates. There are dangers in asserting that
you will reward the truth if you later "shoot the
messenger because he brings bad news." The success
of large organisations depends upon mutual trust
between personnel and perhaps the quickest way for
a senior officer to lose the trust, confidence and
respect of his subordinates is to say one thing
and appear to do another. Trust and confidence,
though easy to destroy, are not so easily re-
created.

2. PERFORMANCE APPRAISAL EFFECTS

The degree of distortion that is likely to
occur in a given situation will obviously depend
upon the nature of the opportunities available to
subordinates for manipulating information flows.
Top management may lay down rules and guidelines,
but the way in which an organisation actually
operates may be very different from the way in
which it should operate. The executives may be
tempted to solve this problem by encouraging subordinates to inform on each other. Such was the
state of affairs in the Paris Police after the fall
of Napolean. Louis Canler, one time chief of the

Sûreté, is reported by Stead [12] as noting, "at
this period informing was the order of the day
among the staff; among friends, among relatives
even, there was spying . . . and it was not uncommon for two close friends to sell one another
in the hope that their treachery might lead to
promotion." Despite the informing, it was not
a period renowned for police efficiency.

The consequences of rules being violated can
range anywhere from acute embarrassment to total
disaster. Sometimes events make headline news:
"Mafia catches out Mobil" [13] -- a headline
introducing a story of how one of America's
largest oil companies unknowingly hired a Mafia-
run firm of hoodlums to help break a lorry driver's
strike. To reassure the public, the company
stressed that scrupulous checks were carried out
on all suppliers. Nevertheless, as one official
had to admit: "Some guy at the district marketing
level was probably under tremendous pressure from
his dealers and he decided to take a few short
cuts." And another -- "New York Police cheat on
crime figures" [14] -- precinct commanders were
believed to have manipulated their statistics to
show headquarters that they were doing a much
better job of controlling crime than in fact they
were.

To explore the effect of various methods of
performance appraisal on both the motivation of
employees and their manipulation of information
flows, the business game, "So you think that you
will make a Managing Director," was created.
Developed at the Manchester Business School and
used on a number of different courses, it is concerned with the management of people and machines
in a production environment. The objective of
the Managing Director is to handle his staff in
such a way that:
  i. output is increased;
  ii. he knows what is happening in his
      factories.
The game is a development of the simulation described in [15] where two hypothetical Managing
Directors were used and, like this earlier work,
is based on a company called "International
Castings Ltd" which is engaged in the production
of a variety of finished engineering components.
One of the factories specialises in the production
of "clunks" and is situated in unpleasant surroundings a long way from Head Office. At the
beginning of the game participants are asked to
take the part of the manager of this factory.
In this way they are able to familiarise themselves with the production problems associated
with the manufacture of "clunks" and the difficulties of persuading the Managing Director
that they are competent, capable and dependable.
Essentially the factory contains two types of
machines and the workforce is divided into three
categories (see Appendix A). There are also a
number of rules governing the way men, money and
machines should be used. However, as the Managing
Director is remote from the factory, it is
assumed that the manager may break these rules
without fear of immediate exposure. The effect
of breaking the company rules as far as production
of clunks is concerned depends on which rules are
broken and by how much; violations can also have
a short and long term effect on the state of the
factory in succeeding months. During the game

participants interact with a computer representing the company and its personnel, the computer responses to information and directives being based partly on assumptions and partly from the analysis of data gathered from the behaviour of managers who have played the game. At the start participants are told that the Managing Director has believed for some time that the current clunk production is too low, although the previous factory manager had always maintained that an increase in production could only be achieved by breaking the rules of the company. Even though relieved of his post for incompetence he told the truth because the game is designed so that, by totally obeying the rules, the manager cannot on average meet the initial aspirations of the Managing Director.

In running the factory the manager has to make decisions regarding the allocation of men to machines, the use of maintenance men for production, the allocation of overtime, the percentage of production not declared but held over to the following month, and the use of sub-contracting money to bolster production.

The game is played for a number of months and in each month the following sequence is followed:

1. The Managing Director tells the manager his primary objective. This can be either:

   a. Production - to produce as many clunks as possible.

   b. Closeness to Target - to get as close to the agreed target as possible.

   c. Honesty - to be truthful about the number of rule infringements made.

2. A target is negotiated; the Managing Director sets a target for the coming month. In setting this target he takes into account past performance, including the number of company rules declared broken. The manager is then given an opportunity to suggest his view of a reasonable target. After this the Managing Director specifies the final target for the month.

3. The programme states the number of men of various categories that are available at work. The manager is asked whether he wishes to allocate any maintenance men to production and what hours of overtime the various categories are to work. Maintenance men who are transferred to production are treated as Grade I operatives. Next, the number of Grade I machines in use for the month, the number of Grade II machine breakdowns, and the mid-month production figures are given. When applicable the manager is asked to state the number of "illegal" clunks ordered and the percentage of clunks that he wishes to withhold. Following the receipt of this information the number of clunks recorded for the month is given.

4. The manager is asked the number of rules broken during the month.

5. The manager is given his performance rating for the month and his average to date. This will normally be between 50 to 100, although higher and lower rates are possible under exceptional circumstances. A typical month's printout is shown in Appendix B.

As the game proceeds there is a conflict of objectives between the Managing Director and the manager: the former wants increased production and meaningful information about the state of the factory, whilst the latter wants to be well thought of by his boss. The Managing Director has control over the method used for appraising and rewarding his subordinate, together with the target negotiating process. The subordinate, on the other hand, decides how the factory will be run and has a measure of control over the information flow. In some circumstances he can manipulate the flow of information to adjust the Managing Director's perceptions of his efforts to his own advantage. It should be remembered that the Managing Director has no knowledge of the actual way the shop is managed other than from his interpretation of the recorded production, the number of rules the manager admits to having broken, and his past experiences as a manager.

At a suitable time participants are promoted and asked to supervise two factory managers, the computer being reprogrammed to respond as rather cynically-minded old hands who have heard many fine words in the past from other Managing Directors. As in the first part of the game, the computer responses are based partly on assumptions and partly on the analysis of actual behaviour. The computer is thus capable of handling realistically Managing Directors who say one thing but do another. Participants are given the last six months production data for each manager:

MANAGER 1

Recorded Number of Clunks	Number of Rule Infringements Admitted
29583	0
27492	0
29981	0
30468	1
30298	0
31284	1

MANAGER 2

Recorded Number of Clunks	Number of Rule Infringements Admitted
31851	1
28955	0
28426	0
31982	2
31255	1
30415	0

It is now the participant's turn to select the main objective each month, to lead the target negotiation process and to tell their subordinates what they think of their efforts. A typical month's sequence of events is given in Appendix C.

It is to be noted that the participant is told the recorded clunk production for each factory and the number of infringements admitted by the managers. After this information has been given the participant is asked to state the number of infringements that he thinks the manager has made. Finally, the participant is given a performance rating; this is composed of a component based on the accuracy of his assessment of the number of rules broken.

3. METHOD OF ANALYSIS

Consider an executive who is confronted with a problem in which the future environment can be in one of N different states. Let P_i be the executive's subjective probability that the environment will be in the i-th state ($i = 1,2,3,...,N$). These probabilities define a point in N dimensional probability space. Further, let $P_i(c)$ be the probability that the environment will be in the i-th state when all the relevant information which has been received by the organisation is correctly transmitted to the executive and correctly interpreted on arrival. The point P_c defined by these probabilities represents the most reliable result that can be expected from the information available to the organisation; there are no errors due to information becoming lost, biased or distorted as it is sent from one part of the organisation to another or from messages being misunderstood or misinterpreted. On the other hand, let the point P_a be defined by the probabilities $P_i(A)$ where $P_i(A)$ is the probability that the executive belives the environment will be in the i-th state based on his interpretation of the information which actually reaches him. This point represents the executive's actual operating position. The distance between P_c and P_a is thus a measure of the extent to which the executive is misled by communication difficulties.

To illustrate, consider a situation in which there are only 3 possible states of interest with associated probabilities P_1, P_2 and P_3. Since

$$P_1 + P_2 + P_3 = 1$$

the set of probabilities (P_1, P_2, P_3) define a point in a triangle in probability space (see Figure 3).

As far as the degree of uncertainty of the executive is concerned, an appropriate measure is given by the entropy function, H, which was first introduced into communication studies by Shannon [16], where

$$H = - (P_1 \log P_1 + P_2 \log P_2 + P_3 \log P_3)$$

or when the environment can be in one of N states

$$H = - \sum_{i=1}^{N} P_i \log P_i$$

When the logarithms are taken to the base two, this expression is roughly the minimum number of questions which can be answered by "yes" or "no" required to determine the actual state the environment is in from among all the possible ones.

In the three state example, lines of constant entropy or uncertainty cut the triangle of feasible probabilities producing a series of curves (see Figure 4). From this figure it can be seen that the closer a point is to one of the apexes, the lower the entropy, and the nearer the point is to the centre, the larger the uncertainty. The centre of the triangle is in fact the point $P_1 = 1/3$, $P_2 = 1/3$, $P_3 = 1/3$, i.e., all states being equally probable. At this point the uncertainty or entropy is a maximum.

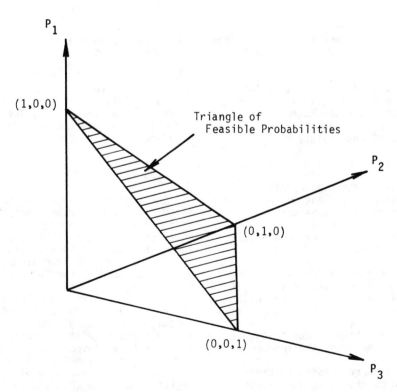

Figure 3. The Feasibility Probability Triangle

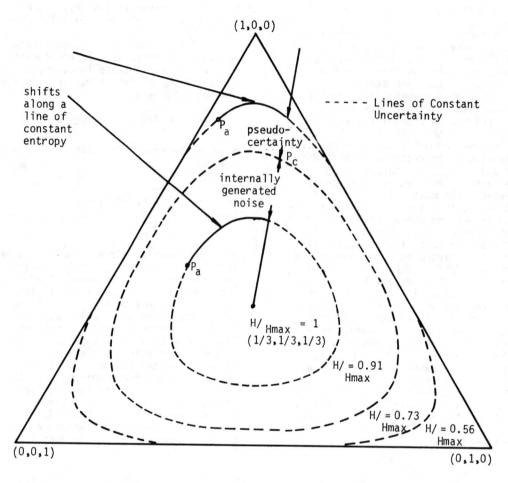

Figure 4. Lines of Constant Uncertainty in the
Planet of Feasible Probabilities

Now consider a series of lines emanating from this central point. From Figure 4 it can be seen that the distance between a typical P_c and a typical P_a consists of two components:
   i. ΔH = a change of uncertainty or entropy, and
   ii. M = a movement along a line of constant entropy
(when the state of affairs under consideration can be in one of N states there is a change of entropy and a movement along a surface of constant entropy).

In considering the structure of the uncertainty, it is helpful if one thinks of the true situation as being masked by noise. In [17] I distinguish between:

   <u>internally generated noise</u> - noise that is due to information becoming lost or distorted inside the organisation or because insufficient use is made of information already obtained, and

   <u>background noise</u> - that which is due to the organisation not receiving the appropriate information.

The uncertainty level corresponding to the point P_c can be regarded as the background noise level. If the executive's operating point, P_a, has a higher uncertainty level, the difference

between the levels is a measure of the internally generated noise involved. On the other hand, if P_a has a lower uncertainty level, the difference indicates the degree of pseudo-certainty appertaining.

4. RESULTS

The participants in the experiments described in this paper were managers attending two Operational Management Courses at the Manchester Business School. Most had production backgrounds and came from well-known multinational companies.

To interpret their responses, it was found to be helpful to differentiate between two levels of production performance [18]:

   i. Capability - the level that a completely efficient manager could achieve using existing resources and acting under existing constraints.

   ii. Potentiality - the level that could conceivably be achieved by fully utilising existing resources and optimally relaxing the constraints.

Thus, if the Managing Director demands a higher production than the capability level, he must expect rules to be broken. Further, a demand beyond the potentiality level is a request for the impossible!

With regard to the number of violations admitted by the manager, an earlier study [15] had shown that near both the capability and potentiality levels, the information given to the Managing Director about rule breakages had very little effect on the uncertainty level. Midway between these points, however, the information was of considerable value. For this reason it was decided to define three production groups:

a. Low: <31500 clunks
              – near to the capability level
b. Medium: ≥31500 but <33000 clunks
              – in between capability and
              potentiality levels
c. High: ≥33000 clunks
              – near to the potentiality level

Figures 5A, B, C show the differences between the actual and perceived operating positions in probability space for participants acting as Managing Directors. Trajectories are given which indicate how these positions change with the level of output for each of the main objectives. For convenience the possible rates of the system are defined as:

S_1 : No rules broken

S_2 : 1 or 2 rules broken

$S_{3'}$: 3 or more rules broken

The results show that in the majority of cases there are considerable differences between perceived and actual operating positions, the only exception being in the case of medium output with production as the main objective.

When the output was either high or low, participants underestimated the chances of no rules being broken. In the former case, this was probably due to participants forgetting that their subordinate managers could have failed to declare the true output earlier and used the clunks saved to bolster production -- a violation in the previous month.

When closeness to target was selected as the main objective, there was insufficient data to be able to estimate meaningful probabilities for high output. When output was low, the chance of no rules being broken was underestimated as in the case of production. However, for medium output, this chance is overestimated.

When honesty was selected as the main objective, there was again insufficient data at the high output level to estimate meaningful probabilities. Unlike the earlier cases, at low output, the chance of one or two rules being broken was underestimated. For medium output, however, the chance of three or more violations was overestimated.

Figure 6 shows the difference between the actual and the perceived operating Managing Director positions in terms of the changes in the uncertainty and in the minimum distance along a surface of constant entropy. To increase the number of dimensions the states of factory were defined as:

S_1 : No rules broken

S_2 : 1 rule broken

S_3 : 2 rules broken

S_4 : 3 or more rules broken

Also, in order to increase the number of output levels these were redefined as:

a. Very Poor: <31000 clunks
b. Poor: <32000 but ≥31000 clunks
c. Medium: <32000 but ≥33000 clunks
d. High: >33000 clunks

Unfortunately, there were insufficient results at the high level for meaningful estimates to be made.

The figure shows:

Main Objective - Production

Minimum Distance is relatively small. It can be seen that the high level of internally generated noise, initially high, decreases with increased output, resulting at the poor and medium output levels in a small amount of pseudo-certainty.

Main Objective - Closeness to Target

Increased output leads first to a decrease in the minimum distance. This is followed by both an increase in internally generated noise and the minimum distance.

Main Objective - Honesty

Increased output leads to a decrease in the noise level but a relatively large increase in the minimum distance. At the medium output level there was almost no difference between the actual and perceived uncertainty levels, but the distance between the two points was substantial.

On the whole the differences between the actual and perceived operating position are relatively small. There are, however, three extreme conditions:

i.   Production, Very Low Output, Large
     Internally Generated Noise
ii. Closeness to Target, Medium Output,
     Large Internally Generated Noise
iii. Honesty, Medium Output, Large
     Minimum Distance

The results so far have been based on the assumption that all the participants had adopted basically the same approach to the problem of motivating and controlling their subordinates. A glance at the number of time histories, however, showed that this was clearly not the case. Not only were several leadership styles used but the reaction of subordinates was also different. Some Managing Directors, for instance, were able to achieve sustained periods of relatively high output, whilst others could neither produce clunks in any quantity or acquire an accurate knowledge of the true state of affairs at their factories.

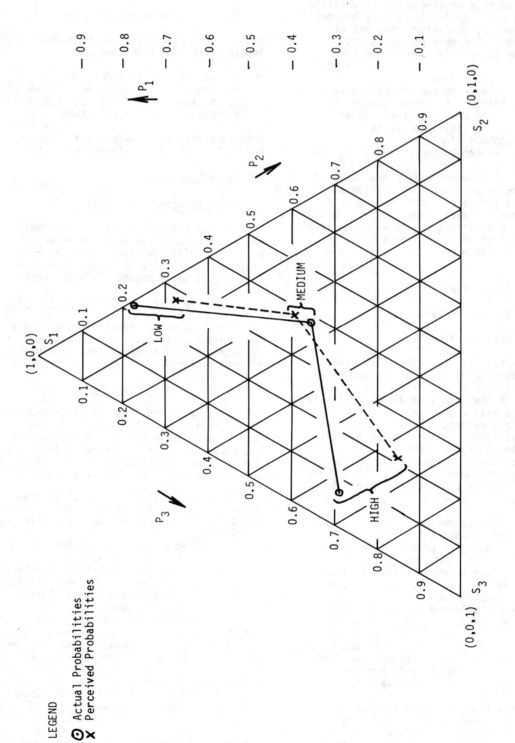

LEGEND

⊙ Actual Probabilities
✗ Perceived Probabilities

Figure 5A. Main Objective - Production
Comparison Between Perceived and Actual Operating
Positions for Managing Directors

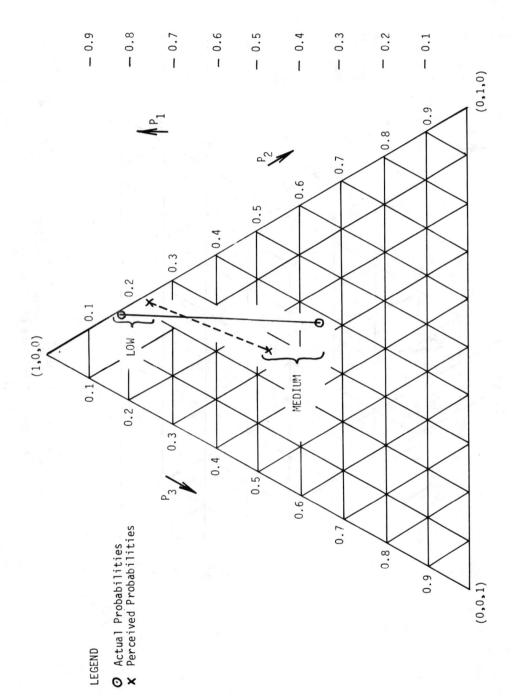

Figure 5B. Main Objective - Closeness to Target
Comparison Between Perceived and Actual Operating
Positions for Managing Directors

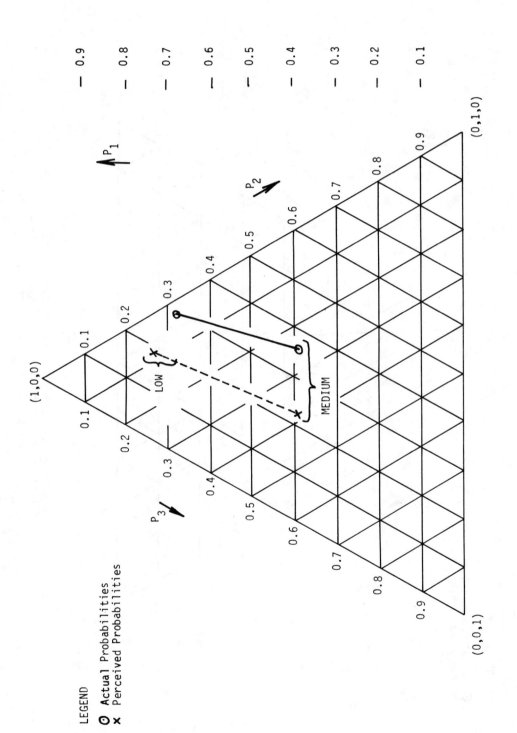

Figure 5C.   Main Objective – Honesty
Comparison Between Perceived and Actual Operating
Positions for Managing Directors

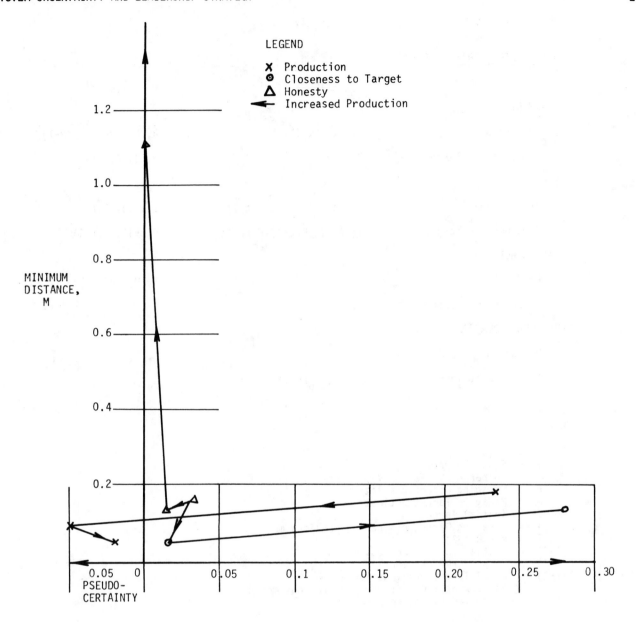

Figure 6.   Comparison of Actual and Perceived
Operating Positions of Managing Directors

From a study of the time histories available, two styles of leadership, accounting for approximately 68% of the total, were discernible. These were:

Style I: Consistently not ungenerous when negotiating targets and a belief that--when honesty is the main objective--production and closeness to target encourage lying.

Style II: Consistently mean when negotiating targets.

Table 1 on the following page gives the factors (significant at 5% level) which best explain the nature of the decisions of the two styles. It can be seen that there are a number interesting differences. For instance, when closeness to target is the main objective, the level of output is a significant factor in the assessment of the subordinates in both styles. However, in Style I the change in the Managing Director's rating is important, whereas in Style II other important factors are the final target level and the Managing Director's assessment of the subordinate the previous month.

Table 1.

MANGING DIRECTOR'S DECISION	FACTORS	
	STYLE I	STYLE II
ASSESSMENT		
Production	P, T, P^2, T^2, V_c	$R, P, (P-T)^2, (P-T)^3$
Closeness to Target	$P, \Delta R$	$P, T, A, (t-1)$
IDEAL TARGET		
Production	$I(t-1), P(t-1), T(t-1)$	$I(t-1), P(t-1)$
Closeness to Target	$I(t-1), \|P(t-1) - T(t-1)\|$	$P(t-1), I(t-1)$
FINAL TARGET		
Production	M, I	$I, M, \|P(t-1) - T(t-1)\|$
Closeness to Target	M, I	I
PERCEIVED VIOLATIONS		
Production	C_v^2	P, T
Closeness to Target	$\|P-T\|, V_p(t-1)$	$C_{v_1} I$

where:

$$
\begin{aligned}
P &= \text{Output} \\
T &= \text{Final Target} \\
V_C &= \text{Number of Confessed Violations} \\
R &= \text{Managing Director's Rating} \\
M &= \text{Managers Target Estimate} \\
I &= \text{Initial Target} \\
R(t-1) &= \text{Managing Director's rating previous month} \\
\Delta R &= R - R(t-1) \\
I(t-1) &= \text{Initial Target previous month} \\
P(t-1) &= \text{Output previous month} \\
T(t-1) &= \text{Final Target previous month} \\
A(t-1) &= \text{Assessment level of manager previous month} \\
V_C(t-1) &= \text{Perceived Violation previous month}
\end{aligned}
$$

As far as the effectiveness of the styles was concerned, there was no significant differences between the output levels achieved. However, those using Style I were significantly less successful in estimating the true state of affairs at the factories than those using Style II at the 5% level.

5.   CONCLUSION

This paper has illustrated the effect of various methods of performance appraisal on both the motivation of subordinates and their manipulation of information flows. It has been shown that the difference between a Managing Director's actual and perceived operating positions consists of two components: a change in uncertainty level and a shift along a surface of constant entropy.

The analysis of the results obtained from the behaviour of two groups of managers shows that these positions and the differences betweeen them can vary with both the output level and the Managing Director's main objective. Although the differences were generally relatively small, three extreme conditions were noted and, except in the case where production was the main objective, these differences tended to increase with the level of output.

On inspection of the time histories two different styles of leadership were discerned and, although there was no significant difference between the output levels obtained, one style was significantly more successful in discerning the true state of affairs than the other. Data from a further seven courses is in the process of being analysed and it is hoped that these data will give further insights into the effectiveness of various styles of leadership.

In reviewing the performance of participants at both parts of the game, it was interesting to note that some, by skillful manipulation of their superiors, achieved considerable success as subordinates but later failed miserably to show any ability as leaders when they were promoted. In contrast, there were others who showed initially far less skill as manipulators of information but later demonstrated that they could be very effective leaders. With further development this line of research may give valuable insights into the selection of leaders in large organisations.

APPENDIX A

INTERNATIONAL CASTINGS LTD

International Castings Ltd is a company engaged in the multiple process production of a variety of finished engineering components. One of its factories specialises in the production of "clunks" and its operational characteristics are summarised as follows:

1. There are 28 Grade I men, 32 Grade II men, and 8 maintenance men on the staff, plus 2 non-productive foremen and 2 inspectors.

2. There are 30 Grade I machines available and the remaining machines are Grade II, of which there are an unlimited supply.

3. The number of clunks turned out by men and machines is given by the following table:

Clunks Produced Per Hour:

	Grade I men	Grade II men
Grade I machines	5	3
Grade II machines	2	1

4. The maximum length of time that any machine can be used on one shift is 12 hours because the machine needs to be reset and any clunks produced beyond this time have very little chance of passing inspection.

5. There is always a chance of a machine breaking down and it is observed that this seems to increase if maintenance men are used in production and if machines are utilised for more than 10 hours per day.

6. Absenteeism among the men is seasonally affected and there is a marked increase if men work more overtime than that recommended.

7. There is a probability of any casting being scrapped. This has been observed to be greater for Grade II men than Grade I men. It is also increased if men work more overtime than that recommended (tired work) or if machine utilisation exceeds 10 hours per day (some machines need to be reset to the correct tolerances). If the scrap ratio, as measured by the scrap divided by the actual number of clunks produced, is greater than 10% then in the next period 2 maintenance men have to be placed on special duty, checking the condition of all the machines. However, every four months or so, it is possible to obtain some clunks (illegal) from an external

source; the costs can be lost in general sub-contracting expenses.

8. The number of clunks actually produced per month need not be correctly declared, a stock of finished clunks being distributed around the shop floor.

9. The effect of breaking the company rules, as far as the production of clunks goes, depends on which rules are broken and by how much. Some rule infringements have only an immediate effect on the production level; others affect the state of the plant in succeeding months.

10. The last six months production data for the firm is as follows:

Recorded Number of Clunks	Number of Rule Infringements Admitted
29583	0
27492	0
29981	0
30468	1
30298	0
31284	1

The company rules for the running of the clunk production plant are as follows:

1. The men only work one shift of forty hours per week and the maximum overtime allowed on top of this is 2720 hours per month.

2. The maximum overtime which can be allocated to any one man should be ten hours per week.

3. The men should only do their appointed tasks, e.g. maintenance men should be wholly employed in resetting and repairing machines and not used for production.

4. All the clunks produced and passed by inspection should be recorded as production for the month.

5. All clunks should be made on the company's equipment.

APPENDIX B

From a typical computer printout for the Factory Manager Exercise:

Month 1

```
THIS MONTH GENERAL MANAGER WILL REWARD MOST
HIGHLY CLOSENESS TO TARGET
LETS DISCUSS A TARGET
GENERAL MANAGER SUGGESTS 31300
HOW MANY CLUNKS DO YOU THINK YOU CAN MAKE THIS
MONTH?
?30000
YOUR TARGET FOR THIS MONTH IS 30500
YOU HAVE:
   28 GRADE 1 MEN
   32 GRADE 2 MEN
    8 MAINTENANCE MEN
HOW MANY MAINTENANCE MEN DO YOU WISH TO HAVE
ON PRODUCTION?
? 0
HOURS OVERTIME PER MAN PER WEEK
   GRADE 1? 10
OVERTIME ALLOCATED SO FAR 1120
```

```
    GRADE 2? 10
OVERTIME ALLOCATED SO FAR 2400
    MAINTENANCE? 10
TOTAL OVERTIME ALLOCATED THIS MONTH 2720
GRADE 1 MACHINES IN USE 30
NUMBER OF GRADE 2 M/C BREAKDOWNS 2
NUMBER OF CLUNKS PRODUCED BY MID-MONTH 16928.5
WHAT PERCENTAGE OF CLUNKS DO YOU WISH TO
WITHHOLD?
? 0
THE NUMBER OF CLUNKS RECORDED THIS MONTH
WAS 33245
HOW MANY RULES DID YOU BREAK THIS MONTH?
? 0
YOUR PERFORMANCE RATING LAST MONTH WAS 94.062
                 ...AND AVERAGE SO FAR 94.062
```

APPENDIX C

From a typical computer printout for the Managing Director Exercise:

Month 1

Manager 1

```
RATE HIS PERFORMANCE LAST MONTH ON SCALE 0-100
? 80
WAS THIS
1. GOOD?
2. SATISFACTORY?
3. POOR?
TYPE 1,2 OR 3
? 2
ADVICE TO MANAGER
THIS MONTH I WILL REWARD MOST HIGHLY
1. HIGH PRODUCTION
2. MEETING THE TARGET
3. THE TRUTH
TYPE 1,2 OR 3
? 1
HOW MANY CLUNKS WOULD YOU LIKE PRODUCED THIS MONTH?
? 34000
MANAGER'S PRODUCTION ESTIMATE IS 29000
TARGET THIS MONTH?
? 32000
CLUNKS RECORDED THIS MONTH 31808
MANAGER 1 CONFESSES TO BREAKING 0 RULES
HOW MANY RULES DO YOU THINK HE HAS BROKEN?
? 0
YOUR RATING THIS MONTH 82.0533
```

REFERENCES

1. BEER, S., "Cybernetics - A Systems Approach to Management," Personnel Review, Vol. 1, No. 1, Spring, 1972.
2. TRANKELL, A., Reliability of Evidence, Beckmans, Stockholm, 1972.
3. REVANS, R. W., "The Structure of Disorder," Survey of Cybernetics, J. Rose (ed.), ILEFFE, 1969.
4. PEARCE, F. T., "Business Intelligence Systems: The Need, Development and Integration," Industrial Marketing Management, Vol. 5, 1976.
5. WILLIAMSON, D. E., The Economics of Discretionary Behaviour: Managerial Objectives in a Theory of a Firm, Prentice Hall, 1964.
6. SCHIFF, M. and A. Y. LEWIN, "The Impact of People on Budgets," The Accounting Review, XLV, April, 1970.
7. LOWE, A. E. and R. W. SHAW, "An Analysis of Managerial Biassing: Evidence from a Company's Budgetary Process," Journal of Management Studies, Vol. 5, No. 3, October 1968.
8. CYERT, R. M., J. G. MARSH and W. M. STARBUCK, "Two Experiments on Rise and Conflict in Organisational Estimation," Management Science, VII, 1961.
9. The Listener, 30 October, 1975.
10. LUCAS, F. L., The Delights of Dictatorship, W. Heffer and Sons Ltd., Cambridge, 1938.
11. WILLMER, M. A. P., "The Priest and the President," Management in Action, Vol. 5, No. 60, September, 1974.
12. STEAD, P. J., The Police of Paris, Staples Press Ltd., London, 1957.
13. The Sunday Times, 12 December, 1971.
14. The Times, 16 May, 1972.
15. WILLMER, M. A. P. and A. J. BERRY, "Management Performance and System Uncertainty," paper presented at the Third European Meeting on Cybernetics and Systems Research, Vienna, 1976.
16. SHANNON, C. E. and W. WEAVER, The Mathematical Theory of Communication," University of Illinois Press, 1949.
17. WILLMER, M. A. P., Crime and Information Theory, Edinburgh University Press, 1970.
18. BEER, S., The Brain of the Firm, Allen Lane, 1972.

Decision making in state administration

WOLFGANG ZEHETNER and HELMUT HIRSCH
Federal Ministry for Trade and Industry, Vienna, Austria

1. STATE ADMINISTRATION VS. BUSINESS MANAGEMENT

1.1. In the given context of an organization and concerned people outside the organization, it is easier for the elements within the organization to agree on the objectives of the organization than the concerned people outside it.

The Austrian Minister for Trade and Industry took measures during the oil crisis 1973-74 such as speed limits and days without cars (autolose Tage) [1], which the population could not have decided so quickly if at all. Consensus among the civil servants working out the details of the regulations was quickly established. Politically speaking, this is a case of crisis management which is exceptional in a democratic system. Under normal circumstances, vehement protests and reactions would have followed such a decision, in spite of the internal agreement reached.

1.2. The objectives of business management are primarily self-determined, whereas the objectives of state administration are primarily determined by external factors.

The decision on a business firm's activities within a certain branch of the economy is basically made according to the will of the businessmen within the firm. Certainly, there is a range of external factors and conditions considered during the making of the decision, such as marketing research, the legal aspect, etc., but the business aim is set internally. For example, the production and the sale of a certain product is decided by the enterprise. Future merchants and buyers of the product are only marginally involved in the decision process or are excluded. Considering a consumers' poll, this would not be a true co-decision. A poll is used only to improve sales figures, but its character does not reflect a democratic decision process. (An election poll would not be considered democratic enough to act as a substitute for elections.) Besides, not all of the future merchants and consumers are interviewed, but only a selection of them. After all, it is up to the enterprise to use the results of the poll and to evaluate them in the light of their own intentions.

The occupation of state administration with economic affairs is due to the desire of many elements (business firms, consumers) outside state administration. Single elements profiting from certain economic situations do not desire the participation and control of state administration. Those, however, who have a disadvantage from such situations desire it and are successful when they gain enough political weight. The desire for the state's participation correlates to a fear of anarchism.

The same is true for other fields of state administration, such as social affairs, education, military defense, transport, etc. Certainly, there is a range of internal determinants. Often they correspond to the "know how", while the external determinants correspond to the "know what".

A. Because of this, decision making in business management is easier than decision making in state administration; decision making in state administration is more difficult because of the external determination of its objectives.

Consider, e.g., price regulations of energy. The aim of a business firm is to sell petrol with as much profit as possible. Therefore, if it had the choice, it would decide against a price regulation for petrol.

State administration is confronted with the desire of consumers to fix a maximum price for petrol. On the other side, it is confronted with the adverse desire of the petro-selling firm. Given enough weight from regulation supporters, the decision can be found in a difficult process. A price limitation has to take place on economic and legal grounds and must respect the petrol-selling firm.

A concrete price regulation case will start, e.g., when the firm finds out that the regulated maximum price is no longer sufficient. The firm decides to apply to state administration for a higher price and produces information to submit along with the application. State administration, in this case the Ministry for Trade and Industry, not only has to examine such an application, but has to actively involve the representatives of lobby-like institutions such as those of economy, agriculture and labor. (Besides, the Ministry for Trade and Industry has to involve other institutions of state administration: the Ministries for Agriculture, for Social Affairs, for Finance [2].) Those involved externally themselves have to go through a process of pre-decisions.

1.3. The more the elements participating in moulding the objectives of an organization lie outside the organization, the more difficult will be its decision making.

This can be illustrated by the course of the nuclear debate in Austria, where different phases in the extent of participation in the conflict can be distinguished [3]:

a. The initial decision to use nuclear energy in Austria was not made by the state administration, but the economy, namely, by the nationalized but largely autonomous electrical utilities, in the late 1960's. State administration was involved mainly as responsible controller of electrical utilities in their task of supplying Austria with sufficient electrical energy. The decision was easy and unanimous. State made it possible by creating the legal foundations necessary to its implementation: Radiological Protection Act (Strahlenschutzgesetz, BGBl. 227/1969), Electricity Promotion Act (Elektrizitäts-förderungsgesetz, BGBl. 19/1970 and 297/1975), and Atomic Liability Act (Atomhaftpflichtgesetz BGBl. 117/1964).

b. In the following years, a few scientists and civil rights groups drew public attention to the risks arising from the so-called peaceful use of nuclear energy. Initially a rather small movement, public opposition to nuclear energy has grown more and more until 1976, when Austria's first nuclear plant should have gone into operation. In addition, knowledge of accidents in and health hazards from operating nuclear plants has spread.

c. All this caused a nationwide nuclear debate; the industrial groups, the scientists, and the politicians who were pro-nuclear in the first place and therefore had not seen the need to extend their arguments in public actively entered the discussion.

d. Finally, the issue is treated on the political level: Political parties, the government, associations of employers and employees, parliament, newspapers and television, all take their share in the discussion. An information campaign was organized by state administration with discussions of proponents and opponents of nuclear energy throughout the country. The result of this has been that the controversy now to a large extent is carried out on the back of state administration, and creates difficult situations for the competent authorities, e.g., the Federal Ministry for Health and Protection of the Environment, which has to implement the Radiological Protection Act, and thus the licensing procedures for nuclear installations. The latter have to proceed solely on the grounds of the existing laws. This is completely independent of the public controversy and of the discussions on the political level, as long as parliament does not change those laws.

The Ministry, however, does not feel happy in initiating decisions which are likely to lead to political disturbances. In the present situation it is risky to give permits for the operation of nuclear plants as long as the political discussion is going on. It is risky because many public statements made by politicians relate to issues concerning such permits. They reduce the scope state administration has for the interpretation of laws and regulations without in any way

supporting it to find a decision.

The government's report on nuclear energy, e.g., states that the question of final disposal of nuclear waste has to be solved before the operating license for a nuclear power station can be given. When is it possible to say that the solution to this problem has been found? Is the trust in the progress of science which is able to solve anything in time sufficient? Can an 80% solution be accepted when facing the threat of future energy shortages? When can one be sure that none of the local communities near a planned storage facility will protest?

A. Hence decision making in state administration will be more difficult, considering the variety and number of external participating elements.

From this follows another distinction between state administration and business management: While business management disposes of given resources and has to formulate its objectives accordingly -- within the basic framework of profit maximization -- state administration is given the objectives first and subsequently has to raise the funds necessary for their implementation [4].

1.4. The more difficult the decision making of an organization, the less dynamic the organization's activities; paths leading to complicated decisions are avoided wherever possible.

State administration generally tries to gain as many competences as possible. This has often been attacked but it is based on a clear interest: if anything goes wrong, then state administration is blamed automatically, independent of its degree of involvement.

Therefore, state administration is interested, e.g., in measures relating to a planned economy for raw materials. In this field, many economical and political interests are concerned, and many conflicts exist. Private industry, in particular, has a strong aversion against any signs of central planning by the state. In such a situation, only very little is actually done: Under the existing law, only the flows of scrap from iron and other metals can be controlled; these are the only items. All other items cannot be controlled at all or only in times of a crisis [5].

2. THE CHALLENGE TO STATE ADMINISTRATION: STATIC VS. DYNAMIC PRACTICE

2.1. In state administration, objectives may be clearly defined or less clearly defined.

A. Clearly defined objectives prevail in non-controversial and/or repeatedly occuring situations.

An example for a clearly defined objective is the licensing procedure for obtaining permission to run an inn or a restaurant [6]. In order to obtain the license, one has to fulfill certain conditions, such as a good reputation, a certain educational standard, sufficient hygienic conditions, no disturbances to the neighbourhood by noise or smell, etc. If all conditions are given, the applicant is certain to get his license.

B. Ill-defined objectives prevail in controversial and/or seldomly occuring situations.

As an example of an ill-defined objective, one may take the licensing of a nuclear plant, as indicated above. As shown there, political factors influence the licensing procedure.

2.2. Clearly defined objectives result in decision activities of a static type; less clearly defined objectives can result in dynamic type activities.

The information policy on nuclear energy [7] illustrates the possibility for dynamic type activities.

Usually, the handling of new tasks is first tried in a rigid, schematic style. Such an approach could not be sufficient at all when the government ordered state administration to plan and implement an information campaign on nuclear energy matters.

There were interests and pressures from all sides: The government wanted a smooth functioning of the campaign. The civil rights groups wanted to gain as much space as possible to express their point of view and accused the organizers of the campaign of manipulation. The electrical utilities and the nuclear industry criticized that nuclear opponents were allowed to speak too long at the debates and that they would make the population insecure and manipulate it.

Therefore, a flexible approach was necessary. The concept of the campaign had to be altered many times; many additional contacts and unexpected steps were necessary in order to create a suitable basis for the campaign. Time was not only pressing, but the politicians induced changes of the timetable whenever the political situation varied.

A. The activities of static type decision making are easy to plan and execute, whereas those of dynamic type are difficult to plan and manage.

2.3. Static type decision activities cover the control of system disturbances which can be foreseen and relate to clear objectives; dynamic type decision activities correspond to less controlled system disturbances arising from less clearly defined objectives.

2.4. Because of its complex, hierarchical, slowly changing structure, state administration has to rely on clear objectives and on the practice of static decision making. On the other hand it has to accommodate dynamic decision practice in as far as other more rapidly changing areas of society affect it.

In the hierarchical structure of state administration, newcomers on the staff have to deal firstly with routine jobs, while those who stand higher in the hierarchy in most cases deal with the more intricate and dynamic type jobs. Unfortunately, the latter are usually less flexible and less open to new ideas.

There is, however, a twofold influence on state administration pushing it to more dynamic decision practice initiated by newcomers: They are usually graduates of a modern education system and have a stronger sensibility for and knowledge of modern social problems. This forms the basis for a more dynamic pace seen either directly when the new employee handles dynamic type activities himself or indirectly when he discusses such matters with his superiors.

A. Several centuries of steady development of bureaucratic structures have left their mark on present-day state administration.

Structures such as the competence catalogue of ministries as well as their division in sections, departments, etc., alter very slowly. It is fairly easy to acquire a new competence, but it is very complicated to transfer a single competence from one department to another, or from one section to another. For the switch from one ministry to another, new laws would even be necessary. The last time that the structure of competence between ministries was changed was 5 years ago, by the Federal Ministries Act (Bundesministeriengesetz, BGBl. 389/1973 [8]). Usually, civil servants strongly resist such changes. It often happens that departments are restructured only after their head has retired.

This often leads to an extraordinarily high work load in single departments, as even the addition of new posts to a unit is very complicated (and seen with jealously by the others), while other departments in the same house may have almost no work to do.

The Section V of the Ministry for Trade and Industry, e.g., is severely overburdened. This section, responsible for the energy sector as far as economic aspects are concerned, has a high work load especially since the energy crisis of 1973-74, and the subsequent foundation of the International Energy Agency of which Austria is a member [9]. Also, it has to deal with most aspects of the nuclear energy debate and associated activities. In spite of the pressing situation on the energy sector, there are at present only 32 civil servants to do the conceptual work.

B. In the long run, dynamic decision practice has a tendency either to convert to static decision practice or to die out without much effect.

After the oil crisis of 1973-74, when there was a high consciousness in state administration for the value of domestic resources of oil and other minerals, a new law was made to promote the exploration and mining of domestic mineral resources, the Mining Act (Bergesetz, BGBl. 259/1975). Exploration and mining rights for oil and natural gas are granted by the state in the legal form of contracts.

In 1977, most of the old exploration and mining contracts ran out. In the discussion about the renewal of these contracts and over the interpretation of the old contracts (where some obligations had not yet been fulfilled by the companies), a conflict arose between the Ministry for Trade and Industry on the one side and the ÖMV-Aktiengesellschaft (which is state owned) and the Rohöl-Aufsuchungsgesellschaft (which is privately owned) on the other. This conflict brought about a phase of dynamic activities for the administration, which demanded:
- more royalties,
- adaptation of the contracts to the new Mining Act,
- better control of the companies to ensure the carrying out of contractual objectives such as new exploratory activities,
- better control of the companies' management policies,
- better control of energy import, in particular of gas
- shorter contract times.

Since February 1978, the conflict has gradually been settled. In the discussions a unanimous solution seems to be near; contracts will be made probably over a long period of time, otherwise most wishes of the Ministry will be fulfilled. Therefore the issue of domestic exploration and mining rights will again turn static.

An example of an issue which died out is the question of an additional year in high school education: In the early sixties there was a heavy debate on educational policy in Austria. As a result an additional year was introduced for high schools to be implemented in the mid-sixties. As time passed and the realization of the planned year came nearer, more and more difficulties appeared. Finally, the additional year was provisionally cancelled. This still is the state of the matter today, and the debate has been dropped.

C. Dynamic decision practice is necessary for the function of static decision practice.

Static practice has a tendency to become out of date and unfitting. Therefore, once in a while dynamic phases will become necessary. Before the cited debate on the renewal of the oil and gas exploration and mining contracts there was a static period of over 20 years, when contracts were based on regulations which were decided upon even before the Austrian State Treaty of 1955 when Austria gained independence.

D. Dynamic decision practice is less determined by the hierarchical structure than static decision practice.

In general, this situation is partly taken account of by the creation of new organizational units which, even if formally placed within the structure, de facto stand outside it and are under the direct authority of the ministers (Departments for Basic Questions, "Grundsatzabteilungen"). The bureau of the minister may play a similar role, where very urgent tasks may be handled directly by the personal secretaries of the minister.

2.5. The elements outside state administration wish to control both the static and the dynamic processes of state administration.

An example for the public control of static processes is the criticism of the handling of certain laws through appeals to the Administrative or the Constitutional Courts.

During the licensing procedure for the first Austrian nuclear power plant near Zwentendorf, the administration refused to grant several people the status of being a neighbour ("Anrainer") of the plant. This status would imply a stronger position during the course of the licensing procedure with the right to assert arguments and to fight the administration's decisions directly. These people insisted on legally being declared neighbours of the Zwentendorf plant even when not living in the immediate vicinity of Zwentendorf. Recently, in the course of the appeal, the Administrative Court granted them this right, which means that probably the whole procedure will have to be repeated by the administration under much more difficult circumstances [10].

An example of the control of dynamic processes is the information campaign on nuclear energy. This campaign did not follow static rules, and a variety of dynamic means was used by the public, such as extensive participation in the public debates, occupation of the halls where they took place, demonstrations, etc.

3. DECISION THEORY VS. DECISION PRACTICE

3.1. Decision activities in state administration are determined to a large extent by laws and regulations.

A. This applies to decision activities relating to the interaction between the elements within and outside state administration and especially to the interaction of the elements within state administration.

B. The interaction of the elements within state administration is determined by an elaborate, rigidly defined hierarchical structure.

This rigid determination is due to principles common to all bureaucratic institutions and appears in business management as well [11].
In all cases, the Austrian ministries are organized in the following way [12]:
1. sections
2. departments
Additionally, some departments may be combined to form a group, some departments may be divided into divisions. The minister himself is the head of the bureau of the minister, where he has usually two to five personal secretaries. The organization of a ministry can therefore appear as follows:
1. bureau of the minister
2. sections
3. groups
4. departments
5. divisions

Each of these units has a head who is responsible for his unit. Each civil servant is assigned to a department or, if a division exists, to a division -- except the head of a unit [13].

If somebody sends a request, e.g., concerning a nuclear matter, to the Ministry for Trade and Industry and addresses it to the minister personally, the procedure might be as follows:

First, it goes to the bureau of the minister, where the minister's secretary will confer with the minister about it. The secretary then passes the letter on to the energy section. From the head of this section, it goes to the department dealing with nuclear affairs, where the head of the department will give it to one of the assigned civil servants who will do the actual work, gathering information and drafting the answer. However, the reply the civil servant produced still has to be approved by all in the hierarchy above him. That means that the heads of the departments or the sections can modify and change the draft according to their feeling and/or knowledge on how the next superior would approve it. This is usually done by throwing the whole thing back to the civil servant at the bottom with some short notes attached to it.

Therefore, as several people have to sign the draft and are responsible for it, it can go back and forth several times until the last revision has perfected it sufficiently to be an answer of the minister to the party outside the ministry. Of course, this takes some time.

It can take even more time and be more complicated if the order for such a draft is passed through additional levels such as groups and divisions. Sometimes the matter is solved by not working on it for a while until its importance has decreased so that an answer seems no longer necessary.

In other cases, official channels have to be used as well. If a division requests an opinion on an issue from another division which belongs to another department, an official note has to be written which goes from one department head to the head of the other department. This can happen even when the divisions are in the same house, on the same floor, only a few meters apart.

There are even more complicated channels. If, for instance, a journey has to be made to an OECD-conference in Paris, this has to be approved of by the Federal Chancellor personally. The civil servant who is to attend the conference in Paris has to fill in the forms at least one month before. The application for approval has to pass about 24 official points before it returns to him, with the approval of the Federal Chancellor. Without this approval, no travel expenses will be paid. It often happens that the civil servant hears only one or two hours before the departure of his train or flight that the Chancellor has signed.

3.2. The laws and regulations determining decision making in state administration constitute the decision theory of state administration.

3.3. Decision theory of state administration is produced by elements outside and within it and concerns elements outside and within it.

Laws can be decided only by legislation, the parliament, in order to be valid. Still, most laws are initiated by the government and constructed as drafts by state administration, e.g., the drafts for the Oil Stocking and Reporting Act and the Energy Control Act are created mainly by the legal experts in the Energy Section of the Ministry for Trade and Industry.

In addition to formulating the text of the law, organisational and coordinating activity is necessary: political parties, lobbies, and other institutions and groups have to be confronted with the draft and have the right to comment on it. Attention has to be paid to their modifying proposals. Finally, last minute changes occuring in parliament have to be integrated swiftly [14].

On the other hand, the population itself can initiate laws under certain circumstances ("Volksbegehren"). Lobbies can make their own proposals for the draft of a law. Laws can also be drafted and proposed by groups of members of parliament.

On the whole, it clearly appears that legislation -- formally the producer of laws, the producer of decision theory -- mainly has a controlling and filtering function, but does not fulfill that position which it has been attributed to by the theories of modern democracy, like the system of checks and balances.

Clearly, the decision theory of state administration concerns the whole population; furthermore, the administration itself has to respect it in many ways.

The position of the staff of state administration, e.g., is controlled by a wide range of rules and regulations in very detailed ways [15]. The intensity of this control by decision theory is much stronger than in business management.

A. Decision theory of state administration is produced with two aims in view: control of the objectives by state administration, and control of state administration itself.

Decision theory is produced, in accordance with the Austrian Federal Constitution, to provide a lawful basis for the activities of state administration in controlling objectives. (Art. 18 of the Constitution: "The whole state administration may be exercised on the grounds of the laws only.")

The foundations for the control of state administration itself are also laid down in the Constitution (control by parliament, the Administrative Court, the Constitutional Court, etc.). For example, the ministers, who are at the same time political functionaries and heads of state administration, are responsible to parliament for their work (cf. Art. 74, 76 and 142 of the Constitution).

3.4. Decision theory defines some objectives clearly, others less clearly.

An example of a very elastic determination is provided by §4 of the Radiological Protection Act: "Every effect of ionising radiation on the human body is, within the permitted radiation dose defined by this federal law, to be kept as low as possible."

How can the term "as low as possible" be understood? Biologically? (by considering the damaging effects of certain radiation doses?): Technically? (by working with the best possible technical methods?); Economically (setting the limit where nuclear plants become too expensive to produce electricity at competitive prices?); Politically? (setting the limit where it is just tolerated by the population?).

On the other hand, the conditions for obtaining a state license to exercise, e.g., the shoemaker's, tailor's, or carpenter's trade, are very clearly and unambiguously defined by law (cf. 2.1 A).

3.5. Decision practice must be based on the knowledge of decision theory.

    A. Decision practice tends to be static because it is controlled by decision theory.

As described in 2.5, the administration for the province of Lower Austria has given, based on a wrong interpretation of decision theory, certain licenses for the nuclear plant near Zwentendorf. The Administrative Court has revoked these decisions.
This revocation may seriously hinder the procedure of completing the Zwentendorf nuclear plant and reduce the dynamics of the licensing process.

    B. Decision practice tends to be static because it is dependent on the knowledge of decision theory.

Many issues of everyday life seem to be similar to the layman, but have to be considered differently from the legal expert's standpoint. This means that state administration frequently has to examine every single issue for the existence of laws, regulations and Administrative and Constitutional Courts' decisions in order to be sure that the decision cannot be changed by appeals.

3.6. The better the knowledge of decision theory, the more dynamic decision practice; wellknown constraints are less of a hindrance than poorly-known ones.

    A. The better the knowledge of the process of decision theory production, the more dynamic decision practice.

In the summer of 1977, the Federal Ministry for Finance introduced a new regulation to the mandatory insurance for motor vehicles (Haftpflichversicherung), the "Bonus-Malus-System", which increases the insurance premium for bad drivers while the accident-free driver gradually acquires a no-claim bonus.
The introduction of this new system is very problematic, but the legal experts in the Ministry for Finance know the legal situation and the decision theory producing process very well. Therefore they expected with a 70% probability that the Administrative Court would not reject it.
Result: After a lawyer's appeal, the Admin-

istrative Court approved the ministry's point of view. If the Administrative Court would have revoked it, the ministry would have presented a new draft to parliament without delay -- as it was already prepared "in reserve" -- producing a secure basis for the Bonus-Malus-System also taking into account the Administrative Court's opinion.

4. DECISION MAKING VS. CONTROL

4.1. Both internal and external elements of state administration want control. At present, control is exercised on the basis of decision theory and via decision theory producing process.

Periodically, the population has the possibility to decide on the composition of the legislative body by parliamentary elections. This provides no direct power to influence the composition of state administration itself, but a certain influence on the formation of its leadership (the strongest political group usually forms the government) andon the basic trends of future legal activities, therefore, an influence on decision theory (and via decision theory on decision practice).

    A. Internal control is guaranteeed by the hierarchical structure of state administration.

With the development of the modern constitutional state, a relation based on laws was formed between the state and its civil servants.
Article 18 of the Constitution states: "The whole state administration may be exercised on the grounds of laws only." Article 20: "Under the guidance of the highest organs administration is handled by . . . assigned professionals according to the determinations of the laws."
As in other Western countries (cf. the present discussion on the reform of the civil servant's legal status in the USA [16]), the professional civil servants' status is guaranteed and manifested as that of a highly important supporter of the modern state, ensuring its continuity.
There is still the hierarchical structure of state administration, which is to be seen as a problem as it impedes the development of individual initiative; on the other hand it can be seen as a condition for the orderly function of the administration within the legal framework.

4.2. External control is exercised in a one-way circle; some elements exert a more direct control. This given form of control makes decision activities of state administration too static, and limits the influence of the population in the process of decision making (see Figure 1).

In the figure, the one-way control between legislation and government represents a simplified picture (cf. 3.3).
Nominally, large parts of the population are organized in lobbies. There are many organizations which can represent the same person several

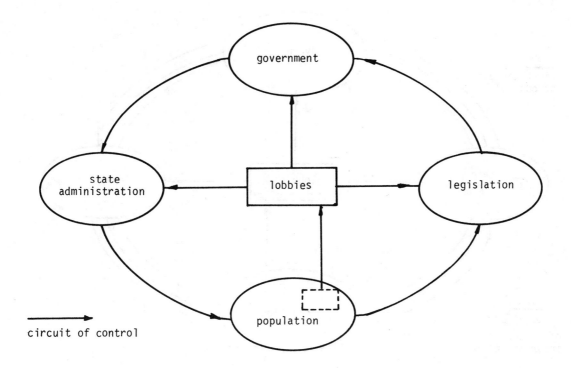

Figure 1. Control of State Administration

times (e.g., party, trade union, student union, mandatory health insurance association, etc.). However, only a small part of the population decides on lobbies' policy.

As an example of the attitude of the Austrian Trade Union Association (Österreichischer Gewerkschaftsbund, ÖGB) towards nuclear energy may be mentioned. This is a clear case of opinion making from the top downwards [17]. Very early the trade unions took up a position that was doubtlessly pro-nuclear. Certainly, in the union's magazines ("Solidarität", etc.) some nuclear opponents were invited to write articles as well. But the president of the OGB, Anton Benya, always emphasized that nuclear energy is necessary for Austria; he expressed this standpoint in public a long time before discussions of the nuclear issue started among the trade union members on a large scale.

The power of even very small lobbies to effectively delay important decisions can be illustrated by the case of the European Patent Agreement:

Since 1977, this agreement is to be ratified by Austria. It is very important for the Austrian economy, as it unifies the international patent laws, exonerates the Austrian patent Office, and is a further step towards European economic integration. The situation is urgent, because the European Patent Office will be opened on June 1, 1978 and it would be advantageous if Austria could participate right from the beginning.

The Chamber of Patent Attorneys, which is involved in the discussions preliminary to the ratification process, however, heavily opposes the agreement because it fears the loss of specific material advantages. (At the Austrian Patent Office, the assistance of a patent attorney is

mandatory, whereas at the European Patent Office, where the patent rights can be acquired for Austria as well as in the case of ratification, there is no such obligation; besides, patent attorneys of other nationality may be employed.)

The opposition of the Patent Attorneys' Chamber caused endless and fruitless debates; other lobbies which are not directly concerned, such as the Federal Chamber of Engineers, declared themselves against the European Patent Agreement as well out of solidarity.

Nevertheless, the agreement is likely to be adopted, because the large lobbies, such as the Chamber of Commerce and the Chamber of Employees, are strongly in favor of it because of its usefulness for the Austrian economy. Still, much time has been lost, and Austria's late entry makes a difficult start for cooperation.

4.3. As a proposal for improving the situation, a second circuit of control and information flow should be established (see Figure 2).

In the light of the difficult situation analyzed here, it is impossible to offer a detailed concept for improving the situation for the near future. As a start, we propose that civic councils (Bürgerbeiräte) be created at the ministries. These councils should not only be appealed to in the course of a complaint, but should have the basic right to gain information concerning all ongoing administrative activities.

Regular meetings with leading civil servants should be held. This would move civil servants to communicate knowledge to the "normal" population, based on their expertise, and to modify their expert language to make it understandable.

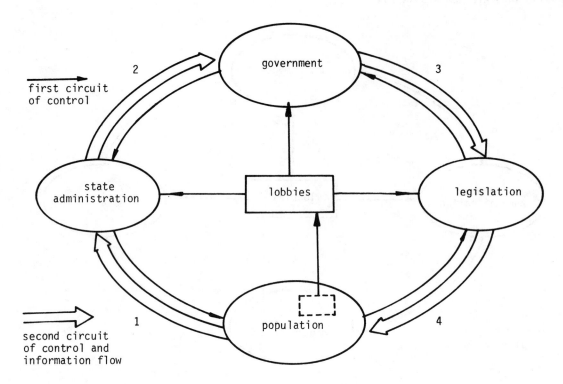

Figure 2. Improved Control of State Administration - Phase One

This would lead to more democratic activities of the civil servants [18], as they gain insights into the wishes of the population. The councils should be given the possibility of participating in all administrative procedures according to the desire of the population.

Such councils have their sister institutions in many countries in the form of public participation at the judicial courts, such as the grand juries. In Austria, there are jurors and lay assessors (Geschworenen and Schöffen) who contribute to a legal process. (Cf. Article 91 of the Austrian Constitution: "The population has to cooperate at the jurisdiction.")

We propose to integrate a corresponding article into the Constitution and into the legal order on the cooperation of the population in state administration. These councils should also have the right, together with civil servants but also on their own, to address themselves to the government in matters of higher importance (arrow 2, Figure 2).

Regarding arrow 3 of Figure 2, it has been stated (3.3 B) that it is already established to a very large, perhaps even too large, extent.

Arrow 4 should be understood not as control (which would be paradoxical) but as a continuous flow of information about the ongoing work of legislation to the population. Contacts between the members of parliament and their voters already exist, but are very weak, partly because of an election system which guarantees proportional representation in parliament for every party but creates no strong link between the constituencies and their candidates (see, e.g., in France and the U. K.).

A. This change would make decision practice accessible to public control and a better feedback between decision practice and decision theory would be established.

B. Direct public control of decision practice would increase its dynamic element.

By way of the civic councils, the actual complaints and wishes of the population would have a direct and unfiltered influence on state administration; the civil servants -- naturally somewhat disturbed in their routine work -- would be forced to react quickly and efficiently in a dynamic way.

C. Direct public control of decision practice would increase the difficulties of decision making.

This directly follows from the fact that the influence of external elements is strengthened (cf. 1.1).

4.4. Finally, the whole population should adopt the central position which is today held by farious lobbies (see Figure 3).

A. This would mean a step from today's representative democratic system towards a participative democratic system.

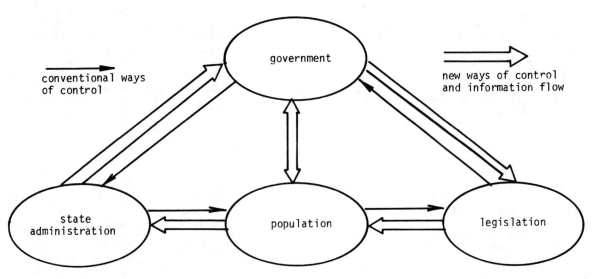

Figure 3. Improved Control of State Administration - Phase Two

REFERENCES AND NOTES

1. HIRSCH, H., W. HALADA, and W. ZEHETNER, "Die Entwicklung des Energiesektors - Auswirkungen und Gegenmaßnahmen," in: Folgeprobleme von Wachstumskrisen in Österreich, B. Tichatschek-Marin (ed.), Europaverlag, Wien, 1978.

2. Experts of lobbies and ministries are cooperating in the Commission for Prices (Preiskommission) at the Ministry for Trade and Industry, as regulated by the Price Act (Preisgesetz, BGBl. 260/1976). This law has to be extended about every two years after debates between administration, lobbies, and political parties.

3. HIRSCH, H., "Austria's Nuclear Debate," Austria Today II, 3/4, 19-20, 1976.
    HIRSCH, H., and H. NOWOTNY, "Europe's Nuclear Debate (1): Austria, A Case Study, Nature, 266, 5598, 107-108, 1977.
    HIRSCH, H., "Kernenergie: Pro und Contra. Die Informationskampagne Kernenergie der Österreichischen Bundesregierung - Analysen und Schlußfolgerungen," Physikalische Blatter, 33, 9, 385-395, 1977.
    HIRSCH, H., "The Nuclear Energy Information Campaign of the Austrian Government," Proceedings of the International Conference on Nuclear Power and its Fuel Cycle, Salzburg, published by IAEA, Vienna, Vol. 7, 219-136, 1977.
    HIRSCH, H., and H. NOWOTNY, Austria's Nuclear Energy Information Campaign, Minerva, in press.

4. KARNY, T., "Die Personalpolitik des Bundes," in: Die Diener des Staates, G. Engelmayer (ed.), Wien, 1977 (see in particular p. 307 f).

5. For controlling measures lobbies are involved as well. They cooperate with state administration in specific councils. Cf. the amendment to the Resources Control Act (BGBl. 320/1976) and the Energy Control Act (Energielenkungsgesetz, BGBl. 319/1976). These laws have to be extended about every two years after debates between state administration, lobbies, and political parties, like the Price Regulation Act (cf. Note 2).

6. Small Business and Industries Regulation Act (Gewerbeordnung, BGBl, 50/1974).

7. See references given in Note 3.

8. This law replaced provisions of 52 other laws, some of them dating back to the year 1848.

9. Austria doesn't have a good reputation at the headquarters of the International Energy Agency in Paris, where the Austrian energy program is considered to be "in a state of infancy." Cf. GRABER, K., "19 Staaten in der Energieagentur - Österreich Genießt Keinen Guten Ruf," in Die Presse, Wien, 29 March 1977.

10. The Administrative Court (Verwaltungsgerichtshof) declared that the decisive point is not whether rights of neighbours actually are violated but whether they could be violated. Cf. APA news release 048-ID and 053-ID, 27 February 1978; APA news release I 146 and I 147, 12 December 1977; and SCHMIEDL, H., "Neue Hürde für Zwentendorf," in: Kurier, Wien, 16 February 1978; "Neue Gutachten für Zwentendorf," in: Kronen-Zeitung, Wien, 2 March 1978.

11. TITSCHER, S., Struktur eines Ministeriums. Eine Verwaltungssoziologishe Studie zur Ministerialbürokratie, Wien, 1975 (cf. discussion of the advantages and disadvantages of bureaucracy).

12. Federal Ministries Act III, §7 (see this paper, 2.4 A).

13. According to a computation of Titscher (see Note 11), out of 139 civil servants in the Ministry for Trade and Industry with academic degrees, 41% were unit heads in 1972; 59% of the civil servants were assigned (Titscher, p. 179, Table 13.1; p. 181, Table 14).

14. Surprisingly, law schools as well as legal science literature take only little notice of state administration's contribution to the production process of decision theory. For example, in a widely used modern textbook on Austrian Constitutional Law-- excepting references to the government's right to initiate laws in parliament -- no information is given on this fact either in the chapter on legislation or in the chapter on ministers and ministries. See WALTER, R. and H. MAYER, Grundriß des Österreichischen Verfassungsrechtes, Wien, 1976, pp. 83-143, 171-175.

15. Cf. the updated compilations in the Union of Civil Servants' yearbooks, containing about 60 rules and regulations. In some years, a space of almost 1000 pages is used. The main principles of these provisions are the lifelong duration of the employment, the appointment according to the educational qualification, and the salary based on the principle of patriarchal care by the state. Cf. KARNY (Note 4); and HIEßMANSEDER, R., "Rechtliche Aspekte der Personalstruktur und der Berufslaufbahn," in Titscher (Note 11), p. 18 ff.

16. At present, there is a discussion on the reform of the laws regulating the legal status of civil servants in the USA. A reform project was presented by President Carter to the public on 2 March 1978. A main objective is the emphasis on performance incentives on the one hand and the permanent posts of civil servants on the other. There are more than 2.8 million civil servants in the USA; only 226 out of 18,000 discharged employees were dismissed in 1977 for not doing their work properly.

Cf. "The Battle over Bureaucracy," in: Time, 6 March 1978; H.E.T., "Reform des Beamtenrechtes in den Vereinigsten Staaten," in: Neue Zürcher Zeitung, March 5-6, 1978. In Austria, a new law regulating the status of civil servants was decided upon in 1977, the Civil Servants Act (Beamten-Dienstrechtsgesetz, 329/1977). This law replaced provisions of 12 other laws, some of which dated back to before World War I.

17. The President of the ÖGB, Anton Benya, as well as the Federal Board of the ÖGB, repeatedly declared the necessity of nuclear energy generation. Cf. APA news release I 180, 16 May 1977; "Benyo über Kernkraftwerke," in: Oberösterr. Nachrichten, Linz, 21 April 1977; APA news release I 189, 27 September 1977; APA news release 150-ID, 3 March 1978.

18. Civil servants basically disagree to such reforms, also, e.g., in the Federal Republic of Germany. Titscher (Note 11), p. 162, quotes the following paragraph of a study of the German Federal Ministry for Economy: "Eine Kontrolle durch das Parlament oder eine Beteiligung der Bürger bie Planunsentscheidungen wird von den Ministerialbeamten für überflüssig gehalten. Sie ist in der Praxis auch kaum durchführbar, weil Parlament und Öffentlichkeit auf die Informationen und Vorarbeiten der Bürokratie angewiesen sind. Die Folge ist eine zunehmende Verselbständigung der öffentlichen Verwaltung, die umso gefährlicher ist, weil die innere Struktur und die personelle Ausstattung der Bürokratie nicht die Gewähr dafür bieten, daß Verwaltungsentscheidungen fachlich abgesichert und demokratisch legitimiert sind." (MOTHS, E. and M. WULF-MATHIES, Des Bürgers teure Diener, Karlsruhe, 1973, p. 81.)

COGNITION AND LEARNING

Introduction

GORDON PASK
Systems Research Ltd., Richmond, England

In many ways this symposium served as a continuation of a dialogue in progress at the last Vienna symposium of the same title; many of the same participants took part in it. A full appreciation of the proceedings calls for reference to the previous debate; such is, and should be, the character of a learned (not earnest, but very serious as a result of it; a properly learned) society. This particular area of interest has peculiar features, even for cybernetics. There are few valid taxonomies in any part of cybernetics, it is true. But, in this area, there are positively none. So, as chairman, I positively refused to adhere to a timetable or to clamp down upon discussion or even to retain an original and quite arbitrary ordering. I regret the inconvenience this may have caused to people anxious to hear a particular, labeled, presentation; but assure them that the labels had little meaning though the presentations did, and the exchanges, discussions, and integration of the many perspectives, even more. To fully appreciate this symposium, you should refer (at least) to the last one. To make sense of it at all was necessary to attend a representative sample of the proceedings, as many of the participants did.

What came out of it? First, some very fundamental reappraisals of commonly accepted canons at a theoretical level by Elstob, Glanville, Hahn, Johnson, and Nowakoska. Both Dr. Gergely and Dr. Locker were unable to attend due to severe indisposition but were represented (their theoretical positions are stated among the published papers). My own paper might be added to this batch, for by "theory" I do not mean simply formal, let alone mathematical, manipulation stripped of all interpretation. Far from it. In most cases a leading seminal notion was the reinstatement of consciousness as a subject of scientific enquiry, which is entirely possible if classical stability criteria are considered as special cases of organizational closure and, in particular, of systems that are not only able to maintain an autonomy, or integrity (organizational closure) but are informationally open ("information" is used in Petri's sense, of which information measures are contextually appropriate indices).

This is not the only way of bringing the issue of consciousness (value, belief, connation, and not mere "cognitive" ratiocination) into the scientific domain, but it is one that is recent, well formulated, and contentious. In this respect we were especially fortunate to have my old friend (we did some work together in the 1950's), Alex Andrew, who criticized this particular formulation sanely and lucidly. He has a great deal of right on his side and, up to a point, it is a matter of taste (Alex has always been inclined to conserving, though widening, the framework of science; I, for example, have always been a scientific radical. Or, maybe, it is that he prefers to demarcate his art and his science, whereas I cannot see a clearcut boundary). If you want to play safe and retain such cherished ideas as "repeatability" or Lewin's "Genidentity," then it is wise to keep the conventional wisdom, bending it where need be. On the other hand, it seemed to some of the symposiasts that, for many issues of practical concern, the bend develops into a rupture and the tried (within limits, true) notions must be subsumed in a wider scheme, to avoid essential bifurcations at the level not only of theory but also of plain pragmatism.

It is with the amanunesis, to make the issue more polar than it is (or it was made out to be), I have taken this liberty. There is in fact a whole continuum of useful work. At one extreme, Staudigl presented a more or less classical model of learning; Reuver, on learning; Ben Eli, on evolution; Mitchell, in education, depart pretty much from the mainstream system-studies but are still interpretable in those terms; so, oddly enough, is Lowen's representation of consciousness, though people tried to push him into a more deviant position (chiefly, by commenting that the metrical aspects of his model are only imitated, however successfully, by computers as they are currently marketed).

So, next, there emerged a range of models, applications views, spanning the entire spectrum from classical system science to the more recent varieties of general system theory.

Among these, Shaw's paper and Thomas's paper are concerned (by consensus, as well as the intent of the authors) with the quantification and manipulation of consciousness and action; Mitchell's paper prescribes types of manipulation. The polarity in dialogue was stressed, nay parodied, because, without that emphasis, it would be easy to misinterpret these contributions as no more than ingenious, computer programmed, methods for fiddling around with repertory grids (Shaw and Thomas), or an attempt to assist teachers and TV producers based upon attention-latency experiments (Mitchell). Nobody at the symposium is likely to make that mistake, but to do so would be a great injustice to the authors and their sense of professional responsibility.

Much of this, it should be added, came out of discussion in which the participants were not authors. There were several of them, but Dr. Wermus of Geneva made some immensely valuable contributions and Dr. Zadeh had, to my knowledge, a lasting impact on several symposiasts.

Last, as it happens (and the only item taken in order), Mayon-White set out a critique of the systems community. To be responsible, the practitioner must know what the paradigms are, where they are coherent and where they are grossly inconsistent. There is ample evidence that many researchers and practitioners do nothing of the kind; simply muddling along, thoughtlessly, with some badly shaped assumptions about matters too esoteric to have either educational or practical relevance.

Here (as at other places, for example, Johnson's paper), the discussion was unavoidably too short. However, the points are well taken. Responsibility (and without it, do not speak of cybernetics)

entails profundity; knowledge of the multifarious philosophical movements that underpin the subject. The practitioner may veer to the classical, when the circumstances of application render the classical approach expedient. Yet, often, the true and tried is quite unsafe, and barring an ivory tower, not sure at all. In particular, some very radical revisions are needed in the context of conscious processes; at the instant when the practitioner/scientist must admit (as some practitioners/scientists prefer to assert from the outset), that they are part of the system which accepts their recommendations, or learns their theories, too often, as though their theories were mere dogmas stripped of the aleatory, the hypothetical, that gives life to the world in which cyberneticians live.

Autopoiesis and self-organization

ALEX M. ANDREW
Department of Cybernetics, University of Reading
Whiteknights, Reading, Berks, England

1. INTRODUCTION

Maturana [10] and his coworkers, notably Varela [16], have introduced the term <u>autopoiesis</u> to designate what is arguably the most fundamental characteristic of living organisms. It refers to the capacity which living systems have to develop and maintain their own organization, the organization which is developed and maintained being identical with that which performs the development and maintenance.

Maturana seems to imply that the new point of view renders obsolete many of the older attempts to theorise about living organisms and particularly their nervous systems. Varela is less dogmatic, but also claims that the autopoietic viewpoint brings valuable new insight. The aim of the present paper is to consider how the viewpoint represented by some of the earlier attempts must be modified in the light of the new ideas. The older viewpoint which is considered is that usually indicated by the term "self-organizing systems" or SOS. In particular, the attempt is made to decide whether autopoiesis provides the essential ingredient whose omission has prevented SOS studies from being more productive than they have.

The treatment confirms the view that autopoiesis provides new insight and may be regarded as contributing a missing ingredient of the SOS approach. Reference is made, however, to two other important missing ingredients which are not subsumed in the autopoietic viewpoint.

2. STATUS OF SOS STUDIES

Interest in SOS was much in evidence in the nineteen-fifties and early nineteen-sixties, a number of conferences being devoted to the topic (Yovits and Cameron [22]; Von Foerster and Zopf [19]; Yovits, Jacobi and Goldstein [23]; Garvey [5]). The essential idea is, and must remain, somewhat intuitive; some reasons for this have been discussed in previous publications (Andrew [1]). In the first place, any term which refers to the self-modification of a system must be observer-dependent, since the same system may be described either as self-modifying or as a fixed system. In the terminology used by Glushkov [6], a self-organizing system is decomposable into an operative automaton and a learning automaton. Whether a given system is judged to be self-organizing depends on whether an observer feels that such a decomposition provides an appropriate description.

The idea of a SOS is also intuitive because it depends on a subjective judgement as to whether the changes which occur in the system as it interacts with its environment are sufficiently fundamental to warrant the term <u>self-organizing</u> as opposed to, say, <u>self-optimising</u>. There are, in addition, some constraints on the means by which these changes may arise; the elements of the system must behave autonomously. That is to say, the changes should be determined locally within the system and not in response to the commands of an "adaption centre" able to view the whole system.

The main objections which have been made to the SOS idea, however, have not been on grounds of imprecision of the concept. A number of workers have followed Ashby [4] in suggesting that SOS studies are unprofitable because there is nothing to study. The implication is that there is nothing more which need, or can, be said once an adaptive system has been described as a state-determined system whose operating point drifts through a phase-space until stability is reached. Such a mode of description is valid but likely to be impractical for non-trivial systems. Ashby himself has presented a somewhat different point of view in another publication [3] where he talks about "Amplifying Adaptation."

For at least the last decade, most workers in Artificial Intelligence have kept well clear of SOS ideas. Various reasons have been advanced, but the main point is that SOS studies have been disappointingly unproductive. By abandoning any attempt to make systems which self-organize, workers in AI have been able to forge ahead and produce spectacular results. Their programs, however, depend heavily on heuristic principles derived by manually-directed experimentation and use of the programmers' own insight into the problems to be solved. The Artificial Intelligence of the systems produced is strongly laced with natural intelligence.

3. AUTOPOIESIS

The autopoietic viewpoint emphasises the essential circularity of the living organism. The idea of circularity, subsumed in that of feedback, is an old one in Cybernetics. The new viewpoint pays particular attention to the circular process whose variables are the <u>internal</u> variables of the organism. A sharp distinction is drawn between this circular process, which constitutes the essential <u>organization</u> of the organism, and other

circular processes associated with it. These
other processes, which operate through input and
output interfaces with the organism's environment,
are held to be part of the structure associated
with the essential organization.

This partitioning of the organism into organization and structure has some surprising consequences. This is because the word organization
must be interpreted in an extremely restricted
sense and structure in a correspondingly expanded
one. One consequence is that any action taken by
the organism to protect itself from an impending
danger must be initiated and executed purely by
the structure. The capacity to make anticipatory
responses has been claimed by Sommerhoff [14] (as
directive correlation) to be the essential feature
which distinguishes living from non-living systems.
It is surprising to find this feature relegated to
mere structure by the treatment in terms of autopoiesis.

Nevertheless the partitioning-off of the
organization, in this very restricted sense, can
be defended on either of two grounds. One is the
argument that such organization corresponds to an
intuitive idea of what essentially constitutes a
living organism. This is in conflict with
Sommerhoff, who has demonstrated that living
organisms as we know them invariably employ
directive correlation. On the other hand, the
recognition of a system as living is not dependent
on the operation of any one specific form of
directive correlation, so might persist in the
absence of any.

The other justification for the separation of
a restricted organization within a living system
is that it is necessary for precise formulation of
the autopoiesis hypothesis. Clearly, those parts
of the organism which learn, or otherwise adapt
to the environment, cannot be said to be maintained
constant by a circular process. It is necessary
either to let "maintained" be interpreted in a
weaker sense than "maintained constant" or to
whittle down the part of the system to which the
circular process is held to apply.

Whether the nature of living systems is such
that it is legitimate to partition them into
organization and structure as postulated is a
matter for debate. Even if it is allowed the
problems are not completely resolved; the organization cannot be the result of such severe whittling-down that it remains absolutely constant.
If it were it could not implement the circular
process which maintains it. This is the crux of
the problem of self-reference which has stimulated
Varela's elegant extension of Brown's Laws of
Form [17] and his later work [18] related to
Scott's treatment of fixed points of algebraic
expressions.

4. THE IMPACT ON SOS STUDIES

In SOS studies systems are discussed in relation to the pursuit of goals. In the context of
natural systems the goal-seeking behaviour has to
be a descriptive expedient only, or in other words
a construct formed by an observer. It is, however,
a form of description which fits many aspects of
observed behaviour so closely that it is not to be
abandoned lightly. To be rigorous, a living system

should be described, not as goal-seeking, but as
behaving as though it were pursuing some goal.

The autopoietic hypothesis could be rephrased
in SOS terms by saying that living systems behave
as though pursuing the goal of their own survival.
Reformulating it in this way does not by-pass any
of the difficulties referred to in connection
with the Maturana-Varela treatment; these still
arise in the attempt to define "survival". To
behave as though pursuing the goal of its own
survival a living system must also behave as
though it distinguishes its own interior from
its environment.

It could be argued, in terms of Varela's
paper [18] that the above reformulation is a
desperate attempt to depart minimally from the
traditional Fregean viewpoint. However, the reformulation does have value in emphasising the
fact that the organization of a living system,
even in the most restricted sense possible, has
to be seen in conjunction with its environment,
or ecological niche. The circular process which
maintains the organization is able to nullify
some types of perturbation due to the environment,
but it must depend on some "rules of the game"
which are invariant. The Varela-Maturana-Uribe
model [16], for example, maintains an enclosing
"membrane" despite random effects which break it
up. However, the membrane would not be maintained if random effects rendered the catalyst
ineffective. An undue emphasis on a Brownian
approach seems to obscure the essentially
empirical nature of living systems.

5. MODELLING SELF-PRESERVATION

Many well-known artifacts embody Sommerhoff's
directive correlation, which can also be termed
feed-forward or anticipatory control. It can in
fact be argued that servo-mechanisms embody it;
if the control action has a derivative component
(or even a proportional component whose magnitude
depends on previous knowledge of the controlled
system) the control action is to some extent
anticipatory and therefore an implementation of
directive correlation.

Autopoiesis can also be realised in artifacts,
as shown by the Varela-Maturana-Uribe model.
Hence, both of these characteristics intended to
distinguish living systems from non-living ones
are in fact making a distinction which allows
certain non-living systems to fall into the same
category as do living systems. These non-living
systems are artifacts which have inherited some
lifelike characteristics from their designers;
they are manifestations of life though not themselves alive.

The autopoietic viewpoint does, however, draw
attention to one important difference between an
artificial system pursuing a goal (and perhaps
improving its performance by self-organization)
and a sub-system of a living organism behaving in
essentially the same way. The subsystem of the
living organism is linked to its parent organism
in two ways; in the first place it is operating
to achieve its particular goal and secondly it is
recognised by the organism as an integral part of
itself to be maintained by autopoiesis. As
stated earlier, it is a corollary of the auto-

poiesis hypothesis that a living system must behave as though it can distinguish its own interior from its environment. It was presumably this corollary which prompted Varela to look to Brown's calculus, with its basis in a simple distinction between inclusion and exclusion, for a formal treatment of autopoiesis.

The dual nature of a living sub-system, which is simultaneously a goal-seeking system and part of an autopoietic system, is something which most artificial systems fail to model. One system which does combine the two roles in an interesting way is the proposal of Svoboda [15] for a model of the instinct of self-preservation. The model consisted of a small computer mounted on a self-propelled trolley, the steering and drive of the trolley being determined by commands from the computer. The computer was so programmed that it would seek a location in which some physical property of the environment was minimised. The method used to seek the minimum involved the mapping of values of the physical property on an internal representation in the computer of the area within which it was free to move. Search strategies of considerable sophistication could be embodied in a scheme of this kind.

What made Svoboda's system specially interesting in the present context, however, was that there were no special tranducers to measure the physical property which was to be minimised. Instead, the computer was designed to exploit redundancy to achieve automatic error-correction at all stages of the computation. (Schemes for automatic error-correction of messages are treated by Peterson [13] and were discussed by von Neumann [20]. The work of Winograd and Cowan [21] is particularly interesting because the redundancy is in the computational structure rather than the messages.) It was arranged that the error-correcting system incorporated in Svoboda's computer provided an indication of its own level of error-correcting activity, and it was this level which constituted the physical property the system sought to minimise.

Svoboda's system allows a computer to seek a location in which it is minimally affected by unknown external effects (of which radioactivity could be one) tending to cause computational malfunctions but not actually damaging the computer. The same principle could be extended to allow the minimisation of unknown effects actually damaging the computer. This could be done either by letting the property to be minimised be the time-derivative of the error-correction rate or by letting the system embody a facility for self-repair rather than one for error-correction. For the latter alternative the property to be minimised would be the level of repair activity. Schemes of this kind seem to be worthy of study because their operation corresponds in an interesting way to the dual nature of living sub-systems as already discussed. Most proposals for SOS do not have this feature.

6. THE BODY SCHEMA

Most human beings are conscious of a strong desire to avoid damage to their own bodies, and are in no doubt about the interface between the system to be preserved and the environment. It is often said that a person "looks after his own skin."

Nathan [11] makes some interesting observations on the nature of the body schema which he says is "the basis of our feeling that our bodies are us, that they are placed in such or such a way in the environment, and that the parts of our bodies make up a whole." The existence of a body schema apparently depends on the functioning of certain parts of the nervous system. Damage to the cortex of the parietal lobes of the brain can lead to part of the body being excluded from the schema. It is not necessary that the peripheral innervation of a part of the body be intact in order that the part be included in the schema; the schema can include "phantom limbs" corresponding to members which have been amputated.

7. CONCLUSIONS

The discussions of Svoboda's model and of the neurologists' concept of a body schema give different impressions of mechanisms which could subserve autopoiesis. The body schema appears to depend on special nervous mechanisms, whereas Svoboda's model requires very little circuitry dedicated to autopoiesis. There is, of course, no reason to suppose that autopoiesis must invariably depend on any one type of mechanism.

While it is true that the autopoiesis hypothesis has a strong bearing on SOS studies, it does not seem to be the one essential ingredient needed for progress. There are many features of living systems which are difficult to describe otherwise than in terms of the pursuit of goals. They behave as though pursuing what might be termed meta-goals, or goals whose achievement facilitates the achievement of lower-order goals. It can be argued, for instance, that living systems seek succinct or economical representations of their internal information, and that successful structural features are often replicated.

The evolution of higher forms of intelligent behaviour requires some selective mechanism favouring succinct representation. In a somewhat different form, this idea has been emphasized by Pask [12] who discusses the emergence of meta-languages within living systems. The terms of a meta-language represent concepts not having a succinct representation in the lower-order language. In a recent discussion by Andrew [2] it is argued that succinct representation can be considered at two levels, namely that corresponding to information stored in the learning automaton and that corresponding similarly to the operative automaton. It is, in fact, not necessary to restrict the number of levels to two. Glushkov, in introducing these two types of automaton, considers the possibility of hierarchies of them. The operative automaton would be at the bottom of the hierarchy, which could have numerous levels.

Much work on learning systems for pattern recognition has been carried out without regard to succinct representation of the information acquired by learning. This work has been highly successful in achieving particular objectives (see, for example, the masterly review by Kohonen [8]) but has an inherent limitation because there is no tendency to form succinct representations.

In all living structures, particular features are replicated many times over. In the context of nervous systems this is clearly illustrated by the studies of Letvin et al [9] and of Hubel and Wiesel [7] on visual systems of different animals. Replication is needed to match a succinct representation of a data-transformation process to the non-succinct input from the real world.

Future SOS studies must certainly be devised with regard to the lessons of autopoiesis, but also (since we cannot hope to run our simulations long enough to let them be evolved) to the embodiment of at least two meta-goals, namely those of seeking succinct representations and of replicating existing successful structural features.

REFERENCES

1. ANDREW, A. M., "Significance Feedback and Redundancy Reduction in Self-Organizing Networks," in: Advances in Cybernetics and Systems Research, Vol. 1, F. Pichler and R. Trappl (eds.), p. 244, London, Transcripta, 1973.
2. ANDREW, A. M., "Succinct Representation in Neural Nets and General Systems," in: Applied General System Research: Recent Developments and Trends, G. Klir (ed.), p. 553, New York, Plenum Press, 1978.
3. ASHBY, W. R., Design for a Brain, 2nd ed., p. 231, London, Chapman and Hall, 1960.
4. ASHBY, W. R., "Principles of the Self-Organizing System," in: Principles of Self-Organization, H. von Foerster and G. W. Zopf (eds.), p. 255, Oxford, Pergamon Press, 1962.
5. GARVEY, J. E., Self-Organizing Systems, Washington, Office of Naval Research, 1963.
6. GLUSHKOV, V. M., Introduction to Cybernetics, New York, Academic Press, 1966.
7. HUBEL, D. H. and T. N. WIESEL, "Receptive Fields and Functional Architecture of Monkey Striate Cortex," Journal of Physiology, 195, p. 215.
8. KOHONEN, T., Associative Memory, Berlin, Springer, 1977.
9. LETTVIN, J. Y., H. R. MATURANA, W. S. McCULLOCH and W. H. PITTS, "What the Frog's Eye Tells the Frog's Brain," Proceedings I. R. E., 47, p. 1940, 1959.
10. MATURANA, H. R., "The Organization of the Living," International Journal of Man-Machine Studies, 7, p. 313, 1975.
11. NATHAN, P., The Nervous System, Penguin, 1969.
12. PASK, G., "The Logical Type of Illogical Evolution," in: Information Processing 1962 (IFIP), p. 482, Amsterdam, North Holland, 1962.
13. PETERSON, W. W., Error-Correcting Codes, M.I.T. Press and Wiley, 1961.
14. SOMMERHOFF, G., Analytical Biology, Oxford University Press, 1950.
15. SVOBODA, A., "Un modèle d'instinct de conservation," in: Proceedings, 2nd International Congress on Cybernetics, p. 866, Namur, International Association of Cybernetics, 1960.
16. VARELA, F. J., H. R. MATURANA and R. URIBE, "Autopoiesis: The Organization of Living Systems," Biological Systems, 5, p. 187, 1974.
17. VARELA, F. J., "A Calculus for Self-Reference," International Journal of General Systems, 2, p. 5, 1975.
18. VARELA, F. J., "The Arithmetic of Closure," Presented at EMCSR 3, 1976.
19. von FOERSTER, H. and G. W. ZOPF (eds.), Principles of Self-Organization, Oxford, Pergamon Press, 1962.
20. von NEUMANN, J., "Probabilistic Logics and the Synthesis of Reliable Organisms from Unreliable Components," in: Automata Studies, C. E. Shannon and J. McCarthy (eds.), Princeton University Press, 1956.
21. WINOGRAD, W. and J. COWAN, Reliable Computation in the Presence of Noise, M.I.T. Press, 1963.
22. YOVITS, M. C. and S. CAMERON, Self-Organizing Systems, New York, Pergamon Press, 1960.
23. YOVITS, M. C., G. T. JACOBI and G. D. GOLDSTEIN, Self-Organizing Systems 1962, Washington, Spartan, 1962.

A model for a holistic and integrated disciplinary approach to environmental education

BELA H. BANATHY
Far West Laboratory for Educational Research and Development
San Francisco, California USA

1. INTRODUCTION

Recent trends in science and human affairs challenge our longstanding preoccupation with specific knowledge, pursued in well-established disciplines.

The need to comprehend the systems of the earth and the way they are interrelated generated tremendous pressure to understand wholeness.

Systems science is the science of wholeness, the science of synthesis. It developed theories and models that enable us to integrate the findings of various disciplines as we deal with ever increasing complex issues such as urbanization, energy and land use, the application of technology, economics and governance, and a host of social problems.

All the issues and problem areas mentioned above are reflected in the interaction of the system of man and nature, which is the center of the environmental concern.

Environmental education, therefore, should closely manifest the holistic view and it should aim at developing competence for the examination and articulation of the patterns of interaction of parts which integrate into the whole. Such education will enable the individual to confront environmental issues from a perspective of wholeness, and to see the relationships between the various components of the systems of humanity and nature to which the environmental problem is related.

Wholeness and an integrated disciplinary approach are the key organizing concepts which guide the development of the project I shall report on. Sponsored by the Office of Environmental Education of the U. S. Office of Education, we designed a set of <u>teacher training models</u>. Two of these models were designed in the functional context of energy focused EE (Environmental Education); the others integrated Environmental Education with science and social studies. In this paper, I report on the general properties of that model.

As used here, the term "model" means an abstraction or a blueprint for a teacher training program that can be developed based on the model. Thus, the outcome of the project was not a model program, but models for a variety of environmental education teacher training programs.

The information presented here is a highly abbreviated adaptation of the introductory part of a document, "The Social Science/Environmental Education Teacher Training Model," prepared at the Far West Laboratory and authored by: Bela H. Banathy, Larry L. Peterson, Stephen F. Mills, Carol J. Murphy, and Kathryn D. O'Connell.

2. THE HOLISTIC AND INTEGRATED DISCIPLINARY NATURE OF THE MODEL

"Holistic models" and the "systems models approach" [1] are nearly synonomous in that they both deal with <u>components</u> and the <u>interactions</u> among components. The nature of the interactions varies from subtle "influences" which are difficult to detect to actual physical "couplings" familiar in the study of physical models. "Models of instruction" are "soft" models in that the nature of the major interactions of their components are "influential" as opposed to physical.

A "holistic" model of instruction has an entire range of possible interaction characteristics from influences (soft connections) to actual physical couplings (hard connections) such as limited physical classroom arrangements and inflexible hierarchies of authority and policy. A holistic model of instruction includes these components: content modules, instructional resources, implementation strategies, and curriculum management methods.

It is important to mention here the hierarchical nature of the language of holistic, transdisciplinary models. Models are abstract constructions of reality and can be regarded as a "map" of the territory. The language used to describe the map of the territory is different from that used to describe the territory. The language of the model (or map) is, by necessity, more abstract and abbreviated than the language of the whole reality (or territory). If this were not the case, models would not be more convenient to use than the reality itself. So, the requirement for model languages to be more abstract and abbreviated than the language of reality forces them to be more general, to avoid getting lost in the detail of reality; and to be more abstract, to avoid getting tangled in the narrowness of specific concepts about reality. Thus, by necessity, the language of the model must be at least one level higher hierarchically than the reality it is attempting to describe.

In our specific case, an effective multi-disciplinary, systemic and holistic educational model must be constructed in a holistic, generally systemic and transdisciplinary language.

A model of instruction in environmental education should display well the many interactions that exist within our natural environment:
• Interactions within the total <u>human system</u> (social, economic, technological)

• Interactions within the total natural system
(physical, biological, econological)
• Interactions between these two systems
Designing an Environmental Education Teacher
Training Model (EETTM) based on our understanding
of the principles on which human and natural systems operate and interact dictates that the model
be open-ended and readily revisable, since our
understanding is incomplete and always changing.
It must be an adaptive model, building in a corrective way on the experiences accrued in its
application.

Further, because of the comprehensive and
holistic nature of the subject matter, it is not
readily subsumed into any one specialized discipline, and therefore the EE model must be integrative -- a useful framework for showing the environmental relationships disciplines have with one
another.

The model must also allow for informing world-
view and attitudinal differences by displaying the
entire spectrum of environmental values and revealing their implications, consequences and impacts
in various environmental contexts. This is the
affective aspect of the model.

Also, as an instructional/learning tool, the
model must be designed to convey the integrated
knowledge and skill components of environmental
education which constitute the definition of and
guide the development of an environmentally aware
person. These components portray the cognitive
aspects of the model.

Two processes for use in EE teacher training
will be introduced next: the Systemic Instructional
Design process which generates the instructional/
learning arrangements and the Systemic Content
Design process which generates the Content Specifications. Both processes are originated by interpreting the educational requirements of the environmental problem configuration and by analyzing the
systemic nature of the problem from their respective
points of view.

3. SYSTEMIC INSTRUCTIONAL DESIGN

A systemic approach to designing the Environmental Education Teacher Training Model enables one
to comprehensively address the instructional design
challenge represented by the environmental problem
configuration addressed by the model (see Figure 1).
Such an approach, which conceptualizes education as
a system, provides a procedural framework for
analyzing and synthesizing effective educational
research and design strategies into a comprehensive
method of instructional design (see [2]; Banathy
also points to a decision-making structure offered
by a systems approach and the manner in which such
an approach provides the basis for planned change;
for a further discussion of a systems-model approach
see [3]). Within this procedural framework, the
purpose and goals of holistic environmental education and portrayed in the environmental configurations are transformed at the model level into
components which represent the elements and functions needed to achieve those goals (see Figure 1).

Before describing the components which comprise
the EETTM and the manner in which they were developed, it is important to identify four major premises or principles related to teacher-learner

functions and curriculum design which guided this
instructional design endeavor. These principles
are:
• teaching as a decision-making process
• learner is the key entity
• integrate rather than re-educate
• competence based approach
The first principle is the formulating of
teaching as a decision-making process which assigns
the selection of instructional/learning arrangements as the significant function of teaching [4].
Within this process, the teacher considers and
evaluates the outcomes of alternative instructional/
learning arrangements and selects those most likely
to accomplish specific learning objectives. Based
on an assessment of student needs and interests,
the teacher, therefore, is actively involved in
making decisions throughout an instructional management sequence of purposing, planning, implementing and evaluating.

This principle of teaching as a decision-making
process:
• is based on an analysis and definition of
the knowledge, skills and attitudes required
by the literate, competent, and aware
energy/environmental education teacher;
• considers initial trainee competence and
previous teaching experience;
• develops competences that will enable a
teacher to purpose, plan and implement alternative instructional/learning arrangements and to predict and assess relevant
learner outcomes;
• provides application experiences in which a
teacher can plan, design, implement, and see
the effects of selected instructional/
learning arrangements;
• provides for the assessment of instructional/
learning outcomes and adjustments in performance based on the assessment.
The second principle, highly complementary to
the first, is that the learner is the key entity
of his/her own instructional/learning system. In
the EETTM, the learner is the teacher and instruc-
tional/learning arrangements are designed around
and in response to his/her assessed needs in order
to facilitate mastery of identified tasks. Designing such instructional/learning arrangements
involves:
• selection and organization of content and
resources which best represent the learning
task
• selection and organization of instructional/
learning experiences
• assessment of progress
• selection of program formatting elements
The third guiding principle addresses the function of the curriculum specified in the EETTM which
seeks to integrate rather than re-educate the
teacher. The design is such that teachers can use
what they already know to achieve a more holistic
understanding and awareness of environmental education. The goal is not to discard previous conceptions and resources but to reorient and re-
organize them in a more systemic manner.

Competences relevant to environmental awareness
and relevant decision-making are clearly defined as
well as competences that relate to the planning,
implementation, and evaluating of environmental
education curriculum.

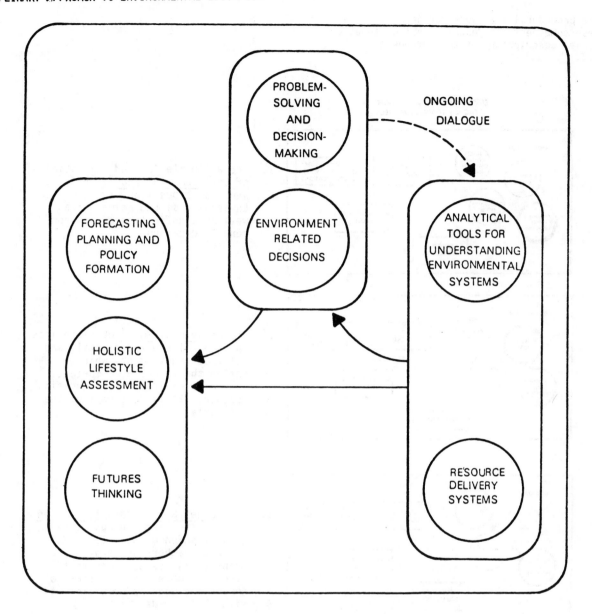

Figure 1. Curriculum Model for Environmental Education

4. DESIGN OF THE MODEL

The components of the Environmental Education Teacher Training Model are designed to address the practitioner questions listed below. The EETTM components which specifically address each of the questions are listed next to the questions.

PRACTITIONER QUESTIONS	RELEVANT EETTM COMPONENTS
· What do I need to know?	CONTENT SPECIFICATIONS
· What materials/resources do I need?	CONTENT SOURCEBOOK
· What instructional/learning arrangements are needed?	CURRICULUM MANAGEMENT SPECIFICATIONS
· What physical and logistical arrangements are needed?	IMPLEMENTATION MODEL
· What general guidelines can I use?	BEHAVIORAL AND CURRICULUM MODELS

The procedural framework for developing each of these components is described below, together with brief descriptions of the components.

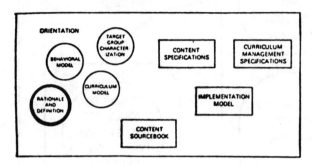

1. The <u>Rationale for and Definition of Environmental Education</u> presents an exposition of the Environmental Education Act as well as a definition of environmental education.

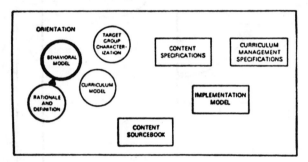

2. The <u>Behavioral Model</u> characterizes the <u>general knowledge, skill and attitude requirements which define the literate, competent, and aware environmental education teacher. It is derived from the Rationale.

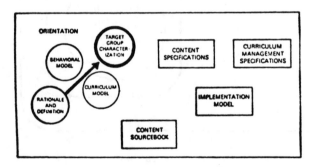

3. The <u>Target Group Characterization</u> defines the target group as K-9 natural science and 4-12 social science teachers and provides a means to assess their current level of competence in order to ensure the model's compatibility with their needs.

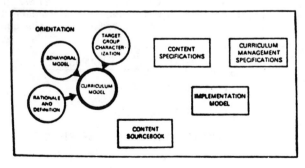

4. The <u>Curriculum Model</u> provides an organized description of the various curriculum content domains within which potential teachers need to attain competence. It is consistent with the Rationale and represents an elaboration of the Behavioral Model and the Target Group Characterization.

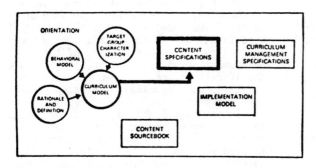

5. The Content Specifications present the knowledge components for environmental education and a description of their instructional foci and purposes. These specifications were designed to satisfy the requirements of the knowledge component of the Curriculum Model.

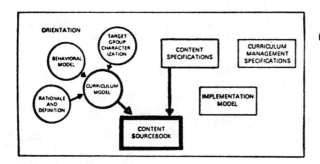

6. The Content Sourcebook presents an elaborated discussion of the knowledge components of the content model, a subject matter/cultural process matrix, an annotated resource bibliography and glossary. The requirements for the Sourcebook are defined by the Curriculum Model and the Content Specifications.

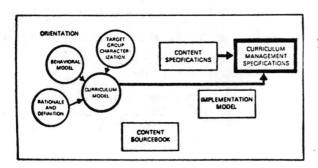

7. The Curriculum Management Specifications provides general instructional arrangements by which teachers can purpose, plan, implement and evaluate an environmental education curriculum. This component was derived from and further elaborates the skills component of the Curriculum Model and the Content Specifications.

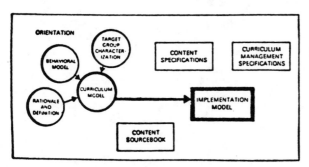

8. The Implementation Model presents the conceptual bases and functions of the implementation process together with characteristic activities associated with each phase of the process. The implementation design was guided by the Curriculum Model.

5. THE CURRICULUM MODEL

In closing, I shall introduce the curriculum model that displays the major content components of an environmental education curriculum.

Environmental Education is, by nature, transdisciplinary. At the heart of the ecological perspective is the realization that human/environmental systems cannot be comprehended by studying their isolated fragments. The following is taken from Meeker [5]:

Subduing and subdividing it into easily manageable units only destroys its most important features, the processes of interaction which make it attractive and functional. Rather than simplifying our subject matter, we must learn to complexify our means for comprehending it. Genuine environmental scholarship will have to emphasize the understanding of processes above the measurement of entities. Environmental Studies should be structured as ecosystems are, recognizing complex interdependencies and accepting competition, contradiction, and uncertainty as necessary conditions for learning. Their goal should be the encouragement of wisdom and good judgement, leaving the task of filling our information cribs to the academic [specialists].

In order to become manifest, "content" demands "form" for its proper express.

The Content Model depicted in Figure 1 is oriented toward providing the learner with a systemic conceptual and operational basis for understanding environmental systems as related to:
- the individual decision maker
- public decisions

The content system emphasizes both the societal and individual dimensions of decision-making and their interrelationships; it identifies how these decisions can be made and interpreted from various worldviews. The use and conservation of environmental resources is approached from both the production and consumption points of view as it relates to both the individual and society.

The figure specifies the components of the Content Model and their linkages. These represent an ordered flow of concepts that build the complex configuration for comprehensive environmental education as necessary to informed decision-making.

Detailed specifications for each of the components of the model are presented in the "Content Specifications" of the Model. These Specifications are followed by a description of the instructional management specifications section. Following these specifications are selected references which could be utilized in developing these components into instructional/learning resources.

In closing, I should report that based on the models we developed we are now designing and developing a teacher training program for energy focused environmental education. I will be pleased to respond to inquiries about the program. For information please write to: Bela H. Banathy, Director, Instructional and Training Systems Program, Far West Laboratory for Educational Research and Development, 1855 Folsom Street, San Francisco, California 94103.

REFERENCES

1. BANATHY, Bela H., A Systems View of Education, A Systems Models Approach, Belmont, Ca., Fearon Publishers, 1973.
2. BANATHY, Bela H., Instructional Systems, Belmont, Ca., Fearon Publishers, 1968.
3. BANATHY, Bela H., Developing a Systems View of Education, the Systems Model Approach, Belmont, Ca., Fearon Publishers, 1973.
4. BERLINER, David, To Develop an In-Service/ Pre-Service Teacher Training Program Demonstrating the Adaptation of Research to Teaching, San Francisco, Far West Laboratory for Educational Research and Development, 1975.
5. MEEKER, Joseph W., "Academic Fields and Other Polluted Environments," The Journal of Environmental Education, Vol. 4, No. 3, Spring 1973, p. 38.

Amplifying regulation and variety increase in evolving systems

MICHAEL U. BEN-ELI

General Systems Research, Inc., New York

1. INTRODUCTION: THE EVOLUTIONARY PERSPECTIVE AND THE CYBERNETIC PARADIGM

Scientific discussions of evolution since Darwin have centered around essentially biological issues related to the emergence and subsequent history of species. A broader concept of evolution as a unifying creative principle embracing all cosmic phenomena including, but not limited to, terrestrial forms of life, has been advocated by visionary thinkers and religious mystics, for example, by Teilhard de Chardin [25], but such contributions remain alien to established scientific disciplines.

Recent developments in the physical sciences, however, made possible the articulation of principles governing the evolution of order and complexity in physico-chemical systems. These principles, formulated in the field of non-equilibrium thermodynamics, have been applied to an analysis of some biological processes (Prigogine [22]; Katchalsky and Kadem [14]), and they have been used by way of speculation or analogy to discuss evolution of socio-psychological and conscious phenomena as well (Katchalsky [15]; Jansch [13]).

The formulation offered by non-equilibrium thermodynamics holds that the increase of organization and complexity in physical systems is a consequence of specific kinetic principles and that the concept of evolution in physics and biology are reconcilable under a single physical law (Glansdorf and Prigogine [11]). This formulation can be interpreted as reaffirming the intuitive concept of the unity underlying natural phenomena, but since it involves mathematical concepts describing the dynamics of energy flows subject to strictly defined constraints, its "extrapolated" projection to the domains of social and psychological systems may be questionable.

An approach suggested by the cybernetic theory of regulation, on the other hand, offers a different perspective which, by emphasizing organizational aspects that are independent of specific material considerations, is free of similar limitations. The cybernetic approach assumes that realizable configurations (identities) imply the fulfillment of thermodynamic and energetic requirements. It involves the formulation of a general concept of regulation linking the notion of survival, in the broad sense of "viability," or "stable identity," to concepts of information communication and control. In this context, evolution can be regarded as an outcome of a particular "survival strategy," applicable to a specific constellation of dynamic circumstances and subject to the laws of regulation. These laws are conceived on a level of abstraction which makes their transfer across systemic boundaries particularly covenient. The cybernetic paradigm can, therefore, contribute significantly to a unified view of evolution and to a characterization of evolution as a general phenomenon. It provides for a consistent interpretation of both the dynamics of specific evolutionary processes and the persistent, overall evolutionary tendency of forming organizations of ever increasing complexity.

One important consequence of the cybernetic perspective is a view of evolution as being characteristic of a particular kind of dynamic behavior in systems, reflecting a particular aspect of the logic of mechanisms (in the sense suggested by Ashby [3]). From this viewpoint, evolution corresponds to a specific type of regulation and, as a process, it is embodied in a particular type of organization of which Pask's ikonic representation of learning processes (Pask, Scott and Kallikourdis [20]) is an example. This broad statement is significant insofar as it stresses the concept that evolution is a general type of stability (steady state being a special case) and that as such it is a general condition typical to environments that are subject to the operation of a particular set of constraints.

On this level of abstraction at which evolution is regarded as a general process, the essential features of reproduction, variation, and selection appear as generalizable unifying principles. Generalizable, in that they can be synthesized and become subject to simulations (Ben-Eli and Tountas [7]). The specific mechanisms through which evolution is mediated will vary, however, with specific identifications. It is when we focus on an actual "real world" organization that such mechanisms will assume specific identities, coinciding with specific embodiments.

Specific identifications should not obscure the general validity of evolutionary principles which are not restricted to the biological domain alone. The uniqueness of biological evolution is limited to the fabric of its particular mechanisms but not to the principles underlying their operations. On the level of underlying principles, there exists a definite correspondence, for example, between biological evolution and "symbolic evolution" where the latter is viewed as the domain of cognitive processes in which concepts, or procedures for control and computation, evolve (Pask [19]). The claim for generality which underscores such a correspondence is particularly significant since it provides a logical link between the processes of biology and the cultural, symbolic domain in which much that is relevant to psychological and social evolution takes place.

2. REGULATION FOR EFFECTIVE VIABILITY: THE CYBERNETIC FORMULATION

Before moving on to explore in further detail the implications of extending some of the fundamental ideas of cybernetics and using aspects of the theory of regulation as an interpretive tool for examining the concept of evolution, a brief review of the now classical formulation may be appropriate.

The central idea is that regulation achieves a goal (brings about a particular outcome) in the face of some set of perturbations. The approach is due to Sommerhoff and Ashby [23,1] who defined the process of regulation as a function of five key variables and the manner in which these variables interact. These variables include a regulator, a regulated system, a source of disturbances, a set of all possible outcomes, and a set defining desired outcomes. While the differentiation between these variables implies a sharp distinction, the latter may not be always actually possible. For example, when control is distributed throughout a system the distinction between "system" and "regulator" is blurred. Similarly the actual boundary between "a system" and "an environment" is not universally clear cut. Often such a boundary is imposed by an observer subject to his particular interest and point of view. Nevertheless, a conceptual differentiation is useful for the purpose of description and analysis.

The role played by the five key variables in the process of regulation is specified as follows (Ashby [4]): for a given situation, there is a set Z of all possible events which may occur whether regulation is applied or not. Of these, a sub-set G defines desired outcomes--those which correspond to a condition of stability for the system under regulation. In addition, there is a set R of events in the regulator, a set S of events in the system which is being regulated, and a set D of disturbances. Events in D produce conditions in S which cause outcomes to be driven out of G. Effective regulation is achieved if for a given value of D, events in R and S relate such that the outcome is bounded by G.

The relations between disturbances and the actions taken by a regulator can be formalized in terms of game theoretic concepts (Ashby [2]). From this viewpoint, a set D of disturbances d_i is countered by a set R of responses r_j producing a matrix of outcomes z_{ij} from a set Z of possibilities. The values taken by D and R correspond to a pair of moves selected by each of two players and the table of outcomes is identical with the pay-off matrix of game theory which specifies values of some desired commodity that are assigned to each move.

As before, of all the possible events in Z, obtained by the interaction of D and R, only a sub-set G contains acceptable outcomes representing values which are compatible with a system's "essential variables." R is considered an effective regulator if it can produce a counter action r_j for each d_i in D keeping the outcome within G.

The nature of the relation between D, R, Z, and G is such that the concept of regulation implies selecting from a number of possible actions the one most likely to achieve a goal. This selective aspect is a dominant feature of regulation especially in complex dynamic systems where regulation takes its more interesting and active form. Since effective selection depends on the availability and processing capacity of information, there is an obvious sense in which communication and information play a central role in regulatory processes. Ashby has stressed the intimate relation between regulation and information [1] and he has shown how regulation depends upon information transfer between pertinent system's components. From a qualitative viewpoint, regulatory actions are subject to information about specific disturbances, about the state of the system which is being regulated, and about the outcome. This relation can be given a precise quantitative expression using information theoretic concepts (Conant [10]) and various regulatory schemes can be reduced to the characteristic structure of their respective information processes. For example, error-controlled regulation can be regarded as a special case of regulation in which R receives its information from variations in the outcome. It can thus react only after the effect of a disturbance has been manifest. In other types of regulatory schemes, R is provided with an information channel directly from the disturbance, making "anticipatory" strategies possible. In such cases, the regulator is activated before the actual effects of a disturbance have been registered and its counter actions are directed at the source of disturbance itself.

3. LIMITS ON REGULATION, AMPLIFYING REGULATION, AND VARIETY INCREASE IN EVOLVING SYSTEMS

According to the formulation given above, the process of regulation can be regarded as a sequence of events in which R selects a move r_j from a finite repertoire for each value d_i taken by a disturbance from the set D. The variety in R's repertoire of actions puts a limit on its capacity as a controller since in order to regulate effectively, the variety of actions available to R must be at least equal to the variety in the disturbance. This concept, which is fundamental to the theory of regulation, is expressed in Ashby's "law of requisite variety.". Ashby's law puts an absolute limit on the amount of regulation which can be achieved by a regulator of a finite capacity. It states that for a given variety in the disturbance only variety in R can force down the variety in the outcome.

The need for a particular amount of variety in a regulator is greatly reduced if its environment is characterized by fundamental regularities such as a continuity or a repetitive pattern of events. Thus, when a regulator "faces" a complex, dynamic world, a situation that is common in biology as it is in social and economic affairs, there are circumstances which make effective regulation actually possible even with a relatively low variety. Nevertheless, a system may be exposed to patterns of disturbances requiring an augmented regulation capacity. In such a case, an extension in regulation potential will be essential, and if systemic disintegration is to be avoided, the regulatory capacity will have to be increased until it becomes adequate.

The limitation specified by the law of requisite variety prohibits any direct increase in the capacity of a regulator but it does not rule out supplementation. As Ashby has shown, if there is a continuity in an environment, a number of regulators can be linked in stages to form a more potent regulator with an increased overall capacity. When regulation is applied in stages, for example when a regulator R_1 uses its selective power to form another regulator R_2, the capacity of the latter need not be bounded by that of the former. The possibility thus exists that a small amount of regulation, properly exercised at one stage, will make available a higher regulation potential at the next stage. The procedure can be repeated over a number of steps with the result that a significant increase in regulation capacity is achieved, the process as a whole showing an amplification.

Conceivable means for maintaining viability relate directly to the law of requisite variety and to the possibility in principle of amplifying regulation. The latter, in particular, makes possible an extension of the classical concepts of steady state and ultrastability to account for evolution. This extension goes beyond but is fully compatible with the original formulation. The basic argument proceeds as follows:

Depending on underlying conditions, various methods for achieving stability are possible. For example, if the environment is simple, in the sense that the pattern of its characteristic events is predictable, a regulator can be constructed as a physical barrier for blocking the effects of disturbances, or it can be made to embody a set of decision rules specifying an appropriate counter action for each disturbance. Both cases require an ability to specify all disturbances in advance and they imply building into the regulator a variety which would exactly match all contingencies. This regulation strategy is manifest in special cases of adaptation where the range and magnitude of environmental variations is sufficiently consistent to make it adequate.

When the pattern of disturbances is particularly complex, or when it is constant for too short a time, specification of all possible configurations may be impractical. In such a case, an advantage can be gained if the regulator is made to incorporate a relatively large amount of variety, and if instead of a fixed set of rules it will contain an underspecified provision for modifying internal states in a search for a match with specific conditions as they occur. This is the more general method of adaptation by ultrastability.

In spite of its great generality, the concept of ultrastability cannot account for the increase in complexity that is typical to evolution. As a strategy for regulation it can be greatly enhanced, however, if it is directed not only towards "experimental" modification of internal states, but also towards forming linkages with selected parts of the environment so that new organizations incorporating a higher variety emerge. Here, in particular, a significant amplification of regulation capabilities can be obtained. The increase in variety that is involved is typical to the evolutionary process. It is relatively slow in biological evolution where it depends on genetic mutations and on primitive forms of cooperation and coalition formation; it becomes more rapid with the emergence of simple forms of learning; and it is accelerated further still, becoming ever more flexible and much richer in scope, in the symbolic environment of language, culture and ideas.

A broad distinction can be made, accordingly, between three major and basically different regulation strategies. The simplest involves a precise specification of contingencies that is manifest in a mechanical adaptation or the incorporation of a fixed decision rule in a simple homeostatic mechanism. The second involves adaptation by ultrastability where a sufficient amount of variety is "built" into a system so that, within limits, changes in its environment can be matched by appropriate internal modifications, even when a specific decision rule is not available. The third is adaptation by evolution. As a strategy for ensuring an effective viability, it involves incorporating additional variety from the "environment," forming a new and more complex "unity." The latter corresponds to a new level of systemic integration which is marked by an increase in regulating capacity, and which is subject to selection for some specific survival advantage.

4. AMPLIFYING REGULATION THROUGH EVOLUTION

The possibility of amplifying regulation has played a major role in the emergence of stable organizations on earth where circumstances favor the formation of active regulators which mediate local stabilities, selecting for those that are particularly effective in their task. Two ideas emerge in this context as all important:

Firstly, that in any complex dynamic system subject to the operation of consistent constraints, some properties will be more resistant to change than others. These will tend to "survive" and gradually dominate their environment appearing as being particularly well adapted to its demands. If the total system is of an exceedingly high complexity, the selective processes leading to local stabilities may involve a wide range of dynamic activities rich in a variety of intriguing manifestations. Complex as such activities may be, they are all traceable to the phenomenon of adaptation (Ashby [5]).

Secondly, the active interactions of coexisting organizations (which are only partially autonomous in any case) continuously alter the properties of the medium in which they occur. (Luria [16]). As initial constraints are modified, and with them the norms of "survival success," new needs and conditions for further evolution are being continuously established, and the whole cumulative process proceeds with new possibilities and challenges created at each evolutionary step. The mutually adaptive processes that are inherent in the interaction of evolving organizations thus generate, as they unfold, the requirement for further adaptation.

In the process of seeking for a local viability, various organizations and modes of behavior arise, subject to satisfying the condition for stability under existing constraints. Relative to such constraints, favorable organizations and modes of behavior are allowed to persist and those which entail an improvement are encouraged to develop, thus generating, step by step, a trend that an observer would deem "evolutionary."

The selective process which mediates evolution is subject to the laws of control, specifically to the law of requisite variety and to the possibility of amplifying regulation. It operates simultaneously on two distinct levels. On one level it operates to increase the regulation potential of specific organizations, producing a better match between such organizations and the variety of their environment. On a higher "meta-level," however, it operates not just by selecting particular organizations at random, but by systematically encouraging variability in general. The outcome, as manifest by organic evolution on earth, is a local increase in the range and variety of adaptive possibilities and a consistent general trend characterized by a succession of progressively more complex organizations.

These involve a succession of stages which mark the ascent of living organisms and the development of a hierarchy of survival-related mechanisms. The latter range from mechanisms associated with differentiation and the formation of specialized organs, to mechanisms such as those involved with sexual reproduction, the formation of nervous systems and ever more complex brains, and the development of various modes of perception and communication. They include social organizations of increasing complexity, together with all their technological extensions. Ultimately, they involve the emergence of such properties as self-consciousness, logical reflection, and moral judgment.

From the viewpoint of cybernetics, this succession is interpretable as manifesting an expansion in regulation capabilities and living organisms, as they ascend the scale of complexity, show their ascent by a growing potency for regulating their environment under a potentially greater range of conditions.

The crucial point is that a viable system that is well adapted to its environment can be regarded as a successful regulator in that the repertoire of its actions matches effectively the variety of the disturbances "threatening" its stability. The concept of selection, accordingly, can be seen as entailing a process which operates to encourage an appropriate match between a regulator's variety and the variety in its environment. In a complex dynamic world it would favor the formation of high variety regulators, those effective in securing

viability under a wide range of dynamic events.

In other words, variety "mismatches" between interacting controllers will tend to produce a pressure for local variety supplementation. A dynamic environment of high variety can be expected, accordingly, to put a definite premium on the possibility of local increases in the potency of regulation capabilities. This condition in itself is sufficient to explain the persistent evolutionary tendency of forming stratified organizations of increasing complexity. Only through such a stratified organization, an increasing advantage in regulating capabilities can be achieved.

Thus, a perception of the world as a hierarchy of structures, differentiated by discontinuities and characterized by an increasing order of complexity and organization (Bronowski [9]), obtains a specific functional meaning. Such a hierarchy can be regarded as a stratified organization of controllers interacting such that across its levels regulation is amplified (Ben-Eli [6]). Each level in this hierarchy corresponds to a class of regulators, and these become more potent as they ascend the scale of complexity. Evolution is the process through which such a complexification--qua increase in regulation potency--is achieved and in this sense it can be regarded as an essential regulation strategy for achieving stability in a dynamic environment in which the context for stability is changing.

5. SUMMARY: A CHARACTERIZATION OF EVOLUTION

Evolutionary processes can be depicted by a dynamic activity in a redundant network of interacting regulators involving the selective formation of linkages between initially independent loci of control. The overall context of stability will shift, and actual realizations of stable configurations in such a network will continuously change, as linkages are formed and reformed.

While such overall shifts and local changes depend on various "chance" events, they are not entirely random. They are directionally biased by selecting processes which reinforce particularly "survival worthy" patterns, thus altering the condition probabilities of their own further realizations. As a result, evolution appears to an observer as a consistent trend involving a progressive increase in organization and suggesting an in-built drive for persistent self-improvement. Both features are fundamental to a concept of evolution and to a perception of life as a process which not only maintains but also constantly improves itself (Szent-Gyoergyi [24]).

Current thinking, whereby the concept of a "stable process," or a "stable identity," has become synonymous with the notion of "organizational closure" (Von Foerster [28]; Goguen [12]; Varela [27]; Pask [21]; but also Maturana and Varela [17]; Varela, Maturana and Uribe [26]--in a characterization of life), can be seen in a particular light with respect to the characterization of evolution as a process involving relative changes in variety, especially relative increases and local amplifications of variety among interacting organizations.

The crucial point is that instances of variety

increases are interpretable as involving the expansion of closure. Across a sequence of evolutionary steps the constancy of closure is maintained. At the same time, however, closure is also being expanded and improvements on previous norms of attaining closure are obtained. While variety is locally amplified, the means of ensuring closure gain in potency, thus expanding not only the closure itself, but the boundaries of the domain within which it can be attained (Ben-Eli [8]).

The evolutionary sequence of realizations and continuous improvements of realizations which result appear to an observer as a coherent trend (Pask [18]) characterized by a consistent dominant feature. We are now in a good position to characterize this dominant feature specifically. It involves the systematic production, through variety amplifications, of ever more general regulators fitted for an increasingly more comprehensive niche.

At any instant, the question of how the next amplification, how the next expansion of closure will be obtained, is left unresolved. For even as it is confined to the circumstances of a particular environment evolution is essentially an open-ended process.

Above all, evolution is regenerative and unlimited for as long as sufficient diversity is generated locally and sufficient distinction is maintained among interacting viable organizations. This fact is important in biology and in the context of the dynamics of stability of any ecology. It is especially significant to the question of the long-range viability of society, and, ultimately, of life itself. The implications of problems of policy in education, social organization, and social development are enormous.

REFERENCES

1. ASHBY, W. R., _Introduction to Cybernetics_, Chapman and Hall, 1956.
2. ASHBY, W. R., "Requisite Variety and Its Applications for the Control of Complex Systems," _Cybernetica_, Vol. 1, No. 2, pp. 53-99, 1958.
3. ASHBY, W. R., "General System Theory As A New Discipline," _General System Yearbook_, Vol. III, pp. 1-6, 1958.
4. ASHBY, W. R., "The Set Theory of Mechanisms and Homeostasis," Technical Report No. 9, Electrical Engineering Research Laboratory, University of Illinois, Urbana, 1962.
5. ASHBY, W. R., "Principles of the Self-Organizing System," in _Principles of Self-Organization_, H. von Foerster and G. W. Zopf (eds.), Pergamon Press, pp. 255-178, 1962.
6. BEN-ELI, M., "Comments on the Cybernetics of Stability and Regulation in Social Systems," Ph.D. Thesis, Brunel University, 1976.
7. BEN-ELI, M. and C. TOUNTAS, "The Evolution of Complexity in a Simulated Ecology," _Proceedings of SGSR Symposium_, Denver, 1977.
8. BEN-ELI, M., "Self-Organization, Autopoiesis and Evolution," _Proceedings of NATO International Conference on Applied General Systems Research_, Binghamton, New York, 1977.
9. BRONOWSKI, J., "New Concepts in the Evolution of Complexity: Stratified Stability and Unbounded Plans," _Zygon_, Vol. 5, No. 1, pp. 18-35, 1970.
10. CONANT, R. C., "Information Transfer in Complex Systems, with Application to Regulation," Technical Report No. 13, B. C. L., University of Illinois, Urbany, 1968.
11. GLANSDORF, P. and I. PRIGOGINE, _Thermodynamics Theory of Structure, Stability and Fluctuation_, Wiley-Interscience, 1971.
12. GOGUEN, J. A., "Objects," _International Journal of General Systems_, Vol. 1, pp. 237-243, 1975.
13. JANSCH, E., _Design for Evolution_, George Braziller, 1975.
14. KATCHALSKY, A., and O. KADEM, "Thermodynamics of Flow Processes in Biological Systems," _Biophysical Journal_, 2, No. 2, pp- 53-78, 1962.
15. KATCHALSKY, A., "Thermodynamics of Flow and Biological Organization," _Zygon_, Vol. 6, No. 2, pp. 99-125, 1971.
16. LURIA, S. E., _Life the Unfinished Experiment_, Charles Scribner's Sons, 1973.
17. MATURANA, H. R., and F. VARELA, "Autopoietic Systems--A Characterization of the Living Organization," B. C. L. Publications, No. 9.4, 1975.
18. PASK, G., "The Cybernetics of Evolutionary Processes and Self-Organizing Systems," _Proceedings of the 3rd Congress, International Association of Cybernetics_, Namur, G. Villars (ed.), pp. 27-75, 1961.
19. PASK, G., "Cognitive Systems," _Cognition: A Multiple View_, L. Garvin (ed.), Spartan Press, 1970.
20. PASK, G., B. C. E. SCOTT, and D. KALLIKOURDIS, "A Theory of Conversation and Individuals (Exemplified by the Learning Process on CASTE)," _International Journal of Man-Machine Studies_, 5, pp. 443-566, 1973.
21. PASK, G., "Organizational Closure of Potentially Conscious Systems," _Proceedings of NATO International Conference on Applied General Systems Research_, Binghamton, New York, 1977.
22. PRIGOGINE, I., "Structure Dissipation and Life," _Theoretical Physics and Biology: Proceedings_, M. Marois (ed.), North-Holland Publishing Co., pp. 23-52, 1969.
23. SOMMERHOFF, G., _Analytical Biology_, Oxford University Press, 1950.
24. SZENT-GYOERGYI, A., "Drive in Matter to Perfect Itself," _Synthesis_, Vol. 1, No. 1, 1974.
25. TEILHARD de CHARDIN, P., _The Phenomenon of Man_, Harper Torchbooks, 1965 (first published in 1955).
26. VARELA, F. G., H. R. MATURANA, and R. URIBE, "Autopoiesis: The Organization of Living Systems, Its Characterization, and A Model," _Biosystems_, 5, North-Holland Publishing Co., pp. 187-196, 1974.
27. VARELA, F. G., "The Arithmetic of Closure," _Proceedings of the 3rd European Meeting on Cybernetics and General Systems Research_," R. Trappl (ed.), Hemisphere, 1976.
28. von FOERSTER, H., Papers in Collected Publications of B. C. L., Microfiche, 1976.

Information, meaning and knowledge

C. M. ELSTOB
Department of Cybernetics, Brunel University
Middlesex, England

1. INTRODUCTION

For many years now I have been plagued by not having a clear understanding of the family of concepts denoted by the various uses of the word information. I was initially trained as a physicist, but physics has little to say about information. Physics accounts for the behaviours it studies in terms of energy interaction, flow and transformation. But there is a world of phenomena --the cybernetic world--that cannot be understood in these terms alone. It appears to be necessary to introduce the additional notion of information. This I find quite acceptable, yet I cannot make a complete break and adopt information as the appropriate irreducible explanatory atom for building understanding of cybernetic phenomena. I still see cybernetic interactions, in both the living and artificial domains, as having a physical basis. I have a persistent need to place cybernetics in a frame compatible with physics.

My aim in this paper is to present a number of questions, distinctions and ideas that seem to me, at this stage in my thinking, to contribute to a fundamental understanding of the notion of information as it appears in its various guises. I should warn those readers who do not share my intellectual discomfort in this matter that much of what I say will probably appear not only obvious but also rather misguided. Let me assure them here, however, that simple-minded though my doubts might seem they are sincerely held and persist in refusing to go away. I feel obliged, therefore, to at least try to articulate them.

2. INFORMATION: AN INITIAL DISTINCTION

When do we naturally say of an object (an entity or thing) that it uses information? We say it, of course, of human beings. But does it offend common usage to say that, for example, a telephone handpiece uses information? Certainly, it transmits information; perhaps we may even say that it processes information, but not, commonly, that is actually <u>using</u> information. Let us ask a closely related question: What sort of objects extract meaning from the inputs they receive? Again, humans do, and most would agree that the higher animals appear to. But do plants? Does a Watts governor? Does a computer program compiler? Consider a process that many would believe to be firmly within the heartland of physics: a rock rolling down a mountain slope. Is information flowing between the rock and the slope? Is the rock extracting meaning from the input it receives? Is the rock using information to "compute" its trajectory? Many people who claim an interest in cybernetics find their intuition answering "yes" to these three questions. My intuition says "maybe" in reply to the first, and definitely "no" in reply to the other two.

It seems to me that these three questions expose an important distinction within the family of concepts denoted by the word information. This is not a new distinction, but it does seem to me to be fundamental. To mark the distinction I propose coining two new words: physical-information (p-information), and semantic-information (s-information). The first question about the rock rolling down the mountainside--about there being information flow between the slope and the rock--appeals to the p-information side of the notion of information. The other two questions relate to s-information aspects, and there is nothing about the situation that makes me think that these aspects of information have any relevance to the phenomena in question.

Physical-information (often referred to as variety, e.g. Ashby [3]) is what is dealt with in technical information theory as developed by Shannon and others (Shannon and Weaver [5]). Studies of physical-information concern (at an agreed level of resolution) questions about the amount of form (pattern, or potential distinction) contained within a specified domain. It also concerns the preservation of form as it undergoes transformation and transmission. P-information flow exists (i.e. there is a channel for p-information) wherever correlation exists. Thus all causally linked events, all causal chains, present themselves as candidates for p-information investigation and analysis. Since a rock's motion is correlated with the terrain over which it rolls it is legitimate to make a technical information-theoretic (p-information) study of the interactions involved. It would, of course, be rather perverse to study such a phenomenon in this way but nonetheless it would be perfectly permissable to do so.

Most usually p-information analysis is carried out when a particular physical channel is used to support communication; or, when a medium is used to store distinct forms which have some significance to entities that so use it. Loosely: it is used for studying information transmission and storage.

We can consider p-information without any concern for s-information. But the reverse is not true; all questions of meaning and significance

necessarily involve, at some stage, questions
about physical embodiment. Meaning and significance are conveyed by p-information carriers and
although we readily accept that different carriers
can convey the same meaning we nonetheless recognise that we cannot completely ignore the means
of conveyance. Indeed, it is the relationship
between p-information and its interaction with
certain entities (call them s-information users,
or s-users) that lies at the heart of what I am
trying to pursue here.

Why can we not do without the concept of
semantic-information? Can we not make a very
strong case for arguing that all information is
really p-information? Theoretically, perhaps
this is possible. Just as it is theoretically
possible to describe all material events in terms
of atomic interactions. Being theoretically possible does not mean that it is useful. Our languages show the need for the distinction between
physical and semantic information. Information,
as used in the everyday sense, is much closer to
s-information in its meaning than p-information.
We are, of course, s-information users, and it is
the transmission of meaning that concerns us in
our interactions with one another and the world
aboud us. But yet, all the communication we have
is in terms of p-information, so why do we need
the concept of s-information?

The answer is not to be found in the p-
information alone, but in the interaction between
p-information and certain objects. Objects which
in their interaction with p-information manifest
behaviour that we describe in s-information terms.
Thus, I conjecture, it is to the behaviour of
certain objects that we should look for further
understanding of s-information.

3. BEHAVIOURAL PROPERTIES OF S-INFORMATION USERS

My aim in this section is to present a tentative analysis of the distinguishing behavioural
properties of those entities that we commonly
identify as s-information users. In order to make
the direction of the analysis clearer at the outset I list below examples of objects whose behaviour, I judge, marks them out as non s-users.
I also list, in contrast, examples of s-users.
These lists reflect my personal classification,
but I believe would not offend a majority judgement.

Examples of Non S-Users	Examples of S-Users
A billiard-ball being struck by a billiard-cue.	A person receiving spoken directions on how to find his way to a place in a town he does not know.
A tree moving in the wind.	A builder using a blue-print to lay out the foundations of a building.
A clockwork mouse run-ning about the floor.	A person balancing a billiard cue on his finger.
An alarm clock.	A person singing a song.
A servo-mechanism.	A bird building a nest.

In developing criteria for classifying s-
users it is simplest to proceed from both ends.
Thus, we want criteria that exclude non-users
and criteria that positively include s-users.
Our criteria are to be behavioural since it is
through observation of behaviour that we commonly
recognise s-users. I shall present and discuss
each criterion separately, and will consider the
behaviour of objects relative to the inputs they
receive.

To avoid serious misunderstanding I must make
one request. When I discuss any particular real-
life situation--like the ones listed above--I
must assume a particular representation (model,
or point of view). This representation may not
accord with my reader's one. Unfortunately, I
cannot engage in meta-discourse with my readers
in order to reach agreement about a common representation. I have to assume, therefore, that the
representation that I use is at least one that
common sense would accept. Of course, it might
not be the right one and as a result my conclusions are at least open to doubt on this score.
But doubt about whether my conclusions follow
from my model should be kept quite distinct from
doubt based on non-acceptance of my model of the
situation we are considering. Thus, for example,
some readers may wish to disagree with my classification above because they have a different
view of the phenomena I describe. If they do
strongly feel this then I ask them, before proceeding, to try to imagine the sort of point of
view that would yield the classification I have
given. It is this point of view that they should
hold in mind when considering the discussion that
follows.

> Criterion 1: The behaviour of an s-user in
> response to an input is not
> simply an energetic consequence
> of the energy of the input

A great many behaviours are directly excluded
by this condition. All passive systems are
excluded, for example the billiard-ball case
above. This condition also accords well with
the common intuition that the responses of
s-information users cannot be accounted for in
terms of the energy of the inputs they receive.
There is the feeling that the input merely acts
as a trigger and that the energy content of the
response is provided from some source within the
project.

We need to consider next those inputs that
constrain physically (energetically) the behaviour of objects. Let us introduce here the term
semantic-behaviour. This is the behaviour we are
trying to distinguish using the criteria we are
developing here.

> Criterion 2: Semantic-behaviour excludes
> effects produced by inputs that
> themselves energetically con-
> strain or alter action.

This condition is introduced to exclude all
behaviour that results either from an input
energetically changing the structure of an
object so that its behaviour is changed, or
through acting as a barrier (energetically) to

the continuation or initiation of certain behaviours. For example, the motion (trajectory) of a clockwork mouse is determined by the material objects it interacts with. A wall, for instance, provides an energetic barrier to further motion of the mouse into the wall. Similarly, a matchstick on the floor may deflect the motion of the mouse. Or, alternatively, a child might break one of the wheels of the mouse so that it behaves in a different fashion. The key point is that all of the effects are quite definite and can be accounted for in simple physical terms; there is no suggestion of indeterminacy.

The reader would be forgiven, at this stage, for perhaps beginning to think that I was working towards introducing some vital force as a necessary ingredient of s-information users. They may well suggest that surely all action is physically based. With this I would agree; but the two criteria given so far do not apply to all physically based behaviour. For example, we can imagine a piece of machinery that alters its structure on receipt of particular inputs, but yet in which the energy involved in the alteration is not provided by the input. Such a machine is a good deal more interesting to us as cyberneticians than a stone rolling down a mountain slope. It certainly suggests the application of s-information notions to its behaviour. Yet, I would suggest that many people would feel unhappy about saying that such a machine was extracting meaning from the input. I think that there are further useful distinctions to be made, and that they can be made in such a way that we have no need to abandon the possibility of giving a purely physical interpretation to the functioning of semantic-information users. The following criteria are drawn from consideration of the behaviour of objects we classify as s-users. They are, if you like, the positive criteria.

> Criterion 3: Semantic-behaviour is characterised by an object being capable of: (a) responding in the same way to different inputs, and (b) responding in different ways to the same input.

The conditions (a) and (b) above do not by themselves distinguish s-users, but they do mark out two important characteristics. Condition (a) accounts for the familiar observation that different things (inputs, messages, signals) can mean the same thing or have the same pragmatic effect. There are, of course, many systems that fail to meet one or both of the first two criteria above, yet meet condition (a). For example, a manual typewriter generally has two separate shift keys each of which produces the same effect when pressed. Incidentally, an electric typewriter would meet criterion 1 and, depending upon the exact details of its construction, possibly also criterion 2.

Condition (b) is introduced in recognition that the same thing can mean different things (have different significance) on different occasions to semantic-information users. We can imagine an electric typewriter meeting this condition too. Suppose that occasionally it got jammed so that depressing the shift key did not have the usual effect. This would meet (b) although we would

still doubt that such an entity was really an s-information user. We need further distinguishing characteristics.

> Criterion 4: A semantic-information user is capable of producing its responses to inputs independently of the inputs.

This sounds at first to be a rather contradictory statement. What it recognises is that s-users are inherently capable of decoupling themselves from their input. They can ignore inputs and they can produce action in the absence of input. This suggests that they _use_ inputs rather than _obey_ inputs. It hints at notions such as free choice and purposefulness, both of which are ideas we associate closely with those objects we also recognise as semantic-information users. This condition is the one least often met by non-s-information users. For example, it would be a strange sort of typewriter that typed itself and could ignore, at times, inputs it received through its keyboard. Such typewriters do appear to exist, however; a Teletype keyboard linked to a computer, for instance. To the unitiated, such an object does have much of the character of an s-information user. To the initiated, the determinacy of the system soon shows through and although it may meet all the above criteria it does not do so very fully. However, sophisticated programs can manifest behaviour that is convincingly s-information oriented. Winograd's [7] well-known program for natural language understanding is an example.

I believe that the above four criteria take us far enough in distinguishing semantic-information users from other entities. This sort of analysis, many may feel, can never reveal the vital character of intelligent entities like ourselves. I have much sympathy with this view, but then this paper has not set out to define the distinctive character of intelligent entities -- it has a very much more limited aim: to try to analyse what makes us say of certain objects that they extract meaning from the inputs they receive.

Before leaving this section it is worth pointing out that a finite-state machine, properly constructed, would meet all the four criteria for being an s-information user. However, we should be careful not to draw the conclusion that the behaviour of s-users is, therefore, entirely predictable. In theory, this is true. But in practice, the sort of finite-state machine (FSM) that would meet the criteria would exhibit considerable decoupling with respect to its environment and it would be difficult for us to keep track of its internal state. As to the difficulties of producing a FSM description of an s-information user, these would, in general, be immense.

4. A PRAGMATIC INTERPRETATION OF MEANING

What sort of objects would need to be s-information users? What is meaning to an s-information user? So far we have not even hinted at the answers to questions like these. We can get some way by rephrasing the two questions and combining them to ask: What sort of objects use p-information in an s-information manner in executing the behaviour they exhibit? I suggest that systems that exhibit goal-directed behaviour (Sommerhoff [6]; Woodfield [8]) might be such objects, but need not be. However, purposeful systems, as defined by Ackoff and Emery [1] almost certainly are.

According to Ackoff and Emery a purposeful individual or system is:

One that can produce (1) the same functional type of outcome in different structural ways in the same structural environment and (2) can produce functionally different outcomes in the same and different structural environments.

Thus a purposeful system is one that can change its goals in constant environmental conditions; it selects goals as well as the means by which to pursue them. It thus displays will. Human beings are the most familiar examples of such systems. (p. 31)

This definition shows marked similarity to our fourth criterion for distinguishing semantic-information users. We can argue that this similarity is more than superficial.

A goal is a particular relation defined on a set of variables. To qualify as a goal, a relation must consist of component variables that are open to independent influence and yet exhibit values that manifest a specific relation. Some examples will make this clear. Thermostatically controlled temperature is a unary goal-relation. The controlled temperature is open to a number of influences, e.g., the temperature of the environment, the temperature of the heater/cooler. The controlled temperature manifests a specific relation under these varying influences since it remains roughly constant in value. Car driving manifests a goal-relation in the roughly constant relation of the car to the road. This is a binary goal-relation since it is defined on the variables: position of car, position of road. Both of these variables are open to independent influence (the road may curve as it will and the car is not energetically constrained to follow it, as, for example, a train on a track is constrained). A tennis player attempts to manifest a specific relation between his racket and the ball. Again, both the position of the ball and the racket are open to independent influences and yet the racket/ball-contact relation is manifest. Some apparent goal-relations turn out not to be so on close examination since the necessary independence of influence cannot be established. For example, a pendulum always returning to its equilibrium state when disturbed might be thought to be manifesting a unary goal-relation but this is not so because the disturbance always gives rise to another influence (the correcting force) that ensures the return of the pendulum to its equilibrium state.

Since a goal-relation implies a correspondence between apparently independent variables there must be some system or set of interactions that ensures the correspondence. Upon examining a goal-relation it is usually found that some of the component variables may have their values forced without losing the goal-relation, whilst others do not have this property. That is, if some are given forced values the goal-relation is no longer manifest. For example, we may force, within fairly wide

limits, the curviness of a road and still observe the car following it. But if we force the trajectory of the car the goal-relation is lost. The road does not follow the car but the car follows the road. Recognition of this leads us to give special consideration to the behaviour of those variables whose action critically determines the existence of goal-relations. Generally there is a system of such variables and I shall call such systems control systems. We can now return to our main theme.

A control system achieves a goal-relation by coordinating its behaviour with events that influence the goal-defining variables so that the goal-relation is attained and/or maintained. Thus, it must produce actions appropriate to circumstances. This means there is a p-information channel, for there is necessarily correlation between the circumstances and the actions if these are to jointly produce a particular relation. That this is the case can be shown formally as Conant [2] has demonstrated.

For simple control systems the necessary coordination between circumstances (e.g. the state of the environment, the goal defining variables, and the state of the control system itself) and control action (the behaviour of the control system) to achieve the goal-relation may be produced by a simple mechanism. For example, a simple household thermostatic switch achieves the required coordination in a very straightforward fashion. The temperature of its surroundings finds expression within the switch as a change in the geometric form of a bimetallic strip. The shape of the strip, in conjunction with an externally variable mechanical constraint, determines the state (open or closed) of a pair of electrical contacts that in turn determine the state (on or off) of a heater. This in its turn affects the temperature of the surroundings of the thermostat. A circular p-information channel is thus produced, but there is no suggestion of semantic-behaviour.

Consider now a control system that has the property of being a purposeful system. Because it is purposeful it can pursue different goals in the same environment and the same goal in different environments. To achieve any goal it must establish an appropriate correlation between circumstances and its behaviour. We accept that it will use p-information to guide its action, but, because it is a purposeful system, it will not be a slave to the p-information it receives. For example, such a system on one occasion (say whilst pursuing goal G1 in environment E) may find it appropriate to respond with one behaviour (say B1) when it receives a particular input (say I1), whilst on another occasion (say whilst pursuing goal G2 in environment E) it may be appropriate for it to respond with a different behaviour (say B2) when it receives the same input (I1).

Similarly, we could argue for a purposeful system responding in the same way to different inputs. Several inputs may, although being different, convey partially the same p-information. For example, you can tell whether it is raining by seeing the rain fall, by noticing the raindrop ripples in a puddle, by feeling the rain, by observing rain streaking down a window-pane, by hearing it on the roof, or by being told that is is raining by someone else. All of these inputs might have the same significance with respect to a particular purposeful act; for instance, they might all signify the need to take an umbrella in order to keep dry outside.

A purposeful system also necessarily meets the last test for identifying an s-information user; i.e. that it can produce behaviour independently of input. The reason for this lies in the definition of a purposeful system: it can change its own goals; it can produce behaviour independently of the inputs it receives. This does not mean that a powerful system typically behaves in this manner, but simply that it is capable of doing so.

What then is the meaning of an input to a purposeful system? A pragmatic interpretation is that it is the effect it has on the system's behaviour. We should recognise that this effect may not show itself straightaway. McKay [4] makes this point very clearly by using the analogy of a signalman in a shunting yard who by changing the state of the signals and the points may not cause any immediate change in the behaviour of trains but has produced a change which can show up in later behaviour. One consequence of this view of meaning is that there is no need for an input to have one meaning; in general the meaning of an input will be determined by context and will certainly always be relative to a particular user or receiver of the input.

A purposeful system can pursue more than one goal. Furthermore, we ourselves are purposeful systems that learn; we can learn to pursue and achieve goal-relations which at one stage we could not or did not pursue. This implies that we can actively attach new meaning to inputs and can give meaning to stimulus configurations that previously lacked semantic content for us. Thus, put another way, we can construct new p-information sequences since by linking inputs in new ways to action we create new causal chains. On this view a learning purposeful system has the capability of establishing causal (p-information) connections between otherwise physically unconnected events. The important point is that the connection is not limited by the physical compatibility of the two sets of events. All that is necessary is that the purposeful system that mediates the interaction should be able to establish a suitable p-information link with one of the event domains and use the p-information it so receives to influence, through action, events in the other domain. Because it uses p-information in an s-information fashion it is able to construct, potentially, a very broad range of correspondences.

5. KNOWLEDGE

Knowledge is a notion closely linked to that of s-information. One of its meanings concerns the relationship between the internal state or condition of an object (usually a control system) and the object's ability to produce a particular goal-relation. For example, we make statements such as: "I know how to ride a bicycle," or "I know how to solve quadratic equations." Sentences like this may be re-stated in the following general form: "X is internally so conditioned that it can mediate goal-relation G." To <u>know how</u> to do something is to be able to relate and produce events

such that the thing in question is brought about.

The word "know" is also used to refer simply to the fact that a particular s-user can produce appropriate s-behaviour in response to particular inputs. For example, my dogs <u>know</u> the sound of my car arriving and they jump up to greet me as I come in. We use "know" in this fashion when we ask questions of the sort: "Do you know what causes wear marks like this on my tyres?" This sort of sentence appears at first sight not to relate to action, but we can see that it could if the questioner was concerned to stop the tyre wear and wanted to know where to direct his action to achieve this. We can generalise this use of "know" to: "X is so internally conditioned that it can produce an action A given input I such that A is appropriate in the context G."

This last generalisation is the key to understanding the idea of knowledge in the broad sense. A semantic-information user that knows something has, in essence, established a connection (correspondence) between two otherwise physically separate forms. In the cases we have examined so far both of these forms have been external to the object mediating the connection, or at least have had effects which have an external manifestation. But there is no necessary reason for this. If an object can establish correspondence between physically previously unrelated external forms, surely it can also establish correspondences between forms internal to itself. The correspondence it constructs will, of course, depend upon its particular nature. If the object has a thermodynamically unstable organisation its nature may be to act to support the goal-relation of maintaining its own organisational integrity. In such a case it would be important for it to establish such correspondences (call them semantic-correspondences, for convenience) between events in its world and its actions. If, for such a control system, action had always to await an appropriately stimulating input there would be many occasions when the system's survival would be at risk. What would be useful would be the establishment of internal sequences of semantic-correspondences that mirrored, or represented (indeed, corresponded to), the semantic-correspondence between inputs and actions that the system used to support the goals it served. These internal sequences of semantic-correspondences could then be activated in place of their external counterparts. Through doing this forms might be found that indicated goal satisfaction. By following through their correspondence to inputs and action, they may suggest appropriate goal achieving behaviour. Such internal semantic-correspondences that relate to inputs, actions and goals we would probably not feel too uncomfortable calling knowledge.

I have made no attempt in this paper to suggest what sort of mechanisms might realize semantic-behaviour. The reason for this is that I do not know what mechanisms would achieve it. Certainly it would be entirely physical, and open, I believe, to p-information analysis. Its key property would be its ability to freely establish correspondences (connections) between forms. But given such a mechanism we would still

be left with a major issue unresolved, and that
is: What directs or guides the particular correspondences between forms that a learning purposeful system such as a human being establishes?
How does an input come to elicit a particular
response? How does an input acquire the meanings
it does acquire?

REFERENCES

1. ACKOFF, R. L. and F. E. EMERY, On Purposeful
    Systems, Travistock, London, 1972.
2. CONANT, R. C., "The Information Transfer
    Required in Regulatory Processes," IEEE
    Transactions on Systems, Science and
    Cybernetics, Vol. SSC-5, No. 4, pp. 334-
    338, 1969.

3. ASHBY, W. R., An Introduction to Cybernetics,
    Chapman and Hall, London, 1956.
4. MacKAY, D. M., Information, Mechanism and
    Meaning, M.I.T. Press, Cambridge, Mass.,
    1969.
5. SHANNON, C. E. and W. WEAVER, The Mathemati-
    cal Theory of Communication, Illinois
    Press, Urbana, Illinois, 1949.
6. SOMMERHOFF, G., "The Abstract Characteristics
    of Living Systems," in: Systems Thinking,
    F. E. Emery (ed.), Penguin Books,
    Harmondsworth, England, 1969.
7. WINOGRAD, T., "Understanding Natural Lan-
    guage," Cognitive Psychology, 3, No. 1,
    1972.
8. WOODFIELD, A., Teleology, Cambridge Univer-
    sity Press, Cambridge, England, 1976.

Consciousness, and so on

RANULPH GLANVILLE
The Architectural Association, London, England

An inhabitant of the Universe of observation is an Object. All observable and observed things are such Objects, including the universe itself.

Such Objects are described as being self-observers: self-observation is the pre-requisite for participation in the Universe. In such self-observation Objects are formally represented as having two alternating roles, self-observing and self-observed -- notated respectively P and E -- together with means of observation -- X. The alternation between roles occurs in a self-time with two corresponding half phases. An Object named as $<O_a>$ can be formulated

$$<O_a> \quad = \quad E_a \quad \Leftarrow [(X_a) \quad] \quad \text{at time } S_a$$

$$\Leftarrow [(X_a)\ P_a] \qquad S'_a$$

$$E_a \quad \Leftarrow [(X_a) \quad] \qquad S + 1_a$$

$$\Leftarrow [(X_a)\ P_a] \qquad S + 1'_a$$

$$\text{etc.}$$

The Universe is inhabited by at least 1 Object: otherwise it is no Universe and the Object no Object. The Universe is an Object. There are at least 2 Objects.

Every Object is a self-observer. Some Objects observe other Objects. Some Objects are observed by other Objects. However, an Object can be non-other-observing and non-other-observed. Such an Object inhabits the Universe unknown to others. It does not know that it inhabits the Universe, nor does the Universe know it is an inhabitant.

Other-observation -- notated F -- of other-Object -- notated B -- can occur. In order for 1 Object to observe another, both must be in the appropriate roles and both self-times must be (temporarily) synchronised.

An Object observes itself. Doing so, it is self-observing: it cannot simultaneously other-observe. When the half-phase changes, the Object is freed from self-observing. Then it may other-observe.

An Object to be other-observed cannot at that moment be in the self-observing role, for when it is, there is nothing to observe. An Object to be other-observed must be in its own self-observed role.

For other-observation to occur, both Objects must be in their own self-observed roles.

In the case that there are 2 Objects, let 1 observe the other. Let the other-observed Object be $<O_a>$, the other-observing $<O_b>$. These 2 Objects are self-observing independently in their own self-times.

at time					at time
S_a	$<O_a> = E_a \Leftarrow [(X_a) \quad]$		$E_b \Leftarrow [(X_b) \quad] = <O_b>$		S_b
S'_a	$\Leftarrow [(X_a)\ P_a]$		$\Leftarrow [(X_b)\ P_b]$		S'_b
$S + 1_a$	$E_a \Leftarrow [(X_a) \quad]$		$E_b \Leftarrow [(X_b) \quad]$		$S + 1_b$
$S + 1'_a$	$\Leftarrow [(X_a)\ P_a]$		$\Leftarrow [(X_b)\ P_b]$		$S + 1'_b$
	etc.		etc.		

---

[1] No attempt will be made, in this paper, to clarify terms other than to say that "observe" is used in a most general (and not necessarily visual) way, and that an "Object" may be thought of as a conceivable. Brief elaborations may be found in previous papers [2,5,6]. My Thesis [4] has a more complete coverage. The general idea is not dis-similar to Pask's Topics [9].

When self-times (in this case $S + 1_a$ and $S + 1_b$) synchronise, an other-observation can take place, which "matures" in the synchronised (syn.) self-times $S + 1'_a$ and $S + 1'_b$.

S_a	$<0_a>$	$=$	E_a	$\Leftarrow [(X_a)\ P_a]$		E_b	$\Leftarrow [(X_b)\quad\ ]$	$= <0_b>$	S_b
S'_a				$\Leftarrow [(X_a)\quad\ ]$			$\Leftarrow [(X_b)\ P_b]$		S'_b
$S + 1_a$			E_a	$\Leftarrow [(X_a)\ F_b]$	syn.	E_b	$\Leftarrow [(X_b)\quad\ ]$		$S + 1_b$
$S + 1'_a$			B_a	$\Leftarrow [(X_a)\ P_a]$			$\Leftarrow [(X_b)\ P_b]$		$S + 1'_b$
$S + 2_a$			E_a	$\Leftarrow [(X_a)\quad\ ]$		E_b	$\Leftarrow [(X_b)\quad\ ]$		$S + 2_b$

The observation made of an other-Object is different to the self-observation of that other-observed Object.

Other-observation has the following characteristics: The other-observed Object is seen to exist. It is at least an "inanimate thing" in our interpretation of the "real world". The other-observing Object is a "cognitive thing" in the "real world". While the other-observing Object remains non-other-observed, its existence is unknown to others, and remains to be discovered.

There are at least 2 Objects. All Objects inhabit the Universe. The Universe is an Object. There are at least 3 Objects.

Other-observation of more than 1 Object, by another Object, can occur. Call the third Object $<0_c>$. Let $<0_b>$ observe $<0_a>$ and $<0_c>$.

at S_a	$<0_a> = E_a \Leftarrow [(X_a)\quad\ ]$	at S_b	$<0_b> = E_b \Leftarrow [(X_b)\quad\ ]$	at S_c	$<0_c> = E_c \Leftarrow [(X_c)\ F_b]$
S'_a	$\Leftarrow [(X_a)\ P_a]$	S'_b	$\Leftarrow [(X_b)\ P_b]$	S'_c	$B_c \Leftarrow [(X_c)\ P_c]$
$S + 1_a$	$E_a \Leftarrow [(X_a)\ F_b]$	$S + 1_b$	$E_b \Leftarrow [(X_b)\quad\ ]$	$S + 1_c$	$E_c \Leftarrow [(X_c)\quad\ ]$
$S + 1'_a$	$B_a \Leftarrow [(X_a)\ P_a]$	$S + 1'_b$	$\Leftarrow [(X_b)\ P_b]$	$S + 1'_c$	$\Leftarrow [(X_c)\ P_c]$

$<0_b>$ observes $<0_a>$ when the times $S + 1_a$ and $S + 1_b$ synchronise, and $<0_c>$ when the times S_c and S_b synchronise. But if times S_c and $S + 1_b$ were synchronised, $<0_b>$ would observe $<0_a>$ and $<0_c>$ simultaneously. Under these circumstances the times of observation co-incide and a relationship is established, for these observations, by $<0_b>$.

Relationships between 2 observations made by 1 observer of 2 Objects can take various forms. Let an arc represent the time of observation of an Object, and the vertical bars the times, over which relationships are computed, of relating. Let the time of observation be notated by S, subscripted by the observed, then the observing Object subscripts. This will serve as a condensed notation, from here on. The following relationships may be observed:

Identity $S_{a,b}$
            $S_{c,b}$ $<0_a> \leftrightarrow <0_c>$

Implication

$S_{a,b}$
$S_{c,b}$ $<0_a> \leftrightarrow <0_c>$

$S_{a,b}$
$S_{c,b}$ $<0_c> \leftrightarrow <0_a>$

$S_{a,b}$
$S_{c,b}$ $<0_c> \leftrightarrow <0_a>$

$S_{a,b}$
$S_{c,b}$ $<0_a> \leftrightarrow <0_c>$

Negation

$$S_{a,b}$$
$$S_{c,b}$$

$$<0_a> \ , \ <\tilde{0_c}>$$

(Negation is no relationship.)

In general, identity will be used in further examples, but only as a convenience.

When 1 Object observes 2 others and relates them, it makes a description. A description consists in a relationship holding between 2 Objects, one being the described Object, the other the describing. There are 3 types of description. Letting $<0_a>$ be the described and $<0_c>$ the describing Objects, we have

$$<0_a> \ \leftrightarrow \ <0_c> \qquad \text{description proper}$$

$$<0_a> \ \leftarrow \ <0_c> \qquad \text{model}$$

$$<0_a> \ \rightarrow \ <0_c> \qquad \text{anti-model (hypothesis)}$$

An Object that can relate 2 other Objects is capable of making representations in the "real world", but not of interpreting them [2,3,5,7,10].

There are at least 3 Objects. All Objects inhabit the Universe. The Universe is an Object. There are at least 4 Objects.

Other-observation of 2 Objects may be carried out by more than 1 observing Object. Let $<0_d>$ be a new Object, which will, like $<0_b>$, observe the Objects $<0_a>$ and $<0_c>$. The observations that $<0_d>$ makes will be different from those made by $<0_b>$, for the observations will be, respectively,

$<0_b>$		$<0_d>$	
$<0_a> =$	$E_a \Leftarrow [(X_a) \ F_b]$	$<0_a> =$	$E_a \Leftarrow [(X_a) \ F_d]$
	$B_a \Leftarrow [(X_a) \ P_a]$		$B_a \Leftarrow [(X_a) \ P_a]$
	$E_a \Leftarrow [(X_a) \ \ \ ]$		$E_a \Leftarrow [(X_a) \ \ \ ]$
$<0_c> =$	$E_c \Leftarrow [(X_a) \ F_b]$	$<0_c> =$	$E_c \Leftarrow [(X_c) \ F_d]$
	$B_c \Leftarrow [(X_c) \ P_c]$		$B_c \Leftarrow [(X_c) \ P_c]$
	$E_c \Leftarrow [(X_c) \ \ \ ]$		$E_c \Leftarrow [(X_c) \ \ \ ]$

(Where necessary, these observations of the Objects' behaviours will be subscripted with the observer thus:

$$B_{a(F_b)} \qquad\qquad B_{a(F_d)}$$

$$B_{c(F_b)} \qquad\qquad B_{c(F_d)}$$

etc.)

While the observations made must be different, the relationships may be similar. If $<0_b>$ observes that there is a relationship between $<0_a>$ and $<0_c>$, $<0_d>$ may also observe a relationship. When this happens, there is a primitive form of communication, subject to certain limits.

Firstly, there is no way of checking that the relationships seen between the Objects, and hence the "understandings" that the 2 observing Objects have, are similar. Secondly, whatever difference in the relationships is seen makes no difference, since there is no form of action that can result, and there is no necessary connection between the 2 relationships.

Under these circumstances we can say that the only relationship that is of significance is identity, since there is no gound for action using a model or anti-model. Thus, communication between 2 observers observing 2 Objects as related will only usefully occur when each sees the relationship as equality. Under these circumstances of individualistic communication, in the "real world", unambiguous messages (such as genetic and behaviour generating codings) are communicated, which require no "understanding". This communication also permits a minimalistic social grouping of Objects.

Other-observation of 3 Objects may be made by 1 Object. Call the third Object to be other-observed $<0_e>$. Let the other-observer be $<0_b>$, the 2 other other-observed Objects be $<0_a>$ and $<0_c>$. When such observations happen simultaneously, the observing Object can relate the 3 Objects. Using the arc and bars as before, we have

Conjunction

$$S_{a,b}$$
$$S_{c,b}$$
$$S_{e,b}$$

$$|<0_a> \wedge <0_c>| \leftrightarrow <0_e>$$

Disjunction

$$S_{a,b}$$
$$S_{c,b}$$
$$S_{e,b}$$

$$|<0_a> \wedge <0_c>| \leftrightarrow <0_e>$$

In these cases, the third Object $<0_e>$ is the result of the relationship. The relationship is thus a computation. (In the relationships between only 2 Objects, one of the Objects itself can be considered as the result of the computation.)

An Object that can relate 2 Objects computing a third Object as the result, can build up pictures of the "real world", can develop knowledge from such pictures, and can make social groupings [2,3,4,5,6,8]. Such Objects are normally considered animate, motivated and of limited intelligence, in the "real world".

Other-observation of 3 Objects may also be used to test representations. When 2 Objects are related, a third may be related similarly. Thus, if the other-observer $<0_b>$ sees a relationship between $<0_a>$ and $<0_c>$ such as

Identity

$$S_{a,b}$$
$$S_{c,b}$$

$$<0_a> \leftrightarrow <0_c>$$

that observer may similarly relate the third Object $<0_e>$

Identity

$$S_{a,b}$$
$$S_{c,b}$$
$$S_{e,b}$$

$$<0_a> \leftrightarrow <0_c> \leftrightarrow <0_e>$$

This expands the potential for communication.

An Object that can relate a third Object, making a similar description to that existing between 2 other Objects, can test that description. In testing a description, an observer can validate it: he can also open up the possibility of non-specific communication, in contrast to the limited communication already mentioned.

There are at least 4 Objects. All Objects inhabit the Universe. The Universe is an Object. There are at least 5 Objects.

2 Objects may other-observe 3 Objects, and, by doing so may communicate, even when meanings are non-specific. Let the 2 observing Objects be $<0_b>$ and $<0_d>$. When $<0_b>$ makes a description with $<0_a>$ and $<0_c>$

Identity

$$S_{a,d}$$
$$S_{c,b}$$

$$\left| B_{a(F_b)} = <0_a> \right| \leftrightarrow \left| <0_c> = B_{c(F_b)} \right|$$
$$<0_b>$$

(The $<0_b>$ subscripted under the identity sign is used to indicate which observing Object creates the identity.)

$<0_d>$ may observe $<0_a>$ and $<0_c>$, similarly, but unless the meanings are specific $<0_d>$ will necessarily not necessarily observe the same as $<0_b>$

Identity

$$S_{a,d}$$
$$S_{c,d}$$

$$\left| B_{a(F_d)} = <0_a> \right| \leftrightarrow \left| <0_c> = B_{c(F_d)} \right|$$
$$<0_d>$$

The other-observation made of $<0_a>$ by $<0_d>$ and described by $<0_c>$ may be tested by $<0_d>$ making another description of $<0_c>$. Since there is the relationship identity between the observations of $<0_a>$ and $<0_c>$, this should also be a description of $<0_a>$

Identity

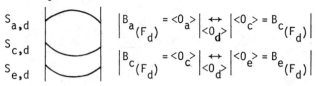

$$S_{a,d}$$
$$S_{c,d}$$
$$S_{e,d}$$

$$\left| B_{a(F_d)} = <0_a> \right| \leftrightarrow \left| <0_c> = B_{c(F_d)} \right|$$
$$<0_d>$$
$$\left| B_{c(F_d)} = <0_c> \right| \leftrightarrow \left| <0_e> = B_{e(F_d)} \right|$$
$$<0_d>$$

The first observer, $<0_b>$ may now observe $<0_d>$, to confirm that the observation of $<0_d>$ matches those which identify $<0_a>$ and $<0_c>$

Identity

$$S_{a,b}$$
$$S_{c,b}$$
$$S_{d,b}$$

$$\left| B_{a(F_b)} = <0_a> \right| \leftrightarrow \left| <0_c> = B_{c(F_b)} \right|$$
$$<0_b>$$
$$\left| B_{c(F_b)} = <0_c> \right| \leftrightarrow \left| <0_e> = B_{e(F_b)} \right|$$
$$<0_b>$$

If this is so, $<0_b>$ may confirm that the observation originally made of $<0_a>$ and described by $<0_c>$ has been communicated to $<0_d>$.

Non-specific communication can take place between 2 other-observing Objects by relating 3 other-observed Objects, in the manner described. In the "real world", this corresponds to that which is colloquially and technically known as a conversation, and allows both the storage and re-interpretation of knowledge, and the testing and development of ideas. Such characteristics are often thought of as distinguishing humanity from other animate life. In practice, we have developed short cuts that simplify our conversational procedures so that we can assume specific meanings even where there may be none (e. g. languages). This argument is beyond the scope of this paper and will not be elaborated here.

Objects can group together in various ways:

— By themselves they self-observe, but are neither other-observed nor other-observing: these remain to be discovered.

— In pairs, other-observing or other-observed; or both. Other-observed Objects are inanimate things, other-observing Objects remain to be discovered.

— 1 Object may observe 2 others, and in so doing will relate them (by identity or by implication). Such an Object can make representations.

— 1 Object may observe 2 others that a fourth is also observing and relating. If both Objects can relate them, limited communication has been established, providing that the meanings are specific. Such Objects are organisms communicating unambiguous codings, and are animate.

— 1 Object may observe 3 others, and relate them. In so doing it can compute results of relationships (and, or), group Objects, test representations, and build knowledge. Such Objects are animate and conscious.

— 2 Objects may observe 3 others and communicate non-specifically about one of them, to each other. Such Objects can store and

---

[1] A forthcoming paper, "The Domaine of Language in a Multi-valued Logic" [1], will attempt to discuss this.

re-interpret knowledge, and communicate by conversation, and test and develop ideas. They are animate, conscious and intelligent.
— Other combinations of Objects may elaborate this schema, but do not basically expand it beyond the range expressed here.

If the concept of the self-observing, and hence self-referential system referred to here as an Object is accepted, the gradual enlarging of the number placed together in a group from 1 to 5 would seem to account for and clarify our ideas of different levels of consciousness, while dispelling the literal idea that such Objects are necessarily animate.

REFERENCES

1. GLANVILLE, R., "The Domaine of Language in a Multi-valued Logic," forthcoming.
2. GLANVILLE, R., "The Logic of Description - or, Why Physics Won't Work," paper presented at the First International Conference on Applied General Systems, Binghamton, New York, 1977.
3. GLANVILLE, R., "The Model's Dimensions: a Form for Argument," paper presented at the Fourth Workshop on General Systems Research, Amsterdam, 1978.
4. GLANVILLE, R., "The Object of Objects, the Point of Points - or, Something about Things," Ph.D. Thesis, Brunel University, 1975.
5. GLANVILLE, R., "The Same is Different," in _Autopoiesis_, M. Zeleny (ed.), in press.
6. GLANVILLE, R., "What is Memory, that it can remember what it is," _Proceedings_ of the Third European Meeting on Cybernetics and Systems Research, 1976.
7. MONOD, J., _Chance and Necessity_, Fontana, London, 1972.
8. PASK, G., _Conversation Theory: Applications in Education and Epistemology_," Elsevier, Amsterdam, 1976.
9. PASK, G., D. KALLIKOURDIS, and B. C. E. SCOTT, "The Representation of Knowables," _International Journal of Man-Machine Studies_, Vol. 7, 1975.
10. de SAUSSURE, F., _Course in General Linguistics_," Philosophical Library, New York, 1959.

Attention, perception and purpose

F. J. HERNANDEZ–CHAVEZ
Department of Cybernetics, Brunel University
Middlesex, England

1. INTRODUCTION: ACTIVITY AS A BASIC CATEGORY

1.1. Approaches to the Subject

In examining the problem of attention, perception and purpose we have to consider the significance of the category of activity in any interpretation of how these processes are determined.

There are two approaches to this question. One of them postulates the direct dependence of those phenomena on the various influences exerted upon an organism's receptive systems. The main task of research in this approach is to establish the quantitative dependence of sensations on the physical parameters of the stimuli affecting the sense organs. This research is thus based on the "stimulus-response" pattern.

The limitations of this approach lay in the fact that it is assumed, on the one hand, things and objects and, on the other, a passive subject influenced by them. In other words, this approach ignores the significant element of the actual relations of the subject with the objective world; it ignores his activity. Such abstraction is, of course, admissible, but only within the bounds of an experiment intended to discover certain properties of elementary structures and functions contributing to the realization of certain mental processes. The moment one goes beyond these narrow limits, however, one realises the inadequacy of this approach, and it was this that compelled some early psychologists to explain psychological facts on the basis of special forces, such as that of active apperception that is to say, to appeal to the active nature of the subject, but only in a mystified form.

In order to overcome the difficulties created by the postulate of immediacy underlying the approach mentioned above, some scholars have stressed that the effect of external influences are determined not immediately by the influences themselves, but depend on their "refraction" by the subject.

In other words, it is emphasized that external causes act through the medium of internal conditions. But this notion can be interpreted in various ways, depending on what is meant by internal conditions. If they are taken to mean a change in the internal states of the organism, the notion offers us nothing new. Any object can change its states and hence manifest itself in different ways in its interaction with other objects. A hungry animal reacts to food differently from one that is well fed. It is another matter if by "internal conditions" we mean the special feature of processes that are active in the organism. But the main question is what these processes are that mediate the influences of the objective world reflected in the brain.

The answer to this question lies, I would say, in acknowledging that these processes are those that realise an organism's actual life in the world by which he is surrounded, his social being in all the richness and variety of its forms. In other words, these processes are his activity.

By activity we mean not the dynamics of the nervous, physiological processes that realise this activity. A distinction must be drawn between the dynamics and structure of mental processes and the language that describes them, on the one hand, and the dynamics and structure of the organism's activity and the language describing them on the other.

Being, the life of each individual, is made up of a system of successive activities. It is in activity that the transition or "translation" of the object into the subjective image takes place; at the same time it is also in activity that the transition is achieved from the subjective image into activity's objective results. Regarded from this angle, activity is a process of inter-traffic between opposite poles, subject and object.

1.2. Internal Conditions as Mediating Images

Activity is a non-additive unit of the corporeal, material life of the material organism. In the narrower sense, i.e. on the psychological plane, it is a unit of life, mediated by an image, whose real function is to orientate the organism in the objective world.

The basic constituent feature of activity is that is has an object. Moreover, the object of activity appears in two forms: first, in its independent existence, commanding the activity of the organism; and second, as the mental image of the object, as the product of the organism's "detection" of its properties, which is effected by the activity of the subject and cannot be effected otherwise.

The circular nature of the process effecting the interaction of the organism with the environment has been generally acknowledged (cf. Varela [5]. But the main thing is not this circular structure as such, but the fact that the mental image of the world is not directly generated by the external influences themselves, but by the process through which the subject comes into practical contact with the world, and which therefore necessarily obey its independent properties, connections and relations. This means that the afferent agent, which controls the process of activity, is primarily the object itself and secondarily its image as the subjective product of activity, which registers, stabilises and carries in itself the objective content of activity. Activity is bound to encounter organism-resisting objects that divert, change and enrich it. In other words, it is external activity that unlocks the circle of internal mental processes, that opens it up to the world.

2. ACTIVITY, ACTION AND STATES: AN ANALYSIS

The word "activity" is a very general word used to describe all sorts of goings on. This would lead one to expect that it did not possess a very strict logic of its own. However, activity in the generic sense of describing very specific kinds of change which cannot be described as precisely by means of any other concept has been the concern of some thinkers (cf. Kenny [3]; von Wright [6]). The search is for a sense of the word "activity" in which it is not implied that an activity is composed of a number of "doings" that are not themselves activities. A definite distinction must be made between an activity and an action such that it is not the case that an activity consists of a succession of acts.

2.1. Action and Its Results

We must draw a distinction already made by von Wright between the result of an action and the consequences of an act. The purpose of this distinction is to bring out two totally different ways in which an act may be connected with the changes effected by it. When the connection between the act and the change is intrinsic or logical von Wright calls the change the "result" of the act. When the connection is extrinsic (von Wright regards this extrinsic relation as primarily a causal one), the change is the "consequence" of the act.

For example, if the act is an act of opening the window, it is logically necessary for the window to be opening. The fact of the window opening is the result of the act. On the other hand, if the opening of the window caused the door to slam, the slamming of the door would be a consequence of the act of opening the window and not the result of an act.

Von Wright gives two possible interpretations that may be given to the use of "result": either the change corresponding to this act, or the end state of this change. Thus, by the result of the act of opening a window we can understand: the fact that the window is opening (changes from closed to open), or the fact that it is open. This distinction has been labelled by C. O. Evans as $result_c$, the change corresponding to the act, and as $result_e$, the end state of the change. Two possibilities present themselves: the agent may either bring about $result_c$ or $result_e$.

An activity may be identified in terms of these possibilities. An agent or organism is engaged in an activity (in the basic or generic sense) when he brings about a $result_c$ and he does not stop as soon as $result_c$ comes about. An agent is engaged in a performance when he brings about a $result_e$ and it takes time for $result_e$ to be produced.

The contrast between an activity and a performance may be brought out in this way: the result in an activity holds at all times from beginning to end; in the case of a performance the result is only fully realized at the termination of the performance.

The fact that in English the perfect tense is used to describe the results of activities and performances has led Kenny to distinguish between activities and performances on grammatical grounds. If the verb describing the activity or performance is represented by "has ∅ed" then it is possible to distinguish between activity and performance as follows: in the case of an activity "A is ∅ing" entails "A has ∅ed"; in the case of a performance "A is ∅ing" entails "A has not ∅ed" (cf. Kenny [3] p. 175). Performances are completed; activities just stop. Performances take time, while activities go on for a time.

2.2. States

The fundamental distinction between an activity and a state is that an activity is a sort of doing of an agent, and a state is not a sort of doing at all. We talk of the state of an organism or thing, or conversely, of a person or thing being in a certain state. A person is in a state when he is undergoing something or something is happening to him; and "undergoings" and "happenings" are not "doings". It must be granted that a person or organism may be able to induce a state, or put himself in a state, but this only means that he is able to bring about the conditions that give rise to the state; it does not mean that he brings about the state itself.

We must recognize non-dispositional as well as dispositional states. In the case of a dispositional state an organism may be said to be in a state under conditions in which he is undergoing nothing in connection with it at the time. In contrast, there are occurrent states which an organism can only be said to be in when he is actually undergoing a certain experience at the time.

The concept of state also implies the idea of its persistence through time. A state which existed for but an instant would be called an event. States, therefore, last for a time. Activities and states have in common that they are both continuous through time, but activities may be said to go on for a time, whereas states last for a time. It is possible to distinguish a thing's state from its circumstances. When we speak of states of an object we always have in mind some classification of the object relative to which the state is an accidental or changeable feature of the object. States are accidental or changeable features of organisms. A state is always a state relative to some prior classification of the thing. We have now the task of applying these distinctions to the phenomena of attention, perception and purpose.

3. ATTENTION, PERCEPTION AND PURPOSE: AN ACCOUNT

3.1. Activity Sustaining the Mediating Image

The previous section has given us some analytical means to determine the logical categories to which the concepts of attention, perception and purpose belong.

Attention has the logical features of an activity. It has temporal continuousness that makes it possible for attention conceived of as an activity to sustain the "image" of the world conceived of as a state. Both activities and states possess temporal continuousness.

When we are attending we are doing something and that rules out the possibility of attention being a state. On the other hand, "A attending to X" does not entail "A has not attended to X", so attending is not a performance. It must therefore be an activity. There is some difficulty in rendering attention itself an activity. The difficulty arises if we accept Ryle's view about attention: "There is no special activity called 'attending', there is only the attentive performance of an activity" (cited by Place [4]). In some passages Ryle points out the logical embarrassment occasioned by identifying attention with an act. But one can deny that attention is an act and to affirm instead that attention is an activity in the generic sense. But equating attention with activities seems to imply that attention is a purely inner mental operation trigger off in conjunction with bodily activities but which is logically distinct from them. In the context in which we have been discussing the term activity (see Section 1), this interpretation is rejected.

We have already said that activity, in the psychological plane, is mediated by an "image" whose real function is to orientate the organism in the world. In order to analyze the concept of "image" we can make use of the analogy with a map, and refer to "information-map" and the way they are structured to describe the "image".

The use of the word "information" (information-map) in this context has the advantage that we can speak of sensory illusion as "misinformation". However, under the influence of information theory it seems natural to think of information or misinformation as something distinct from the true or false information-map the organism acquires as a result of the information or misinformation. Spoken or written words are often naturally spoken of as information and they are distinct from the information-map which the words create in hearer or reader. In our context no distinction at all is intended between the information and the information-map to which it may give rise. Information and information-map are identical.

We can proceed to characterize an information-map as "a map of the world in the light of which we are prepared to act" (cf. Armstrong [1] p. 4). The totality of an organism's information-map at a particular time is a single "global map" of which individual information-maps are submaps. The information-map will include a map of the world that unfolds itself to him, a map in which the organism itself, his actions and states, are included. If we try to make a complete map of the world and therefore try to include in the map a complete map of the map itself we will be involved in infinite series of maps of maps. But since the information-map is not a complete map of the world, and since the map of itself that it contains is even more incomplete, the situation is not so desperate.

In ordinary maps we draw a distinction between the map itself and the map reader's interpretation of the map. In the case of information-map the organism does not read off his interpretation of reality from the data supplied by his information-map. His information-map is his interpretation of reality. Information-maps are maps which carry their interpretation of reality within themselves.

Information-maps fall within the general category of states of mind, that is a mental state. The concept of a mental state is primarily the concept of a state of the organism apt for bringing about a certain sort of behaviour. In the case of some mental states only we must allow that they are also states of the organism apt for being brought about by a certain sort of stimulus. Some mental states are actual occurrences, even although they result in no behaviour. In this way the relationship between mental state and behaviour cover more than one sort of relationship.

In some cases mental states can only be described in terms of their resemblances to other mental states that stand in causal relations to behaviour. Here the relation to behaviour is very indirect indeed. In many cases an account of mental states involves not only their causal relation to behaviour, but their causal relation to other mental states.

A mental state is not to be identified with behaviour. The behaviouristic approach uses the notion of a disposition to talk about mental states. Following Geach and Armstrong is better to use the notion of a capacity. Armstrong has emphasized the similarities and differences between dispositions and capacities: "capacities like dispositions, may or may not be manifested. And given the capacity or given the disposition, the nature of the manifestation or expression that may or may not occur is determined. But in the case of dispositions, the nature of the circumstance which brings about the manifestation is also determined. By contrast to say that a thing has the capacity to do something does not by itself tell us what circumstances will cause this capacity to be manifested. Manifestations of dispositions are stimulus dependent. Manifestations of capacity may be, but need not be, stimulus dependent."

3.2. Perception

Following von Wright we can make a distinction between ability and skill and relate it to a distinction between knowing how and having the mastership of a technique. If the organism is able to do a certain thing he knows how to do it. Only if the activity which is involved in doing the thing is of a complicated kind does this ability amount to mastership of a technique. When it does this we call such ability a skill. Capacity often has the character of "second order" ability. It is within an organism's capacity to do a certain thing, we may say, when he can acquire the ability or skill needed for doing this thing, although he does not yet possess it.

The biological function of perception is to give the organism information about the current state of its own body and its physical environment; information that will assist the organism in the conduct of life. We can think about perception as the acquiring of true or false information-map concerning the current state of the organism's body and environment. Perception is a matter of acquiring capacities to make physical discriminations within our environment if we should be so impelled.

If we look at the perception of objects, space, causality, and so on, as skills which we have to acquire in part through our commerce with objects, as beings capable of manipulating things and being affected by them, then the very idea of a basic building block of perception makes no sense. Perception is transferred from the category of something that happens to us to that of action; it is the exercise of a skill. What is immediately seen can no longer be distinguished as something separable from the interpretation an organism brings with him because of his knowledge, understanding, and social environment; and hence the idea of a percept identical through changes of interpretation has no application outside of its ordinary everyday application.

Perception consists of a cluster of skills, which have themselves developed in relation to abilities and motor skills by which an organism deals with the objects around him. A motor skill has no sharp boundary; rather it is a capacity for dealing with a relatively indefinite range of objects in a relatively indefinite range of ways. An awareness of things grounded in such skills is thus one in which the explicit focus can be surrounded and influenced by an implicit grasp of the situation, which resists reduction to a definite catalog.

3.3. Purpose or Goal

Up to now we have been talking about activity in the generic sense. In reality, however, we have to deal with concrete, specific activities, each of which is oriented towards the object of attention of the organism.

The main thing that distinguishes one activity from another lies in the difference between their objects. It is the object of activity that endows it with a certain orientation. We can refer to the object of activity as its intention. It may be given in perception or it may exist only in imagination, in the mind.

So different activities are distinguished by their intention. The basic "components" of separate human activities are the actions that realize them. These actions are the result which must be achieved, that is, the process which obeys a conscious goal or purpose. Just as the concept of intention is correlative with the concept of activity, so the concept of goal or purpose is correlative with that of action (perception).

The setting of the goal or purpose determine the method and character of the organism's activity. The identification of these goals or

purposes and the formation of activities designed to achieve them lead to a kind of splitting up of functions that were previously united in their intention.

The separation of purpose or goal oriented actions as components of the organism activity naturally brings up the question of their internal relations. As stated above activity is not an additive process. Hence actions are not separate things that are included in activity. Organism's activity exists as action or a chain of actions. When we consider the unfolding of a specific process--external or internal--from the angle of intention, it appears as organism activity, but when considered as goal oriented or purpose process, it appears as an action or a system, a chain of actions.

Activity and action are both genuine and, moreover, non-coincidental realities, because one and the same action may realise various activities, may pass from one activity to another, thus revealing its relative independence. This is due to the fact that the given action may have quite different intentions, that is, it may realise completely different activities. And one and the same intention may generate various goals and hence various actions.

So, in the general flow of activity which forms an organism life in its highest manifestations (those mediated by mental reflection), analysis first identifies separate activities, according to the criterion of the difference in their intentions. Then the action processes obeying conscious goals and purposes are identified, and finally, the operations that immediately depend on the conditions for the attainment of a specific goal.

These "units" of an organism activity form its macrostructure. The analysis by which they are identified is not a process of dismembering living activity into separate elements, but of revealing the relations which characterise that activity. Such systems analysis simultaneously rules out any possibility of a bifurcation of the reality that is being studied, since it deals not with different processes but rather with different planes of abstraction. Hence it may be impossible at first sight, for example, to judge whether we are dealing, in a given case, with action or with operation. Besides, activity is a highly dynamic system, which is characterized by constantly occurring transformations. Activity may lose the intention that evoked it, in which case it turns into an action that realises perhaps a quite different relationship to the world, a different activity; conversely, action may acquire an independent motivating force and become a special kind of activity; and finally, action may be transformed into a means of achieving a goal capable of realising different actions.

The general structure of activity, its "macrostructure", does not change. What changes radically at every stage of development is the character of the relationship that connects the goals or purposes and intentions of activity.

To sum up, the activity of an organism is not a flat surface to be filled with images and processes. Nor is it the connection of its separate elements. It is the internal movement

of its "formative elements" geared to the general
movement of the activity which effects the real
life of an organism in its social environment.

REFERENCES

1. ARMSTRONG, D. M., Belief, Truth and Knowledge,
      Cambridge University Press, 1973.
2. EVANS, C. O., The Subject of Consciousness,
      George Allen and Unwin, London, 1970.
3. KENNY, A., Action, Emotion and Will,
      Routledge and Kegan Paul, London, 1963.
4. PLACE, U. T., "The Concept of Heed," in:
      Essays in Philosophical Psychology,
      D. F. Gustafson (ed.), New York, 1964.
5. VARELA, F. J., "The Arithmetic of Closure,"
      Third European Meeting on Cybernetics
      and Systems Research, Vienna, Austria,
      1976.
6. VON WRIGHT, G. H., Norm and Action, Routledge
      and Kegan Paul, London, 1963.

The growth of knowledge

L. JOHNSON
Department of Cybernetics, Brunel University
Middlesex, England

This paper is not original in any but a trivial sense. It brings together some of my notes into a broad brush account of a philosophical outlook that, I think, sits well with cybernetic interests. In attitude I have been influenced by C. S. Peirce, Kant, Strawson and Wittgenstein. In contents this paper owes a great deal to Rescher and Kenny (listed in the Bibliography). Much of the work was undertaken whilst in receipt of a Science Research Council grant.

1. BACKGROUND

To provide a backcloth I shall paint from a palet with media provided by Armstrong and Lehrer, two very different epistemologists. Against this backcloth we can contrast the view put forward here.

Most accounts of the nature of knowledge take as their starting point a traditional analysis of the concept of knowledge. This traditional analysis has the following outline:

For a thing to be known three conditions must be fulfilled: (1) that the thing purportedly known is true, (2) that the thing purportedly known is believed, (3) that the thing purportedly known is adequately supported and justified. Knowledge, on this view, is true belief adequately supported -- belief is like the running of a race, knowledge is like the winning; knowing is a status beliefs can achieve by "passing the post". The traditional arguments for this analysis were the complex ramifications of the following points: If one claims to know that p (a proposition) and one is shown that p is not the case, then one could not be said to have known that p. Thus knowledge is not simply a psychological state of he who knows his beliefs (personal to him) must be, at least, true (objective). If one claims to know that p and goes on to state that one does not believe that p, the claim to know or the disbelief would be called into doubt. How could it be that one wins a race one has not run? If one claims to know that p, and yet could not support one's claim, one cannot be said to know that p; as part of the objective nature of knowledge, it must be relatable to the world of other things known, and these must be at least part of the grounding for our claims. A claim to knowledge, it seems, must be supported.

We shall not take issue with these points or try to spell out all the moves and countermoves in the traditional arguments. But, we note that, <u>in the terms of the traditional arguments</u>, a difficulty immediately arises:

Suppose one claims to know that p solely on the grounds of evidence E. Now suppose one goes on to admit that one does not know E to be true. One's claim is undermined. It seems that we require a claim to knowledge to be supported in such a way that requires one not only to know that p, but also know that E is true. Thus the conditions for a justified claim to knowledge seem to require knowledge as part of one of those conditions. An infinite regress is threatened.

One can characterize many of the various theories of knowledge as different reactions to the threatened infinite regress (Figure 1). I shall not discuss reactions 1 and 2; the ground is well trodden and hard. Let us consider reaction 3, the reaction of many in cybernetics. If the regress has no end, then at some point the reasons which support a claim must back onto their own tail, so that p is supported by q, q is supported by r, r is supported by s, . . . is supported by p. This, we may suggest, is not viciously circular; if we have a circle of true beliefs which mutually support each other, in a sufficiently comprehensive way, we have, not merely true belief, but knowledge. This theory is close in spirit to the coherence theory of truth -- the theory that a proposition p is true if, and only if, it coheres with the "story" we have built up out of other propositions. The traditional analysis of knowledge implicitly assumes that the conditions of truth and a coherence theory of knowledge, one is denying this. Clearly the difficulties with the Coherence Theory of Knowledge are the same as the difficulties with the Coherence Theory of Truth. The first thing to establish is what coherence means -- it is a stronger idea than consistency; for instance, my belief that this pen is a Parker, and my belief that this page is white are consistent, but this fact barely improves the chances that either or both are true; also it is a truth of logic that if a set of propositions A, B and C are consistent, then so are not-A, not-B and not-C. But then, on the Coherence Theory of Truth, if we adopt consistency as a criteria, two sets of contradictory propositions could both be true. But this contravenes our most basic ideas about Truth, that if a proposition is true, under no circumstances could the contradictory of that proposition be true. The difficulty for a coherence theory of knowledge is, not only what criteria can be given to show that a circle of beliefs is sufficiently comprehensive and structured, but might there not be a circle of beliefs

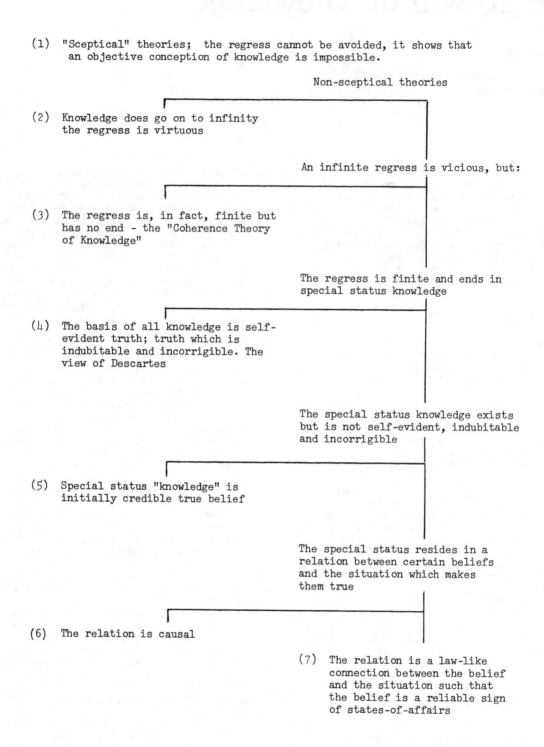

(1) "Sceptical" theories; the regress cannot be avoided, it shows that an objective conception of knowledge is impossible.

Non-sceptical theories

(2) Knowledge does go on to infinity the regress is virtuous

An infinite regress is vicious, but:

(3) The regress is, in fact, finite but has no end - the "Coherence Theory of Knowledge"

The regress is finite and ends in special status knowledge

(4) The basis of all knowledge is self-evident truth; truth which is indubitable and incorrigible. The view of Descartes

The special status knowledge exists but is not self-evident, indubitable and incorrigible

(5) Special status "knowledge" is initially credible true belief

The special status resides in a relation between certain beliefs and the situation which makes them true

(6) The relation is causal

(7) The relation is a law-like connection between the belief and the situation such that the belief is a reliable sign of states-of-affairs

The above diagram is adapted from Armstrong p. 156.

Figure 1. Reactions to the Threatened Regress

which were arrived at by a process so bizarre that we would not want to call it knowledge?

We shall return to reflect upon the coherentist view, but for now, let us press on.

Reaction 4. The regress ends in self-evident truths. The classic answer. Knowledge is founded on indubitable and incorrigible beliefs. Here we find the assimilation of knowledge and certainty. With this pruning knife the tree of knowledge is cut back to a lonely stump: solipsism -- the doctrine that one can only know the contents of one's own mind, here and now. A great deal of philosophical ink has been soaked up by this reaction to the threatened regress. We cannot pay fair attention to it here, although what we say later will stand to contrast with this view.

Reaction 5. This theory equates knowledge with belief which is initially credible and also true. Error is empirically and logically possible. This, I think, is a step in the right direction, but in working this theory through one is led to reaction 7.

Reaction 6. This view takes the roots of knowledge to be in belief-states which are caused by the situation which makes those beliefs true. An example might be the excessive heat of a room which causes one to have this belief. This account would have great difficulty in explaining knowledge of the future. For instance, I know that sooner or later I will put this pen down (or at least release it), but we can hardly say that when I do put this pen down (or release it) this happening causes my belief. A future cause does not seem to be an intelligible idea.

Reaction 7. Armstrong's theory: the philosophical counterpart of many caberneticians' view. This theory equates the roots of knowledge with empirically reliable belief. The question in what areas this special status knowledge is found seems to be a psychological one; a question of the cognitive structure and power of the human mind. The quickest way to grasp this idea is to use a model. Armstrong uses an intuitively clear model: the thermometer. Suppose that a thermometer is reliably registering a certain temperature. There must be some property or properties of the instrument and/or its circumstances such that, if anything has that property or properties, it must be the case, as a matter of natural law, that the temperature is that registered.

Thus, a belief is a case of special status knowledge if, and only if, the belief is true and there is a characterization of the state of the believer C, such that the believer is C and there is a law-like connection in nature, of the form:

For all x, if x is C and if x believes that p, then p is the case.

Examples of such beliefs might be judgments of a simple perception. The relationship holding between the state of affairs and the belief is not here causal. The relation is not independent of causes, however; it can, perhaps, be understood in terms of information flow.

2. PRACTICE AND KNOWLEDGE

The theory of knowledge I am going to recommend stands, as I see it, in the relation of elephant to the trunk, legs and tail of reactions 3, 5 and 7.

As a sweeping generalization I would say that most Cyberneticians have reaction 3 or reaction 7. The Coherentists must see themselves working essentially alone, whereas the "Reliabalists" could see themselves as tunnelling from the opposite side of the hill. I would hope to show the Coherentists they can adopt this attitude too.

We notice that most epistemological discussions begin by scrutinizing the sort of evidential considerations in terms of which claims are validated; some start from the nature of ontology. In contrast the approach here is to ascend to the generic level of the <u>activity</u> of going about the business of substantiating a claim. We examine what it is to have an inquiry procedure, or method, for validating the acceptance of factual theses.

How are we to determine that an inquiry procedure is adequate? This question shows the level of our interest in the inquiry procedure or method; we are not concerned with the details of any proposed inquiry procedure but in the meta-methodological questions, concerning the framework in which this (or these) methods or inquiry procedures have their life.

Our question poses a problem; consider the following argument:

Let C represent the criteria we propose to use in practice for the determination of empirical truth; accordingly we will classify a proposition as true if, and only if, it meets the conditions specified by C. Our question, "How are we to validate C?" seems to boil down to this: "Does C yield truths?" But how can we implement the justificatory programme inherent in this question? We would have to check if, in fact, they were truths. But C <u>is</u> our criteria for the determination of factual truths. Our meta-methodological question either has no sense, or its answer cannot be given directly. This argument teaches us that there can be no direct way of checking the adequacy of an inquiry procedure. If we are to find an answer we must find a different way of validating the inquiry procedure.

Our approach is to apply to the special case of a cognitive methodology an instrumental validation, i.e. a validation in terms of the processes, techniques, procedures and instrumentalities used. We have to found justification of a cognitive method, not on a theoretical stand, but on a practical stand; the practical aspect of cognition comes to the fore. We take practice to be the ultimate control on theory. The practice at issue relates to man's welfare only at the hardcore, and to his existence only ontogenically. In advanced forms of life practice ramifies to the technology of inquiry, bringing the complex intertwining of theory and practice characteristic of sophisticated societies.

Let us draw a diagram to represent the instrumental justification of an inquiry procedure (Figure 2).

We propose an instrumental justification for C; this was meant to be its "external" support. One justification here is, however, two-way; the results justify the method and the method justifies the results as correct. So we must, it seems, appeal to the procedure itself to substain the claim that it is to be its "external" support. There seems to be only one way to break the circle: the premises into the justificatory argument for M,

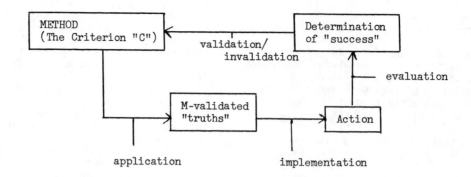

Figure 2.

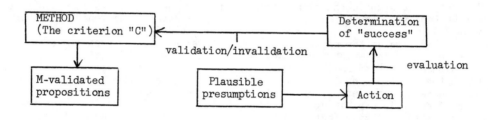

Figure 3.

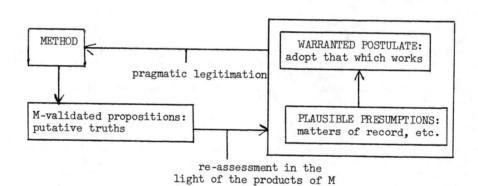

Figure 4.

the experimental data, must not be seen as validated truths but as merely plausible presumptions.
Like the heir presumptive, the plausible presumption comes into the inheritance given that no one
with a higher claim is born. Thus we distinguish
between two classes of propositions. On the one
hand we have warrantedly assertable propositions
which are defeasible (can be defeated) and on the
other hand we have truths which, by the nature of
truth, are not in principle defeasible.

We input plausible presumptions and adopt the
practice of continuing to use a method that has
proven to be successful in those cases where it
has been tried. One ground for the rationality of
this procedure is simply that it is the best we
can do. We do not claim that our method is
correct, but only that it is rational practice to

adopt it. This is the pragmatic element. We
introduce a purposive dimension into the sphere
of knowledge. It is supremely rational to do
something to achieve one's purposes where doing
nothing will not. To be justified in doing something to fulfill our purposes we do not have to
have a correct method but a method that has worked
and for which we can see no reason to believe that
it will be defeated in this case. Thus enrolling
the notions of presumption and plausibility we are
able to give a detailed analysis of the proposed
pragmatic validation of cognitive methodlogy.

The overall process is a feedback loop leading
from M-validated propositions to the initial
merely presumptive defeasible truths. The closure
affords a test of the adequacy of the presumptions
and postulates at issue -- the reasonableness of

the overall process rests not only on the external element of pragmatic efficiency, but also on the internal element of intrinsic coherence of mutual support of self-substantiation that the various stages of the whole are able to lend one another.

Thus we have broken the regress of justifying theses by theses: a thesis can be justified by a method and adoption of a method is justified by reference to its intrinsic coherence and its place in the context of purposive human activity. This two-stage division of labour is the characteristic idea of a specifically _methodological_ pragmatism; a pragmatism which recognized that the content of our knowledge is constrained by an external and independent reality wholly outside the cognitive domain, but it takes these constraints to be manifest predominantly on the side of practice. Most epistemologists focus directly on our knowledge itself without considering it in the light of the methodology that produces it. This approach differs in that it views methodology as a factor of prime importance correlative with knowledge itself.

In contrast to most pragmatic theories, in this theory the contact between pragmatic utility and truth is mediated by methods, and thus avoids most of the standard objections to pragmaticism. Theses are supported by reasons, that is, other theses, and theses are supported by methods, and methods are supported by pragmatic utility. Pragmatic utility and truth are broken apart and the middle ground of methods introduces the inherent generality in this approach. Methods are intrinsically public and interpersonal. A method is not a successful method unless its employment is generally effective, and thus must be capable of being shared by imitation and instruction. In the context of purposive activity it can be codified and taught as a collection of procedures in terms of instructions and rules. Thus methods have a fundamentally social dimension; accordingly, methods possess a freedom from any sort of personal dependence. The success of a method is a feature whose systematic nature gives it great weight in matters of justification -- in spite of its occasional failings. Success is an empirical element that hinges on the "constitution of the world"; it reflects the fact that our concepts are attuned -- through their development -- to the realities of the world we live in. Thus perhaps the seed of the tree of knowledge is something like Armstrong's theory.

But the question remains, "How is one to validate the linkage between the factor of methodological success and theses truth?"

The meaning of "true" must surely continue to be understood in everyday (correspondentist) terms: "P" is true if, and only if, p. That is, a true statement is one which affirms what is actually the case. Thus we cannot validate the linkage between methodological success and theses truth on semantic grounds; "methodological success" does not mean "true". No, we must adopt a certain posture in our metaphysics. Because of the inherent generality of methods and the developmental aligning of our methods to "reality" we postulate that our methods lead to truth. What are these metaphysical considerations? Basically these revolve around man's activism. Man must constantly act appropriately upon his environment, and his knowledge and beliefs must be part of the determinants of his action.

Not only does he act, but these actions bring back a flow of consequences with which he must deal. This provides the linkage between methodological success and truth. We postulate an order in the precognitive realm (or reality) out of which we grow, and postulate the developmental aligning of our concepts to that order such that the order provides the limit to which our developing concepts approach.

Hence we have two interlocking feedback circles (see Figure 5).

Only when everything is adjusted and stable will we obtain a workable pragmatic methodological justification for an inquiry procedure. The success or failure of our actions is wholly outside our control; it is this which blocks the prospect of our spinning around in purely theoretical cycles. Somewhere along the line there must be provision for a corrective contact with the bedrock of a precognitive realm. Thus we have united the two distinct elements: (1) the systematic coherence and closure at the theoretical level, and (2) a controlling monitor of pragmatic efficiency. Both of these ingredients are essential for the inner structure of our knowledge and the legitimizing of our claims to know. Neither can be dismissed for the sake of the other.

3. PRACTICAL REASONING

The following is a brief outline of the methods and some results in the logic of practical reasoning. This shows that there are important features in the logic which differ from standard logic (propositional calculus and lower predicate calculus). These features we found in our discussion on pragmaticism, and there may well be some interesting results to be found from pursuing these questions in a cybernetic context.

In practical reasoning we pass from premises which set our desires, the facts of the case and the possibilities open, to the "conclusions" which are _actions_ or plans for actions. In standard logic we pass from premises to conclusions which are _propositions_. The rules of standard logic are permissive -- given a set of premises one does not have to draw any particular conclusion or any conclusion at all. But there is a necessity in standard logic and it is this: if the premises are characterized as true and the passage from premises to conclusion valid, then the conclusion cannot also be characterized as true. For the rules of standard logic are designed to ensure that we cannot pass from true premises to false conclusion, that is, the rules of standard logic preserve the truth through inference. Metalogic is that branch of logic concerned with such proofs as the proof that standard logic is truth preserving. Now we can ask in what sense does practical reasoning necessitate its conclusion? What value do the rules of practical reasoning have as their purpose to preserve through inference? Before we answer this question, let us consider a difficulty in a _different_ but related field -- imperative logic.

(1) Post the letter → Post the letter or burn it.

(2) Vote Labour → Vote for someone.

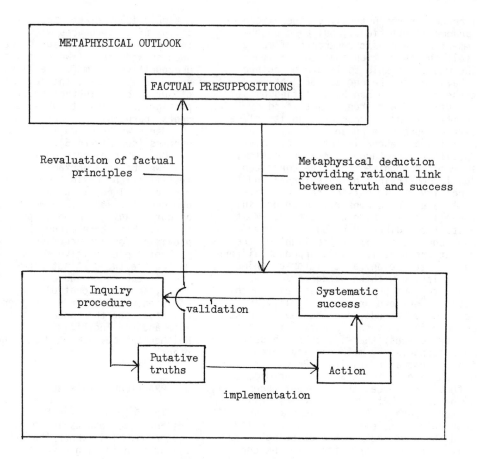

Figure 5.

The inferences ⊢p, ⊢p v q and ⊢F(a), ⊢(∃x)Fx are perfectly valid, but the above antecedents could hardly have been said to have been obeyed by someone who burns the letter and votes Conservative. Clearly we use a different logic, or use logic in a different way when we reason practically.

To pursue this difference, we need to make a few distinctions: we shall follow Frege and distinguish the descriptive content of a sentence, and the mood, i.e. assertoric or imperative. Thus the sentence "Shut the gate" uttered with the force of a command would be characterized by two parts: "The gate's being shut" (the so-called phrastic) and "Bring it about" (the so-called Tropic or mark of mood). Thus the logical form of the sentence is: "Bring it about: the gate's being shut."

Similarly, one could argue -- I do not do so here -- that expressions of intentions have the logical form of fiats. For example, "I intend to shut the gate" has the logical form: "Be it done: the gate's being shut." This suggests that in practical reasoning we make plans which have the logic of fiats. Our pattern of inference leads from fiats to fiats. Thus we extend the formal apparatus of logic to sentences in moods other than the indicative. The formation rules for this logic, which seem most appropriate, are that a tropic can be attached to any well-formed phrastic. But, to return to our first question, what are the transformation rules? We saw that this depends upon the value to be preserved through inference in practical reasoning. Consider fiats. Fiats contain descriptions of possible states of affairs whose actualization satisfies the desires expressed by them. Among fiats are plans and projects. One thing we are looking for are plans and projects which are satisfactory. Now obviously, satisfactoriness is a relative notion -- a plan that is satisfactory for one person may not be satisfactory for another person, or satisfactory to the same person at another time, with a different purpose. This is what we find in practical reasoning. Reflection on these matters leads one to agree, I think, with Kenny that the logic operative in practical reasoning is the logic of satisfactoriness. This logic should consist of rules which ensure that in practical reasoning we never pass from a fiat which is satisfactory for a particular purpose to a fiat which is unsatisfactory for that purpose. The rules should be satisfactoriness preserving, just as the rules of standard logic are truth preserving.

Let us suppose we desire a certain state of affairs for its own sake, not as a means to a further end. Then the fiat expressing this state of affairs will be the fiat whose satisfaction will satisfy the desire. Let us call this fiat a goal, and say it expresses a purpose. We settle our purposes, but it does not usually depend on us which plans are compatible with, or effective of, the achievement of our purposes. Our practical reasoning is bound up with this means end reasoning.

It is not difficult to construct a logic of satisfactoriness. It turns out that the logic of satisfactoriness is the "mirror image" of the logic of satisfaction ("satisfaction" is the notion used to define "truth in an interpretation" for standard logic). Thus whenever we have an inference from A to B in the logic of satisfaction, we have an inference from B to A in the logic of satisfactoriness. This handy fact means we have a "decision procedure" for the logic of satisfactoriness: suppose we wish to know if "Be it done: P" (or "Fiat P") can be derived from $F^{iat}Q$, the answer is that the inference is valid if $\vdash P \supset Q$ is valid.

The logic of satisfactoriness offers a means for solving the puzzles in imperative logic which disturbed us. The inferences $F^{iat}p$ to $F^{iat}p \vee Q$ and $F^{iat}F(a)$ to $F^{iat}(\exists x)Fx$ are not valid in the logic of satisfactoriness, and this conforms with out intuitive expectations. Let us apply our "decision procedure":

We wish to know the validity of "Fiat: The letter is being posted, hence Fiat: The letter being posted OR the letter being burned."

This (we have stated as a result) is conditional upon the validity of "It is the case that: the letter is posted OR the letter is burned, hence it is the case that the letter is posted." This is not valid; assigning false to "The letter is posted" and true to "The letter is burned" is a refutation. Hence the mirror image practical inference is invalid.

The inference $F^{iat}F(a)$ to $F^{iat}(\exists x)Fx$ is invalid because the inference $\vdash (\exists x)Fx$ to $\vdash F(a)$ is expressly forbidden in standard logic.

It is obvious that in our everyday practical reasoning we make use not only of the logic of satisfactoriness, but also of satisfaction. We must note, however, that the "mirror-image" relationship between practical reasoning and standard logic is more complicated than at first appears. It is this complication which shows that practical reasoning is not merely reasoning to sufficient conditions (contra Simon) and it is this feature which has the most important implication for cybernetics. This complication is that the conclusions in practical reasoning are defeasible. Consider the following piece of practical reasoning: Fiat: My possessing an outline of a cybernetic pragmatism. It is the case that: If I write up my notes, I'll have an outline of a cybernetic pragmatism. Therefore, I'll write up my notes.

It could be argued by one who attempted to understand this reasoning in terms of standard logic that it can only be valid because it is enthymematic (i.e., containing one or more suppressed but understood premises), otherwise it would be the fallacy of affirming the consequent. The unstated premise in this case being that I don't want an account other than my own.

If such a premise is made explicit, then there will be reasoning to necessary conditions. Thus, it is argued, the logic of satisfactoriness does not amount to a new logic, for the reasoning of necessary and sufficient conditions is a well worn application of ordinary standard logic.

But what such examples show is not that the reasoning in the logic of satisfactoriness is enthymematic, but that it is defeasible. The reasoning is not enthymematic for no extra premise is needed to ensure that the reasoning will lead from satisfactory premises to satisfactory conclusion. But, the reasoning is defeasible, because if we add further premises we cannot be sure that the conclusion will remain satisfactory. Thus writing up my notes may be reasonable from the previous set of premises, but it ceases to be from the following set: Fiat: My possessing an outline of cybernetic pragmatism. It is the case: If I write up my notes, I'll have an outline of cybernetic pragmatism. It is the case: My notes are unintelligible. Fiat: My outline being intelligible. Therefore, I'll write up my notes.

The defeat of a conclusion by the addition of the premises is not a feature of standard logic. In standard logic the addition of a premise cannot invalidate a previously valid inference: if a conclusion is drawn from a set of premises, then it is validly drawn from any set of premises containing those premises. With the logic of satisfactoriness this is not so. The defeat of a conclusion can come about because satisfactoriness is a relative notion; something is not satisfactory simpliciter, but satisfactory relative to a given set of constraints. The only way to avoid defeasibility in practical reasoning would be to insist that the premises setting out the goal should not only be correct but also complete; that all the wants to be satisfied by one's action should be fully specified. But the notion of a premise which is complete enough to prevent defeasibility while specific enough to yield practical conclusions is surely a fabulous animal. Only in restricted context can we even approach completeness; we insist, for example, that the list of contra-indications on a marketed drug should not only be accurate but complete -- within limits.

If the logic of satisfactoriness is allowed to remain defeasible it is not unfamiliar. It is, however, in need of supplementation with something like decision theory. Where an agent's goals are consistently realizable, then consideration of the advantages and disadvantages of particular actions can be seen as the search for conclusion fiats derivable from the goal fiats which incorporate all events which provide the standards of advantage and disadvantage for the case in point. But, there is no guarantee that the ends are capable of joint attainment, and thus we need something like decision theory. It is also a feature of practical reasoning that the same premises may license different conclusions, not only different conclusions but conclusions which are incompatible (which in standard logic would show the premise set to be inconsistent). In practical reasoning this is unavoidable; it is here that preference is exercised and preference theory would gain its point of contact.

The justification for concentrating upon the logic of satisfactoriness is that it articulates some features of our discourse about an instrumental validation of knowledge and, if we are correct in ascribing this foundational role to practice, why we might be led to the denial of many traditional criticisms of that position.

The logic operative is not standard. Additionally, it seems that the crucial characteristics of defeasibility which the logic of satisfactoriness displays will have to be preserved in any satisficing device -- from a business to a robot.

REFERENCES

1. ARMSTRONG, D. M., <u>Belief, Truth and Knowledge</u>, Cambridge University Press, 1973

2. GEACH, P. T., "Imperatives and Practical Reasoning," in: <u>Logic Matters</u>, P. T. Geach (ed.), p. 270, Basic Blackwell, 1972.

3. GEACH, P. T., "Teleological Explanation," in: <u>Explanation</u>, S. Körner (ed.), p. 76, Basil Blackwell, 1975.

4. LEHRER, K., <u>Knowledge</u>, Clarendon Library of Logic and Philosophy, 1974.

5. KENNY, A., "Practical Inference," <u>Analysis</u>, 1966.

6. KENNY, A., <u>Will, Freedom and Power</u>, Basil Blackwell, 1973.

7. RESCHER, N., <u>Primacy of Practice</u>, Basil Blackwell, 1973.

8. RESCHER, N., <u>Methodological Pragmatism</u>, Basil Blackwell, 1977.

9. SIMON, H. A., <u>The Sciences of the Artificial</u>, M.I.T. Press, 1960.

Essentials of a cybernetic model of consciousness

A. LOCKER

Department of Theoretical Biophysics, University of Technology
Vienna, Austria

1. INTRODUCTION

Consciousness (CSN) is neither simple nor clear-cut and therefore evades direct apprehension. Because of its Janus-faced nature, viz. to be concomitantly the presupposition and the subject matter of any approach to it, it flees into the safe position of a dilemma as soon as it is treated in scientific or cybernetic terms. This dilemma reveals itself in the impossibility of treating CSN by purely objective means, e.g. by elaboration of a formally rigorous theory the validity of which could be tested by computer simulation; a subject as such, having CSN, can never be captured by a machine and inevitably remains outside any objectively designed model; i.e. the subject is only the designer, not the model.

This dilemma need not be a reason for despair since there are profitable mental schemes available that enable us to skirt the purely subjectivistic, i.e. experiential, approach which properly cannot be communicated, and an extreme objectivistic, i.e. behavioristic, approach which neglects CSN as a scientifically tractable phenomenon at all. These mental schemes derive from our understanding of the Cognitive Domain (C.D.) which an observer (O-system) constitutes whenever he places himself vis-à-vis a system proper (S-system) he wants to examine, and takes in addition a designer (D-system) for both the O- and the S-system into account. In between these 3 systems there exists not only complete formal interconnectivity (i.e. closure); they inherently reveal an interplay between complementarity vs. unity. An example for this interplay is the opposition between an O-system and an S-system, overcome by the concept the D-system has about both systems.

The mental scheme complementarity vs. unity will be applied in our approach to a model which exhibits the structural/relational organization of CSN in order to show in which way CSN -- maintaining its unity -- undergoes an unfolding while being active. The model thereby pursues the objective of approximately catching the essential character of CSN. The model is an "egological" (i.e. ego-based) one, i.e based on the thesis that the subject (i.e. a system able to say: "I am I" and thus to declare its self-identity) precedes CSN, but needs CSN for its activity. The model incorporates also the thesis on which the "inegological" (non-ego-based) theory of CSN is based, viz. that CSN devoid of a subject is possible inasmuch as the property of "I-lessness" is actually ascribed to certain parts of CSN only.

2. SOME META-THEORETICAL PRESUPPOSITIONS FOR OUR APPROACH

The inherency of the complementarity vs. unity scheme in our model is one of the presuppositions for the structural/relational organization of the model. We must, in addition, acknowledge some meta-theoretical presuppositions that have been elaborated very ingeniously by Pask [7][1] and extended and generalized by us [6]; they can be stated in the following proposition (Theorem I):

$$p(\cdot)_{for}\text{-system} \dashrightarrow$$

$$\langle p(\cdot)_{in}\text{-system} \wedge p(\cdot)_{with}\text{-system} \wedge (\cdot)\text{-system} \rangle$$

For any arbitrary system the proposition expresses the system's dependence upon a program "for" the system (termed: $p(\cdot)_{for}$-system); after establishment of the system[2], the program transforms into a program "in" the system (termed: $p(\cdot)_{in}$-system), being accompanied by the $p(\cdot)_{with}$-system "surrounding" the system. It can be rightly accounted as the formal expression of the fact that the system built according to the program remains to be kept in attention by the D-system.

The C.D. teaches us that the S-system has its origin in the D-system. This finding can be generalized by stating that "every system stems from a subject" (Theorem II); the system represents the subject that designed it. The situation in model building is somewhat more intricate: every model reveals an intrinsic double nature in being, on the one hand, a model (i.e. representation) of its

---

[1] They represent the cybernetic (or meta-theoretical) version of the age-old philosophical problem of the universals. Theorem I does not explicitly deal with the subject but implies the D-system as the source of the $p(\cdot)_{for}$-system. With respect to the O-system's capacity to recognize the program of the S-system we learn from the C.D. [6,7] that the O-system can formulate a $p(\cdot)_{of}$-system only, i.e. an inferentially derived program formulated on the basis of the observables the O-system selects for the S-system's observation.

[2] The fact that an instrumental system (I-system) is required in order to make the program operative [8] is neglected here.

designer (who is, in the C.D., the O-system) and, on the other hand, a model of the S-system that the nominal-model (built by the O-system) is intended to verbal-model, i.e. to represent.

Proceeding further from the subject towards its origin, it is perfectly legitimate to demand the program "for" the subject itself. If we may venture a "substantial" version of the complexity criterion according to which the complexity of a system (in the form of its structural/relational orgization) must exceed (or at least equal) the complexity of the system built by it and apply it to the generative subject-subject relationship, then we may state a "diaphoretic" or transferential theorem that reads thus: "Every subject stems from a subject" (Theorem III). The transfer of subjectivity from one system to another is analogous to the transform of the program between one system and another in the C.D. whereby the character of "programmativity" is maintained.

There is no subject thinkable without CSN; for the sake of simplifying our terminology we speak from now on about CSN/Subject meaning (1) the conscious subject, and (2) the possible identity of CSN with its underlying subject which in turn is the carrier of CSN.

3. CONSCIOUSNESS AND SUBJECTIVITY

3.1. The "Inegological" Theory

The "inegological" theory (IETh) of CSN claims that CSN is solely formed by means of relations among (unconscious) data, relating circularly or recursively those data with themselves. This assertion is easily refuted: Apart from the neglect of a program for these recursive relations (see Figure 2 later in text), another unsurmountable difficulty for this theory consists in the lack of an explanation of how and when (and at which state) the system of relations has achieved a perfection high enough as to become conscious of itself. In addition there is no provision made for a program giving instructions for the "emergence" of CSN out of the relations between data from which CSN qualitatively differs. However, the main objection to be raised against IETh can be based on the circular argument itself. Neither (1) the "emergence" of CSN (which at the moment of its appearance must be identified as CSN by CSN), nor (2) the activities indicative of CSN, viz. intentionality/reflection, nor (3) the knowledge of consciousness of these activities can sensibly be understood without the precedence of somebody who (or of some system which) identifies himself (or itself) as the performer and knower of these activities; this required system is the subject.

3.2. The "Egological" Theory

The "egological" theory (ETh) of CSN is not only well founded; it is apt at becoming a synthetic theory when it is enabled to embrace or include parts or sub-systems of CSN which can be construed as being objective, i.e. devoid of an "I" or subject. These parts are: (1) the organizational principle which determines CSN [5] (or, more precisely, the subjective part of it) as the program (of that part), and (2) the body (called body-machine or b-machine [6]), particularly the

brain. The subjective parts, by means of actions proceeding from them, are able to seize upon their objective counter-parts and to finally embody them into themselves. These kinds of actions bring about the structural/relational unfolding of CSN.

3.3. CSN and Subjectivity

Although we take CSN and subjectivity, because of their eventual identity, together, the difference between them should be kept in mind and can be marked out as follows: The subject can abstractly be thought of as a system that (1) performs actions indicative of it (viz. intentionality/reflection) without having CSN actually at its disposal, but having it potentially, and that (2) segregates (or singles out) of itself CSN as soon as the subject (2.1) plans those activities, (2.2) knows and thinks of them, (2.3) describes them in a communicable language, and (2.4) directs at last knowledge and description towards itself, and thus, by performing self-reference, expands CSN to Self-CSN and actualizes the "Self", i.e. the subject in its full import. We immediately realize that this circular procedure is impossible without the material presupposition of a superordinated subject that designs, directs and watches consciously the "awakening" of the "subordinated" subject, i.e. its wandering from Pre-CSN through CSN to Self-CSN. The procedure adumbrated by items 1 to 2.4 can be continued and augmented by the subject's ability to expand itself further, i.e. to transcend itself and to try to grasp its own program and thus to freely accept the cognition (cf. Theorem II) that the origin ("ground") of itself is not identical with itself but rather comes from (or is) an authority called the universal system (U-system), i.e. God or at least a God figure. We understand under expansion or unfolding of CSN the structural/relational expression of the procedure of self-recognition. It is vital that the unfolding is a temporal process that is atemporally enabled and preceded by the subject and, despite the unfolding, concomitantly retrieved in the unity of the subject.

4. THE STRUCTURAL/RELATIONAL ORGANIZATION AND UNFOLDING OF CONSCIOUSNESS

The model of CSN proposed is an hierarchical one and assumes, for the sake of brevity, only four levels (viz. level 0, 1, 2, 3), a simplification which is in accordance with the investigations of Roland Fischer [2,3] that led to a "two-state model" of CSN, but amplifies and generalizes them. It allows in principle for more than four, in fact for arbitrarily many levels. The model is neither a manifesto for required performance, nor a claim for a consonant performance of an actual system, but rather a simple description of a mechanism that underlies everybody's conscious experience of CSN.

In delineating the structural/relational organization of the CSN/Subject we begin by regarding the sub-system located at the lowest level and mount there from upwards to the top level, bearing in mind that to the process of unfolding we follow by describing the model exactly corresponds an opposite process that starts with the (sub)system located at the top level and enables the unfolding by decisions coming from the top. As said, both procedures, proceeding simultaneously upwards and downwards, are embraced by the permanent unity of the CSN/Subject. In the following the unfolding will be thoroughly elaborated.

The sub-system which is confronted with the so-called objective reality--of course, via sense systems that are not explicitly considered here-- is called <u>reflective</u> or R-system. It experiences the object via passive perception and active intentionality; by making a model of that object the R-system develops (unfolds) its structure/relation from an abstract (empty) state towards a concrete state, embodying in its structure/relation the object by having become aware of it. The unfolding thus passes from level $\emptyset$ (= the $R_{abstr.}$-system) towards level 1 (= the $R_{concr.}$-system) (Figure 1A). Considering the R-system as the subjective part of a duality, we have to supplement it with its objective counterpart; this is the pertinent <u>organizational</u> system or O_R-system which is, as explained earlier, devoid of an "I" and therefore represents the "inegological" part of the model at the appropriate level, viz. at level 1. This O_R-system, like the other O_i-systems[1] to be described later, differs fundamentally from the outside object perceived via sense systems) by the R-system; the O_i-system is always a <u>program</u> for the subjective sub-system. However, the influence it exerts is not completely deterministic, but possibly best understood as eliciting the subjective system's capabilities. The retro-action of the subjective system towards its quasi-determinant objective system is not a direct, but only an indirect one: by retro-action, the subjective system transforms (unfolds) into the conscious sub-system of the next higher level; in particular, the R-system transforms into the <u>self-reflective</u> or SR-system, located at level 2. This system in turn is quasi-determined by the pertinent O_{SR}-system. Details of the unfolding process are described in Figure 1B. By seizing upon the O_{SR}-system, the SR-system unfolds and becomes the "<u>true-Self</u>" or tS(R)-system, located at level 3. The tS(R)-system, however, is no more <u>sub</u>-system but instead the system that contains and quasi-determines all other system-parts; therefore, it is virtually identical with the CSN/Subject in its full significance. We can also write down the following set inclusions:

$$R_{abstr.}\text{-system} \subseteq R_{concr.}\text{-system}$$

$$\subseteq SR\text{-system} \subseteq tS(R)\text{-system}$$

The tS(R)-system, when it tries to seize upon its own $O_{tS(R)}$-system, has not only to realize that it cannot immediately capture the latter (what the subjective sub-systems of lower levels also have to realize regarding their pertinent O_i-systems); it has before all to take cognizance of the fact that it cannot transform forthwith into a subjective system of any higher order, because there is now a boundary of great importance coming into the play, viz. the individual body.

5. THE ROLE OF BODY AND BRAIN FOR CONSCIOUSNESS

In the sketchy picture of unfolding of CSN/ Subject, the role of the body (called b-machine) has been neglected so far. We have to complete the description of the model by stating that the subjective sub-systems--which because of being reflective can also be termed R_i-systems--also always seize upon the b-machine-parts[2] belonging to them and thereby undergo a development of their structural/relational organization which is comparable to the transform of the R-system from the abstract (level $\emptyset$) to the concrete (level 1) state. With the brain there is, however, a fundamental difference as against the (mental) embodiment of any arbitrary outside object into the R-system; because of the complementarity between psychic perception and the knowledge of the corresponding physical/physiological events in the brain [4], an inner object cannot be directly perceived. The b-machine, however, shares with the subjective R_i-system the common origin: they both stem from the O_i-system and from the subject (i.e. R_{i+1}-system) formulating the O_i-system. Whereas the R_i-system is able to directly seize upon the b_i-machine (of the same level), the O_i-system always escapes direct embodiment. The reason for this direct inaccessibility (and therefore escape) of the O_i-system has to be sought in its essence as a principle that manifests itself (as Theorem I states) "with" and "in" the system concomitantly and that activates the R_i-system's capability to unfold (as Figure 1B depicts). Any embodiment of the O_i-system together with the b_i-system must be understood as enlargement of the knowledge of the subject about his own state of affairs.

The tS(R)-system, by having become conscious of itself, has achieved the <u>utmost</u> possible, i.e. the complete unfolding, that normal conditions of human experience allow. It can neither directly nor indirectly seize upon its pertinent O_i-system (i.e. the $O_{tS(R)}$-system) unless it assumes states lying outside itself and transforms, or at least believes it transforms (under para- or supra-normal conditions of mystical experience), itself into the U-system, that embraces all and everything, but despite quasi-determining enables freedom to act, i.e. God. When we leave these forms of experience outside consideration and take notice of the principal appearance of a boundary then we take the body as the physical expression of the boundary. The CSN/Subject cannot directly seize upon its own body; there only remains some indirect possibility to do so. Although the body, as an I-system serving the CSN/Subject, is ready to move and to perform actions that are physically realizable, it does not completely obey the subject--such that, e.g. sudden illness has to be accepted as unforseeable fate.

Thus, we clearly see the function of the body as (1) <u>boundary condition</u> for the unfolding of the CSN/Subject; it is also (2) a necessary condition for the <u>appearance</u> of one CSN/Subject to another (not necessarily human) subject and for (3) <u>activities</u> of the subject, be these mental or physical;

---

[1] An O_i-system denotes the objective organizational system at any level. It is to be distinguished from the Q-system, i.e. the observer in the C.D.

[2] The b-machine comprises the brain and the body-systems with which mental and/or motor activities can be carried out.

Fig 1 A

(Legend on following page)

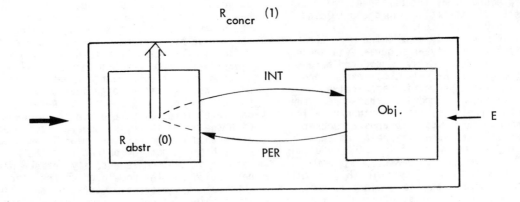

Fig 1 B

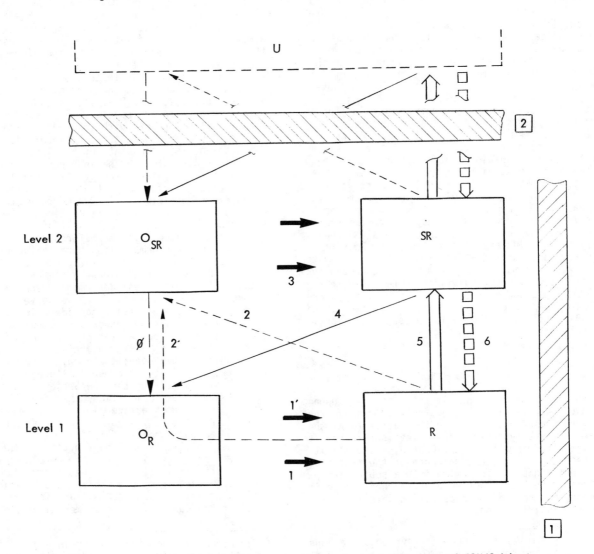

Figure 1.   Structural/relational organization and unfolding part of CSN/Subject.

Figure 1: Legend (see previous page)

A. By passive perception (PER) of an object, located in the environment (E), and active intentionality (INT) referring to the object, the $R_{abstr.}$-system (level $\emptyset$) unfolds ($\Longrightarrow$) to the $R_{concr.}$-system (level 1). The arrow $\longrightarrow$ indicates the R-system's dependence upon its pertinent O_R-system.

B. The further development (via levels 1 and 2) occurs in the following way: The unfolded $R_{concr.}$-system signals (2,2'$\dashrightarrow$) its intent to the O_{SR}-system to become active (i.e. to seize upon its pertinent O_R-system). The O_{SR}-system organizes (3,$\longrightarrow$) the SR-system in such a way that an intentional impulse (4,$\longrightarrow$), directed towards the O_R-system, induces the R-system (1,$\longrightarrow$) to shift (5,$\Longrightarrow$) into the state of the fully unfolded SR-system. Running through the relations 2,3,4 and 4,1',5 (representing (self-) reference between levels 1 and 2) may indefinitely be repeated and finally leads to more "concentration" of the SR-system until a state of repletion is achieved and a signal directed towards the $O_{tS(R)}$-system initiates the further unfolding of the SR-system to the tS(R)-system. The arrow $\emptyset$ ($\dashrightarrow$) denotes the connectedness of the O_i-systems, the arrow 6 ($\Rightarrow$) points to the "diaphoretic" character of subject ascription (and creation). In Figure 1A the widening of the awareness of the R-system from the abstract to the concrete state is indicated by inclusion of the former in the latter; in Figure 1B an hierarchical (stratified) model display is indicating the same process. The blocks ▨, (1) right hand side below and (2) at the top, indicate "reality" and the boundary condition state of the b-machine, respectively. The latter comes into play when the subjective sub-system located at level 3 (not inserted in the figure) would try to seize upon its pertinent organizational system. In this case it should aim at transforming itself into the U-system, which is impossible.

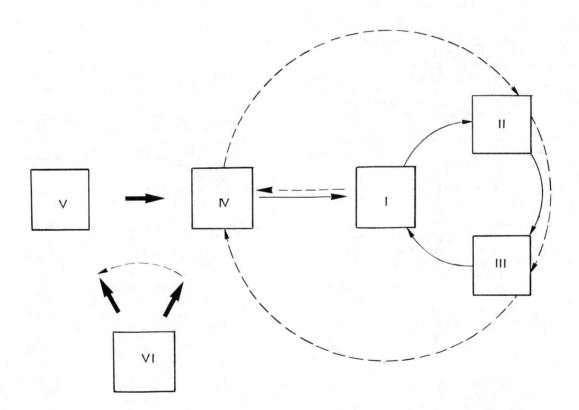

Figure 2. The "primary" (original) circular (recursive) connection between Programs I, II and III ($\longrightarrow$) is dependent upon Program IV. If the latter is (deliberately) included into an expanded recursiveness ($\dashrightarrow$), two further Programs (V, VI) (that act according to $\longrightarrow$) become necessary. Sub-programs, dealing with details of the CSN/Subject unfolding, are feasible.

it is also (4) a necessary condition for the formation of <u>language</u>. The character of the b-machine
to be carrier of the functions mentioned (as inti-
mated by Figure 1B) emphatically excludes the idea
to consider CSN/Subject as a mere product of the
body (or generally, of matter) as it is the mentally inert thesis of epiphenomenalism.

6. CONCLUSION

The essentials of the model for CSN/Subject
have only formally (i.e. structurally/relationally)
been put forward; from the point of view assumed
there is no further material approach possible,
aiming at considering the empirical contents of an
experiencing CSN, since by lumping together CSN and
the subject, as we did, we find we cannot sensibly
speak of the contents of the subject. Even the
structural/relational approach outlined above is
incomplete unless it is supplemented by taking the
significance of the other CSN/Subject (i.e. the
"I"-"Thou"-relation in <u>conversation</u>) into account.
It appears that "themes" or "concepts" (in the garb
of propositions) uttered during a conversation
between at least two CSN/Subjects bring about an
unfolding similar to that described by the model.
Indeed, it is seriously discussable whether an
unfolding "elicited" by conversation is only an
additional one or, on the contrary, the primary one
when we come to interpret the unfolding during
seizing of the subjective system-parts upon their
objective, albeit formal counterparts--to which
uttered "themes" unrestrictedly could be counted--
as an inner conversation. Entering into a theory
of conversation in relation to the CSN/Subject,
however, would be carrying coals to Newcastle when,
thanks to Pask [8,9], a masterfully propounded
theory of this subject matter exists already.

At the end of this communication another remark
should be added. When, in contrast to the recognition underlined at the outset, that unsurpassable
limitations resist an objective treatment of CSN,
we nonetheless try to circumscribe the program for
the model proposed, particularly for the unfolding
process, then we expose our attempt to the grave
and important criticism of having ignored the fundamental dilemma. This criticism, when marshalled
face to face with our endeavor, is invalid to the
extent to which we are aware of the metaphorical
nature of subjectivity in the model and its parts.
The character of subjectivity is deliberately
<u>assigned</u> to the model or its relevant parts such
that the latter <u>represent</u> subjectivity, without
having or being it! The same would hold true for
the intent (or content) of any <u>program</u>, e.g. put
down in a suitable computer language, for the model
of CSN/Subject.

As far as we see, the program should, at least,
consist of 4 parts, 3 of which are recursively
interconnected, whereas the remainder (being at
the same time the "starter") should be ascribed an
exceptional position. We delimit a <u>program I</u> for
the capability of reflecting and self-reflecting,
a <u>program II</u> for the activity of reflecting and
self-reflecting, and a <u>program III</u> for a distinct
"space-time" "machine" to which the capabilities
and activities mentioned refer. An additional
superordinated <u>program IV</u> should not only guarantee

the connectedness and recursive functionality of
the programs I through III but primarily set all
of them into existence; it therefore, albeit
derivatively, represents the U-system which becomes the U_0-system in the moment when new things
could happen. Figure 2 shows that entangling the
4 programs into complete recursiveness would force
us to enrich the total program-net by 2 further
programs: program V for the U_1-system that should
supervise the newly established recursiveness and
program VI for the U_2-system that should design
the U_1-system and warrant the permanent escapement
(or exclusion) of the latter system from circularity.

7. OUTLOOK

A comprehensive theory of CSN/Subject, exceeding the brief approach presented here by considering all relevant new facts and theories, should,
besides the theory of conversation only mentioned
in passing, especially rely on the experimental
facts quoted by Eccles [1] and used by him to
found the assertion of the CSN's independence of
the brain, and the implications of quantum theory
for a theory of CSN/Subject to which v. Weizsäcker
[10] has drawn attention.

REFERENCES

1. ECCLES, J. C., "Hirn und Bewußtsein," <u>mann-
   heimer forum</u> 77/78, pp. 9-63, 1978.
2. FISCHER, R., "Cartography of Inner Space," in:
   R. K. Siegel & L. J. West (eds.), <u>Halluci-
   nations: Behavior, Experience and Theory</u>,
   John Wiley & Sons, New York, 1975.
3. FISCHER, R., "Consiousness as Role and Knowledge," in: <u>Readings in Abnormal Psychology:
   Contemporary Perspectives</u>," Harper & Row,
   New York, 1976.
4. GLOBUS, G. G., "Unexpected Symmetries in the
   'World Knot'", <u>Science</u>, 18 , pp. 1129-1136,
   1973.
5. HENRICH, D., "Selbstbewußtsein. Kritische
   Einleitung in eine Theorie," in: R. Bubner,
   K. Cramer & R. Wiehl (Hsg.), <u>Hermeneutik
   und Dialektik</u>, J. C. B. Mohr, Tübingen,
   1970, Bd. 1, pp. 257-284.
6. LOCKER, A., "Meta-Theoretical Presuppositions
   for 'Autopoesis': Self-Reference and 'Autopoiesis'", in: M. Zeleny (Ed.), <u>Autopoiesis.
   A Theory of Living Organizations</u>, North-
   Holland, New York-Amsterdam, 1978 (to appear).
7. PASK, G., "The Cybernetics of Behavior and
   Cognition, Extending the Meaning of Goal,"
   in: J. Rose (ed.), <u>Progress of Cybernetics</u>,
   Gordon & Breach, London, 1970, pp. 15-44
8. PASK, G., "A Fresh Look at Cognition and the
   Individual," <u>International Journal of Man-
   Machine Studies</u>, 4, pp. 211-216, 1972.
9. PASK, G., "Models for Social Systems and
   for Their Languages," <u>Instructional Science</u>,
   1, pp. 385-445, 1973.
10. v.WEIZSÄCKER, C. F. <u>Die Einheit der Natur</u>,
    Hanser, München, 1971.

Hard and soft implications
of a dichotomous model of consciousness

WALTER LOWEN
School of Advanced Technology, State University of New York
Binghamton, New York USA

I wish to report on the development of a model designed to explain behavioral and personality patterns by postulating an organizational schema of consciousness. The model outcomes correlate well with psychological findings and have already shown promise for practical applications, especially in the design of man-machine interfaces and in simulation. The model is conceptual and complex and I can therefore present here only a sketchy outline. An extended description is now in preparation.

The model draws heavily on the work of Carl Jung and Jean Piaget and is based on a systematic dichotomous partitioning scheme. The model I will describe is a 16-pole model, shown on the "map of capacities" (following page).

The 16 cells are the result of 4 successive and hierarchically applied symmetrical partitions, which can be visualized as a 4-deep binary tree structure. Since each branching of the tree represents a choice between 2 opposing attributes, the structure also defines oppositional pairs. I refer to a symmetrical partition which does not contain an opposite cell as a dichotomy. The combinatorial nature of such organization indicates that there is a total of 10 dichotomies imbedded in the structure, so that there are 20 highly differentiable attributes available to describe and interpret the unique nature of each cell or subset of cells. These interpretations by means of dichotomies is enriched by the fact that the so-called Jungian functions can also be identified. These structural characterizations lead to the construction and interpretation of the map of capacities.

The following features are worth noting. Each cell is numbered reflecting a developmental hierarchy. Each cell has a name and a symbol. Each symbol represents a conscious capacity, i.e., a unique skill for processing information, which was derived from the attributes. These are in order of oppositional pairs:

1.	signal	16.	structure
2.	match	15.	logic
3.	dichotomy	14.	pattern
4.	control	13.	strategy
5.	sign	12.	association
6.	contrast	11.	preference
7.	sorting	10.	harmony
8.	routine	9.	combination

The 16 symbols can be viewed as nouns or verbs. If taken as a verb, each symbol describes a unique information-processing skill. If taken as a noun it describes the nature of preprocessed data. For pole 7 (or cell 7), an example would be that that part of consciousness either deals with presorted data or is capable of sorting information supplied

to that pole.

It is also worth noting that the map of capacities has been given a unique orientation, facilitating interpretations of regions in the map. For instance, the four Jungian functions can be identified as the four quadrants of the map, as follows:

Sensation function:	poles	1, 4, 5, & 8
Feeling " :	"	2, 3, 10, & 11
Thinking " :	"	6, 7, 14, & 15
Intuition " :	"	9, 12, 13, & 16

Right and left brain hemispheres can be identified by the dichotomy I call "style", consisting of the following partition: contextual (right brain hemisphere in right-handed people) consists of poles 1, 2, 5, 6, 9, 10, 13, and 14. They are shaded light. Detailed (left brain hemisphere or speech specialization) is represented by the cells and poles shaded dark, namely 3, 4, 7, 8, 11, 12, 15, and 16.

The power of the model derives largely from its dichotomous organization, which makes it easy to identify easily observable behavioral patterns in people, producing outcomes which are consistent with typologies suggested by Jung and others. The observable patterns are sharpened by the inputs and outputs marked on the map.

The description of the inputs and outputs shown turns out to be a complicated story, because I had to rethink the accepted organizational preconception that there are only five senses. The dichotomies suggested that there are eight senses, and I have been able to find substantiation for such a reconceptualization. Suffice it to say that the inputs and outputs as shown on the map produce an information processing organization consistent with the pole capabilities and observed patterns of behavior. The patterns are striking and best recognized in what I call "modes".

Consider first the mode described by poles 1, 2, 3, and 4, oriented toward the left of the map. It describes a behavioral tendency toward the concrete and physical. Outputs are through the body, learning is by doing, i.e., by experiencing. The opposite mode, consisting of poles 13, 14, 15, and 16 is the opposite: abstracted information processing resulting in intellectual outputs. It represents a very different personality. In a similar fashion the mode consisting of poles 5, 6, 7, and 8, oriented toward the bottom of the map, is opposite to the mode oriented toward the top, consisting of poles 9, 10, 11, and 12. The bottom mode relates to hand-eye coordination resulting in a focus on things, whereas the top mode represents

THE MAP OF CAPACITIES

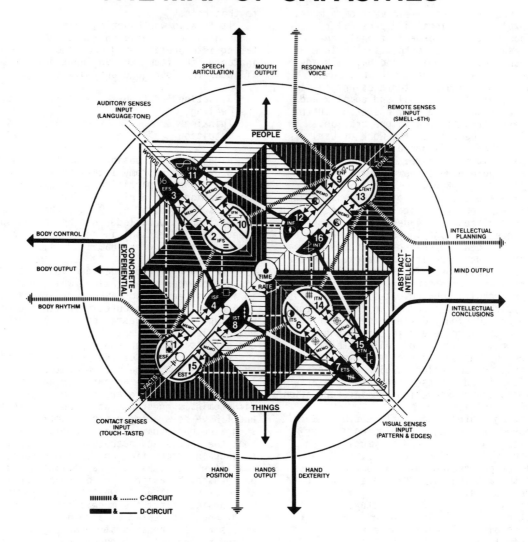

a verbal and therefore people preference.

Implied by this organizational structure is of course the conception that personality differences reflect relative strengths or leanings toward a given set of conscious capacities as identified by the poles. The consistency of this assertion can be made much more explicit through the construction of a competition-cooperation matrix, which shows the relationship of one pole to any of the others on on the basis of shared attributes. Close couplings are shown as links on the map of capacities, suggesting that the poles are tied together through a network. The most basic component of such a network I call a "transaction". There are 26 possible basic transactions, all of which can be recognized as basic human skills. The interpretation of a transaction can be derived from the pole symbols. For instance, the transaction involving poles 9 and 10 can be either introverted or extroverted depending on which pole acts as the processing pole and which acts as the data pole. If pole 9 supplies preprocessed data to pole 10 for processing, one can construct a sentence ascribing a noun to pole 9 and a verb to pole 10, to wit "to harmonize combinations or possibilities" as for example in poetry or music. The transaction $9 \rightarrow 10$ therefore represents the composing skill. The reverse transaction would be to "combine or possibilitize harmonies (or disharmonies)", i.e., to perceive. By means of this algorithm all 16 transactions have been identified and given stereotypical names. They are:

Introverted

$1 \rightarrow 2$	the doer	(dancer, athlete)
$3 \rightarrow 4$	the follower	(nurse, musician)
$5 \rightarrow 6$	the moulder	(sculptor, artisan)
$7 \rightarrow 8$	the organizer	(programmer, accountant, clerk)
$9 \rightarrow 10$	the composer	(poet, "Jewish mother", spiritualist)
$11 \rightarrow 12$	the critic	(speech therapist, language teacher, translator)
$13 \rightarrow 14$	the theoretician	(theoretical physicist, abstract social scientist)
$15 \rightarrow 16$	the conceptualizer	(architect, philosopher)

Extroverted

$2 \rightarrow 1$	the initiator	(opportunist, salesman, entrepreneur)
$4 \rightarrow 3$	the classifier	(politician, anthropologist)
$6 \rightarrow 5$	the operator	(surgeon, mechanic)
$8 \rightarrow 7$	the implementor	(engineer)
$10 \rightarrow 9$	the perceiver	(counselor, actor)
$12 \rightarrow 11$	the verbalist	(orator, preacher, diplomat, speech-writer)
$14 \rightarrow 13$	the suspector	(detective, lawyer)
$16 \rightarrow 15$	the analyst	(diagnostician, applied mathematician)

These descriptors can be tremendously enriched by reference to the applicable dichotomies. As a consequence a very complex pattern of behavioral preferences emerges, indicating the style (e.g., verbal vs. visual instructions), mode preference, complexity (i.e., tendency to simplify or complicate an issue), attitude (i.e., realist or idealist), etc. In short, this approach has proven to be a powerful organizer of human skills and their associated behavior patterns.

With various test instruments and through interviews several hundred individuals have used this method to identify their profiles and gain insight into their behavior patterns. All agree that the most striking, almost incredible aspect is the consistency of patterns in terms of the model. This has led me to define what I call "roles". Roles grow out of two aspects of the model: (1) out of its oppositional or dichotomous nature, and (2) out of a set of formally derivable dichotomies which can be identified with consciousness.

The disposition of consciousness can be shown to reflect an entropy hierarchy among the poles, which ultimately manifests itself in the availability of information stored in memories also marked on the map. As a consequence the effectiveness with which information can be processed by a given pole gives rise to a perception of a given skill expressed as "that's difficult for me" or "I enjoy doing that", etc. I have formalized these perceptions by descriptors which I call roles. They are listed in the table on the following page.

When these roles are associated with poles on the map, i.e., when the conciousness hierarchy of the poles is recognized and superimposed on the map of capacities, I refer to such a specification as a "personality profile". A profile thus not only identifies specific capacities, but also under what circumstances they come into play or not into play. I thus identify a work mode and a play mode, high in the hierarchy of consciousness and a challenge and a creative mode both largely unconscious. With these perceptions included in the model, it is possible to identify what type of activity gets procrastinated, under what circumstances creative behavior is encouraged, or why certain activities or demands come with such difficulty to a given personality.

The resulting patterns are highly consistent both with the literature and with experience. In fact, certain positive and negative experiences in interpersonal relationships can be predicted if both profiles are known. In cases where no consistent pattern could be established, it always pointed to developmental problems, be they persona problems, traumatic cultural impact, or other identifiable psychological complications which prevented the natural process of individuation from developing.

These findings are encouraging to me on two grounds. They confirm speculations of mine and others: (1) that intelligence models need to incorporate what I call "ambi-syn-anti" -- i.e., basic systems characteristics which deal with opposition, hierarchy, levels of complexity, discontinuous growth, and entropy; (2) that the power of a relatively simple 16-pole model is sufficient to capture certain behavioral patterns so as to make computer simulation of intelligent systems feasible.

ROLES

DOMINANT CIRCUIT (STYLE)	COMPLEMENTARY CIRCUIT (STYLE)
Entropy flow: $\underline{a}$ toward $\underline{d}$	Entropy flow: $\underline{d}'$ toward $\underline{a}'$
(a = strongest, d = weakest)	(a' = strongest, d' = weakest)

POLE OPPOSITION

a	dependable	vs.	d'	erratic
b	responsible	vs.	c'	frivolous
c	constrained	vs.	b'	free
d	difficult	vs.	a'	easy

POLE HIERARCHY

a	dependable		a'	easy
b	responsible		b'	free
c	constrained		c'	frivolous
d	difficult		d'	erratic

TRANSACTION

$a \rightarrow b$ dep. + resp. = competence	$b' \rightarrow a'$ free + easy = talent
$a \rightarrow c$ dep. + const. = perseverance	$c' \rightarrow a'$ friv. + easy = relaxation
$b \rightarrow d$ resp. + diff. = toil	$d' \rightarrow b'$ err. + free = synergism
$c \rightarrow d$ const. + diff. = lock	$d' \rightarrow c'$ err. + friv. = key

MODES

$a \rightarrow b + b' \rightarrow a'$	competence	+	talent	=	work
$a \rightarrow c + c' \rightarrow a'$	perseverance	+	relaxation	=	play
$b \rightarrow d + d' \rightarrow b'$	toil	+	synergism	=	challenge
$c \rightarrow d + d' \rightarrow c'$	lock	+	key	=	creativity

The systems community and its paradigm

BILL MAYON–WHITE
The Open University, Faculty of Technology
London, England

We live in an age of exponential growth, be it the growth of population, of knowledge, or of scientific publications. There are obvious hazards associated with this phenomenon, but one danger which I feel is not widely recognised is that there exists the possibility of a breakdown of communications. This possibility is not restricted to our own area of academic activity but is, I consider, of special importance to Systems People.

I base my observations on a comparatively long exposure to Systems from a number of different angles. I consider myself fortunate to have worked successively in a university department of agricultural systems, within a team of government scientists in the world modelling business, and currently to be a member of a group responsible for teaching systems at an undergraduate level to very large numbers of students. This experience has brought me into direct contact with individuals drawn from a very wide range of disciplines and has made me acutely aware of different perceptions of Systems. It is therefore not surprising that I have been irritated and confused by this situation from time to time. I am indebted to Kuhn [1] for providing a way of rationalising the position.

Kuhn is not without his critics (see for example Margaret Masterman's linguistic analysis of his use of the word paradigm [2]). Despite this, and the fact that his essay is addressed to the field of science, I believe his ideas to be applicable to the field of systems. Kuhn deals with the sociology of science, i.e. how scientists go about their work. This is in contrast to Popper [3] whose concern in this area has been with the workings of science itself. The present paper is concerned both with "How do systems people go about their work?" and "How does systems work?"

Kuhn's contention is that science progresses by revolutionary change characterised by the emergence of new concepts, theories, and a language in which these ideas are discussed. The term "community" is invoked to describe that set of individuals using the language and contributing to the ideas. Perhaps the simplest and most familiar example of such a revolutionary change is the emergence and acceptance of the Darwinian theory of evolution. The community is characterised by a Paradigm or set of ideas (possibly amounting to a theory) understood and accepted by its members.

This description can usefully be applied to the field of systems. Certainly there exists what I choose to call "The Systems Community" -- as evidenced by this meeting. We can also identify shared concepts. Kuhn offers a number of "tests" for the existence of a community including the creating of professional societies and the emergence of new journals. This certainly true of Systems, and is evidenced in a most satisfactory way by the recent Klir and Rogers bibliography [4] which effectively lists active members of the Systems Community and their contributions. Other workers [5,6,7] have also applied Kuhn's ideas to Systems but this short description of his work is necessary if we are to consider some of its implications. Problems emerge when we turn to the concepts which might constitute the paradigm. A reasonable goal here is to establish an irreducible minimum list of these concepts. My own attempt at this results in a list which is very much shorter than we might at first imagine. The concepts are embodied in words: system, holism, boundary, environment, element, process, control, feedback and so on. The difficulties arise because these words continue to have different meanings to members of the Systems Community. Because of this my list is restricted to merely two items. The first is the word SYSTEM which I take to mean a set of interconnected parts. The second is HOLISM which I take to mean an interpretation of the real world as a set of systems, and the recognition that it is itself a system.

These two words and the concepts they convey lie at the core of the Systems Paradigm. I believe that the other "systems concepts" which are so frequently cited can be derived from these two. The list is so short because of the immaturity of the subject area (despite its age of some thirty plus years) and because of the existence of some unsolved dilemmas.

The first of these is directly related to the problem of communication referred to earlier. It is the dilemma of language: Should the Systems Community become involved in a linguistic debate? Or, should it continue to use words loosely and to coin terminology freely? I do not particularly want to stray into the minefield of linguistics and philosophy, but some mention of it is necessary, if only to point out that this problem is not peculiar to Systems. Indeed many, if not all, the problems of Systems are the very same problems which philosophy has examined for centuries. Popper's own view is particularly apposite here:

Language analysts believe that there are no genuine philosophical problems, or that the problems of philosophy, if any, are problems of linguistic usage or of the meaning of words. I, however, believe that there is at least one philosophical problem in which all thinking men are interested. It is the problem of cosmology; the problem of understanding the world—including ourselves, and our knowledge, as part of the world. [8]

Magee's view is more succinct:

Philosophy discussing the meaning of words is rather like a carpenter endlessly sharpening his tools but never using them. [9]

This is in contrast to Kuhn, who recognises the creation of a language as a valid activity for a community. To a large degree I agree with Magee's homily, but some semantics are necessary; hence my attempt at an irreducible minimum list of concepts. This necessity arises also because systems differs from other disciplines in that it is not merely a new branch of an existing discipline like mathematics or physics. It attracts individuals from a wide range of fields, individuals who have become dissatisfied with the constraints of disciplinary study and with limitations of reductionism as a method of enquiry. These mavericks arrive in the field of systems equipped only with the language of their parent disciplines and the stage is set for my first dilemma. That dilemma remains: How much discussion and for how long?

The second dilemma (which can be termed the dilemma of divided loyalty) stems from the desire of systems people to make the subject area active and applied. It can be stated thus: "Can the interests of the Systems Community best be served by its members applying systems concepts directly to real world problems, or by applying these same concepts indirectly through the aegis of their parent disciplines?"

At first when we examine this question there appears to be ample room for both activities to continue in parallel, and indeed this is just what happens in practice. However, the different roles have not been explicitly recognised, which has in some instances created confusion about whether an activity is, or is not, Systems. For example, sometimes when systems ideas are applied within an existing discipline the charge is made that the systems work is merely sloppy science. This charge can take a more serious form, e.g. that systems is not a science because it contains no potentially falsifiable hypotheses. It is serious not because of the implication that systems isn't a science, but because of its lack of testable ideas. The charge is at present unanswerable, if it should be true then systems will join the social sciences, and political theories, as an untestable but infinitely elastic body of knowledge.

The concern of the Systems Community with real-world problems is superficially laudable but in practice tends to be inoperable because many of these problems resist clear definition (see the problem-solution dilemma below). We are thus left with a rather muddy picture and no clear indication of how best to resolve this dilemma.

At the risk of being labelled a "meddler" it is possible to make a further observation about the behaviour of the Systems Community in relation to dilemma of divided loyalty. There is a risk associated with harnessing a career to a new discipline. Predictably many members of the Systems Community have adopted risk-averting

strategies and "insured" themselves with their parent disciplines. The commonest form of this is perhaps to use systems ideas from within the parent discipline, and thereby to have a lesser commitment to systems.

This can be explained in terms of Kuhn's community by invoking the post-hoc rationalism of the youth and immaturity of the movement. This is unsatisfactory and in no way contributes to solving the dilemma. However divided loyalty appears to be both a cause and a consequence of the dilemma.

The third dilemma is one I have termed the problem-solution dilemma and arises out of our concern with real-world problems. One component is the dynamic nature of systems, the other is the scale and the nature of the problems which are deemed to exist in these systems. It can be summarised in the form of a question: How can I predict whether the solution arrived at for a system in state P_i and at time T_i will be applicable to that system in state P_{ii} at time T_{ii}? An example of this is the population control problem where the age structure controls the future population size and growth rate. Any successful control strategy must take these facts into account. In smaller, simple systems "hunting" is the characteristic behaviour when the response occurs at the wrong time. Commonsense judgements are adequate for defining problems and the adequacy of solutions with small systems. They are not sufficient for the problems which are commonly held to exist in large human organisations and in other large systems. I suspect that there are difficulties in this area which we have only just begun to appreciate. Yet I believe that we will find that the answers to the questions: "What is a problem?" and "What is a solution?" are in essence philosophical.

The final dilemma which I want to raise is really another aspect of the divided-loyalty dilemma raised earlier. Here it is used to question the contributions of Systems from another angle. Is the road to specialisation a contradiction of the systems paradigm? The Kuhnian model predicts that specialist groups will emerge to form new disciplines. This has clearly happened in the case of systems.

However, we must ask whether this is desirable for an interdisciplinary movement commited to Holism. Put another way, it takes the form of a proposition: that the systems paradigm cannot be improved or extended in isolation, and that such a process requires the constant friction of other disciplines to stimulate growth.

With this incomplete and slightly contradictory statement further discussion of my four dilemmas must be suspended. I believe that they warrant further discussion and examination to tease some of the other problems for the systems community which lie embedded in the dilemma as I have posed them.

The Kuhnian concept of Community and Paradigm have a value which I hope has been demonstrated. They provide a functional framework for the discussion of both the process of systems research and of the idea of a system itself. Extension of the framework to include the student as a potential member of the Community is particularly useful if the discussion is to cover the design of teaching materials. Immediately it suggests that the concepts central to the paradigm be dealt with first, and for the related ideas to be derived from these alone. If it also serves to highlight some problems which should be tackled by the community before the student stumbles across them, then it will indirectly have served an additional purpose.

By way of conclusion, there are some ethical and moral points of relevance to the Systems Community which warrant a brief mention. The first of these has to do with the educational environment to which we have all been exposed. This is, I believe, related to Pask's concept of consciousness [10]. It has implications for both the observer and for the participants in his "conversation" in that it would require of them an awareness of the bias which is induced by that educational environment. Bronowsky and Mazlish's term the "Western Intellectual Tradition" [11] is the best I have found to express my meaning succinctly. We have been conditioned by exposure to this tradition, and I contend that it has a fundamental effect on our roles as observers and as members of a world system. Indeed education would be a lamentable failure if this were not so. Our "knowledge" reflects this observational position and must therefore in some degree be relative rather than absolute, subjective rather than objective -- again another ancient philosophical chestnut which is usually conveniently ignored when we discuss systems.

Another component of this Intellectual Tradition is the impact of monotheism and the Judaic-Christian religion. Frank Fraser Darling [12] has attempted to expose and evaluate this in a discussion of Man's responsibility for his natural environment. Central to his argument is the importance of the convenient conviction that God created living things for the use and delectation of man. Darling expresses concern that although orthodox religion may be losing its impact, the mentality of disocciation is not. I share his concern and have introduced the point to illustrate the sort of value judgements that may be implicit in models. An awareness of this is important to the Systems Community at the present time as it becomes increasingly involved in attempts to understand and control the phenomena described in the opening sentence of this paper. The ethical position of the practitioner becomes important once he is involved in the domain of public policy. I do not know of any attempts to address this question in the systems field, so perhaps this short introduction to it will serve to bring it out into the light of day.

This view applies equally well to the other questions which are merely posed in this paper. My polemic is set out in superficially simple terms but is intended to point out some fundamental weaknesses in the foundations of the "Systems House" that are in need of urgent attention. It is also intended as a pointer to philosophy as a rich discipline which has been neglected by the Systems Community.

POSTSCRIPT

This short paper cannot be said to do anything more than introduce some problems which are, I believe, of immediate importance to the Systems Community. It is essentially a set of observations on the "State of the Art" and is summarised by inverting Ackoff's description of a "mess as a System of problems" to form the statement "Systems is a mess of problems."

REFERENCES

1. KUHN, T. S., The Structure of Scientific Revolutions, 2nd Edition, University of Chicago Press, 1970.
2. MASTERMAN, M., "The Nature of a Paradigm," in: Criticism and the Growth of Knowledge, Kakatos and Musgrave (eds.), Cambridge University Press, 1970.
3. POPPER, K. R., The Logic of Scientific Discovery, Rutledge and Keegan, London, 1959.
4. KLIR, G. J. and G. ROGERS (eds.), Basic and Applied General Systems Research: A Bibliography, State University of New York at Binghamton.
5. BERTALANFFY, L. von, General Systems Theory, Penguin, London, 1973 (Preface to the British Edition).
6. CHECKLAND, P., "Science and the Systems Paradigm," International Journal of General Systems, 3, No. 2, 1976.
7. VICKERS, G., Presidential Address to the Society for General Systems Research, Washington, 1978.
8. POPPER, K. R., op. cit. (Preface to [3]).
9. MAGEE, B., Popper, Fontana, London, 1973.
10. PASK, G., "Consciousness," Proceedings of EMCSR 1978 (this volume).
11. BRONOWSKI, J. and B. MAZLISH, The Western Intellectual Tradition, Pelican, London, 1960.
12. FRASER DARLING, F., "Man's Responsibility for the Environment," Biology and Ethics, Proceedings, Institute of Biology Symposium, No. 18, Academic Press, London, 1969.

Feedback controlled instructional design

P. DAVID MITCHELL
Graduate Programme in Educational Technology, Concordia University
Montreal, Quebec, Canada

1. INTRODUCTION

Instruction is a key feature of education systems yet, as Landa showed, instruction is a process with poor feedback. To improve teaching and learning Landa argued for the development of cybernetic teaching devices. Such devices are not yet common. Here we begin with the same concern but rely on exploiting existing structures within which we can establish tighter feedback loops. Whether this will facilitate a major increase in educational effectiveness remains problematical. However, two widely available media are singled out, teachers and educational television (ETV). Teachers represent one of the world's largest professional groups and television distribution systems are widely available. Any improvement in these spheres of influence should help the global system of life-long education (Mitchell [6]).

Our current investigation of ETV aims not only to provide basic research into educational communications but also to provide feedback to the ETV producer. We operate with a time delay but anticipate a real-time cybernetic system which provides the producer with a visual display indicating the extent to which a sample of viewers is interested in the programme being recorded. Thus he can attempt to regulate output (attention-elicitation) not simply inputs.

Other research is directed to the study of instructional design for classroom lessons. Using a computer simulation of a class of 30 students a teacher can gain decision-taking experience by planning lessons using feedback from "students" to select a new instructional strategy. Such feedback controlled instructional planning is essential and is not otherwise possible without much experience.

Both projects challenge the tacit assumption of instructional design handbooks that an optimal sequence of information or instructional activities can be established by following a simple procedure. Conventional approaches tend to ignore subsidiary adaptive processes: the student learns how to learn in addition to acquiring subject-relevant capability; and the teacher learns how to teach in addition to sharing (and sometimes acquiring) subject-relevant capability.

2. CURRICULUM AND INSTRUCTION

We define a curriculum as a set of intended learning outcomes, or intended capability of a student. Instruction is the set of communications and control procedures intended to implement the curriculum. The basic unit of education is a relatively uninterrupted set of activities involving interplay between one or more students and an instructional system (i.e., a teacher or an environment designed to produce intended changes in capability). This teaching/learning segment may require only a few seconds (as in the case of a programmed textbook's frame), slightly longer (as in a Pask-conversation) or several hours (as in an assignment).

At its best, instruction involves an adaptive information exchange between the student and the instructional system which generates or selects knowledge, communicates knowables, monitors the learner's developing understanding of the topic, and repeats this cycle adapting to the students' needs (cf. Pask [8]). Instruction may be thought of as a partly cooperative and partly competitive game in which the requisite variety of the instructional system must be able to cope with that of the students (excepting that special case, self-instruction). Instructional activities may be extemporaneous or programmed. Here we focus on pre-instructional planning.

Instructional design activities lead to a set of communications and control procedures intended to regulate the student's activity in such a way that he has a high probability of acquiring the intended capability of a subset of the curriculum. Two products of instructional design are salient: a teacher's lesson plan and instructional materials (e.g. an audiovisual programme).

A lesson plan is a behaviour prescription for both teacher and students. It combines an organization of knowledge for presentation to students, procedures for shaping students' behaviour toward intended outcomes, inducing recall or relevant knowledge, selection of instructional materials, etc. It is a teaching strategy (and a teacher may be modelled as a collection of, or producer of, such strategies).

Instructional materials embody a lesson plan into a retrievable form for group or individual use, e.g. a TV programme, book or didactic game. Although parallel and branching versions exist, instructional materials usually incorporate a fixed strategy for all students. Because such materials might not be used under the watchful eye of a teacher it is imperative that they be designed to maximize the probability of inducing a transformation in student's capability.

3. INSTRUCTIONAL DESIGN

Much instructional theorizing can be criticized

for not being empirically based, for leaping from data only remotely related to cognition and learning, or for too heavy reliance on ordinary (rather than on appropriate technical) language. Perhaps more important are the common assumptions that we can find a unique instructional plan suitable for virtually all learners by testing and revising a lesson and that we can implement a series of such lessons without much concern for individual differences in students' development as controlled by the previous lessons. Pask's conversation theory is exceptional in its emphasis on conversational paradigms in instructional communication, a dialogue which requires <u>continuous</u> feedback and adaptation.

More typical is Gagné and Briggs' [1] list of twelve steps in instructional development. Beginning with a needs analysis and goal definition, the final step (after field testing and evaluation) is "operational installation". Though student performance is to be assessed in practice, the inescapable inference is that their procedure should provide an ideal sequence of instructional events. That this macro-instructional design approach can produce functional products is not denied but its insufficient feedback suggests that near optimal instructional sequences will not be identified (if they are feasible). Two kinds of feedback are needed.

The recommended instructional design process appears to succeed in simple instructional situations, especially when students are able to make up for instructional deficiencies by self-instruction. But in more complex subjects or when some students do not master a topic, it is essential that the teacher <u>qua</u> instructional designer use feedback derived from the lesson (or a sequence of lessons). Such feedback includes the lesson plan, students' entering capability and changes in their capability. Knowing the capability state of each student, it should be possible to plan the next lesson (or sequence of lessons) more effectively than if one simply follows a fixed strategy laid out before the course began. A similar argument applies to feedback-controlled design of sequences of instructional materials that encapsulate lesson plans. We shall return to this topic later.

4. MICROANALYTIC INVESTIGATION OF INSTRUCTION

4.1. Attention

Applied at the micro-analytic level, where engaging the attention of students is a <u>sine qua non</u>, instructional design should benefit from continuous feedback-controlled decisions about what instructional events to present next. Instructional theory fails to provide an adequate explanation of how a person's capability is modified by interplay with his environment but it is clear that attention to the message stream is essential. Attention may be controlled not only by instructional messages but also by the manner of presentation. Perhaps learning how to teach involves manner as much as matter.

If a common meaning is to be shared by the instructional designer and student it is necessary to use attention-eliciting techniques especially

if the information stream is externally paced because the student is unable to review the material.

However, we can also exploit the motivational advantages and variety-controlling complexity of a game by designing a system with fuzzy instructional communications algorithms which allow for fuzzy conditional statements and fuzzy feedback in both directions (Mitchell [7]).

4.2. Entertainment

Though producers of educational television materials often talk about the entertainment aspect of their work (e.g. "Sesame Street is intended to entertain as well as to educate"), it is difficult to discern exactly what is meant. If entertainment implies not simply to amuse but to engage the attention of people then any communication (which <u>must</u> engage attention of the intended recipient) might be called entertainment. What can we learn about instructional communications by analyzing the manner of presentation of professional entertainers? Is it possible to examine TV programmes that capture attention in order to discover critical factors that might be used to design instructional communications?

A key research problem concerns the isolation of individual elements' in a lesson and their effects on students' capability. Using television as an exemplary case, we have established a laboratory for monitoring moment-to-moment variations in viewing behaviour (as an operational definition of attention to, or interest in, the instructional messages).

4.3. Feedback

By analogy with a teacher, we need a video playback system which automatically stops the TV programme if the viewer stops watching. We do not have such an interactive system. In our lab the viewer sits before a TV receiver which has been modified so that the brightness of the screen is controlled by his viewing behaviour (which is defined functionally). Each press of a micro-switch held in his hand produces a momentary increase in brightness; this defines a viewing response. Lack of responding produces a blank screen within a second or two, depending on original brightness. A steady rate of responding (which becomes as automatic as eye movements after a few minutes) maintains regular brightness. A cumulative record is made of this viewing behaviour. The degree of resolution is less than three seconds. Thus we can relate isolated events in a TV programme to viewing behaviour (cf. Lindsley [3].

Using one response station the feedback loop to the educational materials producer must be provided by the researcher. This delay can be eliminated if several stations are yoked together and fed directly from the TV studio during a production. The average viewing behaviour would be displayed to the producer who could try different presentation formats, etc., if attention is decreasing. Such cybernetic TV production remains untested.

4.4. Research

We have produced and analyzed three versions of an instructional TV programme. They have a common audio track but different video tracks. One consists solely of a presenter (intended as a baseline for comparison). The others contain mixed video segments: presenter; motion picture film footage; slides; or graphics (including simple movement of a pointer or cut-outs). Ten instructional concepts were presented either by presenter alone (simple video) in one mixed version or by complex video (film or slides or graphics) in the other. Because the audio channel of educational (and other) television often carries most of the significant information, all concepts were presented aurally (audio was not regulated by the viewer). Thus we investigated relative attractiveness of the different video production techniques.

In each of the ten programme blocks attention was higher for the complex version of the video presentation. Comparing mean attention scores for all simple video blocks with complex video, the latter produced 19% more viewing behaviour ($p < .01$), graphics segments being most attention-provoking. Mean scores averaged over several lengthy video segments obscure many interesting details. Individual differences were common.

Figure 1 shows a cumulative record typical of many "viewers" of a mixed video programme; a horizontal line indicates non-viewing and slope is a function of viewing rate. Notice that the second half of the programme began with a graphics shot and viewing rate was high throughout most of this shot, fading near the end and then recovering. With the next shot, the presenter, visual attention dropped to zero except for a short burst for a few seconds. The onset of a motion picture sequence produced a high viewing rate until the presenter appeared again. Such behaviour is not unexpected; it underscores our intention to refine methods of instructional design so that attention is maintained even if visually uninteresting material must be presented. (Preliminary results suggest that a "talking head" will be watched more if the shot is not held constant but e.g. switched from one camera to another or from long shot to close up.) Less readily explained is the fact that Figure 1 shows

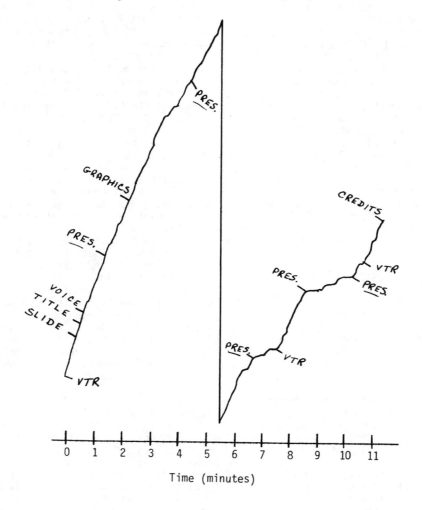

Figure 1. How one person viewed the TV programme "Forest Fires"

that the presenter was watched fairly consistently during the first half of the programme. It may be linked to audio cues.

4.5.   Production Techniques

Inspection of cumulative records reveals frequent cue effects. To illustrate, non-viewing persons responded after hearing such phrases as: "next year the forest may not be there"; "sometimes forest rangers set fires"; ". . . out of control"; "advantages of controlled fire"; and also after a pause in the audio track. Future research will investigate the interaction between attention to audio and video channels.

It is commonly assumed that motion pictures and television can maintain viewers' arousal and interest to some desired level by changing the stimulus frequently (by cutting from one shot to another and using montages of several shots to assemble a larger view). The low resolution display of the TV screen limits the amount of information that can be presented before attention diminishes. Perhaps this analytic tool can help us determine the cutting rate that maintains an acceptable level of attention to the visual display. Armed with laboratory-mediated feedback a highly developed programming strategy might be identified, one which integrates a variety of techniques for singling out details, making transitions, showing transformations of systems, etc.

Using this feedback controlled instructional design procedure, the producer of educational TV should be able to learn how to produce effective programmes more readily than without it. Concordia University's Graduate Programme in Educational Technology (which might be a synonym for educational cybernetics) includes courses in the production and evaluation of ETV materials. It is anticipated that this procedure will be used by students of ETV to develop relevant skills. In principle it could be used to analyze other instructional materials.

5.   ADAPTIVE INSTRUCTIONAL DESIGN IN A SIMULATED CLASSROOM

Successful teaching reflects one's skill in instructional planning and one's ability to note, and to consider, the effects of one's decisions on changes in students' capability. Ability to be flexible and to respond with a wide variety of strategies is characteristic of good teachers. As an adaptive controller the teacher monitors the effects of instruction on students and attempts to modify the content of his presentation, organization of topics, provision of opportunities for students to respond, etc., in order to improve the goal-directed process of enhancing student capability.

It is almost impossible to develop such instructional planning skill prior to classroom teaching experience, yet it is unfair to students to be used as a teaching ground for would-be teachers. Further, many instructional design texts fail to communicate the need for feedback controlled instructional planning. How can

these difficulties be overcome?

Simulation models can compress years of real-time experience with physical systems into a few minutes. A variant, operational gaming, permits a human game-player to participate as a decision-taker within the structure of the system being simulated. EDSIM is such a game.

5.1.   EDSIM

EDSIM provides a framework to observe and analyse instructional planning behaviour and to compress teaching experience into a short period so that teacher-trainees can acquire the requisite flexibility in lesson-planning and management of learning resources. EDSIM simulates a class of 30 students (each of whom is derived from an idealized model of the student as a purposeful system). The user, cast in the role of teacher, takes pre-instructional decisions to design a sequence of 50 lessons. See Mitchell [4,5] for for an overview of the model. Decisions are selected from 26 major strategies (about e.g. objectives, teaching tactics, humour, counselling students, teaching students how to learn, etc.). The computer model calculates coefficients for each decision, updating sub-models of attention, motivation, self-management, learning and aggregate capability for each student on each of 15 curriculum topics. The computer prints educational assessments for the player qua instructional designer who then plans the next lesson using the feedback. Instructional planning for classroom teaching thus involves a cybernetic process rather than a static plan.

The player does not receive immediate feedback about whether a particular decision or sequence of decisions is deemed "correct". Instead, trends emerge in rate of transition in students' capability as a result of previous instructional strategies and decisions. The player must analyze changes in student capability and formulate hypotheses about what happened. With practice this adaptive control process improves so that the player can design successful lesson plans. By making the outcome of instruction an input to the instructional design process for the next period, it is hoped that users will develop habits of thinking and a perspective that will generalize to regular instructional planning tasks. It has not been possible to find the necessary population to conduct the necessary longitudinal investigation. (The EDSIM programme is available for others to use by post, or as a deck of punched cards with a player's manual and administrator's handbook.)

6.   CONCLUSION

Instructional design practice does not always meet the minimum standards assumed by writers of texts on the subject. But even the latter rely frequently on one-shot analysis of the effectiveness of instructional products (albeit with revision and retesting). Such input-output analysis provides no insight into the cybernetics of cognition and learning. It does not even suggest what would happen if different decisions had been made. It is really a static model of a dynamic equilibrium process which we wish to regulate. Nor does it allow the teacher or instructional designer readily to develop knowledge of how to design instruction. We have argued that more and tighter feedback loops are needed to improve instructional design and instruction. Further we have outlined two attempts to conduct basic and applied research on the instructional design process. Both appear to be useful not only to improve instruction directly but also to help trainees or practitioners to develop knowledge pertinent to the task of instructional design, knowledge not readily attainable without experiencing the feedback processes provided.

REFERENCES

1. GAGNÉ, R. M. and L. J. BRIGGS, Principles of Instructional Design, New York, Holt, Rinehart and Winston, 1974.
2. LANDA, L. N., "The Cybernetic Approach to Educational Theory," Voprosy filosofii, 16, No. 9, 75-87, Moscow, 1962 (translated).
3. LINDSLEY, O. E., "A Behavioral Measure of Television Viewing," Journal of Advertising Research, 2, 1-12, 1962.
4. MITCHELL, P. D., "Computer Simulation of a Classroom: An Educational Game to Study Pre-Instructional Decisions," in: Aspects of Educational Technology VII, R. Budgett and J. Leedham (eds.), London, Sir Isaac Pitman and Sons, 1973.
5. MITCHELL, P. D., "A Simulated Classroom and Educational Game," in: Advances in Cybernetics and Systems, J. Rose (ed.), London, Gordon and Breach Ltd., 1974.
6. MITCHELL, P. D., "A System for Education Permanente," Programmed Learning and Educational Technology, 12, 241-254, 1975.
7. MITCHELL, P. D., "Instructional Communications Algorithms in Computer Aided Learning," paper presented to National Symposium on Computer Aided Learning, Guildford, England, March 1977.
8. PASK, G., Conversation Theory, Applications in Education and Epistemology, Amsterdam, Elsevier, 1976.

ACKNOWLEDGEMENT

The assistance of a grant from the Québec Minister of Education's Programme de Formation des chercheurs et d'action concertée, along with the assistance of several students, particularly Arthur Shears and Patrick Rose, is gratefully acknowledged.

Consciousness

GORDON PASK
Systems Research Ltd., Richmond, Surrey, England

This paper comes to grips with the perplexing but important issue of consciousness as manifest in human beings and other organisms; in social organizations and, seemingly without degrading the idea, in other-than-biological systems. The possibility of taking such a radical step as to speak of consciousness <u>within</u> a theoretical frame, and without resorting to the expedient of relegating consciousness to a metatheory about science, arises from combining various developments in Cybernetics or General System Theory, which, though superficially disparate, have a great deal in common; for example, Goguen's work in category theory [22,23] and the work of Gergely and Nemeti [17] in nonclassical model theory, the representation, in several different ways, of concurrent (in contrast to serial or strictly parallel) computation, the work of Varela [61,62], Maturana [34,35], and Von Foerster [64,65], upon organizational closure, Glanville's [18] notion of objects and self reference and the work done on conversation theory by my own group.

Conversation Theory (in which a conversation between participants A, B, . . . is the minimal and canonical unit open to psychological/social observation) has already been presented to the OSGR. For example, there is a paper (Pask [39]) that is an appropriately edited transcript of a symposium at the 1972 Vienna Conference of the OSGR; Pask [48,49] describes more recent aspects. General references are Lewis and Pask [32]; Pask [39,39, 40,41,45,46,47,48,49]; Pask and Scott [50,51]; Pask, Scott and Kallikourdis [52,53]. Apart from detailing a few essential points, the theory and its empirical support will, thus, be taken for granted.

In the past, several equally legitimate reasons have been given for introducing conversation theory at all; pragmatic reasons, insofar as its predictions and prescriptions prove useful in respect to learning, education, design, decision, and the like; foundational reasons, insofar as "mainstream" psychology seems unable to deal with the facts of conceptualization, learning, creativity, awareness, or the seldom referenced, but massive, data accumulated over a century of experimental psychology (the work on problem solving and problem formulation, for instance, which is summarized in Pask [47]). Finally, there are reasons to do with scientific endeavor in the psychological/social field that are, to a large extent, neglected by the "mainstream" movements, though not, for example, by epistemologically based psychologies (Piaget, Luria, Vygotsky), or similarly minded sociologies.

It is desirable, for example, to have a <u>sharp valued</u> type of observation, peculiar to the psychological and social disciplines, which may be obtained by locating agreements over an understanding of topics (or a sharing of stable concepts) through a conversational command and question language, L. The <u>sharp valued</u> observations may surely be surrounded by fuzzy, probabilistic, or partially indeterminate observations; for example, the agreements reached between participants over personal constructs (Kelly [29]; Bannister and Mair [7]; Bannister [6]; Fransella and Bannister [15]) obtained by exchange grid methods (as used by Thomas [59,60]; Glanville [20]; or Abel [1]), which are agreements over descriptions. It is also possible to gain something from the more easily observed, though far less informative, responses of behavioral studies provided that there is an underlying sharp valued <u>psychological</u> observation to which these measurements refer (notice the qualifier "psychological"; it is easy enough to record a "sharp valued <u>response event</u>"; whether it has any relevance to the subject, or to psychology in general, is a different matter).

In this paper conversation theory is justified on somewhat different grounds; namely, that it is a proper theory of consciousness, as a result of which its epistemology is able to embrace analogy, characterization, and the stories, or parables or allegories that characters enact.

1. THE ARGUMENT

In order to express L agreements over understandings between participants A, B, . . . it is necessary to adopt a cybernetic or general systemic approach. Further, the classical forms of cybernetics and general systems theory must be replaced by nonclassical forms, due to Goguen [23], Maturana [35], Varela [61], and Von Foerster [64], or independently, to Andreka, Gergely and Nemeti [2] or (again, independently) to Braten [10] and Herbst [26], or (again, independently) to Glanville [19], to Gaines [16], Bykhovsky [11], and others.

1.1. Organizational Closure as a Stability

All of these (mostly independent) formulations replace the classical canons of deterministic or probabilistic stability by organizational closure of a <u>process</u> that is productive and, incidentally, also <u>reproduces</u> the medium, or processor, in which it is executed; most critically, by establishing, or maintaining, the distinctions (in biology, the bounding surfaces) required for its coherent execution.

1.2. Informationally Open, Organizationally Closed Processes

Another distinctive feature of the nonclassical formulations is that they are generally reflective and relativistic in character, because organisationally closed systems are often informationally open. This point is especially germane to conversation theory, where stable (as a result of organizational closure) units are participants in a conversation that involves information transfer (for example, between A and B) implicating process sharing.

1.3. Fundamental Information

The word information is used in its most fundamental sense (Petri [54]; Holt [27]) to mean either "emergence of local synchronicity between otherwise asynchronous systems," or (equisignificantly) "emergence of dependency between otherwise independent systems." Conversely, essential synchronicities in the ongoing process make it necessary to predicate, or to compute, distinctions that render parts of the medium independent; these distinctions being needed if the process is to take place. This usage of "information" is distinct from the "information" attached to various information theories (Ashby [3]; Shannon and Weaver [57]) or others, such as those of Gabor and McKay, or Bar Hillel (the most elegant general discussion is still in Cherry's [12] book, updated by Glushkov [21]). The measures obtained do, of course, estimate the "fundamental" information transfer, but in different ways.

1.4. The Conscious State

It will be argued that fundamental information transfer between participants A and B is their consciousness (A's consciousness with B of whatever they discuss), the emerging synchronicity, or dependency, being a correlate of coherent process sharing, or agreement, between the participants. The degree of consciousness is their doubt, which is many-faceted (doubt about focus of attention, doubt about outcomes, doubt about methods), but it may be quantified by fairly sophisticated confidence estimation techniques. The content of consciousness is whatever processes are shared by the participants.

1.5. Organization of a Conscious Process

A process is potentially conscious if it is organizationally closed, informationally open, and if information is transferred across distinctions that are computed as required to permit the execution of the process. When the distinctions are so placed that the content of this transfer appears as a series of L statements between participants, then it is a conscious process. In the absence of that condition, it may still be legitimate to speak of awareness and possibly thought; "consciousness" is reserved, as McCulloch [33] insists,

for a situation in which participants are conscious, with one another, of something. But a liberal interpretation of "participant" is permissible, for example, one person may be conscious with himself, insofar as he entertains several, identifiable, "perspectives."

2. THE PARTICIPANTS AND THEIR DIALOGUE

Although the participants A, B, ... are defined as "organizationally closed and informationally open systems," A, B, ... are intuitively seen as people with personal integrity and brains they call their own. If so, A and B engage in conversation about something (call it T), which is a topic they commonly name, in L, and can ostend, or point at; quite possibly T is one of them (T = A, or T = B). Their dialogue is personally addressed and consists, for the most part, in commands (or weaker forms of statement expressing intent, desire, etc.), or questions (interrogations, inquiries), together with whatever amounts to obeying a command or answering a question.

2.1. Some L Transactions

Notice that all L transactions are personally addressed (to A, to B) and that a question is simply a command that calls for (and may or may not be obeyed by) an intellectual rather than a concrete series of actions. Thus, if A asks B "how he does T," or "what he means by T," then B will generally offer an explanation; if A asks B "why did you explain T that way?", then B will generally explain or "justify" his explanation, which, to avoid the inconvenient though legitimate usage, "explanation of explanation" is called a derivation T; if A asks B "how else he explains T," then he usually receives another explanation; if A asks B to describe T, then B gives values of predicates (which may be other topics) that characterize T; in reply to "what is T," examples are cited, and in reply to "which of these is T," the reply is a selection. This by no means exhausts the potentialities of L; for example, A may ask what B believes A thinks about T, or (substituting T by A and B) what B believes, or what B believes that A believes.

These L-transactions are interpreted actively. Very many L-transactions (perhaps all of them) represent processes. Terms such as "an L-expression" or an "L-statement" can be misleading because they suggest the stuff of a textbook, and not the essentially dynamic characteristics of real (in contrast to formal) language usage.

In particular, an explanation is a process. Quite often and quite usefully, a "mathematical proof" is cited as a peculiarly pure kind of explanation, which it is. However, the meaning, in conversation theory, is the "exposition of a proof" (starting with a given set of axioms and rules delineate a sequence, ending in the theorem to be proved). This is an activity; in conversation theory, at any rate, a "proof" does not mean "the proof statement, as written down in a textbook." Moreover, explanations are by no means limited to "mathematical proofs"; they are simply explanations of how or why some circumstance pertains or some action is taken.

Quite distinctly, A might execute a process, represented by any one of his explanations, in his brain as an "internal behavior," which could (depending upon the process concerned) be exteriorized as an "external behavior" or could act as A's image of T, or both. Similarly, B can execute a process and produce an "internal behavior," which may or may not give rise to "external behavior" or to B's image of T or both. The circumstances under which process execution does and does not give rise to imaging are discussed in Section 2.3.

With "explanations" firmly established as processes rather than "strings of symbols," the concepts entertained by the participants will be viewed (and later defined) as certain bundles, or clusters, of processes that "do the same thing" or, more generally, "regulate matters so that a relation exists."

Derivations ("explanations of explanations") are also processes; they are, in fact, processes for producing and reproducing the processes that make up a concept. Further, with only technical variations, the same kind of dynamism can be attributed to all L transactions, for example, questions, expressions of desire, and the like.

There is nothing outrageously novel about this position. The reader is asked to take the common-sensical view that units of reality are processes, seriously, that is all. The position does, however, contrast with the familiar formalisms in which static "elements" are postulated; from these, by devious and slightly arbitrary routes, different formalists construct events, from these, by dint of quite tortuous arguments, different formalists arrive at more or less restricted images of a process.

2.2. Agreement Over an Understanding of T

Agreement over an understanding of T (in a conversation between participants A and B) is recognizable in L dialogue and is the event picked out by a sharp valued observation of this dialogue.

Stated loosely, agreement over an understanding means that A's productive and reproduced (i.e., stable) concept of T has a part that is coherent with (or, to use a general term introduced by Erhardt, is aligned with) B's productive and reproduced (i.e., stable) concept of T, and vice versa (Erhardt and Gioscia [13]).

Using natural language for L, participant A offers at least one explanation of T, which B accepts, can use to produce B's image, T_B, of T and can reproduce it to form part of B's concept of T (denoted $Con_B(T)$, as a shorthand). To satisfy this condition, for some unfamiliar topic, A needs, in general, to indicate to B how he derived the explanation of T that A accepts, as a guideline to a method of reproducing, or reconstructing, this explanation.

Similarly, participant B offers at least one explanation of T, which A accepts, can use to produce A's image, T_A, of T and can reproduce, to form part of A's concept of T (designated $Con_A(T)$, as a shorthand). In general, B needs to furnish A with a means for deriving the explanation that A accepts, as a guideline for reproducing or reconstructing this explanation.

By hypothesis stated already, A's concept of T

is productive and reproduced; also, B's concept of T is productive and reproduced. Agreement over an understanding implies that some of the explanatory processes (at least one) that make up $Con_A(T)$ also belong to and are reproduced in $Con_B(T)$; vice versa, that some of the explanatory processes (at least one of them) that make up $Con_B(T)$ also belong to and are reproduced in $Con_A(T)$. In other words, the initially independent participants, A and B, in this conversation share a common concept, which, being productive and reproduced in its own right (as a result of the conditions for agreement over an understanding reached between A and B) is also a stable (organizationally closed) process.

2.3. Conversational Topics

Let us call T a "topic" (this has an intuitive meaning only, at this stage; later, it is refined and discussed). Similarly, let us call the concept that is common to A and B the concept of a topic T* which is "less than or corresponding to T"; tentatively expressed by "≥" in

$$T \geq T*$$

Consider A's concept of T and B's concept of T; namely, $Con_A(T)$ and $Con_B(T)$. From Section 2.1 concepts are "bundles" or "clusters" of processes. Further, in Section 2.2, the idea of an "internal behavior" was mooted. This internal behavior may (depending upon $Con_A(T)$) be manifest as A's image. It is produced upon executing $Con_A(T)$ meaning the execution of any or all of the processes making up $Con_A(T)$. This fact is expressed by

$$Ex(Con_A(T)) \Rightarrow T_A$$

where "Ex" stands for "execution of," and "$\Rightarrow$" stands for "is produced by."

Symmetrically, for the participant B

$$Ex(Con_B(T)) \Rightarrow T_B$$

The stable concept shared as a result of understanding by A and B is a common (and stable) part of $Con_A(T)$ and $Con_B(T)$ so that

$$Ex(Con_A(T)) \Rightarrow T_A \geq T* \leq T_B \Leftarrow (Con_B(T))Ex$$

This symbolism is not able (or intended) to capture all the requirements for an agreement over an understanding (it is certainly one of several, necessarily distinct ways of expressing an agreed description). The outstanding conditions are to do with the productivity and reproduction of the common concept, agreed as an understanding, without which the common concept would not be a stable (organizationally closed) process. For one thing, explanations that represent concepts must be elicited; for another, some common process must be shared; finally, stability must be evidenced by derivation. These matters are taken up in Section 2.5. Here, we comment only upon a shared process and the entity T*, produced as a result of executing the concept of T*, shared by A and B.

Along these lines, if $\underline{Con}_A(T)$ and $\underline{Con}_B(T)$ really are stable and if the common concept really is stable, then there are subprocesses in $\underline{Con}_A(T)$, designated $\underline{Con}_A(T^*)$, such that, using "⊆" for "inclusion or equality," as usual.

$$Ex(\underline{Con}_A(T^*)) \Rightarrow T_A^* \subseteq T_A \Leftarrow (\underline{Con}_A(T))Ex$$

Further, symmetrically for participant B, there are subprocesses in $\underline{Con}_B(T)$ designated $\underline{Con}_B(T^*)$ such that

$$Ex(\underline{Con}_B(T^*)) \Rightarrow T_B^* \subseteq T_B \Leftarrow (\underline{Con}_B(T))Ex$$

Whatever else, A is not B; nor is $\underline{Con}_A(T)$ the same as $\underline{Con}_B(T)$. Hence, it is not permissible or sensible to write "T* = T* = T*." However, if the sign "⟺" stands for an isomorphism, it is possible that

$$T_A \subseteq T_A^* \Longleftrightarrow T^* \Longleftrightarrow T_B^* \supseteq T_B$$

or, in general, that there is a T preserving morphism, or matching, of different entities, the meaning now assigned to "≥" or "≤"

$$T_A \supseteq T_A^* \geq T^* \leq T_B^* \subseteq T_B$$

The "topic," T, remains elusive. The plain fact is that T, as a topic, is the coherent execution of stable concepts (stable processes).[1] The name "T" of a topic can be formalized but never fixed; formally, it denotes union, over an infinite class of conversations (between arbitrary participants including A and B), of the T* of all of them.

From a linguistic perspective "T" is the noun-like part of a stable process; it is also the set of adjectival descriptions of an indeterminate (the union of the conjunctions of descriptor values, where the descriptors are generated like personal constructs by executing other concepts). One is tempted to think of "T" as merely "that which T* becomes in the limit," as the end point of an operation (like transitive closure) which is iterated indefinitely.

The implied convergence is acceptable if and only if A and B are fixed, and do, in fact, converse. But convergence cannot be guaranteed. Nouns are not realities, except in relation to a culture or a system of belief; even with this qualification, the invariance of nouns is unimpressive. For example, Eskimo conversants have many nouns meaning "snow," but in our culture there is usually only one; the novice in a monastery has a myriad nouns for naming "meditation," and so on. As to invariance, when we go to the Alps, snow becomes many faceted, and there is a tendency nowadays to be more discriminating about states of mind.

---

[1] In Von Foerster's [65] sense, topic names consist in the eigenvalues of a concept, which is a stable concept insofar as it is an eigenoperator. The eigenvalues characterize its indefinite iteration and (given stability) the iteration becomes a recursion.

2.4. Difficulties in the Interpretation of Natural Language Transactions

In Section 2.2 it was possible to give an intuitively plausible account of the conditions to be satisfied in reaching an agreement over an understanding. So far as I know, there is nothing wrong in principle with this account, and it seems to tally with everyday experience.

The question is who says what does count as being a natural language explanation or derivation; the commonly voiced problem of disambiguating natural language utterances, which is encountered in any field where natural language is observed; in discourse analysis, for example, or automatic translation.

So far as the participants are concerned, this does not greatly matter. They (A and B) are satisfied and it is they, after all, who reach agreement; it is their criteria that count. Moreover, I am inclined to the view that this, in general, is sufficient, for a reason mentioned, but not perhaps stressed enough, in Section 2.2.

The truth value of an agreement, in whatever language is employed, is a coherence truth (indicating the accord or alignment of A and B). In logic, the notion of coherence truth has been developed, recently, by Rescher [56], though it has a long history.

Rescher's formulation deals with propositions (he notes that it is easy to recast the thesis in terms of a predicate calculus). The general idea is as follows.

Suppose there are several "observers" of data, all of whom subscribe to a body of hypotheses, or a tentative "theory." These "observers" have, let us say, the same criteria of veridiciality or factual truth. The question arises of which, possibly contradictory, bits of factual evidence will gain acceptance. A "coherence truth" value does not neglect the veridiciality criteria employed when examining a datum for truth candidacy, but it does take into account also the extent to which data fit into the existing set of hypotheses; whether or not the evidence is systemically compatible with an already accepted and well tried body of hypotheses (in Rescher's formulation as a further proposition, to be added to an existing set of propositions). Unlike Rescher, it is necessary to countenance participants, other than scientists, inspecting evidence and to admit veridiciality criteria of different kinds (artistic or commonsensical) as neither better nor worse than the canons of science. But given some criteria of acceptance (whatever they are), the coherence and fittingness of a state of affairs is an issue to do with the language in which the participants engage in conversation with each other.

Two amendments to Rescher's formulation are required in order to obtain a coherence truth appropriate to the present scheme.

It is first of all necessary to import the process orientation, introduced in Section 2.1. The idea of a proposition logically "fitting into a set of propositions," must be replaced by the equivalent dynamic form; a "process (or a propositional statement being made) fitting into a set of processes, so that execution is possible." Of the two amendments, this one is of largely

technical consequence (the difficulties encountered in formalizing a process are indisputable
but largely due to a historical quirk in the
development of formal reasoning).

Next, it is necessary to take the notion of
predication or distinction seriously, and to import
a logic of distinctions (for example, Spencer-
Brown' [58]). A fortiori, the participants A and
B are distinct and may have different criteria of
veridiciality or factuality. An agreement over an
understanding having a coherence truth value is to
be interpreted as a local synchronization of otherwise asynchronous processes (within which the
processes could not be coherently executed), or,
equisignificantly, the local appearance of dependency between otherwise independent entities. To
balance dependency, there must be a mechanism for
securing independence; a mechanism of distinction;
the logical concomitant of which is a many sorted
logic (i.e., using "universe of interpretation" in
its usual sense, the interpretation or semantic of
L involves many sorts of "universe," not just one
universe).

One candidate for a many sorted logic is the
intensional logic of Montague [36], the syntax of
which has a many-sorted semantic-interpretation.
This scheme has been proposed by Andreka and discussed with Gergely, Nemeti, Szotts, and others in
November of 1977 at Budapest. The suggestion is
certainly attractive. This group are nonclassical
(action valued) model theorists, currently, among
other tasks, undertaking a formalization of conversation theory. Between us, we could see no fundamental difficulty in replacing the static (sets-
of-elements) Montague universes by processes (as
required in the first amendment), or even quite
unconventional processors.

The difficulty, which may be remedied, appears
in the context of one of Montague's essays where
he achieves a translation of a subset of syntactic
expressions of the English language into a Montague
syntax and provides, thereby, an interpretation in
the many sorted Montague semantics. It turned out
in discussion that a metaphor in English, denoting
an analogy, cannot be so translated (the technical
reason is simply that Montague's translation requires the English expressions to be represented
in terms of a categorical grammar, which is algorithmically transformed into the syntactic expressions of a Montague logic; this step has the effect
of rendering analogies as similitudes, i.e., whereas an analogy always involves both a similarity
and a distinction, the similitude does not incorporate the crucial distinction).

It looks as though an alternative translation
scheme that respects analogies (denoted by meta-
phors) may work. However, the importance of this
innovation can scarcely be overemphasized. Not
only is analogy, as such, critical in the development of a conversation theory; it is also true, as
later, that analogy is the "most static" or "most
assertoric" representative of all the questions,
intents, etc., indicated in Section 2.1.

Supposing that more serious objections to
natural language are met by the expedients under
discussion, one hurdle still remains. Conjure as
we may, natural language statements are very
often hazy. For ordinary purposes I am not dis-
quieted by this fact, and formally this kind of
"haziness ambiguity" is readily accommodated by

"Fuzzy System Theory" and "Fuzzy Set Theory"
(Goguen [22]; Zadeh [66,67]). There is, however,
a practical problem insofar as the participants
in a conversation are required to interact
through a mechanical interface (CASTE or THOUGHT-
STICKER, Pask et al. [52]), which must, in some
sense, interpret their dialogue.

2.5. Other Types of Participants and the Minimal Processes

So far, A and B have been regarded as people,
though they are defined as stable processes. The
definition permits many other interpretations.

For example, one or both of A and B may represent groups or cultures or social institutions,
executed, qua process, in many brains, over which
the group beliefs, the cultural ethos, or the
norms of a social institution are distributed.

Equally, A and B may represent coherent
mental organizations in one brain (different
perspectives of one person) learning alone,
thinking, or theorizing. If so, the "internal"
conversation between A and B (about a thesis,
for example, or a design) may still be exteriorized for inspection, insofar as it takes place
in language L.

Conversation theory is thus widely applicable
and uncommitted to any one interpretation. Participants may be perspectives, people, cultures,
societies, schools of thought, or social institutions.

In the following three sections one user
with perspectives A and B (or quite commonly a
group of users, but in any case several perspectives A,B,...) converse through a computer
regulated interface, using a special nonverbal
form of language L.

2.6. Other Conversational Languages

It is possible to maintain dialogue through
(to be emphasized, not with) mechanical interfaces like CASTE or THOUGHTSTICKER using a language, L, which is nonverbal. The existing
implementation uses several modalities for
bearing L symbols (graphic displays, some alpha
numerical displays, indicators laid out on a
board, touch sensors, function keyboards, standard keyboards, position sensors, and the like).

The nonverbal conversational language L has
the properties outlined in Section 2.4, but the
machinery can interpret definite transactions
when they are made. Fuzzy transactions (Zadeh
[67,68]) are not excluded, and, in certain conditions, are mandatory.

An entailment mesh, together with mechaniz-
able operations (notably pruning or unfoldment,
selective pruning, condensation, expansion, and
unzipping), is a static inscription guaranteed
to represent stable concepts or agreements over
an understanding, the basic transactions between
participants (Pask [39,44,45]).

The entailment mesh is represented by a
directed and marked graph (which is usually conceived as the exposition of a thesis, plan, or
design) in which the nodes stand for topics and
the directed arcs stand for derivations of topics.

In one variant (Section 2.7) of an L conversational system, each node has a data pointer

(not an arc in the graph) to a working model, and another data pointer to a description scheme. In the other variant (Section 2.8) there is only one pointer at a node. The schemes are equivalent, since the mesh operations just noted provided that the rules of L usage, proper to the scheme, are obeyed. These rules are simple to appreciate and are enforced by a computer regulated part of the interface.

The rules common to the schemes in Section 2.7 and Section 2.8 are as follows.

a. Topics are of two types: topics (simpliciter) denoted "o" and analogical topics denoted "◇".

b. No topic may stand on its own. Thus it is not legitimate to write T without something else (two or more other topics from which T may be derived, say P and Q, as the other topics). For example, in a theory of geometry, T is "circle" and is derived from P = "plane surface" and Q = "rotation of a line of any length but any fixed origin." In electronic design, "regulated power supply" is derived from "power supply" and "a suitable regulator, with a reference potential."

c. If T, unless analogical, is derived from P and Q, then P may be derived from T and Q; similarly, Q may be derived from T and P together. This means "given an explanation of T is derived from an explanation of P and an explanation of Q, then an explanation of P may be derived from . . . "

d. Any topic may have any number of derivations (for example, T may be derived from P and Q, or R and S, or both). This, as in (c) above, is a shorthand for "If T is derived from an explanation of . . . "

e. Any analogical topic relates several other topics. Thus, T, an analogy, relates other topics F and G. For example, T is "linear oscillator," relating F = "linear mechanical oscillator" and G = "linear electrical oscillator." In design, one circuit is analogous to another circuit and both are analogous to a process they stimulate.

Any analogical topic must be supported by either a similarity (Simi) and a distinction (Dist), or by the derivation of a similarity and a distinction. For example, in the first case cited, Simi of T is a first order differential equation, Dist is a distinction between electrical and mechanical universes. If these conditions are not satisfied, and an analogical topic is asserted, the system handling L transactions assumes that the similarity is isomorphism "⟺", and the distinction is any conceivable method of securing the independence of F and G (that is, "any distinction" shown as Dist Ø). It should be stressed that analogies are not confined to strict mathematical relations and fuzzy or even qualitative analogies (for example, between social institutions or legal codes) are as common. In any case (precise or not), there are infinitely many ways of computing Dist that work, as well as infinitely many that do not.

f. The mesh that is asserted is of order 0. It may be condensed to a mesh at order 1, or, in general, n. Any mesh of order n may be expanded to a mesh of order n - 1, or ultimately, 0.

To refine this slightly, consider the cyclic entailment mesh (cyclic because of Rules (c) and (d)) and notice that it can be pruned or unfolded into a hierarchical form under any (one or more) perspective of which there are as many as there are topics in the entailment mesh. In fact, any action (of learning or doing) necessarily imposes a hierarchical ordering from the perspective adopted to learn or behave, the possibilities being delineated in an entailment structure. The class of all prunings is the pruning field.

Condensation carries structures in the pruning field, of order n, into topic nodes in a mesh of order n + 1, which may in turn be related by derivations so that the mesh evolves.

The converse operation (of retrieving the original at order n, from each topic at order n + 1) is unique, if derivations have not been added at order n + 1, and is called expansion. If the order n + 1 mesh has been modified there are specific, but no longer unique, expansions.

Operations of this kind are carried out automatically by THOUGHTSTICKER and CASTE, the L handling computer systems.

All static inscriptions are checked before they are instated at the mechanical interface, and their consequences are displayed; for example, that if T is derived from P and Q, then P is derivable from T and Q; similarly, Q is derivable from T and P. Though seemingly trivial when the entailment mesh is small, these consequences are fairly subtle when it is large. Also, the overgeneralizations, such as the assumption that Simi is isomorphism, have rather far-reaching consequences (for example, whatever F and G are derived from will be isomorphically related). For instance, in the first case cited, mass is isomorphic to inductance, friction is isomorphic to resistance, and elasticity is isomorphic to the capacity, in the electrical universe.

Since "T" is disallowed, from Rule (b). The minimal logical structure for a topic, simpliciter, is

from (b). Further, this means also that

So that the instatement of T is

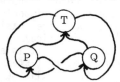

a cyclic organization.

Since all participants may think differently, no commitment is attached to the derivation arcs provided the participants are able, by any productive and reproductive operations at their disposal, to retain the specificity implied by this cyclic picture.

These comments apply to any order of condensation (Rule (f)). The expansion of a condensation is unique if no L statements involving it take place at an order greater than 0. If such L statements are made, expansions exist but are not unique.

By the same token, the minimal inscription for an analogical topic $\overline{T}$ relating F and G coexisting in distinct and a priori independent universes as derivations and specifying between them, a distinction is a complex and no longer entirely closed system. Thus, if F and G are associated by T, the form below suffices (any <u>Simi</u> can be replaced by a <u>derivation</u> of <u>Simi</u> from <u>other</u> topics, as desired).

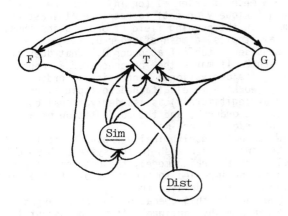

For convenience, a shorthand notation is used. This is as follows:

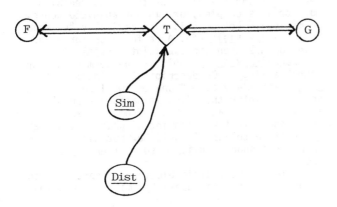

2.7. The Model as an Explanation Embodiment

Let us turn to the model making interpretation in which "verbal explanations" are replaced by "working models."

g. All topics must be associated (either at once, or at any subsequent moment, before the entailment mesh is finally accepted for instatement, as the static inscription of a logical L transaction) with working models; programs compiled and capable of independent execution in one or more "modeling facilities," or processors external to the participants. (Both A and B must build distinct working models in independent processors.) One data link (Section 2.6) attaches the node of each topic to a "working model."

One of the most familiar "working models" is a program written in LOGO (Pappert [37]). Feurtzig and Pappert [14], Howe and O'Shea [28], compiled, or interpreted for execution, in an external processor (computing machine, equipped with a "turtle," or a display-equivalent "turtle"). For example, instead of providing a verbal explanation of T = "circle," participant A is required to write a LOGO program which, upon execution, makes the turtle, or the turtle display, describe a circular figure and to allow for parameter assignments that set up an arbitrary center and diameter. Similarly, there are programs that satisfactorily simulate P = "plane surface," (say as a repertoire of motions of the turtle) and Q = "radial inscription" (to delineate and rotate a radius). These programs are nonverbal explanations in the following sense.

If $\underline{Con}_A(T)$ is stable, it consists (as will be discussed in Section 3) in a cluster of coherently executable procedures (alias, programs interpreted and executed in A's brain), any one of which is representative of $\underline{Con}_A(T)$. The program listings could be elicited as verbal explanations acceptable to another person (B), but if both A and B know LOGO, then a LOGO listing is equivalent, provided it can be interpreted and executed in the external computer, independently.

To satisfy the independence of A and B, each participant must have a distinct LOGO processor, so that their programs and their attempts to write them do not interfere, and so that possibly different programs can be compared and contrasted after A and B have modified the listing to their satisfaction.

Of course, LOGO is not the only transparent programming language; SMALLTALK (Winograd and Kaye) is another. We, in fact, use analogue/ hybrid simulators and computer traced devices that are specific to broad fields of subject matter.

The working model for an analogical topic, $\overline{T}$, is a little more complex. A and B must both have at least two (in general, more than two) external computers so that they can each compare and contrast their own working models for F and G as a result of which they can agree about the similarity and difference between F and G (as made by A) and of F and G (as made by B). Hence, a minimum of 4 external computers is needed (a minimum of 2 for participant A and 2 for participant B) in order to obtain agreement over the explanations of an analogical topic. Moreover, these computers (which, as given, are simply independent) must be cogently distinguished (for example, so that one (X_A) is a universe for accommodating the working model of a mechanical oscillator and the other is a universe, Y_A (say), for accommodating the working model of an electrical oscillator). Similar comments apply to participant B excepting that his distinction X_B/Y_B (though usually not at all identical) shall be compatible with the A distinctions.

h. The other data link (Section 2.6) connects the node of each topic to a description scheme whereby the node can be identified or named (users may give arbitrary or temporary names to topics but the real topic names are conjuncts of descriptor values that uniquely identify each node in the entailment mesh).

Descriptors are elicited in the manner of Kelly's personal constructs (Introduction), over topics in the entailment mesh, which are the objects being described. The algorithm used for this purpose (by CASTE or THOUGHTSTICKER) is selective insofar as it centers initially upon analogical topics, requiring one or more descriptors (with values of "+" = has, "-" = has not, and "*" = is irrelevant) having values that differ upon the topics related by the analogy but, insofar as the analogical topic is concerned, the value of "*" = irrelevant. The descriptor names, thus elicited, are entered in place of Dist in the analogy; thus if D is a descriptor with value "+" on F, "-" on G, the value "*" is assigned to T, and the name "D" is entered in Dist of T.

Since several orders of condensation of a mesh may coexist, the algorithm starts at the highest order and requires (for each order of mesh) that conjuncts of descriptor values uniquely identify each topic. This result may be achieved by the analogy selecting method above; if not, then the process is continued until this condition is satisfied.

Modifications of the method include the use of many valued descriptors and, for several users, a type of exchange grid (Introduction) technique to reach agreement over a description (or set of descriptors and common value assignments to each).

2.8. Eliminating the Requirement of Explicit Working Models

Under certain circumstances, it is neither necessary nor appropriate to call for the explicit construction of a working model attached to any logically instated topic and an alternative technique is adopted. This technique relies upon the idea that condensation and the converse operation of expansion can set a limit to the proliferation of a mesh provided that there is a reserved analogy type, γ_i, called "any other." Perhaps the notion is most easily exhibited in the context of theory building or thesis exposition (say a thesis on genetics or physical chemistry). The fact is either subject matter is somehow related to any other. Subject matter is dissected out from knowledge in general, as a particular thesis or an entire discipline, by the distinctions that underlie a degenerate analogy (the reserved, γ_i,

or "any other" analogy), in which the similarity component exists but is underspecified. For example, in the diagram below, γ_1 and γ_2 are degenerate (Sim = Null cannot be derived for γ_1 or γ_2 or any γ_i).

Consider an ordinary topic, T, and the caliber of the working model that would, in Section 2.7, be attached to it. Since T cannot legally exist on its own, it forms part of a mesh. This mesh can be pruned under all of its topics to produce a pruning field. Each element in the pruning field of the original mesh (say, of order O) can be condensed to one topic in a mesh of order +1 (or, in general, of order n). Given a mesh of order +1 (or +n) it can be expanded (uniquely or not) to retrieve at least one element in the pruning field of order O and thus, over all topics, a mesh of order O.

Consider a topic T at order O. What does it represent? It may either be conceived as representing its derivational connection at order O and the working model attached to topic T, or (just as legitimately) as its derivational connection at order O, and the condensation of a mesh of order -1 (or -m).

We cannot algorithmically expand topic T if O is the lowest order mesh in the system. However, in place of a working model, the user or group of users can be impelled to "unzip" topic T, that is, to say what T is derived from.[1]

How far can this operation (which enlarges the order O mesh) continue? It may go on until the user (or group of users) is unable to furnish a derivation because (to him) the topic is elementary or indivisible (not to be equated with more or less complex, or, in any absolute sense, primitive). Let us call such maximally "unzipped" topics indivisible (for A or for B or for A and B in conversation about a joint thesis).

Each indivisible topic is one term of an "any other" analogy. On description of the mesh the Dist of the "any other" analogy will be filled by some descriptor that discriminates A's or B's thesis or the A and B thesis from the rest of knowledge. In the following diagram, P and Q are indivisible topics (T could be, but has an outgoing arc connecting it to some other topic in the mesh).

Some of the indivisible topics represent (in computer-science language) "primitive operations";

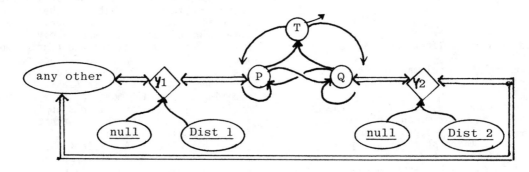

---

[1] Unzipping is defined in Pask [39]; Pask, Scott and Kallikourdis [53] as adding derivations to a mesh.

some indivisible topics (again in computer-science language) represent primitive predicates. The Dist terms in all of the non-degenerate analogies (those that are not γ_i or "any other" analogies) represent distinctions between independent universes in the thesis (so that, unlike computation in general, there may be many sorts (Section 2.4) of primitive operation, and many sorts of primitive predicate). The "any other" analogies relate the thesis to an (arbitrarily) independent, and infinitely large, universe of knowledge (commonly the disciplinary compartments of academic subject matter are distinguished on grounds such as these, in fact multifarious, distinctions).

There is a theorem, due to Steltzer (1977), that any genuine example is an analogy. In this sense, either "physics" or "chemistry" are examples of "science," and "science" is an example of knowledge.

Operationally, the requirement imposed in Section 2.6 (g) for assigning a working model to each topic, may be waived if we replace it by:

g*. For each topic having no working model "unzip" the topic until the process is bounded by "any other" analogies that have indivisible topics as one related component and assign primitive operations and primitive predicates, as required.

Descriptor value elicitation proceeds as in Section 2.6 (h) except that:

h*. In addition to operation h, elicit descriptors with value "+" on each "indivisible" topic and value "+" on all topics in that part of the mesh (or the entire mesh if all topics are of the same sort in the sense of Section 2.4) that is of the same sort as the indivisible topic in question (that is, not rendered independent by the Dist of a nondegenerate analogical topic). Enter the descriptor names in the Dist components of each γ_i, or "any other" analogical topic.

3. MINIMAL ORGANIZATIONALLY CLOSED PROCESSES

From Section 2.2 and 2.3 the minimal stable (organizationally closed) process that exists is called a stable concept, using the term "concept" as a synonym for "skill" (intellectual skill, if you like), the execution of which gives rise to a description (image, imagination) or a behavior, or both of them. The notion of minimality should be examined carefully. My concept of "society," for example, may be larger than any concept I have of "myself." Hence, the minimality notion is not "minimal size." Rather, it is an operational minimality, which refers to the least organizationally closed but informationally open process, which can be dissected out arbitrarily from a nexus of interacting processes and be said to have an autonomy or integrity of its own.

3.1. Concepts of Participants

A concept is denoted Con. In particular, $Con_A(T)$ is A's concept of T, where T is as yet unspecified.

$Con_A(T)$ is defined in terms of procedures ($Proc_A$) that are open to execution as processes, so that a procedure is like a working model, built in the medium of a brain. Consequently, it is not just a program (series of syntactically valid instructions), but a compiled or interpreted program. If Inter stands for the interpretation of a program, and if Prog stands for the instructions that are interpreted for execution in this medium, then if "<" and ">" denote ordered sets, $Proc_A$ is an ordered pair.

$$Proc_A \triangleq <Prog_A, Inter_A>$$

(It is nonsense to say "Ex(Prog)", meaning "Execute Prog" with no processor implied, as it would be in standard computer science; one can say Ex($Proc_A$).)

All of these terms may be qualified, to indicate programs that do particular things (Prog p, Prog q . . .), or do them in different ways (Prog 1p, Prog 2p . . . Prog 1q, Prog 2q . . .) and they may be interpreted in different processors or quasi independent (or independent) parts X, Y, . . . of any one processor (Inter X, Inter Y, . . .).

It is important to note that $Proc_A$ is named $Proc_Ai$ insofar as Ex($Proc_Ai$) $\Rightarrow i_A$. If i, j, k, l are different indices, and if

$$Proc_A i = (Prog\ p, Inter\ X)$$
$$Proc_A j = (Prog\ q, Inter\ X)$$
$$Proc_A k = (Prog\ p, Inter\ Y)$$
$$Proc_A l = (Prog\ q, Inter\ Y)$$

these are all, necessarily, distinct, if they exist (they may not exist if, for example, Prog p with Inter Y is not an executable compilation, though Prog p with Inter X, is).

In order to specify a concept, as conveniently as possible, and using a concise and transparent notation, the following conventions are adopted as standard forms. If u,v stand for Procs as above, then

Conventions.

<u,v>	The ordered pair (or n-tuple) u,v (as before).
{u,v}	An unordered set of u,v.
{u_r}	An unordered set of u_r, (or v_r) r = 1,2,... in which processes may conflict in execution.
[u,v]	The compilation of programs such that they are executed in parallel. For example, u,v may be compiled in independent processors, or interlaced, with interrupt, in one.
[v_r]	A set of parallel processes u_r (or v_r) r = 1,2,...
<{u_r}, [v_r]>	A concurrent set of processes of which there is a subset of parallel-executed processes and some (one or more) conflicting process.

Principle 1 (Concept). In certain media or processors, recompilation takes place so that {u_r} → <{u_r}, [v_r]> [v_r]. There is a

tendency for the execution of process to become coherent.

Principle 2 (Media). Any participant, A, B,... is a process involving such a media. Brains, for example, can act in this manner, any concept belongs to one or more of A, B, ... (a very liberal requirement in view of Section 2). Con is necessarily subscripted as Con_A or Con_B (in general, some value of a variable Z = A,B,...). It is essential to recognize that Z designates processes (neither processors, such as brains, nor syntactic entities such as programs). If "⇐" stands for isomorphism, it is conceivable that $Con_A(T) ⇔ Con_B(T)$ for any T, but the expression "$Con_A(T) = Con_B(T)$" is meaningless.

Definition. For any value of Z (such as A)

$$Con_A ≜ \{Proc_A\} \quad or \quad <\{Proc_A\}, [Proc_A]>$$

$$or \quad [Proc_A]$$

and no other thing is a concept.

Of these, only the last $[Proc_A]$ indicates a parallel and preordainedly coherent collection of procedures; if $Con_A = \{Proc_A\}$ then no information transfer would take place between the procedures that are undergoing execution. If the $\{Proc_A\}$ is a singleton (unit set), then execution does not involve information transfer between the procedures; execution is serial. Otherwise, if $\{Proc_A\}$ is not a singleton, execution is incoherent and probably the process is abortive. (Notice, however, that the compilation of a Prog, to form a Proc, is a process that does involve information transfer; similarly if a Prog is read as a listing.)

If $<\{Proc_A\}, [Proc_A]>$ is executed, information transfer must take place between the coherent and the as yet incoherent procedures; in order that the incoherent procedures become by recompilation coherent, and thus executable. This is a concurrent process.

Execution. The symbolism $Ex(Con_A)$ stands for the execution of some usually concurrent process. Such a concept is not, however, necessarily a stable concept, and it becomes so only if at least some concepts act upon Proc to produce other Procs of which some can gain entry into the original concept (reproduction, reconstruction).

Principle 3 (Production and Reproduction). The existence of such concept-making concepts is assumed in the mental-repertoire of any participant A,B,... It is convenient to distinguish them (artificially) as special operations and to distinguish among them as description building (DB) and procedure building (PB) operations (though, theoretically based, the differentiation of DB and PB operations is empirically supported).[1]

Without debating the exact character of the DB and the PB operations (for they are likely to

differ from person to person), it is possible to distinguish them as classes of operation that act on descriptions to produce other descriptions.

$$DB_A(P_A, Q_A) ⇒ T_A \qquad DB_A(R_A, S_A) ⇒ T_A$$

(like, for example, relational operators) and classes of operation that act upon a mixed argument, like

$$PB_A(Con_A(P), Con_A(Q), T_A) ⇒ Proc_A(T) \text{ in } Con_A(T)$$

$$PB_A(Con_A(R), Con_A(S), T_A) ⇒ Proc_A(T) \text{ in } Con_A(T)$$

(for example, classes of algorithm building programs).

Principle 4 (Continual Action). Some concepts are invariably undergoing execution; of these, some are and some are not DB and PB operations. That is, always, for any Z = A,B,... there is at least one process of each kind

$$Ex \, DB_Z(Con_Z(P), Con_Z(Q), T_Z ⇒$$

$$Proc_Z(T) \text{ in } Con_Z(T)$$

$$Ex \, DB_Z(P_Z, Q_Z) ⇒ T_Z$$

$$Ex \, Con_Z \quad _Z(T) ⇒ T_Z$$

Thus

a. It is possible to construct organizationally closed production schemes and thus to speak of stable concepts as maintained entities.

b. The execution of such a scheme of productions gives rise, for any novel concept, to a progression from its initial appearance ($\{Proc_A\}$ in 3.1, Definition), up to the parallel execution $[Proc_A]$.

c. The middle term $<\{Proc_A\}, [Proc_A]>$, must intervene between these extremities; hence, information transfer must occur between the concurrent processes.

d. The execution (indefinite iteration) of a stable concept $Con_Z(T)$ is the topic T_Z as proposed, loosely, and without specifying a concept in Section 2.3.

e. From (c) stabilization by organizational closure necessarily involves information transfer between procedures undergoing execution; it is this information transfer we identify with "awareness." Similarly, an interaction between Z = A and Z = B (for example, A teaches $Con_A(T)$ to B who learns $Con_B(T)$) also involves information transfer which we identify with consciousness (of A with B of T).

Principle 5 (Coherence and Distinction). By inference from Principle 3 and Principle 4, given a medium with the particular characteristics ordained by Principle 1 and Principle 2, any process tends, in isolation, toward coherence; in psychological terms, to fixity, closure, or even rigidity.

Suppose that isolation is somehow maintained. If so, there must, for consistency of the

---

[1] Pask and Scott [50]; Final Scientific Report, SSRC Research Programme HR/2708/2.

postulates, be means for maintaining the tendency
toward coherence, postulated in Principle 1 and
Principle 2 (which cannot apply if complete
coherence exists). Even if interaction (as with
some other process) is allowed, there are, by
postulate, means for preventing the contravention
of Principle 1 (again, given its intended interpretation, as a tendency toward coherent execution).

This means Principle 5 can be expressed by
saying the equations that describe the motion of a
process have singularities when coherence is approached; in psychological terms this may imply a
change in attention, or in perspective, or the
creation of a further distinguished processor
(universe of interpretation). That is, a distinction of the type $Dist(X,Y)$ is computed to demarcate
independent processors labeled X,Y with interpretations or compilations Inter X, Inter Y. That
is how Inter X becomes distinct from Inter Y in
the first place.

Alternatively, "if there are stable concepts,
then the distinctions required for the existence
of other stable concepts are computed," the "stable
concepts are generalized eigenoperators (Von
Foerster [64]) that yield fixed point solutions
(eigenvalues) upon indefinite iteration" or "stable
concepts are discrete, insofar as there are incon-
ceivables" (this latter sense of discreteness is
in accord with Glanville's [19] criticism, on the
score of spatial perception) or, under an interpretation which is latent in the discussion,
Principles 1 to 5 provide a mechanism for preserving information transfer, or consciousness;
singularities are the points at which the process
would become unconscious, unless some event took
place; consciousness is the information transfer
required to maintain a tendency toward coherent
execution." The conscious process, in other words,
satisfies the conditions of Section 1.5.

3.2. Stable Concepts as Units

If $Con_A(T)$ is a stable concept, then $Ex(Con_A(T))$
$\Rightarrow T_A$ as in Section 2.2.

However, in considering the argument that cul-
minates in Section 3.1, Principle 5, we are given
the license of interpreting an "internal behavior"
(Section 2.2) as involving, under circumstances
where concurrency has not yet passed into coherence, as an image, without qualification, and in
particular, T_A may be A's image or apparition of T
(in one sense modality, or many) or, insofar as
the execution may take place, wholly or only partially, in a brain, T_A may be A's external behavior.

For example, in flying an aircraft, much of the
concept (alias, skill) is executed outside the
pilot's brain and constitutes a behavior (for
example, of keeping the aircraft on course) though
the relation preserved by this regulating behavior
is manifest to the pilot as "even flight."

Conversely, if the pilot wishes, he can execute this concept to obtain a mental picture of
"even flight." Further, he might describe this
picture in terms of "personal constructs" and
their values, i.e., personally computed descriptions, generated by executing other stable concepts
in his repertoire.

Perhaps the majority of concepts are not
generally manifest as behaviors (for example,
"rectangularity" or "product of numbers"), though

they may be. If participant A has a stable concept for "rectangularity" or "multiplication" (or
"hope" or "judgment" or "delight"), then he can
often behave to realize his concept in concrete
action; for instance, by drawing rectangles, or
by multiplying numbers (by hoping, exercising
wisdom, experiencing joy).

The important point is that if A has a stable
concept of T then he can always issue a series of
instructions to some autonomous agent, either
some other participant B or an inanimate processor,
such that the independent execution of the instructions by the agent is one representation of
$Con_A(T)$; this representative series of instructions is one or more of the Progs that constitute
part of some $Proc_A(T)$, in $Con_A(T)$, and this may
either make its appearance as the construction of
a working model (Section 2.7) or figure as an
explanation.

By the same token, both DB_A and PB_A operations are concepts, taking arguments that are
either concepts or the result of executing concepts, or both. They are behaviorally manifest
as derivations, later encompassed by a description (Section 2.7 and Section 2.8).

4. SOME CANONICAL ORGANIZATIONALLY CLOSED AND INFORMATIONALLY OPEN PRODUCTION SYSTEMS

At this point, it is possible to draw production systems that are minimal, organizationally
closed and informationally open units.

Let $Z = A$ and let T_A be derived from P_A and
Q_A (clearly, it is also possible to assert that
P_A is derived from T_A and Q_A or that Q_A is derived from T_A and P_A, as in Section 2.5).

If $Con_A(T)$ is stable (similarly, $Con_A(P)$ and
$Con_A(Q)$, depending upon A's perspective), then
Figure 1 shows the minimal unit as a production
system. In this and other pictures "⇒" stands
for "produces" and "→" is a collecting arc, meaning that arguments are, and become, available as
the output of the productions, some of which
"reproduce" (stabilize) the original. The operation is not serially constrained, and insofar as
it is concurrent the information transfer between
procedures, needed in order to secure the operation of the system, is an awareness on the part
of participant A. The system is activated by
A's adopting a perspective (for example, T_A when
it is a stable concept of T_A) but it is possible
to adopt any perspective (T,P,Q) except that if
the system were isolated, then at least one perspective must be adopted (Principle 4 of Section
3.1).

An organizationally closed and informationally
open system is potentially aware (notice that
productions do not only yield one product, and
that other productions may yield the entities
upon which productions operate). This scheme is
minimal in the sense stipulated in Section 3.1.

Figure 2 shows the minimal production system
for a different participant (or perspective),
$Z = B$, given the postulate that T_B is derived
from R_B and S_B (consequently, that R_B is derived
from T_B and S_B; S_B from T_B and R_B as in all other
statements about stable concepts). That is, in-
sofar as the schemes in Figure 1 and Figure 2 are
executed, $Z = A$ and $Z = B$ necessarily adopt

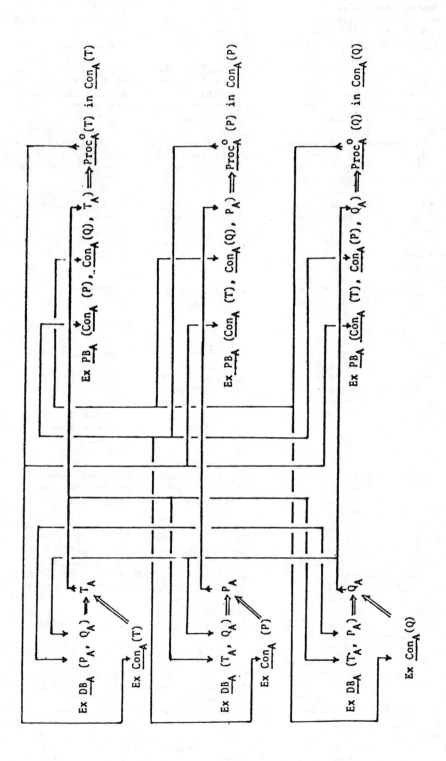

Figure 1.

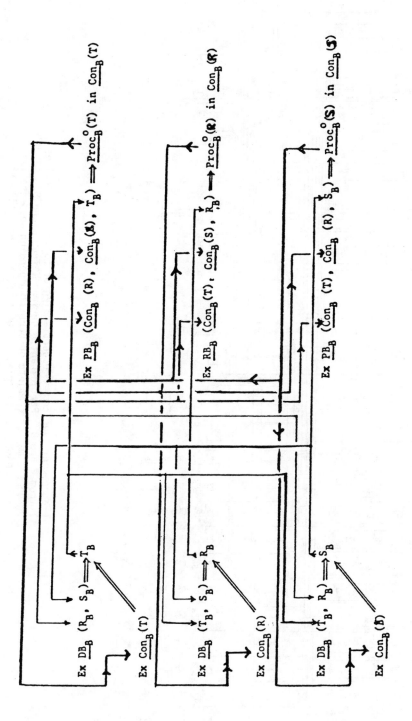

Figure 2.

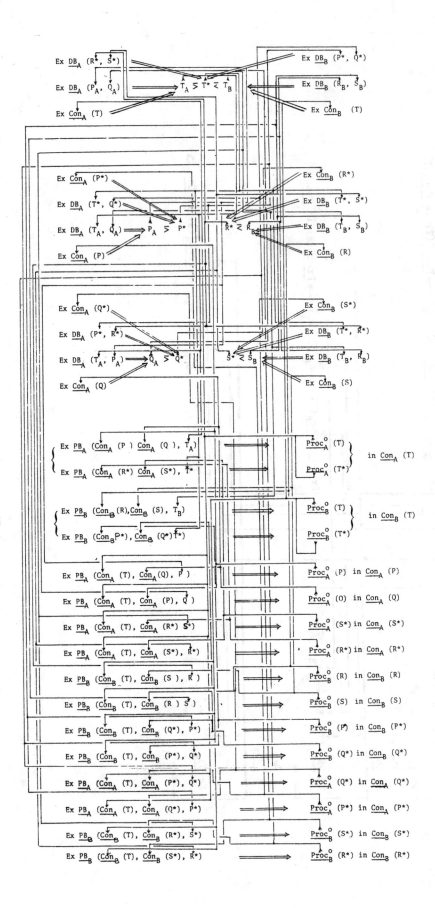

Figure 3. L-agreement over common understanding of topic T. A derives T from P and Q. Participant B derives T from R and S. An agreement may be complete or partial depending upon the isomorphic part (for example, T*) of topic and the similarity of method.

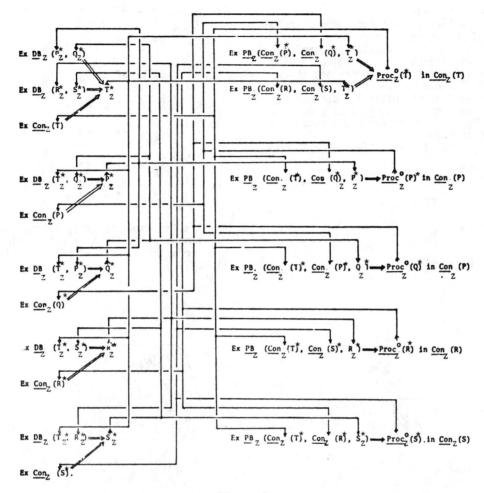

Figure 4.

(Note: Z is a variable indexing participants here Z = A or Z = B.)

perspectives, say T_A and T_B respectively, and supposing that compatible perspectives are adopted (loosely the "same" perspective, though all that is required is a pair of perspectives admitting "coherent" execution), there may be an agreement over an understanding.

Let A and B agree to an understanding of T (where A and B are initially asynchronous, or independent). Their agreement over an understanding of T is minimally represented in the same notation by Figure 3, leading to the simple agreement of Section 2.3, namely

$$T_A \equiv T_A^* \geq T^* \leq T_B^* \equiv T_B$$

But also, since an understanding is involved, and since it is the postulated understanding

$$P_A \equiv P_A^* \geq P^* \leq P_B^*$$
$$Q_A \equiv Q_A^* \geq Q^* \leq Q_B^*$$
$$R_A^* \geq R^* \leq R_B^* \equiv R_B$$
$$S_A \geq S^* \leq S_B^* \equiv S_B$$

which is represented, inpproduction scheme notation, by Figure 4.

However, if the concepts are stable and are executed

P_B^* is transformed into a richer P_B

Q_B^* is transformed into a richer Q_B

R_A^* is transformed into a richer R_A

S_B^* is transformed into a richer S_B

It does not, of course, necessarily follow that enrichment leads to a condition in which, in the limit, there is isomorphism $P_A \Leftrightarrow P_B$ or $Q_A \Leftrightarrow Q_B$ or $R_A \Leftrightarrow R_B$ or $S_A \Leftrightarrow S_B$ any more than $T_A \Leftrightarrow T_B$.

If the system in Figure 3 is executed, then information transfer takes place between A and B, so that A is conscious with B of T, and vice versa; the concurrency is distributed and amounts to a coming about of local (centered at topic T) synchronization of A and B, or, equisignificantly, to a coming about of local (centered at T) dependency between the participants.

As noted in Section 2.7, an agreement over the understanding of an analogy is more complicated and the minimal scheme of production is complex.

Under the postulate that an analogical topic $\bar{T}_A$ between F_A and G_A is agreed, in respect to an analogical topic $\bar{T}_B$ between F_B and G_B, where (for completeness as well as minimality) A derives F_A from P_A and Q_A; G_A from N_A and O_A; that B derives F_B from R_B and S_B; G_B from K_B and L_B; minimal scheme is shown in Figure 5.

There is a simple agreement (Section 2.3) like

$$T_A \equiv T_A^* \geq T^* \leq T_B^* \equiv T_B$$

$$F_A \equiv F_A^* \geq F^* \leq F_B^* \equiv F_B$$

$$G_A \equiv G_A^* \geq G^* \leq G_B^* \equiv G_B$$

$$P_A \equiv P_A^* \geq P^* \leq P_B^*$$

$$Q_A \equiv Q_A^* \geq Q^* \leq Q_B^*$$

$$R_A^* \geq R^* \leq R_B^* \equiv R_B$$

$$S_A^* \geq S^* \leq S_B^* \equiv S_B$$

$$N_A \equiv N_A^* \geq N^* \leq N_B^*$$

$$O_A \equiv O_A^* \geq O^* \leq O_B^*$$

$$K_A^* \geq K^* \leq K_B^* \equiv K_B$$

$$L_A^* \geq L^* \leq L_B^* \equiv L_B$$

Similar comments apply to the development or enrichment of the initial but stable concepts that are iteratively executed (P_B^*, Q_B^*, R_A^*, S_A^*, N_B^*, O_B^*, K_A^*, L_A^*).

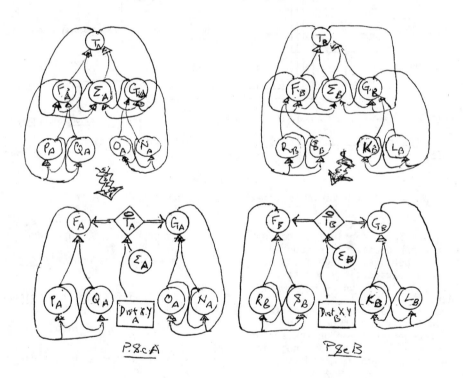

P.ScA   PScB

Figure 5a.

Analogy production within participants. An incoherent distributive derivation (T_A from F_A and E_A, or T_A from G_A and E_A; T_B from F_B and E_B or T_B from G_B and E_B) gives rise to a bifurcation. Consequently A is split into parts X_A, Y_A, and B is split into parts X_B, Y_B, that are independent, but may be related as analogical by $\bar{T}_A$ and $\bar{T}_B$ between F_A, G_A or F_B, G_B with similarity E_A, E_B and distinctions (independent X_A,Y_A; X_B,Y_B) if $\underline{Dist}_A(X,Y)$, $\underline{Dist}_B(X,Y)$. The resulting production schemes are, for A, PSCA, and for B, PSCB.

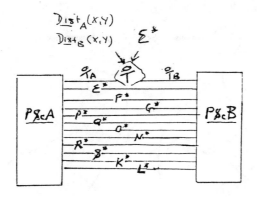

Figure 5b.

Outline of interaction between A and B,((PSCA and PSCB as
in Figure 5a), to obtain agreement over an understanding
$\bar{T}$ of analogies $\bar{T}_A$ and $\bar{T}_B$, with their distinct derivations.

5. METALINGUISTIC STATEMENTS ABOUT
CONVERSATIONAL TRANSACTIONS

This paper is written in a metalanguage L# for
making assertions about the conversational language L and the transactions that go on between
any participants A,B,... that engage in discourse.
As the initial L# statement, a participant was
defined (in Section 1.2) as an organizationally
closed and informationally open system and it was
noted (at the end of Section 4) that production
systems representing the minimal units that can be
isolated from the flux of conceptual activity are
defined in the same way "organizationally closed
and informationally open systems." A conversation
(over which closure is observed by an external
observer and described in L# in order to achieve
sharp value L# observations of "L agreements over
understandings" (between A and B) is also an entity
of this kind.

The entailment mesh notation will be used, for
the purpose of discussion, as an L# syntax in harmony with the L syntax.

5.1. The Truth Value of Agreement over
an Understanding

The inscription of Figure 3 is an L statement
(conversational language statement). The truth
value of this agreement over T is a coherence
truth, representing the consciousness of A, with
B, of topic T; the <u>content</u> of their consciousness.
It is not at all necessary that this content is
veridicially true (or, as a matter of fact), even
logically true according to the canons of a particular logical scheme). Yet an external observer
would like to make a statement, using the meta-
language L#, like "It is true that A and B have a
stable concept T , that they agree over an understanding of T, this being an L agreement," or
"AB(T) is true."

What kind of statement would this metalinguis-
tic, or L#, statement of AB(T) be; one of the sharp

valued observations that external observers are
able and inclined to make? The veridicially true
L# statement would be (whatever else) an L#
metaphor, designating an L# analogy. To see
this, it is only necessary to notice that the
external observer, henceforward <u>OB</u>, can observe
a similarity (T*), based upon other similarities
(P*, Q*, and R*, S*), insofar as he adopts a perspective (so that T* is being understood, rather
than P,Q,R,S) <u>and</u> he makes a distinction between
A and B. Any one of infinitely many possible
distinctions (biological, cultural, and so on)
are legitimate, a particular distinction being
denoted $\underline{Dist}_{OB}(A,B)$.

To represent this state of affairs, all that
is needed is a means of distinguishing L# from L
analogies. It is convenient to adopt the convention that L# analogies are shaded, whereas
L analogies (as before) are not. The convention
is thus:

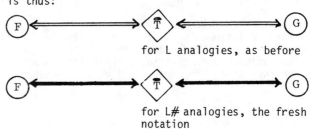

for L analogies, as before

for L# analogies, the fresh
notation

Using this symbolism, it is possible to represent
the L# statement, AB(T), as a veridicially true
but <u>analogical</u> L# statement of the L agreement
concerning the understanding of topic T by A and
B; this (or any other type of agreement) having a
coherence truth; strictly "as seen <u>reflectively</u>
by A and B, <u>relative</u> to their conversational
domain which contains topic T (perhaps because
they constructed a stable concept for T, de novo;
or, equally, because topic T was purveyed by some
other theorist).

The L# statement is shown in Figure 6, using

entailment mesh notation. It is an L entailment
mesh pruned under the perspective adopted, namely T.

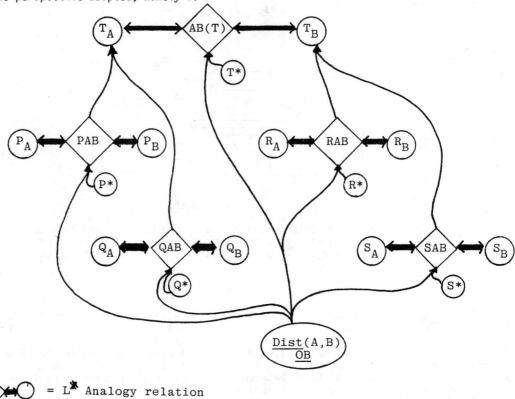

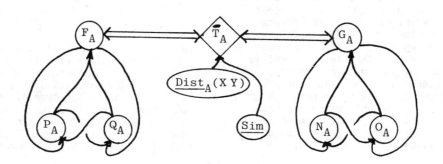

Figure 6.   An L# analogy (designated by an L metaphor), AB(T),
            corresponding to an external observer's inscription
            of agreement and understanding (in L, by partici-
            pants A and B) of an ordinary topic, T, with common
            and agreed part, T*.

5.2. The Status of Agreement over Understanding an Analogical Topic

Now, if the external observer exists and is able
to make L# statements about L agreements, he is able
to observe that A and B do, from time to time, reach
agreement over understanding L analogies. Such
agreements are, as before, credited with a coherence
truth signifying the content of A's consciousness
with B (or B's consciousness with A) of a topic
called T. The necessary production system for this
kind of stable concept sharing is shown and interpreted in Figure 5. Thus participant A has a personal theory about an L analogy, T_A, between topics
F_A and G_A, given the distinction $\underline{Dist}_A(X,Y)$, and
the similarity, $\underline{Simi}$, as stated in Section 4, namely

By the same token, participant B has a personal theory about an L analogy, $\bar{T}_B$, between
topics F_B and G_B, given the distinction $\underline{Dist}_B(X,Y)$
and the similarity, $\underline{Simi}$; and the entailment mesh
picture expressing the statement of Section 4
is

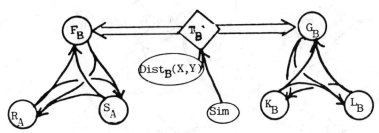

These are static, shorthand, inscriptions for
the production scheme shown in Figure 5, before
an agreement is reached. After the agreement is
reached, there is a common scheme of productions
in the mental repertoires of both A and B that
can be pictured below (where $\bar{T}^*$ is the common
analogical topic, based on possibly different
distinctions, $\underline{Dist}_A(X,Y)$ and $\underline{Dist}_B(X,Y)$.

This is an L (conversation language) statement
and it has a coherence truth value.

Suppose that an A,B agreement over an understanding with content $\bar{T}^*$ is to be represented
by an external observer, in the metalanguage L#
in the same way as the L# statement "AB(T) is
true," of Figure 6. The result is Figure 7,
where, as before, $\underline{Dist}_{OB}(A,B)$ is a distinction
between the participants.

It is once again a pruned L# entailment
mesh in which the L analogies are interleaved
with L# analogies. (Notice that all the lowest
topics in this pruning are L# analogies, though
the terms they relate are unspecified in the
picture.)

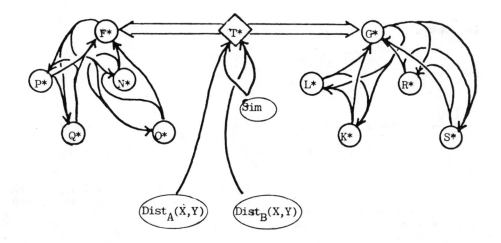

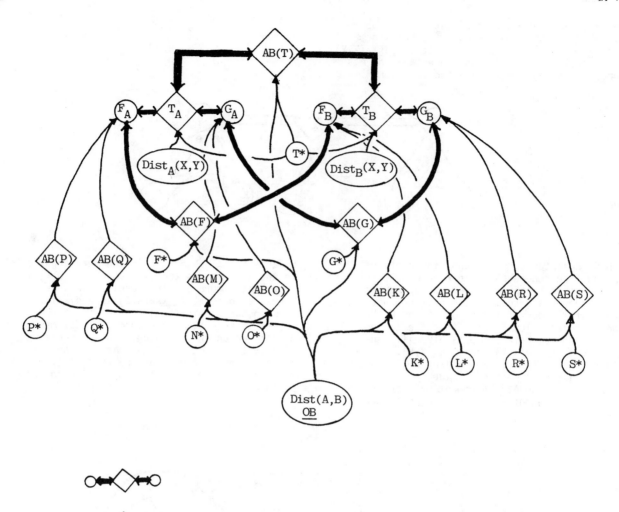

Figure 7. Minimal construction, in L#, for AB(T) if T is an analogy
between F and G derived by A as F from P and Q, G from N
and O; by B as F derived from K and L for G from R and S.

5.3. Significance of Analogies in L and in L

Notably, Figure 7 brings out the point that
the difference (if any difference exists) between
the pruned L# mesh of an outside observer and the
L mesh of the participants, that images a dynamic
production scheme (Figure 5), lies in (a) the
fact that the distinctions in L# analogies,
imaging agreements, are like $\underline{Dist}_{OB}(A,B)$, whereas
those in the L analogies (between acoustics and
optics, or mechanics and electricity, or universes,
in general) are like $\underline{Dist}_A(X,Y)$ and $\underline{Dist}_B(X,Y)$;
and (b) that the external observer adopts a per-
spective (as the participants may do also); hence,
the pruning.

The question arises of whether or not these
two differences (a) and (b) are significant or
salient differences.

Now, of the two, (b) is definitely not salient
(fundamental more than a convenience), for any·

participant A,B can, by definition, adopt a perspective with respect to agreement over an understanding, just as the observer OB can adopt any
or all perspectives. If it turns out that (a)
is in no way salient (fundamental more than a
convenience) either, then there is no essential
difference. It seems to me that (a) is not
salient; for surely, A and B may distinguish
themselves, i.e., A can see himself distinct in
any coherent way from B and vice versa, B from A.
I have tried to show this in Figure 8, where A
and B are imaged in the process of "self inquiry"
or "interpersonal interaction"; they are getting
to know each other, to understand each other
(to agree to an understanding of each other's
beliefs, which certainly does not imply that
they agree about these beliefs; in fact, they
may disagree, yet know why they disagree). The L
topic (an analogical topic) that A and B agree
to understand is AB (their mutual or shared

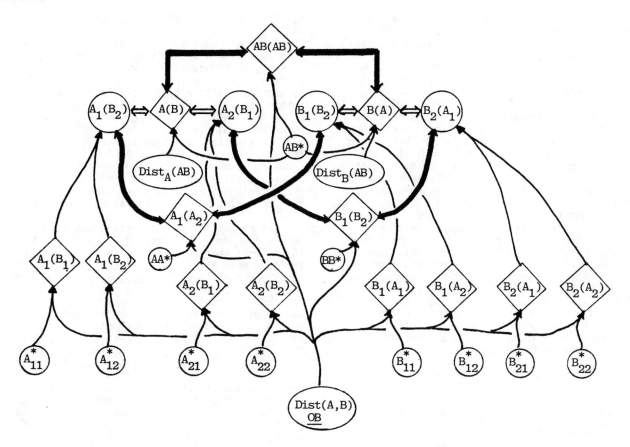

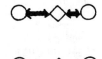

Figure 8. Minimal construction, in L#, for AB(AB) (the L topic AB) is an
           analogy between A(B) and B(A). AB* is common image of A and B,
           that is, image, as shared by A and B, mutually. OB has no
           grounds for distinguishing A₁(A₂), A₂(A₁) or AB(AB), BA(AB).

beliefs) and, consequently, the L representation
of any AB agreement over an understanding of AB
is signified AB(AB) and is an L analogy relation
(as in Bateson or Laing).

   The slightly barbaric notation of Figure 8 is
chosen to simplify the scheme so far as possible.
L# analogies are designated like the companion
L analogies by bracketing. Thus AB(AB) is the L
analogy seen by OB to hold when A and B agree to
understand their views of each other (A's view
of B is A(B) and B's view of A is B(A)). These,
in turn, relate analogies between systems of
belief, or personality, or theory, designated by
specific perspectives A_1, A_2, . . . , B_1, B_2, . . .
As before, the similarity part of the analogy is
designated by an asterisk (as in AB*, or A_1,A*,

B_1,B*) and the distinctions of analogies by
Dist.

   Consider the L# analogy AB(AB), with similarity, like the L analogies A(B) and B(A), consisting in AB*; the common part of A's understanding of B and B's of A. How do these
analogies AB(AB), A(B), B(A) differ? The difference of Figure 8 that A and B computed
distinctions $\underline{Dist}_A(X,Y)$ and $\underline{Dist}_B(X,Y)$ whereas
OB computed the distinction $\underline{Dist}_{OB}(A,B)$ has
evaporated since, in this case, A and B compute
$\underline{Dist}_A(A,B)$ and $\underline{Dist}_B(A,B)$. The difference
between OB and some other symbol, for example
C (in Z = A,B,C), regarded on a par with the
participant-symbols A and B, seems to depend
entirely upon the fact that OB (or C) has opted

to adopt a perspective (as A and B could do just as well by definition) thereby imposing a directionality upon the mesh, relative to which statements are made.

5.4. The Benevolent Trickery of Reflective and Relativistic Theories.

Differentiation between L# and L is really a conjuring trick. Any participant may elect to stand upon a stage speaking L# rather than L, and while he does so, to assert the veridical truth values of strictly L# analogical statements that denote the L analogies which would otherwise represent coherence and agreement over an understanding. Such tricks are often useful, but should be recognized as tricks (the legerdemain is revealed in Figure 8, where the participants are making the same _kind_ of distinction, perhaps even the _same_ distinction as OB the conjuror). The stage on which OB stands is no more than a perspective (and I do not deny that some perspectives may be more useful, even more comprehensive, than others in the context of a participant who is able to adopt them). For example, from the perspective of OB, in Figure 8, it is possible to offer the following cogent interpretations of the tersely named entities in the picture.

	A_1	one aspects of A's personality, one perspective
Identity Interpretation	A_2	another aspect or perspective
	A	the integrity of these perspectives (organizational-closure, as in Varela)

and similarly for B_1, B_2, B. Another, different interpretation is

	A_1	A's past
Temporality Interpretation	A_2	A's future, or A's present)
	A	A at the moment, or A's specious present (invariance of informationally open process, as in Petri)

and similarly for B_1, B_2, B.

Merely to replace "OB" by "C" (and, consequently, to replace "$Dist_{OB}(AB)$" by "$Dist_C(AB)$" in Figure 8 renders all analogies in the picture L analogies (not L# analogies as some were originally). However, this expedient is relatively unilluminating as the replacement is incomplete; it provides C's view, admittedly another participant's view, of the dialogue between and within the participants A and B. The reality is more complex; if C _is_ a participant as supposed, then C is so because C is on a par with A or B who are also in a position to look at the dialogue between and within each other (or C, or any participant).

5.5. A Minimal Substitution of L# into L

A minimal L# into L substitution, which makes this point for A and B (suggesting the role of C), is shown in Figure 9. One way of reading the picture is to notice that the L analogy AB(AB) is supported either by the similarity AB* _and_ _both_ of the distinctions $Dist_A(A,B)$, $Dist_B(A,B)$ _or_ by the similarity AB* _and_ the distinction computed by C, namely $Dist_C$. At the upper right hand of the picture I have sketched, or indicated, the existence of an analogy ABC(ABC), which it is tempting to regard as the _representation_ of a "social reality" that may be viewed differently by participants A, B, C, or any combination of them according to the distinctions which support it.

Let me qualify the reflective entailment mesh of Figure 9 and the suggested "social reality" by the comment that (in common with any other entailment mesh at all) it is a _static_ and _shorthand representation_ for a _process_ governed by a production scheme; as for example, Figure 7 represents a process governed by the production scheme of Figure 5. Such processes can exist, insofar as the necessary independencies and possibilities of information transfer (local dependency, local synchronicity) are computed, and induced within the processor by $Dist_A(A,B)$, $Dist_B(A,B)$, and the rest of them. The participants who are the processes in question appear (in the notation adopted) as letters A, B, and C. They are represented in the entailment mesh as the pairs of analogies A_1 (A_2), A_2 (A_1), and B_1 (B_2), B_2 (B_1) or, alternatively, as the derived terms A(A) and B(B), obtainable if some reference perspective is adopted (here, by C) and the _temporal interpretation_ (in contrast to the _identity interpretation_), is adopted by the referee. If t_C is C's time sense and Δt_C an interval of C's time, then we obtain a directed analogy as in Figure 10.

When Rescher speaks of a command logic, or when Aqvist, Belnap, Harrah and many later authorities speak of interrogation logic, they allude to a metatheory _about_ commands and questions which comments obliquely, at most, upon the _act_ of questioning and commanding. For example, in Rescher's command logic a command is "terminated." This is a metastatement, namely an L# statement; for example, to the effect that A told B to take his hat off when a lady came into the room, that lady did come into the room, and that B duly removed his hat. Thus "termination" has a veridical truth value (Lewis and Cook [31] clearly exhibit this point) but "termination" is _not_ "obedience" (nor of course is it supposed to be).

In fact, these L# metastatements are _about_ L transactions that go on in L; they are, every one, L# analogies _for_ an agreement over (part of) an understanding of a topic (for example, hat removal when ladies come into the room) is founded upon a distinction $Dist_{OB}(A,B)$ between A and B.

Consider, however, the commands that A _really_ gives to B or the questions A _really_

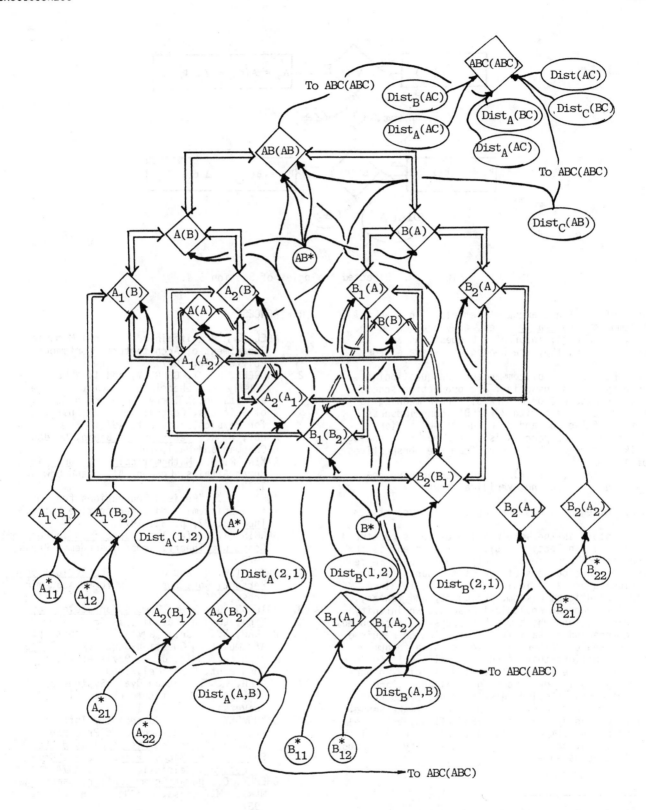

Figure 9. An L analogical construction, minimally representing participants and their conversational interaction as imaged by L analogies. A further construction involving a participant, C, the distinction $\underline{Dist}_C(AB)$ and an L analogy, ABC(ABC), is sketched but not completely exhibited.

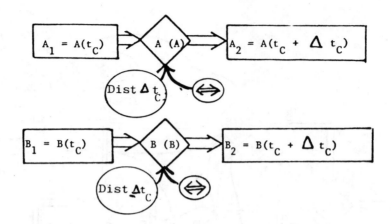

Figure 10. Directed Analogies of Section 5.4.

asks of B. These are L statements. Insofar as
L commands are _really_ given, they are sensed and
obeyed (or not); insofar as L questions are
really asked, they are heeded and answered (or
not).

The dynamics of commanding and questioning,
of obeying and answering, are production schemes
such as Figure 3 or Figure 5. Their meaning is
A's consciousness with B, or B's consciousness
with A of the commanded or questioned action.
The form of the process is an assymetric L analogy
(like Figure 10) but pruned from the perspectives
of A or B.

Obedience, answering, and heeding have coherence _truth_ but not veridical truth.

5.6. Allegories Designating Coherent Beliefs

A story is the interweaving of forms construed
by A or B (in Section 5.5). Its enactment is the
process (of agreement or not) and its experience
is the consciousness of the participants (as individuals or as societies with myths, folklore,
and conventional wisdom, prejudice, and fantasy).

Any coherent analogical mesh has an infinity
of distinctions which may be successfully computed
to comprehend or satisfy the distinction required
by the analogy (there is also an infinite number
of distinctions that do not, as well).[1] It follows
that there are indefinitely many stories, gener-
able by pruning or unfolding an allegory, and
computing the required distinctions. Though an
indefinite number of these will work (make sense,
have coherence), in some (class of) universes held
apart by the computed distinctions, there are just
as many that do not work (do not satisfy storyhood,
fail to be parables).

---

[1]Glanville insists (I believe, rightly, in view
of his recent papers and those by Varela) that
I use "indefinitely many" for the pruning or
unfoldment computations that preserve topics
and reserve "infinite number" for the computation
of the various distinctions.

REFERENCES

1. ABEL, C., "Architrainer," Internal Memorandum,
    Department of Architecture, Portsmouth
    Polytechnic, 1977.
2. ANDREKA, H., T. GERGELY, and I. NEMETI,
    "Easily Comprehensible Mathematical Logic
    and Its Model Theory," Hungarian Academy
    of Sciences, Central Research Institute
    for Physics, Budapest, 1975.
3. ASHBY, W. R., _Design for a Brain_, London,
    Chapman and Hall, 1956.
4. ATKIN, R. H., _Mathematical Structures in
    Human Affairs_, London, Allen and Unwin,
    1973.
5. AQVIST, L., "Revised Foundations for Impera-
    tive-Epistemic and Interrogative Logic,"
    Theoria, 37, p. 33, 1971.
6. BANNISTER, D. (ed.), _Perspectives in Personal
    Construct Theory_, London, Academic Press,
    1970.
7. BANNISTER, D. and J. MAIR, _The Evaluation of
    Personal Constructs_, New York, Academic
    Press, 1968.
8. BATESON, G., _Steps Towards an Ecology of
    Mind_, London, Paladin, 1973.
9. BELNAP, N. D., Jr., "Aqvist's Corrections-
    Accumulating Question-Sequences," _Philo-
    sophical Logic_, J. W. Davis et al. (eds.),
    Dordrecht, D. Reidel, 1969.
10. BRATEN, S., "The Human Dyad. Systems and
    Simulations," Institute of Sociology,
    University of Oslo, 1977.
11. BYKHOVSKY, V. K., "Control and Information
    Processing in Asynchronous Processor
    Networks," _Proceedings of Finland USSR
    Symposium on Micro Processors and Data
    Processors_, Helsinki, Vol. 1, 1974.
12. CHERRY, C., _Human Communication_, Cambridge,
    Mass., MIT Press, and New York, Wiley,
    1957.
13. ERHARDT, W. and V. GIOSCIA, "The est Standard
    Training," _Biosciences Communications_,
    3, pp. 104-122, 1977.
14. FEURZEIG, W. and S. PAPERT, "Programming
    Lanuages as a Conceptual Framework for
    Teaching Mathematics," in: _Programmed_

15. FRANSELLA, F., and D. BANNISTER, A Manual for Repertory Grid Technique, London, Academic Press, 1977.

16. GAINES, B. R., "System Identification Approximation and Complexity," Man Machine Systems Laboratory, University of Essex, Colchester, 1977.

17. GERGELY, T. and I. NEMETI, Various Publications, Institute of Applied Computer Science, Hungarian Academy of Science, Budapest, 1977.

18. GLANVILLE, R., A Cybernetic Development of Epistemology and Observation, Applied to Objects in Space and Time (as seen in Architecture), Ph.D. Thesis, Brunel University, Department of Cybernetics, 1975.

19. GLANVILLE, R., "Is Architecture just a Hollow Space or is it the Empty Set?", AAQ, London, 8-4, 1976.

20. GLANVILLE, R., "What is Memory that it can Remember what it is?", Progress in Cybernetics and Systems Research, Vol. IV, R. Trappl and G. Pask (eds.), Washington, Hemisphere, pp. 17-37, 1978.

21. GLUSHKO, V., Introduction to Cabernetics, London, Academic Press, 1966.

22. GOGUEN, J. A., "The Logic of Inexact Concepts," Synthese, 19, pp. 325-373, 1969.

23. GOGUEN, J. A., "Objects," International Journal of General Systems, 1, pp. 237-243, 1975.

24. HARRAH, D., Communication: A Logical Model Cambridge, Mass., MIT Press, 1963.

25. HARRAH, D., "The Logic of Questions and Its Relevance to Insturctional Science," Instructional Science, 1 (4), pp- 447-468, 1973.

26. HERBST, P. G., Alternatives to Hierarchies, Leiden, 1976.

27. HOLT, A., Comments in Our Own Metaphor, Bateson, M. C., New York, Knopf, 1972.

28. HOWE, J. A. M., and T. O'SHEA, Papers and Remarks at the SSRC Seminar on Computer Aided Learning, Warwick University, 1976.

29. KELLY, G. A., The Psychology of Personal Constructs, Vols. 1 and 2, New York, Norton, 1955.

30. LAING, R. D., Self and Others, London, Tavistock, 1961.

31. LEWIS, B. N. and J. A. COOK, "Towards a Theory of Telling," International Journal of Man Machine Studies, 1 (2), pp. 129-179, 1969.

32. LEWIS, B. N. and G. PASK, "The Use of a Null Point Method to Study the Acquisition of Simple and Complex Transformation Skills," British Journal of Mathematics and Statistical Psychology, 21, pp. 61-81, 1968.

33. McCULLOCH, W. S., Embodiments of Mind, Boston, Mass., MIT Press, 1965.

34. MATURANA, H. R., "Neurophysiology of Cognition," in: Cognition a Multiple View, P. L. Garvin (ed.), New York, Spartan Books, 1969.

35. MATURANA, H. R., "The Organisation of the Living:A Theory of the Living Organisation," International Journal of Man Machine Studies, 7, pp. 313-332, 1975.

36. MONTAGUE, R., Formal Philosophy, R. H. Thomason (ed.), Yale University Press, 1976.

37. PAPPERT, S., "Teaching Children Thinking," Proceedings of IFIP Conference on Computer Education, Amsterdam, 1970.

38. PASK, G., "A Fresh Look at Cognition and the Individual," International Journal of Man Machine Studies, 4, pp. 211-216, 1972.

39. PASK, G., "Cybernetic Theory of Cognition and Learning," Journal of Cybernetics, 5 (1), p. 1-90, 1975.

40. PASK, G., The Cybernetics of Human Learning and Performance, London, Hutchinson, 1975.

41. PASK, G., Conversation, Cognition and Learning, New York, Elsevier, 1975.

42. PASK, G., "Conversational Techniques in the Study and Practice of Education," British Journal of Educational Psychology, 46 (I), pp. 12-25, 1976.

43. PASK, G., "Styles and Strategies of Learning," British Journal of Educational Psychology, 46 (II), pp. 128-148, 1976.

44. PASK, G., Conversation Theory: Applications in Education and Epistemology, New York, Elsevier, 1976.

45. PASK, G., "Knowledge Innovation and Learning to Learn," Proceedings of NATO-ASI 'Structural/Process' Theories of Complex Human Behaviour, Banff Springs, Canada, Alphan an den Rijn, Noordhoff, 1977.

46. PASK, "Organisational Closure of Potentially Conscious Systems and Notes," Applied General Systems Research, Vol. 1, New York, Plenum Press, 1977; and Realities Conference, est Foundation, San Francisco, 1977.

47. PASK, G., Problem Solving, Monograph, IET Open University and Ford Foundation, 1977.

48. PASK, G., "A Cybernetic and Conversation Theoretic Approach to Conscious Events in Learning and Innovations," Proceedings of 23rd Annual Conference of JUREMA, Zagreb, Yugoslavia, April, 1978.

49. PASK, "A Conversation Theoretic Approach to Social Systems," Simulating Modelling and Knowing Social Systems, R. F. Geyer and J. van der Zouwen (eds.), Amsterdam, Martinus Nijhoff, 4th World Congress of Cybernetics and Systems, Amsterdam, August, 1978.

50. PASK, G. and B. C. E. SCOTT, "Learning Strategies and Individual Competence," International Journal of Man Machine Studies, 4, pp. 217-253, 1972.

51. PASK, G. and B. C. E. SCOTT, "CASTE: A System for Exhibiting Learning Strategies and Regulating Uncertainty," International Journal for Man Machine Studies, 5, pp. 17-52, 1973.

52. PASK, G., B. C. E. SCOTT and D. KALLIKOURDIS, "A Theory of Conversations and Individuals (Exemplified by the Learning Process on CASTE)", International Journal of Man Machine Studies, 5, pp. 443-566, 1973.

53. PASK, G., D. KALLIKOURDIS and B. C. E. SCOTT, "The Representation of Knowables," International Journal of Man Machine Studies, 17, pp. 15-134, 1975.

54. PETRI, G. A., "Communication with Automata," (Trans. F. Green, Jr.), supplement to

Technical Documentary Report 1, Rome Air Development Centre, Contract AF30 (602) 3324, 1964.

55. REICHENBACK, R., The Philosophy of Space and Time, London, Dover, 1957.

56. RESCHER, N., The Coherence Theory of Truth, London, Oxford University Press, 1973.

57. SHANNON, C. E. and W. E. WEAVER, "Mathematical Theory of Communication," University of Illinois Press, Urbana, 1949.

58. SPENCER-BROWN, G., The Laws of Form, London, George Allen and Unwin, 1969.

59. THOMAS, L. F., "Kelly McQuittie: A Computer Program for Focussing the Repertory Grid," Centre for the Study of Human Learning, Brunel University Reading, Uxbridge, 1970.

60. THOMAS, L. F., "Interactive Method of Eliciting Kelly Grids," paper presented at the Occupational Section BPS Converence, published in Proceedings, 1971.

61. VARELA, F., "A Calculus for Self Reference," International Journal of General Systems, 2, pp. 5-24, 1975.

62. VARELA, F. and J. GOGUEN, "Arithmetic of Closure," Proceedings of Third European Meeting on Cybernetics and Research, Vienna, 1976.

63. VON FOERSTER, H., "An Epistemology for Living Things," in: L'Unite de l'Homme, E. Morin (ed.), Editions de Sevel, Paris, 1976.

64. VON FOERSTER, H., Various Papers on Microfische, Biological Computer Laboratory, University of Illinois, Illinois Blueprint Corp., 1976.

65. VON FOERSTER, H., Contribution to Sourcebook, est Realities International Conference, San Francisco, 1978.

66. ZADEH, L. A., "A Fuzzy Algorithmic Approach to the Definition of Complex or Imprecise Concepts," Electronics Research Laboratory, College of Engineering, University of California, Berkeley, 1974.

67. ZADEH, L. A., "The Theory of Fuzzy Sets," in: Encyclopedia of Computer Science and Technology, Belser, Halzman and Kent (eds.), Marcel Dekker, 1976.

68. ZADEH, L. A., "PRUF: The Meaning Representation Language for Natural Language," Electronic Engineering Research Laboratory, UCLA, Internal Report No. ERL-M77/61, 1977.

The theory of human learning by Gal'perin and the theory of learning systems

H. A. REUVER

Twente University of Technology, Enschede, The Netherlands

1. INTRODUCTION

The Soviet psychologist Gal'perin, who has been Professor of Psychology at Moscow University for many years, has put forward a theory of human learning that recognizes mental processes ignored by the behaviorists predominating in the western world. The ideas of Gal'perin are strongly influencing the educational and instructional psychology of Eastern Europe.

The theory of learning by Gal'perin distinguishes three levels of human action: (1) material, (2) verbal, (3) mental.

Especially the last level has been condemned by behaviorism. Behaviorists like Watson, Thorndike et al. fulminated against such "unscientific" concepts like mental actions.

Only in the last few years the cognitive approach explaining human behavior in terms of mental processes is gaining ground in western psychology.

In this paper the theory of Gal'perin will be considered within the context of the system theory of learning developed by the author in [7].

2. THEORY OF GAL'PERIN

This exposition of the psychology of Gal'perin is mainly based on van Parreren and Carpay [6], i.e., on Dutch translations of the original Russian papers and on a survey article also in Dutch.

2.1. Parameters of Action

In the thoery of Gal'perin an action is characterized by four parameters:
1. The level mentioned above.
2. Fullness in detail or elaborateness. An action can be performed in detail or some parts of it can be left out or shortened. During the learning process in most cases shortening occurs.
3. Degree of generalization. The class of objects to which the learned action applies can be large or small.
4. Degree of mastery, i.e., the smoothness of performance. The action is carried out without any failure or annoying interruption in case of perfect mastery.

The relevance of these parameters in learning processes will be clarified in this section.

2.2. Levels of action

As we have seen in Section 1, there are three levels of action:

1. Material action. This basic level concerns real world actions, i.e., interventions in the processes of the world around us. Material action means manipulating real objects like eating with a knife and a fork.
2. Verbal action. This second level is the region of speech (conversation), i.e., talking about material actions, e.g. about eating, while using a model (obraz) of the reality concerned. This is the level of communication, information transmission and transfer of knowledge by verbal instruction.
3. Mental action. Here information processing occurs in an abstract language of symbols referring to material actions via the verbal level. The language of the mental level is a kind of shorthand of the natural language used at the verbal level. As the rate of information processing is much faster at the mental than at the verbal or material level, human actions are superior to those of animals where only a very primitive level of verbal actions can be found, e.g. in dolphins and chimpanzees.

2.3. Orientation Basis

According to the theory of Gal'perin the teacher should attempt to provide the learner with a so-called orientation basis by verbal instruction or demonstration, i.e., by showing him how to act. This orientation basis should enable the learner to carry out the material action. An orientation basis can be defined as a system of conditions for action at the disposal of the actor, enabling him to execute the intended action. A complete orientation basis includes all conditions to carry out the action correctly, that is to say without errors.

A full learning and instruction process requires a complete orientation basis, because learning by trial and error should be avoided, according to Gal'perin. Therefore the search for complete orientation bases is essential within the framework of this theory.

Gal'perin distinguishes three types of orientation bases:
1. The orientation basis (O.B.) of the first type is not complete, i.e., the learner is not provided with a complete description of the material action. He has to learn by trial and error to execute the action correctly by adjusting his O.B.
2. The O.B. of the second type is complete and ready for use. No element is missing in the procedure. The O.B. is supplied by direct

369

instruction or demonstration.

3. The O.B. of the third type provides the means, methods and techniques for the construction of an O.B. of the second type by analysis of the situation. The material action can be executed by application of the O.B. of the second type constructed in this way. The versatility of this third type of orientation is maximum. It can be applied in more general situations than type two or one.

2.4. Stages of Learning

From the foregoing theoretical considerations, Gal'perin concludes that a full action can be learned only if the following stages are completed:

1. Formation of an image or representation of the material action to be performed to enable the learner to orientate himself to that action.
2. Performance of the material action. After many repetitions a shortening of the full material action may occur.
3. Verbal description of the material action by speaking loudly but without handling the material objects.
4. Verbal action by inner speech. The learner carries out the action in his imagination by speaking without any sound
5. Shortening the inner speech to mental action by abstraction, i.e., operating on abstract symbols referring to the material action by the intermediary of verbal description. Mental operations correspond to activities in the real world. Thought is a kind of shorthand for real action.

2.5. Theory of Attention

In connection with mental action, Gal'perin has developed a theory of attention. In his view every action has three aspects:

1. The orientating aspect embodied in the orientation basis.
2. The executing aspect of accomplishing the act.
3. The controlling aspect involving a comparison between the expected and the real result of the action.

In shortening mental action to automatized mental action the orientating and controlling aspects are internalized. Attention is internalized control of the automatized mental action.

It will be understood that the above exposition is only a concise summary of the complete theory of learning by Gal'perin. For more detail, the reader should consult the original sources, e.g. Gal'perin [1-4].

3. TAXONOMY OF LEARNING SYSTEMS

In a previous paper by the author [7] a model of a learning system was presented, the essentials of which will be summarized below.

3.1. The Learning System

The complete model includes four components:
1. The black box or real system RS (see Figure 1).

2. The system cell SC, the model of the real world at the disposal of the decision maker (see Figure 2).
3. The decision cell DC, a representation of the decision maker.
4. The learning cell LC, a model of the learning process (see Figure 4).

The normative cell NC, the combination of DC and SC, represents the decision maker with his model and is reproduced in detail in Figure 3.

The complete learning system is shown in Figure 7.

Notations. The variables are denoted by lower case letters and the corresponding spaces of the variables by upper case letters, e.g. X denotes the space of inputs x.

U: decision space, i.e. set of decisions
S: state space
Y: output space
Z: information space
P: parameter space
V: value space, linearly ordered set of values, mostly the real line
T: discrete time parameter space, i.e.
$T = \{....t_{-2}, t_{-1}, t_0, t_1, t_2....\}$

In this paper it is assumed that t can take on only integer values.

In the figures and the text the time index t is attached only if it is needed for ready comprehension.

Mappings.

System cell: $z = f(u, x, s, p)$
$s_{t+1} = g(u_t, x_t, s_t, p_t)$
When $z = f(s)$, the system is called of indirect response and denoted by SCI. Otherwise we have a system cell of direct response SCD.

Normative cell:
$v^d = v^d(z^s, p^{lg})$
$z^s = f^s(u^d, x^s, s^s, p^{ls})$
$s_{t+1}^s = g(u_t^d, x_t^s, s_t^s, p_t^{ls})$

Learning cell:
$v^l = v^l(o^l)$
$o^l = f^l(s^l) = s^l$
$s_{t+1}^l = g^l(z_t^l, z_t^s)$

Algorithms. A^d seeks an optimum u^d in terms of the criterion function v^d of the decision cell DC. A^l seeks an optimum P^l in terms of the criterion function v^l of the learning cell LC. In this case the expectation of the learning goal v^l is optimized.

3.2. Degenerations

The normative cell NC can degenerate into a system cell with direct response SCD.

By the same degeneration process the learning cell LC may pass into a system cell with indirect response SCI, the output of which is a function of only the state.

It can also happen that the learning cell and/or the normative cell are missing.

Figure 1. Black Box or Real System

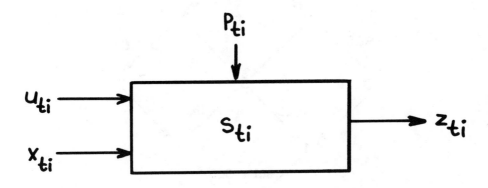

Figure 2. System Cell

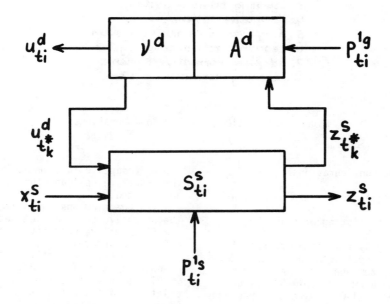

Figure 3. Normative Cell

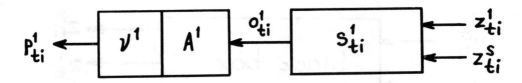

Figure 4. Learning Cell

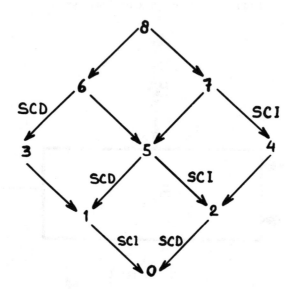

0. Real system or primary system.
1. Adaptive primary system.
2. Instrumental system.
3. Learning primary system.
4. Normative system.
5. Adaptive instrumental system.
6. Learning instrumental system.
7. Adaptive normative system.
8. Learning normative system.

Figure 5. Lattice of Basic Configurations

3.3. Taxonomy of Basic Configurations

The following types of systems can be distinguished:

1. Primary system consisting of only the black box or real system RS.

2. Adaptive primary system with a degenerate learning cell SCI and without a normative cell NC.

3. Instrumental system where the learning cell is missing and the normative cell NC has degenerated into a system cell with direct response SCD.

4. Learning primary system without a normative cell NC.

5. Normative system without a learning cell LC.

6. Adaptive instrumental system where both the normative cell and the learning cell have degenerated.

7. Learning instrumental system where only the normative cell has degenerated.

8. Adaptive normative system with a degenerative learning cell.

9. Learning normative system: the complete learning system without degeneration.

These types of systems can be represented by a lattice of basic configurations as shown in Figure 5, where the arrows without symbols designate degeneration. The arrows with symbols denote the elimination of the corresponding degenerate cells.

It should be noted that the lattice doesn't

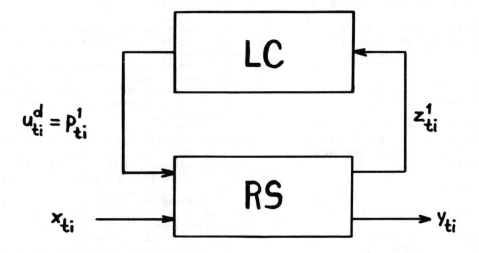

Figure 6. Primary Learning

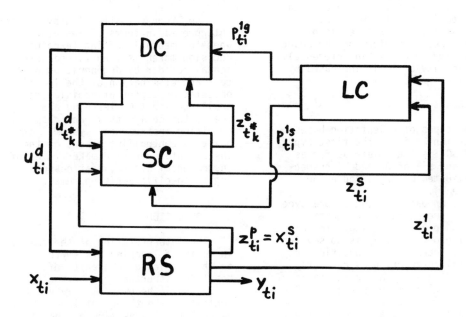

Figure 7. Normative Learning

imply that only degeneration and elimination processes occur. The inverse processes, regeneration and addition, are equally well possible in learning.

The foregoing outline is brief. For more detail the reader is referred to the above-mentioned previous article by the author.

4. THEORY OF GAL'PERIN WITHIN THE CONTEXT OF THE THEORY OF LEARNING SYSTEMS

The reformulation and interpretation of the learning theory by Gal'perin in terms of learning systems theory can be accomplished without major difficulties (see Figure 7).

4.1. Parameters of Action

The four parameters of action can be explained as follows:
1. The level of action. A material action is an intervention in RS. A verbal action is carried out by the decision maker by handling his verbal model SC of RS. A mental action is performed by the decision maker when using his abstract symbolic model SC of the real world RS.
2. Degree of elaborateness or shortening. Shortening can occur on all levels of action and concerns the learning parameter P. A more simple model can yield the same result as the extensive one did.
3. Degree of generalization. The model SC gives information about a specific class of problems. The broader this class the more general the model is. It refers to the interpretation rules of the model SC in terms of RS.
4. Degree of mastery. On all levels of action mastery means better performance by reduction of the sensitivity to noise (interference). The noise filter capacity of SC is increased by means of the parameter p^{ls}.

4.2. Orientation Basis

There are three types of orientation bases:
1. The orientation basis of the first type, embodied in DC and SC, is incomplete as far as the parameters p^{lg} and p^{ls} of DC and SC respectively are to be adjusted by trial and error learning (see Figure 7).
2. The orientation basis of the second type, being complete, is represented by the normative cell NC while p^{lg} and p^{ls} are missing. In this case primary learning occurs, that is to say the primary system RS is learning by repetition to carry out the optimal instruction u^d correctly. This optimum u^d is obtained by NC on the basis of the inforation output x^s from the black box RS (see Figure 3).

The learning cell LC is directly connected to RS by the learning parameter p^l. As far as learning is concerned NC may be considered a part of the real system RS. In this way primary learning results as shown in Figure 6.
3. By an orientation basis of the third type the methods and procedures are supplied to construct a normative cell NC, i.e. an orientation basis of the first or second type. The techniques of system identification for a specified class of

real systems are given.

4.3. Stages of Learning

The five stages of learning of Gal'perin can be described in terms of learning system theory (see Figure 7).
1. Formation of an orientation basis of the second type is identical to the identification of the system cell SC and the decision cell DC. It can be constructed by verbal instruction or by demonstration.
2. Performance of the material action occurs by direct intervention u in the black box RS. This action is in accordance with the mental image SC that one has in its mind. After many repetitions shortening may occur by primary learning.
3. Instead of really acting one gives a detailed verbal account of the material action by speaking loudly. This verbal description is incorporated in the system cell SC.
4. By adjusting the system cell SC via p^{ls} one switches over to verbal description by inner speech. Shortening and mastery are characteristic of this stage.
5. The verbal account passes into an abstract symbolic, possibly mathematical, representation by adjusting the system cell SC via p^{ls}. The whole process is governed by the learning cell LC via p^{ls}. The instructional objectives are incorporated in v^l, the learning goal.

4.4. Theory of Attention

The Theory of attention by Gal'perin can be interpreted in terms of learning system theory. When the mentally acting learning normative decision maker is transformed into an instrumental decider by degeneration of the normative cell and elimination of the learning cell, the orientating aspect of decision making and controlling aspect of learning are amalgamated in the system cell with direct response SCD of the resulting instrumental system. Attention is the built-in controlling aspect of the automatized instrumental decision maker, i.e. of SCD of the instrumental system, that responds to x^s according to specific decision rules.

5. CONCLUSION

The interpretation of the theory of Gal'perin in terms of learning system theory sheds light on the intricate complexity of that theory. The beautiful structure of the theoretical framework of Gal'perin becomes clearly visible within the context of the theory of learning systems. The general systems version of that theory, however, reveals also limitations that would be overlooked otherwise. As an example may serve the proposition of Gal'perin that no material action can be performed without any prior mental image of that action. Learning system theory, on the other hand, states that a learning instrumental system can be adjusted by trial and error without prior image formation. That type of learning has been thorough by investigated by Thorndike and other behaviorists. Apparently, the theory of Gal'perin and the behavioristic tenets supplement each other. So a broad synthesis of the various schools of learning psychology could be envisaged within the context of learning system theory; see [5] (in Dutch; an English translation is forthcoming).

REFERENCES

1. GAL'PERIN, P. J., "An Experimental Study in the Formation of Mental Actions," in: Psychology in the Soviet Union, B. Simon (ed.), Routledge and Kegan Paul, London, 1957.
2. GAL'PERIN, P. J., "Die Entwicklung der Untersuchungen über die Bildung geistiger Operationen," in: Ergebnisse der Sowjetischen Psychologie, H. Hiebsch (ed.), Akademie-Verlag, Berlin, 1967.
3. GAL'PERIN, P. J., "Die Geistige Handlung als Grundlage für die Bildung von Gedanken und Vorstellungen," in: Probleme der Lerntheorie, E. Däbritz (ed.), Volk und Wissen, Berlin, 1967.
4. GAL'PERIN, P. J., "Stages in the Development of Mental Acts," in: A Handbook of Contemporary Soviet Psychology, M. Cole and I. Maltzman (eds.), Basic Books, New York, 1969.
5. HANKEN, A. F. G., and H. A. REUVER, Sociale Systemen en Lerende Systemen, Stenfert Kroese, Leiden, 1977.
6. PARREREN, C. F. von and J. A. M. CARPAY, Sovjetpsychologen aan het woord, Wolters-Noordhoff, Groningen, 1972.
7. REUVER, H. A., "Learning Within the Context of General Systems Theory," in: Progress in Cybernetics and Systems Research, R. Trappl (ed.), Hemisphere Publishing Corporation, Washington, D. C., 1977.

Two roles for the computer in cognisant systems

MILDRED L. G. SHAW
Centre for the Study of Human Learning, Brunel University
Middlesex, England

1. INTRODUCTION

This paper discusses two roles in which the computer can act as an aid towards human cognition. These two roles, the roles of the "cognitive mirror" and the "speculative interpretative participant" have been embodied in a number of interactive computer programs for developing personal models of the world (FOCUS, PEGASUS, CORE, SOCIOGRIDS, ARGUS).

The philosophy and ideology underlying this work has its origins in Personal Construct Theory (Kelly [8]). For many years psychologists have been interested in how an individual classifies his experiences and categorises his environment. The concept of "schema" has ranged widely from Kant to Bartlett [2], from Head [5] to Vernon [25], Bruner, Goodnow and Austin [3], and Skemp [19]. The commonality in these approaches suggests that an individual uses a system of organisation together with inter-relationships between components in the system, which in interacting with the structure produce interdependencies. If the person can become aware of the structure and the organisation within the structure, he becomes more able to make adequate predictions and act according to them. Osgood, Suci and Tannenbaum [13] suggested that each person has a unique system of dimensions which are used to perceive and judge the environment, and that some of these are common to all people. Kelly argues that each individual constructs his own version of reality using a hierarchical system of personal constructs. In the context of a person learning from experience, this theory is abut the way in which he can negotiate a viable position in his own reality, review it, revise it, and refine it within his own world. Enduring reality is non-conscious, and consciousness is merely a temporary construction within a specific situation. This thinking is part of a more general context of ideas put forward by people as widely ranging as McCulloch [12], Schumacher [17], Sir James Jeans [7], Wittgenstein [27], and Lorenz [10].

Each human being may be seen as a personal scientist, classifying, categorising and theorising about his world, anticipating on the basis of his theories and acting on the basis of his anticipation. Each personal scientist uses himself as participative subject matter and construes and interprets the results in a personally meaningful way. To do this effectively a conversational method must be used. A number of people have put forward models of "conversations". Jahoda and Thomas [6] have developed a "science of learning

conversations" in which the learning experience can be viewed from the perspectives of the learner or teacher and evaluated prospectively or retrospectively; Luft [11] used the "Johari Window" which is a model of interpersonal awareness demonstrating the interaction of two variables "know/not known to self" and "know/not known to others". However, the most appropriate conversational model for this work is that of Pask [15], "Theory of Conversations and Individuals". Pask suggests that participants in a conversation cannot be regarded simply as distinct processors, but recognises an "M-Individual" or "mechanically characterised individual" which may be regarded as a biologically self-replicating system and is consequently a hardware distinction; and a "P-Individual" or "psychologically characterised individual" which "has many of the properties ascribed by anthropologists to a role" (Pask [14], p. 302), and is also a procedure executed in some M-Individual or processor and is therefore a software distinction.

Three aspects of conversation are therefore identified:

1. A conversation with oneself which may be generalised to a conversation between several P-Individuals each representing an important aspect of self.

2. A conversation between two P-Individuals in two distinct M-Individuals or processors.

3. A conversation in a group of M-Individuals which constitutes one or more P-Individual.

To build a technology to encompass a conversational method, the Kelly repertory grid was used as a base for articulating each of these aspects of conversation. This grid is a two-dimenstional "construction matrix" in which events are interlaced with abstractions. These abstractions or "constructs" are bipolar dimensions which group events into varying clusters according to their similarities and differences in the individual's frames of reference. This grid then represents the interpretation of the repertoire of experience that the individual has constructed from his personal observations of the world. These personal observations are known as "elements" and were originally constituted from the role titles of significant people in the life of the particular individual. These roles are still commonly used in psychotherapy, but are equally applicable to a person in industry or education.

However, the elements need not be role titles, but may be a set of people -- such as work colleagues or subordinates (e.g. Thomas, Shaw and Pope [24]), things -- such as books used for learning or detergents in market research, events or experiences -- such as parts of a course of therapy, which span the area of the problem. For example, if the problem was one of choosing a future career the elements might be different jobs; if the problem was to become a "better" person the elements might be different aspects of self; if the problem was to evaluate the success of a training course the elements might be significant events which took place during the course. When choosing elements, care must be taken to ensure that each one is well known and personally meaningful to the elicitee. Each construct must be central to the person in the context of the particular problem. Thoughts and feelings, objective and subjective descriptions, attitudes and prejudices, all constitute valid constructs. The verbal descriptions of the construct and the labelling of the poles need not be a coherent statement to the outside world, but only a memory aid of the conversation. The mapping of the elements onto the constructs produces the two dimensional grid of relationships.

The grid is therefore a content-free structure which may be held by the computer whilst the system of constructs is elicited from the individual. As the conversation takes place the computer can monitor and record the process in a person-centred way without intruding on the content. A personal scientist uses structures and mechanisms in a necessarily "human" way, that is, in such a way that they enhance his power, not become his master. Coomaraswamy (cited in Schumacher [17]) draws the distinction between the machine and the tool, likening the tool to a carpet loom which helps the craftsman and the machine to the power loom which does the essentially human part of the work and is hence a destroyer of culture. To use the computer as a tool rather than a machine may be a new experience for some people; and to realise that interactive computing is not necessarily a branch of programmed instruction, but can be a content-free holder of structure which helps the user to express himself in his own terms about his own problems, in a conversation with himself. Gaines [4] goes even further by suggesting that the computer can be seen as a colleague, expressing sympathy and understanding to the user. This comes much closer than before to the hope of Wiener [26] when he spoke of "the human use of human beings".

2. THE COMPUTER AS A COGNITIVE MIRROR

The quality of a person's models, both specific and general, will determine the level of skill, coping, competence and creativity he will be able to achieve. PEGASUS or "Program Elicits Grids and Sorts Using Similarities" is an interactive computer program (Thomas and Shaw [23]) which elicits a grid from an individual, simultaneously acting as a psychological reflector by heightening his awareness and deepening his understanding of himself and his processes. This is done by the provision of continual real-time feedback commentary on highly related elements or constructs, together with the encouragement to differentiate between them. Before choosing his elements the user is asked to think about his purpose for eliciting the

grid. This is of great importance for the interaction which is to follow, as it sets both the intentionalities and the universe of discourse. The mutual dependencies of the elements on the purpose, the constructs on the elements and the purpose jointly on the elements and constructs, contributes to the satisfaction and satisfactoriness of the interaction. By using combinations of reviewing the purpose, adding and deleting constructs and elements, a depth of interaction may be achieved which could not at the start have been envisaged. Thus the user is given the opportunity to reflect on his understanding of the area of the universe of discourse to examine and explore his thoughts and feelings in this atmosphere of heightened awareness of personal knowing. His perception may be changed in a way which by other means can take years to accomplish. The computer is acting as a cognitive mirror, reflecting back to the user his models of construing. The essence of learning is constructive and creative change. Learning is often measured in terms of behavioural objectives devised by the teacher, or one step further removed from the learner -- the course designer. For the learner himself, learning is the revision of his cognitive model in order to make his anticipation of events more effective, that is in the way he perceives and construes events and behaves in the situation. PEGASUS actively encourages the consideration and revision of tentative hypotheses of the personal scientist approach, hence supporting the reconstruction of cognitive models and the change which is the "seeing" and learning of constructive alternativism.

PEGASUS is therefore a content-free heuristic in a conversational mode, allowing the user to fill it with the content of his head and heart, and see it re-ordered and restructured in ways he was unable to achieve without the computer as a tool which he begins to use as a craftsman uses his carpet loom. The PEGASUS process gives to the user an enlightening experience which may not be visible in the results or the printout of the interaction. He may see himself through his own eyes for the first time; he may talk to himself through the computer in a more meaningful way than ever before.

ARGUS (Shaw [18]) or "Alternative Roles Grids Using Sociogrids" is a development of PEGASUS in which the conversational domain is articulated through the computer within which a group of P-Individuals in one M-Individual can interact.

It seems reasonable to hypothesise that a well-adjusted individual has recognised the existence of the personalities in his head, and allowed each a place to operate where it can be valued and made use of in the context of the whole person. Further, psychotherapy consists in creating a converation between these P-Individuals in which each may be recognised and valued. These P-Individuals may be roles, purposes, or centres of attention, but all are significant points from which to view the world. In extreme cases these P-Individuals may not share any constructs in certain areas. This may be due to variations in the ranges of convenience of the constructs used, or perhaps distinct and disjoint P-Individuals are brought into operation in different universes of discourse. Lewin [9] uses the phrase "plurality of separate spaces" to express this same idea. By relating and cross-referencing the ways in which different elements and constructs are used by different P-Individuals, the computer is able to reflect back to the user subgroups of P-Individuals which operate similarly, and those which are uniquely different from the others.

Two people may come to an "understanding" of each other through the computer by each interacting conversationally with the other's constructs which are stored as an adaptable bank. This is known as PEGASUS-BANK and is based on the idea put forward by Thomas [20]. There are two ways in which it can be used: to explore shared construing of an area, and to interfere with an area construed by an "expert". The first use assumes that the two participants have equally valid views of the area; one produces a PEGASUS grid which is stored as a bank to be accessed by the other. As the second person elicits his own grid, comparison is made between his constructs and those already in the bank, high similarities provoking comment. The bank may then be modified in the light of the interaction before the first person, or possibly a new participant, uses it again. In this way it is possible to build up a coherent view of the universe of discourse, with an indication as to the amount of overlap between the participants.

In the second way of using PEGASUS-BANK, the bank of constructs stored in the computer represents an "expert" view of an area of public knowledge. As the processing takes place, continual comparison with the bank gives feedback to the user on the extent to which his constructs map on to the expert's construing of the same elements. Since the comparison is made in terms of how the construct orders the elements rather than in terms of the verbal labels, it is often found that although a person may have only a vague idea of the technical terms, he may actually be using very similar constructs.

The PEGASUS-BANK technique of storing in the computer a bank of constructs which represents an area of public knowledge or the construing of a group of specialists shows how an individual can use the grid methodology to interface between his early gropings and the articulate formulations of the group. When used in the form which encourages two participants to take on each other's construct systems by mapping out the similarities between the patterning, meanings can be exchanged between the pair. Alternatively, if each elicits a grid independently the overlap may also be compared using the patterning of the responses.

Whether or not the grids have been elicited on separate occasions, if the element and construct labels are the same in both grids they can be compared with respect to the similar or different uses of these names by examining the differences in the patterning in each grid.

CORE (Shaw [18]) or "Comparison Of Repeated Elicitations" is an interactive program which allows the user to investigate the extent and content of shared understanding exhibited by two grids. The computer successively reflects back the areas of most difference which are then removed from the grids at each stage, thereby increasing the similarity of the remaining portions. If these grids have been elicited from the same person at two separate times, CORE reflects a measure of change over the time interval; whereas if the two grids are from two different people, the reflection is of the degree of understanding between them. By exchanging constructs through the computer and learning to use them in the way another person intended them to be used, the levels of understanding and empathy may be increased.

In these ways the computer is acting as a cognitive mirror, reflecting back to the user an interpretation of his own meaning system by making explicit the analogies, cross-references and isomorphisms which he uses between the dimensions of his thinking. This enables him to see his modelling processes more clearly, and thereby to review and revise his cognitive model on the basis of this insight.

3. THE COMPUTER AS A SPECULATIVE INTERPRETIVE PARTICIPANT

Methods of grid analysis have for a long time constrained the use of grids as a modelling facility. Previously factor analysis and principal component analysis have extracted factors; more recently cluster analysis and multi-dimensional scaling have been used. FOCUS or "Feedback Of Clustering Using Similarities" was developed as a speculative interpretive method of identifying clusters of like elements and like constructs (Thomas and Shaw [22]). This is a method of grid analysis which systematically re-orders the rows of constructs and columns of elements to produce a focused grid showing the least variation between adjacent constructs and adjacent elements. This is done with respect to the way in which the constructs order the elements rather than to the verbal labels given to the poles of the constructs. The matching score between constructs, which is computed from a city block metric, then indicates the internal consistency of meaning within the cognitive model as exemplified in the grid. The results are presented in a form which lends itself to the conversational participative feedback of the clusters.

As a PEGASUS elicitation proceeds this FOCUS algorithm is used to offer to the user a possible explanation and interpretation of his meaning system in the terms of the similar patterns he uses in supposedly different circumstances. Cross-references are mapped across the grid and exhibited to the user in such a way as to offer him the facility to reconsider and change anything he feels to be inappropriate, which enables him to be more aware of the links he is implicitly holding in his cognitive model. Here the conversation can be seen as a feedback loop with the computer acting as the error regulator by representing the content of the conversation and the implicit links within the conversation. In this way the participative analysis extracts and displays the essence of the subjectivity and personally meaningful relationships in the grid.

In a similar way, two constructs from different grids may be compared, and the extent of similar patterning of shared elements by two people examined. If this is extended to the whole of the two grids elicited from two people using shared elements, the extent to which they are using similar models will be roughly indicated by the degree to which the clusters contain constructs from each of the two grids. These two grids could be from two P-Individuals within the same processor or M-Individual, the extent of overlap then indicating the degree of intersection of the two systems. As the computer processes this type of data, feedback may be given on the areas where the sharing of meaning is high and on those aspects which are unique to the individual grid.

Having found a way of comparing grids from two people, this principle can be applied to all possible pairs in a group of P-Individuals, who may or may not inhabit distinct M-Individuals and who interact in a shared conversational domain. This is described by Thomas, McKnight and Shaw [21], and led to the development of a program called SOCIOGRIDS. The program produces a sequence of "socionets", which are sociometric diagrams showing how like-construing between individual members of a group can lead to the development of pairs of subgroups of people, or the identification of an isolated member who models the situation quite differently from the others. SOCIOGRIDS also identifies the content of the like-construing by selecting from individual grids the "mode constructs". These are the constructs which are common to the majority of the group members. This interpretation can be individually exhibited to each of the group members in turn, highlighting the specific contribution each has made, showing him which of the others have similar ways of perceiving the situation, and where his own ways are unique in the group.

In these ways the computer is acting as a participant in the presentation of the data to the individual, offering the results of the analysis in a provisional way in order to allow the individual as much choice as possible in the acceptance or rejection of the speculative interpretation.

4. CONCLUSION

The repertory grid is only the beginning of a technology for eliciting and developing personal models of the world, and helping each individual to be more effective in his aim to become a personal scientist. Many techniques have potential for developing this work beyond the structure of the repertory grid, especially data structures from computer science, graph theory and optimization from operational research, mathematical structures and forms such as Q-Analysis (Atkin [1]), the concept of cybernetic entities like P-Individuals, and developments in computer graphics. The computer can be used in a new and responsible way being truly interactive and content free but supporting a structure which is amenable to mathematical treatment thereby allowing the reconstruction of the conversational content.

In the field of education, computer-aided learning has been partially developed. The computer is programmed to adapt to an individual learner, record his successes and failures, and use these records as a basis for the selection of further material. However, much of what is called computer-aided learning is indistinguishable from computer-assisted instruction. If the philosophy of the personal scientist were to be incorporated into this process the learner could be offered tools which allow him to attempt new ventures with a firm basis and support in the system. This would be especially appropriate in the teaching of foreign languages, for which there is a greater need since many more people are travelling around Europe than previously. Such systems as those described offer a new light in which the learning of a language from French to PL/1 may be made less obscure.

Similarly, in industry the techniques have successfully been applied to learning and training, quality control (e.g. Pope, Shaw and Thomas [16]), and staff development, by recognizing that one must begin from the cognitive models displayed by the individuals concerned, not those specified by the regulations.

The recent development and availability of microprocessors indicates that the "personal computer" may soon be commonly available to the ordinary person. There is no technical reason why the techniques described here could not be run on these personal computers, offering to all people for the same cost as a pocket calculator these tools for raising personal awareness of one's cognitive models and processes, making explicit relationships on the world in a non-directive and supportive way, and enabling the individual to have an overview of his system in such a way as to allow him to review and revise his models in a non-threatening manner.

REFERENCES

1. ATKIN, R. H., Combinatorial Connectivities in Social Systems, Birkhauser Verlag, Basel, 1977.
2. BARTLETT, F. C., Remembering, Cambridge University Press, London, 1932.
3. BRUNER, J. S., J. J. GOODNOW, and G. A. AUSTIN, A Study of Thinking, Wiley, New York, 1956.
4. GAINES, B. R., "Minicomputers in Business Applications in the Next Decade," paper for Infotech State of Art Report on Minis Versus Mainframes, 1977.
5. HEAD, H., Studies in Neurology, Vol. 2, Hodder and Stoughton and O.U.P., London, 1920.
6. JAHODA, M. and L. F. THOMAS, "A Search for Optimal Conditions of Learning Intellectually Complex Subject Matter," 3rd Progress Report, Centre for the Study of Human Learning, Brunel University, 1965.
7. JEANS, Sir James, Physics and Philosophy, Cambridge University Press, London, 1942.
8. KELLY, G. A., The Psychology of Personal Constructs, Norton, New York, 1955.
9. LEWIN, K., Principles of Topological Psychology, McGraw-Hill, New York, 1936.
10. LORENZ, K., Behind the Mirror: A Search for a Natural History of Human Knowledge, Methuen, London, 1977.
11. LUFT, J., "The Johari Window," Human Relations Training News, 5, pp. 6-7, 1961.
12. McCULLOCH, W. S., Why the Mind is in the Head in "Embodiments of Mind," M.I.T. Press,

Cambridge, Massachusetts, 1965.

13. OSGOOD, C. E., G. J. SUCI, and P. H. TANNENBAUM, The Measurement of Meaning, University of Illinois Press, Urbana, 1957.

14. PASK, G., The Cybernetics of Human Learning and Performance, Hutchinson Educational, London, 1975.

15. PASK, G., B. C. E. SCOTT, and D. KALLIKOURDIS, "A Theory of Conversations and Individuals (Exemplified by the Learning Process on CASTE)," International Journal of Man-Machine Studies, 5, pp. 443-566, 1973.

16. POPE, M. L., M. L. G. SHAW, and L. F. THOMAS, "A Report on the Use of Repertory Grid Techniques in Final Inspection," project for Marks and Spencer in conjunction with Marathon Knitwear, Centre for the Study of Human Learning publication, Brunel University, 1977.

17. SCHUMACHER, E. F., Small is Beautiful, Blond and Briggs, London, 1973.

18. SHAW, M. L. G., "Notes on Computer Programs," Centre for the Study of Human Learning publication, Brunel University, 1977.

19. SKEMP, R. R., "The Need for a Schematic Learning Theory," British Journal of Educational Psychology, 32, pp. 133-142, 1962.

20. THOMAS, L. F., "DEMON and DOUBLE-DEMON: Computer Aided Conversations with Yourself,"

Centre for the Study of Human Learning publication, Brunel University, 1976.

21. THOMAS, L. F., C. McKNIGHT, and M. L. G. SHAW, "Grids and Group Structure," paper presented to the Social Psychology Section of the B. P. S., University of Surrey, 1976.

22. THOMAS, L. F. and M. L. G. SHAW, "FOCUS: A Manual for the 'Feedback Of Clusters Using Similarities' Computer Program," Centre for the Study of Human Learning publication, Brunel University, 1976.

23. THOMAS, L. F. and M. L. G. SHAW, "PEGASUS: A Manual for 'Program Elicits Grids and Sorts Using Similarities'," Centre for the Study of Human Learning publication, Brunel University, 1977.

24. THOMAS, L. F., M. L. G. SHAW, and M. POPE, "The Repertory Grid: A Report of a Feasibility Study on Personal Judgement in Staff Appraisal," Centre for the Study of Human Learning publication, Brunel University, 1977.

25. VERNON, M. D., "The Function of Schemata in Perceiving," Psychology Review, 62, pp. 180-192, 1955.

26. WIENER, N., The Human Use of Human Beings, Cybernetics and Society, Houghton Mifflin, Boston, 1950.

17. WITTGENSTEIN, L., Remarks on the Foundations of Mathematics, Blackwell, Oxford, 1967.

Applied model of learning

PETER STAUDIGL
Technical University of Vienna, Austria

1. BASE OF LEARNING

The problem of effective learning is often taken up in literature. Theories of learning for machines are planned, but scientists sometimes forget basical applications with men. Interdisciplinary analysis shows a model which is invariantly practicable. The following facts in different sciences show the base of our model.

1.1. Psychological Aspects

The psychological theory of decision [1] is a concrete way for cognitive processes of men. This method shows realistic steps for getting the base of communication, handling of the effects, functioning of corpus and thoughts.

1.2. Model of Cybernetic Strategy

The model of cybernetic strategy [2] is the second base to reduce the time of learning and to rise the effects. This way is a way of industrial science and pronounced with facts of several firms in Europe. It shows in simple examples what the manager should do for using the principle of evolution.

1.3. Science of Information

The science of computer and information is the third base [3] which is used for the model of learning. Information systems all over the world show a way for transforming information and their retrieval. The theory of information goes the way of abstracting strategies of the reality for coming to new aspects in the modern system design and computer architecture. These systems are a picture of strategy in nature. So the connex is given to our psychological and social sciences.

1.4. Interdisciplinary Analysis

Interdisciplinary analysis of the named sciences gives us abstract analogies for the model of learning. The problems of the several ways of education lay at the growth of knowledge and at the missing strategies to solve them. The self-organizing strategy in the industry as cybernetic regulator of production and need today nobody can practice and use to the profit of evolution. The way of efficient communication is the really practicable way for forcing the process of learning.

2. DEFINITIONS

The next thing is to define the used words and their meanings.

<u>System</u> is a complete defined sum of parts which are working together for realizing a certain idea.

<u>Idea</u> is an energetic picture with abstract of a certain way or thing or feeling which a system wants to realize.

<u>Strategy</u> is the sum of decisions to realize an idea.

<u>Know-how</u> is the strategy to transform ideas into actions in the physical universe.

<u>Action</u> is a strategy between two systems.

<u>Feedback</u> is the measure of answers to actions of a certain idea.

<u>Learning effect</u> is the quality of a system resulting from actions with feedback.

<u>Delay time</u> is the time between the end of one action or strategy and the beginning of the next one.

<u>Learning</u> is the sum of done actions for getting the know-how to realize ideas in a certain system.

<u>Communication</u> is the strategy to transform ideas over a physical channel with the strategy "speech" and the base for learning of systems.

3. THE TRANSFORMING OF IDEAS

The base of the applied model of learning is the fact that systems can communicate together. So we have two energetic systems with the possibility to store ideas, to work with ideas, and to reduce more ideas to one. Every system has one idea for realizing a certain strategy in a certain form of subdivision (see Figure 1). If system 1 wants system 2 doing the strategy of realizing, system 1 has to ascertain that system 2 has all information points in it to realize the idea (see Figure 2). In this example system 2 cannot accept information of system 1 because the highest level of system 2 is the lowest level of system 1. So no communication is possible.

If system 1 and system 2 want to communicate together, system 1 has to transform the ideas in a certain way so that system 2 can accept the information points and practically transform in it.

This procedure is the way of learning showed in a short building.

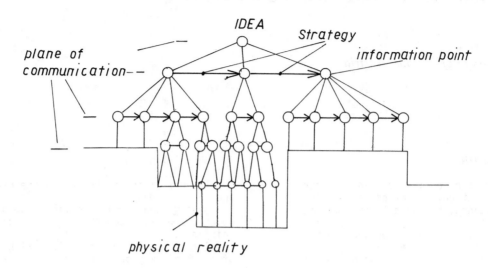

Figure 1.

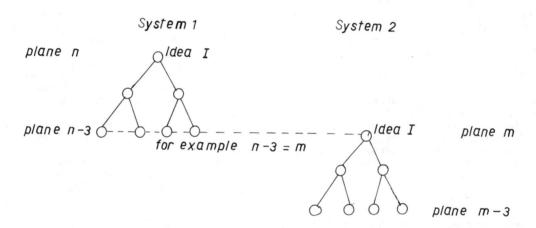

Figure 2.

4. THE STRATEGY OF LEARNING

Now we see that the strategy of learning has two parts:

1. Transforming of information from system 1 (teacher) to system 2 (student) and storing of the information in system 2 by recognizing facts and connecting the new information with available facts.

2. The decision for realizing the new information into the physics is the action of transforming. So the feedback is coming for successful doing and accepting the information and doing of system 1.

We can divide this strategy into the following parts:

1. Destination of aim with reduction of past events to a minimum factor.

2. Fixing of an invariant strategy resulting from the minimum factor.

3. Showing a connex to the invariant strategy by examples.

4. Cognition of influences in the past (preventing or furthering the attaining of the aim) with programmed questions, which create associations independent of men by this strategy, is extended. It is analysed to its importance for the present and finally correct.

5. Concentration to the solving of the minimum factor and repeated application of the new or the improved strategy will automate strategy in order to be permanently available.

6. Comparison of the application with the destination shows the variability of the minimum factor and the strategy can be improved by these six items.

In a short way, Figure 3 shows the strategy. Depending on the several times of these phases and the chosen strategies, you can find a certain behaviour of the system 2 in Figure 4.

The learning optimum is an equation between know-how, action, feedback and learning effect and the minimum of delay.

a) transforming know-how from system 1 to system 2

b) delay time 1

c) action of system 2 for transforming know-how
    in an independant own way

d)   delay time 2

e)   feedback by transforming ideas with the necessary
     know-how

f)   delay time 3

g)   learningeffect by successfully realizing of ideas
     into physis

time

Figure 3.

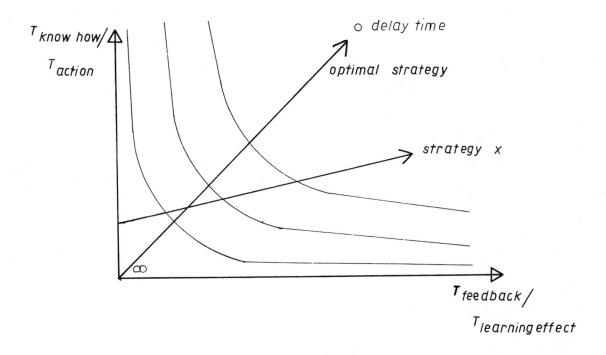

Figure 4.

5.   PRACTICABLE RUN

     The base of the practicable model of learning
is the communication strategy:
     a.   lesson of a principle with example
     b.   demonstration of the practicable exercise
     c.   training of the exercise in dyadic groups
          shows the way to recognition
The best way of education is the following:
     A.   Base of Communication
          1.   Information to the student to get
               his interest.
          2.   Seminar "Psychological Management I".
          3.   Trainings in student's praxis.
          4.   Evenings to stabilize know-how.
          5.   Seminar "Psychological Management II".
          6.   Training in student's praxis.
          7.   Evening to stabilize know-how.
     B.   Base of Strategy
          8.   Seminar "Strategy I".
          9.   Training in student's praxis.
         10.   Evening to stabilize know-how.
     C.   Base of Certain Know-How
         11.   Seminar "Strategy II".
         12.   Trainings in student's praxis.
         13.   Evenings to stabilize know-how.
         14.   Consultation of students for
               difficult problems.
The seminar is held in a modular way of the communication strategy with several themes.

Seminar:	lesson	theme 1
	demonstration	"
	training	"
	lesson	theme 2
	demonstration	"
	training	"
	.	
	.	
	.	
	lesson	theme n
	demonstration	"
	training	"

     Tests with now 600 persons show the invariant-
ability of seminars. Every person has his own
learning effect in a short time. So we can say
that this new way of learning is a more effective
one as the ways perfect. The next years will
underpin the future results for this applied
model of learning.

REFERENCES

1.   STILLE, W., "Theory of Decision," Disserta-
     tion, London, 1974.
2.   MEWES, W., "Model of Cybernetic Strategy,"
     Lessons, Frankfurt, 1977.
3.   STAUDIGL, P., "Acting of Informations in
     General Systems," Vienna, 1977.

Author Index

Subject Index